D1405819

Training Guide: Configuring Advanced Windows Server 2012 R2 Services

Orin Thomas

PUBLISHED BY
Microsoft Press
A Division of Microsoft Corporation
One Microsoft Way
Redmond, Washington 98052-6399

Library of Congress Control Number: 2014935077
ISBN: 978-0-7356-8471-3

Printed and bound in the United States of America.

First Printing

Microsoft Press books are available through booksellers and distributors worldwide. If you need support related to this book, email Microsoft Press Book Support at mspinput@microsoft.com. Please tell us what you think of this book at http://www.microsoft.com/learning/booksurvey.

Acquisitions Editor: Anne Hamilton
Developmental Editor: Karen Szall
Editorial Production: Troy Mott, Backstop Media LLC
Technical Reviewer: Telmo Sampaio
Copyeditor: Christina Rudloff
Indexer: Joe Wizda, Martin Murtonen
Cover: Twist Creative • Seattle

Contents at a glance

Introduction   *xviii*

CHAPTER 1   Advanced Active Directory infrastructure   1

CHAPTER 2   Active Directory sites and replication   59

CHAPTER 3   Advanced DHCP and DNS   119

CHAPTER 4   Active Directory Certificate Services   205

CHAPTER 5   Backup and recovery   301

CHAPTER 6   Advanced file services and storage   373

CHAPTER 7   High availability   441

CHAPTER 8   Virtual machine and site resilience   505

CHAPTER 9   DAC and AD RMS   567

CHAPTER 10   Active Directory Federation Services   657

Index   *715*

Contents

Introduction   **xviii**

Chapter 1   Advanced Active Directory infrastructure   1

Before you begin. 1

Lesson 1: Configuring domains and forests 1

    Multidomain Active Directory environments   2

    Multiforest Active Directory environments   8

    Upgrading existing domains and forests   9

    User principal name (UPN) suffixes   10

    Lesson summary   11

    Lesson review   12

Lesson 2: Configuring trusts 13

    Trusts   13

    SID filtering   21

    Name suffix routing   22

    Lesson summary   23

    Lesson review   24

Practice exercises 25

    Exercise 1: Prepare a domain controller to host a
child domain with a contiguous namespace   25

    Exercise 2: Create a child domain with a contiguous namespace   27

    Exercise 3: Prepare domain controller to host the
wingtiptoys.com tree in the contoso.com forest   30

    Exercise 4: Promote domain controller for
new tree in contoso.com forest   31

What do you think of this book? We want to hear from you!

Microsoft is interested in hearing your feedback so we can continually improve our
books and learning resources for you. To participate in a brief online survey, please visit:

www.microsoft.com/learning/booksurvey/

Exercise 5: Prepare a domain controller to host a new forest   32

Exercise 6: Create new forest   33

Exercise 7: Prepare to configure a forest trust relationship   34

Exercise 8: Begin creating a forest trust relationship   37

Exercise 9: Complete the creation of the forest trust relationship between contoso.com and margiestravel.com   40

Exercise 10: Configure name suffix routing   43

Exercise 11: Configure selective authentication   45

Exercise 12: Configure additional UPN suffixes   50

Exercise 13: Configure a shortcut trust   50

Suggested practice exercises 54

Answers. 55

Lesson 1   55

Lesson 2   56

Chapter 2   Active Directory sites and replication   59

Before you begin. 59

Lesson 1: Configuring sites 59

Configure sites and subnets   60

Manage SRV record registration   68

Moving domain controllers   69

Lesson summary   70

Lesson review   71

Lesson 2: Active Directory replication. 72

Active Directory partitions   72

Understanding multi-master replication   73

RODC replication   76

Configure RODC password replication   77

Monitor and manage replication   81

Repadmin   83

Upgrade SYSVOL replication   85

Lesson summary   86

Lesson review   86

Practice Exercises 88

Exercise 1: Create Active Directory sites   89

Exercise 2: Create Active Directory subnets   91

Exercise 3: Create site links   93

Exercise 4: Modify site link cost and replication schedule   94

Exercise 5: Configure MEL-DC as an additional domain controller 96

Exercise 6: Verify site placement and trigger replication   101

Exercise 7: Configure ADL-DC as an RODC   102

Exercise 8: Configure RODC replication   105

Exercise 9: View account passwords replicated to ADL-DC   107

Exercise 10: Monitor replication with repadmin   110

Exercise 11: Remove the RODC and reset accounts   113

Suggested practice exercises 114

Answers. 115

Lesson 1   115

Lesson 2   116

Chapter 3   Advanced DHCP and DNS   119

Before you begin. 119

Lesson 1: Implementing an advanced DNS solution 119

DNSSEC   120

DNS event logs   122

GlobalNames zones   124

Advanced DNS options   126

Delegated administration   129

Analyze zone level statistics   131

Lesson summary   132

Lesson review   132

Lesson 2: Implementing an advanced DHCP solution 134

Superscopes   134

Multicast scopes   135

Split scopes   136

DNS registration   137

Name Protection   138

DHCP failover   139

Lesson summary   141

Lesson review   142

Lesson 3: Deploying and managing IPAM 143

Introduction to IPAM   144

Deploy IPAM   144

Configure IPAM database storage   144

Configure server discovery   145

Managing the IP address space   148

IP address tracking   150

IPAM administration   152

Lesson summary   153

Lesson review   153

Practice exercises 154

Exercise 1: Configure MEL-DC   155

Exercise 2: Configure DNSSEC   156

Exercise 3: Configure the name resolution policy   158

Exercise 4: Increase the size of the DNS socket pool   161

Exercise 5: Modify DNS Cache Locking   161

Exercise 6: Create and manage a GlobalNames zone   163

Exercise 7: Configure and view the DNS event log   165

Exercise 8: Verify netmask ordering and disable recursion   167

Exercise 9: Install and activate the DHCP role   168

Exercise 10: Create a DHCP superscope   173

Exercise 11: Create a split scope   177

Exercise 12: Configure DHCP Name Protection   180

Exercise 13: Create new multicast scopes   182

Exercise 14: Configure DHCP failover   184

Exercise 15: Install the IPAM feature   186

Exercise 16: Configure IPAM GPOs and server discovery   187

Exercise 17: Configure servers to be managed by IPAM   189

Exercise 18: Manage servers using IPAM   194

Exercise 19: Use IPAM to create a DHCP scope   196

Exercise 20: Use IPAM to manage IP addresses   197

Suggested practice exercises 199

Answers. 200

    Lesson 1   200

    Lesson 2   202

    Lesson 3   203

Chapter 4   Active Directory Certificate Services   205

Before you begin. 205

Lesson 1: Installing and configuring
    Active Directory Certificate Services 205

    Installing certificate authorities   *206*

    CRL distribution points   212

    Online Responders   214

    Administrative role separation   215

    CA backup and recovery   216

    Lesson summary   218

    Lesson review   219

Lesson 2: Manage certificates. 220

    Certificate templates   221

    Certificate revocation   222

    Certificate renewal   224

    Autoenrollment   225

    Key archiving and recovery   227

    Lesson summary   229

    Lesson review   230

Practice exercises 231

    Exercise 1: Deploy and configure an enterprise root CA   232

    Exercise 2: Deploy an enterprise subordinate CA   241

    Exercise 3: Install a standalone subordinate CA   246

    Exercise 4: Configure a standalone CA   250

    Exercise 5: Configure a CRL distribution point   253

    Exercise 6: Configure an Online Responder   257

    Exercise 7: Configure administrative role separation   264

    Exercise 8: Configure a key recovery agent certificate template   268

    Exercise 9: Request a key recovery agent certificate   273

    Exercise 10: Configure key recovery   277

Exercise 11: Configure a certificate template for autoenrollment and
key recovery   279

Exercise 12: Configure Group Policy to support autoenrollment,
credential roaming, and automatic renewal   282

Exercise 13: Configure a certificate template to support private key
archival and recovery and reenroll all certificate holders   287

Exercise 14: Perform certificate revocation   288

Exercise 15: Perform certificate recovery   292

Suggested practice exercises 296

Answers. 297

Lesson 1   297

Lesson 2   299

Chapter 5 Backup and recovery   **301**

Before you begin. 301

Lesson 1: Configuring and managing backups 301

Windows Server Backup   302

Windows Azure Backup   306

Role-specifc and application-specific backups   312

Vssadmin   313

Data Protection Manager   316

Lesson summary   317

Lesson review   317

Lesson 2: Recovering servers 318

Restore from backups   318

Recover servers using Windows Recovery Environment   321

Safe mode and Last Known Good Configuration   322

Configure the Boot Configuration Data store   324

Lesson summary   325

Lesson review   325

Practice exercises 326

Exercise 1: Prepare MEL-DC and CBR-DC for exercises   326

Exercise 2: Install Windows Server Backup   327

Exercise 3: Configure CBR-DC for local backup   330

Exercise 4: Perform a backup to a local volume   334

Exercise 5: Perform a backup over the network 336

Exercise 6: Use Vssadmin 338

Exercise 7: Perform a full volume recovery using
Windows Server Backup 341

Exercise 8: Prepare for Windows Recovery Environment 344

Exercise 9: Perform full server recovery over the network 345

Exercise 10: Boot into Safe Mode 348

Exercise 11: Modify Boot Configuration Data store 350

Exercise 12: Configure a standalone computer for use with Windows
Azure Backup 354

Exercise 13: Configure Windows Azure Backup 358

Exercise 14: Backup data to Windows Azure Backup 362

Exercise 15: Restore data from Windows Azure Backup 367

Suggested practice exercises 369

Answers. 370

Lesson 1 370

Lesson 2 371

Chapter 6   Advanced file services and storage   373

Before you begin. 373

Lesson 1: Configuring advanced file services. 373

File screens 374

Quotas 377

Server for NFS 379

BranchCache 380

File classification 384

File access auditing 385

Lesson summary 387

Lesson review 387

Lesson 2: Configuring and optimizing storage 388

iSCSI target and initiator 389

iSNS server 392

Thin provisioning and trim 394

Features on Demand 396

Tiered storage 398

Lesson summary   398

Lesson review   399

Practice exercises 400

Exercise 1: Prepare MEL-DC and ADL-DC   400

Exercise 2: Deploy FSRM   401

Exercise 3: Configure quota templates and quotas   402

Exercise 4: Create file groups, file screen templates, apply file
screens, and apply file screen exceptions   407

Exercise 5: Configure file classification   410

Exercise 6: Verify the classification   413

Exercise 7: Configure file access auditing   414

Exercise 8: Create and assign an iSCSI target   417

Exercise 9: Connect to an iSCSI target   421

Exercise 10: Create a new storage pool and thin provisioned virtual
disk   423

Exercise 11: Install the iSNS server and register the initiator   426

Exercise 12: Remove feature files   429

Exercise 13: Configure BranchCache policies   431

Exercise 14: Deploy BranchCache on Windows Server 2012 R2   435

Suggested practice exercises 437

Answers. 438

Lesson 1   438

Lesson 2   439

Chapter 7   High availability   441

Before you begin. 441

Lesson 1: Configuring and managing failover clustering. 441

Failover clustering   442

Cluster quorum modes   443

Cluster storage and cluster shared volumes   445

Cluster Shared Volumes   446

Shared virtual hard disks   447

Cluster networks   448

Cluster-Aware Updating   449

Migrating and upgrading clusters   451

Failover and preference settings 452

Continuously available shares 454

Active Directory detached clusters 454

Lesson summary 455

Lesson review 455

Lesson 2: Understanding Network Load Balancing 456

Network Load Balancing 457

Network Load Balancing prerequisites 458

NLB cluster operation modes 459

Managing cluster hosts 461

Port rules 462

Filtering and affinity 463

Upgrading an NLB cluster 464

New NLB PowerShell cmdlets 465

Lesson summary 466

Lesson review 466

Practice exercises 467

Exercise 1: Prepare ADL-DC, MEL-DC, and CBR-DC for exercises 468

Exercise 2: Install the Network Load Balancing feature
on ADL-DC, CBR-DC, and MEL-DC   469

Exercise 3: Create a three-node NLB cluster   470

Exercise 4: Configure port rules and affinity   473

Exercise 5: Remove an NLB cluster   475

Exercise 6: Create shared storage for failover clustering   477

Exercise 7: Connect potential cluster nodes to shared storage 479

Exercise 8: Install failover cluster features   483

Exercise 9: Validate cluster configuration   484

Exercise 10: Create a two-node failover cluster   485

Exercise 11: Add a cluster node   486

Exercise 12: Change the quorum configuration   488

Exercise 13: Install and configure a highly available file server 489

Exercise 14: Configure a highly available file share   491

Exercise 15: Configure failover settings, failback settings,
and move node   493

Exercise 16: Simulate unplanned failure   495

Exercise 17: Cluster-Aware Updating   496

Suggested practice exercises 501

Answers. 502

Lesson 1   502

Lesson 2   503

Chapter 8   Virtual machine and site resilience   505

Before you begin. 505

Lesson 1: Virtual machine movement 505

Virtual machine failover clustering   506

Shared Nothing Hyper-V live migration   509

Storage migration   512

Virtual machine import and export   515

Lesson summary   516

Lesson review   517

Lesson 2: Site-level fault tolerance. 518

Hyper-V Replica   518

Hyper-V Replica Broker   525

Multisite clustering   526

Lesson summary   528

Lesson review   528

Practice exercises 529

Exercise 1: Install the Hyper-V role on MEL-HV-1 and MEL-HV-2 531

Exercise 2: Configure identical virtual switches
on MEL-HV-1 and MEL-HV-2   536

Exercise 3: Prepare servers for live migration   538

Exercise 4: Prepare servers for replication   541

Exercise 5: Create two virtual machines on MEL-HV-1   544

Exercise 6: Configure TEST-ONE for replication   547

Exercise 7: View replication health and perform planned failover of
TEST-ONE to MEL-HV-2   550

Exercise 8: Configure Hyper-V to support live migration   552

Exercise 9: Perform live migration of TEST-TWO   553

Exercise 10: Perform storage migration   556

Exercise 11: Perform a virtual machine export   558

Exercise 12: Create a copy of a running virtual machine   558

Exercise 13: Enable reverse replication   559

Exercise 14: Perform an unplanned failover   561

Suggested practice exercises 563

Answers. 564

Lesson 1   564

Lesson 2   565

Chapter 9 DAC and AD RMS   567

Before you begin. 567

Lesson 1: Implementing Dynamic Access Control (DAC). 567

Introduction to Dynamic Access Control   568

Configuring Group Policy to support DAC   569

Configuring user and device claims   569

Configuring resource properties   571

Central access rules   573

Central access policies   575

Staging   576

Access Denied Assistance   577

Lesson summary   578

Lesson review   579

Lesson 2: Installing and configuring
Active Directory Rights Management Services (AD RMS) 580

Installing AD RMS   580

AD RMS certificates and licenses   582

AD RMS templates   583

AD RMS Administrators and Super Users   586

Trusted user and publishing domains   587

Exclusion policies   589

Apply AD RMS templates automatically   590

Backing up AD RMS   591

Lesson summary   592

Lesson review   592

Practice exercises 593

Exercise 1: Prepare MEL-DC and ADL-DC   594

Exercise 2: Enable group policy support for DAC   595

Exercise 3: Create users and groups   598

Exercise 4: Configure user and device claims   602

Exercise 5: Configure resource properties   607

Exercise 6: Prepare server for file classification   609

Exercise 7: Create a file classification rule   611

Exercise 8: Run and verify the file classification   619

Exercise 9: Create central access rules   621

Exercise 10: Create a central access policy   624

Exercise 11: Configure Access Denied Assistance   627

Exercise 12: Configure staging   629

Exercise 13: Prepare infrastructure for an AD RMS deployment   632

Exercise 14: Install and configure the AD RMS server role   635

Exercise 15: Create the AD RMS Super Users group   641

Exercise 16: Create AD RMS templates   642

Exercise 17: Configure template distribution   647

Exercise 18: Configure application exclusions   648

Exercise 19: Apply RMS templates using file classification   649

Suggested practice exercises 652

Answers. 653

Lesson 1   653

Lesson 2   654

Chapter 10   Active Directory Federation Services   657

Before you begin. 657

Lesson 1: Implementing Active Directory Federation Services. 657

AD FS Components   658

Claims, claim rules, and attribute stores   658

Claims provider   659

Relying party   660

Relying party trust   660

Claims provider trust   661

Configuring certificate relationship   662

Attribute stores   663

Claims rules   664

Configure Web Application Proxy   666

Workplace Join   669

Multi-factor authentication   671

Lesson summary   672

Lesson review   672

Practice exercises 673

Exercise 1: Prepare separate forests   673

Exercise 2: Configure DNS forwarding   675

Exercise 3: Deploy AD CS in each forest   678

Exercise 4: Prepare SYD-DC for certificate publication   680

Exercise 5: Prepare MEL-DC for certificate publication   684

Exercise 6: Configure CA trust in each forest   689

Exercise 7: Acquire certificates for each server   691

Exercise 8: Deploy AD FS in each forest   694

Exercise 9: Configure relying party trust   699

Exercise 10: Configure a claims provider trust   702

Exercise 11: Prepare claim data   703

Exercise 12: Configure claim rules   705

Suggested practice exercises 713

Answers. 714

Lesson 1   714

Index   *715*

What do you think of this book? We want to hear from you!

Microsoft is interested in hearing your feedback so we can continually improve our
books and learning resources for you. To participate in a brief online survey, please visit:

www.microsoft.com/learning/booksurvey/

Introduction

This Training Guide is designed for information technology (IT) professionals who support, or plan to support, Windows Server 2012 R2 networks, and are ramping up on the latest technology. It is assumed that before you begin using this guide, you have a solid, foundation-level understanding of Microsoft Windows client and server operating systems, and common Internet technologies. This guide provides job-role training for the job role that is covered by the Microsoft certification exam 70-412. Use this book to enhance your job skills or to prepare for an upgrade to Windows Server 2012 R2. You can also use it to complement your exam preparation plan if you are preparing for certification.

When Microsoft Learning puts together exam objectives, it doesn't randomly select pages from TechNet. Instead, in conjunction with subject matter experts and representatives of the product team, it puts together a list of tasks and areas of knowledge that represents what someone in a specific job role would do and need to know on a day-to-day, a weekly, or even a monthly basis.

Each exam maps to a different job role. The objectives for the 70-412 exam are a list of tasks and areas of knowledge that describe what an advanced administrator of the Windows Server 2012 and Windows Server 2012 R2 operating systems with several years of on-the-job experience (managing other server operating systems as well as Windows Server 2012 and Windows Server 2012 R2) does and understands. These topics include some that experienced administrators may not have encountered before or have limited experience with, such as Active Directory Rights Management Services and Active Directory Federation Services.

This book covers the majority of the topics and skills that are the subject of the Microsoft certification exam 70-412. The idea behind this book is that by reading it and by performing the extensive practice exercises at the end of each chapter in your own lab, you can learn how to perform tasks with the technologies addressed by the exam. By performing the tasks yourself in a test environment you'll learn enough about how these technologies work that you'll be able to leverage that knowledge in your real-world role as a Windows Server 2012 or Windows Server 2012 R2 administrator. Reading and performing the practice exercises in this book will assist you in preparing for the exam, but it's not a complete exam preparation solution. If you are preparing for the exam, you should use additional study materials, such as practice tests and the *70-412 Configuring Advanced Windows Server 2012 Services Exam Ref* to help bolster your real-world experience.

By using this training guide, you will learn how to do the following:

- Configure and manage high availability
- Configure file and storage solutions
- Implement business continuity and disaster recovery
- Configure network services
- Configure the Active Directory infrastructure
- Configure access and information protection solutions

System requirements

The following are the minimum system requirements your computer needs to meet to complete the practice exercises in this book. This book is designed assuming you will be using Hyper-V—either the client version available with some editions of Windows 8.1, or the version available in Windows Server 2012 R2. You can use other virtualization software instead, such as VirtualBox or VMWare Workstation, but the practice setup instructions later in this introduction assume that you are using Hyper-V. The exercises in Chapter 8 require the version of Hyper-V available in Windows Server 2012 R2 and involve functionality specific to this version of the product.

Hardware requirements

If you choose to use virtualization software, you need only one physical computer to perform the exercises in this book, except for in Chapter 8, which requires two identical computers. The physical host computer must meet the following minimum hardware requirements:

- x64-based processor that includes both hardware-assisted virtualization (AMD-V or Intel VT) and hardware data execution protection. (On AMD systems, the data execution protection feature is called the No Execute or NX bit. On Intel systems, this feature is called the Execute Disable or XD bit.) These features must also be enabled in the BIOS. (Note: You can run Windows Virtual PC without Intel-VT or AMD-V.) If you want to use Hyper-V on Windows 8 or Windows 8.1, you need a processor that supports Second Layer Address Translation (SLAT).
- 8 gigabytes (GB) of RAM (more is recommended).
- 250 GB of available hard disk space.
- Internet connectivity.

Software requirements

The following software is required to complete the practice exercises:

- Windows Server 2012 R2 evaluation. You can download an evaluation edition of Windows Server 2012 R2 in iso format from the Windows Server and Cloud Platform website at *http://www.microsoft.com/server*.

Virtual machine setup instructions

This set of exercises contains abbreviated instructions for setting up the SYD-DC, MEL-DC, ADL-DC, and CBR-DC computers used in the practice exercises in all chapters of this training kit. To perform these exercises, first install Windows Server 2012 R2 Standard edition using the default configuration, setting the administrator password to **Pa$$w0rd.**

Exercise 1: SYD-DC to function as a Windows Server 2012 R2 domain controller

1. Log on to the first computer on which you have installed Windows Server 2012 R2 using the Administrator account and the password **Pa$$w0rd**.

2. Open an elevated PowerShell prompt and issue the following command:

   ```
   cmd
   ```

3. Enter the following command:

   ```
   Netsh interface ipv4 set address "Ethernet" static 10.10.10.10
   ```

4. Enter the following command:

   ```
   netdom renamecomputer %compuvvtername% /newname:SYD-DC
   ```

5. Restart the computer and log back on using the Administrator account.

6. Open an elevated PowerShell prompt and issue the following command:

   ```
   Add-WindowsFeature AD-Domain-Services -IncludeManagementTools
   ```

7. Open the Server Manager console. Click the Refresh icon.

8. Click the Notifications icon and then click Promote This Server To Domain Controller.

9. On the Deployment Configuration page, choose Add A New Forest. Type **Contoso.com** as the root domain name and then click Next.

10. On the Domain Controller Options page, configure the following settings and then click Next:

   - Forest Functional Level: **Windows Server 2012 R2**
   - Domain Functional Level: **Windows Server 2012 R2**
   - Specify Domain Controller Capabilities: **Domain Name System (DNS) Server And Global Catalog**
   - DSRM Password: **Pa$$w0rd**

11. On the DNS Options page, click Next.

12. On the Additional Options page, click Next.

13. Accept the default settings for the Database, Log Files, and SYSVOL locations, and click Next.

14. On the Review Options page, click Next.

15. On the Prerequisites Check page, click Install.

16. The computer will restart automatically.

Exercise 2: Prepare Active Directory Domain Server (AD DS)

1. Log on to server SYD-DC using the Administrator account.

2. Using Active Directory Users And Computers, create a user account named **don_funk** in the Users container and assign the account the password **Pa$$w0rd**. Configure the password to never expire. Add this user account to the Enterprise Admins, Domain Admins, and Schema Admins groups.

3. Open the DNS console and create a primary IPv4 Reverse Lookup Zone for the subnet 10.10.10.x. Ensure that the zone is stored within AD DS and is replicated to all DNS servers running on domain controllers in the forest and allows only secure dynamic updates.

Exercise 3: Prepare ADL-DC

1. Ensure that computer SYD-DC is turned on and connected to the network or virtual network to which the second computer is connected.

2. Log on to the second computer on which you have installed Windows Server 2012 R2 using the Administrator account and the password **Pa$$w0rd**.

3. Open an elevated PowerShell prompt and issue the following commands:

   ```cmd
   Netsh interface ipv4 set address "Ethernet" static 10.10.10.20
   Netsh interface ipv4 set dnsservers "Ethernet" static 10.10.10.10 primary
   ```

4. Enter the following command:

   ```
   netdom renamecomputer %computername% /newname:ADL-DC
   ```

5. Restart the computer and then log on again using the Administrator account.

6. Shut down the computer.

Exercise 4: Prepare CBR-DC

1. Ensure that computer SYD-DC is turned on and connected to the network or virtual network to which the second computer is connected.

2. Log on to the third computer on which you have installed Windows Server 2012 R2 using the Administrator account and the password **Pa$$w0rd**.

3. Open an elevated PowerShell prompt and issue the following commands:

   ```cmd
   Netsh interface ipv4 set address "Ethernet" static 10.10.10.30
   Netsh interface ipv4 set dnsservers "Ethernet" static 10.10.10.10 primary
   ```

4. Enter the following command:

   ```
   netdom renamecomputer %computername% /newname:CBR-DC
   ```

5. Restart the computer and then log on again using the Administrator account.

6. Shut down the computer.

Exercise 5: Prepare MEL-DC

1. Ensure that computer SYD-DC is turned on and connected to the network or virtual network to which the second computer is connected.

2. Log on to the third computer on which you have installed Windows Server 2012 R2 using the Administrator account and the password **Pa$$w0rd**.

3. Open an elevated PowerShell prompt and issue the following commands:

```cmd
Netsh interface ipv4 set address "Ethernet" static 10.10.10.40
Netsh interface ipv4 set dnsservers "Ethernet" static 10.10.10.10 primary
```

4. Enter the following command:

```
netdom renamecomputer %computername% /newname:MEL-DC
```

5. Restart the computer and then log on again using the Administrator account.

6. Shut down the computer.

Exercise 6: Checkpoint all virtual machines

1. Checkpoint all virtual machines. This is the state that they need to be in prior to performing exercises. Checkpoints were termed snapshots in prior versions of Hyper-V.

Acknowledgments

I'd like to thank the following people for their dedication and help in getting this book written: Telmo Sampaio, Troy Mott, and Christina Rudloff. I'd also like to thank Oksana and Rooslan for their patience with me during the writing process.

Errata, updates, and book support

We've made every effort to ensure the accuracy of this book and its companion content. You can access updates to this book—in the form of a list of submitted errata and their related corrections—at:

http://aka.ms/TG412R2

If you discover an error that is not already listed, please submit it to us at the same page.

If you need additional support, email Microsoft Press Book Support at *mspinput@microsoft.com*.

We want to hear from you

At Microsoft Press, your satisfaction is our top priority, and your feedback is our most valuable asset. Please tell us what you think of this book at:

http://aka.ms/tellpress

The survey is short, and we read every one of your comments and ideas. Thanks in advance for your input!

Stay in touch

Let's keep the conversation going! We're on Twitter: *http://twitter.com/MicrosoftPress*.

CHAPTER 1

Advanced Active Directory infrastructure

If you are the administrator of a medium to large organization, it is likely that you are responsible for managing multiple domains, perhaps even multiple forests, rather than managing a single domain forest. In this chapter you discover how and why you would configure forests with multiple domain trees and the benefits of each functional level. You also find out how to configure and manage different types of trust relationships to ensure users in one forest or domain are granted appropriate access to resources in another forest, domain, or Kerberos realm.

Lessons in this chapter:

- Lesson 1: Configuring domains and forests
- Lesson 2: Configuring trusts

Before you begin

To complete the practice exercises in this chapter, you need to have deployed computers SYD-DC, MEL-DC, CBR-DC, and ADL-DC as described in the Introduction, using the evaluation edition of Windows Server 2012 R2.

Lesson 1: Configuring domains and forests

As an experienced administrator you're probably quite familiar with the configuration of single domain Active Directory forests. In this lesson, you find out more about multidomain and multiforest environments. You discover how to upgrade an existing domain and forest so that it uses only Windows Server 2012 R2 domain controllers, and you find out how to configure UPN suffixes.

> **After this lesson, you will be able to:**
>
> - Understand multidomain Active Directory environments
> - Understand multiforest Active Directory environments
> - Upgrade existing domains and forests
> - Configure multiple user principal name (UPN) suffixes
>
> **Estimated lesson time: 45 minutes**

Multidomain Active Directory environments

The majority of current Active Directory deployments in small-sized and medium-sized enterprises have a single domain. This hasn't always been the case because earlier versions of the Windows Server operating system, such as Windows NT 4.0, supported far fewer accounts. Supporting a smaller number of accounts often necessitated the use of multiple domains, and it wasn't unusual to see medium-sized organizations that used complicated domain structures.

Each Windows Server 2012 and Windows Server 2012 R2 domain controller can create approximately 2.15 billion objects during its lifetime, and each domain supports the creation of up to approximately 2.15 billion *relative identifiers (RIDs)*. Given this, however, few administrators implement multiple domain forests because they need to support a large number of users. Of course, in very large organizations, the replication load between sites might make a domain with several hundred thousand user accounts problematic, but site and replication considerations are covered in Chapter 2, "Active Directory Sites and Replication."

There are many reasons why organizations implement multidomain forests. These can include but are not limited to:

- **Historical domain structure**   Even though newer versions of the Windows Server operating system handle large numbers of objects more efficiently, some organizations have retained the forest structure that was established when the organization first adopted Active Directory.

- **Organizational or political reasons**   Some organizations are conglomerates, and they might be comprised of separate companies that share a common administrative and management core. An example of this is a university faculty in Europe or Australia, such as a Faculty of Science, that is comprised of different departments or schools, such as the school of physics and the department of botany. For political or organizational reasons it might have been decided that each department or school should have its own domain that is a part of the overall faculty forest. Active Directory gives organizations the ability to create domain namespaces that meet their needs, even if those needs might not directly map to the most efficient way of accomplishing a goal from a strict technical perspective.

- **Security reasons**   Domains enable you to create authentication and authorization boundaries. You can also use domains to partition administrative privileges so that you can have one set of administrators who are able to manage computers and users in their own domain, but who are not able to manage computers and users in a separate domain. Although it's possible to accomplish a similar goal by delegating privileges, many organizations prefer to use separate domains to accomplish this goal.

Domain trees

A *domain tree* is a set of names that share a common *root domain* name. For example contoso.com can have pacific.contoso.com and atlantic.contoso.com as child domains, and these domains can have child domains themselves. A forest can have multiple domain trees. When you create a new tree in a forest, the root of the new tree is a *child domain* of the original root domain. In Figure 1-1, adatum.com is the root of new domain tree in the contoso.com forest.

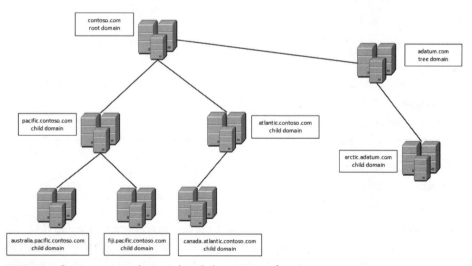

FIGURE 1-1 Contoso.com as the root domain in a two-tree forest

The depth of a domain tree is limited by a domain having maximum fully qualified domain name (FQDN) length for a host of 64 characters.

Intraforest authentication

All domains within the same forest automatically trust one another. This means that in the environment shown in Figure 1-1, you can assign a user in the Australia.pacific.contoso.com permissions to a resource in the arctic.adatum.com domain without performing any extra configuration.

Because of the built-in automatic *trust relationships*, a single forest implementation is not appropriate for separate organizations, even when they are in partnership with one another. A single forest makes it possible for one or more users to have administrative control. Most organizations aren't comfortable even with trusted partners having administrative control over their IT environments. When you do need to allow users from partner organizations to have access to resources, you can configure trust relationships or federation. You read more about trust relationships in Lesson 2 of this chapter and more about federation in Chapter 10, "Active Directory Federation Services."

Domain functional levels

Domain functional levels determine the Active Directory functionality and features that are available. The higher the domain functional level is, the more functionality and features are available.

You can use Windows Server 2012 domain controllers with the following domain functional levels:

- Windows Server 2003
- Windows Server 2008
- Windows Server 2008 R2
- Windows Server 2012

You can use Windows Server 2012 R2 domain controllers with the following domain functional levels:

- Windows Server 2003
- Windows Server 2008
- Windows Server 2008 R2
- Windows Server 2012
- Windows Server 2012 R2

The limiting factor on a domain functional level is the domain controllers used to host Active Directory. If your organization has Windows Server 2003 domain controllers, you aren't able to raise the functional level until you replace or upgrade those domain controllers to a more recent version of the Windows Server operating system.

You can alter the domain functional level using the Active Directory Users And Computers console, the Active Directory Domains And Trusts console as shown in Figure 1-2, or the SetADDomainMode Windows PowerShell cmdlet. Your account needs to be a member of the Domain Admins or Enterprise Admins groups to perform this operation.

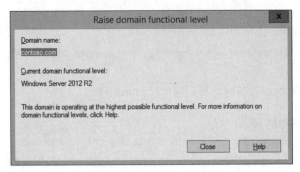

FIGURE 1-2 Raise or verify the domain functional level

WINDOWS SERVER 2003 FUNCTIONAL LEVEL

The Windows Server 2003 domain functional level is the lowest level at which you can introduce domain controllers running the Windows Server 2012 or Windows Server 2012 R2 operating system. You can set this functional level if you have domain controllers running the Windows Server 2003, Windows Server 2003 R2, Windows Server 2008, Windows Server 2008 R2, Windows Server 2012, or Windows Server 2012 R2 operating systems. The Windows Server 2003 domain functional level includes the following features, which are also available at higher domain functional levels:

- The LastLogonTimestamp attribute records a user's last domain logon.
- *Constrained delegation* enables applications to securely delegate user credentials.
- *Selective authentication* enables you to configure specific resources in the forest so that only certain users and groups can authenticate. The default is to allow all users in the forest to authenticate before permissions to those resources are checked.
- Support for storing DNS zones in custom application partitions enables you to selectively replicate DNS zones to specific domain controllers that are enrolled in the custom partitions, rather than requiring that you configure replication to all domain controllers in the domain or the forest.
- Attribute-level replication for group and other multivalued attributes. Rather than replicating the whole Active Directory object, only altered attributes will be replicated.

WINDOWS SERVER 2008 FUNCTIONAL LEVEL

The Windows Server 2008 domain functional level requires that all domain controllers be running the Windows Server 2008, Windows Server 2008 R2, Windows Server 2012 or Windows Server 2012 R2 operating systems. The Windows Server 2008 domain functional level includes all of the features available at the Windows Server 2003 functional level as well as the following:

- Improvements in Distributed File System (DFS) replication that make it possible for replication to occur more efficiently

- Support for fine-grained password policies, which enables you to apply multiple separate password policies within the same domain

- Support for personal virtual desktops through RemoteApp and Remote Desktop when used with Hyper-V

- AES (Advanced Encryption Services) 128 and 256 Kerberos support

WINDOWS SERVER 2008 R2 FUNCTIONAL LEVEL

The Windows Server 2008 R2 domain functional level requires that all domain controllers are running the Windows Server 2008 R2, Windows Server 2012 or Windows Server 2012 R2 operating systems. This functional level supports the features of the Windows Server 2003 and Windows Server 2008 domain functional levels as well as:

- Managed service account support, which enables you to automatically manage service account passwords rather than manually managing them

- Support for command-line-based Active Directory Recycle Bin if the forest functional level is raised to Windows Server 2008 R2

WINDOWS SERVER 2012 FUNCTIONAL LEVEL

The Windows Server 2012 domain functional level requires that all domain controllers be running the Windows Server 2012 or Windows Server 2012 R2 operating system. This functional level supports the features of all the lower functional levels as well as:

- **Group Managed Service Accounts**   Enables you to install a single managed service account on multiple computers.

- **Fine-Grained Password Policies**   Supports the Active Directory Administrative Center rather than by editing them using ADSI Edit.

- **Active Directory Recycle Bin**   Supports through Active Directory Administrative Center rather than through command-line utilities if the forest is configured at the Windows Server 2012 forest functional level.

- **Key Distribution Center (KDC)**   In addition to support for claims, compound authentication, and Kerberos armoring is set to always provide claims or fail unarmored authentication requests, and they aren't available unless the domain is raised to the Windows Server 2012 functional level.

WINDOWS SERVER 2012 R2 FUNCTIONAL LEVEL

The Windows Server 2012 R2 domain functional level requires that all domain controllers be running the Windows Server 2012 R2 operating system. This functional level supports the features of all the lower functional levels as well as:

- **Domain controller side protection for Protected Users**   Protected Users authenticating against a Windows Server 2012 R2 domain controller are not able to use NTLM authentication, DES or RC4 cipher suites, cannot be delegated with constrained or unconstrained delegation, and cannot renew user tickets beyond the initial four-hour lifetime.

- **Authentication policies** These are new forest-based policies, which you can apply to accounts in domains that control the member computers that a user or service account can sign-on from. These policies also allow you to apply access control conditions for authentication to services running as an account.

- **Authentication policy silos** These silos allow you to create relationships between user, computer, and managed service accounts for the purposes of applying authentication policies or implementing authentication isolation.

Forest functional levels

A forest can host domains running at different domain functional levels. *Forest functional level* is dependent on the minimum domain functional level of any domain in your forest. For example, if your organization has one domain running at the Windows Server 2008 functional level and all other domains running at the Windows Server 2012 functional level, you can't raise the forest functional level beyond Windows Server 2008. After you raise that one domain from the Windows Server 2008 functional level to the Windows Server 2012 domain functional level, you're also able to raise the forest functional level to Windows Server 2012. When you raise the forest functional level, you limit the domain functional levels that can be added to the forest in the future. For example, if the forest functional level is set to Windows Server 2012 R2, all new domains added to the forest must also be set to the Windows Server 2012 R2 domain functional level. The Windows Server 2012 and Windows Server 2012 R2 forest functional levels don't introduce any new features beyond those that were available at the Windows Server 2008 R2 functional level. The Windows Server 2008 R2 functional level introduced the ability to implement the Active Directory Recycle Bin, but otherwise has the same features as the Windows Server 2003 and Windows Server 2008 forest functional levels.

> **MORE INFO FUNCTIONAL LEVELS**
>
> To learn more about functional levels, consult the following article: *http://technet. microsoft.com/en-us/library/understanding-active-directory-functional-levels(v=ws.10). aspx.*

You can raise the forest functional level using the Active Directory Domains and Trusts console, as shown in Figure 1-3, or using the Set-ADForestMode Windows PowerShell cmdlet. You need to use a user account that is a member of the Enterprise Admins group to perform this task. In general you can't lower the forest functional level after you've raised it. The exception to this rule is that you can lower the forest functional level from Windows Server 2012 to Windows Server 2008 R2 if you haven't enabled Active Directory Recycle Bin.

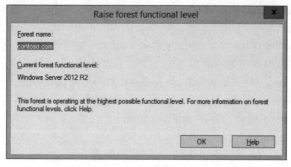

FIGURE 1-3 Raise the forest functional level

Although Active Directory Recycle Bin becomes available at the Windows Server 2008 R2 forest functional level, you need to have configured your organization's forest to be running at the Windows Server 2012 or Windows Server 2012 R2 forest functional level to be able to use the Active Directory Administrative Center interface as opposed to the command-line interface.

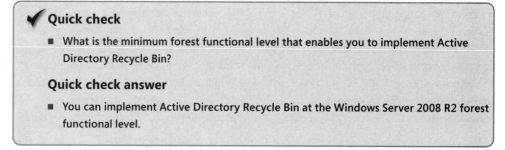

Quick check

- What is the minimum forest functional level that enables you to implement Active Directory Recycle Bin?

Quick check answer

- You can implement Active Directory Recycle Bin at the Windows Server 2008 R2 forest functional level.

Multiforest Active Directory environments

Not only do many organizations have more than one domain in their forest, but some organizations have multiple Active Directory forests. Multiple forests often result when organizations merge, during the period before the acquiring organization has subsumed the acquired organization's infrastructure.

Other reasons for having multiple Active Directory forests within a single organization include:

- **Security requirements** You can ensure that administrators of one part of the organization have no rights over another part of the organization by having each part of the organization in a separate forest.

- **Incompatible schemas** All domains in a forest share a schema. If two separate schemas are required for two different parts of the organization, it is necessary to implement multiple forests.

- **Political requirements** Multinational organizations might have to deal with different jurisdictional requirements. It might be simpler to meet these requirements by having separate forests with trust relationships than it is to attempt to configure domains within the same forest to meet these different compliance benchmarks.

Upgrading existing domains and forests

You can use one of two strategies when upgrading an existing domain so that you can configure it at the Windows Server 2012 R2 functional level:

- The first strategy is to upgrade the operating systems on each domain controller to Windows Server 2012 R2. This method can be problematic because many organizations are running Windows Server 2003 on domain controllers, and you can't directly upgrade Windows Server 2003 to Windows Server 2012 R2. It's also likely that existing domain controllers are running an x86 version of a Windows Server operating system. Windows operating systems never support direct upgrades from x86 versions to x64 versions.

- You can introduce Windows Server 2012 R2 domain controllers into an existing domain and then decommission existing domain controllers running earlier versions of the Windows Server operating system. This method is less complex than performing a direct upgrade. If the hardware supports it, you can repurpose the existing hardware so that the decommissioned domain controllers have a new purpose as Windows Server 2012 R2 domain controllers (although an increasing number of organizations have domain controllers run on virtual machines).

Unlike previous domain controller upgrades, you don't need to run adprep.exe directly to prepare Active Directory for the introduction of domain controllers running Windows Server 2012 or Windows Server 2012 R2. Instead, if you promote the first Windows Server 2012 or Windows Server 2012 R2 domain controller using an account that is a member of the Schema Admins and Enterprise Admins group, the schema upgrade occurs automatically. You need to run adprep.exe separately only if you are performing an in-place upgrade of a domain controller running an x64 version of Windows Server 2008 or Windows Server 2008 R2 and if this upgraded domain controller will be the first Windows Server 2012 or Windows Server 2012 R2 domain controller in the domain.

> *NOTE* **ACTIVE DIRECTORY MIGRATION TOOL**
>
> The Active Directory Migration Tool can assist you in migrating from an existing Active Directory environment rather than upgrading an existing environment. Version 3.2 of the Active Directory Migration Tool isn't supported on Windows Server 2012 or Windows Server 2012 R2.

User principal name (UPN) suffixes

User principal name (UPN) suffixes are the part of a user's UPN that trails the @ symbol. For example, in the UPN don_funk@contoso.com, the UPN suffix is the domain name contoso. com. UPN suffixes enable users to sign on using an account name that includes the name of their domains. Because UPN suffixes look like email addresses, users find them easy to remember. This is useful in complex environments where users might be logging on to computers that are members of domains that are different from the domains that host their accounts. For example, Kim Aker's user account might be located in the accounts.contoso.com domain, but she needs to sign on to a computer that is a member of the computers.contoso. com domain. Rather than having to sign on as accounts\kim_akers as her user name, or selecting the accounts domain from a list, she can instead sign on using the UPN of kim_akers@contoso.com.

By default, all users use the UPN suffix that is the name of the forest root domain, even if their accounts are in a child domain. You configure UPN suffixes using the Active Directory Domains And Trusts console as shown in Figure 1-4.

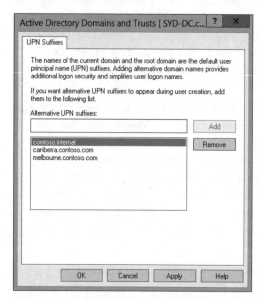

FIGURE 1-4 Configure alternative UPN suffixes

You can configure the UPN suffix associated with a specific user account on the Account tab of the user account's properties through the Active Directory Users And Computers console as shown in Figure 1-5. When you are configuring forest trusts, you can block or allow user authentication based on the UPN suffix.

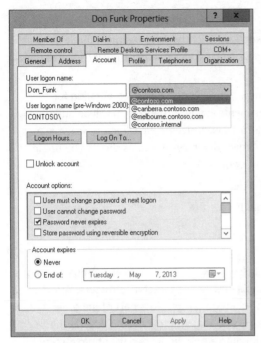

FIGURE 1-5 Configure a specific UPN suffix

MORE INFO UPN SUFFIXES

To learn more about UPN suffixes, consult the following article:
http://technet.microsoft.com/en-us/library/cc772007.aspx.

Lesson summary

- A forest can contain multiple domains. Domain trees build on the same namespace. A forest can contain multiple domain trees.
- No hostname in an Active Directory forest can exceed 64 characters.
- The domain functional level is dependent on the earliest version of the Windows Server operating system used on a domain controller in a domain.
- A domain functional level defines the minimum version of the Windows Server operating system that can be used on domain controllers.
- Each domain in a forest can have a different functional level. The forest functional level depends on the lowest domain functional level in the forest.
- You can configure custom UPN suffixes to simplify the sign-on process for users in multidomain and multiforest environments.

Lesson review

Answer the following questions to test your knowledge of the information in this lesson. You can find the answers to these questions and explanations of each answer choice in the "Answers" section at the end of this chapter.

1. You are in the process of designing a new Active Directory implementation for your organization. Two different departments in your organization will be adopting applications that have separate and mutually exclusive Active Directory schema requirements. Which of the following Active Directory structures should you use in your design to accommodate these requirements?

   A. A single forest with a single domain tree

   B. A single forest with multiple domain trees

   C. Multiple forests

   D. A single domain forest

2. You are the systems administrator for Tailspin Toys and its subsidiary company Wingtip Toys. You are in the process of designing a new Active Directory structure. You've been asked to ensure that employees who work in the Tailspin Toys part of the organization log into a domain named tailspintoys.com and that employees who work in the Wingtip Toys part of the organization log into a domain named wingtiptoys.com. You want to do this in the simplest way possible and minimize the creation of trust relationships. Which of the following Active Directory structures should you use in your design to accommodate these requirements?

   A. A single domain forest

   B. Multiple forests

   C. A single forest with multiple domain trees

   D. A single forest with a single domain tree

3. You want to deploy several domain controllers running the Windows Server 2012 R2 operating system. You will eventually decommission existing domain controllers and bring the domain up to the Windows Server 2012 R2 domain functional level. What is the minimum domain functional level required to support the introduction of domain controllers running the Windows Server 2012 R2 operating system?

   A. Windows Server 2003 domain functional level

   B. Windows Server 2008 domain functional level

   C. Windows Server 2012 domain functional level

   D. Windows Server 2012 R2 domain functional level

4. At which forest functional levels is the Active Directory Recycle Bin available? (Choose all that apply.)

   A. Windows Server 2012 forest functional level

   B. Windows Server 2008 R2 forest functional level

C. Windows Server 2008 forest functional level

D. Windows Server 2003 forest functional level

Lesson 2: Configuring trusts

From time to time it's necessary to connect two different domains so that users who have accounts in one domain are able to access resources in another domain. If those domains are owned by the same organization, the simplest way of doing this is by configuring a trust. In this lesson, you find out how to configure trusts between two different forests, between two separate domains in different forests, and between a domain and a Kerberos realm.

> **After this lesson, you will be able to:**
> - Configure external, forest, shortcut, and realm trusts.
> - Configure trust authentication.
> - Configure SID filtering.
> - Configure name suffix routing.
>
> **Estimated lesson time: 45 minutes**

Trusts

Trusts make it possible for users in one domain to be authenticated by domain controllers in a separate domain. For example, if there is a bidirectional trust relationship between the domains contoso.local and adatum.remote, users with accounts in the contoso.local domain are able to authenticate in the adatum.remote domain. By configuring a trust relationship, it's possible to allow users in one domain to access resources in another, such as being able to use shared folders and printers or being able to sign on locally to machines that are members of a different domain than the one that holds the user's account.

 Some trusts are created automatically. For example, domains in the same forest automatically trust each other. Other trusts, such as *external trusts*, *realm trusts*, *shortcut trusts*, and forest trusts must be created manually. Trusts use the Kerberos V5 authentication protocol by default, and they revert to NTLM if Kerberos V5 is not supported. You configure and manage trusts using the Active Directory Domains And Trusts console or the netdom.exe command-line utility with the /trust switch.

To understand trusts, you need to understand the difference between a *trusting domain or forest* and a *trusted domain or forest*. The trusting domain or forest contains the resources to which you want to grant security principals from the trusted domain or forest access. The trusted domain or forest hosts the security principals that you want to allow to access resources in the trusting forest. For example, if you want to grant users in the adatum.remote domain access to resources in the contoso.local domain, the adatum.remote domain is the trusted domain and the contoso.local domain is the trusting domain. In bidirectional trust relationships a domain or forest is both trusting and trusted.

Trust transitivity

A *transitive trust* is one that extends beyond the original trusting domains. For example, if you have a trust between two domain forests and that trust is transitive, all of the domains in each of the forests trust each other. Forest trusts are transitive by default. External trusts are not transitive by default. When you create a trust, keep in mind that there may be domains beyond the one you are establishing the relationship with that may be included. You might trust the administrator of adatum.remote not to allow access by nefarious users, but do you trust the administrator of subdomain.adatum.remote?

Trust direction

When you create a new trust, you specify a trust direction as shown in Figure 1-6. You can choose a two-way (or bidirectional) trust or a unidirectional trust, which is either one-way incoming or one-way outgoing.

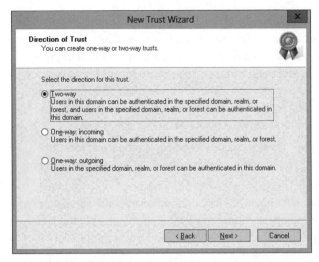

FIGURE 1-6 Specify the trust direction

When you configure a one-way incoming trust, users in the local are authenticated in the remote domain, realm, or forest. Remember that if you are configuring a one-way incoming trust between the single domain forests contoso.local and adatum.remote, users with accounts in contoso.local are able to access resources in adatum.remote. Similarly if you are configuring a one-way outgoing trust between the single domain forests contoso.local and adatum.remote, users with accounts in adatum.remote are able to access resources hosted in contoso.local.

The terminology around trusts can be a little confusing. The key thing to remember is that the direction of trust is the opposite of the direction of access, as shown in Figure 1-7. An outgoing trust allows incoming access, and an incoming trust allows outgoing access.

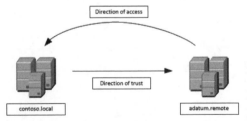

FIGURE 1-7 The direction of trust and direction of access

> **MORE INFO** **TRUST DIRECTION**
>
> To learn more about trust direction, consult the following article:
> *http://technet.microsoft.com/en-us/library/cc731404.aspx.*

Forest trusts

When you configure a forest trust, one Active Directory forest trusts the other one. Forest trusts are transitive. When you configure a forest trust, you can allow any domain in the trusting forest to be accessible to any security principal in the trusted forest. Forest trusts require that each forest be configured to run at the Windows Server 2003 forest functional level or higher. Forest trusts can be bidirectional or unidirectional. You are most likely to configure forest trusts if your organization has two or more Active Directory forests.

You can configure one of two authentications scopes when you configure a forest trust. The type of authentication scope that you configure depends on your security requirements. The options are:

- **Forest-wide authentication** When you choose forest-wide authentication, users from the trusted forest are automatically authenticated for all resources in the local forest. You should use this option when both the trusted and trusting forests are part of the same organization. Figure 1-8 shows a forest trust configured with this type of authentication.

- **Selective authentication** When you configure this option, Windows does not automatically authenticate users from the trusted forest. You can then configure specific servers and domains within the forest to allow users from the trusted forest to authenticate. Use this option when the two forests are from different organizations, or you have more stringent security requirements.

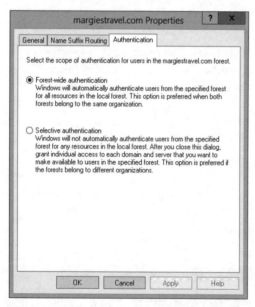

FIGURE 1-8 Configure the authentication type

Configuring selective authentication

Configuring *selective authentication* means granting specific security principals in the trusted forest the Allowed to authenticate (allow) permission on the computer that hosts the resource to which you want to grant access. For example, assume you had configured a forest trust with selective authentication. You want to grant users in the Research universal group from the trusted forest access to a Remote Desktop Services (RDS) server in the trusting forest. To accomplish this goal, you can configure the properties of the RDS server's computer account in Active Directory Users and Computers and grant the Research universal group from the trusted forest the Allowed to authenticate permission as shown in Figure 1-9. Doing this only allows users from this group to authenticate; you still have to grant them access to RDS by adding them to the appropriate local group on the RDS server.

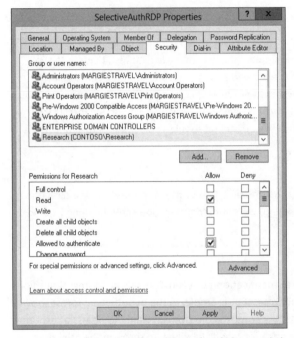

FIGURE 1-9 Configure the Allowed To Authenticate permission

External trusts

External trusts enable you to configure one domain in one forest to trust a domain in another forest without enabling a transitive trust. For example, you configure an external trust if you want to allow the auckland.fabrikam.com domain to have a trust relationship with the wellington.adatum.com domain without allowing any other domains in the fabrikam.com or adatum.com forests to have a security relationship with one another.

You can use external trusts to configure trust relationships with domains running unsupported Windows Server operating systems, such as Windows 2000 Server and Windows NT 4.0, because these operating systems do not support forest trusts. Even though these operating systems are well beyond their supported lifespan, there are still organizations out there with servers, and even domains, running these operating systems. It's possible, however unlikely, that you might need to configure a trust relationship between a domain running these operating systems and one running Windows Server 2012 domain controllers.

 Quick check

- You are the administrator of the single domain contoso.local forest. Users in the adatum.remote single domain forest need to access resources in the contoso.local domain. Users in contoso.local should not have access to resources in adatum.remote. You are configuring an external trust between these two single domain forests from the contoso.local domain. Which trust direction should you configure to support this configuration?

Quick check answer

- One-way outgoing. Remember that the direction of trust is opposite to the direction of authentication. To have incoming users authenticated, you configure an outgoing trust.

Shortcut trusts

 Shortcut trusts enable you to speed up authentication between domains in a forest that might be in separate branches or even separate trees. For example, in the hypothetical forest shown in Figure 1-10, if a user in the canada.atlantic.contoso.com domain wants to access a resource in the arctic.adatum.com domain, authentication needs to travel up through the atlantic. contoso.com and contoso.com domains before passing across to the adatum.com domain and finally back to the arctic.adatum.com. If you implement a shortcut trust between the canada.atlantic.contoso.com and arctic.adatum.com domains, authentication traffic instead travels directly between these two domains without having to traverse the two domain trees in the forest.

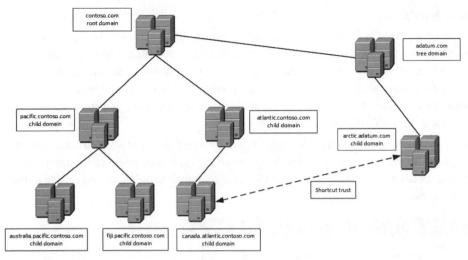

FIGURE 1-10 Shortcut trust

You configure a shortcut trust using the Active Directory Domains And Trusts console by editing the properties of one domain and triggering the New Trust Wizard on the Trusts tab. When the trust is created, it is listed as a shortcut trust as shown in Figure 1-11. Shortcut trusts can be unidirectional or bidirectional. As is the case with the creation of other trusts, ensure that you have name resolution working properly between the trusting and the trusted domains either by having the Domain Name System (DNS) zones propagate through the forest, by configuring conditional forwarders, or by configuring stub zones.

FIGURE 1-11 Trusts tab

Realm trusts

You use a realm trust to create a relationship between an Active Directory Services domain and a Kerberos V5 realm that uses a third-party directory service. Realm trusts can be transitive or nontransitive. They can also be unidirectional or bidirectional. You're most likely to configure a realm trust when you need to allow users who use a UNIX directory service to access resources in an Active Directory domain or users in an Active Directory domain to access resources in a UNIX Kerberos V5 realm.

You can configure a realm trust from the Active Directory Domains And Trust console. You do this by selecting the Realm trust option as shown in Figure 1-12. When configuring a realm trust, you specify a realm trust password that you use when configuring the other side of the trust in the Kerberos V5 realm.

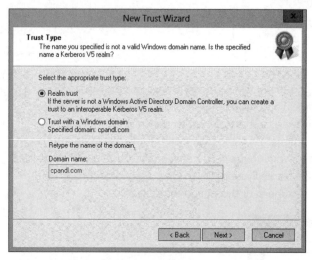

FIGURE 1-12 Configure the Realm Trust

> **MORE INFO REALM TRUSTS**
>
> To learn more about realm trusts, consult the following link: *http://technet.microsoft.com/ en-us/library/cc731297.aspx.*

Netdom.exe

You use Netdom.exe with the /trust switch to create and manage trusts from the command line. When using Netdom.exe, you specify the trusting domain name and the trusted domain name. You can use Netdom.exe with the /trust switch to create and manage forest, shortcut, realm, and external trusts.

The syntax of the Netdom.exe command with the trust switch is shown in Figure 1-13.

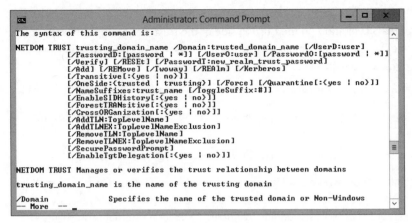

```
                     Administrator: Command Prompt                _ □ X
The syntax of this command is:

NETDOM TRUST trusting_domain_name /Domain:trusted_domain_name [/UserD:user]
            [/PasswordD:[password : *]] [/UserO:user] [/PasswordO:[password : *]]
            [/Verify] [/RESEt] [/PasswordT:new_realm_trust_password]
            [/Add] [/REMove] [/Twoway] [/REAlm] [/Kerberos]
            [/Transitive[:<yes : no>]]
            [/OneSide:<trusted : trusting>] [/Force] [/Quarantine[:<yes : no>]]
            [/NameSuffixes:trust_name [/ToggleSuffix:#]]
            [/EnableSIDHistory[:<yes : no>]]
            [/ForestTRANsitive[:<yes : no>]]
            [/CrossORGanization[:<yes : no>]]
            [/AddTLN:TopLevelName]
            [/AddTLNEX:TopLevelNameExclusion]
            [/RemoveTLN:TopLevelName]
            [/RemoveTLNEX:TopLevelNameExclusion]
            [/SecurePasswordPrompt]
            [/EnableTgtDelegation[:<yes : no>]]

NETDOM TRUST Manages or verifies the trust relationship between domains

trusting_domain_name is the name of the trusting domain

/Domain              Specifies the name of the trusted domain or Non-Windows
-- More --  _
```

FIGURE 1-13 The command syntax for Netdom.exe

At release, Windows PowerShell in Windows Server 2012 and Windows Server 2012 R2 does not include much in the way of cmdlets for creating and managing trust relationships beyond the Get-ADTrust cmdlet.

SID filtering

In a trusted domain, it's possible, though extremely difficult, for you to configure an account in your domain to have SIDs that are identical to those used by privileged accounts in a trusting domain. If you use this configuration, then the accounts from trusted domains gain the privileges of the accounts in the trusting domain. For example, you can configure the SIDs of an account in a trusted domain so that it has domain administrator privileges in the trusting domain.

To block this type of configuration, Windows Server 2012 and Windows Server 2012 R2 enable *SID filtering*, also known as *domain quarantine*, on all external trusts. SID filtering blocks users in a trusted forest or domain from being able to grant themselves elevated user rights in the trusting forest domain by discarding all SIDs that do not have the domain SID of the trusting domain.

It's possible to verify SID filtering settings on a trust using the Get-ADTrust cmdlet in a Windows PowerShell session run by a user with administrative privileges. For example, to verify that SID filtering is enabled on the trust with the margiestravel.com forest, issue the command:

```
Get-ADTrust margiestravel.com | fl *SID*
```

To disable SID filtering for the trusting forest, use the netdom trust command with the following option:

```
/enablesidhistory:Yes
```

Enabling SID history allows SIDs that don't have the domain SID of the trusting domain. You enable or disable SID filtering on the trusting side of the trust. For example, if you are an administrator in the contoso.com domain and you want to disable SID filtering, you can issue the following command from an elevated command prompt:

```
Netdom trust contoso.com /domain:margiestravel.com /enablesidhistory:Yes
```

In the same scenario, if you want to re-enable SID filtering, you can issue the following command:

```
Netdom trust contoso.com /domain:margiestravel.com /enablesidhistory:Yes
```

The default configuration, where SID filtering is enforced by default on trusts, is something that you should probably leave as it is. In the past it was necessary to allow SID history when trusts were created with forests running Windows 2000 Server domain controllers. As Windows 2000 is no longer supported by Microsoft, and SID history is not necessary for trust relationships with Windows Server 2003, Windows Server 2003 R2, Windows Server 2008, Windows Server 2008 R2, Windows Server 2012 or Windows Server 2012 R2 domain controllers, you probably won't need to disable it.

> **MORE INFO** **SID FILTER QUARANTINING ON EXTERNAL TRUSTS**
>
> To learn more about SID filtering, consult the following link: *http://technet.microsoft.com/ en-us/library/cc794757(v=ws.10).aspx.*

Name suffix routing

Name suffix routing enables you to configure how authentication requests are routed when you configure a forest trust between two Active Directory forests. When you create a forest trust, all unique name suffixes are routed. Name suffix routing assists users when they sign on with a UPN, such as don_funk@contoso.com. Depending upon the UPNs that are configured, you might want to allow or disallow the use of specific UPN suffixes. You do this by configuring name suffix routing on the Name Suffix Routing tab of the trust's properties as shown in Figure 1-14.

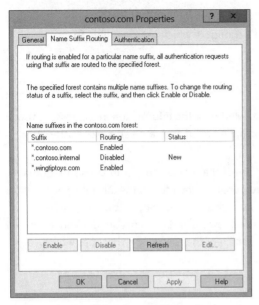

FIGURE 1-14 Configure name suffix routing

> **MORE INFO** **NAME SUFFIX ROUTING**
>
> To learn more about name suffix routing, consult the following link: *http://technet. microsoft.com/en-us/library/cc731648.aspx.*

Lesson summary

- Trusts can be unidirectional or bidirectional. A one-way outgoing trust allows users in the remote domain to access resources in the local domain. A one-way incoming trust allows users in the local domain to access resources in the remote domain.

- Trust transitivity allows access to resources in child domains of the trusting domain.

- A forest trust allows one forest to trust another forest. This means that all domains in the first forest have a trust relationship with all domains in the second forest.

- Selective authentication in a forest trust enables you to limit which users and groups from the trusted domain are able to authenticate.

- An external trust is a trust between domains in different forests. External trusts are not transitive. You can configure external trusts to connect to Windows 2000 Server and Windows NT 4 domains.

- You use a realm trust when you want to configure a trust between an Active Directory domain and a Kerberos V5 realm.

- You can use a shortcut trust between domains in the same forest to speed the authentication process.

- SID filtering is enabled by default on all new external and forest trusts.
- You can configure name suffix routing to configure which users are able to authenticate in a forest.

Lesson review

Answer the following questions to test your knowledge of the information in this lesson. You can find the answers to these questions and explanations of each answer choice in the "Answers" section at the end of this chapter.

1. You have a 30-domain Active Directory forest that has contoso.com as its root domain. This forest has five separate domain trees. Users in the Melbourne.australia.pacific. contoso.com domain report that there are substantial authentication delays when they try to access resources in the Auckland.newzealand.adatum.com domain. Both domains are located in the same forest. Which of the following trust types would you configure to resolve this problem?

   A. Forest trust

   B. External trust

   C. Realm trust

   D. Shortcut trust

2. You are a systems administrator at a local university. The university has a deployment of Linux servers and workstations that are members of a Kerberos V5 realm. You want to allow users of the Linux workstations to have access to several file shares hosted in one of your organization's Active Directory domains. Which of the following trust types would you implement to accomplish this goal?

   A. Shortcut trust

   B. Realm trust

   C. Forest trust

   D. External trust

3. Your organization recently acquired a subsidiary company. Your organization currently has a 10-domain Active Directory forest running at the Windows Server 2012 R2 functional level. The subsidiary company has a five-domain Active Directory forest running at the Windows Server 2008 functional level. The subsidiary company has implemented a number of schema modifications to support a custom application. You want to allow users in the subsidiary company to be able to access resources hosted in your organization's forest. Users in your organization's forest should also be able to access resources in the subsidiary company's forest. Which of the following trust relationships should you configure to accomplish this goal?

   A. External trust

   B. Forest trust

C. Realm trust

D. Shortcut trust

4. You are the senior systems administrator of the contoso.com forest. Users in the australia.pacific.contoso.com domain need access to resources hosted in one domain of a partner organization's Active Directory forest. These users shouldn't have access to any other domain in the partner organization's forest. Users from other domains in your organization's forest should also not have access to resources in the partner organization's forest. Which of the following trust types would you configure in this scenario?

A. External trust

B. Realm trust

C. Shortcut trust

D. Forest trust

Practice exercises

The goal of this section is to provide you with hands-on practice with the following:

- Creating a forest trust
- Configuring name suffix routing
- Configuring selective authentication
- Configuring UPN suffixes
- Configuring a shortcut trust

To perform the exercises in this section, you need access to an evaluation version of Windows Server 2012 R2. You should also have access to virtual machines SYD-DC, MEL-DC, CBR-DC, and ADL-DC, the setup instructions for which are described in the Introduction. You should ensure that you have a checkpoint of these virtual machines that you can revert to at the end of the practice exercises.

Exercise 1: Prepare a domain controller to host a child domain with a contiguous namespace

In this exercise, you prepare CBR-DC to function as a domain controller for a child domain of the contoso.com domain. To complete this exercise, perform the following steps:

1. Power on SYD-DC and log in as **contoso\don_funk** with the password **Pa$$w0rd**.

2. Click the Tools menu in the Server Manager console, and click DNS.

3. In the DNS Manager console, expand SYD-DC and Forward Lookup Zones.

4. Verify that the following lookup zones are present as shown in Figure 1-15:

   - _msdcs.contoso.com
   - contoso.com

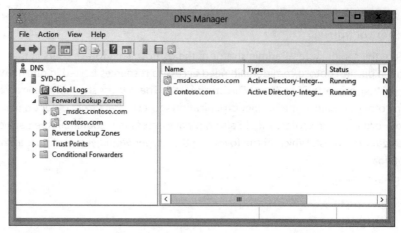

FIGURE 1-15 Verify the DNS configuration

5. Power on CBR-DC and sign on as **Administrator** with the password **Pa$$w0rd**.

6. In Server Manager, click the Local Server node.

7. In the Properties area, click 10.10.10.30 next to Ethernet.

8. In the Network Connections window, right-click Ethernet and click Properties.

9. In the Ethernet Properties dialog box, click Internet Protocol Version 4 (TCP/IPv4) and click Properties.

10. Verify that the Preferred DNS Server is set to 10.10.10.10, as shown in Figure 1-16, click OK, and then click Close.

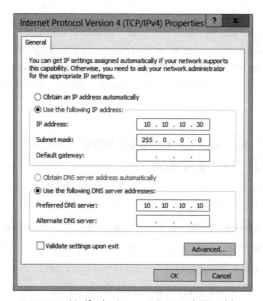

FIGURE 1-16 Verify the Internet Protocol (IP) address configuration

11. In the Server Manager console, click Manage and then click Add Roles And Features.

12. On the Before You Begin page of the Add Roles And Features Wizard, click Next three times.

13. On the Select Server Roles page, click the Active Directory Domain Services check box as shown in Figure 1-17.

14. On the Add Roles And Features Wizard, click Add Features.

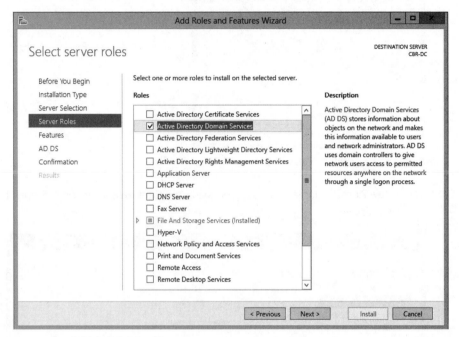

FIGURE 1-17 Add the AD DS role

15. On the Select Server Roles page, click Next three times and click Install. When the installation completes, click Close.

Exercise 2: Create a child domain with a contiguous namespace

In this exercise, you configure CBR-DC to host the Canberra.contoso.com child domain. To complete this exercise, perform the following steps:

1. In the Server Manager console on CBR-DC, click the Notifications item and then click Promote This Server To A Domain Controller.

2. On the Deployment Configuration page, click Add A New Domain To An Existing Forest.

3. On the Select Domain Type drop-down menu, select Child Domain.

4. Click Select next to Parent Domain Name.

5. In the Windows Security dialog box, type the user name **contoso\don_funk**, type the password **Pa$$w0rd**, and click OK.

6. In the Select A Domain From The Forest dialog box, click Contoso.com as shown in Figure 1-18 and then click OK.

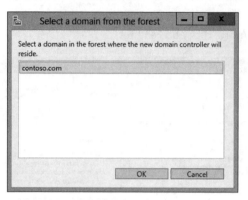

FIGURE 1-18 Select the domain in the forest

7. In the New Domain Name text box, type the name **Canberra** as shown in Figure 1-19 and then click Next.

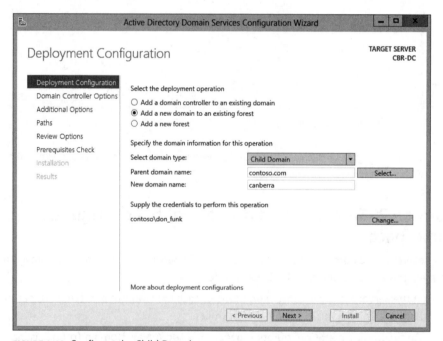

FIGURE 1-19 Configure the Child Domain

8. On the Domain Controller Options page, set the DSRM password as **Pa$$w0rd** in both the Password and Confirm Password dialog boxes and click Next.

9. On the DNS Options page, ensure that the settings match those in Figure 1-20 and click Next.

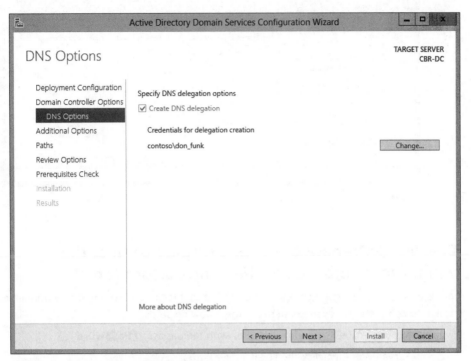

FIGURE 1-20 Configure the delegation credentials

10. On the Additional Options page, verify that the NetBIOS domain name is set to CANBERRA, click Next three times, and click Install.

11. After CBR-DC restarts, sign on as **Canberra\Administrator** with the password **Pa$$w0rd**.

12. Switch to SYD-DC. In the DNS console, expand the contoso.com zone and verify the presence of the canberra.contoso.com zone as shown in Figure 1-21.

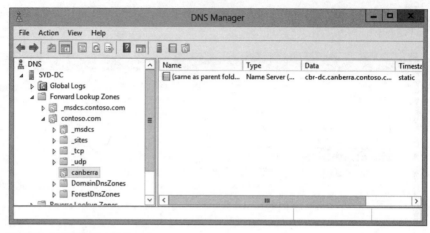

FIGURE 1-21 Verify the DNS zone

Exercise 3: Prepare domain controller to host the wingtiptoys.com tree in the contoso.com forest

In this exercise, you prepare computer ADL-DC so that it can be promoted to a domain controller. To complete this exercise, perform the following steps:

1. Sign on to ADL-DC as **Administrator** with the password **Pa$$w0rd**.

2. In Server Manager, click the Local Server node.

3. In the Properties area, click 10.10.10.20 next to Ethernet.

4. In the Network Connections window, right-click Ethernet and click Properties.

5. In the Ethernet Properties dialog box, click Internet Protocol Version 4 (TCP/IPv4) and click Properties.

6. Verify that the Preferred DNS server is set to 10.10.10.10 and then click OK. Click Close.

7. In the Server Manager console, click Manage and then click Add Roles And Features.

8. On the Before You Begin page of the Add Roles And Features Wizard, click Next three times.

9. On the Select Server Roles page, click the Active Directory Domain Services check box.

10. On the Add Roles And Features Wizard, click Add Features.

11. On the Select Server Roles page, click Next three times and click Install. When the installation completes, click Close.

Exercise 4: Promote domain controller for new tree in contoso.com forest

In this exercise, you promote ADL-DC to domain controller of a new domain tree in an existing Active Directory forest. To complete this exercise, perform the following steps:

1. In the Server Manager console on ADL-DC, click the Notifications item and then click Promote This Server To A Domain Controller.

2. On the Deployment Configuration page, click Add A New Domain To An Existing Forest.

3. On the Select Domain Type drop-down menu, click Tree Domain.

4. In the Forest Name textbox, type **contoso.com**.

5. In the New Domain Name textbox, type **wingtiptoys.com**.

6. Next to <No Credentials Provided>, click Change.

7. On the Windows Security dialog box, type the user name as **contoso\don_funk**, type the password as **Pa$$w0rd**, and click OK.

8. Verify that the Deployment Configuration page matches Figure 1-22 and then click Next.

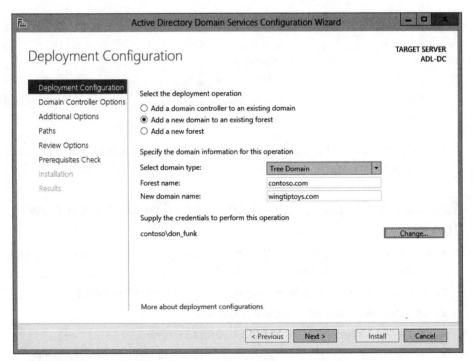

FIGURE 1-22 Add a domain tree

9. On the Domain Controller Options page, type the DSRM password **Pa$$w0rd** in both the Password and Confirm Password text boxes and then click Next.

10. On the DNS Options page, review the warning and click Next.

11. On the Additional Options page, verify that the NetBIOS name is set to WINGTIPTOYS as shown in Figure 1-23. Click Next three times and then click Install.

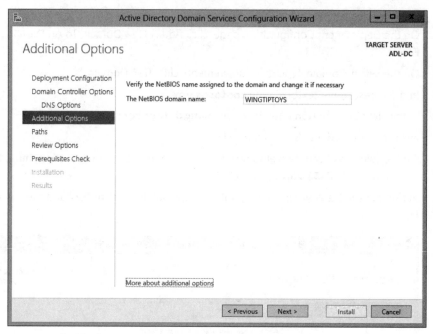

FIGURE 1-23 Verify the NetBIOS name

12. After the computer restarts, sign in as **WINGTIPTOYS\Administrator** with the password **Pa$$w0rd**.

Exercise 5: Prepare a domain controller to host a new forest

In this exercise, you configure MEL-DC so that it is able to host the new forest margiestravel. com. To complete this exercise, perform the following steps:

1. Sign on to MEL-DC as **Administrator** with the password **Pa$$w0rd**.

2. In Server Manager, click the Local Server node.

3. In the Properties area, click 10.10.10.40 next to Ethernet.

4. In the Network Connections window, right-click Ethernet and click Properties.

5. In the Ethernet Properties dialog box, click Internet Protocol Version 4 (TCP/IPv4) and click Properties.

6. Verify that the Preferred DNS server is set to 10.10.10.10, click OK, and then click Close.

7. In the Server Manager console, click Manage and then click Add Roles And Features.

8. On the Before You Begin page of the Add Roles And Features Wizard, click Next three times.

9. On the Select Server Roles page, click the Active Directory Domain Services checkbox.

10. On the Add Roles And Features Wizard, click Add Features.

11. On the Select Server Roles page, click Next three times and then click Install. When the installation completes, click Close.

Exercise 6: Create new forest

In this exercise, you configure MEL-DC as the first domain controller in a new forest. To complete this exercise, perform the following steps:

1. In the Server Manager console on MEL-DC, click the Notifications item and then click Promote This Server To A Domain Controller.

2. On the Deployment Configuration page, click Add A New Forest.

3. In the Root Domain Name textbox, type **margiestravel.com** as shown in Figure 1-24 and click Next.

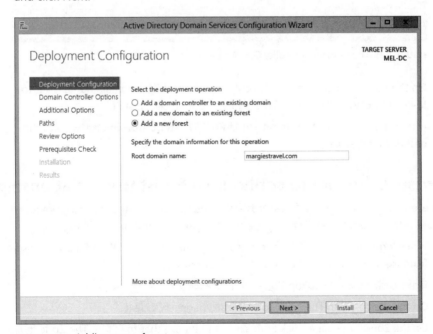

FIGURE 1-24 Adding a new forest

4. On the Domain Controller Options page, ensure that Domain Name System (DNS) server is selected and that you type the DSRM password of **Pa$$word** twice as shown in Figure 1-25. Click Next twice.

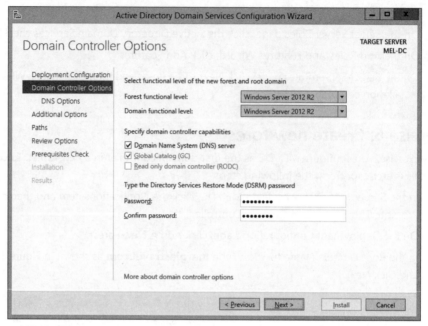

FIGURE 1-25 The Domain Controller Options page

5. On the Additional Options page, verify that the NetBIOS domain name is set to MARGIESTRAVEL, click Next three times, and then click Install.

6. After the server restarts, sign on as **MARGIESTRAVEL\Administrator** with the password **Pa$$w0rd**.

Exercise 7: Prepare to configure a forest trust relationship

In this exercise, you configure a forest trust relationship between the contoso.com forest and the margiestravel.com forest. To complete this exercise, perform the following steps:

1. While logged onto SYD-DC as contoso\don_funk, open the DNS Manager console from the Tools menu in the Server Manager console.

2. Right-click Forward Lookup Zones and click New Zone.

3. On the Welcome To The New Zone Wizard page, click Next.

4. On the Zone Type page, click Stub Zone and ensure that the Store The Zone In Active Directory check box is selected as shown in Figure 1-26. Click Next.

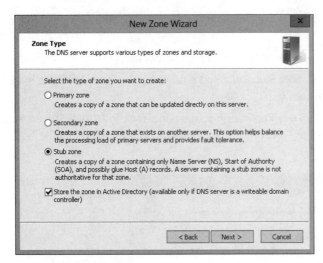

FIGURE 1-26 Configure the zone type

5. On the Active Directory Zone Replication Scope page, click To All DNS Servers Running On Domain Controllers In This Forest: contoso.com and click Next.

6. In the Zone Name text box, type **margiestravel.com** and click Next.

7. On the Master DNS Servers page, type the IP address **10.10.10.40** in the list of master servers as shown in Figure 1-27, click Next, and then click Finish.

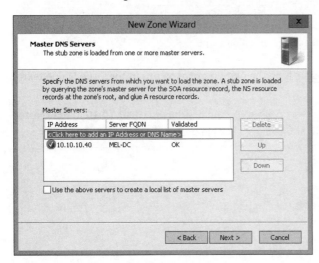

FIGURE 1-27 Configure the stub zone master servers

8. On MEL-DC, ensure that you are signed in as **MARGIESTRAVEL\Administrator** with the password **Pa$$w0rd**.

9. Open the DNS Manager console from the Tools menu in the Server Manager console.

10. In the DNS Manager console, right-click on Forward Lookup Zones and click New Zone.

11. On the Welcome To The New Zone Wizard page, click Next.

12. On the Zone Type page, click Stub Zone and ensure that the Store The Zone In Active Directory check box is selected. Click Next.

13. On the Active Directory Zone Replication Scope page, click To All DNS Servers Running On Domain Controllers In This Forest: Margiestravel.com as shown in Figure 1-28. Click Next.

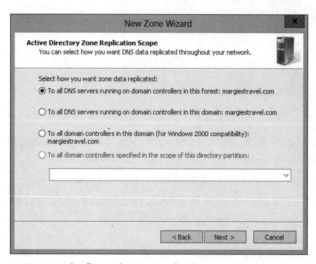

FIGURE 1-28 Configure the zone replication scope

14. On the Zone Name page, type the name **contoso.com in** the Zone Name textbox and click Next.

15. On the Master DNS Servers page, type the IP address **10.10.10.10** in the Master Servers list as shown in Figure 1-29, click Next, and click Finish.

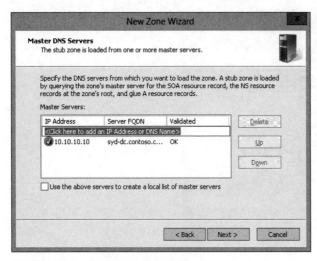

FIGURE 1-29 Configure the master DNS servers

Exercise 8: Begin creating a forest trust relationship

In this exercise, you configure the contoso.com side of a forest trust relationship between the contoso.com and margiestravel.com forests. To complete this exercise, perform the following steps:

1. On the Tools menu of the Server Manager console on SYD-DC, click Active Directory Domains And Trusts.

2. In the Active Directory Domains And Trusts console, right-click Contoso.com and click Properties.

3. On the Trusts tab of the Contoso.com Properties dialog box, shown in Figure 1-30, click New Trust.

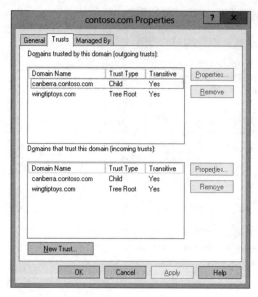

FIGURE 1-30 Create the new trust

4. On the Welcome To The New Trust Wizard page, click Next.

5. On the Trust Name page, type **margiestravel.com** as shown in Figure 1-31, and click Next.

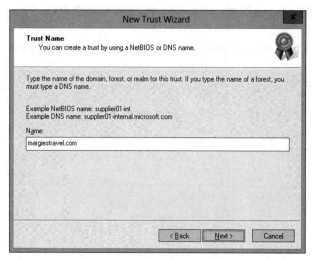

FIGURE 1-31 Set the trust name

6. On the Trust Type page, select the Forest Trust option as shown in Figure 1-32 and click Next.

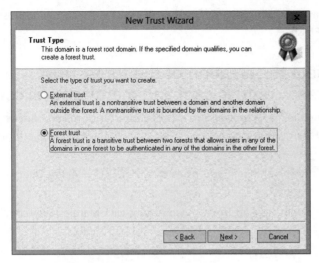

FIGURE 1-32 Configure the trust type

7. On the Direction Of Trust page, click Two-Way and click Next.

8. On the Sides Of Trust page, click This Domain Only and then click Next.

9. On the Outgoing Trust Authentication Level page, click the Forest-Wide Authentication option as shown in Figure 1-33 and click Next.

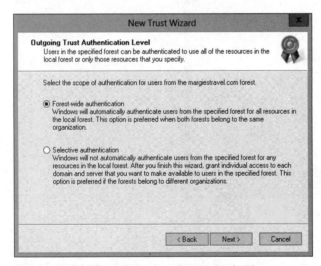

FIGURE 1-33 Configure the trust authentication level

10. On the Trust Password page, type **Pa$$w0rd** in the Trust Password and Confirm Trust Password text boxes. Click Next three times.

11. On the Confirm Outgoing Trust page, click No, Do Not Confirm The Outgoing Trust and click Next.

12. On the Confirm Incoming Trust page, click No, Do Not Confirm The Incoming Trust, click Next, and click Finish.

Exercise 9: Complete the creation of the forest trust relationship between contoso.com and margiestravel.com

In this exercise, you configure the margiestravel.com side of a forest trust relationship between the contoso.com and margiestravel.com forests. To complete this exercise, perform the following steps:

1. In the Tools menu of the Server Manager console on MEL-DC, click Active Directory Domains And Trusts.

2. In the Active Directory Domains And Trusts console, right-click Margiestravel.com and click Properties.

3. On the Trusts tab of the Margiestravel.com Properties dialog box, shown in Figure 1-34, click New Trust.

FIGURE 1-34 View the current trusts

4. On the Welcome To The New Trust Wizard page, click Next.

5. On the Trust Name page of the New Trust Wizard, type **contoso.com** in the Name text box and click Next.

6. On the Trust Type page, click Forest Trust and click Next.

7. On the Direction Of Trust page, click Two-Way as shown in Figure 1-35 and click Next.

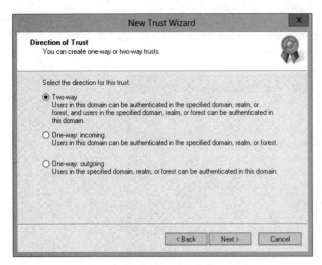

FIGURE 1-35 Configure the direction of the trust

8. On the Sides Of Trust page, click This Domain Only and click Next.

9. On the Outgoing Trust Authentication Level page, click Forest-Wide Authentication and click Next.

10. On the Trust Password page, type **Pa$$w0rd** in the Trust Password and Confirm Trust Password text boxes. Click Next three times.

11. On the Confirm Outgoing Trust page, click Yes, Confirm the Outgoing Trust as shown in Figure 1-36, and click Next.

FIGURE 1-36 Confirm the outgoing trust

12. On the Confirm Incoming Trust page, click Yes, Confirm The Incoming Trust. In the User Name text box, type **contoso\don_funk** and in the Password text box type **Pa$$w0rd** as shown in Figure 1-37. Click Next.

FIGURE 1-37 Confirm the incoming trust

13. On the Completing The New Trust Wizard page verify that the trust is successfully created as shown in Figure 1-38 and click Finish. Click OK to close the Margiestravel.com Properties dialog box.

FIGURE 1-38 Confirm the trust creation

Exercise 10: Configure name suffix routing

In this exercise, you configure the forest trust between the margiestravel.com forest and the contoso.com forest so that name suffix routing is supported for the wingtiptoys.com domain tree. To complete this exercise, perform the following steps:

1. In the Active Directory Domains and Trusts console on MEL-DC, right-click Margiestravel.com and click Properties.

2. On the Trusts tab of the Margiestravel.com Properties dialog box, click Contoso.com in the Domains Trusted By This Domain (Outgoing Trusts) area, as shown in Figure 1-39, and then click Properties.

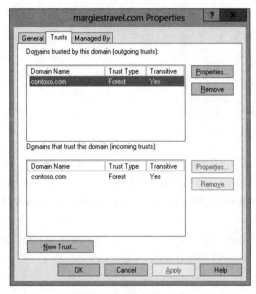

FIGURE 1-39 Editing the properties of trusts

3. On the Name Suffix Routing tab of the Contoso.com Properties dialog box, click *.wingtiptoys.com and then click Enable as shown in Figure 1-40.

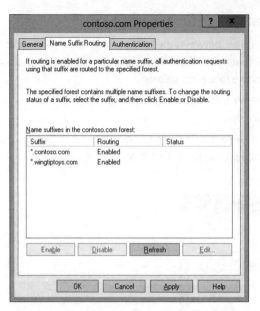

FIGURE 1-40 Configure the Name Suffix Routing

4. On the General tab of the Contoso.com Properties dialog box, click Validate.

5. On the Active Directory Domain Services dialog box, click Yes, Validate The Incoming Trust by entering the user name **contoso\don_funk** and the password **Pa$$w0rd,** and click OK.

6. Click OK on the Active Directory Domain Services dialog box and then click Yes on the second Active Directory Domain Services dialog box.

7. Click OK to close the Contoso.com Properties dialog box.

8. Click Contoso.com on the list of Domains That Trust This Domain (Incoming Trusts) dialog box as shown in Figure 1-41 and then click Properties.

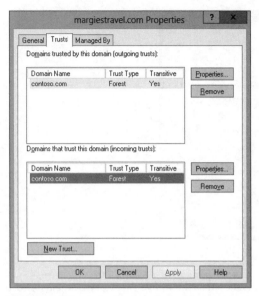

FIGURE 1-41 Trusts for the margiestravel.com domain

9. On the Name Suffix Routing tab of the Contoso.com Properties dialog box verify that both *.contoso.com and *.wingtiptoys.com are enabled and then click OK.

10. Click OK to close the Margiestravel.com Properties dialog box.

Exercise 11: Configure selective authentication

In this exercise, you configure selective authentication. You configure the trust to use selective authentication, create a user group in one forest, and create a computer account in the other forest. You then configure the computer account so that members of the user group in the trusted forest can authenticate when connecting to that computer. To complete this exercise, perform the following steps:

1. When signed on to SYD-DC as **contoso\don_funk**, click Active Directory Users And Computers on the Tools menu of the Server Manager console.

2. In Active Directory Users And Computers, right-click the Users container, click New, and click Group.

3. On the New Object – Group dialog box, type the group name as **Research**, set the group scope to Universal as shown in Figure 1-42, and click OK.

FIGURE 1-42 Create a new universal group

4. On MEL-DC, right-click Margiestravel.com in the Active Directory Domains And Trust console and click Properties.

5. On the Trusts tab of the Margiestravel.com Properties dialog box, click Contoso.com in the Domains That Trust This Domain (Incoming Trusts) list and click Properties.

6. On the Authentication tab of the Contoso.com Properties dialog box, click Selective Authentication as shown in Figure 1-43.

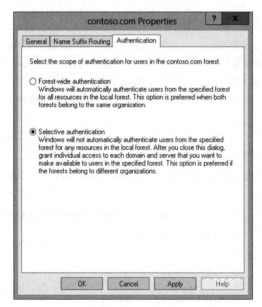

FIGURE 1-43 Configure selective authentication

7. On the General tab of the Contoso.com Properties dialog box, shown in Figure 1-44, click Validate.

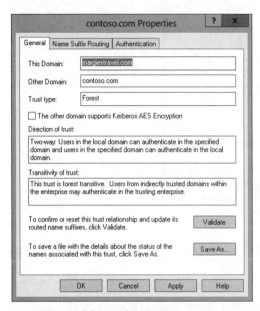

FIGURE 1-44 Validate authentication

8. On the Active Directory Domain Services dialog box, click Yes to validate the incoming trust. Enter the user name as **contoso\don_funk**, type the password as **Pa$$w0rd**, and then click OK twice.

9. Click Yes on the Active Directory Domain Services dialog box and then click OK twice to close the Contoso.com Properties and Margiestravel.com Properties dialog boxes.

10. Click Active Directory Users And Computers in the Tools menu of the Server Manager console.

11. Right-click the Computers node and click New and then click Computer.

12. In the New Object – Computer dialog box, type the name **SelectiveAuthRDP** as shown in Figure 1-45 and click OK.

FIGURE 1-45 Create new computer object

13. Enabled Advanced Features on the View menu of the Active Directory Users And Computers console.

14. Right-click the SelectiveAuthRDP computer object and click Properties.

15. On the Security tab of the SelectiveAuthRDP Properties dialog box, shown in Figure 1-46, click Add.

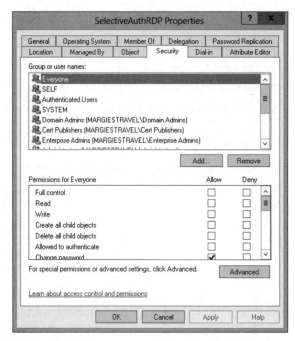

FIGURE 1-46 Add a user

16. On the Select Users, Computers, Service Accounts, Or Groups dialog box, click Locations.

17. On the Locations dialog box, click Contoso.com as shown in Figure 1-47 and then click OK.

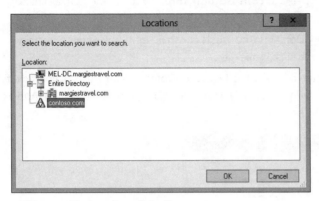

FIGURE 1-47 The Locations dialog box

18. In the Select Users, Computers, Service Accounts, Or Groups dialog box, type **Research**, click Check Names, and click OK.

19. On the SelectiveAuthRDP Properties dialog box, click Research (Contoso\Research) and click the Allow check box next to the Allowed To Authenticatepermission as shown in Figure 1-48. Click OK.

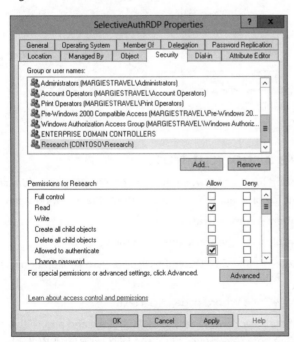

FIGURE 1-48 Configure Allowed to authenticate permission

Exercise 12: Configure additional UPN suffixes

In this exercise, you configure additional UPN suffixes. To complete this exercise, perform the following steps:

1. When signed on to SYD-DC as **contoso\don_funk**, switch to the Active Directory Domains And Trusts console.

2. In the Active Directory Domains And Trusts console, right-click Active Directory Domains And Trusts and click Properties.

3. On the UPN Suffixes tab of the Active Directory Domains And Trusts dialog box, type **contoso.internal** in the Alternative UPN suffixes dialog box and then click Add as shown in Figure 1-49. Click OK.

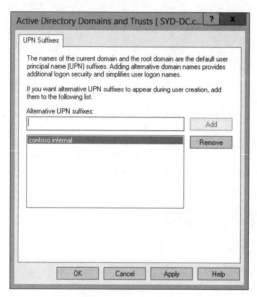

FIGURE 1-49 Configure a UPN suffix

Exercise 13: Configure a shortcut trust

In this exercise, you configure a shortcut trust between the Canberra.contoso.com domain and the wingtiptoys.com domain. To complete this exercise, perform the following steps:

1. Sign on to CBR-DC as **canberra\administrator**.

2. In the Server Manager console, click the Tools menu and then click DNS.

3. In the DNS Manager console, expand CBR-DC, right-click Forward Lookup Zones, and click New Zone.

4. On the Welcome To The New Zone Wizard page, click Next.

5. On the Zone Type page of the New Zone Wizard, click Stub Zone and ensure that the Store The Zone In Active Directory (Available Only If The DNS server Is A Writable Domain Controller) check box is selected as shown in Figure 1-50 and click Next twice.

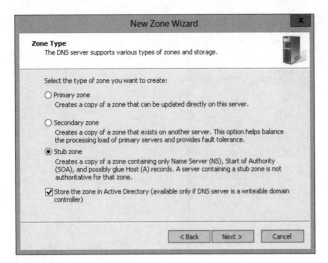

FIGURE 1-50 Create a stub zone

6. On the Zone name page, type **wingtiptoys.com** and click Next.

7. On the Master DNS Servers page, type **10.10.10.20** in the list of master DNS servers and press Enter as shown in Figure 1-51. Click Next and then click Finish.

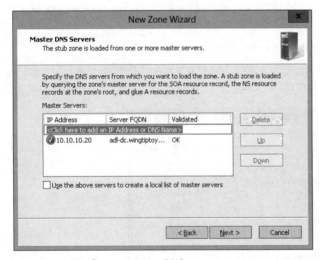

FIGURE 1-51 Configure a master DNS server

8. In the Server Manager console, click the Tools menu and then click Active Directory Domains And Trusts.

9. In the Active Directory Domains And Trusts console, expand the Contoso.com node, right-click Canberra.contoso.com, and click Properties.

10. On the Trusts tab of the Canberra.contoso.com Properties dialog box, show in Figure 1-52, click New Trust.

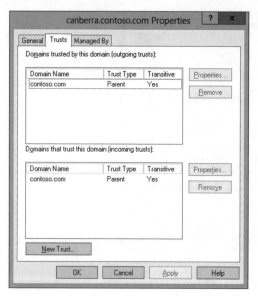

FIGURE 1-52 Create a new trust

11. On the Welcome To The New Trust Wizard page, click Next.

12. On the Trust Name page of the New Trust Wizard, type **wingtiptoys.com** and click Next.

13. On the Direction Of Trust page, click Two-Way and click Next.

14. On the Sides Of Trust page, click Both This Domain And The Specified Domain as shown in Figure 1-53 and click Next.

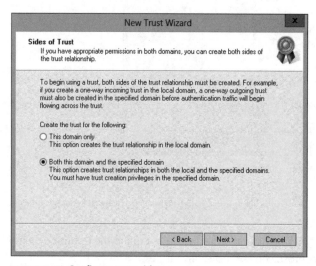

FIGURE 1-53 Configure trust sides

15. On the User Name And Password page, type **wingtiptoys\administrator** in the user name text box, type **Pa$$w0rd** in the password text box, and click Next three times.

16. On the Confirm Outgoing Trust page, click Yes, Confirm The Outgoing Trust as shown in Figure 1-54, and click Next.

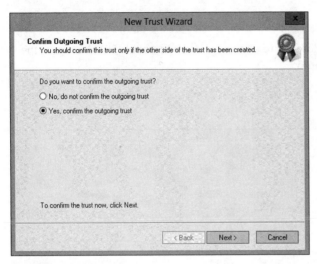

FIGURE 1-54 Confirm the trust

17. On the Confirm Incoming Trust page, click Yes, Confirm The Incoming Trust and click Next.

18. Verify that the trust relationship was successfully created and click Finish.

19. Verify that the Wingtiptoys.com trust is listed as a shortcut trust as shown in Figure 1-55 and then click OK.

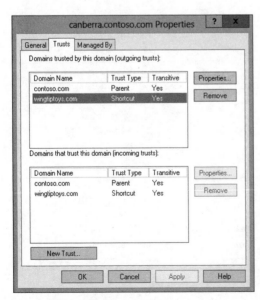

FIGURE 1-55 Verify the trust type

Suggested practice exercises

The following additional practice exercises are designed to give you more opportunities to practice what you've learned and to help you successfully master the lessons presented in this chapter.

- **Exercise 1:** Configure additional UPN suffixes for the margiestravel.com forest.
- **Exercise 2:** Use Netdom.exe to disable and then re-enable SID filtering on the margiestravel.com forest.

Answers

This section contains the answers to the lesson review questions in this chapter.

Lesson 1

1. **Correct answer:** C

   A. **Incorrect.** This structure does not support the two different departments that have mutually exclusive Active Directory schema requirements. This structure supports only one Active Directory schema.

   B. **Incorrect.** This structure does not support the two different departments that have mutually exclusive Active Directory schema requirements. This structure supports only one Active Directory schema.

   C. **Correct.** This structure supports the two different departments that have mutually exclusive Active Directory schema requirements because each forest has a separate schema.

   D. **Incorrect.** This structure does not support the two different departments that have mutually exclusive Active Directory schema requirements. This structure supports only one Active Directory schema.

2. **Correct answer:** C

   A. **Incorrect.** You need more than one domain to support the two separate domain names.

   B. **Incorrect.** Implementing this solution requires the creation of additional trust relationships when compared to using a single forest with multiple domain trees.

   C. **Correct.** You can accomplish this objective with a design that uses two domain trees, one for wingtiptoys.com and one for tailspintoys.com.

   D. **Incorrect.** With a single domain tree, a child domain of the root domain needs to use a contiguous namespace. The requirements are that two domains with noncontiguous namespaces be available, which means at least two domain trees.

3. **Correct answer:** A

   A. **Correct.** You can add domain controllers running the Windows Server 2012 R2 operating system to a domain running at the Windows Server 2003 functional level.

   B. **Incorrect.** You can add domain controllers running the Windows Server 2012 R2 operating system to a domain running at the Windows Server 2003 functional level.

   C. **Incorrect.** You can add domain controllers running the Windows Server 2012 R2 operating system to a domain running at the Windows Server 2003 functional level.

D. Incorrect. You can add domain controllers running the Windows Server 2012 R2 operating system to a domain running at the Windows Server 2003 functional level.

4. **Correct answers:** A and B

   A. Correct. The Active Directory Recycle Bin is available at the Windows Server 2008 R2 and Windows Server 2012 forest functional levels.

   B. Correct. The Active Directory Recycle Bin is available at the Windows Server 2008 R2 and Windows Server 2012 forest functional levels.

   C. Incorrect. The Active Directory Recycle Bin is available at the Windows Server 2008 R2 and Windows Server 2012 forest functional levels.

   D. Incorrect. The Active Directory Recycle Bin is available at the Windows Server 2008 R2 and Windows Server 2012 forest functional levels.

Lesson 2

1. **Correct answer:** D

   A. Incorrect. A forest trust is created between two forests when you want users in each forest to access resources in the counterpart forest. In this instance you need to create a shortcut trust between two domains in the same forest.

   B. Incorrect. You configure an external trust between two domains in different forests, often when you don't want to allow the trust to be transitive. In this instance you need to create a shortcut trust between two domains in the same forest.

   C. Incorrect. You configure a realm trust between an Active Directory domain and a Kerberos V5 realm. In this instance you need to create a shortcut trust between two domains in the same forest.

   D. Correct. In this instance you need to create a shortcut trust between two domains in the same forest.

2. **Correct answer:** B

   A. Incorrect. In this instance you need to create a shortcut trust between two domains in the same forest. You configure a realm trust between an Active Directory domain and a Kerberos V5 realm.

   B. Correct. You configure a realm trust between an Active Directory domain and a Kerberos V5 realm.

   C. Incorrect. A forest trust is created between two forests when you want users in each forest to access resources in the counterpart forest. You configure a realm trust between an Active Directory domain and a Kerberos V5 realm.

   D. Incorrect. You configure an external trust between two domains in different forests, often when you don't want to allow the trust to be transitive. You configure a realm trust between an Active Directory domain and a Kerberos V5 realm.

3. **Correct answer:** B

   A. **Incorrect.** You configure an external trust between two domains in different forests, often when you don't want to allow the trust to be transitive.

   B. **Correct.** A forest trust is created between two forests when you want users in each forest to access resources in the counterpart forest.

   C. **Incorrect.** You configure a realm trust between an Active Directory domain and a Kerberos V5 realm.

   D. **Incorrect.** In this instance you need to create a shortcut trust between two domains in the same forest.

4. **Correct answer:** A

   A. **Correct.** You configure an external trust between two domains in different forests, often when you don't want to allow the trust to be transitive.

   B. **Incorrect.** You configure a realm trust between an Active Directory domain and a Kerberos V5 realm.

   C. **Incorrect.** In this instance you need to create a shortcut trust between two domains in the same forest.

   D. **Incorrect.** A forest trust is created between two forests when you want users in each forest to access resources in the counterpart forest.

CHAPTER 2

Active Directory sites and replication

Even though large organizations can be spread out over countries or continents, that same large organization might only have one Active Directory domain. Branch offices might be located in the same city or in cities that are hundreds of miles or kilometers from each other. As any user in the organization might be signing on in any of these locations, it's important to ensure that each domain controller has an up-to-date version of the Active Directory database. This is where Active Directory sites and replication become important. Active Directory sites enable you to enter representations of physical locations into the Active Directory database. These sites and the links between them are used to automatically create an efficient replication topology. An efficient replication topology ensures that when a user's password is changed by the service desk on a domain controller in a remote city city the updated password is available for the user at the domain controller in at the user's branch office. In this chapter you find out how to configure Active Directory sites and how to manage and monitor Active Directory replication.

Lessons in this chapter:

- Lesson 1: Configuring sites
- Lesson 2: Active Directory replication

Before you begin

To complete the practice exercises in this chapter, you need to have deployed computers SYD-DC, MEL-DC, CBR-DC, and ADL-DC as described in the Introduction, using the evaluation edition of Windows Server 2012 R2.

Lesson 1: Configuring sites

Sites enable you to map physical locations, such as branch offices, into Active Directory. Sites make it possible for Active Directory clients to locate the closest instance of a particular resource, for example ensuring that a user signing on to a computer in the Sydney office isn't authenticated by a domain controller in the New York office. In this lesson you will find out how to configure *sites* and *subnets*, move domain controllers between sites, and ensure that service (SRV) records are correctly configured.

Configure sites and subnets

Active Directory sites enable you to configure Active Directory so that it understands which network locations have a fast local network connection. Generally this means the computers are in the same building, although if your organization has a group of buildings in the same area that are connected by a high-speed network, you use a single Active Directory site configuration.

You configure sites by associating them with IP address ranges. For example, you might associate the subnet 192.168.10.0 /24 with the Active Directory Site BNE-Site. (The standardized international three-character abbreviations for capital cities/airport codes are used in these examples to ensure a consistent naming scheme.) Any computers that have an Internet Protocol (IP) address in this range would be located in that site. You can configure network addresses using IPv4 or IPv6 networks. When you install Active Directory for the first time, a default site, named Default-First-Site-Name is created. You configure sites using the Active Directory Sites and Services console shown in Figure 2-1.

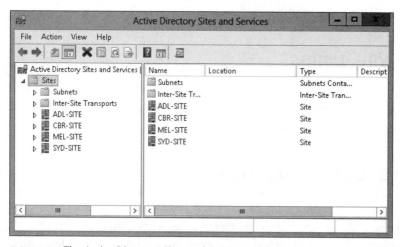

FIGURE 2-1 The Active Directory Sites and Services console

It's important that you add sites for each separate location in your organization. If you don't, Active Directory assumes that all computers are located on the same fast network and this might cause problems with other products as well as with Active Directory. Microsoft Products, such as System Center 2012 R2 Configuration Manager and Exchange Server 2013 use Active Directory site information when generating network topologies.

- Separate different locations that are connected by a slow wide-area network (WAN) or expensive WAN link. For example, if your organization has a branch office in Sydney and another branch office in Melbourne, and these branch offices are connected by a WAN link that is rated at 512 kilobits per second (Kbps), you configure the Sydney and Melbourne branch offices as separate sites.

- Control which domain controllers are used for authentication. When users log on to the network, they perform authentication against an available domain controller located in their Active Directory site. Although users are still able to sign on and authenticate against a domain controller in another site if one isn't available in their local site, you should strongly consider placing a domain controller at any site with a sufficient number of users. What counts as "a sufficient number of users" varies depending on the speed and reliability of the site's connection to the rest of the organization's network. In some cases you might deploy a read only domain controller (RODC) to aid authentication at some branch office sites.

- Control service localization. As mentioned earlier, many Microsoft products, such as System Center 2012 R2 Configuration Manager, Exchange Server, and technologies such as BranchCache and DFS (Distributed File System), use Active Directory sites as a way of determining network topology. To ensure that these products and technologies work well, you should ensure that each Active Directory site is configured properly.

- Control Active Directory replication. You can use Active Directory sites to manage domain controller replication. The default settings make it possible for replication to occur 24 hours a day, 7 days a week. You can use Active Directory site configuration to instead configure replication to occur according to a specific schedule. You read more about replication in Lesson 2.

Quick check

- What is the name of the first Active Directory site created when you promote the first domain controller in a new forest?

Quick check answer

- The name of the first Active Directory site created when you promote the first domain controller in a new forest is Default-First-Site-Name.

Creating sites

To create a site using the graphical user interface, perform the following steps:

1. In the Active Directory Sites and Services console, click the Sites node.
2. On the Action menu, click New Site.

3. In the New Object – Site dialog box, shown in Figure 2-2, enter a name for the site and specify the site link for the site. Selecting DEFAULTIPSITELINK is fine at this point because you can alter things later after you've configured some site links. Click OK to create the site.

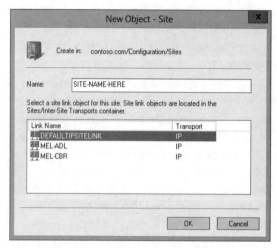

FIGURE 2-2 Create a new Active Directory site

You can use the New-ADReplicationSite Windows PowerShell cmdlet to create a new site. For example, to create a new site named HBA-SITE that is associated with the default IP site link, issue the command:

```
New-ADReplicationSite HBA-SITE
```

After you've created a site, you need to associate it with IP address ranges. You can't do that until you've added IP address ranges as subnets. When you create a subnet, you specify an IPv4 or IPv6 network prefix. For an IPv4 network you specify the network address and the subnet in CIDR notation. For example, you specify network 192.168.15.0 with a subnet mask of 255.255.255.0 as 192.168.15.0 /24.

> **REAL WORLD ASSUMED KNOWLEDGE**
>
> In the distant past there were specific Microsoft exams that tested your ability to subnet TCP/IP networks. These days the ability to create subnets and supernets and calculate the number of hosts on the resultant network is an assumed skill.

Creating subnets

To create a subnet, perform the following steps:

1. In the Active Directory Sites and Service console, click Subnets under the Sites node.
2. On the Action menu, click New Subnet.

3. In the New Object – Subnet dialog box, specify the network prefix of the subnet and specify the site associated with the subnet as shown in Figure 2-3. Click OK to create the subnet.

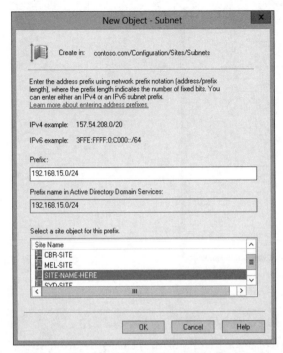

FIGURE 2-3 The New Object – Subnet dialog box

You can create a new subnet from Windows PowerShell with the New-ADReplicationSubnet cmdlet. For example, to create a new subnet that has the address 192.168.16.0/24 and associate it with the HBA-SITE site, issue the command:

```
New-ADReplicationSubnet –Name "192.168.16.0/24" –Site HBA-SITE
```

You can verify which subnets are associated with a particular Active Directory site by viewing the properties of that site. You can't change which subnets are associated with a site by editing the site properties. You can only change which site is associated with a specific subnet by editing the subnet properties. You do this using the Site drop-down menu shown in Figure 2-4. You can associate multiple subnets with an Active Directory site, but you can't associate multiple Active Directory sites with a specific subnet.

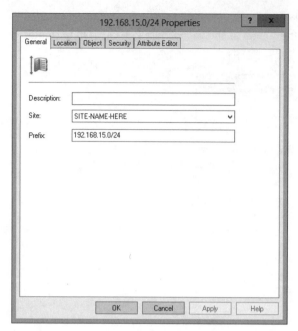

FIGURE 2-4 Configuring the subnet properties

> **REAL WORLD** **ALL ROADS LEAD TO ROMA**
>
> A few years back I was discussing replication issues with a guy I met at TechEd Australia who worked for a big company, which had branch offices scattered across the state of Queensland. The guy was telling me how the company found the cause of some replication issues with its site in Cairns. Apparently site replication had always been problematic, and no one had been able to figure out why until someone looked at the subnets associated with the Cairns site and discovered that someone had accidentally associated the subnet for the Roma branch office with the Cairns site. Driving from Cairns to Roma takes about 15 hours. To complicate things further, the two locations didn't have a direct link to each other, but they were instead both directly connected to the Brisbane site. A drive from Cairns to Roma through Brisbane would probably take about 25 hours, assuming you didn't need to make any stops. After the subnet was associated with the correct site, the problem resolved itself.

Creating site links

Site links enable you to specify how different Active Directory sites are connected to each other. When you add a site, you're asked to specify the site link, and the DEFAULTIPSITELINK site link is the default option even if another site link is available. Sites that are connected to the same site link are considered to be able to replicate with each other directly. For example, if all of the sites in Figure 2-5 are associated with the DEFAULTIPSITELINK site link, each site assumes that it could replicate directly with the others. For example, a domain controller in the Melbourne site attempts to replicate directly with a domain controller in the Canberra site. With this topology, you instead configure site links for Melbourne-Sydney, Adelaide-Sydney, and Canberra-Sydney. This way, domain controllers in Canberra, Melbourne, and Adelaide only replicate with the Sydney site rather than attempting to directly replicate with each other.

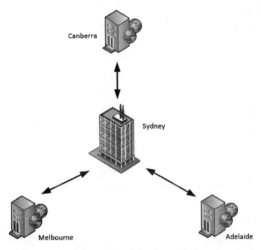

FIGURE 2-5 Configure site links that mirror network topology

You can create a new IP site link using the Active Directory Sites and Services console. When you create a site link, you specify the sites that use the link as shown in Figure 2-6.

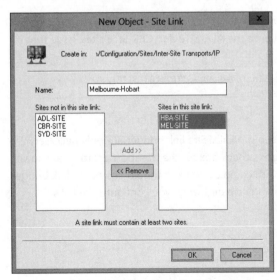

FIGURE 2-6 The New Object – Site Link dialog box

You can configure the cost and replication schedule of a site link after it is created by editing the site link properties as shown in Figure 2-7. The default Cost is 100, and site links that have lower costs are preferred for replication over site links that have a higher cost. Replication occurs every 180 minutes by default, 24 hours a day. You can modify when replication occurs by configuring a replication schedule.

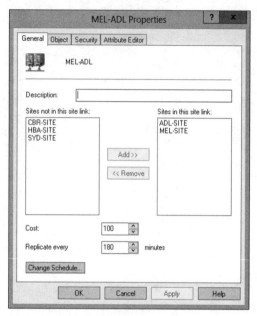

FIGURE 2-7 The Site Link properties dialog box

You can create a site link using the New-ADReplicationSiteLink cmdlet. For example, to create a new site link named ADL-CBR that links the ADL-SITE and CBR-SITE sites, issue the command:

```
New-ADReplicationSiteLink "ADL-CBR" –SitesIncluded ADL-SITE, CBR-SITE
```

Creating site link bridges

Site link bridges create transitive links between site links. Site link bridges are only necessary when you have cleared the Bridge All Site Links check box for the transport protocol as shown in Figure 2-8. It's only necessary to do this with complex network topologies as site link bridges are automatically created based on the topology created when you configure site links.

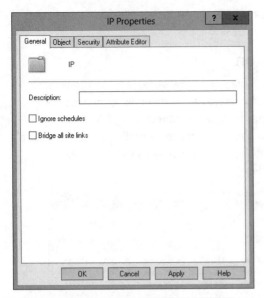

FIGURE 2-8 The transport protocol properties

You can create a site link bridge using the Active Directory Sites and Services console by specifying the two site links that will be in the bridge as shown in Figure 2-9. A site link bridge must contain at least two site links.

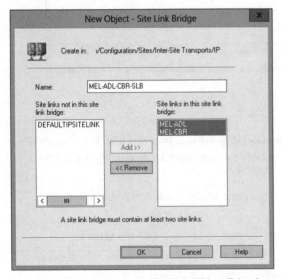

FIGURE 2-9 The New Object – Site Link Bridge dialog box

You can create a new site link bridge in Windows PowerShell using the New-ADReplicationSiteLinkBridge cmdlet. For example, to create a new site link bridge named MEL-ADL-CBR using the MEL-ADL and MEL-CBR site links, issue the command:

```
New-ADReplicationSiteLinkBridge "MEL-ADL-CBR" -SiteLinksIncluded "MEL-ADL", "MEL-CBR"
```

Manage SRV record registration

Domain controllers use special Domain Name System (DNS) resource records, known as SRV records to enable clients to locate them. *SRV records* are sometimes termed locator records because they make it possible for clients to locate resources using DNS queries. SRV records map to existing host records. For example, each domain controller in a domain has a _kerberos and an _ldap SRV record as shown in Figure 2-10 that maps to the domain controller's fully qualified domain name (FQDN).

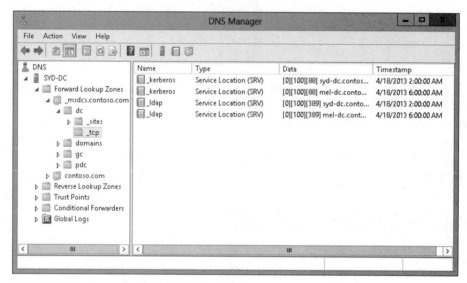

FIGURE 2-10 The domain controller SRV records

As Figure 2-11 shows, SRV records contain the following information:

- **Service** Whereas domain controllers provide the kerberos and ldap services, an SRV record can also provide information about servers that host Finger, Ftp, Http, Msdcs, Nntp, Telnet, or Whois services.

- **Protocol** The protocol that is available depends on the service, although this is usually TCP or UDP.

- **Port number** This specifies the port number to be used with the service.

- **Weight** This setting makes it possible to indicate preference of one record over another. By default this is set to 100.

- **Priority** This setting enables you to configure service priority for services that support prioritization. It is set to 0 for the kerberos and ldap SRV records used by domain controllers.

FIGURE 2-11 The SRV resource record properties

Unless something goes wrong, you are unlikely to need to modify the default SRV resource records. By default, the Netlogon service on domain controllers running Windows Server 2012 and Windows Server 2012 R2 reregisters SRV records every 60 minutes. You can manually reregister a domain controller's SRV records by restarting the Netlogon service.

> **MORE INFO REAL-LIFE DIAGNOSIS**
>
> The following TechNet blog post from a Microsoft Premier Field Engineer (PFE) describes diagnosing and resolving problems with SRV records: *http://blogs.technet.com/b/ askpfeplat/archive/2012/07/09/the-case-of-the-missing-srv-records.aspx.*

Moving domain controllers

When you deploy a new domain controller, the domain controller promotion process performs a lookup to determine which Active Directory site the domain controller should be a member of based on its IP address. If you haven't created a subnet in the Active Directory Sites and Services console that maps to the IP address of the server that you are promoting to the domain controller, the domain controller is instead assigned to the first Active Directory site, which is Default-First-Site-Name unless you have changed it.

The domain controller does not automatically reassign itself to a new site if you create the subnet and site objects in the Active Directory Sites and Services console if it has already been added to the Default-First-Site-Name site. In this instance, you need to manually move the domain controller to the new site. You can move the domain controller using the Active Directory Sites And Services console by right-clicking the domain controller that you want to move, clicking Move, and selecting the destination site on the Move Server dialog box, as shown in Figure 2-12.

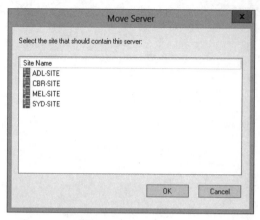

FIGURE 2-12 The Move Server dialog box

You can also move a domain controller to a different site using the Move-ADDirectoryServer powershell cmdlet. For example, to move the server PERTH-DC to the Perth-Site Active Directory site, execute the following command:

```
Move-ADDirectoryServer -Identity "PERTH-DC" -Site "Perth-Site"
```

> **MORE INFO** **MOVE-ADDIRECTORYSERVER**
>
> To learn more about the Move-ADDirectoryServer cmdlet, consult the following article: *http://technet.microsoft.com/en-us/library/ee617235.aspx.*

Lesson summary

- Subnets enable you to associate IP addresses in either IPv4 or IPv6 format with network locations.
- Sites enable you to connect one or more subnets to represent a location where all the hosts on those subnets share a high-speed network.
- Site links enable you to connect sites.
- Site link bridges enable you to connect site links. You should only do this if you want to override the replication topology automatically generated by Active Directory.
- SRV records make it possible for clients to use DNS to locate servers that provide services, such as LDAP and Kerberos, to the network.
- You might need to move domain controllers to different sites if you installed them before you configured sites and subnets.

Lesson review

Answer the following questions to test your knowledge of the information in this lesson. You can find the answers to these questions and explanations of each answer choice in the "Answers" section at the end of this chapter.

1. You want to manually reregister a specific domain controller's SRV records. Which service should you restart to accomplish this goal?

   A. Netlogon

   B. Secondary Logon

   C. Active Directory Domain Services

   D. DNS Server

2. You installed two domain controllers at a new branch office site before you created the appropriate objects using the Active Directory Sites and Services console. You have since created the appropriate subnet and site objects. Which of the following Windows PowerShell cmdlets could you use to move these domain controllers to the newly created appropriate site?

   A. New-ADReplicationSubnet

   B. New-ADReplicationSiteLink

   C. Move-ADDirectoryServer

   D. New-ADReplicationSite

3. Your organization has just opened a new branch office in the city of Hobart. You have assigned this branch office the IPv4 address range 10.100.10.0/24. Which of the following Windows PowerShell cmdlets would you use to add this IPv4 address range to Active Directory so that it is used when determining replication topology?

   A. New-ADReplicationSiteLink

   B. Move-ADDirectoryServer

   C. New-ADReplicationSite

   D. New-ADReplicationSubnet

4. Your organization has just opened a new branch office in the city of Hobart. You have used the Active Directory Sites and Services console to enter the IP address range used at the site into Active Directory. You now want to create an Active Directory site called HBA-SITE and to associate it with this IP address range. Which of the following Windows PowerShell cmdlets could you use to accomplish this goal?

   A. New-ADReplicationSite

   B. New-ADReplicationSubnet

   C. Move-ADDirectoryServer

   D. New-ADReplicationSiteLink

5. Your organization has just opened a new branch office in the city of Hobart. You want to associate the newly created HBA-SITE site with the SYD-SITE site as these two sites are connected to each other by a high-speed broadband link. Which of the following Windows PowerShell cmdlets could you use to accomplish this goal?

   A. New-ADReplicationSite

   B. New-ADReplicationSubnet

   C. New-ADReplicationSiteLink

   D. Move-ADDirectoryServer

Lesson 2: Active Directory replication

Replication makes it possible for changes that are made on one Active Directory domain controller to be replicated to other domain controllers in the domain and in some cases to other domain controllers in the forest. This lesson explains Active Directory replication, and in it you find out how to configure password replication for Read Only Domain Controllers, discover how to monitor and manage replication using a variety of tools, and see how to upgrade SYSVOL replication so that it uses DFS.

> **After this lesson, you will be able to:**
> - Configure replication to RODCs
> - Configure password replication to RODCs
> - Monitor and manage replication
> - Upgrade SYSVOL replication
>
> **Estimated lesson time: 45 minutes**

Active Directory partitions

Rather than replicating the Active Directory database in its entirety, the *replication* process is made more efficient by splitting the database into logical *partitions*. Replication occurs at the partition level, with some partitions only replicating to domain controllers within the local domain, some partitions replicating only to enrolled domain controllers, and some partitions replicating to all domain controllers in the forest. Active Directory includes the following default partitions:

- **Configuration partition**   This partition stores forest-wide Active Directory structure information including domain, site, and domain controller location data. The configuration partition also holds information about DHCP server authorization and Active Directory Certificate Services certificate templates. . The configuration partition replicates to all domain controllers in the forest.

- **Schema partition** The schema partition stores definitions of all objects and attributes as well as the rules for creating and manipulating those objects. There are a default set of classes and attributes that cannot be changed, but it's possible to extend the schema and add new attributes and classes. Only the domain controller that holds the Schema Master FSMO role is able to extend the schema. The schema partition replicates to all domain controllers in the forest.

- **Domain partition** The domain partition holds information about domain-specific objects such as organizational units, domain-related settings, user, group, and computer accounts. A new domain partition is created each time you add a new domain to the forest. The domain partition replicates to all domain controllers in a domain. All objects in every domain partition are stored in the global catalog, but these objects are stored only with some, not all, of their attribute values.

- **Application partitions** Application partitions store application-specific information for applications that store information in Active Directory. There can be multiple application partitions, each of which is used by different applications. You can configure application partitions so that they replicate only to some domain controllers in a forest. For example, you can create specific application partitions to be used for DNS replication so that DNS zones replicate to some, but not all, domain controllers in the forest.

Domains running at the Windows Server 2008 and higher functional level support *attribute-level replication*. Rather than replicate the entire object when a change is made to an attribute on that object, such as when group membership changes for a user account, only the attribute that changes is replicated to other domain controllers. Attribute-level replication substantially reduces the amount of data that needs to be transmitted when objects stored in Active Directory are modified.

Understanding multi-master replication

Active Directory uses *multi-master replication*. This means that any writable domain controller is able to make modifications of the Active Directory database and to have those modifications propagate to the other domain controllers in the domain. Domain controllers use pull replication to acquire changes from other domain controllers. A domain controller may pull changes after being notified by replication partners that changes are available. A domain controller notifies its first replication partner that a change has occurred within 15 seconds and additional replication partners every 3 seconds after the previous notification. Domain controllers also periodically poll replication partners to determine whether changes are available so that those changes can be pulled and applied to the local copy of the relevant partition. By default, polling occurs once every 60 minutes. You can alter this by editing the properties of the connection object in the Active Directory Sites and Services console as shown in Figure 2-13.

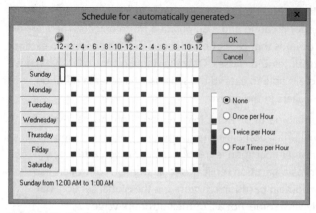

FIGURE 2-13 Configure the replication-polling schedule

Knowledge Consistency Checker (KCC)

The *Knowledge Consistency Checker (KCC)* runs on each domain controller. The KCC is responsible for creating and optimizing the replication paths between domain controllers located at a specific site. In the event that a domain controller is added or removed from a site, the KCC automatically reconfigures the site's replication topology. The KCC topology organization process occurs every 15 minutes by default. Although you can change this value by editing the registry, you can also trigger an update using the repadmin command-line tool with the KCC switch.

> **MORE INFO KCC**
>
> To learn more about the KCC, consult the following article:
> *http://technet.microsoft.com/en-us/library/cc961781.aspx.*

Store and forward replication

Active Directory supports *store and forward replication.* For example, the Canberra and Melbourne branch offices are enrolled in a custom application partition. These branch offices aren't connected to each other, but they are connected to the Sydney head office. In this case, changes made to objects stored in the application partition at Canberra can be pulled by the domain controller in Sydney. The Melbourne domain controller can then pull those changes from the domain controller in Sydney as shown in Figure 2-14.

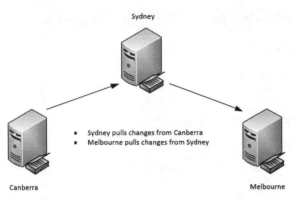

Sydney

- Sydney pulls changes from Canberra
- Melbourne pulls changes from Sydney

Canberra

Melbourne

FIGURE 2-14 An example of store and forward replication

Conflict resolution

In an environment that supports multi-master replication, it's possible that updates may be made to the same object at the same time in two or more different places. Active Directory includes sophisticated technologies that minimize the chance that these conflicts will cause problems, even when conflicting updates occur in locations that are distant from each other.

Each domain controller tracks updates by using update sequence numbers (USNs). Each time a domain controller updates, either by processing an update performed locally or by processing an update acquired through replication, it increments the USN and associates the new value with the update. USNs are unique to each domain controller as each domain controller processes a different number of updates to every other domain controller.

When this happens, the domain controller that wrote the most recent change, known as the last writer, wins. Because each domain controller's clock might not be precisely synchronized with every other domain controller's clock, last write isn't simply determined by a comparison of timestamps. Similarly because USNs are unique to each domain controller, a direct comparison of USNs is not made. Instead the conflict resolution algorithm looks at the attribute version number. This is a number that indicates how many times the attribute has changed and is calculated using USNs. When the same attribute has been changed on different domain controllers, the attribute with the higher attribute version number wins. If the attribute version number is the same, the attribute modification timestamps are compared, with the most recent change being deemed authoritative.

If you add or move an object to a container that was deleted on another domain controller at the same time, the object is moved to the LostAndFound container. You can view this container when you enable the Advanced Features option in the Active Directory Users and Computers console as shown in Figure 2-15.

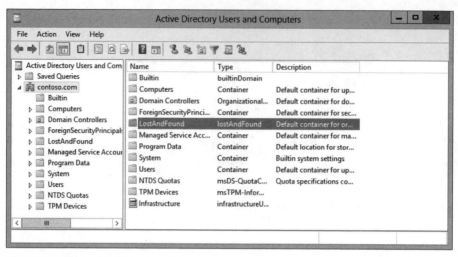

FIGURE 2-15 The LostAndFound container

RODC replication

Read-only domain controllers (RODCs) are a special type of domain controller that are suitable for branch office locations that require a local domain controller for authentication but don't have a secure location where the server can be stored. The key difference between an RODC and a writable domain controller is that RODCs aren't able to update the Active Directory database and that they only host password information for a subset of security principals.

> **REAL WORLD SERVERS AND BISCUITS**
>
> I once visited a branch office of a company where the two local servers were stored in a locked wardrobe in the staff break room. Although it's reasonable to object to this arrangement because of the security implications, it was redeemed by the presence of a large jar with chocolate biscuits.

When a client in a site that only has RODCs needs to make a change to the Active Directory database, that change is forwarded to a writable domain controller in another site. When considering replication, remember that all RODC-related replication is incoming and that other domain controllers do not pull updates from the AD DS database hosted on an RODC.

RODCs use the usual replication schedule to pull updates from writeable domain controllers except in some special cases. In certain cases, RODCs perform inbound replication using a replicate-single-object (RSO) operation. These cases include:

- The password of a user whose account password is stored on the RODC is changed.
- A DNS record update occurs where the DNS client performing the update attempts to use the RODC to process the update and is then redirected by the RODC to a writable DC that hosts the appropriate Active Directory Integrated DNS zone.

- Client attributes including client name, DnsHostName, OsName, OsVersionInfo, supported encryption types, and LastLogonTimeStamp are updated.

These updates occur outside the usual replication schedule as they involve objects and attributes that are important to security. For example, a user at a site that uses RODCs calls the service desk to have his or her password reset. The service desk staff member, located in another site, resets the password using a writable domain controller. If a special RSO operation isn't performed, it is necessary to wait for the change to replicate to the site before the user is able to sign-on with the newly reset password.

Configure RODC password replication

If a writable domain controller is compromised then it's possible that any of the user accounts that were stored on that domain controller might be compromised. If it's a writable domain controller then every account in the domain is at risk. RODCs ameliorate the risk by only allowing specific accounts to be stored on the RODC. If the RODC is compromised then only a fraction of the accounts in the domain are at risk. Rather than having to reset all of the accounts in the organization, you can delete the RODC computer account and automatically reset all of the user and computer accounts stored on the RODC in a simple action. You configure which accounts can be stored on the RODC by configuring RODC *password replication*.

Members of the Allowed RODC Password Replication security group are able to have their passwords replicated to the RODC as long as they aren't members of a group that has a Deny setting in the Password Replication Policy. The following groups have a Deny setting by default:

- Account Operators
- Administrators
- Backup Operators
- Denied RODC password replication group
- Server Operators

The Password Replication Policy tab of an RODC's computer account properties dialog box displays the configuration of allowed and denied security groups for password replication to that RODC. This tab is shown in Figure 2-16. The Password Replication Policy is unique to each RODC, and it enables you to ensure that the passwords that are replicated to each RODC are unique to that RODC. For example, if you have an RODC in the Perth site and one in the Hobart site, it's unlikely that users in the Perth site will be authenticating in the Hobart site and that users from the Hobart site will authenticate using the RODC in Perth. Configuring separate password replication policies for each RODC ensures that only the passwords of users in Perth are replicated to the Perth RODC and that only the passwords of users in Hobart are replicated to the Hobart RODC. The easiest way to ensure that only relevant account passwords replicate to a site is to create a separate security group for each location, populate it with the relevant accounts, and add that group to that site's RODC Password Replication Policy.

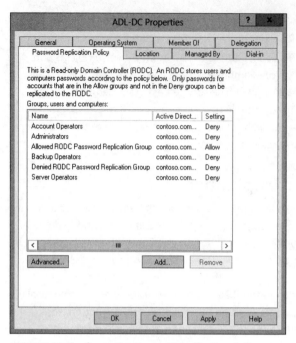

FIGURE 2-16 Configure the Password Replication Policy

You can check which passwords have replicated to a specific RODC by clicking the Advanced button on the Password Replication Policy tab of the RODC's computer account's Properties. You can also use the dialog box shown in Figure 2-17 to populate the RODC with passwords. When you populate an RODC with passwords, authentication is faster the first time a user signs on at the site because the authentication can be performed locally and doesn't need to occur against a writable domain controller in another site.

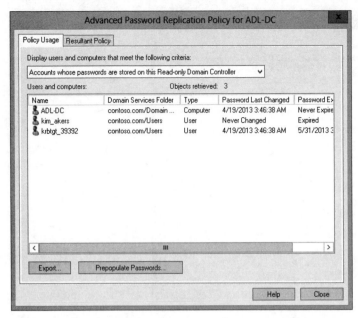

FIGURE 2-17 View the stored account passwords

Rather than figure out a user's group membership to determine whether a user's password can be replicated to an RODC, you can use the Resultant Policy tab of the Advanced Password Replication Policy dialog box, shown in Figure 2-18, to determine whether a specific user's password will be replicated to the RODC. This dialog box doesn't tell you which group membership is blocking the password replication, but it enables you to verify that a sensitive user's account is blocked from replication.

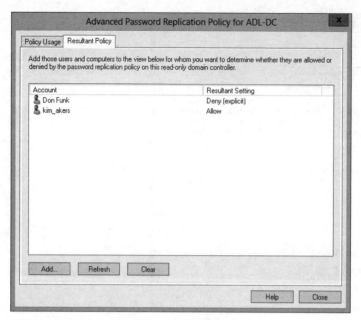

FIGURE 2-18 The Resultant Password Replication Policy

In the event that an RODC is compromised, you can automatically configure Active Directory to reset the passwords of all of the user and computer accounts by deleting the RODC's computer account. When you attempt to delete the RODC's computer account, you are prompted with the Deleting Domain Controller dialog box, shown in Figure 2-19. When you use this dialog box, you can also choose to export the list of accounts that were cached on the RODC, which enables you to perform follow-up activities such as contacting users to inform them why their account password has been reset. If you reset computer account passwords, you need to rejoin the computers to the domain.

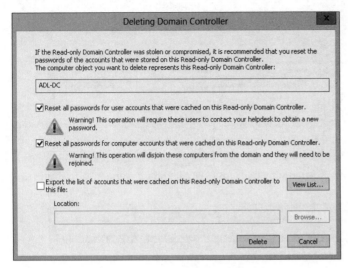

FIGURE 2-19 The Deleting Domain Controller dialog box

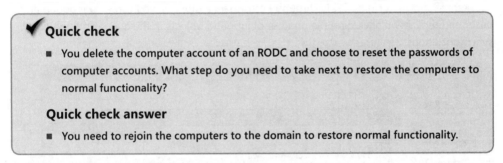

Quick check

- You delete the computer account of an RODC and choose to reset the passwords of computer accounts. What step do you need to take next to restore the computers to normal functionality?

Quick check answer

- You need to rejoin the computers to the domain to restore normal functionality.

Monitor and manage replication

You can use the Active Directory Sites and Services console to trigger replication. You can trigger replication on a specific domain controller by right-clicking the connection object and clicking Replicate Now as shown in Figure 2-20. When you do this, the domain controller replicates with all of its replication partners.

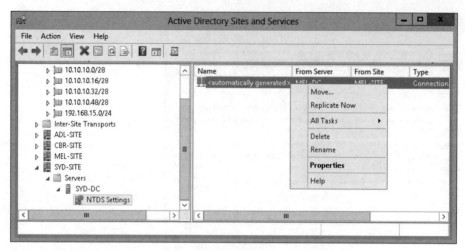

FIGURE 2-20 Trigger domain controller replication

You can also monitor replication as it occurs using DirectoryServices performance counters as shown in Figure 2-21. Through Performance Monitor, you can view inbound and outbound replication, including the number of inbound objects in the queue and pending synchronizations.

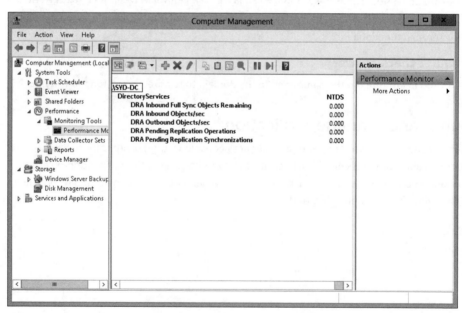

FIGURE 2-21 Use Performance Monitor to view replication performance

Repadmin

You can use the repadmin command-line tool to manage and monitor replication. This tool is especially useful at enabling you to diagnose where there are problems in a replication topology. For example, when you use repadmin with the replsummary option, as shown in Figure 2-22, you can generate information showing when replication between partners has failed. You can also use this option to view information about the largest intermission between replication events.

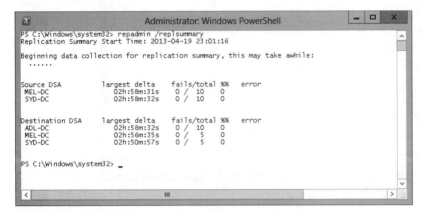

FIGURE 2-22 Use repadmin to view a replication summary

REAL WORLD FINDING LOST DOMAIN CONTROLLERS

Sometimes, for undetermined reasons, a domain controller stops replicating with the other domain controllers. The reason might be that the domain controller picks up accounts created on other domain controllers but changes made on this specific domain controller don't replicate to the rest of the organization. Or it might be something much odder. If you're investigating a quirky issue related to Active Directory, it always helps at the start to run repadmin /replsummary as a quick method of determining whether all of the domain controllers are playing along or one of them has wandered off the track without anyone noticing.

You can view specific inbound replication traffic by using the /showrepl switch. Figure 2-23 shows detail about inbound replication traffic, including the objects that were replicated and the date stamps associated with that replication traffic.

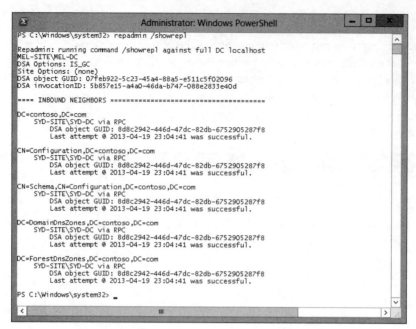

FIGURE 2-23 View the inbound replication traffic

Rather than viewing the properties of an RODC's computer account in the Active Directory Administrative Center or the Active Directory Users and Computers console when you want to determine which users have had their password replicated to the RODC, you can instead use repadmin with the /prp switch to determine this information. Figure 2-24 shows how to use repadmin to determine which account passwords are being stored on the RODC named ADL-DC.

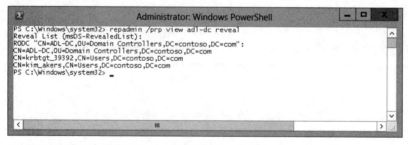

FIGURE 2-24 View the RODC Password Replication Policy

Using repadmin with the /kcc switch, as shown in Figure 2-25, enables you to force the KCC to recalculate a domain controller's inbound replication topology. Although this process happens automatically, you might want to manually trigger this operation in cases where the replication topology has changed radically and you don't want to wait for your organization's domain controllers to recalculate the topology as they would normally.

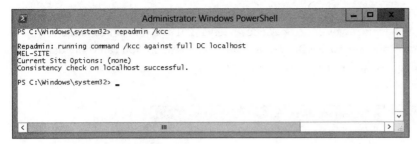

FIGURE 2-25 Recalculate the topology

In addition to this functionality, you can use repadmin to perform the following tasks:

- The /queue switch enables you to display inbound replication requests that a domain controller must make to reach a state of convergence with source replication partners.

- Use the /replicate switch to force replication of a specific directory partition to a specific destination domain controller.

- Use the /replsingleobj switch when you need to replicate a single object between two domain controllers.

- The /rodcpwdrepl option enables you to populate RODCs with the passwords of specific users.

- Use the /showutdvec to display the highest USN value recorded for committed replication operations on a specific DC.

> **MORE INFO** **REPADMIN.EXE**
>
> For more information about Repadmin, consult the following TechNet article:
> *http://technet.microsoft.com/en-us/library/cc770963(v=ws.10).aspx.*

Upgrade SYSVOL replication

SYSVOL is a special folder located on each domain controller in the %SystemRoot%\SYSVOL folder. This folder hosts logon scripts, group policy templates, and other Active Directory items. SYSVOL is replicated to all domain controllers in a domain. Prior to the introduction of Windows Server 2008, SYSVOL used File Replication Service (FRS) to perform replication. With the introduction of Windows Server 2008, Distributed File System (DFS), a much more efficient replication technology became available to replicate the contents of SYSVOL.

If your organization has upgraded from a Windows Server 2003 Active Directory environment, SYSVOL may still be configured to use FRS rather than DFS. After you have upgraded all domain controllers so that the minimum domain functional level is Windows Server 2008, you can use the Dfsrmig.exe utility to migrate SYSVOL replication so that it uses DFS rather than FRS.

If your domain was deployed from the beginning using Windows Server 2008, Windows Server 2008 R2, Windows Server 2012, or Windows Server 2012 R2 domain controllers, SYSVOL is already configured to use DFS rather than FRS replication. You can verify that SYSVOL is using DFS using the dfsrmig.exe command with the /getglobalstate switch as shown in Figure 2-26.

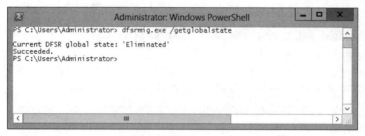

FIGURE 2-26 Upgrade SYSVOL replication

MORE INFO **DFSRMIG.EXE**

For more information about dfsrmig.exe, consult the following TechNet article: *http://technet.microsoft.com/en-au/library/dd641227(v=ws.10).aspx.*

Lesson summary

- Active Directory domain controllers perform multi-master replication.
- Domain controllers pull updates from replication partners.
- RODCs are unable to update Active Directory.
- The Password Replication Policy is unique to each RODC and determines which account passwords are stored on the RODC.
- When you remove an RODC from the domain, you can configure an automatic password reset for all account passwords stored on the RODC.
- You can use repadmin to manage and monitor Active Directory replication.
- You can use dfsrmig.exe to migrate a domain that uses FRS for SYSVOL replication so that it uses DFSR.

Lesson review

Answer the following questions to test your knowledge of the information in this lesson. You can find the answers to these questions and explanations of each answer choice in the "Answers" section at the end of this chapter.

1. As a part of a security audit, you are attempting to verify which user accounts have replicated to the RODC named ADL-RO DC. This RODC is running on the server core version of Windows Server 2012 R2. Which of the following commands could you use to accomplish this goal?

A. Repadmin /prp view ADL-RODC Reveal

B. Repadmin /replsummary ADL-RODC

C. Repadmin /kcc ADL-RODC

D. Repadmin /showrepl ADL-RODC

E. Repadmin /syncall ADL-RODC

2. You have just substantially changed the structure of your organization's WAN links. You want to trigger an update on SYD-DC of the inbound replication topology. Which of the following commands could you use to accomplish this goal?

A. Repadmin /prp view SYD-DC Reveal

B. Repadmin /syncall SYD-DC

C. Repadmin /showrepl SYD-DC

D. Repadmin /kcc SYD-DC

E. Repadmin /replsummary SYD-DC

3. You are in the process of diagnosing replication problems to a DC named CBR-DC, which is located in your organization's Canberra branch office. You want to view information about the failure and success percentages of both inbound and outbound replication operations. Which of the following commands could you use to accomplish this goal?

A. Repadmin /showrepl CBR-DC

B. Repadmin /syncall CBR-DC

C. Repadmin /kcc CBR-DC

D. Repadmin /prp view CBR-DC Reveal

E. Repadmin /replsummary CBR-DC

4. You want to force the domain controller MEL-DC to immediately perform synchronization with all its replication partners. Which of the following commands would you use to accomplish this goal?

A. Repadmin /showrepl MEL-DC

B. Repadmin /syncall MEL-DC

C. Repadmin /kcc MEL-DC

D. Repadmin /replsummary MEL-DC

E. Repadmin /prp view MEL-DC Reveal

5. You are attempting to diagnose some replication problems with the domain controller BNE-DC. You want to show status information on this domain controller's most recent attempts to perform inbound replication. Which of the following commands would you use to accomplish this goal?

A. Repadmin /syncall MEL-DC

B. Repadmin /kcc MEL-DC

C. Repadmin /showrepl MEL-DC

D. Repadmin /replsummary MEL-DC

E. Repadmin /prp view MEL-DC Reveal

6. Up until last night, the Perth site has had an RODC that was kept in a locked cupboard. This RODC was used to authenticate computer and user accounts in the Perth site. In the early hours of the morning, the Perth site was robbed and the RODC was stolen. As a part of your response to this incident, you are in the process of deleting the computer account of the Perth site RODC. Which of the following steps might you need to take after removing this account? (Choose all that apply.)

A. Assign users new passwords.

B. Enable user accounts.

C. Rejoin computers to the domain.

D. Enable computer accounts.

7. What is the minimum domain functional level required before you can update SYSVOL replication to use DFS instead of FRS?

A. Windows Server 2003

B. Windows Server 2008

C. Windows Server 2008 R2

D. Windows Server 2012

8. You have recently transitioned from a Windows Server 2003 domain functional level to a Windows Server 2012 R2 domain functional level. Which of the following utilities would you use to determine whether FRS or DFS is being used to support SYSVOL replication?

A. dfsrmig.exe

B. repadmin.exe

C. dcdiag.exe

D. dnscmd.exe

Practice exercises

The goal of this section is to provide you with hands-on practice with the following:

- Creating Active Directory sites
- Creating Active Directory subnets
- Creating site links

- Modifying site link cost and replication schedule
- Deploying an RODC
- Configuring an RODC replication
- Monitoring replication
- Removing an RODC and resetting accounts

To perform the exercises in this section, you need access to an evaluation version of Windows Server 2012 R2. You should also have access to virtual machines SYD-DC, MEL-DC, CBR-DC, and ADL-DC, the setup instructions for which are as described in the Appendix. You should ensure that you have a checkpoint of these virtual machines that you can revert to at the end of the practice exercises. You should revert the virtual machines to this initial state prior to beginning these exercises.

Exercise 1: Create Active Directory sites

In this exercise, you create Active Directory sites in the Contoso.com domain named ADL-SITE, CBR-SITE, and MEL-SITE. You also rename the default first site to SYD-SITE. To complete this exercise, perform the following steps:

1. Power on SYD-DC and sign on as contoso\don_funk with the password **Pa$$w0rd**.

2. In the Server Manager console, click the Tools menu and then click Active Directory Sites And Services.

3. In the Active Directory Sites And Services console, right-click Default-First-Site-Name and click Rename.

4. Rename the Default-First-Site-Name site SYD-SITE as shown in Figure 2-27.

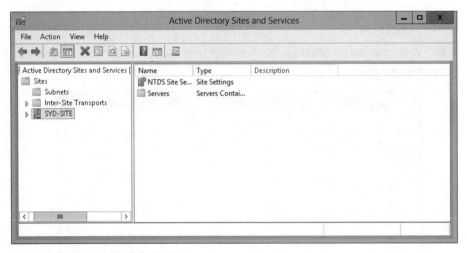

FIGURE 2-27 Rename the default site

5. Right-click the Sites node and click New Site.

6. In the New Object – Site dialog box, type **ADL-SITE**, click the DEFAULTIPSITELINK item as shown in Figure 2-28, and then click OK. In the Active Directory Domain Services dialog box, click OK.

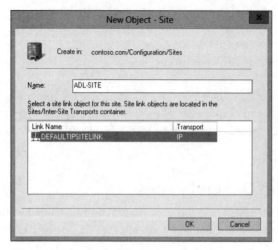

FIGURE 2-28 Create the ADL-SITE

7. Right-click the Sites node and click New Site.

8. In the New Object – Site dialog box, type **MEL-SITE**, click the DEFAULTIPSITELINK item, and click OK.

9. In the Active Directory Domain Services dialog box, click OK.

10. Right-click the Sites node and click New Site.

11. In the New Object – Site dialog box, type **CBR-SITE**, click the DEFAULTIPSITELINK item, and click OK.

12. Verify that the list of sites in the Active Directory Sites And Services console matches Figure 2-29.

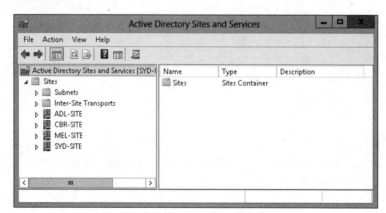

FIGURE 2-29 The Active Directory Sites And Services configuration

Exercise 2: Create Active Directory subnets

In this exercise, you create IPv4 subnets and associate them with different Active Directory sites. To complete this exercise, perform the following steps:

1. In the Active Directory Sites And Services console on SYD-DC, right-click the Subnets node and click New Subnet.

2. In the Prefix text box of the New Object – Subnet dialog box, type **10.10.10.0/28** and click SYD-SITE as shown in Figure 2-30. Click OK.

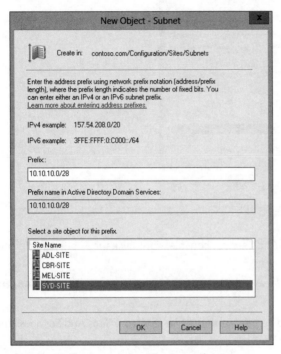

FIGURE 2-30 Create an Active Directory subnet

3. In the Active Directory Sites And Services console, right-click the Subnets node and click New Subnet.

4. In the Prefix text box of the New Object – Subnet dialog box, type **10.10.10.16/28**, click ADL-SITE, and click OK.

5. In the Active Directory Sites And Services console, right-click the Subnets node and click New Subnet.

6. In the Prefix text box of the New Object – Subnet dialog box, type **10.10.10.32/28**, click MEL-SITE as shown in Figure 2-31, and click OK.

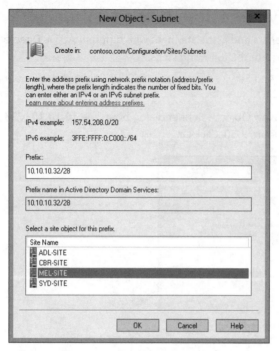

FIGURE 2-31 Create another subnet

7. In the Active Directory Sites And Services console, right-click the Subnets node and click New Subnet.

8. In the Prefix text box of the New Object – Subnet dialog box, type **10.10.10.48/28**, click CBR-SITE, and click OK.

9. Select the Subnets node and verify that the Active Directory Sites And Services console matches Figure 2-32.

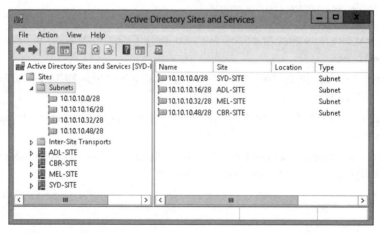

FIGURE 2-32 Verify the subnet configuration

Exercise 3: Create site links

In this exercise, you create two new IP Site Links. To complete this exercise, perform the following steps:

1. On SYD-DC in the Active Directory Sites And Services console, expand the Sites\Inter-Site Transports node.

2. Right-click the IP node and click New Site Link.

3. On the New Object – Site Link dialog box, type **MEL-ADL** in the Name text box. Hold the Ctrl key, click ADL-SITE and MEL-SITE, and click Add as shown in Figure 2-33. Click OK.

FIGURE 2-33 Create a site link

4. Right-click the IP node and click New Site Link.

5. On the New Object – Site Link dialog box, type **MEL-CBR** in the Name text box. Hold the Ctrl key, click MEL-SITE and CBR-SITE, click Add, and then click OK.

6. Select the IP node of the Active Directory Sites and Services console and verify that the site links listed match those in Figure 2-34.

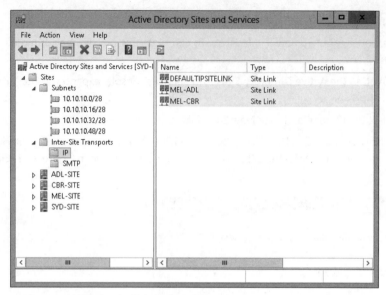

FIGURE 2-34 Verify the site link configuration

Exercise 4: Modify site link cost and replication schedule

In this exercise, you modify the site link cost and replication schedule of the MEL-CBR site link. To complete this exercise, perform the following steps:

1. In the Active Directory Sites And Services console on SYD-DC, expand Sites\Inter-Site Transports and click on the IP node.

2. In the list of site links, right-click MEL-CBR and click Properties.

3. On the MEL-CBR Properties dialog box, set the Cost to 150 and set the Replicate Every option to 240 as shown in Figure 2-35.

FIGURE 2-35 View the site link properties

4. On the General tab, click the Change Schedule button.

5. On the Schedule for MEL-CBR, select all of the hours on Sunday and click Replication Not Available as shown in Figure 2-36. Click OK twice.

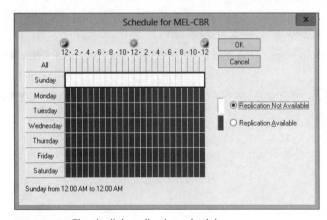

FIGURE 2-36 The site link replication schedule

Exercise 5: Configure MEL-DC as an additional domain controller

In this exercise, you configure MEL-DC as an additional domain controller in the contoso.com domain. To complete this exercise, perform the following steps:

1. Sign on to MEL-DC as Administrator with the password **Pa$$w0rd**.

2. In the Server Manager console, click Local Server and verify that the IP address listed for Ethernet is set to 10.10.10.40 as shown in Figure 2-37.

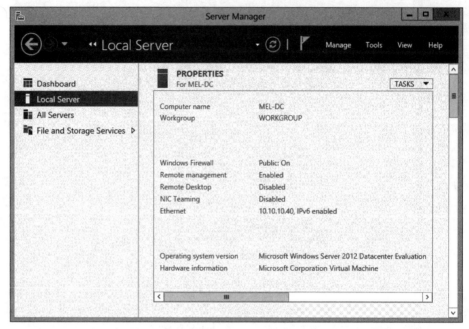

FIGURE 2-37 Verify the IP address configuration

3. On the Manage menu, click Add Roles And Features.

4. On the Before You Begin page of the Add Roles And Features Wizard, click Next three times.

5. On the Select Server Roles page, click Active Directory Domain Services as shown in Figure 2-38.

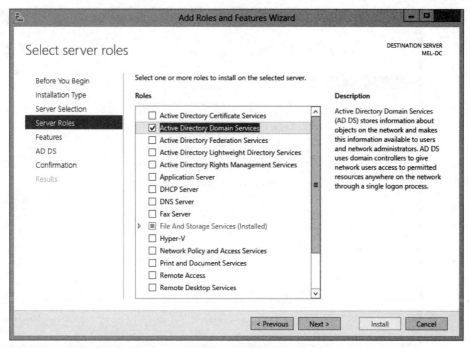

FIGURE 2-38 Add the Active Directory Domain Services role

6. On the Add Roles And Features Wizard pop up, click Add Features.

7. Click Next three times and click Install.

8. Click Close to close the Add Roles And Features Wizard.

9. Click the alert item next to the notification flag and click Promote This Server To A Domain Controller.

10. On the Deployment Configuration page of the Active Directory Domain Services Configuration Wizard, click Add A Domain Controller To An Existing Domain and click Select.

11. In the Credentials for Deployment Operation, type **contoso\don_funk** in the User Name text box, **Pa$$w0rd** in the Password text box, and click OK.

12. In the Select A Domain From The Forest dialog box, click Contoso.com and click OK.

13. Verify that the Deployment Configuration page matches Figure 2-39 and click Next.

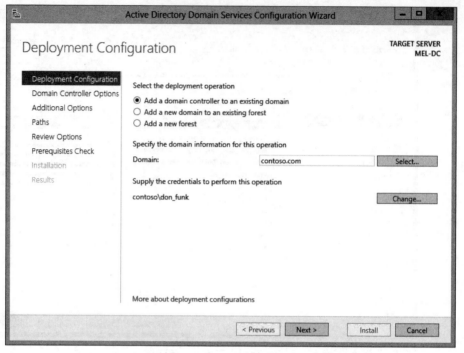

FIGURE 2-39 The Active Directory Domain Services deployment configuration

14. On the Domain Controller Options page, type the DSRM password **Pa$$w0rd** in both the Password and Confirm Password text boxes. Verify that the site name is set to MEL-SITE as shown in Figure 2-40 and then click Next twice.

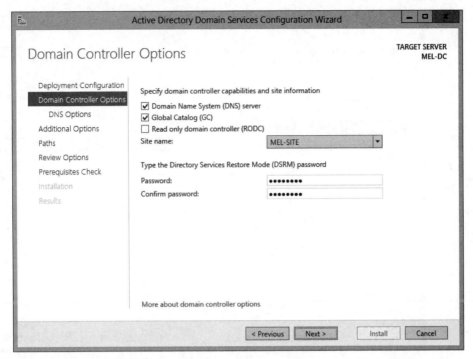

FIGURE 2-40 Configure the domain controller options

15. On the Additional Options page, set the Replicate From drop-down menu to SYD-DC. contoso.com as shown in Figure 2-41 and then click Next three times.

FIGURE 2-41 Configure the domain controller to replicate from

16. On the Prerequisites Check page, click Install.

17. After MEL-DC restarts, sign on as contoso\don_funk with the password **Pa$$w0rd**.

Exercise 6: Verify site placement and trigger replication

In this exercise, you verify that MEL-DC is located in the MEL-SITE Active Directory site. To complete this exercise, perform the following steps:

1. When signed on to MEL-DC as contoso\don_funk, click Active Directory Sites And Services in the Tools menu of the Server Manger console.

2. Expand the MEL-SITE node, expand Servers and click MEL-DC as shown in Figure 2-42.

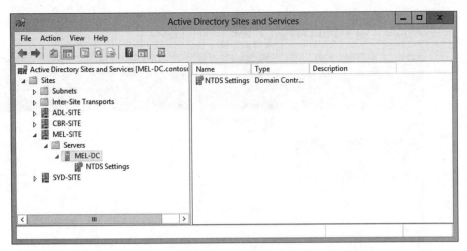

FIGURE 2-42 View the domain controller in the Active Directory Sites And Services console

3. Click NTDS Settings under MEL-DC.

4. In the Actions pane, click <Automatically Generated> and then click Replicate Now on the Action menu.

5. In the Replicate Now dialog box, shown in Figure 2-43, click OK.

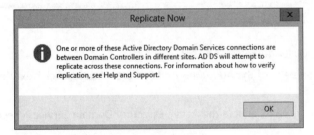

FIGURE 2-43 The Replicate Now dialog box

6. In the Active Directory Sites And Services console, click the Sites\SYD-SITE\Servers\SYD-DC\NTDS Settings node.

7. In the Actions pane, click <Automatically Generated> and then click Replicate Now on the Action menu.

8. In the Replicate Now dialog box, click OK.

Exercise 7: Configure ADL-DC as an RODC

In this exercise, you configure ADL-DC as an RODC in the ADL-SITE Active Directory site. To complete this exercise, perform the following steps:

1. Sign on to ADL-DC as Administrator with the password **Pa$$w0rd**.

2. In the Local Server node of the Server Manager console, verify that the Ethernet address is set to 10.10.10.20 as shown in Figure 2-44.

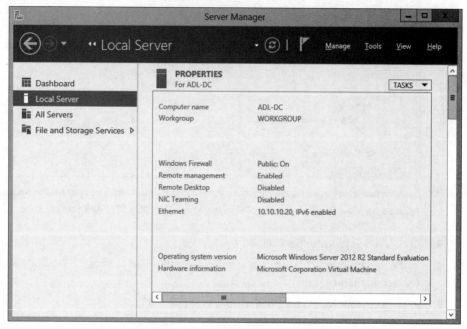

FIGURE 2-44 Verify the ADL-DC IP address

3. On the Manage menu, click Add Roles And Features.

4. On the Before You Begin page of the Add Roles And Features Wizard, click Next three times.

5. On the Select Server Roles page, enable the Active Directory Domain Services check box.

6. On the Add Roles And Features Wizard pop-up, click Add Features.

7. On the Select Server Roles page, click Next three times and click Install. Click Close to close the Add Roles And Features Wizard.

8. Click the Notification icon next to the Manage menu on the Server Manager console and click Promote This Server To A Domain Controller as shown in Figure 2-45.

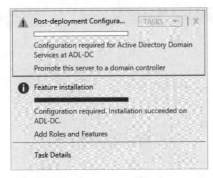

FIGURE 2-45 Promote this server to a domain controller

9. On the Deployment Configuration page of the Active Directory Domain Services Configuration Wizard, click Select.

10. On the Credentials For Deployment Operation dialog box, type **contoso\don_funk** and **Pa$$w0rd** as shown in Figure 2-46 and then click OK.

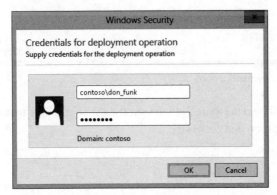

FIGURE 2-46 Provide deployment credentials

11. On the Select A Domain from the Forest dialog box, click Contoso.com and then click OK.

12. On the Deployment Configuration page, click Next.

13. On the Domain Controller Options page, click the Read Only Domain Controller (RODC) check box, type the DSRM password as **Pa$$w0rd**, and ensure that the site name is set to ADL-SITE as shown in Figure 2-47. Click Next.

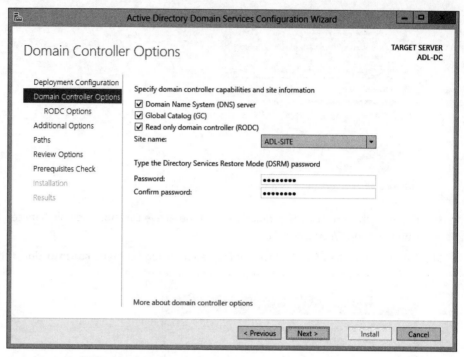

FIGURE 2-47 Verify the RODC deployment options

14. On the RODC Options page, shown in Figure 2-48, review the list of accounts that are blocked from password replication and click Next.

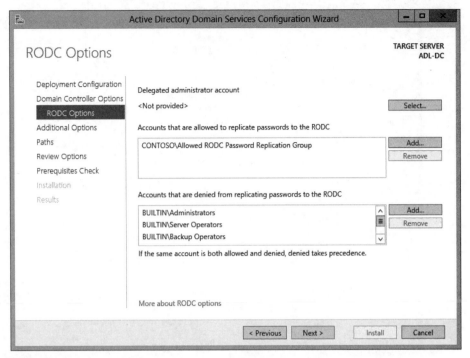

FIGURE 2-48 The RODC password replication options

15. On the Additional Options page, use the Replicate From drop-down menu to specify that replication should occur from SYD-DC.contoso.com, click Next three times, and click Install.

16. After ADL-DC restarts, sign on as Contoso\don_funk with the password **Pa$$w0rd**.

Exercise 8: Configure RODC replication

In this exercise, you configure replication for ADL-DC, which you configured as an RODC in the previous exercise. To complete this exercise, perform the following steps:

1. Sign on to SYD-DC as Contoso\don_funk with the password **Pa$$w0rd**.

2. On the Tools menu, click Active Directory Administrative Center.

3. In the Active Directory Administrative Center, click Contoso (Local).

4. In the details pane of the Active Directory Administrative Center, double-click the Users container.

5. Under the Users section in the Tasks pane, click New and then click Group.

6. In the Create Group dialog box, type the group name as **ADL-Replicated-Accounts** as shown in Figure 2-49 and click OK.

FIGURE 2-49 Create a security group

7. Double-click the Contoso (Local) node and then double-click the Domain Controllers node.

8. In the Details pane, click ADL-DC and click Properties.

9. In the ADL-DC dialog box, click Extensions, click the Password Replication Policy tab, and click Add.

10. In the Add Groups, Users And Computers dialog box, select the Allow Passwords For The Account To Replicate To This RODC option as shown in Figure 2-50 and click OK.

FIGURE 2-50 Specify the password replication options

11. On the Select Users, Computers, Service Accounts, Or Groups dialog box, type **ADL-Replicated-Accounts**, click Check Names, and click OK.

12. Verify that the ADL-DC dialog box matches Figure 2-51 and click OK.

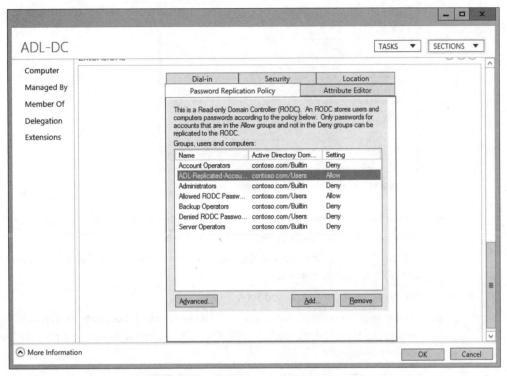

FIGURE 2-51 Verify the password replication options

Exercise 9: View account passwords replicated to ADL-DC

In this exercise, you create a user account and add it to the group that has its password replicated to ADL-DC. You also add the account of a user who should not have his or her password replicated to the RODC to this group. You then trigger replication and verify which accounts have had password information replicated. To complete this exercise, perform the following steps:

1. While signed on to SYD-DC as Contoso\don_funk, click Active Directory Users And Computers in the Tools menu of the Server Manager console.

2. In the Active Directory Users And Computers console, expand Contoso.com and click the Users container.

3. On the Action menu, click New and click User.

4. On the New Object – User dialog box, type **kim_akers** in the Full Name and User Logon Name text boxes as shown in Figure 2-52 and click Next.

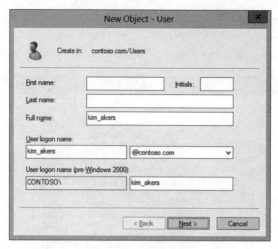

FIGURE 2-52 Create a new user account

5. On the New Object – User dialog box, type **Pa$$w0rd** in the Password and Confirm Password dialog boxes, click Next, and click Finish.

6. In the Active Directory Users And Computers console, click Don Funk. Hold down the Ctrl key and click kim_akers.

7. On the Action menu, click Add To A Group.

8. On the Select Groups dialog box, type **ADL-Replicated-Accounts** as shown in Figure 2-53, click Check Names, and click OK. Click OK to dismiss the Active Directory Domain Services dialog box.

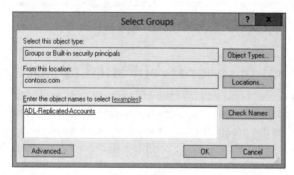

FIGURE 2-53 Add a user to a group

9. In the Active Directory Users And Computers console, click the Domain Controllers node.

10. Right-click ADL-DC and click Properties.

11. On the Password Replication Policy tab, click Advanced.

12. In the Advanced Password Replication Policy for ADL-DC dialog box, click Prepopulate Passwords.

13. In the Select Users Or Computers dialog, type **Don Funk;kim_akers**, click Check Names, and then click OK.

14. In the Prepopulate Passwords dialog box, shown in Figure 2-54, click Yes.

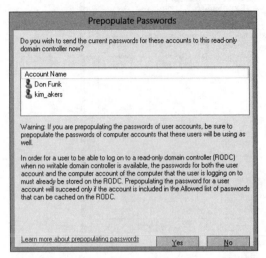

FIGURE 2-54 Prepopulate the passwords

15. On the Prepopulate Password Errors list, verify that Don Funk is listed as shown in Figure 2-55. This is because the Don Funk account belongs to a group that restricts its password from being replicated to the RODC. Click OK.

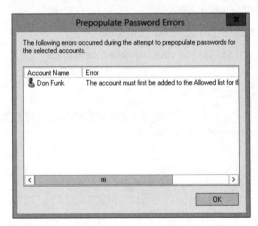

FIGURE 2-55 Verify the account prepopulation error

16. Verify that the kim_akers account password has been replicated to the RODC as shown in Figure 2-56 and click Close.

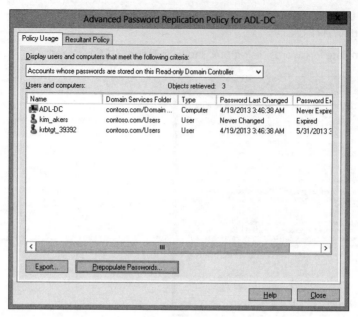

FIGURE 2-56 Verify the password replication

Exercise 10: Monitor replication with repadmin

In this exercise, you monitor replication settings from the command prompt with repadmin. To complete this exercise, perform the following steps:

1. Ensure that you are signed on to MEL-DC as contoso\don_funk.

2. Right-click the Windows PowerShell item on the task bar and click Run As Administrator.

3. In the User Account Control dialog box, click Yes.

4. In the Windows PowerShell window, type the following command as shown in Figure 2-57 and press Enter to generate a replication summary:

```
repadmin /replsummary
```

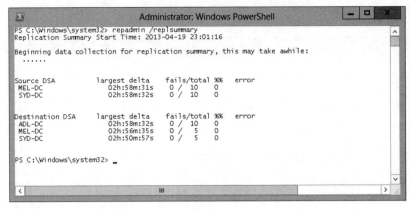

FIGURE 2-57 The output of repadmin /replsummary

5. In the Windows PowerShell window, type the following command as shown in Figure 2-58 and press Enter to generate a list of accounts that have passwords replicated to RODC ADL-DC:

```
repadmin /prp view adl-dc reveal
```

FIGURE 2-58 The output of the repadmin /prp command

6. In the Windows PowerShell window, type the following command as shown in Figure 2-59 and press Enter to force the KCC to recalculate the inbound replication topology:

```
repadmin /kcc
```

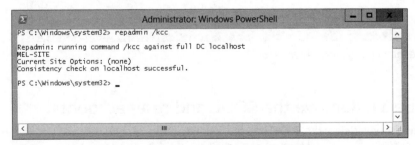

FIGURE 2-59 Trigger the recalculation of the replication topology

7. In the Windows PowerShell window, type the following command as shown in Figure 2-60 and press Enter to display the most recent inbound replication activity:

```
repadmin /showrepl
```

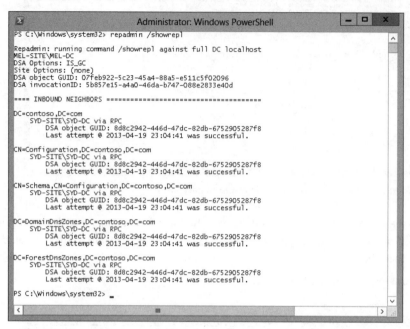

FIGURE 2-60 View the recent replication

8. In the Windows PowerShell window, type the following command as shown in Figure 2-61 and press Enter to force the domain controller to replicate with all replication partners:

```
repadmin /syncall
```

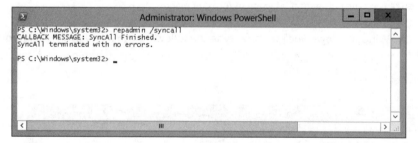

FIGURE 2-61 Trigger synchronization

Exercise 11: Remove the RODC and reset accounts

In this exercise, you delete the RODC and configure all computer and user accounts on the RODC to be reset. To complete this exercise, perform the following steps:

1. Ensure that you are signed on to SYD-DC as Contoso\don_funk.

2. On the Tools menu of the Server Manager console, click Active Directory Users And Computers.

3. In the Active Directory Users And Computers console, expand the Contoso.com\ Domain Controllers node.

4. Right-click ADL-DC and click Delete.

5. In the Active Directory Domain Services dialog box, click Yes.

6. In the Deleting Domain Controller dialog box, click Browse.

7. Configure the Save As dialog box so that you save the file as **reset_accounts.csv** on the Desktop.

8. Ensure that the Reset All Passwords For User Accounts That Were Cached On This Read-Only Domain Controller, Reset All Passwords For Computer Accounts That Were Cached On This Read-Only Domain Controller, and Export The List Of Accounts That Were Cached On This Read-Only Domain Controller check boxes are selected as shown in Figure 2-62 and click Delete.

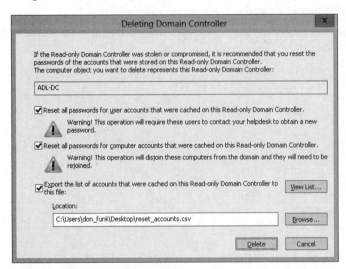

FIGURE 2-62 Delete the RODC account

9. In the Delete Domain Controller dialog box, review the warnings and click OK.

10. In the Delete Domain Controller dialog box, shown in Figure 2-63, click Yes.

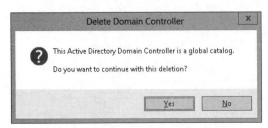

FIGURE 2-63 Verify the domain controller deletion

11. Verify that ADL-DC is no longer listed as a domain controller.

12. On the desktop of SYD-DC, right-click Reset_accounts.csv and click Edit.

13. Review the list of reset accounts.

Suggested practice exercises

The following additional practice exercises are designed to give you more opportunities to practice what you've learned and to help you successfully master the lessons presented in this chapter.

- **Exercise 1** Use Windows PowerShell to create a subnet for use with an Active Directory site that uses the 10.10.100.0/24 IP address range.

- **Exercise 2** Use Windows PowerShell to create a site named LON-SITE that is associated with the subnet created in the previous exercise.

- **Exercise 3** Use Windows PowerShell to create a site link that joins LON-SITE with MEL-SITE.

Answers

This section contains the answers to the lesson review questions in this chapter.

Lesson 1

1. **Correct answer:** A

    A. **Correct.** Restarting this service will reregister a specific domain controller's SRV records in DNS.

    B. **Incorrect.** This service allows for processes to start under alternate credentials. Restarting this service will not reregister a specific domain controller's SRV records.

    C. **Incorrect.** Although this service allows a domain controller to function as a domain controller, restarting this service does not reregister a specific domain controller's SRV records.

    D. **Incorrect.** Although a DNS server hosts SRV records, restarting this service does not reregister a specific domain controller's SRV records.

2. **Correct answer:** C

    A. **Incorrect.** You use the New-ADReplicationSubnet cmdlet to create a new Active Directory subnet.

    B. **Incorrect.** You use the New-ADReplicationSiteLink cmdlet to create site link connecting sites.

    C. **Correct.** You use the Move-ADDirectoryServer cmdlet to move a domain controller to a different Active Directory site.

    D. **Incorrect.** You use the New-ADReplicationSite cmdlet to create a new Active Directory site.

3. **Correct answer:** D

    A. **Incorrect.** You use the New-ADReplicationSiteLink cmdlet to create site link connecting sites.

    B. **Incorrect.** You use the Move-ADDirectoryServer cmdlet to move a domain controller to a different Active Directory site.

    C. **Incorrect.** You use the New-ADReplicationSite cmdlet to create a new Active Directory site.

    D. **Correct.** You use the New-ADReplicationSubnet cmdlet to create a new Active Directory subnet. Active Directory subnets enable Active Directory to recognize IP address ranges and to use those ranges when calculating replication topologies.

4. **Correct answer:** A

    A. **Correct.** You use the New-ADReplicationSite cmdlet to create a new Active Directory site. When creating the site, you can associate it with an existing subnet.

B. Incorrect. You use the New-ADReplicationSubnet cmdlet to create a new Active Directory subnet.

C. Incorrect: You use the Move-ADDirectoryServer cmdlet to move a domain controller to a different Active Directory site.

D. Incorrect. You use the New-ADReplicationSiteLink cmdlet to create site link connecting sites.

5. **Correct answer:** C

A. Incorrect. You use the New-ADReplicationSite cmdlet to create a new Active Directory site.

B. Incorrect. You use the New-ADReplicationSubnet cmdlet to create a new Active Directory subnet.

C. Correct. You use the New-ADReplicationSiteLink cmdlet to create site link connecting sites.

D. Incorrect. You use the Move-ADDirectoryServer cmdlet to move a domain controller to a different Active Directory site.

Lesson 2

1. **Correct answer:** A

A. Correct. Repadmin /prp view [DC Name] reveal lists all of the accounts that have replicated to a specific RODC. You can't use this command with a writable domain controller.

B. Incorrect. Repadmin /replsummary provides information about the failure percentages of inbound and outbound replication in the form of a report.

C. Incorrect. Repadmin /kcc forces the KCC to recalculate inbound replication topology.

D. Incorrect. Repadmin /showrepl shows the status of the domain controller's last attempt to perform inbound replication.

E. Incorrect. Repadmin /syncall forces the local or targeted domain controller to sync with all replication partners.

2. **Correct answer:** D

A. Incorrect. Repadmin /prp view [DC Name] reveal lists all of the accounts that have replicated to a specific RODC. You can't use this command with a writable domain controller.

B. Incorrect. Repadmin /syncall forces the local or targeted domain controller to sync with all replication partners.

C. **Incorrect.** Repadmin /showrepl shows the status of the domain controller's last attempt to perform inbound replication.

D. **Correct.** Repadmin /kcc forces the KCC to recalculate inbound replication topology.]

E. **Incorrect.** Repadmin /replsummary provides information about the failure percentages of inbound and outbound replication in the form of a report.

3. **Correct answer:** E

   A. **Incorrect**. Repadmin /showrepl shows the status of the domain controller's last attempt to perform inbound replication.

   B. **Incorrect.** Repadmin /syncall forces the local or targeted domain controller to sync with all replication partners.

   C. **Incorrect.** Repadmin /kcc forces the KCC to recalculate inbound replication topology.

   D. **Incorrect**. Repadmin /prp view [DC Name] reveal lists all of the accounts that have replicated to a specific RODC. You can't use this command with a writable domain controller.

   E. **Correct.** Repadmin /replsummary provides information about the failure percentages of inbound and outbound replication in the form of a report.

4. **Correct answer:** B

   A. **Incorrect.** Repadmin /showrepl shows the status of the domain controller's last attempt to perform inbound replication.

   B. **Correct.** Repadmin /syncall forces the local or targeted domain controller to sync with all replication partners.

   C. **Incorrect.** Repadmin /kcc forces the KCC to recalculate inbound replication topology.

   D. **Incorrect.** Repadmin /replsummary provides information about the failure percentages of inbound and outbound replication in the form of a report.

   E. **Incorrect.** Repadmin /prp view [DC Name] reveal lists all the accounts that have replicated to a specific RODC. You can't use this command with a writable domain controller.

5. **Correct answer:** C

   A. **Incorrect.** Repadmin /syncall forces the local or targeted domain controller to sync with all replication partners.

   B. **Incorrect.** Repadmin /kcc forces the KCC to recalculate inbound replication topology.

   C. **Correct.** Repadmin /showrepl shows the status of the domain controller's last attempt to perform inbound replication.

   D. **Incorrect.** Repadmin /replsummary provides information about the failure percentages of inbound and outbound replication in the form of a report.

**E.	Incorrect.** Repadmin /prp view [DC Name] reveal lists all the accounts that have replicated to a specific RODC. You can't use this command with a writable domain controller.

**6.	Correct answer:** C

**A.	Correct.** When you delete the computer account of an RODC, you have the option of resetting the passwords of all user accounts that had passwords stored on the RODC. If you do this, you need to assign users new passwords and inform them of the change.

**B.	Incorrect.** Although you can reset the passwords of user accounts, removing an RODC does not give you the option of disabling computer accounts.

**C.	Correct.** When you delete the computer account of an RODC, you have the option of resetting computer account passwords of computer accounts that had passwords stored on the RODC. If you do this, you need to rejoin these computers to the domain.

**D.	Incorrect.** Although you can reset the passwords of computer accounts, removing an RODC does not give you the option of disabling computer accounts.

**7.	Correct answer:** B

**A.	Incorrect.** The Windows Server 2003 domain functional level does not support upgrading SYSVOL replication so that it uses DFS instead of FRS.

**B.	Correct.** The Windows Server 2008 domain functional level is the minimum required to support upgrading SYSVOL replication so that it uses DFS instead of FRS.

**C.	Incorrect.** The Windows Server 2008 domain functional level, rather than the Window Server 2008 R2 domain functional level, is the minimum required to support upgrading SYSVOL replication so that it uses DFS instead of FRS.

**D.	Incorrect.** The Windows Server 2008 domain functional level, rather than the Window Server 2012 domain functional level, is the minimum required to support upgrading SYSVOL replication so that it uses DFS instead of FRS.

**8.	Correct answer:** A

**A.	Correct.** You can use dfsrmig.exe to determine if FRS or DFS is being used for SYSVOL replication. You can also use dfsrmig.exe to migrate from using FRS to using DFS to support SYSVOL replication.

**B.	Incorrect.** Although you use repadmin.exe to manage Active Directory replication, you can't use repadmin.exe to determine if FRS or DFS is being used to support SYSVOL replication.

**C.	Incorrect.** Although dcdiag.exe provides domain controller diagnostics, it cannot be used to determine if FRS or DFS is being used to support SYSVOL replication.

**D.	Incorrect.** You use dnscmd.exe to manage DNS. You can't use dnscmd.exe to determine if FRS or DFS is being used to support SYSVOL replication.

CHAPTER 3

Advanced DHCP and DNS

Windows Server 2012 and Windows Server 2012 R2 include several tools that increase the functionality, security, and manageability of name and Internet Protocol (IP) address spaces. It is important to be able to efficiently manage the name and address space because of the increase in computers on organizational networks that use dynamically assigned names and addresses. This chapter discusses IP address management (IPAM), a technology that simplifies the centralized management of Dynamic Host Control Protocol (DHCP) and Domain Name System (DNS) servers. Maintaining the integrity of the DNS is also important, and in recent years there have been an increase in attacks against DNS infrastructure. In this chapter you discover several different methods that enable you to harden your organization's DNS infrastructure.

Lessons in this chapter:

- Lesson 1: Implementing an advanced DNS solution
- Lesson 2: Implementing an advanced DHCP solution
- Lesson 3: Deploying and managing IPAM

Before you begin

To complete the practice exercises in this chapter, you need to have deployed computers SYD-DC, MEL-DC, CBR-DC, and ADL-DC as described in the Introduction, using the evaluation edition of Windows Server 2012 R2.

Lesson 1: Implementing an advanced DNS solution

DNS is one of those core network services to which many administrators pay little attention. It's possible to manage a Windows Server 2012 R2 Active Directory implementation without having to open the DNS Manager console. In some environments, especially those that have stricter than average security requirements, you might need to go beyond the default configuration to make your organization's DNS implementation more secure. In this lesson, find out about Domain Name System Security Extensions (DNSSEC), how to log DNS traffic, and how to configure a GlobalNames Zone. You read about several steps that you can take to harden a DNS server against attack by nefarious third parties.

DNSSEC

DNSSEC provides clients with a way of verifying the integrity of the results of a DNS query. DNSSEC accomplishes this by cryptographically signing DNS zone data. When a client queries a record in a zone signed using DNSSEC, the DNS server returns both the record and the record's digital signature that enables the client to validate that record as shown in Figure 3-1.

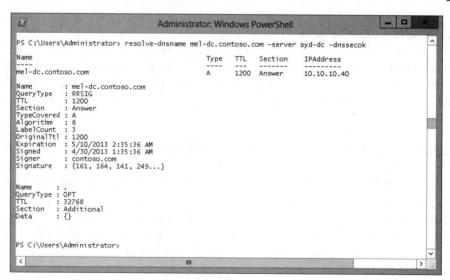

FIGURE 3-1   View the Resource Record Signature (RRSIG) record

When you sign a zone, the following new resource records are created:

- **Resource Record Signature (RRSIG) record**   This record is stored in the DNS zone, and each one is associated with an individual zone record. When a DNS query against the secure zone is performed, the DNS server returns both the record queried and the associated RRSIG record.

- **DNSKEY**   This special record allows for cryptographic verification of the RRSIG records.

- **Next Secure (NSEC/NSEC3) record**   This record provides proof that a queried record does not exist. For example, if a DNS client is querying the record unicorn. contoso.com and there is no unicorn.contoso.com host record hosted in the contoso. com zone, the DNS server returns an NSEC record.

When you implement DNSSEC, the following additional cryptographic keys are created:

- **Trust anchor**   This is a special public cryptographic key associated with a specific zone. The DNSKEY record is validated against this key. When you use DNSSEC with an Active Directory Integrated Zone, the trust anchor is replicated to all DNS servers hosted on domain controllers in the forest.

- **Key Signing Key (KSK)**   This special cryptographic key is used to sign all DNSKEY records. This key is created by a computer that hosts the DNSSEC Key Master role. The DNSSEC Key Master is a computer, usually the first DNS server on which DNSSEC is implemented, that generates and manages signing keys for a DNSSEC protected zone. A single DNS server can function as a DNSSEC Key Master for multiple zones.

- **Zone Signing Key (ZSK)**   This special cryptographic key is used to sign zone data, such as individual host records. The ZSK is created using the DNSSEC Key Master.

You can configure the Group Policy to ensure that clients only accept records from a DNS server for a specific zone if those records have been signed using DNSSEC. You do this by configuring the Name Resolution Policy Table (NRPT), which is located in the Computer Configuration\Policies\Windows Settings\Name Resolution Policy node of a GPO. Figure 3-2 shows configuring Group Policy in such a way that clients who are querying records in the contoso.com zone only accept those records as valid if they are correctly signed using DNSSEC.

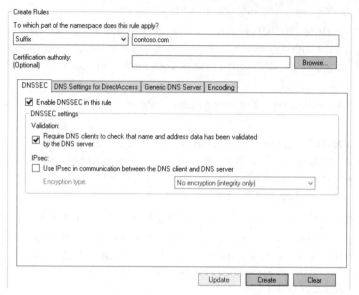

FIGURE 3-2 Require DNSSEC for a specific DNS suffix

DNSSEC is appropriate for high-security environments, such as those where Internet Protocol Security (IPSec) and authenticating switches are also in use. DNSSEC protects against attacks where clients are fed false DNS information. In many small-sized to medium-sized environments, the likelihood of such an attack is minimal. In high-security environments, enabling DNSSEC is a prudent precaution.

> **MORE INFO   DNSSEC**
>
> To learn more about DNSSEC zone, consult the following article:
> *http://technet.microsoft.com/en-us/library/jj200221.aspx.*

DNS event logs

The DNS server log is located in the Applications And Services Logs folder in Event Viewer. Depending upon how you configure event logging on the Event Logging tab of the DNS server's properties, as shown in Figure 3-3, this event log records information including:

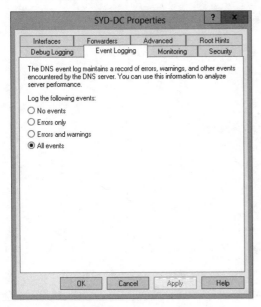

FIGURE 3-3 Configure the DNS event logs

- Changes to the DNS service. For example when the DNS Server service is stopped or started.
- Zone loading and signing events.
- Modifications to DNS server configuration.
- DNS warning and error events.

By default the DNS server records all of these events. It's also possible to configure the DNS server to only log errors, or errors and warning events. The key with any type of logging is that you should only enable logging for information that you might need to review at some time. Many administrators log everything "just in case" even though they will only ever be interested in a specific type of event.

In the event that you need to debug how a DNS server is performing, you can enable debug logging on the Debug Logging tab of the DNS server's properties dialog box as shown in Figure 3-4. Debug logging is resource intensive, and you should only use it when you have a specific problem related to the functionality of the DNS server. You can configure debug logging to use a filter so that only traffic from specific hosts is recorded, rather than traffic from all hosts that interact with the DNS server.

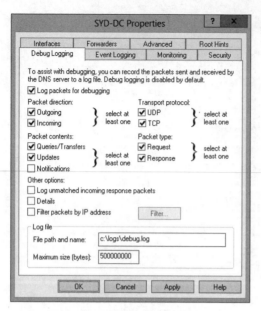

FIGURE 3-4 Configure debug logging

GlobalNames zones

GlobalNames zones provide single-label name resolution. Single-label name resolution allows single names to be translated to IP addresses, such as Windows Server Update Services (WSUS), rather than requiring fully qualified domain names (FQDN) such as wsus.contoso. com. In the past, single-label name resolution has been handled by Windows Internet Name Service (WINS), a service that translates NetBIOS names to IPv4 addresses. GlobalNames zones are hosted on DNS servers and are intended as a replacement technology for WINS. You use alias (CNAME) records when populating a GlobalNames zone, which maps the single-label name to an existing FQDN as shown in Figure 3-5.

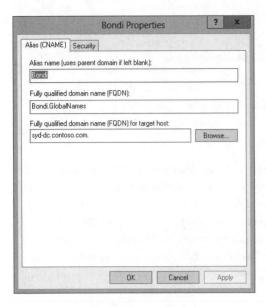

FIGURE 3-5 A CNAME record

Consider using GlobalNames zones in the following circumstances:

■ You need to provide single-label name resolution when your network uses IPv6 addressing. WINS does not support IPv6, whereas a single-label record in the GlobalNames zone are mapped to A or AAAA records, allowing both IPv4 and IPv6 name resolution.

■ You need to provide single-label name resolution for a small number of hosts. An advantage of WINS is that it's dynamically populated. You must populate the GlobalNames zone manually by creating CNAME records.

> **MORE INFO** **GLOBALNAMES ZONE**
>
> To learn more about the GlobalNames zone, consult the following article:
> *http://technet.microsoft.com/en-us/library/cc731744.aspx.*

To deploy the GlobalNames zone, you need to do the following:

■ Create a new Active Directory integrated forward lookup zone named GlobalNames that you have configured to replicate throughout the forest.

■ Manually activate the GlobalNames zone on each DNS server in the forest by running the following Windows PowerShell command (substituting DNSServerName name for the FQDN of the DNS server):

```
Set-DNSServerGlobalNameZone –ComputerName DNSServerName –Enable $True
```

Advanced DNS options

In high-security environments there are a number of steps that you can take to make a DNS server more secure from attackers who attempt to spoof the server so that it provides records that redirect clients to malicious sites. Although DNSSEC provides security for zones hosted on the server, most DNS server traffic involves retrieving information from remote DNS servers and then passing that information on to clients. In this section you find out about settings that you can configure to ensure that the information relayed to clients retains its integrity in the event that a nefarious third party attempts to spoof your organization's DNS servers.

DNS socket pool

DNS socket pool is a technology that makes cache-tampering and spoofing attacks more difficult by using source port randomization when issuing DNS queries to remote DNS servers. To spoof the DNS server with an incorrect record, the attacker needs to guess which randomized port was used as well as the randomized transaction ID issued with the query. A DNS server running on Windows Server 2012 or Windows Server 2012 R2 uses a socket pool of 2,500 by default. You can use the dnscmd command-line tool to vary the socket pool between 0 and 10,000. For example, to set the socket pool size to 4,000, issue the following command:

```
dnscmd /config /socketpoolsize 4000
```

You must restart the DNS service before the reconfigured socket pool size is used.

> **MORE INFO** **DNS SOCKET POOL**
>
> To learn more about the DNS socket pool, consult the following article:
> *http://technet.microsoft.com/en-us/library/ee683907(v=ws.10).aspx.*

DNS cache locking

DNS *cache locking* enables you to control when information stored in the DNS server's cache can be overwritten. For example, when a recursive DNS server responds to a query for a record that is hosted on another DNS server, it caches the results of that query so that it doesn't have to contact the remote DNS server if the same record is queried again within the TTL (Time to Live) value of the resource record. DNS cache locking prevents record data in a

DNS server's cache from being overwritten until a configured percentage of the TTL value has expired. By default, the DNS cache locking value is set to 100, but you can reset it using the Set-DNSServerCache cmdlet with the LockingPercent option. For example, to set the cache locking value to 80 percent, issue the following command and then restart the DNS server service:

```
Set-DNSServerCache -LockingPercent 80
```

> **MORE INFO DNS CACHE LOCKING**
>
> To learn more about the DNS Cache Locking zone, consult the following article:
> *http://technet.microsoft.com/en-us/library/ee683892(v=ws.10).aspx.*

DNS recursion

DNS servers on Windows Server 2012 or Windows Server 2012 R2 perform *recursive queries* on behalf of clients by default. This means that when the client asks the DNS server to find a record that isn't stored in a zone hosted by the DNS server, the DNS server goes out and finds the result of that query and passes it back to the client. It's possible for nefarious third parties to use recursion as a denial-of-service (DoS) attack vector, slowing a DNS server to the point where it becomes unresponsive. You can disable recursion on the Advanced tab of the DNS server's properties as shown in Figure 3-6.

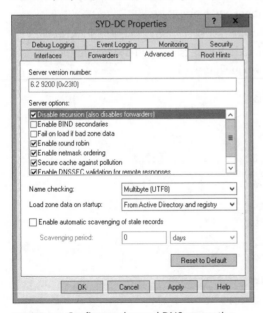

FIGURE 3-6 Configure advanced DNS properties

MORE INFO DNS RECURSION

To learn more about the DNS recursion, consult the following article:
http://technet.microsoft.com/en-us/library/cc771738.aspx.

Netmask ordering

Netmask ordering ensures that the DNS server returns the host record on the requesting client's subnet if such a record exists. For example, imagine that the following host records existed on a network that used 24-bit subnet masks:

- 10.10.10.105 wsus.contoso.com

- 10.10.20.105 wsus.contoso.com

- 10.10.30.105 wsus.contoso.com

If netmask ordering is enabled and a client with the IP address 10.10.20.50 performs a lookup of wsus.contoso.com, it is always returned the record 10.10.20.105 because this record is on the same subnet as the client. If netmask ordering is not enabled, then the DNS server returns records in a round robin fashion. If the requesting client is not on the same network as any of the host records, then the DNS server also returns records in a round robin fashion. Netmask ordering is useful for services such as Windows Server Update Services (WSUS) that you might have at each branch office. When you use it, the DNS server redirects the client in the branch office to a resource on the local subnet when one exists.

Netmask ordering is enabled by default on Windows Server 2012 and Windows Server 2012 R2 DNS servers. You can verify that netmask ordering is enabled by viewing the advanced properties of the DNS server as shown in Figure 3-7.

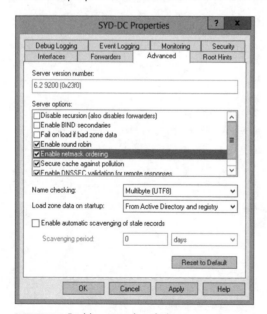

FIGURE 3-7 Enable netmask ordering

Delegated administration

In some larger environments, you might want to separate administrative privileges so that the people who are responsible for managing your organization's DNS servers don't have other permissions, such as the ability to create user accounts or reset passwords. By default, members of the Domain Admins group are able to perform all DNS administration tasks on DNS servers within a domain. Members of the Enterprise Admins group are able to perform all DNS administration tasks on any DNS server in the forest.

You can use the DNSAdmins domain local group to grant users the ability to view and modify DNS data as well as server configuration of DNS servers within a domain. You add users to this group when you want to allow them to perform DNS administration tasks without giving them additional permissions. You can assign permissions that allow users or security groups to manage a specific DNS server using the Security tab of the server's properties as shown in Figure 3-8.

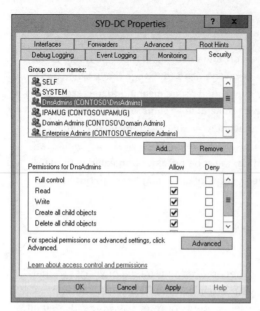

FIGURE 3-8 The DnsAdmins security group

You can also configure permissions at the zone level. You do this by assigning a security principal permissions on the Security tab of the zone's properties as shown in Figure 3-9. You might do this when you want to allow a specific person to manage host records without assigning them any other permissions. Today most organizations allow DNS records to be updated dynamically. This means that the only zones where you might need to configure special permissions to allow manual management are special ones, such as those that are accessible to clients on the Internet.

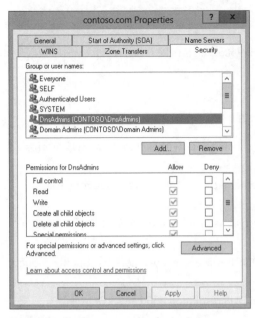

FIGURE 3-9 Configure zone-level permissions

Analyze zone level statistics

You can understand how a DNS zone is being utilized by clients, by viewing DNS statistics. You can do this on computers running the Windows Server 2012 R2 operating system by using the Get-DnsServerStatistics cmdlet. Some of the information that you can view using this cmdlet includes:

- **Cache statistics** View information about the number of requests that the DNS server satisfies from cache.

- **DNSSEC statistics** Provides data about successful and failed DNSSEC validations.

- **Error statistics** Detailed information about the number of errors, including bad keys, bad signatures, refusals, and unknown errors.

- **Master statistics** Contains information about zone transfer statistics.

- **Query statistics** Information about queries made to the DNS server.

- **Record statistics** Data about number of records in the cache and memory utilization.

- **Recursion statistics** Information about how the DNS server solves recursive queries.

You can view statistics related to a specific zone by using the –Zonename parameter. For example, if you wanted to view the statistics of the australia.adatum.com zone, you would issue the following command from an elevated Windows PowerShell prompt on a computer that hosts the DNS server role:

```
Get-DnsServerStatistics -Zonename australia.adatum.com
```

MORE INFO **DNS STATISTICS**

To learn more about DNS statistics, consult the following article: *http://technet.microsoft. com/en-us/en-us/library/dn305898.aspx.*

Lesson summary

- DNSSEC uses digital signatures to allow clients to verify the integrity of DNS records returned from a DNS server.
- The NRPT enables you to configure whether a client requires a specific zone to be signed using DNSSEC.
- A DNS event log records DNS events such as service startup and shutdown as well as errors.
- Debug logging enables you to record DNS traffic and events more thoroughly, though this has an effect on performance.
- GlobalNames zone provides single-label DNS resolution and can serve as a replacement for WINS.
- The DNS socket pool allows for port randomization with DNS requests as a way of protecting against spoofing attacks.
- DNS cache locking blocks a record stored in the DNS server's cache from being overwritten until a specified percentage of the record's TTL has expired.
- You can enable DNS recursion as a way of hardening a DNS server against attacks that use recursion as a way of denying service.
- Netmask ordering allows the DNS server to return a DNS record that is on the same IP subnet as the client, if such a record exists.
- You can analyze zone level statistics using the Get-DnsServerStatistics cmdlet.

Lesson review

Answer the following questions to test your knowledge of the information in this lesson. You can find the answers to these questions and explanations of each answer choice in the "Answers" section at the end of this chapter.

1. The contoso.com zone hosts DNS records that map FQDNs of hosts in the zone to their IPv6 addresses. You have configured a GlobalNames zone and want to allow single-label name resolution of the name WSUS to the appropriate IPv6 address. Which type of record should you create in the GlobalNames zone to accomplish this goal?

   A. Host (AAAA)

   B. Alias (CNAME)

   C. Mail Exchanger (MX)

   D. Pointer (PTR)

2. You have deployed WSUS servers to each of your organization's branch offices. Each branch office is located on its own subnet. You have created DNS records that use the same name, wsus.contoso.com, for each of the WSUS servers in these different branch offices. You want to ensure that when a client makes a name request for the record wsus.contoso.com, the DNS server returns the record that corresponds to an IP address on the client's local subnet. Which of the following DNS options do you configure to accomplish this goal?

   A. Socket pool

   B. Cache locking

   C. Recursion

   D. Netmask ordering

3. The DNS server that hosts your organization's external address space is under attack from nefarious third parties who are slowing it down by constantly launching DNS queries against the server for hosts in zones not hosted on the server. The DNS server should only return data for zones that it hosts directly. Which of the following settings should you configure to stop it responding to queries for hostnames located in zones that it does not host?

   A. Recursion

   B. Netmask ordering

   C. Cache locking

   D. Socket pool

4. You want to ensure that a record stored in the DNS server's cache cannot be overwritten until 90 percent of its TTL period has expired. Which of the following DNS server settings would you configure to accomplish this goal?

   A. Netmask ordering

   B. Recursion

   C. Socket pool

   D. Cache locking

5. You want to increase the number of ports available that can be used when the DNS server makes a query. Which of the following DNS server settings should you configure to accomplish this goal?

   A. Socket pool

   B. Netmask ordering

   C. Recursion

   D. Cache locking

Lesson 2: Implementing an advanced DHCP solution

Like DNS, DHCP is another network service that most administrators barely pay attention to after they've configured it. The main concern that most administrators have with DHCP is that up until the release of Windows Server 2012, it's been difficult to configure as a highly available service. Although DNS became highly available through being able to be hosted on any domain controller, the problem with making DHCP highly available was ensuring that when multiple DHCP servers were in play, duplicate addresses weren't assigned to separate clients. In this lesson you find out about superscopes and multicast scopes. You also see how you can make DHCP more fault tolerant by implementing split scopes or by deploying DHCP failover.

> **After this lesson, you will be able to:**
>
> - Create and manage DHCP superscopes
> - Implement and maintain multicast scopes
> - Create DHCP split scopes
> - Configure DHCP Name Protection
> - Implement DHCP failover
> - Configure DNS registration
>
> **Estimated lesson time: 30 minutes**

Superscopes

A *superscope* is a collection of individual DHCP scopes. You might create a superscope when you want to bind existing scopes together for administrative reasons. For example, you might have a subnet in a building that is close to fully allocated. You add a second subnet to the building and then bind them together into a superscope. The process of binding several separate logical subnets together on the same physical network is known as multinetting. Figure 3-10 shows a superscope.

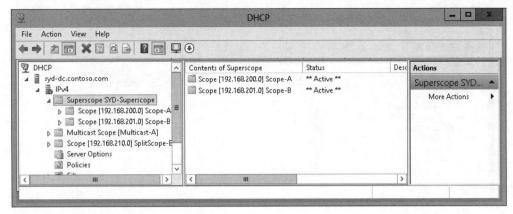

FIGURE 3-10 A superscope

There needs to be at least one existing scope present on the DHCP server before you can create a superscope. After you have created a superscope, you can add new subnets to, or remove subnets from, that scope. It's also possible to deactivate subnets within a scope, while keeping others active. You might use this technique when migrating clients from one IP address range to another, having both the source and destination scopes part of the same superscope, activating the new scope, and deactivating the original scope as necessary when performing the migration.

> **MORE INFO SUPERSCOPES**
>
> To learn more about superscopes consult the following article: *http://technet.microsoft. com/en-us/library/dd759168.aspx.*

Multicast scopes

A *multicast address* is an address that allows many communications on a network. When you use multicast, multiple hosts on a network listen for traffic on a single multicast IP address. Multicast addresses are in the IPv4 range of 224.0.0.0 through to 239.255.255.255. *Multicast scopes* are collections of multicast addresses. You can configure a Windows Server 2012 or Windows Server 2012 R2 DHCP server to host multicast scopes. Multicast scopes are also known as MADCAP (Multicast Address Dynamic Client Allocation Protocol) scopes as applications that require access to multicast addresses support the MADCAP application programming interface (API). Figure 3-11 shows a multicast scope.

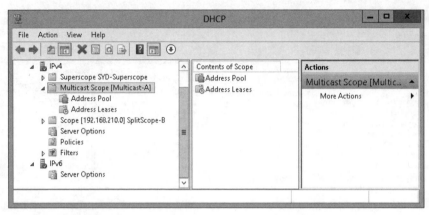

FIGURE 3-11 A multicast scope

Windows Deployment Services are the most common use of multicast addresses in infrastructures that use the default configurations of Windows Server 2012 or Windows Server 2012 R2. You can, however, configure the Windows Deployment Services (WDS) server with its own set of multicast addresses, and you don't need to configure a special multicast scope in DHCP to support this role.

✔ **Quick check**

- What is the range of multicast IP addresses?

Quick check answer

- Multicast IP addresses are in the range of 224.0.0.0 through 239.255.255.255

Split scopes

Split scope is one method of providing fault tolerance for a DHCP scope. The idea behind a split scope is that you host one part of the scope on one DHCP server, and a second smaller part of the scope on a second DHCP server. Usually this split has 80 percent of the addresses on the first DHCP server, and 20 percent of the addresses on the partner server. In this scenario, the DHCP server that hosts the 20 percent portion of the address space is usually located on a remote subnet. In this scenario you use a DHCP Relay Agent configured with a delay so that the majority of addresses are leased from the DHCP server that hosts 80 percent of the address space. Split scopes are most likely to be used in scenarios where your DHCP servers aren't running on the Windows Server 2012 operating system. If you want to provide fault tolerance for scopes hosted on servers running Windows Server 2012 or Windows Server 2012 R2, you should instead implement DHCP failover.

> **MORE INFO** SPLIT SCOPES
>
> To learn more about split scopes, consult the following information. This information deals with Windows Server 2003 configurations, but is still relevant to Windows Server 2012 and Windows Server 2012 R2: *http://technet.microsoft.com/en-us/library/cc757346(v=ws.10).aspx.*

DNS registration

You can configure a DHCP server running the Windows Server 2012 or Windows Server 2012 R2 operating system to register a host's name in DNS when that DHCP server leases an address to a client. When you do this, you ensure that addresses stored in the DNS zone match the IP addresses leased by the DHCP server. This is useful in environments where hosts are often changing IP addresses because it ensures that the DNS server has the most up-to-date name/IP address mapping. You configure DNS registration at the DHCP server level or at the individual DHCP scope level. Figure 3-12 shows the DNS registration page of a DHCP scope named ALPHA where dynamic registration is configured.

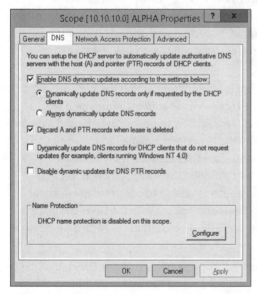

FIGURE 3-12 DNS registration

You can configure the following DNS registration options:

- **Enable DNS Dynamic Updates According To The Settings Below**   This setting allows you to configure the DHCP server to only update DNS records when requested by the client (the default value). You can also configure registration to always dynamically update DNS records each time the DHCP server leases an address.

- **Discard A And PTR Records When Lease Is Deleted**   Enabled by default, the DHCP server will instruct the DNS server to remove any associated host and reverse lookup records when a DHCP lease expires and is deleted. Use this option in scopes that support transient clients, such as those that only infrequently connect to a specific network.

- **Dynamically Update DNS Records For DHCP Clients That Do Not Request Updates**   Enabling this setting will ensure that DNS records are always updated when the DHCP server leases an address. Selecting this option configures the DHCP server to perform registration in a manner similar to when the Always Dynamically Update DNS records option is enabled.

- **Disable Dynamic Updates For DNS PTR Records**   This option configures the DHCP server to update host (A) records, but does not update records in a reverse lookup zone. This option is useful for organizations that haven't configured reverse lookup zones where attempts to register PTR records cause errors in the event log.

Name Protection

DHCP *Name Protection* is a feature that enables you to ensure that the hostnames that a DHCP server registers with a DNS server are not overwritten in the event that a non-Windows operating system has the same name. DHCP Name Protection also protects names from being overwritten by hosts that use static addresses that conflict with DHCP-assigned addresses.

For example, in the contoso.com domain there is a computer running the Windows 8.1 operating system that has the name Auckland. It receives its IP address information from a Windows Server 2012 DHCP server. The DHCP server registers this name in DNS, and a record associating the name Auckland.contoso.com with the IP address assigned to the computer running Windows 8.1 is now present in the contoso.com DNS zone. A newly installed computer running on a distribution of Linux is also assigned the name Auckland. Because Name Protection has been enabled, this new computer is unable to overwrite the existing record with a record associating the name Auckland.contoso.com with the Linux computer's IP address. If Name Protection had not been enabled, it's possible that the record would have been overwritten.

You can enable Name Protection on a scope by clicking Configure on the DNS tab of the IPv4 or IPv6 properties dialog box as shown in Figure 3-13. You can also do this using the Set-DhcpServerv4DnsSetting or the Set-DhcpServerv6DnsSetting cmdlet. For example, to configure the DHCP server on computer MEL-DC so that Name Protection is enabled on all IPv4 scopes, issue the command:

```
Set-DhcpServerv4DnsSetting -Computer MEL-DC -NameProtection $true
```

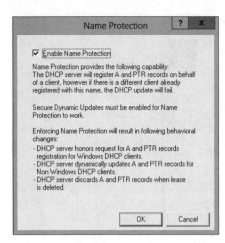

FIGURE 3-13 Configure Name Protection

MORE INFO **NAME PROTECTION**

To learn more about Name Protection, consult the following article:
http://technet.microsoft.com/en-us/library/dd759188.aspx.

DHCP failover

DHCP failover enables you to configure DHCP to be highly available without using split scopes. DHCP failover is a feature new to Windows Server 2012. You have two options when configuring DHCP failover:

- **Hot standby mode**   This relationship is a traditional failover relationship and is shown in Figure 3-14. When you configure this relationship, the primary server handles all DHCP traffic unless it becomes unavailable. You can configure DHCP servers to be in multiple separate relationships, so it's possible that a DHCP server can be the primary server in one relationship and a hot standby server in another relationship. When configuring this relationship, you specify a percentage of the address ranges to be reserved on the standby server. The default value is 5 percent. This 5 percent of addresses is available as soon as the primary server is unavailable. The hot standby server takes control of the entire address range when the figure specified by the state switchover interval is reached. The default value for this interval is 60 minutes.

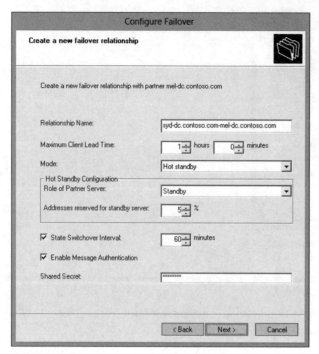

FIGURE 3-14 Configure a hot standby relationship

- **Load sharing mode** This is the default mode when you create a DHCP failover relationship. In this mode both servers provide IP addresses to clients according to the ratio defined by the load balance percentage as shown in Figure 3-15. The default is for each server to share 50 percent of the load. The Maximum Client Lead Time is used to renew DHCP leases issued by the failed partner.

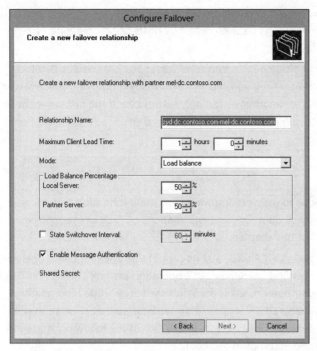

FIGURE 3-15 Configure load balanced DHCP

Prior to configuring DHCP failover, you need to remove any split scopes between the potential partners. You can also choose a shared secret to authenticate replication traffic, although you won't have to enter this secret on the partner DHCP server.

> **MORE INFO DHCP FAILOVER**
>
> To learn more about DHCP failover consult the following article:
> *http://technet.microsoft.com/en-us/library/hh831385.aspx*.

Lesson summary

- Superscopes enable you to combine existing DHCP scopes for the purpose of administration.
- Multicast scopes enable you to provide multicast address ranges to applications that require multicast addresses.
- Split scopes enable you to host parts of the same scope on different DHCP servers. Split scopes provide high availability if DHCP servers don't run the Windows Server 2012 operating system.
- DNS registration allows you to have the DHCP server update DNS with the DHCP client's name and IP address information.

- Name Protection enables you to configure DHCP so that names registered on behalf of Windows clients in DNS can't be overwritten by hosts using operating systems unrelated to Microsoft.

- DHCP failover is a technology new to Windows Server 2012. It enables DHCP servers to be configured in a partner relationship. In hot standby mode, one DHCP server serves as a hot standby for another server, only taking over if the first server becomes unavailable. In load sharing mode, the DHCP servers share IP address allocation duties for the same scope.

Lesson review

Answer the following questions to test your knowledge of the information in this lesson. You can find the answers to these questions and explanations of each answer choice in the "Answers" section at the end of this chapter.

1. Your organization has two DHCP servers at its central site. The first one is hosted on a computer running the Windows Server 2012 operating system. The second DHCP server is hosted on a computer running the Windows Server 2008 R2 operating system. You want to make a DHCP scope highly available so that clients can still obtain address leases if one of these DHCP servers fail. Which of the following strategies should you implement to accomplish this goal?

   A. Configure DHCP failover. Use hot standby mode.

   B. Configure DHCP failover. Use load sharing mode.

   C. Configure a split scope.

   D. Configure a superscope.

2. Your organization has two DHCP servers at its central site. Both DHCP servers are running on the Windows Server 2012 operating system. One DHCP server also hosts the company's intranet site. You want to configure DHCP so that one DHCP server handles the majority of the organization's DHCP traffic and the other DHCP server, installed on the server that hosts the intranet site, only leases addresses if the first one becomes unavailable. The second DHCP server should be able to lease addresses from the entire scope until such time as the first DHCP server is returned to service. Which of the following strategies should you implement to accomplish this goal?

   A. Configure DHCP failover. Use load sharing mode.

   B. Configure a split scope.

   C. Configure DHCP failover. Use hot standby mode.

   D. Configure a superscope.

3. You are about to add a large number of users and computers to one of the existing buildings at your company. Unfortunately the existing DHCP scope used at this building is close to exhaustion. You want to configure DHCP so that clients on this physical network can be leased addresses from either the original or an additional

address range, but allow these ranges to be administered as a single combined entity. Which of the following strategies should you implement to accomplish this goal?

A. Configure a superscope.

B. Configure a split scope.

C. Configure DHCP failover. Use load sharing mode.

D. Configure DHCP failover. Use hot standby mode.

4. Your organization's head office has two DHCP servers that are hosted on computers running the Windows Server 2012 operating system. You want to configure these DHCP servers so that they share scopes and respond to client requests in a load-balanced manner. In the event that one server fails, the other server should be able to lease addresses from the entirety of any scope that it hosts after the partner server has been unavailable for a preconfigured amount of time. Which of the following strategies should you implement to accomplish this goal?

A. Configure a split scope.

B. Configure DHCP failover. Use load sharing mode.

C. Configure DHCP failover. Use hot standby mode.

D. Configure a superscope.

Lesson 3: Deploying and managing IPAM

IP Address Management (IPAM) is a technology introduced with the release of Windows Server 2012 that simplifies the process of managing multiple DHCP and DNS servers. Rather than having to keep detailed records to track scopes and DHCP servers, IPAM enables you to view and manage this information centrally. In this lesson you find out about the functionality of the IPAM feature and how you can deploy IPAM to manage your organization's DHCP and DNS servers.

After this lesson, you will be able to:

- Configure IPAM
- Configure server discovery
- Create and manage IP blocks and ranges
- Track IP addresses
- Delegate IPAM administration
- Configure IPAM database storage

Estimated lesson time: 45 minutes

Introduction to IPAM

IPAM enables you to centralize the management of DHCP and DNS servers. Rather than managing each server separately, you can use IPAM to manage them from a single console. You can use a single IPAM server to manage up to 150 separate DHCP servers and up to 500 individual DNS servers. A single IPAM server is able to manage 6,000 separate DHCP scopes and 150 separate DNS zones. You can perform tasks such as creating address scopes, configuring address reservations, and managing DHCP and DNS options globally, rather than having to perform these tasks on a server-by-server basis.

You can also use IPAM to search stored IP address lease data, MAC address data, and corresponding user sign on and sign off information. Microsoft estimates that the Windows Internal Database (WID) used by IPAM is able to store three years of IP address utilization data for an organization that has 100,000 users before data must be purged.

> **MORE INFO IPAM**
>
> To get more of an overview of IPAM, consult the following article: *http://technet.microsoft.com/en-us/library/jj878343.aspx.*

Deploy IPAM

You can only install the IPAM feature on a computer that is a member of an Active Directory domain. IPAM is also limited so that you can only use it to manage DHCP and DNS servers that are members of the same Active Directory forest. You can't use IPAM to manage standalone servers or servers that are members of different forests. You can have multiple IPAM servers within a single Active Directory forest. You are likely to do this if your organization is geographically dispersed.

It's important to note IPAM cannot manage a locally installed DHCP or DNS server. For this reason you should install the IPAM feature on a server that doesn't host the DNS or DHCP roles. IPAM is also not supported on computers that host the domain controller server role. Additionally, if you want to use the IPAM server to manage IPv6 address ranges, you need to ensure that IPv6 is enabled on the computer that will host the IPAM server.

> **MORE INFO DEPLOYING THE IPAM SERVER**
>
> To learn more about deploying the IPAM server, consult the following TechNet document: *http://technet.microsoft.com/en-us/library/jj878327.aspx.*

Configure IPAM database storage

You could only use the version of IPAM that shipped with Windows Server 2012 with the Windows Internal Database (WID). The version of IPAM available in Windows Server 2012 R2 supports using a SQL Server 2012 instance for hosting IPAM data. This allows you to host the

IPAM database on a host that is separate from the IPAM server. Microsoft recommends that the SQL Server instance be devoted to hosting the IPAM database. You should not host other databases on this instance.

Configure server discovery

Server discovery is the process where the IPAM server checks with Active Directory to locate domain controllers, DNS servers, and DHCP servers. You select which domains to discover in the Configure Server Discovery dialog box, as shown in Figure 3-16.

FIGURE 3-16 Configure server discovery

After you've completed server discovery, you need to run a special PowerShell cmdlet that creates and provisions Group Policy objects that allow the servers to be managed by the IPAM server. When you set up the IPAM server, you choose a GPO name prefix as shown in Figure 3-17. You use this prefix when executing the Invoke-IpamGpoProvisioning Windows PowerShell cmdlet that creates the appropriate GPOs.

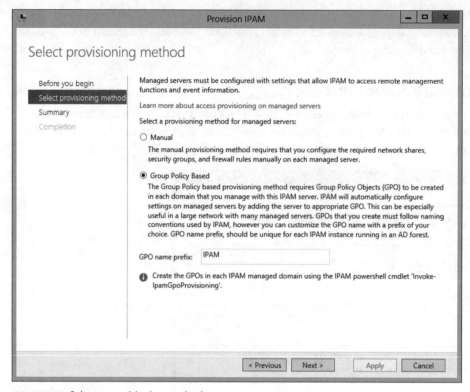

FIGURE 3-17 Select a provisioning method

If you use the GPO prefix IPAM, the three GPOs are named:

- IPAM_DC_NPS
- IPAM_DHCP
- IPAM_DNS

Until these GPOs apply to the discovered servers, these servers are listed as having an IPAM Access Status of Blocked. After the GPOs are applied to the discovered servers, the IPAM Access Status changes to Unblocked as shown in Figure 3-18.

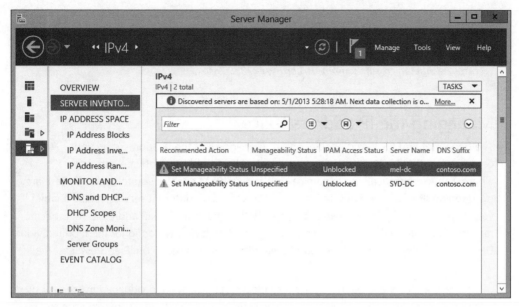

FIGURE 3-18 Server inventory

When the discovered service has an IPAM Access Status set to Unblocked, you can edit the properties of the server and set it to Managed as shown in Figure 3-19. After you do this, you can use IPAM to manage the selected services on the server.

FIGURE 3-19 Configure server manageability

MORE INFO **SERVER DISCOVERY**

To learn more about server discovery, consult the following article:
http://technet.microsoft.com/en-us/library/jj878355.aspx.

Managing the IP address space

The benefit of IPAM is that it enables you to manage all of the IP addresses in your organization. IPAM supports the management of IPv4 public and private addresses whether they are statically or dynamically assigned. IPAM enables you to detect if there are overlapping IP address ranges defined in DHCP scopes on different servers. It also enables you to determine IP address utilization and whether there are free IP addresses in a specific range, and create DHCP reservations centrally without having to configure them on individual DHCP servers. IPAM also enables you to create DNS records based on IP address lease information.

IPAM separates the IP *address space* into blocks, ranges, and individual addresses. An IP *address block*, shown in Figure 3-20, is a large collection of IP addresses that you use to organize the address space used in your organization at the highest level. An organization might only have one or two address blocks: one for its entire internal network and another smaller block that represents the public IP address space used by the organization.

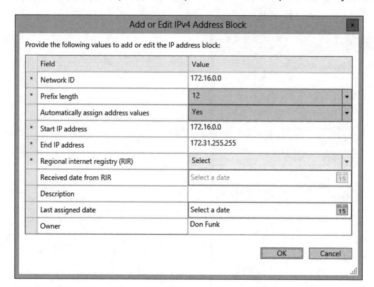

FIGURE 3-20 An IPv4 address block

An IP *address range* is part of an IP address block. An IP address range cannot map to multiple IP address blocks. Generally an IP address range corresponds to a DHCP scope. Figure 3-21 shows an IP address range.

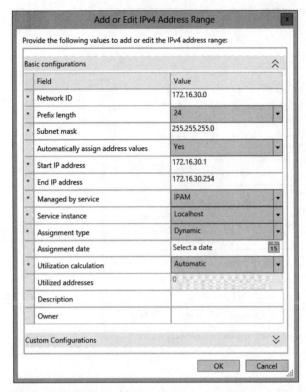

FIGURE 3-21 An IPv4 address range

An IP address maps to a single IP address range. As Figure 3-22 shows, an IP address includes information about an associated MAC address, how the address is assigned, and when that assignment expires.

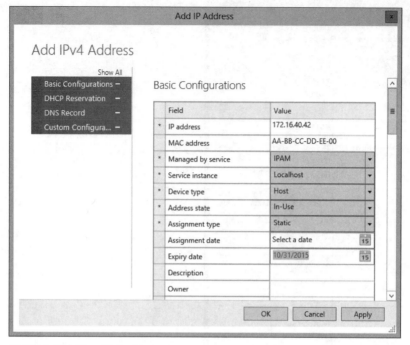

FIGURE 3-22 Add an IPv4 address

> **MORE INFO** **MANAGING IP ADDRESS SPACE**
>
> To learn more about managing IP address space, consult the following article:
> *http://technet.microsoft.com/en-us/library/jj878303.aspx.*

IP address tracking

One of the most important features of IPAM is its ability to track IP addresses by correlating DHCP leases with user and computer authentication events on managed domain controllers and Network Policy Servers (NPS). IP address tracking enables you to figure out which user was associated with a specific IP address at a particular point of time, something that can be important when trying to determine the cause of unauthorized activity on the organizational network.

As Figure 3-23 shows, you can search for IP address records using one of the following four parameters:

- **IP address** Track by IPv4 address, but IPAM does not support tracking on the basis of IPv6 address.

- **By client ID** Track IP address activity on the basis of media access control (MAC) address.

- **By host name** Track by the computer's name as registered in DNS.

- **By user name** Track a user name by providing a host name.

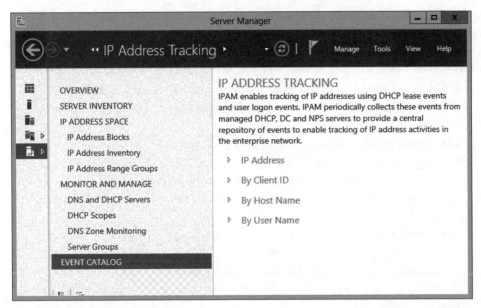

FIGURE 3-23 IP address tracking

MORE INFO **IP ADDRESS TRACKING**

To learn more about IP address tracking, consult the following article:
http://technet.microsoft.com/en-us/library/jj878332.aspx.

You can track only data that has been recorded since IPAM has been deployed. So although it is possible to store several years of data in the Windows Internal Database that IPAM uses, you're limited to being able to retrieve only events that have been recorded after IPAM was configured.

✔ **Quick check**

- You want to determine which IP addresses a computer with a particular MAC address was assigned to over a specific period. What IP address tracking category would you use to determine this information?

Quick check answer

- You would track by client ID when you have a computer's MAC address and want to extract additional information from IPAM address tracking.

IPAM administration

You can delegate administrative permissions by adding user accounts to one of five local security groups on the IPAM server. By default, members of the Domain Admins and Enterprise Admins groups are able to perform all tasks on the IPAM server. The five local security groups, shown in Figure 3-24, enable you to delegate the following permissions:

- **IPAM Users**   Members of this group are able to view IPAM server information such as address space and operational event information, but they are unable to view IP address tracking information.

- **IPAM MSM Administrators**   MSM stands for multi-server management. Users added to this group have all the rights of the IPAM Users group and are able to perform common IPAM management tasks such as managing server inventory. They have read-only access to the IP address space. They are unable to view or perform IP address tracking tasks.

- **IPAM ASM Administrators**   ASM stands for address space management administrator. Users added to this group are able to perform all tasks that can be performed by members of the IPAM Users group, but they are also able to manage the IP address space. They cannot perform monitoring tasks and are unable to perform IP address tracking tasks.

- **IPAM IP Audit Administrators**   Members of this group are able to manage server inventory and perform common management tasks, but they have read-only access to the IP address space and IP address tracking information.

- **IPAM Administrators**   Members of this group are able to perform all tasks on the IPAM server including viewing IP address tracking information.

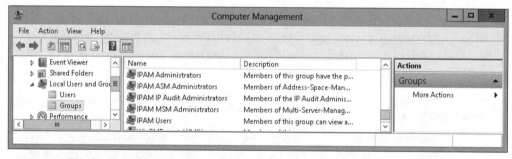

FIGURE 3-24 IPAM local user groups

***MORE INFO* IPAM ADMINISTRATION**

To learn more about IPAM administration, consult the following article:
http://technet.microsoft.com/en-us/library/jj878348.aspx.

Lesson summary

- IPAM enables you to centrally manage DHCP and DNS servers.
- You cannot deploy the IPAM server on a domain controller. You should not deploy a DNS or DHCP server on the IPAM server if you want to manage those servers using IPAM.
- The IPAM server must be a member of an Active Directory domain and can only manage DHCP and DNS servers that are members of the same forest.
- You can use IP address tracking to search the IPAM database on the basis of IP address, MAC address, computer name, or user name.
- Members of the Domain Admins and Enterprise Admins groups have full administrative access to the IPAM server. There are five local security groups on the IPAM server that you can use to delegate administrative privileges.
- The IPAM role available with Windows Server 2012 R2 can use a SQL Server 2012 instance to host the IPAM database.

Lesson review

Answer the following questions to test your knowledge of the information in this lesson. You can find the answers to these questions and explanations of each answer choice in the "Answers" section at the end of this chapter.

1. You need to give a user the ability to view IP address tracking information stored in your organization's IPAM server without adding him or her to the IPAM Administrators group. To which of the following IPAM-related security groups could you add this user to grant this privilege?

   A. IPAM Users

   B. IPAM IP Audit Administrators

   C. IPAM MSM Administrators

   D. IPAM ASM Administrators

2. You need to give a user the ability to manage the IP Address Space on an IPAM server without adding the user to the IPAM Administrators group. To which of the following IPAM-related security groups could you add this user to grant this privilege?

   A. IPAM MSM Administrators

   B. IPAM Users

   C. IPAM ASM Administrators

   D. IPAM IP Audit Administrators

3. You want to use IPAM's IP address tracking feature to determine which IP addresses a computer with a specific MAC address was assigned by your organization's DHCP servers during a particular week. Which of the following categories should you search on to accomplish this goal?

A. IP address

B. Client ID

C. Host name

D. User name

4. You are in the process of configuring IPAM. You have run the discovery process and discovered three servers that host the DHCP server role. The server's IPAM Access Status is listed in the IPAM Server Inventory as Blocked. Which of the following steps should you take so that this status changes to unblocked? (Choose two.)

A. Ensure that you have provisioned the GPOs using the Invoke-IpamGPOProvisioning cmdlet.

B. Verify that Group Policy is applied correctly to the server hosting the IPAM server role.

C. Verify that Group Policy is applied correctly to the three servers hosing the DHCP server role.

D. Restart the IPAM server.

Practice exercises

The goal of this section is to provide you with hands-on practice with the following:

- Configuring DNSSEC
- Configuring NRPT
- Creating GlobalNames zone
- Configuring advanced DNS server options
- Configuring a DHCP superscope
- Deploying a split scope
- Configuring DHCP Name Protection
- Setting up a multicast scope
- Enabling DHCP failover
- Configuring and deploying IPAM

To perform the exercises in this section, you need access to an evaluation version of Windows Server 2012 R2. You should also have access to virtual machines SYD-DC, MEL-DC, CBR-DC, and ADL-DC, the setup instructions for which are described in the Introduction. You should ensure that you have a checkpoint of these virtual machines that you can revert to at the end of the practice exercises. You should revert the virtual machines to this initial state prior to beginning these exercises.

Exercise 1: Configure MEL-DC

In this exercise, you configure MEL-DC to be a member of the contoso.com domain. To complete this exercise, perform the following steps:

1. Ensure that SYD-DC is started.

2. Start MEL-DC and sign on as Administrator with the password **Pa$$w0rd**.

3. On the Local Server node of the Server Manager console, verify that the local IP address is set to 10.10.10.40 and then click on the WORKGROUP link next to Workgroup.

4. On the Computer Name tab of the System Properties dialog box, click Change.

5. In the Computer Name/Domain Changes dialog box, click Domain and type **contoso.com** as shown in Figure 3-25 and then click OK.

FIGURE 3-25 Join the domain

6. In the Windows Security dialog box, type the user name **don_funk** and the password **Pa$$word** and then click OK.

7. On the Computer Name/Domain Changes dialog box, shown in Figure 3-26, click OK.

FIGURE 3-26 Verify the domain join

8. In the dialog box that informs you that you need to restart the computer to apply changes, click OK.

9. Click Close on the System Properties dialog box.

10. Click Restart Now on the Microsoft Windows dialog box.

11. When MEL-DC restarts, sign in as contoso\don_funk with the password **Pa$$w0rd**.

Exercise 2: Configure DNSSEC

In this exercise, you configure DNSSEC on the contoso.com zone. To complete this exercise, perform the following steps:

1. Ensure that you are signed on to SYD-DC as contoso\don_funk.

2. From the Tools menu of the Server Manager console, click DNS.

3. In the DNS Manager console, expand the SYD-DC\Forward Lookup Zones node and click the Contoso.com node.

4. Verify that the records present in the Contoso.com zone match those shown in Figure 3-27.

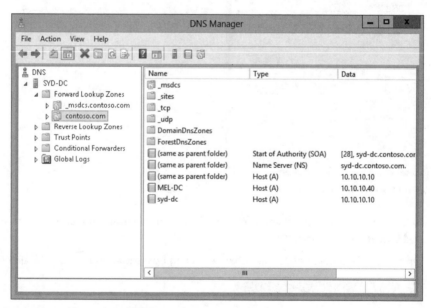

FIGURE 3-27 The unsigned DNS zone

5. On the Action menu, click DNSSEC and click Sign The Zone.

6. On the DNS Security Extensions (DNSSEC) page of the Zone Signing Wizard, click Next.

7. On the Signing Options page, click Use Default Settings To Sign The Zone as shown in Figure 3-28 and click Next.

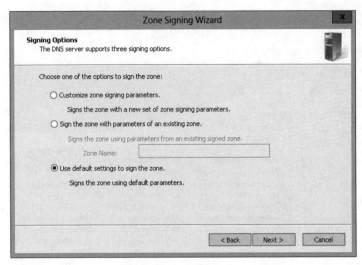

FIGURE 3-28 Configure zone signing options

8. On the DNS Security Extensions (DNSSEC) page, verify that the Key Master is set to SYD-DC as shown in Figure 3-29 and click Next.

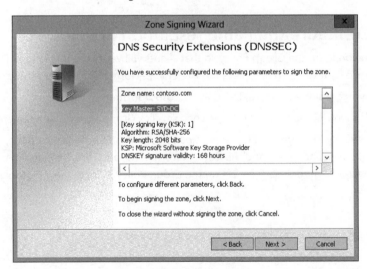

FIGURE 3-29 Verify the Key Master is SYD-DC

9. On the Signing The Zone page of the Zone Signing Wizard, click Finish.
10. On the Action menu of the DNS Manager console, click Refresh and verify the presence of the new DNS records as well as the DNSSEC icon on the zone as shown in Figure 3-30.

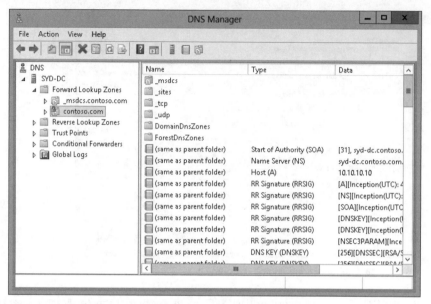

FIGURE 3-30 View the signed DNS zone

Exercise 3: Configure the name resolution policy

In this exercise, you configure the Group Policy so that clients will verify the integrity of DNS records in the contoso.com zone. To complete this exercise, perform the following steps:

1. Ensure that you are signed on to SYD-DC as contoso\don_funk.

2. On the Tools menu of the Server Manager console, click Group Policy Management.

3. In the Group Policy Management Console, expand the Forest: Contoso.com node, expand the Domains node, expand the Contoso.com node, and click Default Domain Policy as shown in Figure 3-31. Click OK on the Group Policy Management Console dialog box.

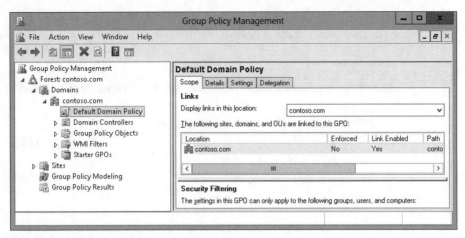

FIGURE 3-31 Configure the Name Resolution Policy

4. On the Action menu, click Edit.

5. In the Group Policy Management Editor, expand the Computer Configuration\Policies\ Windows Settings node and click Name Resolution Policy.

6. In the Name Resolution Policy area, type **contoso.com** in the text box next to the Suffix drop-down menu, select the Enable DNSSEC in This Rule check box, and select the Require DNS Clients To Check That Name And Address Data Has Been Validated By The DNS Server as shown in Figure 3-32. Click Create.

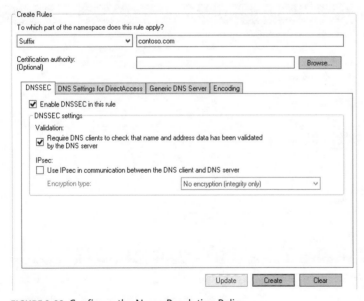

FIGURE 3-32 Configure the Name Resolution Policy

7. In the Group Policy Management Editor, scroll down to view the Name Resolution Policy Table and verify that the settings match those shown in Figure 3-33. Click Apply.

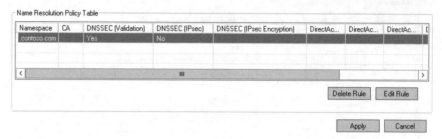

FIGURE 3-33 Verify the Name Resolution Policy

8. Close the Group Policy Management Editor and the Group Policy Management Console.

9. On the taskbar, click the Windows PowerShell icon.

10. Type the following command and press Enter to force a Group Policy update

    Gpupdate /force

11. Type the following command and press Enter to verify that an RRSIG record exists for mel-dc.contoso.com as shown in Figure 3-34:

    resolve-dnsname mel-dc.contoso.com –server syd-dc –dnssecok

FIGURE 3-34 Verify the DNS record

12. Close the Windows PowerShell window.

Exercise 4: Increase the size of the DNS socket pool

In this exercise, you increase the size of the DNS socket pool. To complete this exercise, perform the following steps:

1. When signed on to SYD-DC as contoso\don_funk, right-click the Windows PowerShell icon on the taskbar and click Run As Administrator. Click Yes in the User Account Control dialog box.

2. Type the following command and press Enter to view the currently configured DNS socket pool site:

   ```
   (Get-DNSServer).ServerSetting.SocketPoolSize
   ```

3. Type the following command and press Enter to change the DNS socket pool size to 4,000:

   ```
   Dnscmd /config /socketpoolsize 4000
   ```

4. Type the following command and press Enter:

   ```
   Restart-Service DNS
   ```

5. Type the following command and press Enter to verify the new DNS socket pool size:

   ```
   (Get-DNSServer).ServerSetting.SocketPoolSize
   ```

Exercise 5: Modify DNS Cache Locking

In this exercise, you verify the current DNS Cache Locking setting, change this setting, and then verify the change. To complete this exercise, perform the following steps:

1. Ensure that you are signed on to SYD-DC as contoso\don_funk and have an elevated Windows PowerShell window open.

2. Type the following command and press Enter to verify the size of the current DNS cache locking setting as shown in Figure 3-35:

   ```
   get-DNSServerCache
   ```

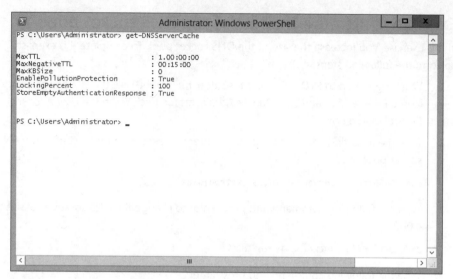

FIGURE 3-35 View the DNS Server cache settings

3. Configure the cache locking percentage to 80 percent by typing the following command and pressing Enter:

   ```
   Set-DNSServerCache –LockingPercent 80
   ```

4. Restart the DNS Server service to apply the changes by typing the following command and pressing Enter:

   ```
   Restart-Service DNS
   ```

5. Verify the alterations to the cache locking by typing the following command as shown in Figure 3-36 and pressing Enter:

   ```
   get-DNSServerCache
   ```

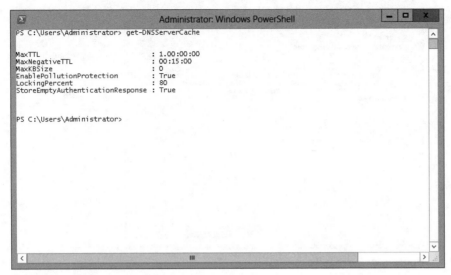

```
Administrator: Windows PowerShell

PS C:\Users\Administrator> get-DNSServerCache

MaxTTL                           : 1.00:00:00
MaxNegativeTTL                   : 00:15:00
MaxKBSize                        : 0
EnablePollutionProtection        : True
LockingPercent                   : 80
StoreEmptyAuthenticationResponse : True


PS C:\Users\Administrator>
```

FIGURE 3-36 Verify the DNS server cache settings

Exercise 6: Create and manage a GlobalNames zone

In this exercise, you configure single-name resolution by configuring a GlobalNames zone. You then create a record in the GlobalNames zone. To complete this exercise, perform the following steps:

1. While signed on to SYD-DC as contoso\don_funk, open the DNS Manager console by clicking DNS in the Tools menu of the Server Manager console.

2. In the DNS Manager console, click the Forward Lookup Zones node under SYD-DC.

3. On the Action menu, click New Zone.

4. On the Welcome page of the New Zone Wizard, click Next.

5. On the Zone Type page, click Primary Zone, ensure that Store The Zone In Active Directory is selected, and click Next.

6. On the Active Directory Zone Replication Scope page, click To All DNS Servers Running On Domain Controllers In This Forest: Contoso.com and click Next.

7. In the Zone Name page, type **GlobalNames**, as shown in Figure 3-37, and click Next.

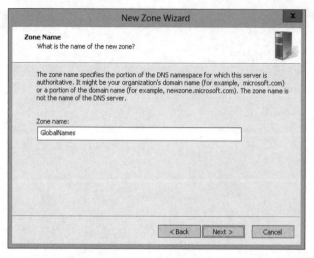

FIGURE 3-37 The zone name

8. On the Dynamic Update page, click Do Not Allow Dynamic Updates and click Next.

9. On the Completing The New Zone Wizard page, click Finish.

10. Switch to the elevated Windows PowerShell window, type the following command, and press Enter.

```
Set-DNSServerGlobalNameZone -ComputerName SYD-DC -Enable $True
```

11. Type the following command and press Enter to verify that the GlobalNameZone is enabled as shown in Figure 3-38:

```
Get-DNSServerGlobalNameZone
```

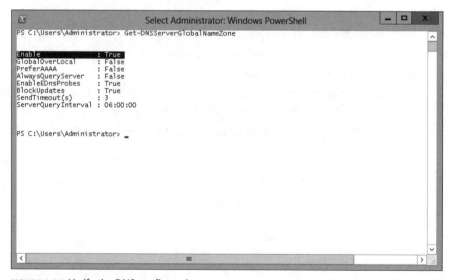

FIGURE 3-38 Verify the DNS configuration

12. Switch to the DNS Manager console and click the GlobalNames zone under Forward Lookup Zones.

13. On the Action menu, click New Alias (CNAME).

14. In the New Resource Record dialog box, configure the following information, as shown in Figure 3-39, and click OK:

- Alias Name (Uses Parent Domain If Left Blank): **Bondi**
- Fully Qualified Domain Name (FQDN) For Target Host: **syd-dc.contoso.com**

FIGURE 3-39 The CNAME record

Exercise 7: Configure and view the DNS event log

In this exercise, you configure event logging for the DNS service. To complete this exercise, perform the following steps:

1. While signed on to SYD-DC as contoso\don_funk, open the DNS Manager console.

2. In the DNS Manager console, right-click SYD-DC and click Properties.

3. On the SYD-DC Properties dialog box, click the Event Logging tab.

4. On the Event Logging tab, ensure that All Events are selected as shown in Figure 3-40 and click OK.

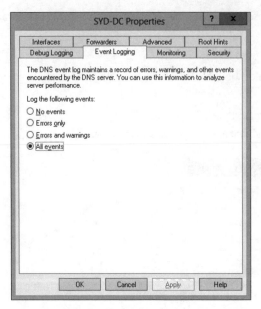

FIGURE 3-40 The DNS event log settings

5. In the Tools menu of the Server Manager console, click Event Viewer.

6. In the Event Viewer Console, expand the Applications And Service Logs node and click DNS Server.

7. In the DNS Server log, look for Event ID 7646 which confirms that the zone contoso.com is now signed with DNSSEC as shown in Figure 3-41.

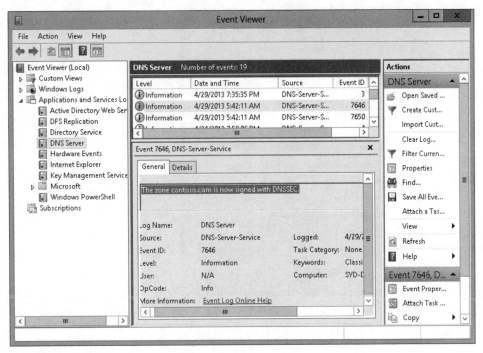

FIGURE 3-41 The DNS event

8. View the DNS event in the event log.

Exercise 8: Verify netmask ordering and disable recursion

In this exercise, you verify that netmask ordering is enabled on the DNS server hosted on SYD-DC. You also disable recursion. To complete this exercise, perform the following steps:

1. While signed on to SYD-DC as contoso\don_funk, switch to the DNS Manager console.

2. In the DNS Manager console, right-click the SYD-DC node and click Properties.

3. On the SYD-DC Properties dialog box, click the Advanced tab.

4. On the Advanced Tab of the SYD-DC Properties dialog box, select Disable Recursion (Also Disables Forwarders) and verify that Enable Netmask Ordering is enabled as shown in Figure 3-42.

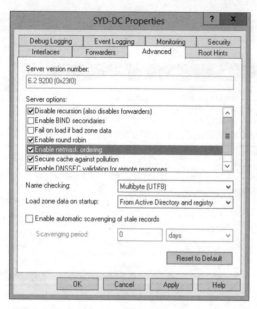

FIGURE 3-42 Enable netmask ordering

5. Click OK to close the SYD-DC Properties dialog box.

6. Close the DNS Manager console.

Exercise 9: Install and activate the DHCP role

In this exercise, you install the DHCP role on MEL-DC and SYD-DC. To complete this exercise, perform the following steps:

1. Ensure that you are signed on to SYD-DC as contoso\don_funk.

2. In the Server Manager console on SYD-DC, click the All Servers node.

3. On the Manage menu, click Add Servers

4. In the Add Servers dialog box, click Find Now.

5. In the Add Servers dialog box, click MEL-DC and click the arrow to add it to the Selected box as shown in Figure 3-43. Click OK.

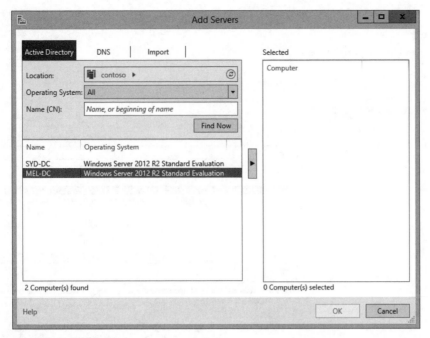

FIGURE 3-43 Add servers

6. Right-click SYD-DC and click Start Performance Counters.

7. Right-click MEL-DC and click Start Performance Counters.

8. In the Manage menu of the Server Manager console, click Add Roles And Features.

9. On the Before You Begin page of the Add Roles And Features Wizard, click Next.

10. On the Select Installation Type Page, click Role-Based or Feature-Based Installation and click Next.

11. On the Select Destination Server page, click MEL-DC.contoso.com as shown in Figure 3-44 and click Next.

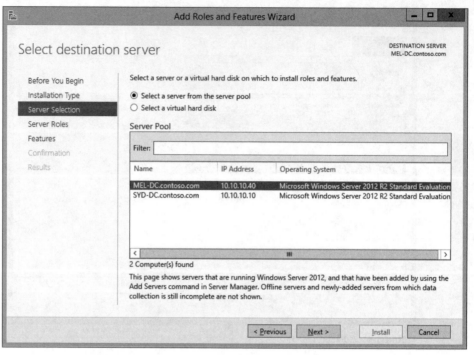

FIGURE 3-44 Select a server to manage

12. On the Select Server Roles page, click the DHCP Server check box.

13. In the Add Roles And Features Wizard dialog box, click Add Features.

14. On the Select Server Roles page, click Next three times and then click Install.

15. When the installation completes, click Close on the Installation Progress page of the Add Roles And Features Wizard.

16. On the Manage menu, click Add Roles And Features.

17. On the Before You Begin page of the Add Roles And Features Wizard, click Next twice.

18. In the Select Destination Server page, click SYD-DC.contoso.com and click Next.

19. On the Select Server Roles page, click the DHCP Server check box as shown in Figure 3-45.

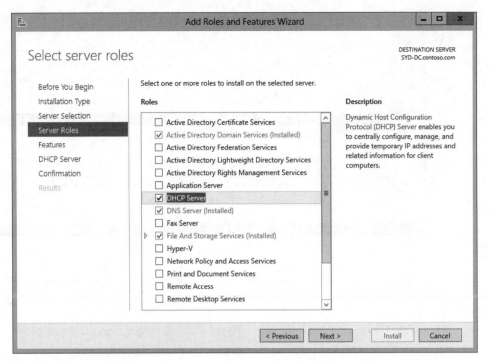

FIGURE 3-45 Add the DHCP server role

20. On the Add Roles And Features Wizard dialog box, click Add Features and then click Next three times. Click Install and then click Close.

21. In the Server Manager console on SYD-DC, click the DHCP Server node.

22. Next to the There Are 2 Jobs With New Notifications message, click More.

23. In the All Servers Task Details dialog box, shown in Figure 3-46, click the Complete DHCP Configuration link next to MEL-DC.

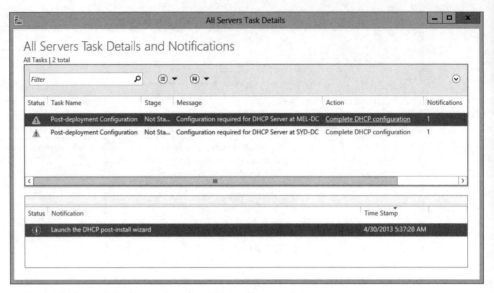

FIGURE 3-46 The post-deployment configuration notice

24. On the Description page of the DHCP Post-Install Configuration Wizard, click Next.

25. On the Authorization page, verify that the user credentials are set to CONTOSO\don_funk as shown in Figure 3-47, click Commit, and then click Close.

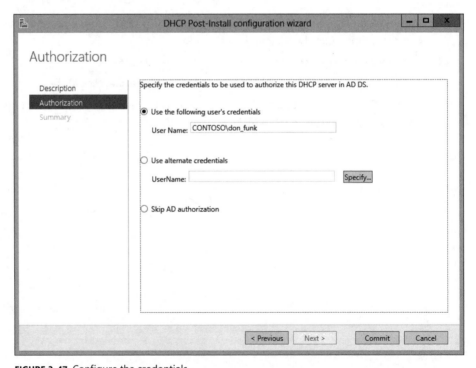

FIGURE 3-47 Configure the credentials

26. In the All Servers Task Details dialog box, click the Complete DHCP Configuration link next to SYD-DC.

27. On the Description page of the DHCP Post-Install Configuration Wizard, click Next.

28. On the Authorization page, verify that CONTOSO\don_funk is listed as the credentialed user, click Commit, and then click Close.

29. Verify that the Stage is listed as complete on the All Servers Task Details And Notifications dialog box as shown in Figure 3-48 and then click the close icon on the title bar.

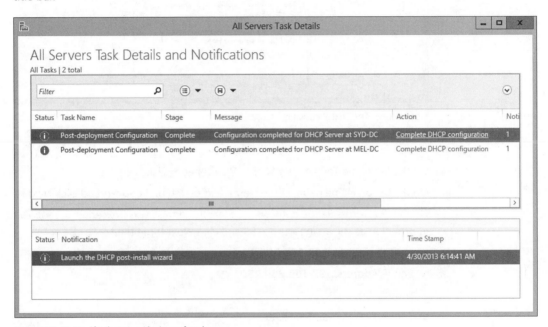

FIGURE 3-48 Verify the completion of tasks

Exercise 10: Create a DHCP superscope

In this exercise, you create a DHCP superscope. To complete this exercise, perform the following steps:

1. Ensure that you are signed on to SYD-DC with the contoso\don_funk user account.

2. On the Tools menu of the Server Manager console, click DHCP.

3. In the DHCP console, expand Syd-dc.contoso.com and click IPv4 as shown in Figure 3-49.

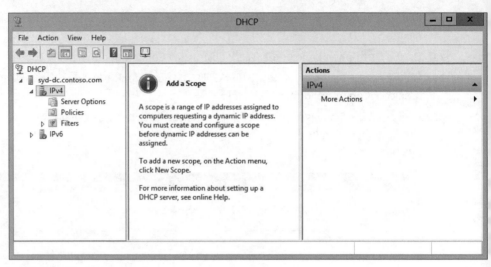

FIGURE 3-49 The DHCP console

4. On the Action menu, click New Scope.

5. On the Welcome To The New Scope Wizard page, click Next.

6. On the Scope Name page, in the Name text box, type **Scope-A** and click Next.

7. On the IP Address Range page, in the Start IP Address text box, enter the following information as shown in Figure 3-50 and click Next three times:

   ■ Start IP Address: **192.168.200.10**

   ■ End IP Address: **192.168.200.230**

   ■ Length: **24**

   ■ Subnet Mask: **255.255.255.0**

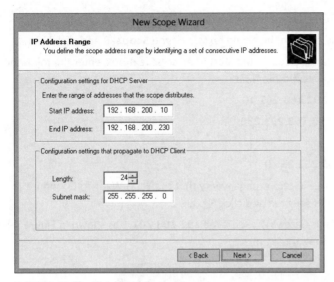

FIGURE 3-50 The IP Address Range

8. On the Configure DHCP Options page, verify that Yes, I Want To Configure These Options Now is selected and click Next.

9. On the Router (Default Gateway) page, type **192.168.200.1** as shown in Figure 3-51 and click Add. Click Next three times.

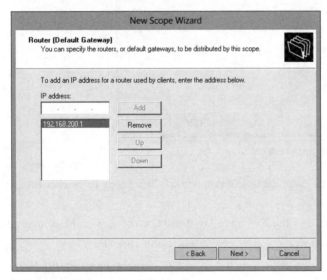

FIGURE 3-51 Configure the default gateway

10. On the Activate Scope page, click No, I Will Activate This Scope Later, click Next, and then click Finish.

11. In the DHCP console, click the IPv4 node, and on the Action menu click New Scope.

12. On the Welcome To The New Scope Wizard page, click Next.

13. On the Scope Name page, in the Name text box, type **Scope-B** and click Next.

14. On the IP Address Range page, in the Start IP Address text box, enter the following information and click Next three times:

 - Start IP Address: **192.168.201.10**

 - End IP Address: **192.168.201.230**

 - Length: 24

 - Subnet Mask: **255.255.255.0**

15. On the Configure DHCP Options page, verify that the Yes, I Want To Configure These Options Now option is selected and click Next.

16. On the Router (Default Gateway) page, type **192.168.201.1** as shown in Figure 3-52 and click Add. Click Next three times.

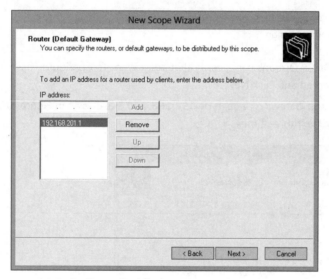

FIGURE 3-52 Configure the default gateway

17. On the Activate Scope page, click No, I Will Activate This Scope Later, click Next, and click Finish.

18. In the DHCP console, click the IPv4 node. On the Action menu, click New Superscope.

19. On the Welcome To The New Superscope Wizard page, click Next.

20. On the Superscope Name page, type the name **SYD-Superscope** and click Next.

21. On the Select Scopes page, hold the Ctrl key and click [192.168.200.0] Scope-A and [192.168.201.0] Scope-B as shown in Figure 3-53. Click Next.

FIGURE 3-53 Create a superscope

22. On the Completing The New Superscope Wizard page, click Finish.

23. In the DHCP console, click Superscope SYD-Superscope as shown in Figure 3-54, and, on the Action menu, click Activate.

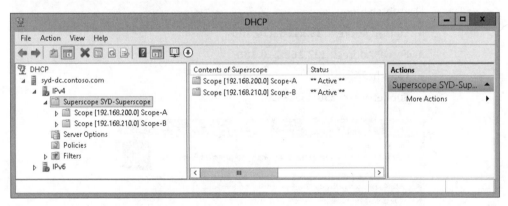

FIGURE 3-54 Verify the superscope creation

Exercise 11: Create a split scope

In this exercise, you configure a split scope that is hosted on SYD-DC and MEL-DC. To complete this exercise, perform the following steps:

1. In the DHCP console on SYD-DC, click the DHCP node, and on the Action menu click Add Server.

2. In the Add Server dialog box, click This Authorized DHCP Server and click Mel-dc. contoso.com as shown in Figure 3-55. Click OK.

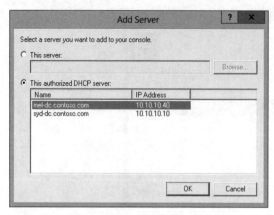

FIGURE 3-55 Add an additional DHCP server

3. In the DHCP console, expand Mel-dc.contoso.com and click the IPv4 node.

4. On the Action menu, click New Scope.

5. On the Welcome To The New Scope Wizard page, click Next.

6. On the Scope Name page, type **SplitScope-A** and click Next.

7. On the IP Address Range page, enter the following as shown in Figure 3-56 and click Next three times:

   ■ Start IP Address: **192.168.210.100**

   ■ End IP Address: **192.168.210.180**

   ■ Length: **24**

   ■ Subnet Mask: **255.255.255.0**

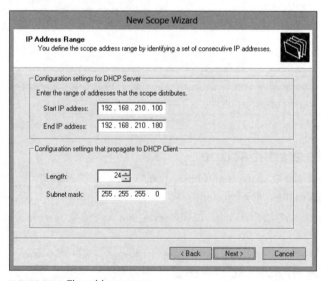

FIGURE 3-56 The address range

8. On the Configure DHCP Options page, verify that the Yes, I Want To Configure These Options Now option is selected and click Next.

9. On the Router (Default Gateway) page, type **192.168.210.1** as shown in Figure 3-57 and click Add. Click Next three times.

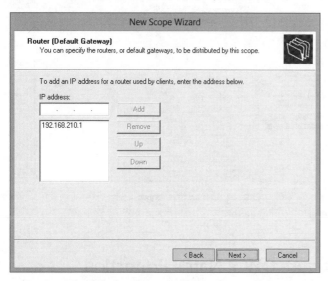

FIGURE 3-57 The default gateway address

10. On the Activate Scope page, select the Yes, I Want To Activate This Scope Now option, click Next, and then click Finish.

11. In the DHCP console, click the IPv4 node under Syd-dc.contoso.com.

12. On the Action menu, click New Scope.

13. On the Welcome To The New Scope Wizard, click Next.

14. On the Scope Name page, type **SplitScope-B** and click Next.

15. On the IP Address Range page, enter the following and click Next three times:

   - Start IP Address: **192.168.210.181**
   - End IP Address: **192.168.210.200**
   - Length: **24**
   - Subnet Mask: **255.255.255.0**

16. On the Configure DHCP Options page, verify that the Yes, I Want To Configure These Options Now option is selected and then click Next.

17. On the Router (Default Gateway) page, type **192.168.210.1** and click Add. Click Next three times.

18. On the Activate Scope page, select the Yes, I Want To Activate This Scope Now option, click Next, and then click Finish.

19. Verify that the DHCP console appears as shown in Figure 3-58.

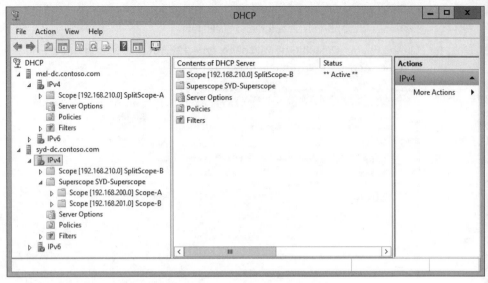

FIGURE 3-58 Verify the DHCP configuration

Exercise 12: Configure DHCP Name Protection

In this exercise, you configure DHCP Name Protection using the graphical user interface (GUI) and using Windows PowerShell. To complete this exercise, perform the following steps:

1. In the DHCP console on SYD-DC, click the IPv4 node under the Syd-dc.contoso.com node.

2. On the Action menu, click Properties.

3. In the IPv4 Properties dialog box, click the DNS tab.

4. On the DNS tab, shown in Figure 3-59, click Configure.

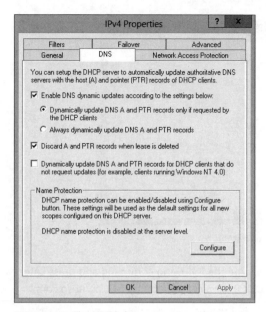

FIGURE 3-59 The DNS tab

5. On the Name Protection dialog box, check the Enable Name Protection check box as shown in Figure 3-60 and click OK.

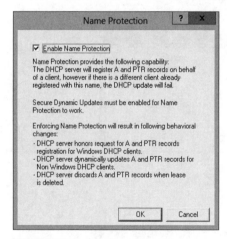

FIGURE 3-60 Enable Name Protection

6. Click OK to close the IPv4 Properties dialog box.

7. In an elevated Windows PowerShell window, type the following command as shown in Figure 3-61 and press Enter to verify the status of Name Protection on the DHCP server running on MEL-DC:

```
Get-DhcpServerv4DnsSetting –Computer MEL-DC
```

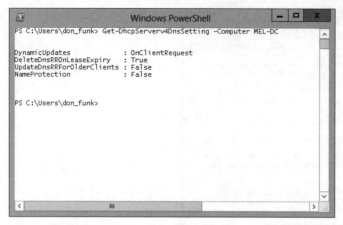

FIGURE 3-61 Verify the Name Protection status

8. In a Windows PowerShell window, type the following command and press Enter to enable Name Protection on the DHCP server hosted on mel-dc.contoso.com:

```
Set-DhcpServerv4DnsSetting -Computer MEL-DC -NameProtection $true
```

9. Verify that Name Protection is now enabled on MEL-DC by reissuing the following command as shown in Figure 3-62:

```
Get-DhcpServerv4DnsSetting -Computer MEL-DC
```

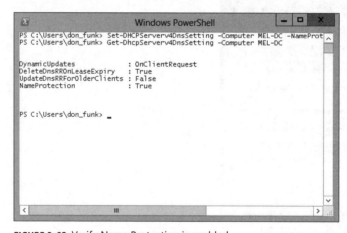

FIGURE 3-62 Verify Name Protection is enabled

Exercise 13: Create new multicast scopes

In this exercise, you create a new multicast scope that will be hosted on the DHCP server SYD-DC. To complete this exercise, perform the following steps:

1. In the DHCP console on SYD-DC, click the IPv4 node under Syd-dc.contoso.com.

2. In the Action menu, click New Multicast Scope.

3. On the Welcome To The New Multicast Scope Wizard page, click Next.

4. On the Multicast Scope Name page, enter the name **Multicast-A** and click Next.

5. On the IP Address Range page, configure the following settings as shown in Figure 3-63 and click Next three times:

   ■ Start IP Address: **230.100.0.10**

   ■ End IP Address: **230.100.0.230**

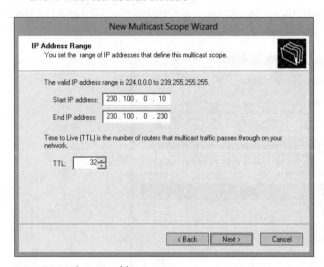

FIGURE 3-63 A new multicast range

6. On the Activate Multicast Scope page, shown in Figure 3-64, click Yes, click Next, and click Finish.

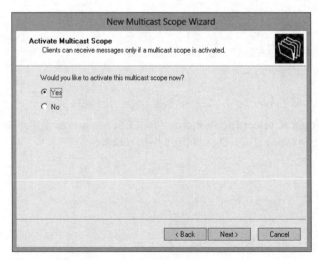

FIGURE 3-64 Activate a multicast scope

Exercise 14: Configure DHCP failover

In this exercise, you configure DHCP failover. To complete this exercise, perform the following steps:

1. In the DHCP console on SYD-DC, expand the Syd-dc.contoso.com node and click the IPv4 node.

2. On the Action menu, click Configure Failover.

3. On the Introduction To DHCP Failover page of the Configure Failover Wizard, clear the Select All check box, hold down the Ctrl key and click 192.168.200.0 and 192.168.201.0 as shown in Figure 3-65. Click Next.

FIGURE 3-65 Configure the scopes for failover

4. On the Specify The Partner Server To Use For Failover page, click Add Server.

5. In the Add Server dialog box, select This Authorized DHCP Server and click Mel-dc. contoso.com as shown in Figure 3-66. Click OK and then click Next.

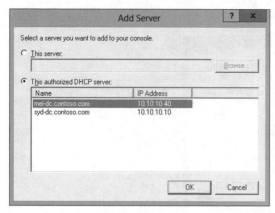

FIGURE 3-66 Add a failover server

6. On the Create A New Failover Relationship page, click the Mode drop-down menu and set it to Hot Standby. Enable the State Switchover Interval and set it to 60 Minutes as shown in Figure 3-67. Type the Shared Secret as **Pa$$w0rd**. Click Next, click Finish, and click Close.

FIGURE 3-67 Create a failover relationship

7. In the DHCP console, click the IPv4 node under Syd-dc.contoso.com, and on the Action menu, click Properties.

8. On the Failover tab, verify that the settings listed match Figure 3-68 and click Delete.

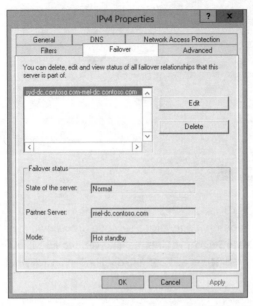

FIGURE 3-68 Delete a failover relationship

9. On the Delete Failover Relationship dialog box, click OK and click Close.

10. Click OK to close the IPv4 Properties dialog box.

Exercise 15: Install the IPAM feature

In this exercise, you join server ADL-DC to the domain and install the IPAM feature. To complete this exercise, perform the following steps:

1. Ensure that SYD-DC and MEL-DC remain powered on.

2. Turn on ADL-DC and sign on as Administrator with the password **Pa$$w0rd**.

3. Open a Windows PowerShell window by clicking the Windows PowerShell icon on the Desktop taskbar.

4. Type the following command and press Enter to join ADL-DC to the contoso.com domain.

   ```
   Netdom join ADL-DC /domain:contoso.com
   ```

5. Restart ADL-DC and sign on as contoso\don_funk.

6. Click on Add Roles And Features on the Manage menu of the Server Manager console.

7. On the Before You Begin page of the Add Roles And Features Wizard, click Next twice.

8. On the Select Destination Server page, ensure that ADL-DC.contoso.com is selected and click Next twice.

9. On the Select Features page, click IP Address Management (IPAM) Server as shown in Figure 3-69.

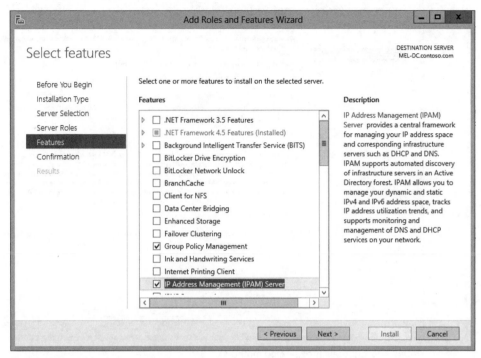

FIGURE 3-69 Add the IPAM feature

10. On the Add Roles And Features Wizard dialog box, click Add Features, click Next, and then click Install. When the installation completes, click Close.

Exercise 16: Configure IPAM GPOs and server discovery

In this exercise, you configure IPAM-related GPOs. To complete this exercise, perform the following steps:

1. While signed on to ADL-DC, click the IPAM node in the Server Manager console.

2. On the IPAM Server Tasks section, click Provision The IPAM Server.

3. On the Before You Begin page of the Provision IPAM Wizard, click Next.

4. On the Select Provisioning Method page, click Group Policy Based, and in the GPO Name Prefix box type **IPAM** as shown in Figure 3-70. Click Next.

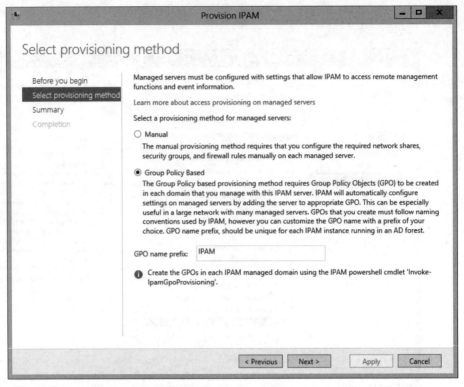

FIGURE 3-70 Choose a provisioning method

5. On the Summary page, click Apply and then click Close.

6. On the IPAM Server Tasks section of the Server Manager console, click Configure Server Discovery.

7. In the Configure Server Discovery dialog box, click Add as shown in Figure 3-71 and click OK.

FIGURE 3-71 Configure discovery

8. On the IPAM Server Tasks section of the Server Manager console, click Start Server Discovery.

9. Wait 15 minutes for server discovery to complete before starting Exercise 17.

Exercise 17: Configure servers to be managed by IPAM

In this exercise, you configure servers so that they can be managed centrally by IPAM. To complete this exercise, perform the following steps:

1. On the IPAM Server Tasks section, click Select Or Add Servers To Manage And Verify IPAM Access.

2. Both SYD-DC and MEL-DC should be present as shown in Figure 3-72.

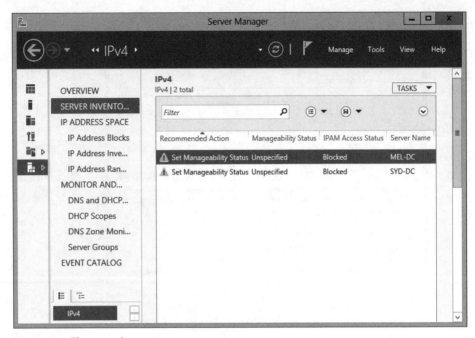

FIGURE 3-72 The server inventory

3. Right-click the Windows PowerShell icon on the taskbar and click Run As Administrator.

4. On the User Account Control dialog box, click Yes.

5. In the Windows PowerShell window, type the following command and press Enter:

```
Invoke-IpamGpoProvisioning –Domain contoso.com –GpoPrefixName IPAM –IpamServerFqdn
ADL-DC.contoso.com –DelegatedGpoUser "contoso\don_funk"
```

6. When prompted, type **Y** for Yes, and press Enter.

7. Switch to SYD-DC and ensure that you are signed on as contoso\don_funk.

8. Open an elevated Windows PowerShell prompt, type the following command, and press Enter:

```
gpupdate /force
```

9. On SYD-DC, on the Tools menu of the Server Manager console, click Active Directory Users And Computers.

10. Expand the Contoso.com domain and click the Computers container.

11. On the Action menu, click New, and click Group.

12. On the New Object – Group dialog box, enter the following information as shown in Figure 3-73 and click OK:

   - Group Name: **IPAM_Managed_Servers**
   - Group Scope: **Universal**
   - Group Type: **Security**

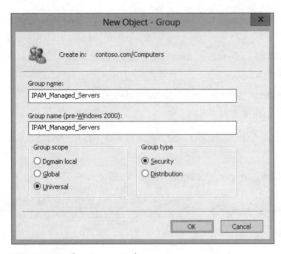

FIGURE 3-73 Create a security group

13. Right-click the IPAM_Managed_Servers group and click Properties.

14. On the Members tab of the IPAM_Managed_Servers Properties dialog box, click Add.

15. On the Select Users, Contacts, Computers, Service Accounts, Or Other Objects dialog box, click Object Types.

16. On the Object Types dialog box, select the Computers check box and click OK.

17. In the Select Users, Contacts, Computers, Service Accounts, Or Other Objects dialog box, type **SYD-DC; MEL-DC**, click Check Names, and click OK.

18. Verify that both MEL-DC and SYD-DC are listed as members of the group as shown in Figure 3-74 and click OK.

FIGURE 3-74 Verify group membership

19. On the Tools menu of the Server Manager console on SYD-DC, click Group Policy Management.

20. In the Group Policy Management Console, expand Forest: Contoso.com, Domains, Contoso.com, and click IPAM_DNS.

21. On the Group Policy Management Console pop-up box, click OK.

22. Under Security Filtering, click Add.

23. In the Select User, Computer, Or Group dialog box, type **IPAM_Managed_Servers** and click OK.

24. Verify that the Group Policy Management Console matches Figure 3-75.

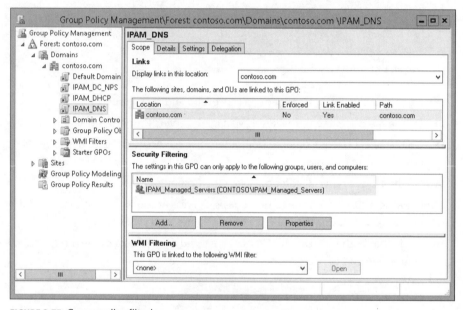

FIGURE 3-75 Group policy filtering

25. Click the IPAM_DHCP policy and click OK to dismiss the Group Policy Management Console.

26. Under Security Filtering, click Add.

27. In the Select User, Computer, Or Group dialog box, type **IPAM_Managed_Servers** and click OK.

28. Click the IPAM_DC_NPS policy and click OK to dismiss the Group Policy Management Console.

29. Under Security Filtering, click Add.

30. In the Select User, Computer, Or Group dialog box, type **IPAM_Managed_Servers** and click OK.

31. Restart SYD-DC and MEL-DC to refresh the group membership of these computers.

32. Sign on to each computer as contoso\don_funk, open an elevated Windows PowerShell prompt and type the following command:

```
Gpupdate /force
```

33. After you have updated the Group Policy, run the following command on SYD-DC and MEL-DC to verify that the IPAM-related Group Policy Objects apply to the computer as shown in Figure 3-76:

```
Gpresult /r /scope computer
```

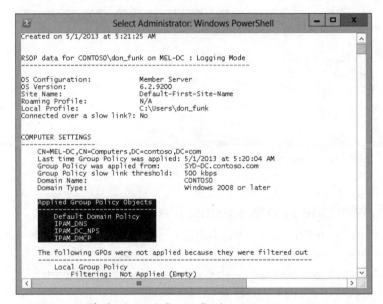

FIGURE 3-76 Verify the Group Policy application

34. On ADL-DC, open the Server Manager console, click the IPAM node, and when Overview is selected, click Select Or Add Servers To Manage And Verify IPAM Access.

35. When IPv4 is selected, right-click SYD-DC, and click Refresh Server Access Status.

36. Right-click MEL-DC and click Refresh Server Access Status.

37. Wait until the task completes and then click the Refresh icon on the taskbar and verify that both servers are listed as Unblocked, as shown in Figure 3-77.

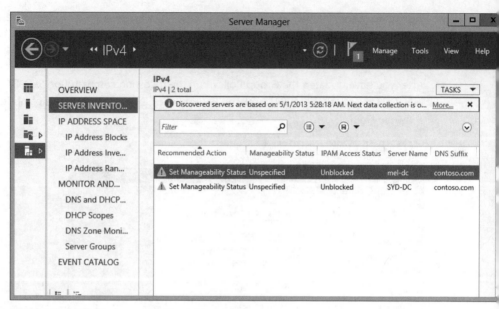

FIGURE 3-77 Verify the manageability status

Exercise 18: Manage servers using IPAM

In this exercise, you configure SYD-DC and MEL-DC to be managed by IPAM. To complete this exercise, perform the following steps:

1. On ADL-DC, in the Server Manager console, with the Server Inventory section of the IPAM area selected, right-click Mel-dc, and click Edit Server.

2. In the Add Or Edit Server dialog box, set the Manageability Status to Managed as shown in Figure 3-78 and click OK.

FIGURE 3-78 Configure the server manageability

3. Right-click SYD-DC, and click Edit Server.

4. In the Add Or Edit Server dialog box, set the Manageability Status to Managed, and click OK.

5. Verify that both servers now have the status of Managed and Unblocked as shown in Figure 3-79.

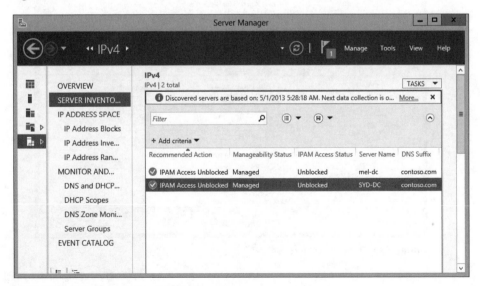

FIGURE 3-79 Verify successful configuration

Exercise 19: Use IPAM to create a DHCP scope

In this exercise, you use IPAM to create a DHCP scope on MEL-DC. To complete this exercise, perform the following steps:

1. While signed on to ADL-DC as contoso\don_funk, click the IPAM node in the Server Manager console, and then click DNS and DHCP under Monitor and Manage.

2. Right-click Mel-dc.contoso.com, and click Create DHCP Scope.

3. In the Create DHCP Scope dialog box, enter the following information as shown in Figure 3-80 and click OK:

   - Scope Name: **IPAM_Scope_A**
   - Start IP Address: **192.168.250.10**
   - End IP Address: **192.168.250.230**
   - Subnet Mask: **255.255.255.0**

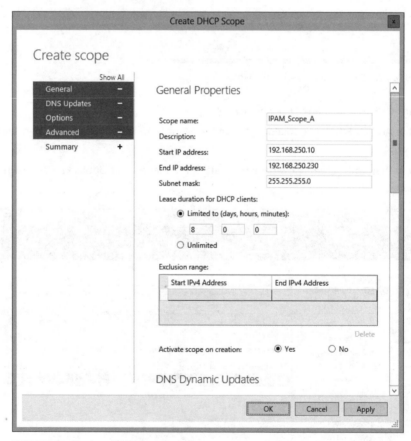

FIGURE 3-80 Create a DHCP scope

Exercise 20: Use IPAM to manage IP addresses

In this exercise, you use IPAM to manage IP addresses, including creating address blocks, creating reservations, and managing DNS records. To complete this exercise, perform the following steps:

1. While signed on to ADL-DC as contoso\don_funk, click the IPAM node in the Server Manager console, and then click IP Address Blocks under IP Address Space.

2. Click Tasks, and click Add IP Address Block.

3. In the Add Or Edit IPv4 Address Block dialog box, enter the following information as shown in Figure 3-81 and click OK:

   - Network ID: **172.16.10.0**
   - Prefix Length: **24**
   - Description: **Perth Office**

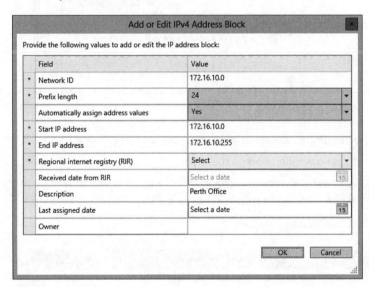

FIGURE 3-81 Add an IPv4 address block

4. Click the IP Address Inventory node. In the Tasks menu, click Add IP Address.

5. In the Add IPv4 Address dialog box shown in Figure 3-82, enter the following information and click OK:

   - IP Address: **172.16.10.20**
   - MAC Address: **AA-BB-CC-DD-EE-00**
   - Device Type: **Host**
   - Device Name: **PER-DC**
   - Forward Lookup Zone: **Contoso.com**
   - Forward Lookup Primary Server: **SYD-DC.contoso.com**

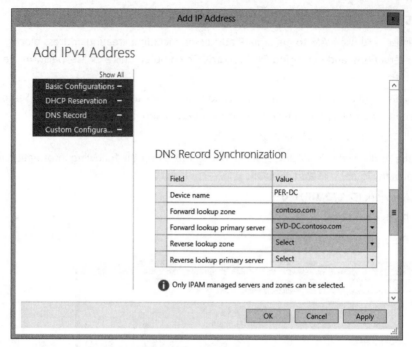

FIGURE 3-82 Configure a DNS record

6. Right-click the PER-DC IP Address Inventory Record, and click Create DNS Host Record.

7. Click the Windows PowerShell icon on the taskbar.

8. In the Windows PowerShell window, type the following command to verify that the DNS record has been created as shown in Figure 3-83:

```
Resolve-dnsname per-dc.contosoc.com
```

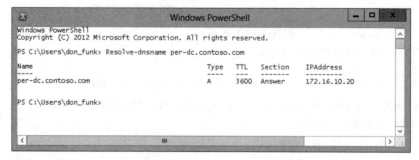

FIGURE 3-83 Verify the DNS record

Suggested practice exercises

The following additional practice exercises are designed to give you more opportunities to practice what you've learned and to help you successfully master the lessons presented in this chapter.

- **Exercise 1**   Use IPAM to create a DHCP scope on SYD-DC for the 172.16.10.0 /24 IP Address Range.

- **Exercise 2**   Reset the DNS socket pool on SYD-DC to its original value.

- **Exercise 3**   Create a new DNS zone named Margiestravel.com and configure it to use DNSSEC.

Answers

This section contains the answers to the lesson review questions in this chapter.

Lesson 1

1. **Correct answer**: C

   A. **Incorrect**. This method cannot be used with a DHCP server hosted on the Windows Server 2008 R2 operating system. Hot standby mode has the primary DHCP server respond to DHCP clients except in the case when the primary server is unavailable, at which point the hot standby server begins leasing addresses.

   B. **Incorrect**. This method cannot be used with a DHCP server hosted on the Windows Server 2008 R2 operating system. Load sharing has each partner DHCP server lease addresses from the scope to DHCP clients. In the event that one DHCP server fails, the other DHCP server utilizes the whole scope after the maximum client lead time period has elapsed.

   C. **Correct**. In a split scope, part of the scope is hosted on one DHCP server, and a smaller part is hosted on a second DHCP server. Traditionally the split between the first and second DHCP servers is 80/20. Use this option when one or both DHCP servers are not running the Windows Server 2012 operating system.

   D. **Incorrect**. Superscopes enable you to combine existing scopes for administrative purposes. They are often implemented when there are multiple logical subnets used on the same physical network. Superscopes do not provide high availability.

2. **Correct answer**: C

   A. **Incorrect**. Load sharing has each partner DHCP server lease addresses from the scope to DHCP clients. In the event that one DHCP server fails, the other DHCP server utilizes the whole scope after the maximum client lead time period has elapsed. This does not meet the requirement that the second server not lease addresses unless the first is unavailable.

   B. **Incorrect**. In a split scope, part of the scope is hosted on one DHCP server, and a smaller part is hosted on a second DHCP server. Traditionally the split between the first and second DHCP servers is 80/20. Use this option when one or both DHCP servers are not running the Windows Server 2012 operating system. This does not meet the requirement that the second server be able to lease addresses from the entire scope if necessary.

   C. **Correct**. Hot standby mode has the primary DHCP server respond to DHCP clients except in the case when the primary server is unavailable, at which point the hot standby server begins leasing addresses.

D. Incorrect. Superscopes enable you to combine existing scopes for administrative purposes. They are often implemented when there are multiple logical subnets used on the same physical network. Superscopes do not provide high availability.

3. **Correct answer**: A

A. Correct. Superscopes enable you to combine existing scopes for administrative purposes. They are often implemented when there are multiple logical subnets used on the same physical network. Superscopes do not provide high availability.

B. Incorrect. Split scopes are high-availability solutions. In a split scope, part of the scope is hosted on one DHCP server, and a smaller part is hosted on a second DHCP server. Traditionally, the split between the first and second DHCP servers is 80/20. Use this option when one or both DHCP servers are not running the Windows Server 2012 operating system.

C. Incorrect. Load sharing mode is a high-availability solution. Load sharing has each partner DHCP server lease addresses from the scope to DHCP clients. In the event that one DHCP server fails, the other DHCP server utilizes the whole scope after the maximum client lead time period has elapsed.

D. Incorrect. Hot standby mode is a high-availability solution. Hot standby mode has the primary DHCP server respond to DHCP clients except in the case when the primary is unavailable at which point the hot standby server begins leasing addresses.

4. **Correct answer**: B

A. Incorrect. In a split scope, part of the scope is hosted on one DHCP server, and a smaller part is hosted on a second DHCP server. Traditionally the split between the first and second DHCP servers is 80/20. Use this option when one or both DHCP servers are not running the Windows Server 2012 operating system. This solution does not distribute IP addresses in a load-balanced manner.

B. Correct. Load sharing has each partner DHCP server lease addresses from the scope to DHCP clients. In the event that one DHCP server fails, the other DHCP server utilizes the whole scope after the maximum client lead time period has elapsed.

C. Incorrect. Hot standby mode has the primary DHCP server respond to DHCP clients except in the case when the primary server is unavailable, at which point the hot standby server begins leasing addresses. This solution does not distribute IP addresses in a load-balanced manner.

D. Incorrect. Superscopes enable you to combine existing scopes for administrative purposes. They are often implemented when there are multiple logical subnets used on the same physical network. Superscopes do not provide high availability.

Lesson 2

1. **Correct answer**: B

    A. **Incorrect**. Members of the IPAM Users group are unable to view IP address tracking information. This information can only be viewed by users that are members of the IPAM IP Audit Administrators and IPAM Administrators local groups.

    B. **Correct**. This information can only be viewed by users that are members of the IPAM IP Audit Administrators and IPAM Administrators local groups.

    C. **Incorrect**. Members of the IPAM MSM Administrators group are unable to view IP address tracking information. This information can only be viewed by users that are members of the IPAM IP Audit Administrators and IPAM Administrators local groups.

    D. **Incorrect**. Members of the IPAM ASM Administrators group are unable to view IP address tracking information. This information can only be viewed by users that are members of the IPAM IP Audit Administrators and IPAM Administrators local groups.

2. **Correct answer**: C

    A. **Incorrect**. Only members of the IPAM ASM Administrators group and the IPAM Administrators group are able to manage the IP address space on an IPAM server.

    B. **Incorrect**. Only members of the IPAM ASM Administrators group and the IPAM Administrators group are able to manage the IP address space on an IPAM server.

    C. **Correct**. Members of the IPAM ASM Administrators group are able to manage the IP address space on an IPAM server.

    D. **Incorrect**. Only members of the IPAM ASM Administrators group and the IPAM Administrators group are able to manage the IP address space on an IPAM server.

3. **Correct answer**: B

    A. **Incorrect**. You track by client ID when you know a computer's MAC address to determine which IP addresses the computer was assigned.

    B. **Correct**. You track by client ID when you know a computer's MAC address to determine which IP addresses the computer was assigned.

    C. **Incorrect**. You track by client ID when you know a computer's MAC address to determine which IP addresses the computer was assigned.

    D. **Incorrect**. You track by client ID when you know a computer's MAC address to determine which IP addresses the computer was assigned.

4. **Correct answers**: A and C

    A. **Correct.** These servers need to have the appropriate IPAM-related GPOs apply to them before their status can change to unblocked. This involves creating the GPOs using the Invoke-IpamGPOProvisioning cmdlet and then ensuring that they apply to the servers that host the services that IPAM will manage.

B. **Incorrect**. These servers need to have the appropriate IPAM-related GPOs apply to them before their status can change to unblocked. This involves creating the GPOs using the Invoke-IpamGPOProvisioning cmdlet and then ensuring that they apply to the servers that host the services that IPAM will manage.

C. **Correct**. These servers need to have the appropriate IPAM-related GPOs apply to them before their status can change to unblocked. This involves creating the GPOs using the Invoke-IpamGPOPRovisioning cmdlet and then ensuring that they apply to the servers that host the services that IPAM will manage.

D. **Incorrect**. Restarting the IPAM server does not alter the blocked status of the servers that you want to manage. These servers need to have the appropriate IPAM-related GPOs apply to them. This involves creating the GPOs using the Invoke-IpamGPOPRovisioning cmdlet and then ensuring that they apply to the servers that host the services that IPAM will manage.

Lesson 3

1. **Correct answer**: B

   A. **Incorrect**. Members of the IPAM Users group are unable to view IP address tracking information. This information can only be viewed by users that are members of the IPAM IP Audit Administrators and IPAM Administrators local groups.

   B. **Correct**. This information can only be viewed by users that are members of the IPAM IP Audit Administrators and IPAM Administrators local groups.

   C. **Incorrect**. Members of the IPAM MSM Administrators group are unable to view IP address tracking information. This information can only be viewed by users that are members of the IPAM IP Audit Administrators and IPAM Administrators local groups.

   D. **Incorrect.** Members of the IPAM ASM Administrators group are unable to view IP address tracking information. This information can only be viewed by users that are members of the IPAM IP Audit Administrators and IPAM Administrators local groups.

2. **Correct answer:** C

   A. **Incorrect**. Only members of the IPAM ASM Administrators group and the IPAM Administrators group are able to manage the IP Address space on an IPAM server.

   B. **Incorrect**. Only members of the IPAM ASM Administrators group and the IPAM Administrators group are able to manage the IP Address space on an IPAM server.

   C. **Correct**. Members of the IPAM ASM Administrators group are able to manage the IP address space on an IPAM server.

D. Incorrect. Only members of the IPAM ASM Administrators group and the IPAM Administrators group are able to manage the IP address space on an IPAM server.

3. **Correct answer**: B

   A. Incorrect. You track by client ID when you know a computer's MAC address to determine which IP addresses the computer was assigned.

   B. Correct. You track by client ID when you know a computer's MAC address to determine which IP addresses the computer was assigned.

   C. Incorrect. You track by client ID when you know a computer's MAC address to determine which IP addresses the computer was assigned.

   D. Incorrect. You track by client ID when you know a computer's MAC address to determine which IP addresses the computer was assigned.

4. **Correct answers**: A and C

   A. Correct. These servers need to have the appropriate IPAM-related GPOs applied to them before their status can change to unblocked. This involves creating the GPOs using the Invoke-IpamGPOProvisioning cmdlet and then ensuring that they apply to the servers that host the services that IPAM will manage.

   B. Incorrect. These servers need to have the appropriate IPAM-related GPOs applied to them before their status can change to unblocked. This involves creating the GPOs using the Invoke-IpamGPOProvisioning cmdlet and then ensuring that they apply to the servers that host the services that IPAM will manage.

   C. Correct. These servers need to have the appropriate IPAM-related GPOs applied to them before their status can change to unblocked. This involves creating the GPOs using the Invoke-IpamGPOProvisioning cmdlet and then ensuring that they apply to the servers that host the services that IPAM will manage.

   D. Incorrect. Restarting the IPAM server does not alter the blocked status of the servers that you want to manage. These servers need to have the appropriate IPAM-related GPOs applied to them. This involves creating the GPOs using the Invoke-IpamGPOProvisioning cmdlet and then ensuring that they apply to the servers that host the services that IPAM will manage.

CHAPTER 4

Active Directory Certificate Services

Active Directory Certificate Services (AD CS) can be as important to your organization's network infrastructure as Domain Name System (DNS) and Dynamic Host Control Protocol (DHCP). This is because an increasing number of network services are reliant upon certificate services for authorization and identification, from the smart cards used to sign on to the network, to computer certificates used to identify servers and remote clients. In this chapter you find out how to configure and deploy Active Directory Certificate Services in a variety of ways. You also discover how to configure certificate templates to best meet the needs of your organization.

Lessons in this chapter:

- Lesson 1: Installing and configuring Active Directory Certificate Services
- Lesson 2: Managing certificates

Before you begin

To complete the practice exercises in this chapter, you need to have deployed computers SYD-DC, MEL-DC, CBR-DC, and ADL-DC as described in the Introduction, using the evaluation edition of Windows Server 2012 R2.

Lesson 1: Installing and configuring Active Directory Certificate Services

Active Directory Certificate Services is the role that you install on a computer running the Windows Server 2012 or Windows Server 2012 R2 operating system when you want it to function as a certificate authority. In this lesson you find out how to deploy Active Directory Certificate Services in either enterprise root, or subordinate, or standalone root, or subordinate configurations. You also discover how to configure certificate revocation list distribution points, online responders, and administrative role separation, and how to back up and recover a certificate authority.

Installing certificate authorities

Certificates play an increasingly important role on Windows networks. A *certificate authority* *(CA)*, also known as a certificate server, is a Windows Server 2012 and Windows Server 2012 R2 role service responsible for issuing, revoking, verifying, and managing digital certificates.

You deploy a CA by installing the Active Directory Certificate Services role as shown in Figure 4-1. It is important to remember that even when you are deploying a CA on a computer that is not a member of an Active Directory domain, you install the Active Directory Certificate Services role.

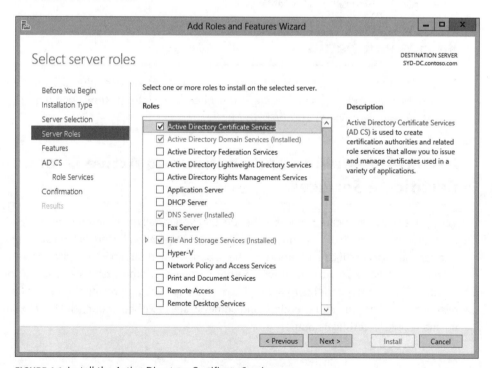

FIGURE 4-1 Install the Active Directory Certificate Services

Active Directory Certificate Services role services

Active Directory Certificate Services is comprised of the following role services as shown in Figure 4-2.

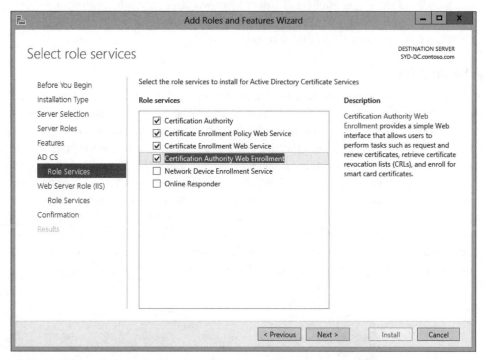

FIGURE 4-2 Active Directory Certificate Services

- **Certification authority** The core component responsible for issuing certificates to computers, users, and services. You can deploy four types of CA: enterprise root, standalone root, enterprise subordinate, and standalone subordinate.

- **Certification Authority Web Enrollment** Provides a web-based interface through which enrollment tasks can be performed. You can use this to perform certificate tasks for computers that are not members of the same forest as the certificate server, including computers running third-party operating systems.

- **Online Responder** A web service that makes the CRL (certificate revocation list) check process more efficient by enabling clients to check the status of a specific certificate without having to download CRLs and delta CRLs in their entirety.

- **Network Device Enrollment Service (NDES)** A service that enables network devices such as routers, switches, firewalls, and hardware-based virtual private network (VPN) gateways to obtain certificates from the CA.

- **Certificate Enrollment Policy Web Service** A service that enables users in a forest running at the Windows Server 2008 R2 or higher functional level to obtain certificate enrollment policy information when enrolling on computers that are not members of the Active Directory domain.

- **Certificate Enrollment Web Service** A service that enables users in a forest running at the Windows Server 2008 R2 or higher functional level to interact with the CA through a web browser to request and renew certificates, retrieve CRLs, and enroll across forest boundaries and the Internet.

CA hierarchies

The *CA hierarchy* determines how CAs are deployed in your organization. A CA hierarchy has two or more CAs. A root CA sits at the top, or apex, of a hierarchy. An issuing CA sits at the base of the hierarchy. You can configure an issuing CA to issue any type of certificate, or configure an issuing CA to only issue certificates from specific templates. For example, you might have an enterprise subordinate CA that issues computer certificates used to authenticate Internet Protocol security (IPSec) communication between domain members and a standalone subordinate CA used to issue web server certificates to computers on your organization's perimeter network. Some organizations use three tiers as shown in Figure 4-3, with a policy tier in between the root CA and the issuing CA. These policy CAs are configured to implement specific certificate policies, such as certificate lifetime, encryption algorithm, key length, and approval requirements on issuing CAs at the third tier of the hierarchy.

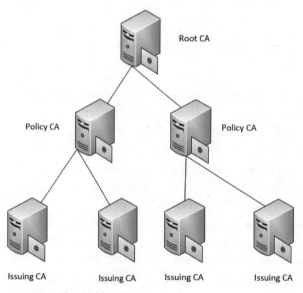

FIGURE 4-3 The CA hierarchy

Cross certification trusts exist where a CA in one hierarchy issues the signing certificate to the root CA of another hierarchy. This usually happens in organizations that have multiple forests.

It enables all clients in the organization to trust each other's certificates even though the users, computers, and services enrolled in those certificates might be located in separate forests.

> **MORE INFO** **CA HIERARCHIES**
>
> To learn more about multilevel certification hierarchies, consult the following article: *http://technet.microsoft.com/en-us/library/cc962078.aspx*.

Enterprise root CA

An *enterprise root CA* is a certificate server that has signed its own certificate, is installed on a computer that is a member of the domain, and can issue certificates based on templates stored in Active Directory. Members of the same Active Directory forest automatically trust the certificates issued from an enterprise CA. The advantage of enterprise CAs is that you can configure issuance policies based on Active Directory properties. This means that an enterprise CA can automatically issue a specific type of certificate to a user, computer, or service without requiring the manual approval of an administrator. Because of the way they integrate into Active Directory, enterprise CAs need to remain online. Enterprise root CAs are suitable for organizations with fewer than 300 users who only need a single CA and do not need to deploy a complex CA hierarchy. You choose whether a CA is a root or subordinate, enterprise or standalone, during setup as shown in Figure 4-4. After you've configured a CA, you can't change its type without removing and reinstalling the role service.

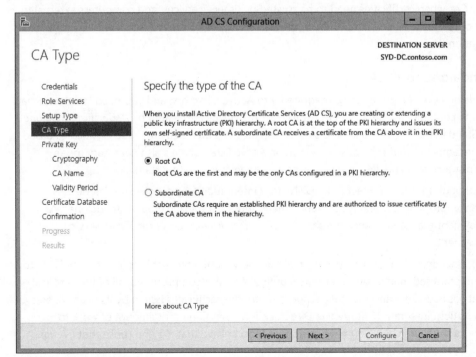

FIGURE 4-4 Configure the CA

Although it is technically possible to deploy multiple enterprise root CAs in an Active Directory forest, Microsoft does not recommend this configuration. Microsoft's guidance is that you don't use an enterprise root CA except in small environments, but instead use an offline root CA as the apex of the CA hierarchy and use enterprise subordinate CAs for the day-to-day deployment and management of certificates. You find out about offline root CAs later in this lesson. A user needs to be a member of both the Enterprise Admins and the root domain's Domain Admins groups to deploy an enterprise root or enterprise subordinate CA.

Enterprise subordinate CA

An *enterprise subordinate CA* can obtain its signing certificate from a standalone root CA or an enterprise root CA. Enterprise subordinate CAs are able to issue certificates based on certificate templates that are stored in Active Directory. This means that enterprise subordinate CAs are able to automatically issue certificates based on certificate template permission and don't require that an administrator approve each certificate request. Enterprise subordinate CAs can be configured as policy CAs or issuing CAs. You read more about certificate templates in Lesson 2, "Manage certificates."

Although it's possible to purchase a signing certificate from a trusted third-party CA, in most cases you should use a certificate from a root CA managed by your organization. You should do this because signing certificates from third-party CAs are expensive and because the vast majority of the certificates issued from an enterprise subordinate CA are used by computers, users, and services that are parts of your environment. You only need to use third-party CAs when certificates need to be trusted by usaers, services, and computers external to your organization—for example, if you want to provide e-commerce services to customers on the Internet.

Standalone root CA

Standalone CAs are not directly integrated into Active Directory, and you need to take special steps to configure all clients in a forest to trust the certificates issued by a specific *standalone CA*. Standalone CAs have a limited set of templates and aren't able to issue certificates based on the templates that enterprise CAs store in Active Directory. It's also necessary for an administrator to manually approve certificate requests issued to a standalone CA.

Although the lack of direct Active Directory integration might make standalone CAs seem inappropriate for enterprise deployment, there is a specific type of standalone CA deployment that can enhance the security of a large organization's certificate service deployment.

To function, enterprise CAs must remain online. A computer that is online is more likely to be compromised than a computer that is offline. If a CA is compromised, all of the certificates that it has issued are automatically suspect, as are the certificates issued by its subordinates. With its tight integration into Active Directory, it takes a significant amount of work to resolve a situation where you have good reason to believe that the enterprise root CA has been compromised and certificates issued from that CA are suspect. For that reason, larger organizations deploy offline root CAs.

> **REAL WORLD** **BACK UP OFFLINE ROOT CA**
>
> Ensure that you back up your offline root CA. One of the participants at the user group I run in Melbourne worked at a company that had a physically deployed offline root CA. When they attempted to bring the CA up after a long period of it being offline, they found that the hard disk that hosted the operating system and the certificate services database had failed. Although they were able to migrate to a new offline standalone root, having a good backup of the original would have saved them a lot of time.

An offline root CA is a standalone CA that you only bring online when you want to perform specific tasks, such as issuing a signing certificate to a subordinate CA or publishing a certificate revocation list (CRL). An offline root CA might be a computer that is not connected to a network and where certificates are transferred using removable media. Offline root CAs have the following properties:

- **Deployed as a standalone root CA** You use this type of CA because its CRL can be published to a location separate from the server, and the CA doesn't need to be online for revocation checks to be successful.

- **Deployed on a computer that is not a member of the domain** As a security precaution, the offline root CA is powered down most of the time. Any computer that spends the vast majority of time powered off is likely to encounter problems retaining domain membership due to synchronization problems.

In addition, you need to configure the CRL and AIA (Authority Information Access) distribution points for offline access. The AIA extension specifies the location of up-to-date certificates for the CA. You also need to export the CA certificate so that it is accessible while the CA is offline. This is because it is necessary for clients to perform successful CRL checks even though the CA is offline. The CRL and AIA distribution points and CA certificate for an offline root CA can be, and usually are, hosted on a computer that is a member of the forest. The CA certificate is usually published to the Active Directory enterprise root store.

> **MORE INFO** **OFFLINE ROOT CA**
>
> To learn more about offline root CAs, consult the following article: *http://social.technet.microsoft.com/wiki/contents/articles/2900.offline-root-certification-authority-ca.aspx*.

Standalone subordinate CA

You can deploy a *standalone subordinate CA* on a computer that is a member of a domain or a computer that is not domain joined. Standalone subordinate CAs are often deployed on perimeter networks. Rather than deploy to a perimeter network, you can also deploy a standalone subordinate CA to a virtual machine running on a cloud provider, such as

Windows Azure. The properties of a certificate issued by a standalone CA are dependent on the contents of the request file. By default all certificate requests made to a standalone CA must be processed manually by an administrator. From an administrative perspective, you should only use standalone CAs where it makes sense that each request must be processed manually. Although it is possible to configure a standalone subordinate to function as an offline CA, it is simpler to revoke the CA's signing certificate if you suspect the CA has become compromised.

> **MORE INFO CA TYPES**
>
> To learn more about the CA types, consult the following article:
> *http://technet.microsoft.com/en-us/library/cc732368.aspx.*

Hardware security module

A *hardware security module (HSM)* is a special hardware device that is specially designed to improve the performance and security of certificate server operations. HSMs contain special hardware for storing CA keys. They also have special hardware that speeds up signature and encryption operations. HSMs are optional components, and you are only likely to see them in environments that have stringent security requirements. HSMs can be attached as Peripheral Component Interconnect (PCI) devices, but are more commonly attached to universal serial bus (USB) ports.

> **MORE INFO HARDWARE SECURITY MODULE**
>
> To learn more about hardware security modules, consult the following article: *http://social. technet.microsoft.com/wiki/contents/articles/10576.hardware-security-module-hsm.aspx.*

CRL distribution points

When a new certificate is encountered, the operating system performs a check against the certificate server that issued the certificate to determine if the certificate has been revoked. This check is performed against a CRL. As the name suggests, this is a list of all the certificates issued by the CA that have been revoked. A CRL distribution point (also known as a CDP) hosts the following lists:

- **CRL**   A list of all certificates that have been revoked on a specific CA. The older the CA, the longer this list is likely to be. By default, a CA publishes a new CRL every 7 days.
- **Delta CRL**   This is a list of all certificates that have been revoked on a specific CA since the publication of the last CRL. By default, these are published daily.

A CA can have multiple CDPs. You specify the CRL distribution points on the Extensions tab of the CA's Properties dialog box as shown in Figure 4-5. By default, CRLs are published to the following locations:

- C:\Windows\system32\CertSrv\CertEnroll\<CaName><CRLNameSuffix><DeltaCRLAllo wed>.crl

- Ldap:///CN=<CATruncadedName><CRLNameSuffix>,CN=<ServerShortName>,CN=CDP ,CN=Public Key Services,CN=Services,<ConfigurationContainer> <CDPObjectClass>

- http://<ServerDNSName>/CertEnroll<CaName><CRLNameSuffix><DeltaCRLAllowed>. crl

- File://<ServerDNSName>/CertEnroll<CaName><CRLNameSuffix><DeltaCRLAllowed>. crl

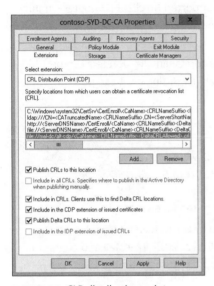

FIGURE 4-5 CLR distribution points

Consider the following when configuring CDPs:

- If you are publishing certificates that will be used by third parties, ensure that a CDP is in a location that is accessible to those third parties.

- You need to configure an alternative AIA point if you are implementing an online responder.

- Consider publishing the CDP to a Distributed File System (DFS) share, especially in distributed environments with a lot of sites.

MORE INFO CRL DISTRIBUTION POINTS

To learn more about CDPs, consult the following article:
http://technet.microsoft.com/en-us/library/cc753296.aspx.

Online Responders

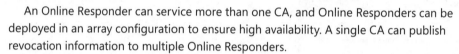

Online Responders allow certificate revocation checks to occur without requiring that the client download the entire CRL and delta CRL. As a CRL stores the details of all certificates that have been revoked on a particular CA, they can become very large over time. Even though they have a lifetime of 7 days, and a delta CRL 1 day, requiring the client to view a list of all revoked certificates to determine if a specific certificate is valid is less efficient than sending a request to the *Online Responder* service querying whether a specific certificate is valid. Rather than check the whole list, the client sends a certificate-specific query. This reduces traffic load on both the CA and the client. Online Responders are supported on client computers running the Windows Vista and later client operating systems and Windows Server 2008, and later server operating systems.

An Online Responder can service more than one CA, and Online Responders can be deployed in an array configuration to ensure high availability. A single CA can publish revocation information to multiple Online Responders.

> **MORE INFO** **ONLINE RESPONDERS**
>
> To learn more about Online Responders, consult the following article:
> *http://technet.microsoft.com/en-us/library/045d2a97-1bff-43bd-8dea-f2df7e270e1f.*

To deploy an Online Responder, you need to complete the following tasks:

- The computer hosting the Online Responder also needs to host Internet Information Server (IIS). Windows Server 2012 and Windows Server 2012 R2 install and configure IIS automatically when you install an Online Responder using the Add Roles And Features Wizard.

- You need to configure the OCSP (Online Certificate Status Protocol) Response Signing Certificate template so that the computer hosting the Online Responder is able to request this certificate. You can request this certificate manually, or you can configure auto enrollment.

- You must configure the CA that will use the Online Responder so that the AIA extension points to the Online Responder. Only certificates issued after the AIA extension points have been configured will be able to use the Online Responder.

- Although optional, you should make the Online Responder highly available.

> ✔ **Quick check**
>
> - What modification do you need to make on the CA if you want to use an Online Responder?
>
> **Quick check answer**
>
> - You need to modify the AIA extensions to point to the Online Responder URL if you want to use an Online Responder.

Administrative role separation

By default, a user that is a member of the Domain Admins or Enterprise Admins group is able to manage a CA. By default, a user that is a member of the local Administrators group is also able to manage a CA. If you are responsible for managing a larger organization, it is likely that you will want to use role-based administration to provide information technology (IT) professionals with specific permissions, such as the ability to revoke permissions or configure CA properties, without making them local, domain, or enterprise administrators.

You configure CA role separation by assigning one of the following permissions on the Security tab of the CA's Properties as shown in Figure 4-6:

- **Read**   This permission allows the user to view the configuration of the CA. This includes CA settings, the list of issued and revoked certificates, and the list of CA templates.

- **Issue and Manage Certificates**   This permission allows the user to approve certificate requests, revoke issued certificates, and trigger CRL publication.

- **Manage CA**   This permission allows the user to manage CA settings, including configuring security, altering recovery agents, and changing certificate server extensions. Users assigned this permission are able to alter security permissions and can delegate themselves the Issue and Manage Certificates permission.

- **Request Certificates**   Users assigned this permission are able to request certificates from the CA. In secure environments, you might want to allow only specific users to request certificates. By default, members of the authenticated users group are able to request certificates.

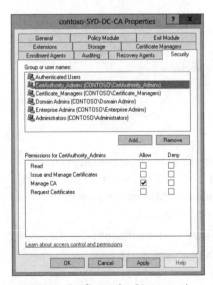

FIGURE 4-6 Configure the CA separation

You can restrict which security principals are able to perform certificate management tasks on the Certificate Managers tab as shown in Figure 4-7. When you restrict certificate managers, any users assigned the Issue and Manage Certificates permission will be listed as certificate managers. You can go further when configuring certificate managers and assign permissions so that specific security groups only have the right to issue certificates based on specific templates. You should use this to ensure that certificates based off sensitive templates (such as those used for key and data recovery) can only be managed by a small group of users.

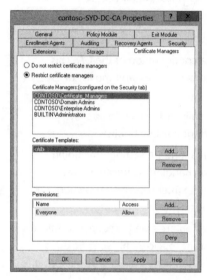

FIGURE 4-7 Restrict the security principals

MORE INFO **ROLE-BASED ADMINISTRATION**

To learn more about role-based administration, consult the following article: *http://technet.microsoft.com/en-us/library/cc732590.aspx.*

CA backup and recovery

Although you automatically back up a CA when you perform a full server or system state backup, you can also perform a backup and recovery of a certificate server from the Certification Authority console. A user needs to be assigned the Manage CA permission or be a member of the Backup Operators group, to be able to back up a CA.

To back up a CA using the Certification Authority console, perform the following steps:

1. In the Certification Authority console, click the CA that you want to back up. On the Action menu, click All Tasks and click Back Up CA.

2. On the Welcome To The Certification Authority Backup Wizard page of the Certification Authority Backup Wizard, click Next.

3. On the Items To Backup page, choose from the following options as shown in Figure 4-8:

- **Private Key and CA Certificate**   Backs up the CA's private and public keys. Enables you to restore the CA on a different computer in the event that the CA fails.

- **Certificate Database and Certificate Database Log**   Enables you to recover the public keys of the certificates that the CA has issued. If key archiving is enabled, this option enables you to recover private keys of these certificates.

- **Location**   Enables you to specify a directory to back up the files.

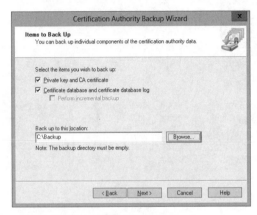

FIGURE 4-8 Select CA keys to back up

4. On the Select A Password page, enter a password. This password will be used to encrypt the backed up data. The password will be required to recover the backup data.

You can also perform a backup using the certutil command. For example, to back up the private key, CA certificate, certificate database, and database log to the C:\backup directory, issue the command:

```
Certutil –backup c:\backup
```

Restoring a CA involves using the Certification Authority Restore Wizard as shown in Figure 4-9. You can choose to restore the private key and CA Certificate, and the certificate database and certificate database log. You can also use the certutil command with the restore option to restore a backup.

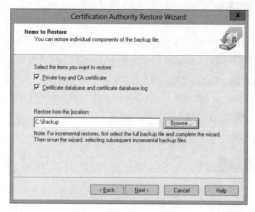

FIGURE 4-9 Restore a CA

MORE INFO **CA BACKUP AND RECOVERY**

To learn more about backing up and recovering a CA, consult the following article:
http://technet.microsoft.com/en-us/library/cc770552.aspx.

Lesson summary

- Enterprise CAs are integrated into Active Directory. You can configure them to automatically enroll certificates based on the requestor's attributes in Active Directory.

- You can install standalone CAs on computers that are both domain joined and not joined to a domain.

- Root CAs are the apex of a certificate services hierarchy. Root CAs use self-signed CA certificates.

- Subordinate CAs must have their CA certificate signed by another CA.

- CDPs host lists of revoked certificates.

- Online Responders provide certificate revocation data that do not require the client to access the whole CRL.

- By configuring CA security, you can allow users to approve and revoke certificates without giving them the permission to manage the CA.

- You can use the Certificate Services console to back up the CA certificate, private key, certificate database, and certificate database log.

Lesson review

Answer the following questions to test your knowledge of the information in this lesson. You can find the answers to these questions and explanations of each answer choice in the "Answers" section at the end of this chapter.

1. You want to deploy an offline CA as the apex of your organization's certificate services hierarchy. You should only bring this CA online to sign the certificates of subordinate CAs. Which of the following solutions should you implement to accomplish this goal?

   A. Enterprise root CA

   B. Enterprise subordinate CA

   C. Standalone root CA

   D. Standalone subordinate CA

2. You have deployed a standalone computer running Windows Server 2012 R2 to Windows Azure. You want to use this computer to provide certificates to partner organizations without having the certificate authority joined to your organization's Active Directory domain. Which of the following CA types could you deploy in this scenario? (Choose all that apply.)

   A. Enterprise root CA

   B. Enterprise subordinate CA

   C. Standalone root CA

   D. Standalone subordinate CA

3. You want to minimize the amount of network traffic caused by clients accessing the CRL of your organization's CA. Which of the following role services could you install to accomplish this goal?

   A. CA Web Enrollment

   B. Online Responder

   C. Network Device Enrollment Service

   D. Certificate Enrollment Policy Web Service

4. You want to allow computers running third-party operating systems to be able to obtain certificates by accessing a web page and submitting a certificate request. Which of the following role services could you install to accomplish this goal?

   A. Certificate Enrollment Policy Web Service

   B. Network Device Enrollment Service

   C. Online Responder

   D. CA Web Enrollment

5. You are in the process of deploying authenticating switches in your organization. You need to provision these switches with certificates. Which of the following role services should you install to support this type of certificate deployment?

   A. Online Responder

   B. Certificate Enrollment Policy Web Service

   C. Network Device Enrollment Service

   D. CA Web Enrollment

6. You are in the process of configuring the permissions on a specific issuing CA. To improve security, you want to limit which users are able to obtain certificates from the CA. Which of the following permissions would you assign to accomplish this goal?

   A. Read

   B. Issue and Manage Certificates

   C. Manage CA

   D. Request Certificates

7. You want to delegate the ability to issue and revoke certificates from a specific certificate server to a specific group of users without giving them permission to modify certificate server settings. Which of the following permissions would you assign to accomplish this goal?

   A. Manage CA

   B. Issue and Manage Certificates

   C. Request Certificates

   D. Read

8. You want to delegate the ability to manage a specific certificate server to a certain group of users. Which of the following permissions would you assign to accomplish this goal?

   A. Request Certificates

   B. Read

   C. Issue and Manage Certificates

   D. Manage CA

Lesson 2: Manage certificates

Certificate templates enable you to configure the properties of certificates, such as how they can be used, who can enroll in the certificate, the validity period of the certificate, and whether the private key is archived on the certificate server. In this lesson you find out how to manage certificate templates, configure certificate autoenrollment, as well as how to archive and recover private keys.

Certificate templates

Certificate templates enable you to configure the properties of certificates that are issued by enterprise CAs. Certificate templates are stored in Active Directory and replicate throughout the forest. You can edit the properties of certificate templates through the Certificate Templates console.

Important certificate template settings include:

- **Validity Period**   Determines how long the certificate is valid once issued.
- **Renewal Period**   Specifies the amount of time before the validity period expires where the certificate might be automatically renewed.
- **Publish Certificate In Active Directory**   Determines whether the public key of the certificate is stored in Active Directory.
- **Compatibility**   Determines minimum CA and client operating system that can issue and use the certificate.
- **Archive Subject's Encryption Private Key**   Makes it possible for the private key to be recovered.
- **Allow Private Key To Be Exported**   Enables the certificate holder to export their private key.
- **Superseded Templates**   Specifies which existing templates the current template supersedes.
- **Security**   Determines which security principals can enroll or use autoenroll with the certificate.

Although a large number of certificate templates are stored within Active Directory, a newly installed enterprise CA only issues certificates based on a subset of these templates. To configure an enterprise CA to issue a certificate off of a template, right-click the Certificate Templates node in the Certification Authority console, click New, and click Certificate Template To Issue. From the list of available templates, shown in Figure 4-10, select the certificate template that you want the CA to be able to issue. When you create a new certificate template, remember to use this method to configure the CA to issue certificates based on that template.

FIGURE 4-10 List of CA templates

> *MORE INFO* **CERTIFICATE TEMPLATES**
>
> To learn more about certificate templates, consult the following article: *http://technet.microsoft.com/en-us/library/cc730826(v=ws.10).aspx.*

Certificate revocation

Revoking a certificate cancels it and makes it invalid. You can revoke a certificate by locating it in the list of issued certificates and then choosing Revoke Certificate on the All Tasks menu of the Action menu. When you revoke a certificate, you need to specify a reason code as well as a date and time as shown in Figure 4-11. You can specify one of the following reasons when revoking a certificate:

- **Unspecified** Doesn't provide a revocation code. The drawback of selecting this code is that it does not provide auditors with a reason as to why you chose to revoke the certificate.

- **Key Compromise** Choose this reason when you believe a key might have been compromised, such as when a user loses their smart card.

- **CA Compromise** Use this reason when you suspect the CA's private key has been compromised. For example, if you have reason to believe that someone has gained remote access to the server that hosts the CA.

- **Change of Affiliation** Use this reason when a person's departure from the organization or change in role requires existing certificates to be revoked.

- **Superseded** Use this reason when you have issued a new certificate and want to revoke the existing certificate.

- **Cease of Operation** The device that the certificate was issued to is no longer in use.

- **Certificate Hold** A temporary state that revokes the certificate but allows you to unrevoke the certificate. Use this when you need to temporarily suspend a certificate. For example, when someone suspects that they have lost their smartcard but might have left it at home.

FIGURE 4-11 Revoke a certificate

MORE INFO **CERTIFICATE REVOCATION**

To learn more about certificate revocation, consult the following article: *http://technet.microsoft.com/en-us/library/cc771079.aspx.*

After you revoke the certificate, you need to publish a new CRL or delta CRL. You can trigger this manually by right-clicking the Revoked Certificates node, clicking All Tasks, and clicking Publish. You then choose to publish either a CRL or a delta CRL as shown in Figure 4-12.

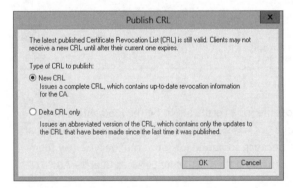

FIGURE 4-12 Choose the type of CRL to publish

It is important to realize that even when you publish a new CRL or a delta CRL, there will be a period before clients will access the new revocation data. This is because each CRL and delta CRL has a validity period, and clients don't check for a new CRL or delta CRL until that validity period has expired. You configure the CRL validity period on the Revoked Certificates Properties dialog box, shown in Figure 4-13. Although it's possible to clear the cache on a client manually using the certutil command, when revoking a certificate you should assume that clients will consider the certificate to be valid for the delta CRL publication interval. If you are in a high security environment where the status change of a certificate needs to propagate quickly, reduce the publication interval and ensure that you have configured an Online Responder. The minimum publication interval for delta CRLs is 30 minutes.

FIGURE 4-13 Configure the CRL validity period

✔ **Quick check**

■ What step do you need to take after revoking a certificate if you want clients to be aware of the certificate's new status?

Quick check answer

■ You need to publish either a CRL or delta CRL.

Certificate renewal

Automatic *certificate renewal* makes it possible for a certificate to be reissued with a new expiry date after a certain period of enrollment has expired. Automatic renewal ensures that certificates are updated and don't expire because someone forgot to manually renew them. You need to enable certificate renewal by enabling the Certificate Services Client – Auto-Enrollment group policy item.

Automatic certificate renewal occurs whenever one of the following occurs:

■ 80 percent of the certificate's lifetime has passed.

■ The renewal period specified on the template has passed.

You configure the validity period and renewal period on the General tab of the certificate template's properties. The renewal period is specified in terms of the certificate's expiration date. In the case of Figure 4-14, the renewal period is 6 weeks before the certificate would expire, which, given the certificate validity of 1 year, would be 46 weeks. However, given that 80 percent of 52 weeks is just under 42 weeks, the 80 percent renewal trigger will occur before the specified renewal period trigger.

FIGURE 4-14 Configure the validity and renewal period

You can also reenroll certificates that have been distributed from an enterprise CA to clients that are subject to Group Policy by selecting the Reenroll All Certificate Holders option on the Certificate Templates console. Certificates that have been revoked will not be renewed.

REAL WORLD REMEMBER YOUR ENTERPRISE ROOT CA'S SIGNING CERTIFICATE

In many organizations, the person who originally set up the CA is long gone by the time the CA signing certificate expires. This can lead to mayhem when every certificate used in an organization expires because their lifetime can't exceed that of the CA signing certificate. If you're responsible for managing the CA infrastructure in your organization, regularly ensure that there is plenty of time left on the CA signing certificate.

Autoenrollment

Autoenrollment allows certificates to be automatically deployed to users, services, and computers from an enterprise CA without requiring the client requesting the certificate. Autoenrollment vastly simplifies the certificate deployment process, especially given the complexity of the certificate request process, which must either be done through an arcane console or through a web interface. With autoenrollment, you can automatically provision users, computers, and services with certificates without them being aware that this has occurred.

To support autoenrollment,key a certificate template must be configured so that the user, computer, or service to be enrolled is assigned the Enroll and Autoenroll permissions as shown in Figure 4-15.

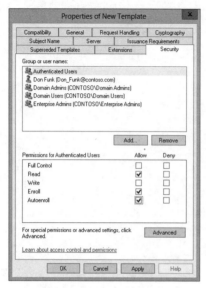

FIGURE 4-15 Assign the Enroll and Autoenroll permissions

After the certificate template is configured for autoenrollment, it's also necessary to configure the Certificate Services Client – Auto-Enrollment Group Policy item in a GPO that applies to the user, service, or computer that you want to automatically enroll in the certificate. This Group Policy item is shown in Figure 4-16. When both the policy and an enterprise CA are configured to deploy an appropriately configured template, autoenrollment will occur the next time the policy refreshes. The simplest way to verify that autoenrollment is working properly is to look at the Issued Certificates node of the CA, and sort by Certificate Template.

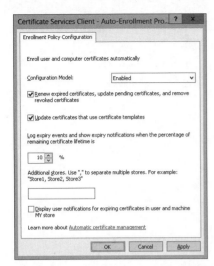

FIGURE 4-16 Configure the Certificate Services Client – Auto-Enrollment Group Policy

> **MORE INFO** **CERTIFICATE AUTOENROLLMENT**
>
> To learn more about certificate autoenrollment, consult the following article: *http://technet.microsoft.com/en-us/library/cc731522.aspx.*

Key archiving and recovery

Key archiving enables you to recover private keys from the certificate server if key archiving is enabled and you know the serial number of the certificate. For example, if you need to recover data that a user has encrypted using Encrypting File System (EFS) and a data recovery agent hasn't been configured. In this scenario, you could use key recovery to recover the user's private key, which would allow you to access the encrypted data.

Key archiving is not enabled by default. You need to enable key archiving on the CA and also on each certificate template that you want to use it with. Before you can enable key archiving on a CA, you need to enroll at least one user with a certificate issued from the key recovery agent template. You need to configure an enterprise CA to issue this template, as this is not a template that is available by default. After you've issued a certificate based on this template to a user, you can configure the user as a recovery agent as shown in Figure 4-17. When a user is configured as a recovery agent, they are able to extract and recover private keys. As private keys allow access to sensitive information, you should limit the distribution of key recovery agents and create a policy for their use.

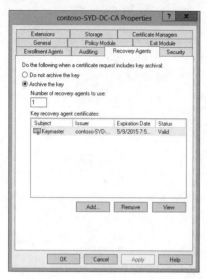

FIGURE 4-17 Configure the user as a recovery agent

When key archiving is enabled on the CA, you need to enable the archive subject's encryption private key on each certificate template where you want to allow for private key recovery. You do this on the Request Handling tab as show in Figure 4-18. In some cases you need to create a new template as only templates that have a minimum compatibility of Windows Server 2008 support key archiving. Only certificates issued off a template with this option enabled will have keys archived. If existing users have certificates issued off this template, you need to reenroll them before the keys for their certificate are archived.

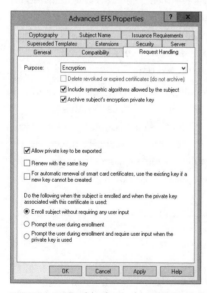

FIGURE 4-18 Enable the Archive Subject's Encryption Private Key

A user that has the private key associated with the key recovery agent (KRA) certificate configured on the certificate server is able to perform recovery from an elevated command prompt using the certutil command. To perform recovery, it's necessary to use the certutil command with the getkey option and to have the serial number of the certificate that needs to be recovered as shown in Figure 4-19.

FIGURE 4-19 Recover a certificate with the certutil command

After the certificate blob has been extracted from the database, you can recover the key using certutil with the recoverkey option as shown in Figure 4-20. When recovering the key, the user with the recovery agent certificate needs to specify a password. This password is required when importing the private certificate for use.

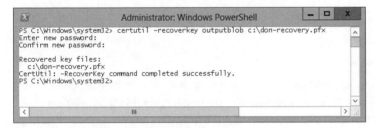

FIGURE 4-20 Recover the key using certutil

MORE INFO **KEY ARCHIVING AND RECOVERY**

To learn more about key archiving and recovery, consult the following article:
http://technet.microsoft.com/en-us/library/cc730721(v=ws.10).aspx.

Lesson summary

- Certificate templates enable you to configure the properties of certificates.
- Certificate template compatibility settings determine the minimum CA and certificate recipient that can be used with the certificate. The more stringent the requirement, the more options available on the template.

- Certificate revocation enables you to deem an existing certificate invalid. The certificate hold option is the only one that allows you to unrevoke a certificate.
- Certificate renewal properties determine the frequency at which the certificate is renewed. You can force renewal on certificates issued by enterprise CAs by reenrolling all certificate holders
- Autoenrollment allows certificates to be automatically requested and deployed.
- Autoenrollment must be enabled through permissions on the certificate template and through the Certificate Services Client – Auto-Enrollment policy.
- You can configure private key recovery if a user has been enrolled in a key recovery agent certificate and the certificate template has been configured so that the private key is archived.

Lesson review

Answer the following questions to test your knowledge of the information in this lesson. You can find the answers to these questions and explanations of each answer choice in the "Answers" section at the end of this chapter.

1. You want to allow specific users the ability to recover private keys, such as those used for encryption. Which certificate template can you use to issue keys to these users so that they can recover private keys from the certificate services database?

   A. Administrator

   B. EFS recovery agent

   C. Key recovery agent

   D. OCSP Response Signing

2. You want to ensure that clients will always recognize that a certificate has been revoked within 30 minutes of an administrator performing the revocation. Which of the following settings must you configure to accomplish this goal?

   A. CRL publication interval

   B. Key recovery agent

   C. Delta CRL publication interval

   D. Certificate templates

3. You want to configure a certificate so that users are automatically in the certificate. Which of the following steps do you need to take to accomplish this goal? (Choose all that apply.)

   A. Configure the users with the Enroll and Autoenroll permissions on the certificate template.

   B. Configure an enterprise CA to issue the template.

   C. Configure the Certificate Services Client – Auto-Enrollment Group Policy item.

D. Configure a standalone CA to issue the template.

4. On Monday morning, Don rings you and tells you that he doesn't have his smart card and might have lost it at the coffee shop, but he suspects that he might have left it at home. He's travelling interstate today and won't get home until Friday. He won't know until then if it is lost or sitting on the kitchen table at home. Policy dictates that you should revoke his smart card certificate. Which of the following reasons should you specify when revoking his certificate to minimize the effort required if the smart card is found at home on Friday?

   A. Certificate Hold

   B. CA compromise

   C. Key compromise

   D. Change of Affiliation

5. You have located Trojan software that allows remote access to a standalone certificate server located on your organization's perimeter network. The CA certificate for the perimeter network CA was issued from your organization's enterprise root CA. You are in the process of revoking the CA certificate of the perimeter network CA. Which of the following reasons should you use when revoking this certificate?

   A. Certificate Hold

   B. Change of Affiliation

   C. CA compromise

   D. Key compromise

6. You have just modified an existing template so that it supports key recovery. The CA already supports key recovery. A large number of users are enrolled in certificates issued based on the template prior to you making this modification. How can you ensure that it will be possible to recover the private keys of these users?

   A. Use the Certificate Templates console to reenroll all certificate holders

   B. Delete the certificate template

   C. Create a new certificate template and configure supersedence

   D. Change the certificate template name

Practice exercises

The goal of this section is to provide you with hands-on practice with the following:

- Deploying an enterprise root CA
- Deploying an enterprise subordinate CA
- Deploying a standalone subordinate CA
- Configuring a CRL distribution point

- Configuring an Online Responder
- Configuring administrative role separation
- Configuring a KRA and key recovery
- Configuring autoenrollment
- Performing certificate revocation
- Performing private key recovery

To perform the exercises in this section, you need access to an evaluation version of Windows Server 2012 R2. You should also have access to virtual machines SYD-DC, MEL-DC, CBR-DC, and ADL-DC, the setup instructions for which are described in the Introduction. You should ensure that you have a checkpoint of these virtual machines that you can revert to at the end of the practice exercises. You should revert the virtual machines to this initial state prior to beginning these exercises.

Exercise 1: Deploy and configure an enterprise root CA

In this exercise, you deploy an enterprise root CA on SYD-DC and perform initial configuration tasks. To complete this exercise, perform the following steps:

1. Sign on to SYD-DC as contoso\don_funk with the password **Pa$$w0rd**.
2. On the Manage menu of the Server Manager console, click Add Roles And Features.
3. On the Before You Begin page of the Add Roles And Features Wizard, click Next three times.
4. On the Select Server Roles page, click the Active Directory Certificate Services check box as shown in Figure 4-21.

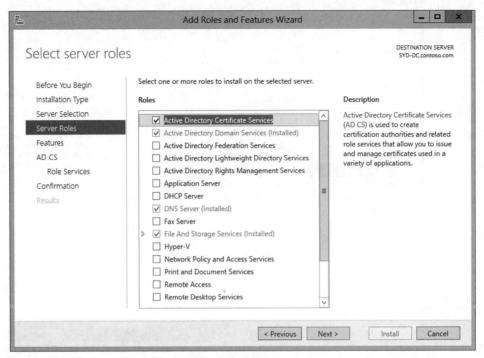

FIGURE 4-21 Choose the Active Directory Certificate Services option

5. On the Add Roles And Features Wizard dialog box, click Add Features, and then click Next three times.

6. On the Select Role Services page, ensure that the following are selected as shown in Figure 4-22, clicking Add Features as necessary on the Add Roles And Features Wizard dialog box, and then click Next three times.

- Certification Authority
- Certificate Enrollment Policy Web Service
- Certificate Enrollment Web Service
- Certification Authority Web Enrollment

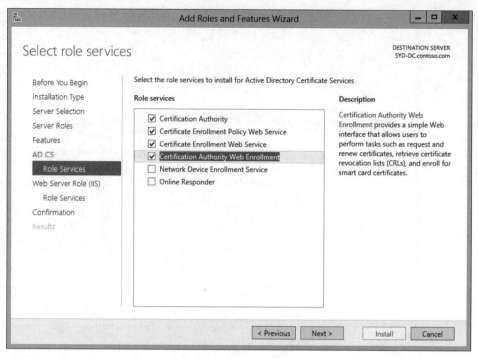

FIGURE 4-22 Select Role Services

7. On the Confirm Installation Selections page, click Install. When the installation completes, click Close.

8. On the Notification menu, click Configure Active Directory Certificate Services on the Destination Computer.

9. On the Credentials page of the AD CS Configuration Wizard, ensure that Contoso\ don_funk is selected as shown in Figure 4-23 and click Next.

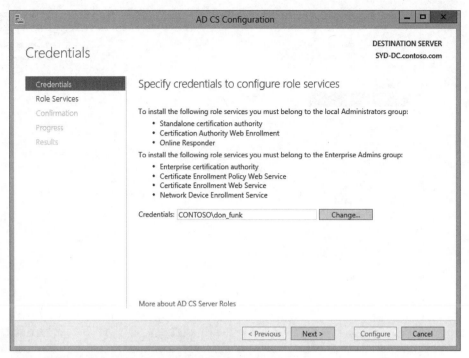

FIGURE 4-23 Set credentials to CONTOSO\don_funk

10. On the Select Role Services To Configure page, select both Certification Authority and Certification Authority Web Enrollment as shown in Figure 4-24, and click Next.

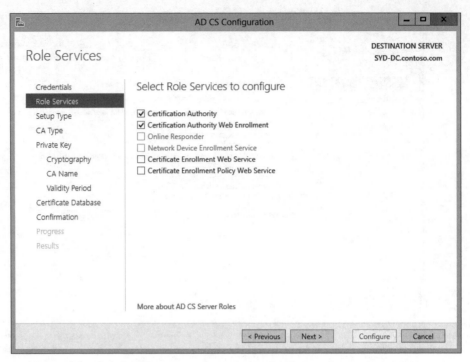

FIGURE 4-24 Select Role Services

11. On the Setup Type page, select Enterprise CA and click Next.

12. On the CA Type page, select Root CA as shown in Figure 4-25, and click Next.

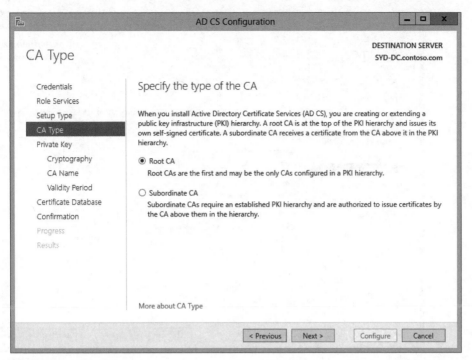

FIGURE 4-25 Select Root CA

13. On the Private Key page, click Create A New Private Key, and click Next.

14. On the Cryptography For CA page, set the Key Length to 4096 and click Next.

15. On the CA Name page, ensure that the name is set to contoso-SYD-DC-CA as shown in Figure 4-26, and click Next.

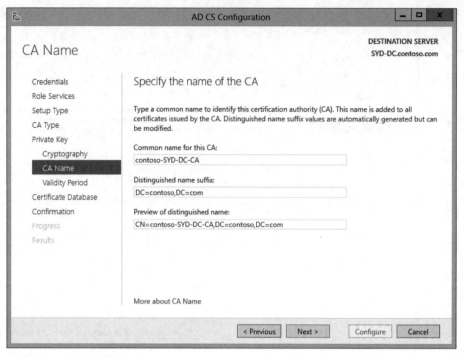

FIGURE 4-26 Set the CA Name

16. On the Validity Period page, set the validity to 10 years and click Next twice.

17. On the Confirmation page, click Configure and then click Close.

18. On the AD CS Configuration dialog box click Yes.

19. On the Credentials dialog box, verify that the credential of CONTOSO\don_funk has been configured and then click Next.

20. On the Select Role Services To Configure page, click Certificate Enrollment Web Service and Certificate Enrollment Policy Web Service as shown in Figure 4-27, and click Next.

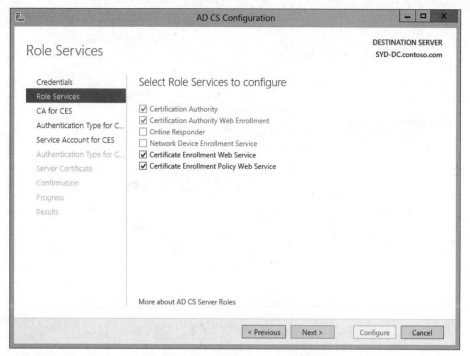

FIGURE 4-27 Select the Certificate Enrollment Web Service and Certificate Enrollment Policy Web Service

21. On the CA For CES page, ensure that CA Name is selected, and click Next.

22. On the Authentication Type For CES page, ensure that Windows Integrated Authentication is selected as shown in Figure 4-28 and click Next.

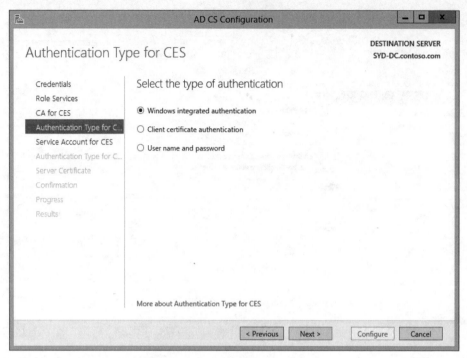

FIGURE 4-28 Select Windows Integrated Authentication

23. On the Service Account For CES page, select Use The Built-In Application Pool Identity, and click Next.

24. On the Authentication Type For CES page, click Next.

25. On the Specify A Server Authentication Certificate page, click Contoso-SYD-DC-CA as shown in Figure 4-29, and click Next.

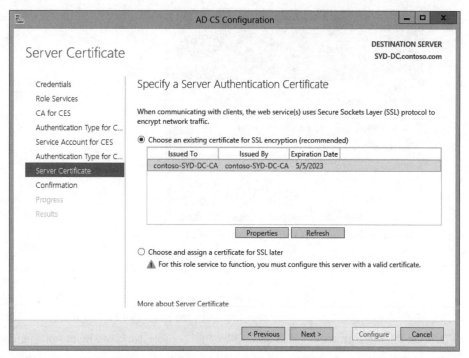

FIGURE 4-29 Click Contoso-SYD-DC-CA

26. On the Confirmation page, click Configure, and when configuration is complete, click Close.

Exercise 2: Deploy an enterprise subordinate CA

In this exercise, you join MEL-DC to the domain and configure the computer as an enterprise subordinate CA. To complete this exercise, perform the following steps:

1. Ensure that SYD-DC is powered on. Sign in to MEL-DC as Administrator with the password **Pa$$w0rd**.

2. On the taskbar, click on the Windows PowerShell icon.

3. In the Windows PowerShell Window, type the following command:

```
Add-computer –Credential contoso\don_funk –DomainName contoso.com
```

4. In the Windows PowerShell Credential pop-up dialog box, ensure that contoso\ administrator is listed as the username as shown in Figure 4-30, type the password **Pa$$word**, and click OK.

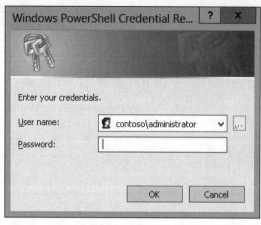

FIGURE 4-30 Listing contoso\administrator as the user name.

5. Type the following command and press Enter to restart the computer:

```
restart-computer
```

6. Sign in to MEL-DC as contoso\don_funk with the password **Pa$$w0rd**.

7. On the Manage menu of the Server Manager console, click Add Roles And Features.

8. On the Before You Begin page of the Add Roles And Features Wizard, click Next three times.

9. On the Select Server Roles page, click Active Directory Certificate Services as shown in Figure 4-31.

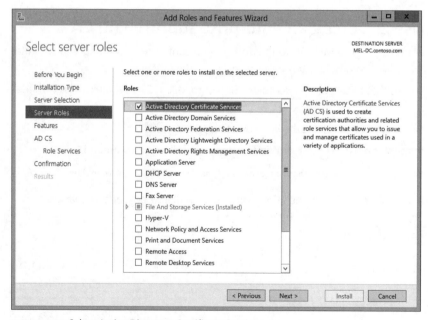

FIGURE 4-31 Select Active Directory Certificate Services

10. On the Add Roles And Features Wizard dialog box, click Add Features, and then click Next four times and click Install. When the installation completes, click Close.

11. Click the Notification item on Server Manager, and click Configure Active Directory Certificate Services on the Destination Computer.

12. On the Credentials page of the AD CS Configuration Wizard, verify that CONTOSO\ don_funk is listed as shown in Figure 4-32, and click Next.

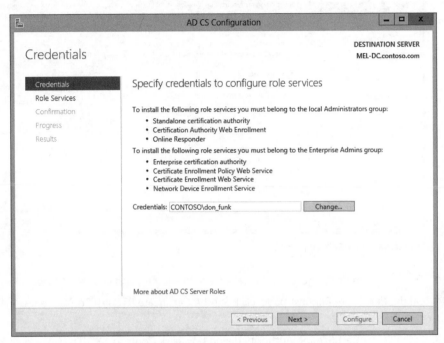

FIGURE 4-32 Verify that CONTOSO\don_funk is listed on the Credentials page

13. On the Role Services page, click Certification Authority and click Next.

14. On the Setup Type, select Enterprise CA, and click Next.

15. On the CA Type page, click Subordinate CA as shown in Figure 4-33, and click Next.

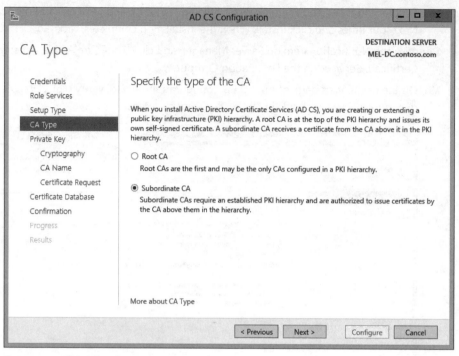

FIGURE 4-33 Click Subordinate CA

16. On the Private Key page, click Create A New Private Key, and click Next three times.

17. On the Certificate Request page, click Send A Certificate Request To A Parent CA, and click Select.

18. In the Select Certification Authority dialog box, click Contoso-SYD-DC-CA and click OK.

19. Verify that the Parent CA text box is set to SYD-DC.contoso.com\contoso-SYD-DC-CA as shown in Figure 4-34, and click Next twice.

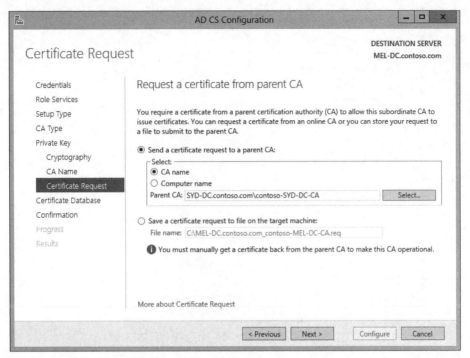

FIGURE 4-34 Send a certificate request from a parent CA

20. On the Confirmation page, click Configure.

21. On the Results page, click Close.

22. On the Tools menu of the Server Manager console, click Certification Authority.

23. In the Certification Authority console, right-click Contoso-MEL-DC-CA and click Properties.

24. On the General tab of the Contoso-MEL-DC-CA Properties dialog box, click Certificate #0 and click View Certificate.

25. On the Certificate dialog box, verify that the certificate is issued by Contoso-SYD-DC-CA as shown in Figure 4-35, and then click OK twice.

FIGURE 4-35 Verify the certificate is issued by Contoso-SYD-DC-CA

Exercise 3: Install a standalone subordinate CA

In this exercise, you install a standalone subordinate CA on ADL-DC. You obtain the CA certificate using a web browser. To complete this exercise, perform the following steps:

1. Sign on to ADL-DC as Administrator with the password **Pa$$w0rd**.

2. On the taskbar, click the Windows PowerShell icon.

3. In the Windows PowerShell Window, type the following command:

   ```
   Add-computer –Credential contoso\don_funk –DomainName contoso.com
   ```

4. In the Windows PowerShell Credential pop-up dialog box, ensure that contoso\ administrator is listed as the username as shown in Figure 4-36, type the password **Pa$$word**, and click OK.

FIGURE 4-36 Verify that Contoso\administrator is listed as the user name

5. Type the following command and press Enter to restart the computer:

```
restart-computer
```

6. Sign on to ADL-DC as contoso\don_funk with the password **Pa$$w0rd**.

7. On the Manage menu of the Server Manager console, click Add Roles And Features.

8. On the Before You Begin page of the Add Roles And Features Wizard, click Next three times.

9. On the Select Server Roles page, click Active Directory Certificate Services, click Add Features in the Add Roles And Features Wizard dialog box, shown in Figure 4-37, and then click Next four times.

FIGURE 4-37 Click Add Features

10. Click Install on the Confirm Installation Selections page of the Add Roles And Features Wizard, and then click Close.

11. Click the Notifications area and click Configure Active Directory Certificate Services on the Destination Server

12. On the Credentials page of the AD CS Configuration Wizard, ensure that CONTOSO\ don_funk is set in the Credentials text box and click Next.

13. On the Role Services page, click Certification Authority in the list of roles to configure and click Next.

14. On the Setup Type page, verify that Standalone CA is selected and click Next.

15. On the Specify The Type Of The CA page, click Subordinate CA as shown in Figure 4-38 and click Next.

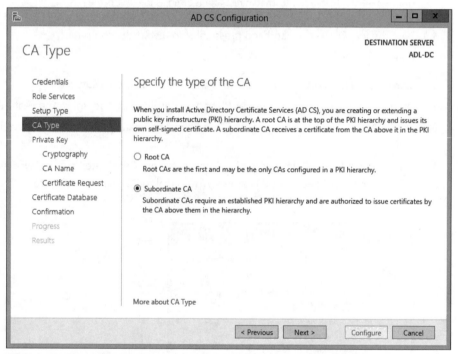

FIGURE 4-38 Click Subordinate CA

16. On the Private Key page, select Create A New Private Key and click Next.

17. On the Cryptography For CA page, set the Key Length to 4096 and click Next.

18. On the CA Name page, verify that the Common Name For This CA is listed as Contoso-ADL-DC-CA as shown in Figure 4-39 and click Next.

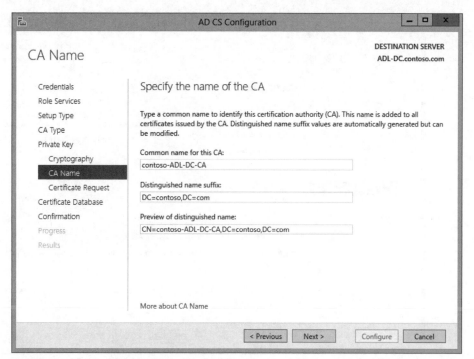

FIGURE 4-39 Verify the common name for the CA

19. On the Certificate Request page, verify that the certificate request will be saved to C:\ ADL-DC.contoso.com_contoso-ADL-DC-CA.req as shown in Figure 4-40 and click Next twice.

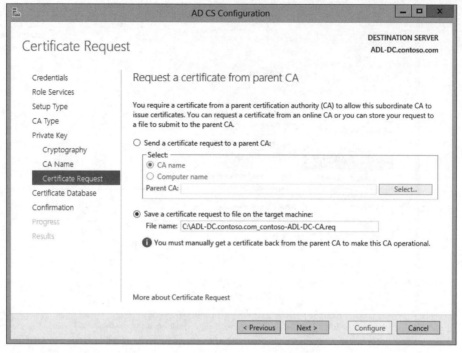

FIGURE 4-40 Verify the certificate request

20. On the Confirmation page, click Configure and then click Close.

Exercise 4: Configure a standalone CA

In this exercise, you complete the standalone CA configuration process. To complete this exercise, perform the following steps:

1. In the Server Manager console of ADL-DC, click the Local Server node.
2. In the Properties area, click the On link next to IE Enhanced Security Configuration. In the Internet Explorer Enhanced Security Configuration dialog box, click Off as shown in Figure 4-41 and then click OK.

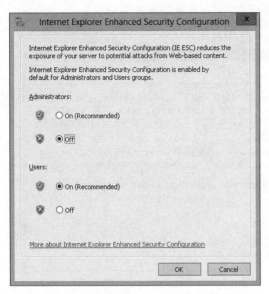

FIGURE 4-41 Set the IE Enhanced Security Configuration

3. In the Search charm, type Internet Explorer.

4. In the list of results for Internet Explorer, click Internet Explorer.

5. In the Windows Internet Explorer 11 dialog box, shown in Figure 4-42, click Use Recommended Security And Compatibility Settings and then click OK.

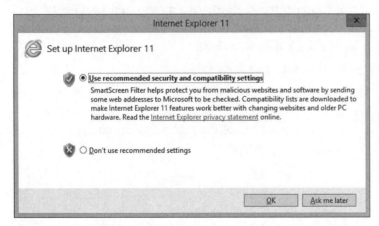

FIGURE 4-42 Choose the IE Use Recommended Security And Compatibility Settings

6. In the address bar, type **http://SYD-DC/certsrv** and press Enter.

7. On the Welcome webpage, shown in Figure 4-43, click Request A Certificate.

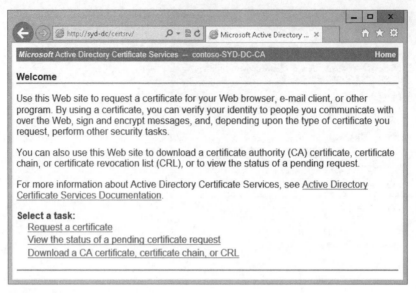

FIGURE 4-43 Request a certificate

8. On the Request A Certificate page, click Advanced Certificate Request.

9. On the Advanced Certificate Request page, click Submit A Request By Using A Base-64-Encoded CMC Or PKCS #10 File, Or Submit A Renewal Request By Using A Base-64-Encoded PKCS #7 File.

10. In the Search charm, type **notepad c:\ADL-DC.contoso.com_contoso-ADL-DC-CA. req**.

11. On the Edit menu of Notepad, click Select All.

12. On the Edit menu of Notepad, click Copy.

13. In Internet Explorer, in the Saved Request text box, right-click and click Paste.

14. On the Certificate Template drop-down menu, select Subordinate Certification Authority as shown in Figure 4-44, scroll down, and click Submit.

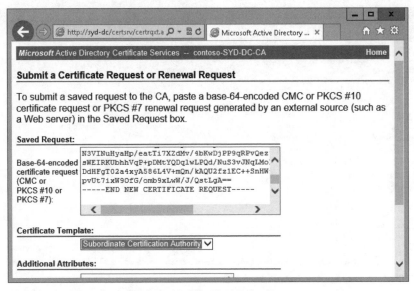

FIGURE 4-44 Select the Subordinate Certification Authority

15. On the Certificate Issued page, click Download Certificate.

16. On the Do You Want To Open Or Save Certnew.cer page, click Save.

17. On the Tools menu of the Server Manager console, click Certification Authority.

18. On the Certsrv – [Certification Authority (Local)] console, click ADL-DC-CA. On the Action menu, click All Tasks and then click Install CA Certificate.

19. On the Select File To Complete CA Installation dialog box, set the file type to X.509 Certificate (*.cer,*.crt), click the Downloads folder, click Certnew, and click Open.

20. Click ADL-DC-CA, and then on the Action menu click All Tasks, and click Start Service.

Exercise 5: Configure a CRL distribution point

In this exercise, you configure a CRL distribution point on SYD-DC. To complete this exercise, perform the following steps:

1. Sign on to MEL-DC as contoso\don_funk with the password **Pa$$word**.

2. On the Taskbar, click File Explorer.

3. In the Libraries window, expand the Computer node and click the Local Disk (C:) node.

4. On the Home ribbon, click New Folder and type the name as **ALT-CDP**.

5. On the Share ribbon, click Specific People as shown in Figure 4-45.

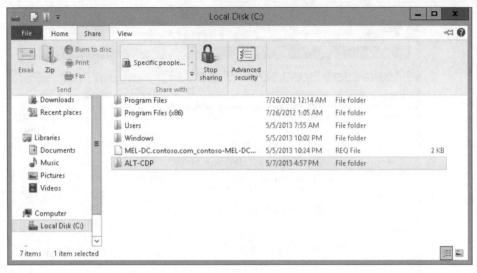

FIGURE 4-45 Click Specific People on the Share Ribbon

6. On the File Sharing dialog box, click the drop-down arrow, click Everyone, and click Add. On the drop-down menu next to Everyone, select Read/Write. Click Share, and click Done.

REAL WORLD **DIFFERENT CDP PERMISSIONS**

In a real-world scenario, you would configure permissions on a share that hosts the CRL so that only the CA would be able to write data to this location.

---

7. Switch to SYD-DC as contoso\don_funk with the password **Pa$$w0rd**.

8. In the Certification Authority console, click Contoso-SYD-DC-CA, and on the Action menu, click Properties.

9. On the Extensions tab, ensure that CRL Distribution Point (CDP) is selected as shown in Figure 4-46, and click Add.

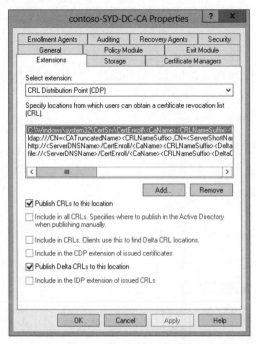

FIGURE 4-46 Verify the CRL Distribution Point (CDP) is selected on the Extensions tab

10. In the Add Location dialog box, type file://mel-dc/alt_cdp/.

11. Ensure that <CaName> is selected as a Variable and click Insert.

12. Ensure that <CRLNameSuffix> is selected as a Variable and click Insert.

13. Ensure that <DeltaCRLAllowed> is selected as a Variable and click Insert

14. Append the location with .crl as shown in Figure 4-47 and click OK.

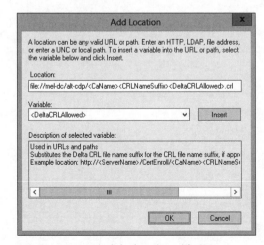

FIGURE 4-47 Append the location with CRL

15. On the Extensions tab, select the following options as shown in Figure 4-48 and click OK.

- Publish CRLs To This Location.

- Include In CRLs. Clients Use This To Find Delta CRL Locations.

- Include In The CDP Extension Of Issued Certificates.

- Publish Delta CRLs To This Location.

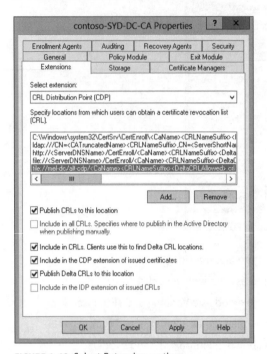

FIGURE 4-48 Select Extension options

16. When prompted to restart the Certification Authority, click Yes.

17. In the Certification Authority console, click the Revoked Certificates node. On the Action menu, click All Tasks and then click Publish.

18. On the Publish CRL dialog box, select New CRL as shown in Figure 4-49 and click OK.

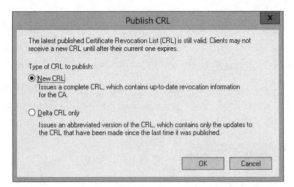

FIGURE 4-49 Select the New CRL option

19. In the Search charm, type **\\MEL-DC\ALT-CDP** and verify that two files are present as shown in Figure 4-50.

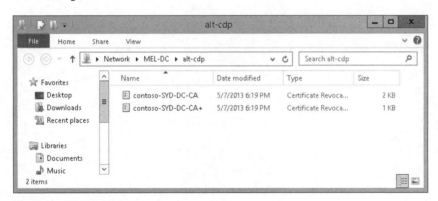

FIGURE 4-50 Verify CA files

Exercise 6: Configure an Online Responder

In this exercise, you configure an Online Responder. To complete this exercise, perform the following steps:

1. On SYD-DC, while signed on as contoso\don_funk, switch to the Certification Authority console.

2. In the Certification Authority console, expand Contoso-SYD-DC-CA and click Certificate Templates.

3. On the Action menu, click Manage.

4. In the Certificate Template console, right-click OCSP Response Signing, and then click Properties.

5. On the Security tab of the OCSP Response Signing Properties dialog box, click Add.

6. In the Select Users, Computers, Service Accounts, Or Groups dialog box, click Object Types, select Computers, click OK, type **SYD-DC**, click Check Names, and then click OK.

7. On the Security tab of the OCSP Response Signing Properties dialog box, set the permissions for SYD-DC$ to Read (Allow), Enroll (Allow), and Autoenroll (Allow) as shown in Figure 4-51. Click OK.

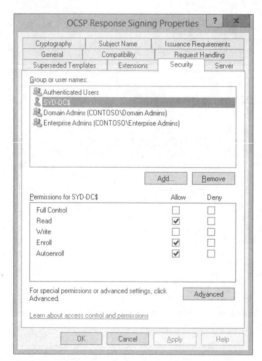

FIGURE 4-51 Set SYD-DC$ permissions

8. Close the Certificate Templates console.

9. In the Certification Authority console, expand Contoso-SYD-DC-CA and click Certificate Templates.

10. On the Action menu, click New, and click Certificate Template To Issue.

11. On the Enable Certificate Templates dialog box, click OCSP Response Signing as shown in Figure 4-52 and click OK.

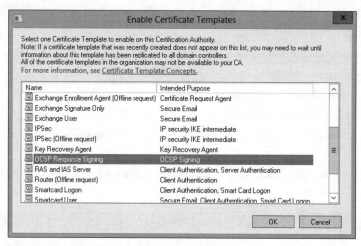

FIGURE 4-52 Click OCSP Response Signing

12. Click Add Roles And Features on the Manage menu of the Server Manager console.

13. On the Before You Begin page of the Add Roles And Features Wizard, click Next three times.

14. On the Select Server Roles page, expand the Active Directory Certificate Services (Installed) node and click Online Responder as shown in Figure 4-53.

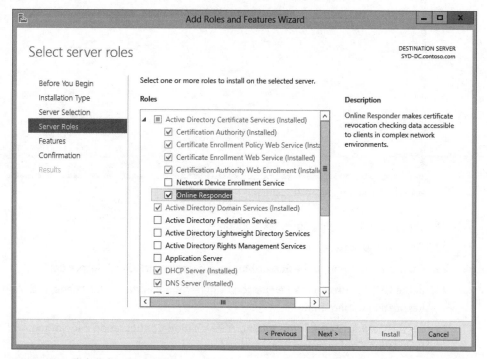

FIGURE 4-53 Click Online Responder

15. On the Add Features That Are Required For Online Responder dialog box, click Add Features, and then click Next twice.

16. On the Confirm Installation Selections page, click Install.

17. When the installation completes, click Close.

18. Click the Notifications menu and then click Configure Active Directory Certificate Services on the Destination Server.

19. On the Credentials page, ensure that CONTOSO\don_funk is selected and then click Next.

20. On the Role Services page, select Online Responder as shown in Figure 4-54, and then click Next.

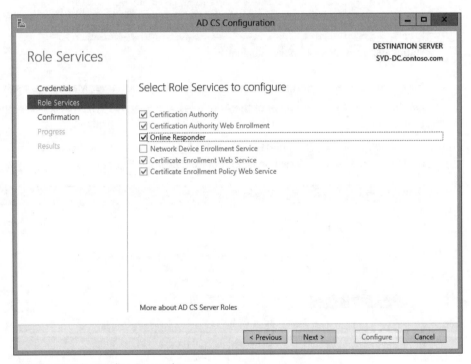

FIGURE 4-54 Select Online Responder

21. On the Confirmation page, click Configure.

22. On the Results page, click Close.

23. On the Tools menu of the Server Manager console, click OCSP Responder.

24. In the OCSP console, click Revocation Configuration. In the Actions pane, click Add Revocation Configuration.

25. On the Getting Started With Adding A Revocation Configuration page of the Add Revocation Configuration Wizard, click Next.

26. On the Name The Revocation Configuration page, type the name **Contoso_OCSP** and click Next.

27. On the Select CA Certificate Location page, click Select A Certificate For An Existing Enterprise CA as shown in Figure 4-55, and click Next.

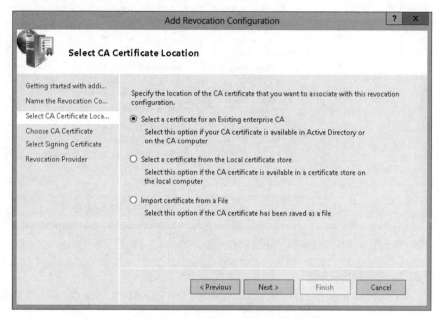

FIGURE 4-55 Select A Certificate For An Existing Enterprise CA location

28. In the Select Certification Authority dialog box, click Contoso-SYD-DC-CA and click OK.

29. On the Choose CA Certificate page, click Next.

30. On the Select Signing Certificate page, select Auto-Enroll For An OCSP Signing Certificate, click Browse, click Contoso-SYD-DC-CA, and click OK. Verify that the Select Signing Certificate page matches Figure 4-56, and then click Next.

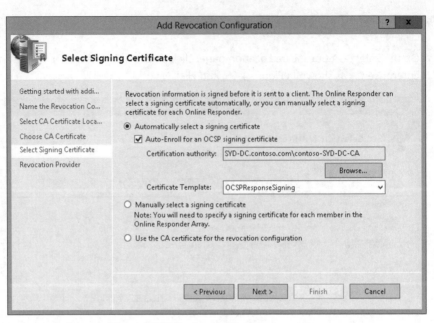

FIGURE 4-56 Autoenroll for an OCSP signing certificate

31. On the Revocation Provider page, click Provider.

32. Verify that the provider is configured as shown in Figure 4-57, click OK and click Finish.

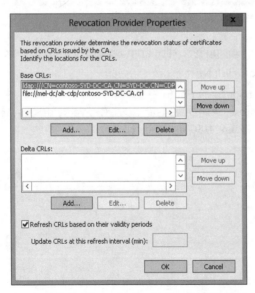

FIGURE 4-57 Configure the Revocation Provider page

33. Verify in the OCSP console that the Revocation Configuration Status is set to Working as shown in Figure 4-58.

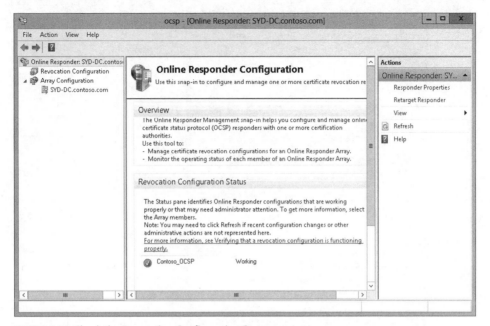

FIGURE 4-58 Check the Revocation Configuration Status

34. In the Certification Authority console, right-click Contoso-SYD-DC-CA and click Properties.

35. On the Extensions tab of the Contoso-SYD-DC-CA Properties dialog box, set the Extension drop-down menu to Authority Information Access (AIA) and click Add.

36. In the Location text box, type **http://syd-dc.contoso.com/ocsp** and click OK.

37. On the Extensions tab of the Contoso-SYD-DC-CA Properties dialog box, click http://syd-dc.contoso.com/ocsp, select Include In The Online Certificate Status Protocol (OCSP) Extension as shown in Figure 4-59, and click OK.

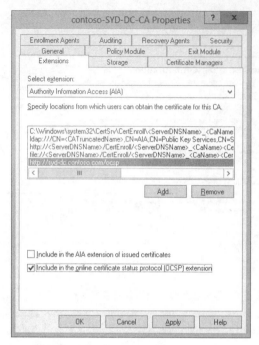

FIGURE 4-59 Set certificate locations

38. When prompted to restart certificate services, click Yes.

Exercise 7: Configure administrative role separation

In this exercise, you configure administrative role separation by delegating different certificate services permissions to different security groups. To complete this exercise, perform the following steps:

1. When signed on to SYD-DC as contoso\don_funk, click Active Directory Administrative Center on the Tools menu of the Server Manager console.

2. In Active Directory Administrative Center, click the Contoso (Local) node and then click the Users container.

3. In the Tasks menu, click New, and click Group.

4. In the Create Group dialog box, type the name **Certificate_Managers**, ensuring that the group type is set to Security and the Group Scope is set to Global as shown in Figure 4-60, and click OK.

FIGURE 4-60 Set Security and Global group types

5. In the Tasks menu, click New and click Group.

6. In the Create Group dialog box, type the name CertAuthority_Admins, ensuring that the group type is set to Security, and the Group Scope is set to Global. Click OK.

7. In the Certification Authority console, click Contoso-SYD-DC-CA and in the Action menu click Properties.

8. On the Security tab of the Contoso-SYD-DC-CA Properties dialog box, click Add.

9. On the Select Users, Computers, Service Accounts, Or Groups dialog box, type **Certificate_Managers; CertAuthority_Admins** as shown in Figure 4-61 and click OK.

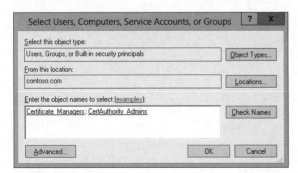

FIGURE 4-61 Type **Certificate_Managers; CertAuthority_Admins**

10. On the Security tab, click CertAuthority_Admins (CONTOSO\CertAuthority_Admins) and configure permissions so that only the Manage CA (Allow) permission is selected as shown in Figure 4-62. Click Apply.

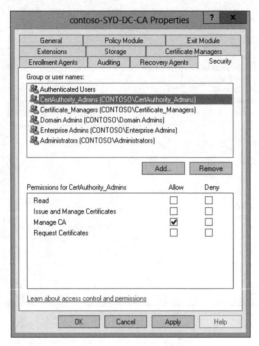

FIGURE 4-62 Configure security permissions

11. On the Security tab, click Certificate_Managers (CONTOSO\Certificate_Managers) and configure permissions so that only the Issue And Manage Certificates (Allow) permission is selected as shown in Figure 4-63 and click Apply.

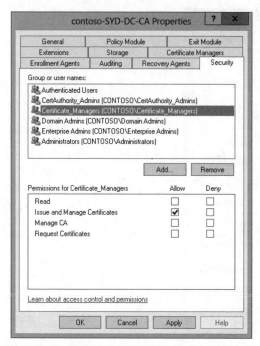

FIGURE 4-63 Select the Issue And Manage Certificates (Allow) permission

12. On the Certificate Managers tab, click Restrict Certificate Managers as shown in Figure 4-64 and click OK.

FIGURE 4-64 Click Restrict Certificate Managers

Exercise 8: Configure a key recovery agent certificate template

In this exercise, you configure a key recovery agent certificate. To complete this exercise, perform the following steps:

1. On SYD-DC while signed in as contoso\don_funk, open the Certification Authority console.

2. In the Certification Authority console, click Certificate Templates. On the Action menu, click Manage to open the Certificate Templates console.

3. In the Certificate Templates console, click the Key Recovery Agent template. On the Action menu, click Duplicate Template.

4. On the Compatibility tab of the Properties Of New Template dialog box, set the Certification Authority to Windows Server 2012 R2.

5. On the Resulting Changes dialog box, click OK.

6. On the Compatibility tab of the Properties Of New Template dialog box, set the Certificate Recipient to Windows 8.1 / Windows Server 2012 R2 as shown in Figure 4-65.

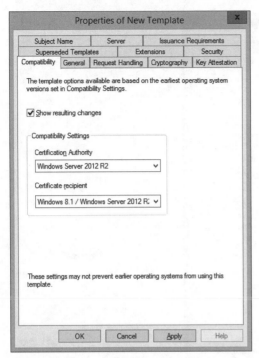

FIGURE 4-65 Set the Certificate Recipient to Windows 8.1 / Windows Server 2012 R2

7. On the Resulting Changes dialog box, shown in Figure 4-66, click OK.

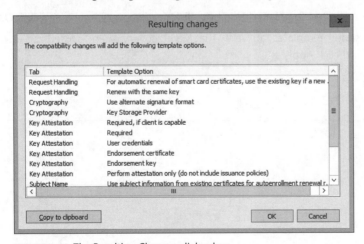

FIGURE 4-66 The Resulting Changes dialog box

8. On the General tab, set the Template Display Name to New Key Recovery Agent and the template name to NewKeyRecoveryAgent. Select the Publish Certificate In Active Directory option as shown in Figure 4-67 and click Apply.

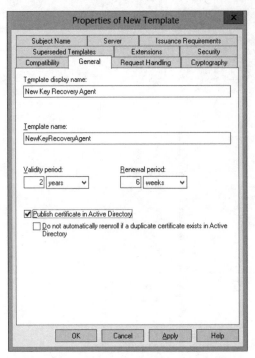

FIGURE 4-67 The Publish Certificate In Active Directory option

9. On the Superseded Templates tab, click Add.

10. In the Add Superseded Template dialog box, click Key Recovery Agent, and click OK.

11. On the Superseded Templates tab, verify that Key Recovery Agent is listed as shown in Figure 4-68, and click Apply.

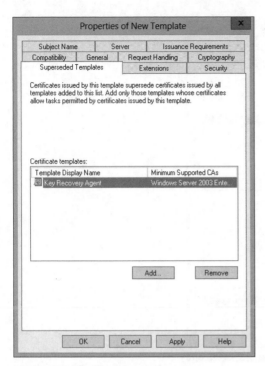

FIGURE 4-68 The Key Recovery Agent

12. On the Security tab, ensure that Domain Admins (CONTOSO\Domain Admins) has the Read (Allow), Write (Allow), and Enroll (Allow) permissions as shown in Figure 4-69 and then click OK.

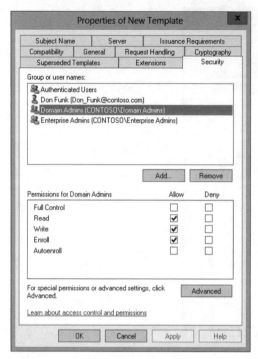

FIGURE 4-69 Ensure that the Domain Admins (CONTOSO\Domain Admins) has the Read (Allow), Write (Allow), and Enroll (Allow) permissions set

13. Close the Certificate Templates console.

14. In the Certification Authority console, click Certificate Templates.

15. On the Action menu, click New and click Certificate Template To Issue.

16. On the Enable Certificate Templates dialog box, click New Key Recovery Agent as shown in Figure 4-70 and click OK.

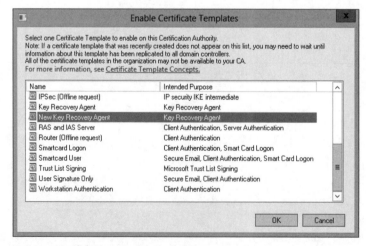

FIGURE 4-70 Click New Key Recovery Agent

17. In the Certification Authority console, refresh the list of Certificate Templates and verify that the New Key Recovery Agent template is visible, as shown in Figure 4-71.

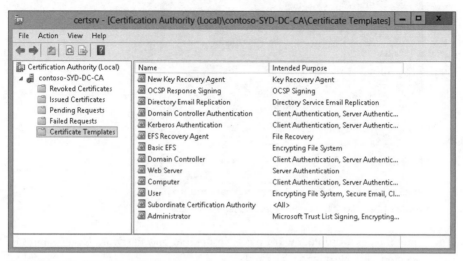

FIGURE 4-71 Verify that the New Key Recovery Agent template is visible

Exercise 9: Request a key recovery agent certificate

In this exercise, you create a user account to be used as a key recovery agent. To complete this exercise, perform the following steps:

1. When signed on to SYD-DC as contoso\don_funk, click Active Directory Users And Computers on the Tools menu of the Server Manager console.

2. In the Users container, click Don Funk. In the Action menu, click Copy.

3. On the Copy Object – User dialog box, enter the following information as shown in Figure 4-72 and click Next:

- Full Name: **Keymaster**
- User Logon Name: **keymaster**

FIGURE 4-72 Fill out the Copy Object - User dialog box

4. Enter the password **Pa$$w0rd** twice. Ensure that only Password Never Expires is selected, click Next, and click Finish.

5. Sign off SYD-DC and sign on as contoso\keymaster with the password **Pa$$w0rd**.

6. In the Search charm, type MMC. Click Mmc in the list of results.

7. On the User Account Control dialog box, click Yes.

8. On the File menu of the Console1 window, click Add/Remove Snap-In.

9. On the Add Or Remove Snap-Ins dialog box, click Certificates as shown in Figure 4-73 and click Add.

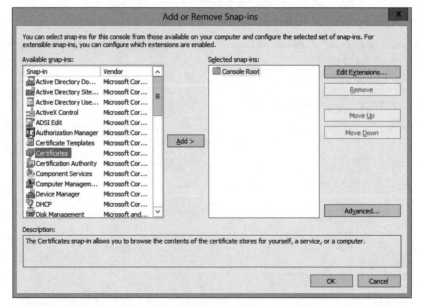

FIGURE 4-73 Click Certificates in the Add Or Remove Snap-Ins dialog box

10. In the Certificates Snap-In dialog box, click My User Account, click Finish, and click OK.

11. In Console1, expand Certificates – Current User and click the Personal node.

12. On the Action menu, click All Tasks and click Request New Certificate.

13. On the Before You Begin page of the Certificate Enrollment Wizard, click Next twice.

14. On the Request Certificates page, select New Key Recovery Agent as shown in Figure 4-74, click Enroll, and click Finish.

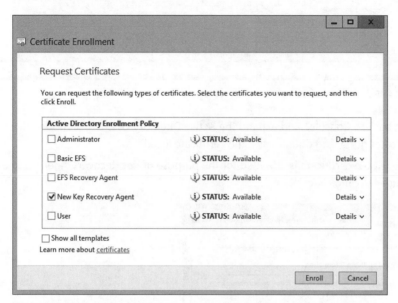

FIGURE 4-74 Select New Key Recovery Agent on the Request Certificates page

15. On the Tools menu of the Server Manager console, click Certification Authority.

16. In the Certification Authority console, expand the Contoso-SYD-DC-CA node and click the Pending Requests node.

17. Click the certificate request listed as shown in Figure 4-75. On the Action menu, click All Tasks and click Issue.

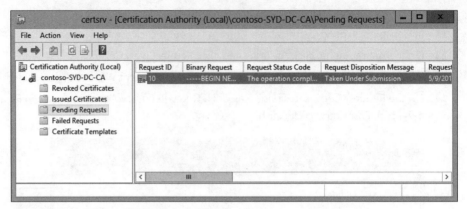

FIGURE 4-75 Pending requests on the Certification Authority

18. Switch back to Console1 and expand the Active Directory User Object node, click the Certificates node, and double-click the certificate listed.

19. Verify that the certificate is intended for the purpose of Key Recovery Agent as shown in Figure 4-76 and click OK.

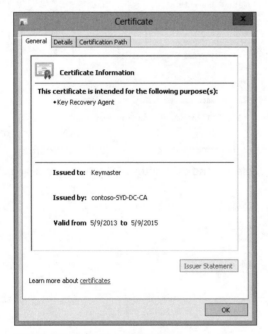

FIGURE 4-76 Verify the certificate

20. Sign off SYD-DC and sign back on as contoso\don_funk with the password **Pa$$w0rd**.

Exercise 10: Configure key recovery

In this exercise, you configure key recovery on SYD-DC. To complete this exercise, perform the following steps:

1. While signed on to SYD-DC as contoso\don_funk, open the Certification Authority console from the Tools menu of the Server Manager console.

2. In the Certification Authority console, click Contoso-SYD-DC-CA. In the Action menu, click Properties.

3. On the Recovery Agents tab of the Contoso-SYD-DC-CA Properties dialog box, click Archive The Key and click Add.

4. In the Key Recovery Agent Selection dialog box, click Keymaster as shown in Figure 4-77 and click OK.

FIGURE 4-77 Select Keymaster in the Key Recovery Agent Selection dialog box

5. On the Contoso-SYD-DC-CA Properties dialog box, click Apply.

6. When prompted to restart Active Directory Certificate Services, click Yes.

7. After Active Directory Certificate Services has restarted, on the Recovery Agents tab, verify that the Keymaster Key Recovery Agent Certificate has the status of Valid as shown in Figure 4-78.

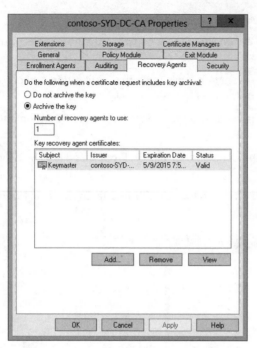

FIGURE 4-78 Verify that the Keymaster Key Recovery Agent Certificate has the status of Valid

8. Click OK to close the Contoso-SYD-DC-CA Properties dialog box.

Exercise 11: Configure a certificate template for autoenrollment and key recovery

In this exercise, you configure a certificate so that it can be configured for automatic enrollment and certificate recovery. To complete this exercise, perform the following steps:

1. On SYD-DC when signed on as contoso\don_funk, switch to the Certification Authority console and click the Certificate Templates node.

2. On the Action menu, click Manage.

3. In the Certificate Templates console, click the Basic EFS template. On the Action menu, click Duplicate Template.

4. On the Compatibility tab of the Properties Of New Template dialog box, set the Certification Authority drop-menu down to Windows Server 2012 R2.

5. On the Resulting Changes dialog box, click OK.

6. On the Compatibility tab, set the Certificate Recipient to Windows 8.1 / Windows Server 2012 R2.

7. On the Resulting Changes dialog box, click OK.

8. Verify that the Properties Of New Template dialog box matches Figure 4-79 and click the General tab.

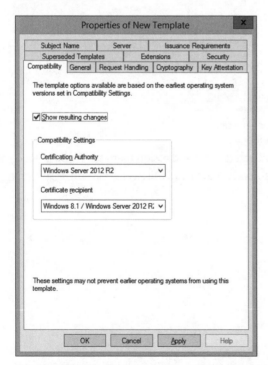

FIGURE 4-79 Verify that the Properties Of New Template dialog box matches

9. On the General tab, set the following properties as shown in Figure 4-80 and click Apply:

- Template Display Name: **Advanced EFS**
- Template Name: **AdvancedEFS**
- Publish Certificate in Active Directory: Enabled

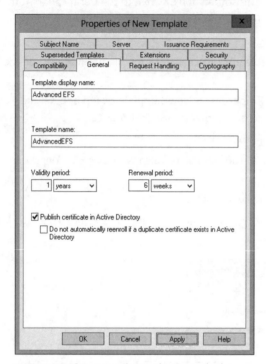

FIGURE 4-80 Set properties on the General tab

10. On the Security tab, click Authenticated Users and assign them the Enroll (Allow) and Autoenroll (Allow) permissions and retain the Read (Allow) permission as shown in Figure 4-81. Click OK.

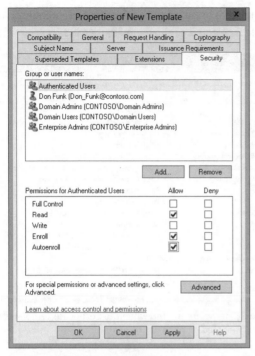

FIGURE 4-81 Click Authenticated Users and assign them the Enroll (Allow) and Autoenroll (Allow) permissions as well as retain the Read (Allow) permission

11. Close the Certificate Templates console.

12. On the Certification Authority console, click the Certificate Templates node. On the Action menu, click New and click Certificate Template To Issue.

13. On the Enable Certificate Templates dialog box, click Advanced EFS as shown in Figure 4-82 and click OK.

FIGURE 4-82 Clicking Advanced EFS

14. Verify that the Advanced EFS template is listed when the Certificate Templates node of the Certification Authority console is selected as shown in Figure 4-83.

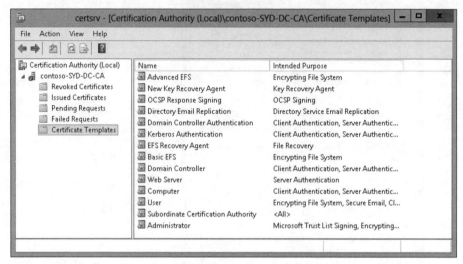

FIGURE 4-83 Verify that the Advanced EFS template is listed when the Certificate Templates node of the Certification Authority console is selected

Exercise 12: Configure Group Policy to support autoenrollment, credential roaming, and automatic renewal

In this exercise, you configure the default domain policy to support autoenrollment and automatic certificate renewal. To complete this exercise, perform the following steps:

1. On SYD-DC when signed in as contoso\don_funk, click Group Policy Management on the Tools menu of the Server Manager console.

2. In the Group Policy Management console, expand Forest: Contoso.com, expand Domains, expand Contoso.com, and click Default Domain Policy.

3. On the Group Policy Management Console dialog box, click OK.

4. On the Action menu, click Edit.

5. In the Group Policy Management Editor, expand User Configuration\Policies\Windows Settings\Security Settings and click the Public Key Policies node as shown in Figure 4-84.

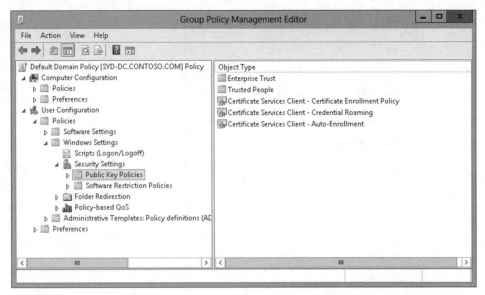

FIGURE 4-84 Expand User Configuration\Policies\Windows Settings\Security Settings and click the Public Key Policies node

6. Click the Certificate Services Client – Auto-Enrollment policy. On the Action menu, click Properties.

7. Set the Configuration Model drop-down menu to Enabled.

8. Select the following options as shown in Figure 4-85 and click OK.

   ■ Renew Expired Certificates, Update Pending Certificates, And Remove Revoked Certificates.

   ■ Update Certificates That Use Certificate Templates.

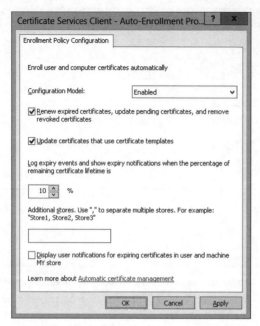

FIGURE 4-85 Configuring the CA Enrollment Policy

9. In the Group Policy Management Editor, click the Certificate Services Client – Certificate Enrollment Policy item. On the Action menu, click Properties.

10. On the Certificate Services Client – Certificate Enrollment Policy dialog box, set the Configuration Model to Enabled and ensure that Active Directory Enrollment Policy is selected as shown in Figure 4-86. Click OK.

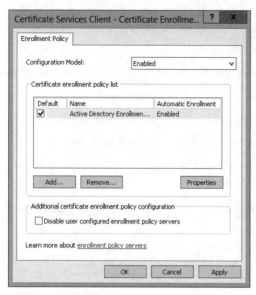

FIGURE 4-86 Set the Configuration Model to Enabled and ensure that the Active Directory Enrollment Policy is selected

11. In the Group Policy Management Editor, click the Certificate Services Client –
Credential Roaming policy. On the Action menu, click Properties.

12. On the Certificate Services Client – Credential Roaming Properties dialog box, click
Enabled as shown in Figure 4-87 and click OK.

FIGURE 4-87 Enable the Certificate Services Client – Credential Roaming Properties dialog box

13. Click OK on the Changing RUP Exclusion List dialog box, close the Group Policy Management Editor, and then close the Group Policy Management console.

14. Click the Windows PowerShell icon on the taskbar.

15. In the Windows PowerShell window, type the following command and press Enter:

    Gpupdate /force

16. Close the Windows PowerShell window when both policies have updated.

17. In the Certification Authority console, click the Issued Certificates node.

18. Verify that a certificate using the Advanced EFS template has been issued to CONTOSO\don_funk as shown in Figure 4-88.

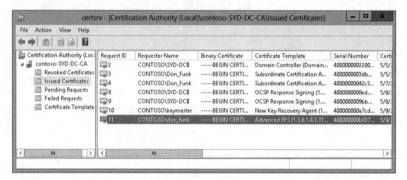

FIGURE 4-88 Verify that a certificate using the Advanced EFS template has been issued to CONTOSO\don_funk

Exercise 13: Configure a certificate template to support private key archival and recovery and reenroll all certificate holders

In this exercise, you modify the properties of the Advanced EFS template so that the private key is automatically archived and then reenroll all certificate holders. To complete this exercise, perform the following steps:

1. On SYD-DC when signed in as contoso\don_funk, select the Certificate Templates node of the Certification Authority console. On the Action menu, click Manage.

2. In the Certificate Templates console, click the Advanced EFS template. In the Action menu, click Properties.

3. On the Request Handling tab of the Advanced EFS Properties dialog box, select Archive Subject's Encryption Private Key.

4. On the Changing Key Archival Property dialog box, click OK.

5. Ensure that the Request Handling tab of the Advanced EFS Properties dialog box is configured as shown in Figure 4-89 and click OK.

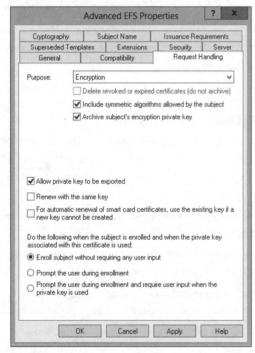

FIGURE 4-89 Ensure that the Request Handling tab of the Advanced EFS Properties dialog box is configured

6. Click the Advanced EFS template and on the Action menu click Reenroll All Certificate Holders.

7. Open a Windows PowerShell window by clicking the Windows PowerShell icon on the taskbar.

8. In the Windows PowerShell window, type the following command and press Enter:

9. Gpupdate /force

10. Switch to the Certificate Authority console and select the Issued Certificates node.

11. Verify that a new certificate using the Advanced EFS certificate template has been issued to CONTOSO\don_funk as shown in Figure 4-90.

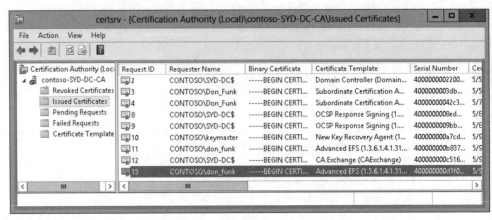

	Request ID	Requester Name	Binary Certificate	Certificate Template	Serial Number	Cer
	2	CONTOSO\SYD-DC$	-----BEGIN CERTI...	Domain Controller (Domain...	4000000002200...	5/5
	3	CONTOSO\Don_Funk	-----BEGIN CERTI...	Subordinate Certification A...	4000000003db...	5/5
	4	CONTOSO\Don_Funk	-----BEGIN CERTI...	Subordinate Certification A...	40000000042c3...	5/7
	8	CONTOSO\SYD-DC$	-----BEGIN CERTI...	OCSP Response Signing (1....	4000000008ed...	5/8
	9	CONTOSO\SYD-DC$	-----BEGIN CERTI...	OCSP Response Signing (1....	4000000009bb...	5/8
	10	CONTOSO\keymaster	-----BEGIN CERTI...	New Key Recovery Agent (1...	400000000a7cd...	5/9
	11	CONTOSO\don_funk	-----BEGIN CERTI...	Advanced EFS (1.3.6.1.4.1.31...	400000000b837...	5/9
	12	CONTOSO\SYD-DC$	-----BEGIN CERTI...	CA Exchange (CAExchange)	400000000c516...	5/9
	13	CONTOSO\don_funk	-----BEGIN CERTI...	Advanced EFS (1.3.6.1.4.1.31...	400000000d1f0...	5/9

FIGURE 4-90 Use the Advanced EFS certificate template

Exercise 14: Perform certificate revocation

In this exercise, you revoke the certificate issued to the subordinate CA hosted on ADL-DC. You would do this if the computer hosting the CA had been compromised by malware and might have been exploited by nefarious third parties. To complete this exercise, perform the following steps:

1. On SYD-DC when signed in as CONTOSO\don_funk, open the Certification Authority console and select the Issued Certificates node.

2. Select the second certificate issued or the one with the higher number in the Request ID column that uses the Subordinate Certification Authority template.

3. On the Action menu, click Open and verify that this certificate has been issued to Contoso-ADL-DC-CA as shown in Figure 4-91. Click OK to close the Certificate Properties dialog box.

FIGURE 4-91 Certificate information

4. With the correct certificate selected, click All Tasks on the Action menu and then click Revoke Certificate.

5. In the Certificate Revocation dialog box, choose Certificate Hold as the reason for the certificate revocation as shown in Figure 4-92 and click Yes.

FIGURE 4-92 The Certificate Revocation dialog box

6. In the Certification Authority console, click the Revoked Certificates node and verify that the certificate is listed with the Revocation Reason set to Certificate Hold as shown in Figure 4-93.

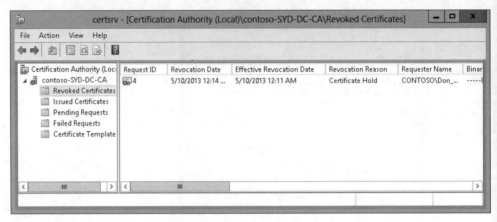

FIGURE 4-93 Verify that the certificate is listed

7. Ensure that the Revoked Certificates node is selected. On the Action menu, click All Tasks and click Publish.

8. In the Publish CRL dialog box, click New CRL as shown in Figure 4-94 and then click OK.

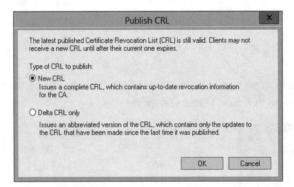

FIGURE 4-94 Select New CRL in the Publish CRL dialog box

9. Switch to ADL-DC and sign in as contoso\don_funk with the password **Pa$$w0rd**.

10. On the Taskbar, click the Windows PowerShell icon.

11. In the Windows PowerShell window, type the following commands and press Enter after each command:

```
Gpupdate /force

Certutil –urlcache crl delete

Certutil –urlcache ocsp delete
```

12. On the Tools menu of the Server Manager console, click Certification Authority.

13. In the Certification Authority console, click the Contoso-ADL-DC-CA node.

14. On the Action menu, click Properties.

15. On the General tab of the Contoso-ADL-DC-CA Properties dialog box, click View Certificate.

16. Verify that the certificate is listed as revoked, as shown in Figure 4-95, and click OK twice.

FIGURE 4-95 Verify that the certificate is listed as revoked

Exercise 15: Perform certificate recovery

In this exercise, you delete the Advanced EFS certificate that has been assigned to Don Funk and then use the keymaster user account to perform key recovery. To complete this exercise, perform the following steps:

1. When signed on to SYD-DC as contoso\don_funk, type **mmc.exe** in the Search charm and click Mmc in the list of results.

2. On the User Account Control dialog box, click Yes.

3. On the File menu of the Console1 console, click Add/Remove Snap-In.

4. On the Add Or Remove Snap-Ins dialog box, click Certificates and click Add.

5. On the Certificates Snap-In dialog box, click My User Account as shown in Figure 4-96, click Finish, and then click OK.

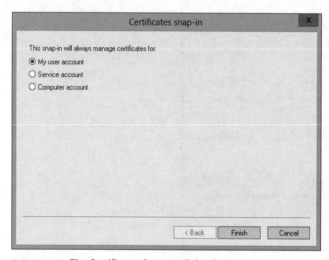

FIGURE 4-96 The Certificates Snap-In dialog box

6. In the Console1 console, expand the Certificates – Current User\Personal\Certificates node and click the certificate with the intended purpose listed as Encrypting File System as shown in Figure 4-97.

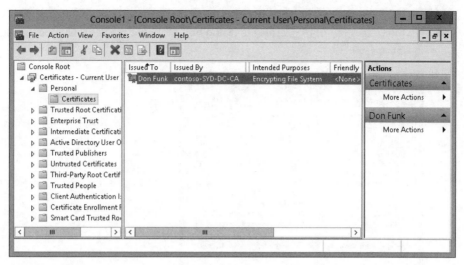

FIGURE 4-97 Click the certificate with the intended purpose of the Encrypting File System

7. On the Action menu, click Delete.

8. On the Certificates dialog box, click Yes.

9. On the File menu, click Save. Save the console on the desktop as **console1.msc**.

10. Sign off SYD-DC and sign on as contoso\keymaster with the password **Pa$$w0rd**.

11. On the Tools menu of the Server Manager console, click Certification Authority.

12. On the Certification Authority console, expand Contoso-SYD-DC-CA and click the Issued Certificates node.

13. Click the most recently issued certificate to CONTOSO\don_funk that uses the Advanced EFS certificate template as shown in Figure 4-98.

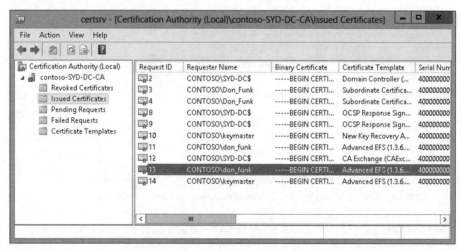

FIGURE 4-98 Click the most recently issued certificate to CONTOSO\don_funk that uses the Advanced EFS certificate template

14. On the Action menu, click Open.

15. On the Details tab of the Certificate dialog box, highlight the Serial Number as shown in Figure 4-99.

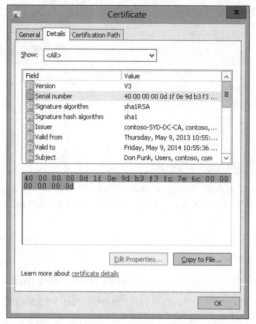

FIGURE 4-99 Highlighting the Serial Number on the Details pane of the Certificate dialog box

16. While the text is highlighted, press Ctrl+C to copy the text.

17. On the Search charm, type Notepad and then click Notepad in the results pane.

18. On the Edit menu of Notepad, click Paste.

19. In Notepad, remove all of the spaces in the serial number so that it appears in a manner similar to that of Figure 4-100.

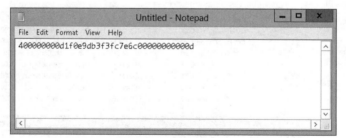

FIGURE 4-100 Remove all of the spaces in the serial number in Notepad

20. In Notepad, select the serial number on the Edit menu, and then click Copy.

21. Open an elevated Windows PowerShell window and type the following command where <serial number> is the pasted serial number from Notepad as shown in Figure 4-101:

```
Certutil -getkey <serial number> outputblob
```

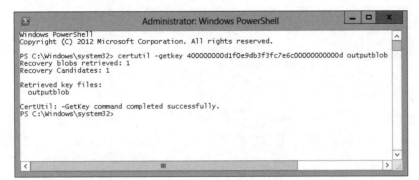

FIGURE 4-101 An elevated Windows PowerShell window

22. Type the following command and press Enter to convert the outputblob to a PFX file. Type the password **Pa$$w0rd** when prompted as shown in Figure 4-102.

```
Certutil -recoverkey outputblob c:\don-recovery.pfx
```

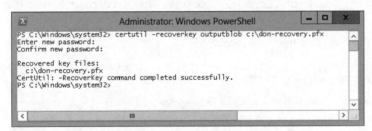

FIGURE 4-102 Convert the outputblob to a PFX file

23. Sign off and sign back on to SYD-DC as contoso\don_funk.

24. Click the File Explorer icon on the taskbar and navigate to Local Disk (C:).

25. Double-click the Don-recovery file.

26. On the Welcome To The Certificate Import Wizard page of the Certificate Import Wizard, click Current User and then click Next twice.

27. On the Private Key Protection page, enter the password **Pa$$w0rd** as shown in Figure 4-103, click Next twice, click Finish, and then click OK.

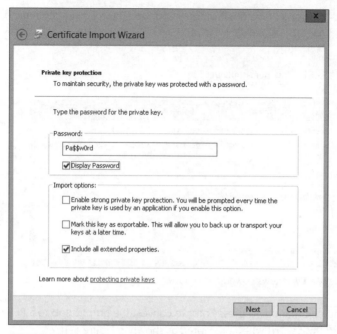

FIGURE 4-103 Enter the password on the Private Key Protection page

28. On the Desktop, double-click Console1. Click Yes on the User Account Control dialog box.

29. Verify that the certificate has been recovered.

> **REAL WORLD** AUTOENROLLMENT POLICY
>
> Because of the autoenrollment policy applied to the Advanced EFS certificate template, a second certificate may also be present. This second certificate will have a different serial number. You can verify that an additional certificate was issued by checking the list of issued certificates in the Certification Authority console.

Suggested practice exercises

The following additional practice exercises are designed to give you more opportunities to practice what you've learned and to help you successfully master the lessons presented in this chapter.

- **Exercise 1** Join CBR-DC to the domain and deploy an enterprise subordinate CA on this computer. Obtain the CA certificate from the enterprise subordinate CA hosted on MEL-DC.

- **Exercise 2** Remove the certificate hold placed on the ADL-DC CA's certificate. Publish a new CRL and then verify that the certificate is now valid.

Answers

This section contains the answers to the lesson review questions in this chapter.

Lesson 1

1. **Correct answer**: C

   A. **Incorrect**. Enterprise root CAs are integrated into Active Directory and cannot be configured as offline root CAs.

   B. **Incorrect**. Enterprise subordinate CAs cannot serve as the apex of a CA hierarchy as they are subordinate to another CA.

   C. **Correct**. Offline root CAs are always standalone root CAs that are only brought online to perform tasks such as renewing the CA certificate of subordinate CAs.

   D. **Incorrect**. Standalone subordinate CAs cannot serve as the apex of a CA hierarchy as they are subordinate to another CA.

2. **Correct answer**: C

   A. **Incorrect**. Enterprise CAs can only be deployed on computers that are members of an Active Directory domain.

   B. **Incorrect**. Enterprise CAs can only be deployed on computers that are members of an Active Directory domain.

   C. **Correct**. You can deploy standalone CAs on computers that are not members of an Active Directory domain, including computers running as virtual machines on Windows Azure.

   D. **Correct**. You can deploy standalone CAs on computers that are not members of an Active Directory domain, including computers running as virtual machines on Windows Azure.

3. **Correct answer**: B

   A. **Incorrect**. This component is a web interface that enables computers that are not members of the Active Directory forest, including those running third-party operating systems, to request and obtain certificates from the CA.

   B. **Correct**. This component publishes certificate revocation data based on published CRLs and delta CRLs. Online Responders enable clients to perform revocation checks without requiring them to download the entire CRL and delta CRL.

   C. **Incorrect**. This component enables network devices such as routers and switches to obtain certificates from the CA.

   D. **Incorrect**. This component enables policy-based certificate enrollment when a computer is not a member of the Active Directory forest.

4. **Correct answer**: D

   A. **Incorrect**. This component enables policy-based certificate enrollment when a computer is not a member of the Active Directory forest.

   B. **Incorrect**. This component enables network devices such as routers and switches to obtain certificates from the CA.

   C. **Incorrect**. This component publishes certificate revocation data based on published CRLs and delta CRLs.

   D. **Correct**. This component is a web interface that enables computers that are not members of the Active Directory forest, including those running third-party operating systems, to request and obtain certificates from the CA.

5. **Correct answer**: C

   A. **Incorrect**. This component publishes certificate revocation data based on published CRLs and delta CRLs.

   B. **Incorrect**. This component enables policy-based certificate enrollment when a computer is not a member of the Active Directory forest.

   C. **Correct**. This component enables network devices such as routers and switches to obtain certificates from the CA.

   D. **Incorrect**. This component is a web interface that enables computers that are not members of the Active Directory forest, including those running third-party operating systems, to request and obtain certificates from the CA.

6. **Correct answer**: D

   A. **Incorrect**. Security principals assigned the Read permission are able to view CA settings.

   B. **Incorrect**. Security principals assigned the Issue And Mange Certificates permission are able to approve certificate requests and revoke issued certificates.

   C. **Incorrect**. Security principals assigned the Manage CA permission are able to modify CA settings.

   D. **Correct**. Security principals assigned the Request Certificates permission are able to request certificates from the CA.

7. **Correct answer**: B

   A. **Incorrect**. Security principals assigned the Manage CA permission are able to modify CA settings.

   B. **Correct**. Security principals assigned the Issue And Mange Certificates permission are able to approve certificate requests and revoke issued certificates.

   C. **Incorrect**. Security principals assigned the Request Certificates permission are able to request certificates from the CA.

   D. **Incorrect**. Security principals assigned the Read permission are able to view CA settings.

8. **Correct answer**: D

  A. **Incorrect**. Security principals assigned the Request Certificates permission are able to request certificates from the CA.

  B. **Incorrect**. Security principals assigned the Read permission are able to view CA settings.

  C. **Incorrect**. Security principals assigned the Issue And Mange Certificates permission are able to approve certificate requests and revoke issued certificates.

  D. **Correct**. Security principals assigned the Manage CA permission are able to modify CA settings.

Lesson 2

1. **Correct answer**: C

  A. **Incorrect**. You cannot use an Administrator certificate to allow private key recovery from the certificate services database.

  B. **Incorrect**. An EFS recovery agent certificate allows for the recovery of EFS encrypted data. You cannot use a certificate based off of this template to perform private key recovery from the certificate services database.

  C. **Correct**. You can configure a certificate server so that users who are enrolled in a specific key recovery agent certificate are able to recover private keys from the certificate services database.

  D. **Incorrect**. The OCSP Response Signing certificate template is used when configuring an Online Responder.

2. **Correct answer**: C

  A. **Incorrect**. The minimum CRL publication interval is 1 hour. You need to configure the delta CRL publication interval to accomplish this goal.

  B. **Incorrect**. Key recovery agents aren't related to certificate revocation but are related to private key recovery.

  C. **Correct**. By configuring the delta CRL publication interval, clients will seek a new delta CRL that will contain the details of the revoked certificate within 30 minutes of the revocation occurring.

  D. **Incorrect**. Although you can configure a renewal period of 1 hour for a certificate, this setting would mean that the previous certificate would expire without renewal without direct client recognition of its revocation.

3. **Correct answers**: A, B, and C

  A. **Correct**. A user must be assigned the Enroll and Autoenroll permissions on the certificate template before they can be issued a certificate based on that template through autoenrollment.

  B. **Correct**. Autoenrollment is only supported from enterprise CAs.

C. Correct. You must configure autoenrollment in Group Policy using the Certificate Services Client – Auto-Enrollment Group Policy item.

D. Incorrect. Standalone CAs don't support autoenrollment.

4. **Correct answer**: A

    A. Correct. This reason enables you to unrevoke the certificate if Don finds it at home.

    B. Incorrect. Use this reason when you suspect that the certificate server has been compromised, not when a user loses their smart card.

    C. Incorrect. Use this reason when you know that Don's card has been lost.

    D. Incorrect. Use this reason when someone leaves the organization or when their role has changed in such a way that you need to revoke their existing certificates.

5. **Correct answer**: D

    A. Incorrect. This reason enables you to unrevoke a certificate when you are unsure if the reason for the revocation might change in future.

    B. Incorrect. Use this reason when someone leaves the organization or when their role has changed in such a way that you need to revoke their existing certificates.

    C. Incorrect. Use this reason when you suspect that the certificate server that issued the CA signing certificate has been compromised. In this case the issuing CA is fine; it's the perimeter network CA that's been compromised.

    D. Correct. Use this reason when you know that a specific certificate might have been compromised. In this case, the certificate issued by your enterprise root CA to the perimeter network CA is suspect.

6. **Correct answer**: A

    A. Correct. Using the certificate templates console to reenroll all certificate holders would trigger the issuance of new certificates based on the updated templates. These newly reissued certificates would have their private keys archived.

    B. Incorrect. Performing this step would not ensure that users' private keys would be archived.

    C. Incorrect. Although you could do this, it wouldn't trigger reenrollment of all certificate holders, which would mean that until certificate reenrollment needed to occur, the private keys would not be archived.

    D. Incorrect. Performing this step would not ensure that users' private keys would be archived.

CHAPTER 5

Backup and recovery

Data protection is a topic that most people find less than interesting until a server fails or data gets corrupted. When you've lost data, being able to recover it becomes the most interesting topic in the universe. Windows Server 2012 and Windows Server 2012 R2 include several different tools that enable you to back up and recover data. Understanding which tool is appropriate for a given situation is important for the 70-412 exam, and it's the topic of this chapter.

Lessons in this chapter:

- Lesson 1: Configuring and managing backups
- Lesson 2: Recovering servers

Before you begin

To complete the practice exercises in this chapter, you need to have deployed computers SYD-DC, MEL-DC, CBR-DC, and ADL-DC as described in the Introduction, using the evaluation edition of Windows Server 2012 R2.

Lesson 1: Configuring and managing backups

Windows Server 2012 and Windows Server 2012 R2 include several different tools that you can use to create and manage backups. The primary tool that most people are familiar with is Windows Server Backup, which enables you to back up everything from a single file to an entire server. Windows Server Backup includes the Wbadmin.exe command-line utility and, with Windows Server 2012 and Windows Server 2012 R2, it also includes more than 45 new Windows PowerShell cmdlets. Another backup option is Windows Azure Backup, which enables you to back up files and folders to the Windows Azure cloud. In this lesson you find out how you can use these different technologies to back up Windows Server 2012 and Windows Server 2012 R2.

> **NOTE NEW NAME!**
>
> Windows Azure is being renamed Microsoft Azure. Expect to see these changes soon.

After this lesson, you will be able to:

- Configure Windows Server Backups
- Configure Windows Online Backups
- Perform role-specific backups
- Use Vssadmin to manage VSS settings

Estimated lesson time: 45 minutes

Windows Server Backup

Windows Server Backup is the default backup application included with Windows Server 2012 and Windows Server 2012 R2. Windows Server Backup is a basic backup solution. It only enables you to back up to disk or network share. Tasks such as export to tape for long-term retention require a more sophisticated solution, such as System Center 2012 R2 Data Protection Manager. Windows Server Backup has a minimal level of reporting functionality and has no native functionality that makes it possible for alerts to be sent to an administrator through email in the event that a backup fails.

Windows Server Backup enables you to back up and recover the following:

- Full server (all volumes)
- Specific volumes
- Specific folders
- System State data

Although you can connect from the Windows Server Backup console to other computers to manage Windows Server Backup remotely, you can only use an instance of Windows Server Backup to back up the local computer. For example, whereas you can back up network shared folders that the computer is able to access, such as a mapped network drive, you can't configure Windows Server Backup on one computer to do a full volume or System State backup of another computer.

You can configure exclusions for backup jobs run on Windows Server Backup. Exclusions are specific file types that you want to exempt from the backup process. You can configure exclusion on the basis of file type, or you can choose to exclude the contents of entire folders and their subfolders. Figure 5-1 shows an exclusion that stops files with the .tmp extension in the C:\shared-docs folder and its subfolders from being written to backup.

FIGURE 5-1 File exclusions

Users who are local Administrators or members of the Backup Operators group are able to use Windows Server Backup to back up the entire computer, volumes, files, or folders, and the System State. You can grant other security principals this right by editing the Back Up Files And Directories Group Policy item. Windows Server Backup does not encrypt backups by default. When you are backing up data, you can configure access control so that only a user with specific credentials are able to access the backup, such as in Figure 5-2, but this does not encrypt the backup.

> **REAL WORLD** **SECURITY OF BACKUPS**
>
> The security of backups is important. Anyone who has access to backed up data can restore it to a separate location where they have complete access to that data. The security of backed up data is as important as the security of the servers being backed up.

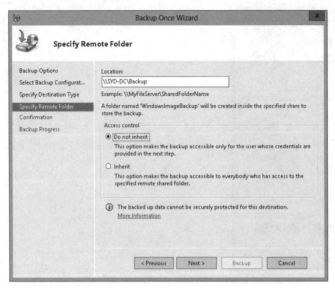

FIGURE 5-2 Configure access control

Backup locations

Windows Server Backup enables you to back up to any locally attached disk, to a volume, to the storage area network (SAN), or to any network folder. When configuring a scheduled backup, you should specify a destination volume or disk that is empty. If the disk is local or connected to the SAN, Windows Server Backup performs a full backup at least once every 14 days and incremental backups on subsequent backups. Incremental backups in Windows Server 2012 and Windows Server 2012 R2 use block-level backups rather than file-level backups, meaning that the incremental backups are much smaller. Rather than back up all of the files that have changed since the last backup, only the data blocks that have changed on the hard disk are backed up. For example, if you changed one image in a 25-megabyte (MB) PowerPoint file after it was backed up, only the data blocks associated with that image would be backed up next time, not the whole 25-MB file.

> **REAL WORLD** **BACK UP TO DIFFERENT DISKS**
>
> Although you can write backup data to a different volume on the same disk, you should back up data to a different disk so that if your disk fails, you don't lose both the data being protected and the backup itself.

The exception to the rule about automatic full and incremental backups when a backup is scheduled is when the backup data is written to a network folder. When you back up to a network folder (as opposed to a SAN-connected disk, which appears as local to Windows Server) each backup is a full backup and the previous full backup that was stored on the network share is erased. As only one backup at a time can be stored on a network share, if you choose to back up to this location, you can't recover data from any backup other than the most recently performed one.

You can modify the performance of full system and full volume backups using the Optimize Backup Performance dialog box, shown in Figure 5-3. You can increase backup performance by using the Faster Backup Performance option. The drawback of selecting this option is that it reduces disk performance on the disks that host the volumes that you are backing up.

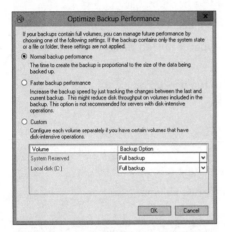

FIGURE 5-3 Optimize backups

Windows Server Backup in Windows Server 2012 and Windows Server 2012 R2 has the following new features:

- Capability to back up and restore individual Hyper-V hosted virtual machines.
- Capability to be configured for how long backups should be stored (backup retention) through Windows PowerShell cmdlets.
- Capability to back up volumes exceeding 2 terabytes (TB) in size.
- Capability to back up volumes with 4 kilobyte (KB) sector size.
- Support for backing up Cluster Shared Volumes.

> **MORE INFO** **WINDOWS SERVER BACKUP**
>
> To learn more about Windows Server Backup, consult the following article:
> *http://technet.microsoft.com/en-us/library/jj614621.aspx.*

Windows Server Backup PowerShell cmdlets

Prior to Windows Server 2012, you used the Wbadmin.exe utility to perform command-line management of Windows Server Backup. Windows Server 2012 and Windows Server 2012 R2 introduce more than 45 new Windows PowerShell cmdlets that can be used for backup and recovery. When using Windows PowerShell, you create backup policies that include all of the settings related to a backup job, such as: what to back up, where to store it, the backup schedule, and backup retention. You can view a list of all Windows Server Backup-related Windows PowerShell cmdlets by typing the following command:

```
Get-Command -Module WindowsServerBackup
```

Important cmdlets in this module include:

- **New-WBPolicy**   Creates a new backup policy
- **Add-WBBackupTarget**   Adds a backup target to a backup policy
- **Add-WBSystemState**   Adds the System State to a backup policy
- **Add-WBVirtualMachine**   Adds one or more Hyper-V hosted virtual machines to the policy
- **Add-WBVolume**   Adds a volume or volumes to the backup policy
- **Start-WBBackup**   Starts a one-time backup
- **Start-WBFileRecovery**   Starts a file recovery
- **Start-WBHyperVRecovery**   Begins the recovery of a Hyper-V virtual machine
- **Start-WBSystemStateRecovery**   Begins System State recovery
- **Start-WBVolumeRecovery**   Begins the recovery of a volume

> *MORE INFO* **WINDOWS SERVER BACKUP POWERSHELL CMDLETS**
>
> To learn more about Windows Server Backup PowerShell cmdlets, consult the following article: *http://technet.microsoft.com/en-us/library/jj902428(v=wps.620).aspx.*

Backing up data with Windows Server Backup

You can back up data using methods with Windows Server Backup. You can configure a scheduled backup, which means a backup occurs according to a scheduled basis. You can also perform a one-off backup. When you perform a one-off backup, you can either use the existing scheduled backup settings, or you can configure a separate set of settings for the one-off backup. For example, you might have configured Windows Server Backup to perform a full server backup twice a day to a locally attached disk. You could connect at any time and perform a one-off backup where you select only specific files and folders and have them written to a location on the network.

Windows Azure Backup

Windows Azure Backup is Microsoft's cloud-based subscription backup service. You run the client on an Internet-connected computer server that you want to back up, and the backup data is stored on the Windows Azure servers in the cloud. Windows Azure Backup functions as an off-site data storage and recovery location. In the event that a site is lost, you'll still be able to recover this important data from Windows Azure. The Windows Azure Backup console is shown in Figure 5-4.

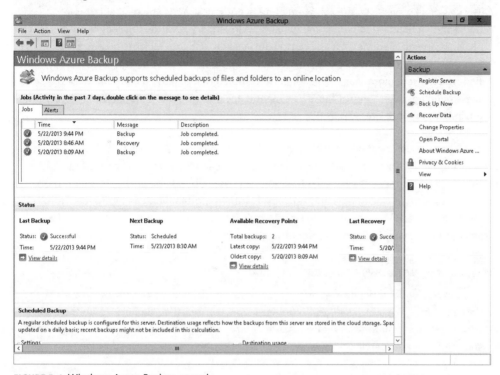

FIGURE 5-4 Windows Azure Backup console

You should back up important settings and data to Windows Azure Backup. You don't need to perform (and Windows Azure Backup doesn't currently support) a full server backup. If your server hosts a shared folder that stores backup images, it's technically possible to back up those images to Windows Azure Backup by treating them like normal files, but this would be a waste of resources.

You can run both the Windows Server Backup and Windows Azure Backup clients in parallel. This approach enables you to perform local backups and backups to Windows Azure on the same server. You can then do frequent full server backups locally with infrequent critical data backups to Windows Azure. When you employ this strategy, you will mostly restore data from your local backups. It's only when something goes drastically wrong that you need to restore data from Windows Azure.

The key to understanding what data to back up to Windows Azure is that if your organization loses a site to some type of disaster, you can always reinstall operating systems and applications from media that you can easily obtain again. The data stored on your servers, such as documents and settings, is something that you can't generate from installation media. By storing it in the cloud, you'll be able to recover it in the event of a disaster after you've rebuilt your server infrastructure.

Preparing for Windows Azure Backup

Before you can start using Windows Azure Backup to back up data from a server running Windows Server 2012 or Windows Server 2012 R2, you need to take several preliminary steps as shown in Figure 5-5. These include performing the following steps:

- Create a backup vault. You create the backup vault within Windows Azure. Backup vaults are the storage locations hosted within Windows Azure that store your backup data. Azure enables you to select a backup vault in an appropriate geographic location.

- Upload a specially configured public certificate that identifies the server to the public vault. This certificate can be self-signed using the Makecert.exe utility, can be obtained from an internal certificate authority (CA), or can be obtained from a trusted third-party CA. This certificate is used to identify the server and to secure the backup process.

- Download and install the Windows Azure Backup agent to the server that you want to protect.

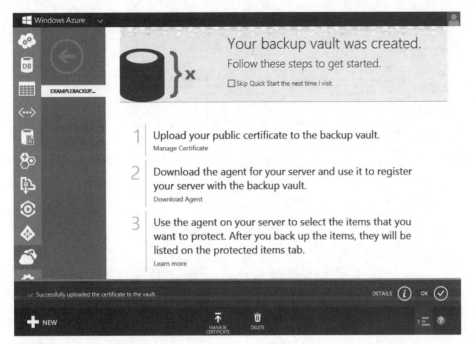

FIGURE 5-5 Creating a backup vault

After you've installed the agent, you need to register the server with Windows Azure Backup. This requires that the private key for the certificate you uploaded to Windows Azure be located in the private certificate store of the computer you are registering. You also need to configure Windows Azure Backup to use a specific backup vault. You select the backup vault on the Vault Identification page of the Register Server Wizard as shown in Figure 5-6. The final step is to configure an encryption passphrase. This *passphrase* is used to encrypt the data stored in the backup vault. You won't be able to restore the data to another location even if you have access to the backup vault without providing the encryption passphrase. The passphrase must be a minimum of 16 characters long, and you can save it to an external location such as a universal serial bus (USB) storage device.

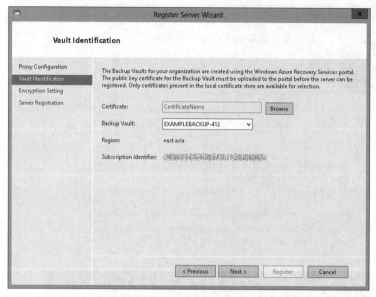

FIGURE 5-6 Specify a backup vault

Backing up data to Windows Azure Backup

Scheduling a backup to Windows Azure Backup involves running a wizard very similar to the Schedule Backup Wizard in Windows Server Backup. When running this wizard you:

- Select which items to back up. This is file and folder based. Although you can select a volume to back up, you don't use Windows Azure Backup to perform full volume recovery in the same manner as you would with Windows Server Backup. Windows Azure Backup has a limit of 850 gigabytes (GB) per volume of data per backup operation. When selecting items to backup, you can configure exclusions for file types, folders, or folder trees.

- Select a backup schedule. Determine how often a synchronization occurs. You can configure Windows Azure Backup to synchronize up to three times per day. You can also configure bandwidth throttling as shown in Figure 5-7. Throttling enables you to limit the utilization of bandwidth and ensures that your organization's Internet connection isn't choked with backup traffic replicating to the recovery vault on Windows Azure during business hours.

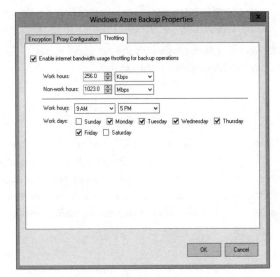

FIGURE 5-7 Configuring backup throttling

■ Configure backup retention. The retention setting, which you configure on the Specify Retention Setting page shown in Figure 5-8, determines how long backup data is stored in Windows Azure before being deleted. You can configure retention for Windows Server Backup when creating a policy in Windows PowerShell.

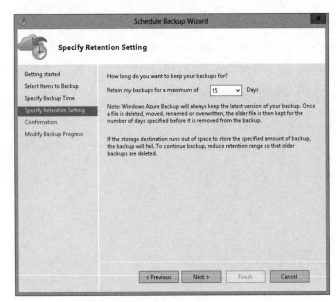

FIGURE 5-8 Configuring retention settings

Role-specifc and application-specific backups

The majority of Windows Server 2012 and Windows Server 2012 R2 roles and features store data in locations that are backed up when you perform a System State backup. System State data is automatically backed up when you perform a full server backup or select it for backup as shown in Figure 5-9. Depending on the roles and features installed on a computer running Windows Server 2012 or Windows Server 2012 R2, the System State can contain the following data:

- Registry
- Local users and groups
- COM+ Class Registration database
- Boot files
- Active Directory Certificate Services (AD CS) database
- Active Directory database (Ntds.dit)
- SYSVOL directory
- Cluster service information
- System files under Windows Resource Protection
- Internet Information Services (IIS) settings

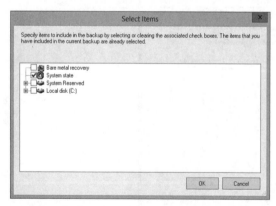

FIGURE 5-9 Back up System State

Increasing numbers of applications, such as Exchange Server 2013, also register themselves with Windows Server Backup. This means when you perform a full server backup, you are able to recover data that is relevant to the application only without having to perform a full system restore. Figure 5-10 shows how you can choose to restore Exchange. Support for application registration depends on the application. You can't select a specific application for back up using Windows Server Backup, but you can restore applications that have registered themselves with Windows Server Backup as long as you've performed a full server backup.

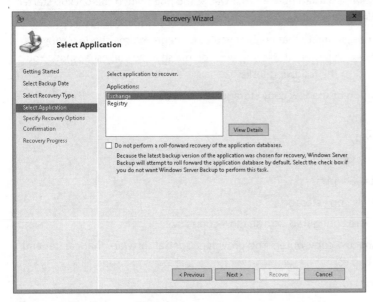

FIGURE 5-10 The Recovery Wizard

✔ Quick check

- What do you need to have configured in Windows Azure before you can install and configure the Windows Azure Backup agent on a computer running Windows Server 2012 R2?

Quick check answer

- You need to have uploaded the computer certificate to Windows Azure and to have configured a Backup Vault on Windows Azure before you can install and configure the Windows Azure Backup agent on a computer running Windows Server 2012 R2.

Vssadmin

Volume Shadow Copy Services (VSS) is a technology that was first introduced with Windows Server 2003 R2 that provides a point-in-time snapshot of the data on a volume as it existed at a specific point in time. VSS enables you to make a consistent backup of a file that is in use, such as a mailbox database or SQL Server database. Prior to the introduction of VSS, you might have needed to take such a database offline to ensure that the backup of that database was consistent. Consistency issues arise when it takes so long to back up a large file or a system that the configuration of the system or the contents of the file have changed during the backup. Windows Server Backup, Windows Azure Backup, and other backup products such as Data Protection Manager use VSS to ensure the data that is backed up is consistent and represents the state of the backed up data as it was at the point when the backup started without having to take files in use offline.

Vssadmin is a command-line utility that enables you to manage volume shadow copy snapshots. Figure 5-11 shows Vssadmin displaying two volume shadow copy snapshots. You can use VSS admin to perform the following tasks:

- Configure the location of shadow copy storage
- Create a shadow copy
- Delete a shadow copy
- Delete shadow copy storage
- View existing shadow copies
- View existing shadow copy storage
- View volumes that are configured with shadow copies
- View subscribed shadow copy writers and providers (special software that creates and manages shadow copies)
- Resize shadow copy storage

FIGURE 5-11 Volume shadow copies

You can also view shadow copy status on a per volume basis through the Previous Versions tab as shown in Figure 5-12. When used with file shares, the VSS snapshots exposed through the Previous Versions functionality enable users to recover previous versions of files and folders without having to restore from backup. To do this, users right-click the parent folder or volume, and click Restore Previous Versions. They are then able to select previous versions of the files that correspond to existing VSS snapshots.

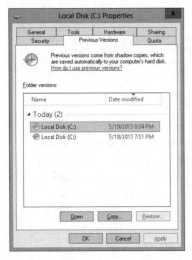

FIGURE 5-12 The Previous Versions tab

Although Vssadmin allows you to create and manage VSS snapshots, you can't use Vssadmin to configure a schedule for the automatic creation of VSS snapshots. You can configure a schedule for the creation of VSS snapshots on a per-volume basis by right-clicking a volume and clicking Configure Shadow Copies. After you enable shadow copies, you can configure a schedule in the Settings dialog box shown in Figure 5-13. By default, when you enable Shadow Copies, a shadow copy is created at 07:00 and noon every weekday. You can modify the schedule so that copies are created more often. When doing this remember that after the space used to store shadow copies is consumed, older shadow copies are removed to store new versions. The amount of space needed to store shadow copies and the retention period depends on the properties of the data stored on the volume.

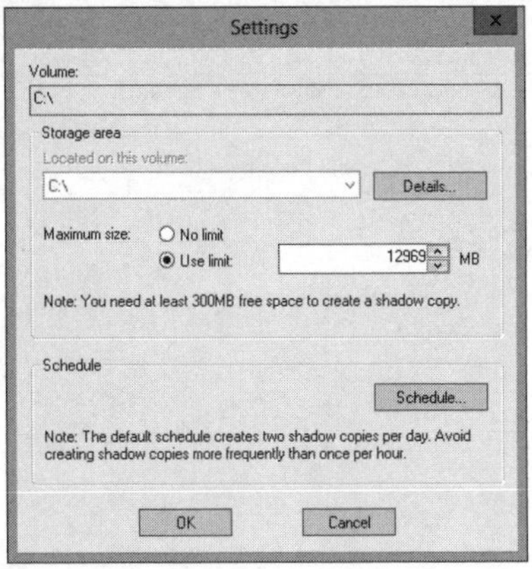

FIGURE 5-13 Shadow copy storage

Data Protection Manager

Windows Server Backup is pretty limited in what it can do. You can back up only the one
server, and you can have only the one schedule. You can't use it to perform sophisticated
backup and recovery tasks, such as backing up servers and clients remotely or recovering
a single user's Exchange Server 2013 mailbox. Microsoft's premium backup and recovery
product is System Center 2012 R2 Data Protection Manager (DPM). DPM enables you to
manage backup and recovery for hundreds of servers and thousands of clients from a single
console. It integrates fully into System Center 2012 R2 Operations Manager so that you
can be alerted if any one backup or recovery job fails anywhere within your organization.
Although the 70-412 exam concentrates on Windows Server Backup and Windows Azure
Backup, in a production environment, you use an enterprise backup product, such as DPM
or one from a trusted third-party vendor, to manage the backup and recovery of servers and
clients.

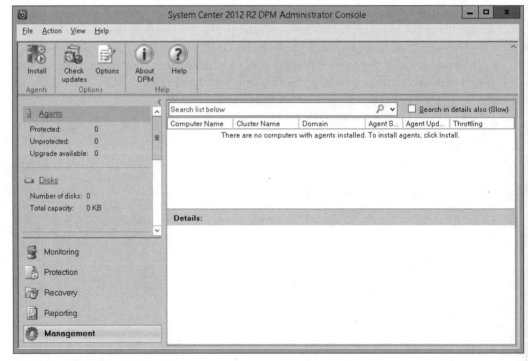

FIGURE 5-14 DPM Administrator Console

Lesson summary

- Windows Server Backup enables you to perform backups of files, folders, the System State, and an entire server.
- Windows Server Backup can write backups to a local disk, volume, or network share.
- Wbadmin.exe is the command-line version of Windows Server Backup. Windows Server 2012 and Windows Server 2012 R2 also include more than 45 Windows PowerShell cmdlets for Windows Server Backup.
- Windows Azure Backup enables you to back up files and folders to Microsoft's public Windows Azure cloud.
- Vssadmin enables you to manage volume shadow copy snapshots.

Lesson review

Answer the following questions to test your knowledge of the information in this lesson. You can find the answers to these questions and explanations of each answer choice in the "Answers" section at the end of this chapter.

1. Which of the following utilities can you use to create a System State backup on a computer running the Windows Server 2012 R2 operating system? (Choose all that apply.)

   A. Windows Azure Backup

   B. Windows Server Backup

   C. Vssadmin.exe

   D. Wbadmin.exe

2. You want to delete two volume shadow copy snapshots that reside on a server that you are responsible for managing. Which of the following tools could you use to accomplish this goal?

   A. Wbadmin.exe

   B. Vssadmin.exe

   C. Windows Server Backup

   D. Windows Azure Backup

3. You need to configure two standalone non-domain-joined computers running the Server Core version of Windows Server 2012 R2 so that they are able to perform

regular full server backups to a special internal hard disk drive. Which of the following tools could you use to accomplish this goal?

A. Vssadmin.exe

B. Wbadmin.exe

C. Windows Azure Backup

D. Windows Server Backup

4. You need to perform regular scheduled backups to an off-site location as a way of ensuring business continuity in the event that all servers in a particular site are lost in a natural or other type of disaster. Which of the following tools could you use to accomplish this goal?

A. Windows Server Backup

B. Wbadmin.exe

C. Windows Azure Backup

D. Vssadmin.exe

Lesson 2: Recovering servers

The true test of any backup is whether you're able to perform a successful recovery. This is why you should hold regular disaster recovery drills. It's one thing to have a console inform you that you've successfully backed up specific data, but you can only be certain that the data was backed up properly after you have successfully recovered it. In this lesson you find out how to recover data backed up using Windows Server Backup and Windows Azure Backup. You also find out when you need to use the Windows Recovery Environment or boot into Safe Mode.

After this lesson, you will be able to:

- Restore from backups
- Recover servers using Windows Recovery Environment
- Recover servers using Safe Mode
- Configure the Boot Configuration Data (BCD) store

Estimated lesson time: 45 minutes

Restore from backups

Windows Server Backup enables you to restore data that has been backed up on the local computer. You can also use it to restore data that was backed up on another computer using Windows Server Backup that is accessible to the local computer, either because it is stored locally or is stored on an accessible shared folder. You can use Windows Server Backup to do the following:

- You can use Windows Server Backup to restore files and folders as well as applications.
- You can use Windows Server Backup to restore the System State data. After the System State data is restored, you'll need to restart the computer.
- You can use Windows Server Backup to restore any volume except the one that hosts the operating system. If you want to restore the volume that hosts the operating system, you need to boot into the Windows Recovery Environment.
- You can use the Windows Recovery Environment to perform a full server restore, also known as a bare metal recovery. When you do this, all existing data and volumes on the server are overwritten with the backed up data.

If multiple backups of the data you want to restore exist, you need to select which version to restore. Figure 5-15 shows the Select Backup Date page of the recovery wizard. If you are unsure which date holds the data you want to restore, you should restore to multiple alternative locations and then perform the comparison. Doing this saves the bother of restoring, figuring out you've restored the wrong data, going and doing another restore, and figuring out that isn't right either.

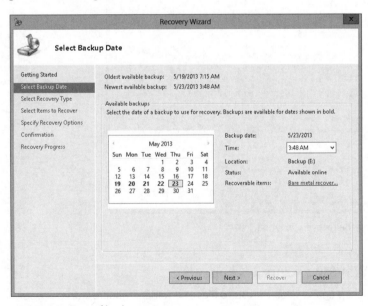

FIGURE 5-15 Date of backup

Windows Server Backup writes backups to .vhdx files, the same type that are used with Hyper-V as well as when creating disks for Internet Small Computer System Interface (iSCSI) targets and disks in storage pools. Windows Server 2012 and Windows Server 2012 R2 enable you to mount the contents of a virtual hard disk (VHD), which allows you to examine those contents without having to perform a full restoration using Windows Server Backup.

Restore to an alternative location

When you are performing a restoration of data, you can choose to restore data to the original location or to an alternative location. It is not uncommon, when restoring data to the original location, for backup administrators to unintentionally overwrite good live data with older restored data. If you restore to an alternative location, it's possible to compare the restored data against the current data. It's important when restoring data that you retain permissions associated with data.

If you choose to restore to the original location, as shown in Figure 5-6, you can configure Windows Server Backup to perform one of the following tasks:

- Automatically create copies if an original exists
- Overwrite existing versions
- Do not recover any item that exists in the recovery destination

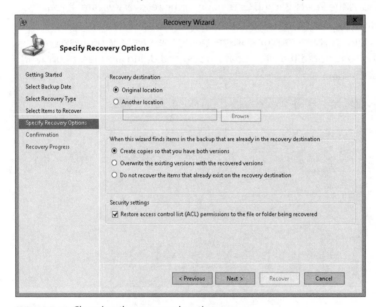

FIGURE 5-16 Choosing the recovery location

Restore from Windows Azure Backup

Windows Azure Backup enables you to restore files and folders that are stored in your Windows Azure recovery vault. You can't perform a full server recovery, System State recovery, or volume recovery using Windows Azure Backup, you can only restore files and folders. Of course if you've backed up all of the files and folders on a volume, you can restore all of them either individually or at one time. Windows Azure Backup also enables you to restore data from another server that you've backed up to Windows Azure. Recovering data using Windows Azure Backup involves performing the following steps:

- Selecting the server from which you will recover data.

- Selecting whether you want to browse or search for files to recover. This functionality differs from Windows Server Backup, which doesn't provide a search option.

- Select the volume that hosts the data you want to recover and the specific backup date and time from which you want to recover data.

- Select the items that you want to recover as shown in Figure 5-17. You can recover files, folders, and folder trees.

- Select Recovery Options, including whether to restore to the original or an alternative location, or to create copies or overwrite original files. You can also use this page of the wizard to choose whether to restore the original permissions.

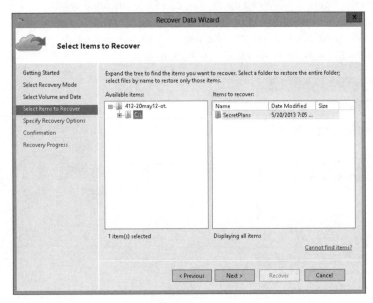

FIGURE 5-17 Selecting Items To Recover

Recover servers using Windows Recovery Environment

Windows Recovery Environment (Windows RE) is a special environment that enables you to perform computer repair tasks or to perform full server recovery. You can enter Windows RE by pressing the F8 key when Windows starts, or by doing the following:

- Issuing the **shutdown /r /o** command from a command prompt or from Windows PowerShell

- Holding the Shift key when clicking Restart on the Settings charm

- Booting using the recovery media

The computer also automatically enters Windows RE under the following conditions:

- There are two successive failed attempts to start Windows Server 2012 or Windows Server 2012 R2.

- Two unexpected shutdowns occur within two minutes of boot completion in succession.
- A secure boot error.

> **MORE INFO WINDOWS RE**
>
> To learn more about Windows RE, consult the following article:
> *http://technet.microsoft.com/en-us/library/hh825051.aspx.*

You can use Windows RE to recover volumes or server images from local disks or from network locations as shown in Figure 5-18. When using Windows RE to restore a system image from a network location, you need to ensure that the computer's network adapter has been assigned an Internet Protocol (IP) address. You also need to provide credentials that enable you to connect to the network share that hosts the backup files.

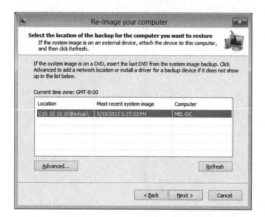

FIGURE 5-18 Selecting a backup of the system

> **Quick check**
>
> - You have backed up a single volume deployment of Windows Server 2012 R2. You want to recover volume C. Can you use Windows Server Backup to perform this task?
>
> **Quick check answer**
>
> - No. You need to use Windows RE when restoring the operating system volume from a backup taken with Windows Server Backup.

Safe mode and Last Known Good Configuration

Safe mode is a boot option that you can access by pressing F8 when you start the computer, or enable through the System Configuration (Msconfig.exe) utility as shown in Figure 5-19. Safe mode enables you to start Windows Server 2012 or Windows Server 2012 R2 with a minimal set of device drivers and services. You can use safe mode to disable drivers or services that are stopping a server from starting normally. There are three types of safe mode:

- **Safe mode**   Boots the computer to a desktop running a minimal number of services and drivers. Enables you access to administrative tools. You need to use an account that has administrative privileges. This can be a local Administrator account or a Domain Administrator account that has cached credentials on the server.

- **Safe mode with networking**   Boots the computer to a desktop running a minimal number of services and drivers, but includes network connectivity.

- **Safe mode with command prompt**   Boots the computer to a special mode where a command prompt is available but the Windows Desktop is not. You can access both the command prompt and Windows PowerShell from this environment (although you have to type **Powershell.exe** from the command prompt to do this). It appears similar to Server Core except that not all services configured to automatically start will have started.

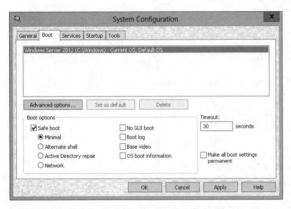

FIGURE 5-19 The System Configuration dialog box

Last Known Good Configuration is also accessible through the boot options menu that is available when you press the F8 key when starting the computer. The Last Known Good Configuration is the most recent set of driver and registry settings that allowed a successful startup and user sign on. Each time a user successfully signs on to a computer after it first starts up, a new Last Known Good Configuration is written. In the event that the server is unable to start to the point where it is not possible to sign on, you can use Last Known Good Configuration. Last Known Good Configuration might allow you to access the desktop to perform troubleshooting tasks in the event that you cannot perform these tasks in Safe Mode.

Configure the Boot Configuration Data store

The Boot Configuration Data (BCD) store hosts information that describes boot applications and boot application settings. You can modify the BCD store using the BCDEdit command-line utility. Figure 5-20 shows the BCD store of a default single volume installation of Windows Server 2012 R2. BCDEdit serves a similar function to the Bootcfg.exe utility that was available in previous versions of the Windows Server operating system including Windows Server 2003. You address entries in the BCD store using the identifier GUID. When working with the currently loaded operating system, you can use {current} in commands instead of the GUID. For example, to create a duplicate BCD store entry of the currently loaded operating system entry, issue the command:

```
Bcdedit /copy {current} /d "Duplicate Entry"
```

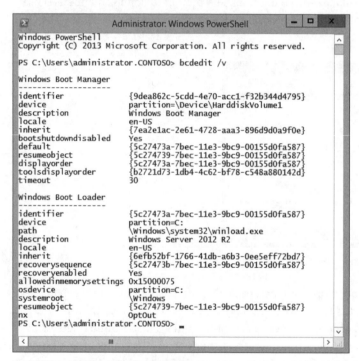

FIGURE 5-20 The Boot Configuration Store

> **MORE INFO** **BCDEDIT**
>
> To learn more about BCDEdit, consult the following article:
> *http://technet.microsoft.com/en-us/library/cc731662.aspx.*

Lesson summary

- You can use Windows Server Backup to restore files, folders, and volumes other than the operating system volume.
- When restoring files, you can restore in the original or an alternative location. When restoring to the original location, you can choose to create copies of duplicate files, overwrite duplicate files, or not restore duplicate files.
- When restoring you have the option of applying the file permissions that existed on the restored items when they were backed up.
- You use Windows RE to perform bare metal recovery and operating system volume restore.
- You can restore files and folders from Windows Azure Backup.
- You can use BCDEdit to configure the boot configuration data store.
- You can boot into Safe Mode when you need to access the operating system with a minimal set of drivers and services.

Lesson review

Answer the following questions to test your knowledge of the information in this lesson. You can find the answers to these questions and explanations of each answer choice in the "Answers" section at the end of this chapter.

1. Which of the following tools could you use to perform a bare metal recovery?

    A. Windows Azure Backup

    B. Windows RE

    C. Windows Server Backup

    D. Wbadmin.exe

2. You are experiencing problems with a computer running Windows Server 2012 R2. You want to boot up the computer, but only load the minimum necessary drivers and start the minimum necessary services. Which of the following strategies should you pursue?

    A. Boot into Last Known Good Configuration.

    B. Boot into safe mode.

    C. Boot into Windows RE.

    D. Perform bare metal recovery.

3. Which of the following can you back up and restore from Windows Azure Backup?

    A. System State

    B. Full server backup

    C. Files and folders

    D. Bare metal recovery

4. Which of the following steps must you take after restoring the System State data on a computer running Windows Server 2012 R2?

   A. Restart the Volume Shadow Copy service.

   B. Restart the server.

   C. Restart the Workstation service.

   D. Restart the Server service.

Practice exercises

The goal of this section is to provide you with hands-on practice with the following:

- Performing a local backup using Windows Server Backup
- Performing a backup over the network using Windows Server Backup
- Using Vssadmin.exe to manage volume shadow copies
- Performing a full server recovery over the network using Windows RE
- Booting into Safe Mode
- Modifying the Boot Configuration Data Store
- Configuring a computer to use Windows Azure Backup
- Backing up data to and restoring data from Windows Azure Backup

To perform the exercises in this section, you need access to an evaluation version of Windows Server 2012 R2. You should also have access to virtual machines SYD-DC, MEL-DC, CBR-DC, and ADL-DC, the setup instructions for which are as described in the Introduction. You should ensure that you have a checkpoint of these virtual machines that you can revert to at the end of the practice exercises. You should revert the virtual machines to this initial state prior to beginning these exercises.

Exercise 1: Prepare MEL-DC and CBR-DC for exercises

In this exercise, you prepare MEL-DC and CBR-DC for later exercises in this chapter by joining them to the contoso domain. To complete this exercise, perform the following steps:

1. Ensure that SYD-DC is powered on.

2. Power on MEL-DC and sign on as Administrator with the password **Pa$$w0rd**.

3. Open a Windows PowerShell window by clicking the Windows PowerShell icon on the taskbar.

4. Type the following command and press Enter to join MEL-DC to the contoso domain:

   ```
   Add-computer -credential contoso\administrator -DomainName contoso.com
   ```

5. When prompted with the Windows PowerShell Credential dialog box, shown in Figure 5-21, type the password **Pa$$w0rd** and click OK.

FIGURE 5-21 Entering the credentials

6. Type the following command and press Enter to restart MEL-DC:

   ```
   Restart-Computer
   ```

7. When MEL-DC restarts, sign in as contoso\don_funk with the password **Pa$$w0rd**.

8. Power on CBR-DC and sign on as Administrator with the password **Pa$$w0rd**.

9. On CBR-DC, open a Windows PowerShell window by clicking the Windows PowerShell icon on the taskbar.

10. Type the following command and press Enter to join CBR-DC to the contoso domain:

    ```
    Add-computer –credential contoso\administrator –DomainName contoso.com
    ```

11. When prompted with the Windows PowerShell Credential dialog box, type the password **Pa$$w0rd** and click OK.

12. Type the following command and press Enter to restart MEL-DC:

    ```
    Restart-Computer
    ```

13. When CBR-DC restarts, sign in as contoso\don_funk with the password **Pa$$w0rd**.

Exercise 2: Install Windows Server Backup

In this exercise, you install Windows Server Backup on SYD-DC, MEL-DC, and CBR-DC. To complete this exercise, perform the following steps:

1. Ensure that you are signed on to SYD-DC as contoso\don_funk.

2. On the Manage menu of the Server Manager console, click Add Roles And Features

3. On the Before You Begin page of the Add Roles And Features Wizard, click Next twice.

4. On the Select Destination Server page, verify that SYD-DC.contoso.com is selected as shown in Figure 5-22 and click Next.

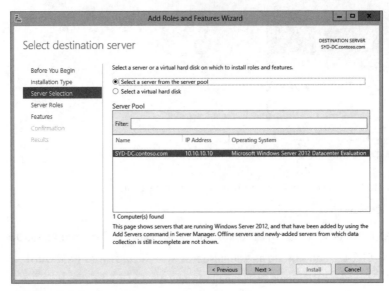

FIGURE 5-22 Selecting a server

5. On the Select Server Roles page, click Next.

6. On the Select Features page, click the Windows Server Backup check box as shown in Figure 5-23 and click Next.

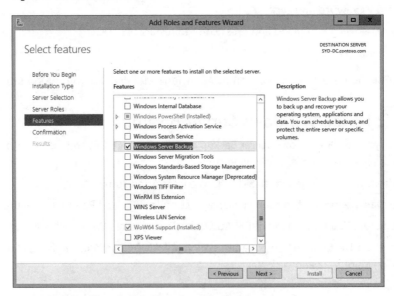

FIGURE 5-23 Installing the Windows Server Backup feature

7. On the Confirm Installation Selections page, click Install. When the installation completes, click Close.

8. On the Tools menu of the Server Manager console, click Windows PowerShell ISE.

9. On the File menu of the Windows PowerShell ISE window, click New Remote PowerShell Tab.

10. In the New Remote PowerShell Tab window, enter the following information as shown in Figure 5-24 and then click Connect:

   ■ Computer: **MEL-DC**

   ■ User Name: **contoso\don_funk**

FIGURE 5-24 The New Remote Windows PowerShell tab.

11. On the second credentials dialog box, type the password **Pa$$word** and click OK.

12. In the Windows PowerShell ISE window, type the following command and press Enter:

```
Install-WindowsFeature –Name Windows-Server-Backup –IncludeAllSubFeature
-IncludeManagementTools
```

13. Verify that the exit code is listed as Success as shown in Figure 5-25.

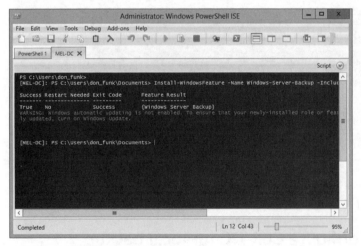

FIGURE 5-25 Verifying the installation

14. On the File menu of the Windows PowerShell ISE window, click New Remote PowerShell Tab.

15. On the New Remote PowerShell Tab dialog box, enter the following information as shown in Figure 5-26 and click Connect:

   ■ Computer: **CBR-DC**

   ■ User Name: **contoso\don_funk**

FIGURE 5-26 The New Remote PowerShell tab

16. On the Windows PowerShell Credentials dialog box, type the following credentials and click OK:

   - User Name: **contoso\don_funk**
   - Password: **Pa$$w0rd**

17. In the Windows PowerShell ISE window, type the following command and press Enter:

   ```
   Install-WindowsFeature –Name Windows-Server-Backup –IncludeAllSubFeature
   -IncludeManagementTools
   ```

18. Verify that the exit code is listed as success as shown in Figure 5-27.

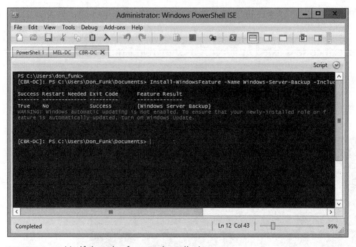

FIGURE 5-27 Verifying the feature installation

Exercise 3: Configure CBR-DC for local backup

In this exercise, you reconfigure CBR-DC for local backup and configure a backup schedule. To complete this exercise, perform the following steps:

1. When signed on to CBR-DC as Contoso\don_funk, click Computer Management on the Tools menu of the Server Manager console.

2. In the Computer Management\Disk Management console, click the (C:) section of disk 0 as shown in Figure 5-28.

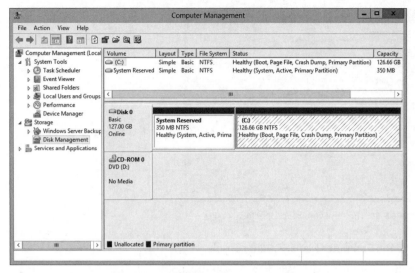

FIGURE 5-28 The Computer Management console

3. Right-click and click Shrink Volume.

4. In the Shrink C: dialog box, type the shrink space as **30000** as shown in Figure 5-29 and then click Shrink.

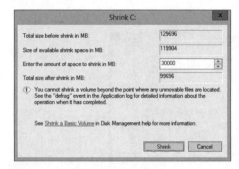

FIGURE 5-29 Shrinking a volume

5. In the Computer Management console, right-click the Unallocated space and click New Simple Volume.

6. On the Welcome To The New Simple Volume Wizard page of the New Simple Volume Wizard, click Next three times.

7. On the Format Partition page, set the volume label as Backup, ensure that the file system is set to NTFS and Perform A Quick Format is selected as shown in Figure 5-30, click Next, and then click Finish.

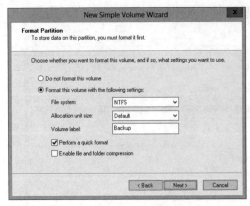

FIGURE 5-30 The new volume properties

8. Close the Computer Management console.

9. On the Tools menu, click Windows Server Backup.

10. In the Windows Server Backup console, click Local Backup.

11. In the Actions pane, click Backup Schedule.

12. On the Getting Started page of the Backup Schedule Wizard, click Next.

13. On the Select Backup Configuration page, click Full Server (Recommended) as shown in Figure 5-31 and then click Next.

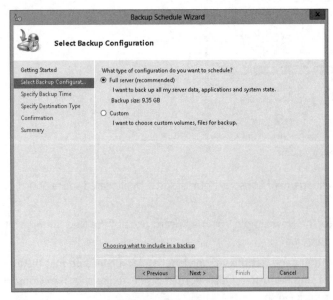

FIGURE 5-31 Choosing the Full Server option

14. On the Specify Backup Time page, configure a backup to run every six hours at 3 A.M., 9:00 A.M., 3:00 P.M., and 9:00 P.M. as shown in Figure 5-32. Click Next.

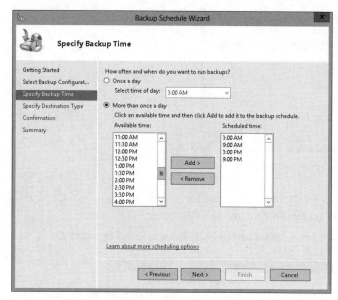

FIGURE 5-32 Choosing the backup times

15. On the Specify Destination Type page, click Back Up To A Volume as shown in Figure 5-33 and click Next.

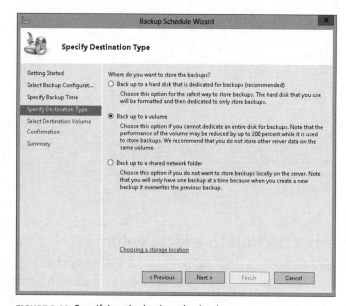

FIGURE 5-33 Specifying the backup destination

16. On the Select Destination Volume dialog box, click Add.

17. In the Add Volumes dialog box, click Backup (E:) as shown in Figure 5-34 and click OK.

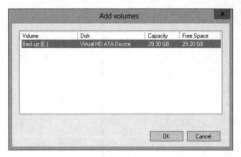

FIGURE 5-34 The Add Volumes dialog box

18. On the Windows Server Backup dialog box, review the warnings, click OK, and then click Yes. On the Select Destination Volume dialog box, click Next.

19. On the Confirmation page, shown in Figure 5-35, click Finish and click Close.

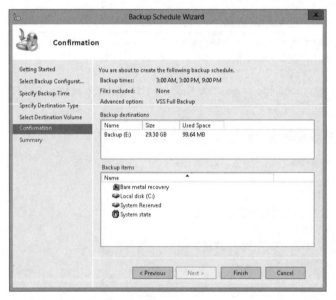

FIGURE 5-35 The Confirmation page

Exercise 4: Perform a backup to a local volume

In this exercise, you perform a backup to a local volume using the Scheduled Backup Options that you configured in the previous exercise. To complete this exercise, perform the following steps:

1. While logged in to CBR-DC as **Contoso\don_funk**, open the Windows Server Backup console.

2. In the Windows Server Backup console, click Local Backup. In the Actions pane, click Backup Once.

3. On the Backup Options page of the Backup Once Wizard, click Scheduled Backup Options as shown in Figure 5-36 and click Next.

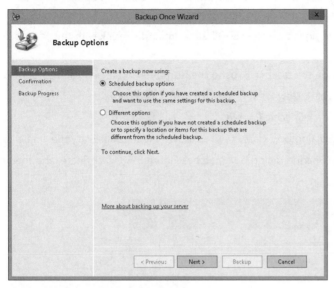

FIGURE 5-36 The Backup Options page

4. On the Confirmation page, click Backup.

5. When the backup is completed, as shown in Figure 5-37, click Close.

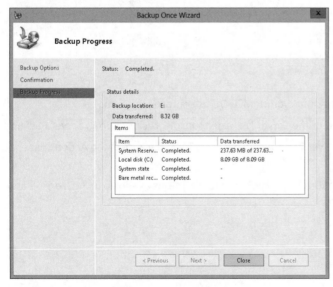

FIGURE 5-37 Verifying the success of the backup

Exercise 5: Perform a backup over the network

In this exercise, you use Windows Server Backup to perform a backup to a network location. To complete this exercise, perform the following steps:

1. Ensure that you are signed on to SYD-DC as contoso\don_funk with the password **Pa$$w0rd**.

1. Click File Explorer on the taskbar. Expand the Computer node and click Local Disk (C).

2. On the Home tab, click New Folder. Type the name as **Backup**.

3. On the Share tab, click Specific People.

4. In the File Sharing dialog box, click the drop-down menu, click Everyone, and click Add.

5. Verify that the File Sharing dialog box matches Figure 5-38, click Share, and then click Done.

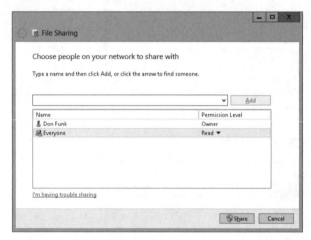

FIGURE 5-38 File Sharing permissions

6. Ensure that you are signed on to MEL-DC as contoso\don_funk.

7. On the Tools menu of the Server Manager console, click Windows Server Backup.

8. In the Windows Server Backup console, click Local Backup. In the Actions pane, click Backup Once.

9. On the Backup Options page, click Different Options as shown in Figure 5-39 and click Next.

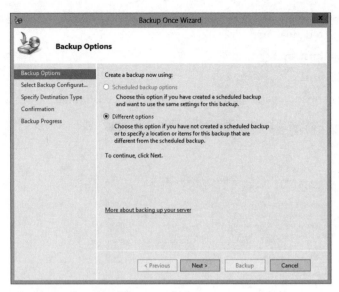

FIGURE 5-39 Choosing different options

10. Ensure that Full Server is selected on the Select Backup Configuration page and click Next.

11. On the Specify Destination Type page, click Remote Shared Folder and then click Next.

12. On the Specify Remote Folder page, type **\\SYD-DC\Backup** in the Location text box and select Do Not Inherit For Access Control as shown in Figure 5-40. Click Next.

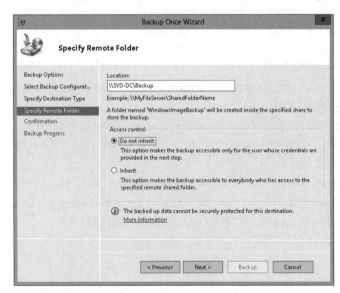

FIGURE 5-40 Specifying the destination folder

13. On the Provide User Credentials For Backup page of the Windows Security dialog box, type the following credentials and click OK:

- User name: **Administrator**
- Password: **Pa$$w0rd**

14. Verify that the Confirmation page matches Figure 5-41 and click Backup.

FIGURE 5-41 The Confirmation page

15. When the backup completes, click Close.

Exercise 6: Use Vssadmin

In this exercise, you use Vssadmin to manage volume shadow copies. To complete this exercise, perform the following steps:

1. When signed on to MEL-DC as contoso\don_funk, open an elevated Windows PowerShell window by right-clicking the Windows PowerShell icon on the taskbar and clicking Run As Administrator.

2. When prompted by the User Account Control dialog box, click Yes.

3. In the Windows PowerShell window, type the following command and press Enter to list the current shadow copy backups on MEL-DC as shown in Figure 4-42:

```
Vssadmin list shadows
```

FIGURE 5-42 Verifying the lack of shadow copies

4. Type the following command and press Enter to list all volumes that are eligible for shadow copies:

   Vssadmin list volumes

5. Type the following command and press Enter to create a new volume shadow copy:

   Vssadmin create shadow /For=C:

6. Type the following command and press Enter to list the volume shadow copy providers as shown in Figure 4-43:

   Vssadmin list providers

FIGURE 5-43 Viewing shadow copy providers

7. Create an additional volume shadow copy snapshot by typing the following command and pressing Enter:

   Vssadmin create shadow /For=C:

8. List available shadow copies by typing the following command and pressing Enter as shown in Figure 5-44:

   Vssadmin list shadows

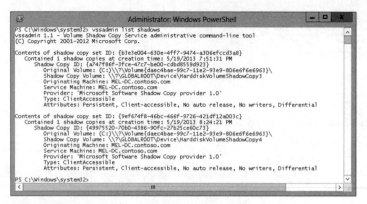

FIGURE 5-44 Verifying the creation of shadow copies

9. On the task bar, click File Explorer.

10. In the File Explorer, expand the Computer node, right-click Local Disk (C), and click Properties.

11. In the Local Disk (C) Properties dialog box, click the Previous Versions tab and verify that two or more shadow copies are present as shown in Figure 5-45.

FIGURE 5-45 Viewing previous versions

12. Click OK to close the Local Disk (C) Properties dialog box.

Exercise 7: Perform a full volume recovery using Windows Server Backup

In this exercise, you perform a System State recovery on CBR-DC. To complete this exercise, perform the following steps:

13. Sign on to CBR-DC as contoso\don_funk with the password **Pa$$w0rd**.

14. On the Tools menu of the Server Manager console, click Computer Management.

15. In the Computer Management console, expand the Local Users And Groups node and click Groups.

16. On the Action menu, click New Group.

17. On the New Group dialog box, type **Kangaroos** as shown in Figure 5-46 and click Create.

FIGURE 5-46 Creating a group

18. In the New Group dialog box, type **Wombats**, click Add, type **Domain Admins**, click OK, click Create, and then click Close.

19. Verify that the Kangaroos and Wombats are listed as local groups.

20. In the Tools menu of the Server Manager console, click Windows Server Backup.

21. In the Actions pane of the Windows Server Backup console, click Backup Once.

22. On the Backup Options page, ensure that Scheduled Backup Options are selected as shown in Figure 5-47, click Next, and click Backup.

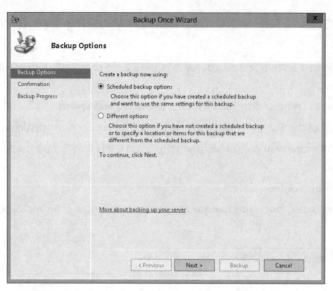

FIGURE 5-47 Selecting scheduled backup options

23. When the Backup completes, click Close. Make sure the backup completes before moving to the next step.

24. Switch back to the Computer Management Console and delete the Kangaroos and Wombats local groups.

25. Switch to the Windows Server Backup console.

26. In the Actions menu, click Recover.

27. On the Getting Started page, shown in Figure 5-48, ensure that This Server (CBR-DC) is selected, and click Next twice.

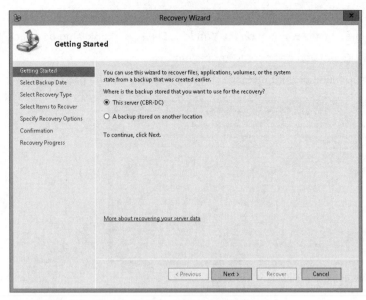

FIGURE 5-48 Selecting where the recovery data is stored

28. On the Select Recovery Type page, click System State as shown in Figure 5-49 and then click Next.

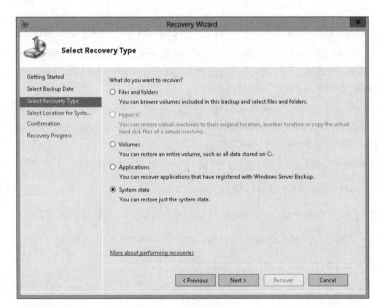

FIGURE 5-49 Choosing the System State data

29. On the Select Location For System State Recovery, ensure Original Location is selected and click Next.

30. On the Confirmation page, click Recover.

31. When prompted by the warning on the Windows Server Backup dialog box, click Yes.

32. Restart CBR-DC and sign on as contoso\don_funk.

33. Review the command prompt message shown in Figure 5-50 and press Enter.

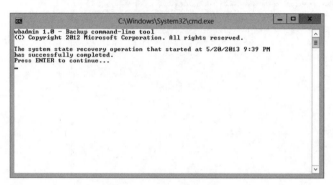

```
wbadmin 1.0 - Backup command-line tool
(C) Copyright 2012 Microsoft Corporation. All rights reserved.

The system state recovery operation that started at 5/20/2013 9:39 PM
has successfully completed.
Press ENTER to continue...
```

FIGURE 5-50 Verifying completion of the recovery

34. Open the Computer Management console from the Tools menu of the Server Manager console.

35. Verify the presence of the Kangaroos and Wombats local groups.

Exercise 8: Prepare for Windows Recovery Environment

In this exercise, you install a DHCP server and configure a scope on SYD-DC so that the network adapter in the Windows Recovery environment can acquire a network address. To complete this exercise, perform the following steps:

1. When signed on to SYD-DC as contoso\don_funk, right-click the Windows PowerShell icon on the taskbar and click Run As Administrator to open an elevated Windows PowerShell window. Click Yes on the UAC warning.

2. Type the following command and press Enter to install a DHCP server:

   ```
   Install-WindowsFeature DHCP -IncludeManagementTools
   ```

3. Authorize the DHCP server by typing the following command and pressing Enter:

   ```
   Add-DHCPServerInDC -DNSName syd-dc.contoso.com -ipaddress 10.10.10.10
   ```

4. Type the following to create a DHCP scope named TEST:

   ```
   Add-DHCPServerv4Scope -Name TEST -StartRange 10.10.10.110 -EndRange 10.10.10.150
   -SubnetMask 255.255.255.0
   ```

5. Type the following to configure the DNS server address for the scope:

   ```
   Set-DHCPServerv4OptionValue -Computername syd-dc.contoso.com -ScopeID 10.10.10.0
   -DNSServer 10.10.10.10
   ```

Exercise 9: Perform full server recovery over the network

In this exercise, you perform a restore of MEL-DC from the Windows Recovery Environment from files that are stored on the network. To complete this exercise, perform the following steps:

1. Shut down MEL-DC.

2. Edit the settings of the MEL-DC virtual machine. Remove the existing Network Adapter and add a Legacy Network Adapter that is connected to the Private Network used for the other virtual machines as shown in Figure 5-51.

FIGURE 5-51 Configuring the virtual machine settings

3. Start MEL-DC and press F8 so that you get the Advanced Boot Options Menu shown in Figure 5-52.

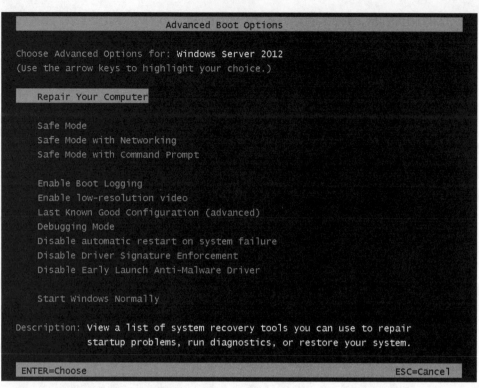

FIGURE 5-52 The Boot Options menu

4. On the Advanced Boot Options menu, use the arrow keys to select Repair Your Computer and press Enter.

5. On the Choose An Option page of the Boot Options menu, click Troubleshoot.

6. On the Advanced Options page, shown in Figure 5-53, click Command Prompt.

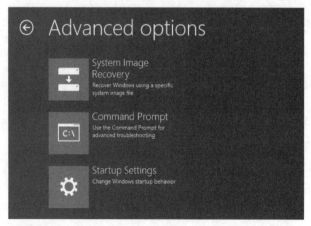

FIGURE 5-53 Advanced Options page

7. On the System Image Recovery menu, click Administrator. Type the password **Pa$$w0rd** and click Continue.

8. In the command prompt window, enter the following command and press Enter:

```
Wpeinit
```

9. Type the following command and press Enter to obtain an IP address:

```
Ipconfig /renew
```

10. Type the following command and press Enter to return to the Choose An Option menu:

```
Exit
```

11. On the Choose An Option page, click Troubleshoot.

12. On the Advanced Options page, click System Image Recovery and then click Windows Server 2012 R2 as the target operating system.

13. In the Re-Image Your Computer dialog box, click Cancel.

14. On the Select A System Image Backup dialog box, shown in Figure 5-54, select the Select A System Image and click Next.

FIGURE 5-54 Choosing a system image backup

15. In the Re-Image Your Computer dialog box, click Advanced.

16. In the Re-Image Your Computer dialog box, click Search For A System Image on the Network.

17. When prompted to choose whether you want to connect to the network, click Yes.

18. In the Re-Image Your Computer dialog box, type the address **\\10.10.10.10\Backup** as shown in Figure 5-55 and click OK.

FIGURE 5-55 Entering the system image location

19. When prompted for credentials, type the following and click OK:

   - User Name: **contoso\administrator**

   - Password: **Pa$$w0rd**

20. On the list of backups, select the most recent system image as shown in Figure 5-56 and click Next.

FIGURE 5-56 Selecting the backup to restore

21. On the Select The Date And Time Of System Image To Restore page, select the most recent available option, click Next twice, and click Finish.

22. When prompted by the warning informing you that data will be replaced, click Yes.

23. MEL-DC restarts automatically when the restore is complete.

24. When MEL-DC restarts, sign in as contoso\don_funk with the password **Pa$$w0rd**.

Exercise 10: Boot into Safe Mode

In this exercise, you configure CBR-DC to boot into Safe Mode. To complete this exercise, perform the following steps:

1. Sign on to CBR-DC as Contoso\don_funk with the password **Pa$$w0rd**.

2. In the Search charm, type **msconfig.** Click System Configuration in the list of results.

3. On the Boot tab, click the Safe Boot option as shown in Figure 5-57 and click OK.

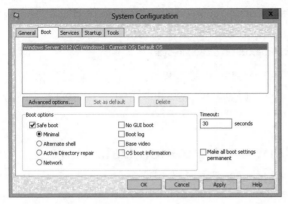

FIGURE 5-57 Configuring the computer to boot in safe mode

4. On the System Configuration dialog box, click Restart.

5. When the server restarts, sign in as CBR-DC\Administrator with the password **Pa$$w0rd**.

6. Verify that the server is in safe mode by identifying the Safe Mode text at each corner of the screen.

7. In the Search charm, type **services** and click on the Services item.

8. Click the Startup Type column and verify that many services that are configured with the Automatic startup type have not started because the server has restarted in safe mode, as shown in Figure 5-58.

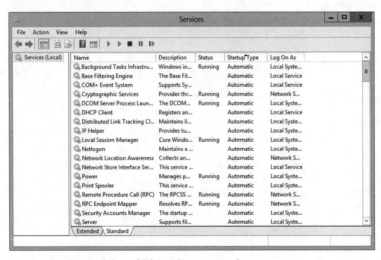

FIGURE 5-58 Determining which services are running

9. In the Search charm, type **msconfig** in the results click System Configuration.

10. On the Boot tab of the System Configuration dialog box, clear the check box next to Safe Boot and click OK.

11. On the System Configuration dialog box, click Restart.

12. When CBR-DC restarts, sign on as contoso\don_funk.

13. From the Tools menu of the Server Manager, open the Services console and verify that all services configured with the Automatic startup type are running.

Exercise 11: Modify Boot Configuration Data store

In this exercise, you modify the boot configuration of CBR-DC using the BCDEdit command-line tool. To complete this exercise, perform the following steps:

1. When signed on to CBR-DC as contoso\don_funk, right-click the Windows PowerShell icon on the Task Bar and click Run As Administrator.

2. Type the following command and press Enter to view the current boot entry as shown in Figure 5-59:

```
bcdedit /v
```

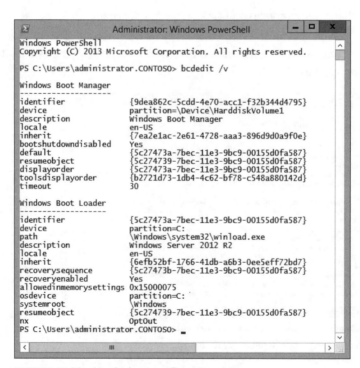

FIGURE 5-59 Viewing the boot configuration data

3. Type the following and press Enter to switch to a command prompt:

   Cmd.exe

4. Create a duplicate of the currently loaded operating system boot entry by executing
   the following command as shown in Figure 5-60:

   Bcdedit /copy {current} /d "Duplicate Entry"

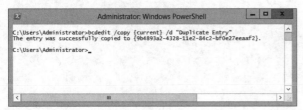

FIGURE 5-60 Copying the boot entry

5. Type the following command to verify that the new duplicate entry is listed:

   Bcdedit /v

6. Type the following command to switch the Windows Server 2012 R2 boot entry to the
   bottom of the list:

   Bcdedit /displayorder {current} /addlast

7. Type the following command to verify that the Windows Server 2012 R2 entry is now
   the last entry on the list:

   Bcdedit /v

8. Type the following command to enable Emergency Management Shell (EMS) for the
   Windows Server 2012 R2 entry:

   Bcdedit /ems {current} on

9. Type the following command to restart the computer and verify the currently
   configured changes as shown in Figure 5-61:

   Shutdown /r /t 0

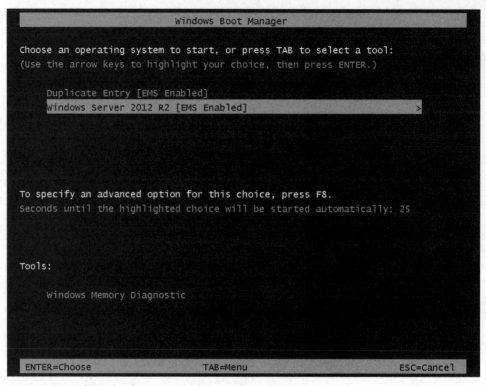

```
                              Windows Boot Manager

Choose an operating system to start, or press TAB to select a tool:
(Use the arrow keys to highlight your choice, then press ENTER.)


      Duplicate Entry [EMS Enabled]
      Windows Server 2012 R2 [EMS Enabled]                              >




To specify an advanced option for this choice, press F8.
Seconds until the highlighted choice will be started automatically: 25




Tools:

      Windows Memory Diagnostic




ENTER=Choose                    TAB=Menu                         ESC=Cancel
```

FIGURE 5-61 Verifying the changes to the boot configuration

10. Leave the Windows Server 2012 R2 [EMS Enabled] option selected.

11. When the computer boots, sign on as contoso\don_funk and launch an elevated Windows PowerShell prompt by right-clicking the Windows PowerShell icon on the taskbar and clicking Run As Administrator. Click Yes when prompted on the User Account Control dialog box.

12. In the Windows PowerShell window, type the following command and press Enter to enter a command prompt:

Cmd.exe

13. Type **bcdedit /v**.

14. Use the marking functionality to mark and copy the identifier GUID associated with the Duplicate Entry as shown in Figure 5-62.

FIGURE 5-62 Locating GUID

15. Use the copied GUID, including the curly braces, in the following command to remove the duplicate entry:

```
Bcdedit /delete {GUID} /cleanup
```

16. Type **bcdedit /v** to verify that the duplicate entry has been removed as shown in Figure 5-63.

FIGURE 5-63 Verifying the entry deletion

Exercise 12: Configure a standalone computer for use with Windows Azure Backup

In this optional exercise, you prepare ADL-DC to use Windows Azure Backup. You rename the computer, connect it to the Internet, and prepare a self-signed certificate that can be used to authenticate the computer with Windows Azure Backup. This exercise and the next three exercises require that you already have a Windows Azure account. You can sign up for a trial account at *http://www.windowsazure.com/en-us/pricing/free-trial/*. This exercise also requires that the virtual machine be configured with Internet Access and that you download approximately half a gigabyte of data. Instructions to configure the virtual machine with Internet Access are provided in the first few steps of the exercise. To complete this exercise, perform the following steps:

1. Prior to powering on ADL-DC, edit the properties of the virtual machine in Hyper-V Manager and configure the network adapter so that it is connected to an external network as shown in Figure 5-64. This allows you to configure ADL-DC to work with Windows Azure Backup.

FIGURE 5-64 Configuring the Network Adapter properties

2. Power on ADL-DC and sign in as Administrator with the password of **Pa$$w0rd**.

3. Click the Windows PowerShell icon on the taskbar and enter the following command to set the IP address so that it is obtained dynamically:

```
Netsh interface ipv4 set address "Ethernet" dhcp
```

4. Enter the following command to set the Domain Name System (DNS) server address so that it is obtained dynamically:

```
Netsh interface ipv4 set dnsservers "Ethernet" dhcp
```

NOTE SETTING DHCP

These commands assume that Dynamic Host Control Protocol (DHCP) is used on your local network. If DHCP is not present, you need to set appropriate IPv4 addresses to ensure connectivity manually.

---

5. Enter the following command to install Windows Server Backup on ADL-DC:

```
Install-WindowsFeature –Name Windows-Server-Backup –IncludeAllSubFeature
-IncludeManagementTools
```

6. In the Server Manager console, click Local Server and click the On link next to IE Enhanced Security Configuration.

7. On the Internet Explorer Enhanced Security Configuration dialog box, click Off for Administrators as shown in Figure 5-65 and then click OK.

FIGURE 5-65 Internet Explorer Enhanced Security Configuration

8. In the Windows PowerShell window, issue the following command where Date is the current date and Initials are your initials:

```
Netdom /renamecomputer ADL-DC /newname:412-Date-Initials
```

For example, Figure 5-66 shows a computer on the date 20May12 with the initials OT.

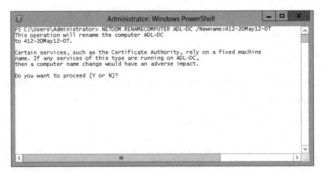

FIGURE 5-66 Rename the computer

9. When prompted, type **Y.**

10. Enter the following command and press Enter to restart the computer:

```
Restart-Computer
```

11. Sign on as Administrator with the password **Pa$$word**.

12. Open Internet Explorer from the Start screen. When prompted, click Use Recommended Security And Compatibility Settings and click OK.

13. Navigate to *http://www.bing.com* to verify that the virtual machine has Internet connectivity.

14. Navigate to the following website to obtain the Windows 8 Software Development Kit (SDK): *http://msdn.microsoft.com/en-us/windows/hardware/hh852363.aspx.*

> **REAL WORLD** **MAKECERT.EXE**
>
> Some Windows Azure documentation intimates that makecert.exe will be made available as a separate standalone download at some point in the future. At present the only way to get the utility for creating self-signed certificates is to download the Windows 8 SDK. Before you perform the next step, search TechNet to determine if the standalone download is available. If it is, download the file into the directory created in step 21.

15. On the Windows Software Development Kit (SDK) for Windows 8 webpage, click Download.

16. Save the sdksetup.exe file on the Desktop. When the download completes, click Run.

17. On the Specify Location page, click Next twice and click Accept.

18. On the Select the Features You Want To Install page, ensure that only Windows Software Development Kit is selected as shown in Figure 5-67 and click Install.

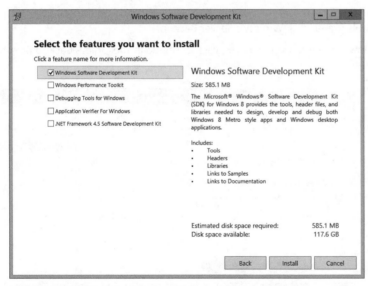

FIGURE 5-67 Installing the Windows Software Development Kit

19. When the install completes, click Close.

20. Click the Windows PowerShell icon on the taskbar.

21. In the Windows PowerShell window, type the following commands, pressing Enter after each:

```
Mkdir c:\certs
Cd c:\certs
Copy "c:\program files (x86)\Windows Kits\8.0\bin\x64\makecert.exe" .
.\makecert.exe -r -pe -n CN=CertificateName -ss my -sr localmachine -eku
1.3.6.1.5.5.7.3.2 -len 2048 -e 01/01/2016 CertificateName.cer
```

22. Close the Windows PowerShell.

REAL WORLD **SELF SIGNING**

When you're doing this in the real world, you would configure a CA to issue the appropriate certificate. When configuring the expiry date, which in the above command is the 1ˢᵗ of January 2016, set it to 36 months from the current date.

Exercise 13: Configure Windows Azure Backup

In this exercise, you configure Windows Azure Backup on ADL-DC. This exercise requires that you already have a Windows Azure account. You can sign up for a trial account at *http://www. windowsazure.com/en-us/pricing/free-trial/*. As you can only get one trial per email account, you might consider creating a new email account for this trial. This exercise requires that you have completed Exercise 12. To configure Windows Azure Backup, perform the following steps:

1. From the Tools menu, click Windows Server Backup.

2. In the Windows Server Backup window, click Continue in the Online Backup box shown in Figure 5-68.

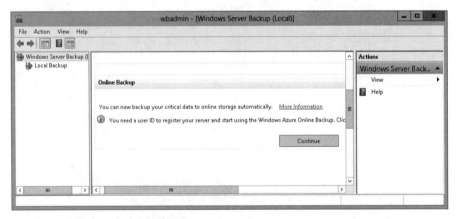

FIGURE 5-68 Windows Server Backup

3. Internet Explorer navigates to the Recovery Services webpage. Click Account and then click Sign In.

4. On the Windows Azure sign in page, sign in with the Microsoft Account associated with your Windows Azure account or trial account.

5. On the Windows Azure page, click Portal.

6. In the Portal, click New, click Data Services and click Recovery Services as shown in Figure 5-69.

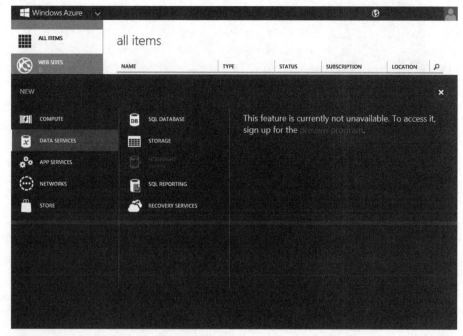

FIGURE 5-69 The Windows Azure portal

7. If prompted, click the Preview Program link, and then on the Preview Features page click Try It Now. Select the check box in the dialog box and then click Manage.

> **MORE INFO** **NOT IN PREVIEW LONG**
>
> Instructions for the preview version are included because this feature was in preview at the time the book was written.

8. In the Management portal, click Recovery Services.

9. In Recovery Services, shown in Figure 5-70, click Create A New Vault.

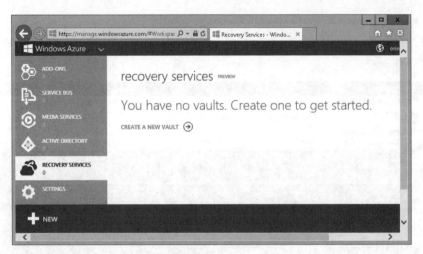

FIGURE 5-70 Creating a recovery vault

10. Click Backup Vault and click Quick Create.

11. In the Name text box type **EXAMPLEBACKUP-412** and select the region that is closest to you geographically. Click Create Vault.

12. With Recovery Services selected, click Manage Certificate.

13. Click Browse For File and select C:\certs\CertificateName.cer and click Open as shown in Figure 5-71. Click the check icon.

FIGURE 5-71 Managing the Certificate File

14. In the Windows Azure Management Console, click Recovery Services and then click EXAMPLEBACKUP.

15. On the EXAMPLEBACKUP-412 screen shown in Figure 5-72, click the Download Agent link.

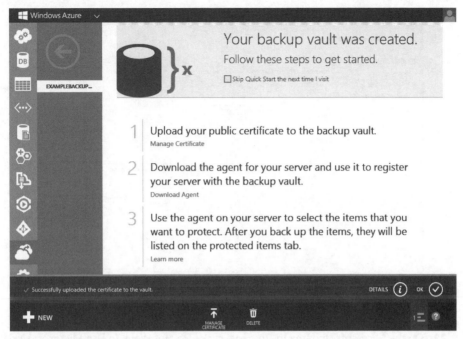

Your backup vault was created.
Follow these steps to get started.

☐ Skip Quick Start the next time I visit

1 | Upload your public certificate to the backup vault.
Manage Certificate

2 | Download the agent for your server and use it to register your server with the backup vault.
Download Agent

3 | Use the agent on your server to select the items that you want to protect. After you back up the items, they will be listed on the protected items tab.
Learn more

✓ Successfully uploaded the certificate to the vault.   DETAILS ⓘ   OK ✓

➕ NEW   ⬆ MANAGE CERTIFICATE   🗑 DELETE   ☰ 1   ?

FIGURE 5-72 Verifying the backup vault creation

16. Click Download Agent under Agent For Windows Server And System Center – Data Protection Manager.

17. Save WABInstaller.exe on the desktop.

18. When WABInstaller.exe has downloaded, click Run.

19. On the Supplemental Notice page of the Windows Azure Backup dialog box, click I Accept The Terms Of The Supplemental Notice and click OK.

20. On the Prerequisites Check page of the Windows Azure Backup Agent Setup Wizard, click Next.

21. On the Installation Settings page, shown in Figure 5-73, accept the default setting and click Next.

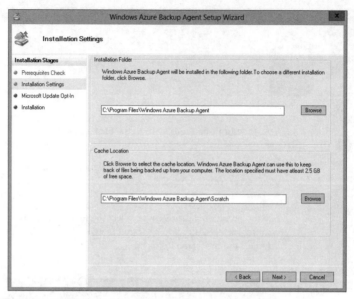

FIGURE 5-73 Installation Settings page

22. On the Microsoft Update Opt-In page, click I Do Not Want To Use Microsoft Update and click Install.

> **REAL WORLD   YOU PROBABLY WOULD**
>
> This option is chosen for this lab environment. In a production environment, you'd make sure that you were regularly applying software updates.

23. Remove the Check For Newer Updates selection and click Finish.

Exercise 14: Backup data to Windows Azure Backup

In this exercise, you back up data to Windows Azure Backup. This exercise requires that you already have a Windows Azure account. You can sign up for a trial account at *http://www. windowsazure.com/en-us/pricing/free-trial/*. You can complete this exercise only if you have performed Exercises 12 and 13. To complete this exercise, perform the following steps:

1. On the Taskbar of the computer that was ADL-DC but now has a new name, click the File Explorer icon.

2. In the File Explorer window, click Computer and then double-click Local Disk (C).

3. On the Home menu, click New Folder. Enter the folder name as **SecretPlans**.

4. Open the SecretPlans folder and create three text files with the following names as shown in Figure 5-74:

- **Global-Domination-Plan.txt**

- **Dance-Robots.txt**
- **Groceries.txt**

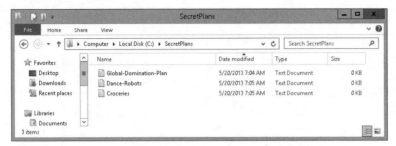

FIGURE 5-74 Create files to be backed up

5. On the desktop, click the Windows Azure Backup icon.

6. In the Actions pane, click Register Server.

7. On the Proxy Configuration page of the Register Server Wizard, click Next.

8. On the Vault Identification page, click Browse, click CertificateName, and click OK.

9. On the Backup Vault drop-down menu, click EXAMPLEBACKUP-412 as shown in Figure 5-75 and click Next.

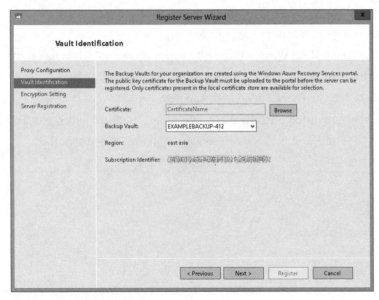

FIGURE 5-75 Vault Identification

10. On the Encryption Setting page, type the following as shown in Figure 5-76 and click Register:

- Enter Passphrase: **S3cr3t W0mb4t N1nj4**

- Confirm Passphrase: **S3cr3t W0mb4t N1nj4**
- Enter A Location To Save The Passphrase: **C:\certs**

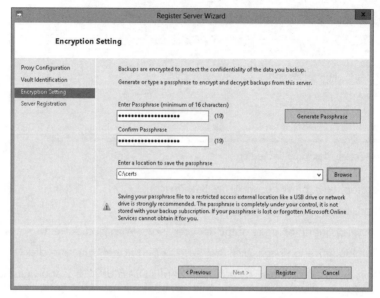

FIGURE 5-76 Configuring the encryption

11. On the Server Registration page, click Close.

12. In the Actions pane of the Windows Azure Backup console, click Schedule Backup.

13. On the Getting Started page of the Schedule Backup Wizard, click Next.

14. On the Select Items To Backup page, click Add Items.

15. On the Select Items dialog box, expand C:, select the SecretPlans folder, and click OK.

16. Verify that C:\SecretPlans\ is selected as shown in Figure 5-77 and click Next.

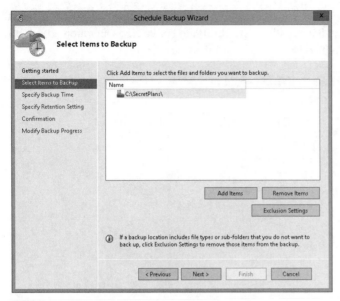

FIGURE 5-77 Selecting items to back up

17. On the Specify Backup Time page, ensure that each day is selected and that backups occur at 8:30 A.M. and 8:30 P.M. as shown in Figure 5-78. Click the Change Properties link.

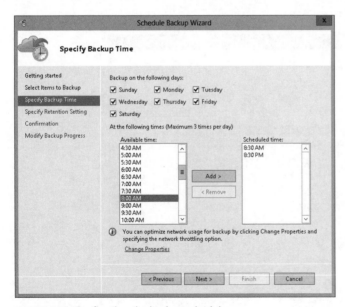

FIGURE 5-78 Configuring the backup schedule

18. On the Throttling tab of the Windows Azure Backup Properties dialog box, select the Enable Internet Bandwidth Usage Throttling For Backup Operations check box as shown in Figure 5-79, click OK twice, and then click Next.

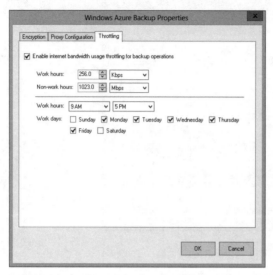

FIGURE 5-79 Configuring backup throttling

19. On the Specify Retention Setting page, set the retention to 15 days as shown in Figure 5-80 and click Next.

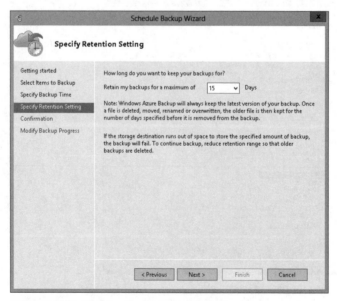

FIGURE 5-80 Configuring the backup retention

20. On the Confirmation page, click Finish and then click Close.

21. On the Windows Azure Backup console, click Back Up Now in the Actions pane.

22. On the Back Up Now Wizard, verify that C:\SecretPlans\ is selected as shown in Figure 5-81 and click Back Up.

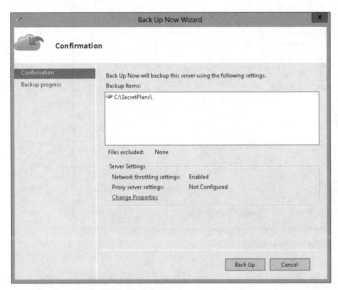

FIGURE 5-81 The backup confirmation

23. When the backup completes, click Close.

Exercise 15: Restore data from Windows Azure Backup

In this exercise, you restore data from Windows Azure Backup. To complete this exercise, perform the following steps:

1. On the renamed computer that was originally ADL-DC, open File Explorer and delete the C:\SecretPlans folder.

2. In the Actions pane of the Windows Azure Backup console, click Recover Data.

3. On the Getting Started page of the Recover Data Wizard, ensure This Server is selected and click Next.

4. On the Select Recovery Mode page, click Browse For Files and click Next.

5. On the Select Volume And Date page, use the drop-down menu to select C:\ as shown in Figure 5-82 and click Next.

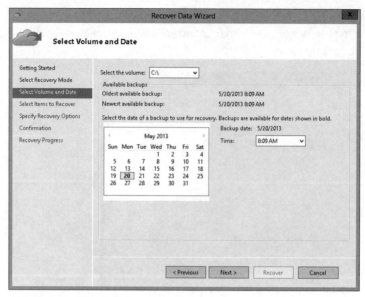

FIGURE 5-82 Selecting the backup date

6. On the Select Items To Recover page, expand C:\ and click SecretPlans as shown in Figure 5-83. Click Next.

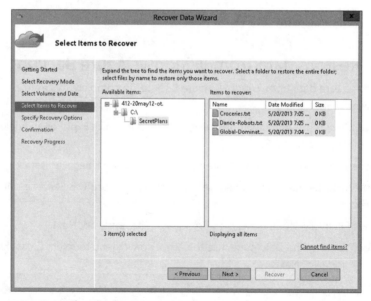

FIGURE 5-83 Choosing items to recover

7. On the Specify Recovery Options page, ensure that Original Location is selected as shown in Figure 5-84 and click Next.

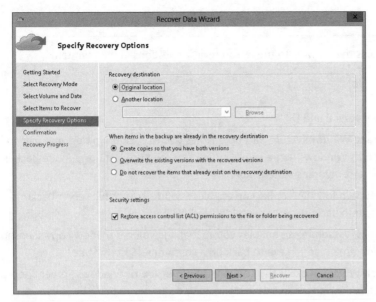

FIGURE 5-84 Choosing the recovery location

8. On the Confirmation page, click Recover. When the recovery completes, click Close.

9. Open File Explorer and verify that the contents of the C:\SecretPlans folder has been recovered.

Suggested practice exercises

The following additional practice exercises are designed to give you more opportunities to practice what you've learned and to help you successfully master the lessons presented in this chapter.

- **Exercise 1**   Use Vssadmin.exe to create a volume shadow copy of a file named Echidna.txt.

- **Exercise 2**   Verify that the shadow copy exists, delete the file, and then use previous versions of files to recover Echidna.txt.

Answers

This section contains the answers to the lesson review questions in this chapter.

Lesson 1

1. **Correct answers**: B and D

   A. **Incorrect**. Windows Azure Backup enables you to back up folders and files to Microsoft's Windows Azure public cloud. You can't use Windows Azure Backup to back up a computer's system state.

   B. **Correct**. Windows Server Backup enables you to perform full server backups, System State backups, volume, folder, and file backups.

   C. **Incorrect**. Vssadmin.exe enables you to manage volume shadow copy snapshots. You can't use Vssadmin.exe to back up a computer's System State.

   D. **Correct**. Wbadmin.exe is the command-line version of Windows Server Backup. You can use Wbadmin.exe on a standalone computer running the server core version of Windows Server 2012 R2 to perform backup and recovery operations.

2. **Correct answer**: B

   A. **Incorrect**. Wbadmin.exe is the command-line version of Windows Server Backup. You can use Wbadmin.exe on a standalone computer running the server core version of Windows Server 2012 R2 to perform backup and recovery operations.

   B. **Correct.** Vssadmin.exe enables you to manage volume shadow copy snapshots.

   C. **Incorrect**. Windows Server Backup enables you to perform full server backups, System State backups, volume, folder, and file backups.

   D. **Incorrect**. Windows Azure Backup enables you to back up folders and files to Microsoft's Windows Azure public cloud.

3. **Correct answer**: B

   A. **Incorrect.** Vssadmin.exe enables you to manage volume shadow copy snapshots.

   B. **Correct.** Wbadmin.exe is the command-line version of Windows Server Backup. You can use Wbadmin.exe on a standalone computer running the server core version of Windows Server 2012 R2 to perform backup and recovery operations.

   C. **Incorrect.** Windows Azure Backup enables you to back up folders and files to Microsoft's Windows Azure public cloud.

   D. **Incorrect**. Windows Server Backup enables you to perform full server backups, System State backups, volume, folder, and file backups. Windows Server Backup requires the full graphical user interface (GUI) version of Windows Server 2012 R2.

4. **Correct answer**: C

   A. **Incorrect**. Windows Server Backup enables you to perform full server backups, System State backups, volume, folder, and file backups.

B. **Incorrect**. Wbadmin.exe is the command-line version of Windows Server Backup. You can use Wbadmin.exe on a standalone computer running the server core version of Windows Server 2012 R2 to perform backup and recovery operations.

C. **Correct**. Windows Azure Backup enables you to back up folders and files to Microsoft's Windows Azure public cloud.

D. **Incorrect**. Vssadmin.exe enables you to manage volume shadow copy snapshots.

Lesson 2

1. **Correct answer**: B

    A. **Incorrect**. Windows Azure Backup cannot be used to perform a full server backup or to perform a bare metal recovery.

    B. **Correct.** You perform a bare metal recovery using a system image in Windows RE.

    C. **Incorrect.** Windows Server Backup can create full server backups, but you can't use Windows Server Backup to perform a bare metal recovery.

    D. **Incorrect**. Wbadmin.exe can create full server backups, but you can't use Windows Server Backup to perform a bare metal recovery.

2. **Correct answer**: B

    A. **Incorrect**. Last Known Good Configuration loads the last known set of good drivers and registry settings.

    B. **Correct**. Safe mode loads a minimum set of drivers and services.

    C. **Incorrect**. Windows Recovery Environment enables you to recover a server. It doesn't load the server with a minimum set of drivers and services.

    D. **Incorrect.** Bare Metal Recover enables you to completely restore a server from backup.

3. **Correct answer**: C

    A. **Incorrect**. You cannot back up or recover system state data from Windows Azure Backup.

    B. **Incorrect**. You cannot perform a full server backup to Windows Azure Backup.

    C. **Correct.** You can back up and recover files and folders from Windows Azure Backup.

    D. **Incorrect**. You cannot perform a bare metal recovery from Windows Azure Backup.

4. **Correct answer**: B

    A. **Incorrect**. You need to restart the server after restoring the system state data.

    B. **Correct**. You need to restart the server after restoring the system state data.

    C. **Incorrect.** You need to restart the server after restoring the system state data.

    D. **Incorrect**. You need to restart the server after restoring the system state data.

CHAPTER 6

Advanced file services and storage

The basics of file servers are simple. Set up a share. Configure permissions. Share files. When you start as a systems administrator, managing file servers is rarely more complicated than performing those tasks and occasionally checking to ensure that the volume that hosts the shared folder hasn't filled up. Windows Server 2012 and Windows Server 2012 R2 offer administrators more options for managing file servers than just setting up shares and configuring permissions. You can go much further, configuring ways to block certain types of files from being written to the share, setting quotas, sharing files to third-party operating systems, and making files more accessible to clients in remote branch offices. You can also use Windows Server 2012 and Windows Server 2012 R2 as an iSCSI target, allowing the server to provide fast storage to other hosts on the network in the same way that you would if provisioning storage from a traditional SAN.

Lessons in this chapter:

- Lesson 1: Configuring advanced file services
- Lesson 2: Configuring and optimizing storage

Before you begin

To complete the practice exercises in this chapter, you need to have deployed computers SYD-DC, MEL-DC, CBR-DC, and ADL-DC as described in the Introduction. You also need to use the evaluation edition of Windows Server 2012 R2.

Lesson 1: Configuring advanced file services

The most commonly deployed server role in the world is the file server. Making file servers work more efficiently saves you time and saves your organization money. In this lesson you find out how to block users from writing certain types of files to folders and file shares as well as how to apply quotas on specific paths. You discover how to configure file classification, configure file access auditing, and speed up access to remote shared folders for clients on branch office networks.

After this lesson, you will be able to:

- Configure and manage file screens
- Create and apply quotas
- Understand when to use Server for NFS
- Manage and deploy BranchCache
- Configure file classification
- Deploy file access auditing

Estimated lesson time: 45 minutes

File screens

File screens enable you to use a file's name to block users from saving specific files in a specific location. You apply file screens to shared folders by applying them to the folder on the file server that is associated with the shared folder. For example, you could create a file screen that blocks all audio and video files from being written to the C:\Share folder, which hosts a file share accessible as \\SYD-FS1\Share. Any time a user attempts to save a file to \\SYD-FS1\ Share that has a file extension on the block list, the user is unable to save the file. File screens enable you to stop users from using file shares to store material other than that for which the file share was intended.

The first step in creating a file screen is to configure a file group, which allows you to create a set of file name patterns. *File Server Resource Manager* (FSRM) on Windows Server 2012 and Windows Server 2012 R2 ship with a number of preexisting patterns based on common file name extensions. You might need to add additional extensions. For example, Figure 6-1 shows how to add the *.mkv extension to the Audio and Video File Group because the *.mkv file extension is not included in the file group by default. When configuring a file group, you can also configure exclusions. For example, you might want to block all video and audio files except for those that fit the pattern manager*.*. You can use file group properties as a way of enforcing a file naming standard. For example, you can block people from saving Excel spreadsheets on a specific file share unless they use a particular file name pattern.

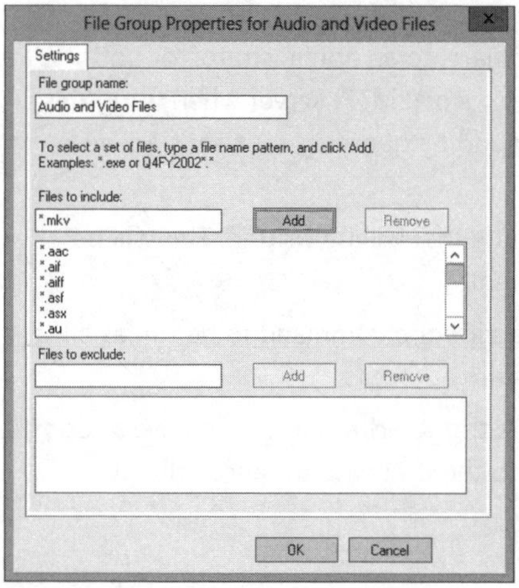

FIGURE 6-1 File group properties

> ***REAL WORLD*** **BLOCK BY NAME**
>
> **At TechEd I met a guy who ran the network for a private boarding school in Canberra. They had a big problem with students at the school using file shares to distribute movies downloaded from the Internet. To resolve the issue, the guy implemented file screens on the shared folders, blocking all files that had extensions associated with popular video formats. This worked until the students figured out that renaming video files with the .txt extension made it possible for them to save the files to the shared folder. It became obvious what was going on when he ran a storage report and found a large number of suspiciously named text files that were larger than 700 MB.**

After you have configured the file groups that you want to use with the file screen, you can configure a file screen template. Although it is possible to create a custom file group and then apply that to a path, from a management perspective it's easier to create a template and then apply the template. That way, if you want to update the file screen across multiple locations, you simply modify the template and those modifications flow on to all locations where the template is applied.

Configuring a template involves performing the following:

- Specify whether the template will use active or passive screening. Active screening blocks configured file groups. Passive screening allows users to save the files, but allows you to configure other components, such as the sending of an email message. You can configure multiple file groups to be blocked when configuring a template. For example, you can select multiple file groups if you want to block users from storing everything except Office files to a file share. Figure 6-2 shows the Settings tab of a file screen template.

- Specify whether an email message should be sent. Email messages can be sent to the user who attempted to write the file to the share, to an administrator, or both. You need to configure a Simple Mail Transfer Protocol (SMTP) server when using this functionality. The email address of the user is found by querying the user's Active Directory attributes.

- Configure the properties of the event log message that will be written. This will be written to the System event log as a warning event.

- Run a script or command. You can configure a script or a command to be run as either the Local Service, Network Service, or Local System accounts.

- Configure report generation. When the screen is triggered, you can also have a report generated and emailed. The email can be sent to the user who triggered the file screen, to an administrator, or both.

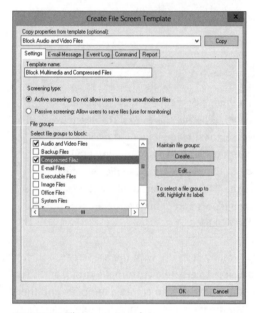

FIGURE 6-2 File screen template

After you have created a file screen template, you can apply it to a path as a file screen. You can also use file screen templates to apply exceptions, which override file screens. For example, you might use a file screen to block all audio and video files on the path C:\Share. You might then create a file screen exception to allow audio and video files to be written to the path C:\Share\audio-video. Figure 6-3 shows a file screen and a file screen exception applied on the C:\research path.

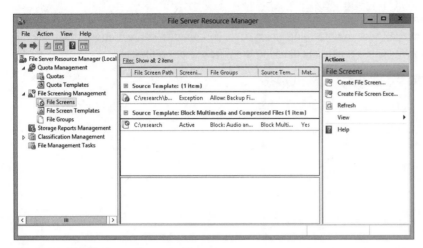

FIGURE 6-3 The File Server Resource Manager

MORE INFO FILE SCREENS

To learn more about file screens, consult the following article:
http://technet.microsoft.com/en-us/library/cc732074.aspx.

Quotas

Quotas enable you to limit the amount of data an individual user can store based upon a quota path. Because quotas are path based, you can have different and separate quotas applied on the same volume. For example, if you have a quota applied to the share hosted off E:\accounting and a quota applied to the share hosted off E:\management, and a user saves data to both shares, the quotas are enforced separately. If a user has access to both shares and reaches his or her limit on one share, he or she is still able to save data to the other share.

REAL WORLD 80/20 RULE

When it comes to quotas, you'll often find that 20 percent of the users store 80 percent of the data. This is true when it comes to file shares, and it's especially true when it comes to Exchange mailboxes.

You can configure quota templates and then apply those templates to specific paths. When you want to change quotas, you simply update the template. When configuring a quota template, you need to choose one of the following options:

- **Hard Quota** When you set a quota as a hard quota, users are unable to exceed the quota limit. A 1 gigabyte (GB) hard quota is shown in Figure 6-4.

- **Soft Quota** When you set a quota as a soft quota, users are able to exceed the limit. You might use these to determine which users you need to contact about their file storage habits without actually blocking them from storing files.

FIGURE 6-4 A quota template

> **MORE INFO QUOTAS**
>
> To learn more about quotas, consult the following article: *http://technet.microsoft.com/en-us/library/cc733029.aspx.*

When configuring a quota template, you can configure thresholds at which an event is written to the event log, a command is run, or a report is generated. For example, you might configure an email to be sent to users after they exceed 90 percent of their quotas, and then send them reports showing their least recently used files when they exceed 95 percent of their quotas. Sending emails is often more effective than writing events to the event log, and if you send an email to a user, the user will probably go and clean up his or her files. If you write an event to the event log, you have to make sure that you check the log regularly, and you still have to notify the users to ensure that they clean out data that they no longer need to store on the file share.

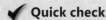

✔ **Quick check**

- You want to be notified if a user is storing more than 1 GB of data on a file share, but you don't want to block the user from storing more than that amount. What type of quota should you configure?

Quick check answer

- You should configure a soft quota. This enables you to configure notification options when a quota threshold is exceeded, but it does not block additional data from being stored.

Server for NFS

Server for NFS Data Store allows clients that use the Network File System (NFS) protocol to access data stored on computers running Windows Server 2012 or Windows Server 2012 R2. NFS is primarily used by UNIX and Linux clients, but it is also used by some third-party hypervisors. Server for NFS Data Store supports continuous availability when it's deployed on a Windows Server 2012 or Windows Server 2012 R2 failover cluster. After it's installed, you configure Server For NFS by editing the properties of the Server For NFS node of the Services For Network File System tool (see Figure 6-5).

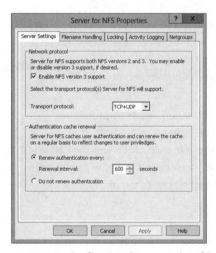

FIGURE 6-5 Configuring the properties of Server For NFS

You use this dialog box to configure the following:

- Support for NFS version 3
- Transport protocol: TCP/UPD, TCP, or UDP
- Authentication cache renewal
- File name translation (for file characters supported by NFS but not supported by NTFS)

- File locking wait period
- Activity logging
- Netgroups for managing access to NFS shares.

> **MORE INFO** **SERVER FOR NFS DATA STORE**
>
> To learn more about Server for NFS Data Store, consult the following article: *http://technet.microsoft.com/en-us/library/hh831653.aspx.*

BranchCache

BranchCache is a technology that speeds file access to files hosted on shared folders for client computers located in remote sites. Where possible, files hosted on shared folders that are hosted on servers in distant sites are retrieved from a cache on the local site network. The BranchCache process performs a series of checks to ensure that the version of the file in the cache is up to date and that even though the file is being taken from a local cache, a file lock is maintained on the file on the remote file server. BranchCache also works with content hosted on Internet Information Server (IIS) and can also be used with Windows Server Update Services and System Center Configuration Manager 2012 distribution points. BranchCache supports the following configurations:

- **Hosted cache mode**   In this mode, the cache is stored on one or more file servers in the branch office. The advantage of this mode is that the cache is always available to clients in the office. The disadvantage is that you need to have a server running Windows Server 2008 R2, Windows Server 2012, or Windows Server 2012 R2 in the branch office.

- **Peer cache mode**   In this mode, the cache is distributed across all properly configured Windows 7, Windows 8, and Windows 8.1 clients in the branch office. In this mode, it's not necessary to deploy a server at the branch office, but the cache is spread across clients in the office, meaning that files stored in the cache might not be accessible if the client that hosts that part of the cache is switched off.

Hosted cache server configuration

When you want to deploy BranchCache in hosted cache mode configuration, you need to install the BranchCache feature as shown in Figure 6-6. Installing this feature configures the computer running Windows Server 2012 or Windows Server 2012 R2 to function as a hosted cache mode server to BranchCache clients in the same Active Directory site. BranchCache hosted cache mode servers no longer require that you install a separate server certificate. BranchCache hosted cache mode servers register their service principal names (SPNs) with Active Directory, allowing Windows 8 and Windows 8.1 clients configured to use the appropriate hosted cache mode to discover them. Unlike Windows Server 2008 R2 hosted cache mode servers, you can deploy multiple hosted cache mode servers running Windows Server 2012 or Windows Server 2012 R2 in a single site.

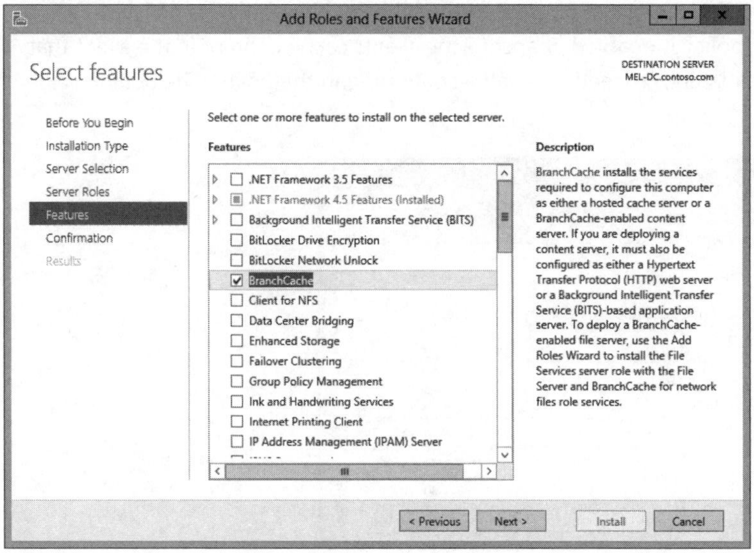

FIGURE 6-6 The BranchCache feature

BranchCache for Network File Server

Installing the BranchCache feature on a server with the web server role makes it possible for BranchCache clients in a remote office to use BranchCache when accessing content hosted on the web server. If you want to allow BranchCache clients in remote offices to utilize BranchCache when accessing content on the file server, you need to install the BranchCache for Network File Server role service as shown in Figure 6-7. After you've done that, you need to Enable BranchCache in the Offline Settings dialog box for the file shares.

FIGURE 6-7 Enabling BranchCache

You also need to configure the Configure BranchCache For Network Files policy shown in Figure 6-8. When this policy is enabled, BranchCache clients cache content in the event that the round-trip network latency exceeds the value configured in the policy. The default value is 80 milliseconds.

FIGURE 6-8 BranchCache For Network Files policy

Client configuration

You can configure BranchCache clients using a Group Policy or through Windows PowerShell. Most of the time you use Group Policy because that simplifies the configuration of large numbers of BranchCache clients. Configuring BranchCache involves enabling the Turn On BranchCache policy shown in Figure 6-9, enabling firewall rules to support BranchCache communication, and configuring the policy settings necessary to support distributed cache mode or hosted cache mode.

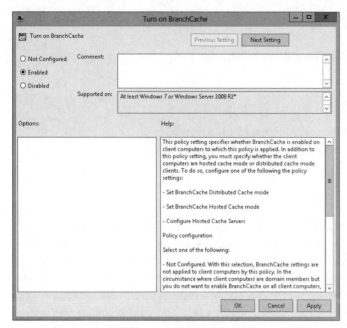

FIGURE 6-9 Turn On BranchCache policy

To enable clients to use distributed cache mode, enable the Set Distributed Cache Mode policy. When configuring BranchCache for clients in environments in which you want to deploy hosted cache mode, you can choose among the following policies:

- **Set BranchCache Hosted Cache Mode** Use this policy to support clients running the Windows 7 operating system. When this policy is enabled, Windows 7 clients use hosted cache mode.

- **Configure Hosted Cache Servers** Use this policy when you are supporting BranchCache clients running the Windows 8 or Windows 8.1 operating system, and you want to specify the address of the hosted cache server.

- **Enable Automatic Hosted Cache Discovery By Service Connection Point** Use this policy if you want computers running the Windows 8 and Windows 8.1 operating system to automatically detect the location of the hosted cache mode server. You can configure this policy in conjunction with the Set Distributed Cache Mode policy. When you do this, clients check for a local hosted cache mode server before falling back to use distributed cache mode.

When configuring clients to use BranchCache, you also need to enable appropriate firewall rules. The firewall for Windows 8 and Windows 8.1 includes the following predefined firewall rules to support BranchCache:

- **BranchCache – Content Retrieval (Uses HTTP)** Use this rule to enable the client to access BranchCache content.

- **BranchCache – Hosted Cache Server (Uses HTTPS)**   Use this rule when using hosted cache mode.
- **BranchCache – Peer Discovery (Uses WSD)**   Use this rule when using distributed cache mode.

> **MORE INFO** **BRANCHCACHE**
>
> To learn more about BranchCache, consult the following article:
> *http://technet.microsoft.com/en-us/library/hh831696.aspx.*

File classification

File classifications enable you to attach custom metadata to files. Classifications are visible on the Classification tab, where you can configure multiple classifications. Classifications can be applied manually or automatically. For example, using FSRM, you can create a classification property named Confidential, which can have a value of Yes or No. You can then create a rule that searches the contents of files for specific keywords. If those keywords are found, the file is then assigned the Yes value for the Confidential property. When used in conjunction with Discretionary Access Control, this makes it possible for the file to be protected by a specific set of NTFS permissions or have a specific Active Directory Rights Management Services (AD RMS) template applied. Figure 6-10 shows a file named Secret where a custom classification property named Confidential has been assigned the value of Yes. Read more about applying NTFS and AD RMS templates based on file classification in Chapter 9, "DAC and AD RMS."

FIGURE 6-10 Confidential classification

File access auditing

File access auditing enables you to track which users access specific files and folders and how those users access those files and folders. For example, by enabling auditing, you can track which users open and make changes to secure files hosted on the management share.

You configure file access auditing by performing two steps. You enable auditing in Group Policy, and then you enable auditing on the objects that you want to track. When configuring auditing in Group Policy, you can either enable the more general Audit Object Access policy, which is located in the Computer Configuration\Policies\Windows Settings\Security Settings\ Local Policies\Audit Policy node, or by configuring the Audit File System policy that is located in the Computer Configuration\Policies\Windows Settings\Security Settings\Advanced Audit Policy Configuration\Audit Policies\Object Access node. The advantage of using the Audit File System policy, shown as enabled for Success And Failure auditing in Figure 6-11, is that it's specific to file and folder access. If you use the more general Audit Object Access policy, all object access events are audited, not just the ones related to file access. Auditing for success and failure ensures that events are written when someone tries to do something they are allowed to do, and also that events are written when someone tries to do something they aren't allowed to do, such as change a file they don't have permission to change.

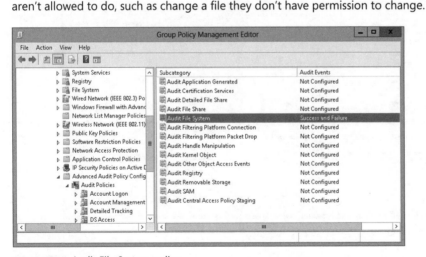

FIGURE 6-11 Audit File System policy

After you have enabled auditing within Group Policy, you enable auditing on the objects that you want to track. When configuring an auditing entry, you specify the following as shown in Figure 6-12:

- The security principal you want to track. You can limit scope later.
- The auditing type, which can be success, failure, or both.
- Whether the auditing applies to a file, a folder, or all folders, subfolders, and files.
- The permissions associated with the auditing.
- Conditions limiting scope. For example, you could use permissions to limit auditing to those cases where the files were accessed from computers that were members of a particular security group.

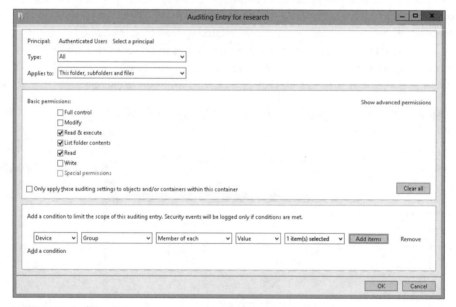

FIGURE 6-12 Auditing Entry

Conditions enable you to implement complex auditing rules. For example, you can track access to files if a user is a member of both group A and group B, but not if the user is a member of group A or group B. You can configure more advanced expression-based audit policies when implementing DAC (Dynamic Access Control). Chapter 9 covers more about DAC.

Lesson summary

- File screens enable you to block files from being written based on file name, including file extension.
- Quotas enable you to limit the amount of data that can be written to a specific path.
- Server for NFS Data Store enables you to share files with clients that access files using the NFS protocol.
- BranchCache allows clients located in branch offices to cache file share files and website data retrieved from servers in remote offices either in a local peer cache or on a host cache.
- File classification makes it possible for files to have classification metadata associated with them based on the file properties.
- File access auditing enables you to track how, and by whom, files are accessed.

Lesson review

Answer the following questions to test your knowledge of the information in this lesson. You can find the answers to these questions and explanations of each answer choice in the "Answers" section at the end of this chapter.

1. You want to provide access to shared files for a collection of computers that run the Linux operating system. Which of the following features or roles would you deploy to accomplish this goal?

   A. Server for NFS

   B. iSNS Server

   C. BranchCache for Network Files

   D. iSCSI Target Server

2. You want to allow clients in a remote branch office to cache content from a file server in the local office. The file server is running the Windows Server 2012 R2 operating system and the appropriate Group Policy settings have been applied. Which role must you install on the file server in the local file server to accomplish this goal?

   A. iSNS Server

   B. iSCSI Target Server

   C. BranchCache for Network Files

   D. Server for NFS

3. Your organization is working on a secret project named Jupiter. You want to have all Microsoft Word files that contain the word Jupiter that are stored on a sensitive file share marked automatically by File Server Resource Manager. Which of the following technologies should you configure to accomplish this goal?

   A. File screen

   B. File access auditing

   C. Quota

   D. File classification

4. You want to block users in your organization from storing audio and video files to a specific file share. Which of the following technologies should you configure to accomplish this goal?

   A. File classification

   B. File screen

   C. File access auditing

   D. Quota

5. You want to track which users are accessing files located on a sensitive share. Which of the following technologies should you configure to accomplish this goal?

   A. Quota

   B. File screen

   C. File access auditing

   D. File classification

Lesson 2: Configuring and optimizing storage

Although iSCSI targets have been available as add-on components for previous versions of the Windows Server operating system, Windows Server 2012 is the first version of the operating system that includes an iSCSI target as a default installable role. In this lesson, you find out how to configure iSCSI targets and iSCSI initiators to work together so that you can access virtual hard disks hosted on other computers, whether those computers are virtual or physical. You also discover how to optimize the role and feature payloads so that your deployment of Windows Server 2012 or Windows Server 2012 R2 only stores the files needed for those roles and features that you actually use, rather than every role and feature that can possibly be installed on the operating system.

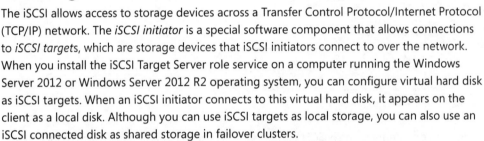

After this lesson, you will be able to:

- Configure the iSCSI initiator
- Create an iSCSI target
- Deploy an iSNS server
- Create thinly provisioned virtual disks
- Configure features on demand
- Configure tiered storage

Estimated lesson time: 45 minutes

iSCSI target and initiator

The iSCSI allows access to storage devices across a Transfer Control Protocol/Internet Protocol (TCP/IP) network. The *iSCSI initiator* is a special software component that allows connections to *iSCSI targets*, which are storage devices that iSCSI initiators connect to over the network. When you install the iSCSI Target Server role service on a computer running the Windows Server 2012 or Windows Server 2012 R2 operating system, you can configure virtual hard disk as iSCSI targets. When an iSCSI initiator connects to this virtual hard disk, it appears on the client as a local disk. Although you can use iSCSI targets as local storage, you can also use an iSCSI connected disk as shared storage in failover clusters.

The iSCSI initiator component is installed by default on all computers running Windows Vista, Windows 7, Windows 8, and Windows 8.1 client operating systems and Windows Server 2008, Windows Server 2008 R2, Windows Server 2012, and Windows Server 2012 R2 operating systems. When you select the iSCSI initiator for the first time in the Tools menu of the Server Manager console, it prompts you to have the service start and to have the service be configured to start automatically in future. After the service has started, you can configure the iSCSI initiator on the iSCSI Initiator Properties dialog box, available when you select the iSCSI Initiator in the Tools menu of the Server Manager console. In most cases, configuration involves entering the fully qualified domain name (FQDN) of the server that hosts the iSCSI target in the Target text box and clicking Quick Connect. The iSCSI Initiator Properties dialog box is shown in Figure 6-13.

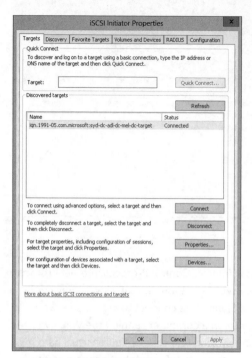

FIGURE 6-13 iSCSI Initiator Properties

You can only connect to an iSCSI target, which has been configured to accept connections from the iSCSI initiator you are attempting to connect with. When creating an iSCSI target, you specify which iSCSI initiators can access the target, as shown in Figure 6-14. You can specify initiators on the basis of International Qualifications Network (IQN), Domain Name System (DNS) name, IP address, or media access control (MAC) address.

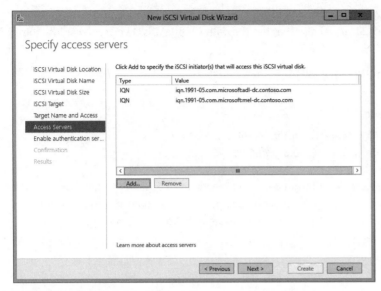

FIGURE 6-14 Configuring Access Servers

If the initiator is running on a computer that has the Windows 8, Windows 8.1, or Windows Server 2012 or Windows Server 2012 R2 operating systems, you can query Active Directory to determine the initiator ID as shown in Figure 6-15. When configuring an initiator ID for a client running a Microsoft operating system, the format is iqn.1991-05.com.microsoft:FQDN. For example, if specifying the initiator ID of cbr.contoso.com, you use iqn.1991-05.com. microsoft:cbr.contoso.com.

FIGURE 6-15 Identifying the initiator

You can create a new iSCSI virtual disk using the New-IscsiVirtualDisk cmdlet. For example, to create a new 10 GB iSCSI virtual disk that has the path E:\Disks\Disk1.vhd, you can use the following command:

```
New-IscsiVirtualDisk -Path "e:\disks\disk1.vhd" -Size 10GB
```

> **MORE INFO** ISCSI TARGET
>
> To learn more about iSCSI targets, consult the following article:
> *http://technet.microsoft.com/en-us/library/hh848272.aspx.*

You can use the New-IscsiServerTarget cmdlet to create an iSCSI server target. For example, to configure an iSCSI target that allows computers syd-a.contoso.com and syd-b. contoso.com to access an iSCSI virtual disk, you can use the following command:

```
New-IscsiServerTarget -Targetname "Syd-A-Syd-B-Target" -InitiatorIDs DNSName:Syd-a.
contoso.com,DNSName:syd-b.contoso.com
```

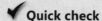

Quick check

- What component do you need to enable and configure to connect to an iSCSI target?

Quick check answer

- You need to enable and configure the iSCSI initiator to connect to an iSCSI target.

iSNS server

The *iSNS server* role enables you to centralize the discovery of iSCSI initiators and targets. Rather than having to enter the address of a server that hosts an iSCSI target when configuring the iSCSI initiator, the iSNS server provides a list of available targets. You can use the iSNS server with both Microsoft and third-party iSCSI initiators and targets. Figure 6-16 shows the iSNS Server Properties dialog box and the addresses of two initiators that have registered with iSNS. Discovery domains enable you to partition initiators and targets into more manageable groups and are useful if your organization uses iSCSI extensively.

FIGURE 6-16 A list of initiators

You can register an iSCSI initiator running on Windows Server 2012 or Windows Server 2012 R2 with an iSNS server through the Discovery tab of the iSCSI Initiators Properties dialog box, shown in Figure 6-17. Using an iSNS server to locate initiators is useful when you have iSCSI initiators running on Windows 7 or Windows Server 2008 R2 and earlier operating systems. With clients running Windows 8, Windows 8.1, Windows Server 2012, and Windows Server 2012 R2 operating systems, you can locate iSCSI IDs through Active Directory.

FIGURE 6-17 Configuring iSNS server

Windows Server 2012 and Windows Server 2012 R2 do not currently support registering iSCSI targets through the graphical user interface (GUI). You can register an iSCSI target associated with a virtual disk with an iSNS server using Windows PowerShell. To register all of the iSCSI targets hosted on a computer running Windows Server 2012 or Windows Server 2012 R2 with an iSNS server, use the following command:

```
Set-WmiInstance –Namespace root\wmi –Class WT_iSNSServer –Arguments @
{ServerName="ISNSservername"}
```

> **MORE INFO** **ISNS SERVER**
>
> To learn more about the iSNS server role, consult the following article:
> *http://technet.microsoft.com/en-us/library/cc772568.aspx*.

Thin provisioning and trim

Thin provisioning enables you to create virtual disks where you specify a total size for the disk, but only the space that is actually used will be allocated. For example, with thin provisioning you might create a virtual hard disk that can grow to 500 GB in size but that is only 10 GB in size because only 10 GB of data is currently stored on the volumes hosted on the disk. Figure 6-18 shows where you select the provisioning type on the New Virtual Disk Wizard.

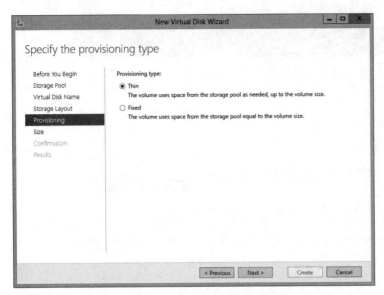

FIGURE 6-18 Thin provisioning

You can view the amount of space that has been allocated to a thin provisioned virtual disk as well as the total capacity in the Virtual Disks area when the Storage Pools node is selected in the Server Manager console as shown in Figure 6-19. When you create a virtual disk, the maximum disk size available is determined by the amount of free space on the physical disks that make up the storage pool rather than the maximum capacity of the existing thin provisioned disks. For example, if you have a storage pool that has two physical disks of 10 terabytes (TB) capacity, you'd be able to create more than two thin provisioned disks that had a maximum size of 10 TB. You'd be able to create thin provisioned disks 10 TB in size as long as the actual allocated space on the storage pool didn't exceed 10 out of the 20 available TB. It is possible to create thin provisioned disks in such a way that the total thin provisioned disk capacity exceeds the storage capacity of the underlying storage pool. If you do over allocate space, you need to monitor how much of the underlying storage pool capacity is consumed and add disks to the storage pool as that capacity is exhausted.

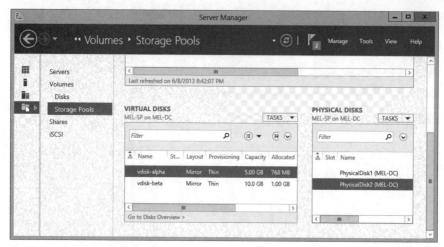

FIGURE 6-19 Capacity and allocation

Trim is an automatic process that reclaims space when data is deleted from thin provisioned disks. For example, if you have a 10 TB thin provisioned virtual disk that stores 8 TB of data, 8 TB is allocated from the storage pool that hosts that virtual disk. If you delete 2 TB of data from that thin provisioned virtual disk, trim ensures that the storage pool that hosts that virtual disk is able to reclaim that unused space. The 10 TB thin provisioned virtual disk would still appear to be 10 TB in size, but after the trim process is complete, it only consumes 6 TB of space on the underlying storage pool. Trim is enabled by default. A drawback of thin provisioning is that you may over-allocate storage space. For example, you might configure 10 5 TB thin provisioned virtual disks on a 30 TB volume hosted on a storage pool. If you don't keep track of the growth of those virtual disks, you may exceed the capacity of the underlying volume.

> **MORE INFO THIN PROVISIONING AND TRIM STORAGE**
>
> To learn more about thin provisioning and trim storage, consult the following article: *http://technet.microsoft.com/en-us/library/hh831391.aspx.*

Features on Demand

When you install Windows Server, almost all roles and features have the payload files present on the system volume. This enables you to add roles and features without having to provide access to the installation media, as was the case in Windows Server 2003 and earlier versions of the Windows Server operating system. An exception to this that you're likely to run into on a frequent basis is the .NET Framework 3.5 features. When you install the .NET Framework 3.5, you have to specify an alternative installation source.

The payload files take up just more than 2 GB of data. If you're deploying a large number of servers where you won't need to add roles and features after initial deployment, needing to store 2 GB of data per server does have a measurable effect on storage costs. For example, if you have 1000 virtual machines running Windows Server 2012 or Windows Server 2012 R2, you might be storing about 2 TB of role and feature payload data that is no longer necessary. *Features on Demand* enables you to add and remove role and feature payload data as necessary. When you've configured a server so that it is no longer necessary to add additional roles and features, you can remove the payload data for those roles and features that won't be used. You can remove the payload data for roles and features that aren't used on a server using the following Windows PowerShell command:

```
Get-WindowsFeature | Where-Object {$_.Installed -eq $False} | Uninstall-WindowsFeature -Remove
```

The first part of this command finds all roles and features that are not currently installed on the server. The second part of the command removes the payload data for those features. You can verify that features have been removed by issuing the following command, which gives the output shown in Figure 6-20:

```
Get-WindowsFeature | Where-Object {$_.Installed -eq $False} | Out-GridView
```

FIGURE 6-20 View removed features

In the figure, if you need to add a role or feature when you've removed the installation files, you can use the -Source option of the Install-WindowsFeature cmdlet to specify the location of the installation files. You can use a mounted .wim image or a shared folder to host the payload installation files.

> **MORE INFO FEATURES ON DEMAND**
>
> To learn more about Features on Demand, consult the following article:
> *http://technet.microsoft.com/en-us/library/jj127275.aspx.*

Tiered storage

Storage tiers are a functionality new to Windows Server 2012 R2 that allows you to create virtual disks that are composed of differently performing storage devices. For example, using solid state drives as one tier to host frequently accessed data and a traditional hard disk drive tier to host less frequently accessed data. Storage space functionality moves data at the subfile level between the faster media and the slower media depending on how frequently that data is accessed.

On most volumes, a small percentage of data is accessed far more frequently than the rest of the data. By implementing storage tiers, the performance of the volume will be greatly increased without the attendant cost of converting all the media that the volume resides on in the storage space to solid state disk.

When creating storage spaces with storage tiers, take the following into consideration:

- When creating a storage space that will use storage tiers, ensure you have an appropriate number of disks to support the layout. Although it will vary depending on the type of data stored, an optimum ratio of solid state to traditional hard disk drives is 1 to 4.

- Create volumes that are the same size as the virtual disk created on the storage space. Virtual disks used with storage tiers use fixed provisioning.

- Although the process of allocating files to faster drives is automatic, you can override the process and pin files using the Set-FileStorageTier Windows PowerShell cmdlet.

> **MORE INFO STORAGE TIERS**
>
> To learn more about storage tiers, consult the following article:
> *http://technet.microsoft.com/en-us/library/dn387076.aspx#bkmk_tiers.*

Lesson summary

- iSCSI targets on Windows Server 2012 and Windows Server 2012 R2 enable you to provide storage across the network to Windows computers through iSCSI initiators.

- The iSCSI initiator component enables Windows clients and servers to connect to iSCSI targets.

- The iSNS server role enables a computer running the Windows Server 2012 or Windows Server 2012 R2 operating system to function as a repository for information about iSCSI targets and initiators.

- Thin provisioning enables you to create virtual disks by specifying a maximum size but where the virtual disks only consume storage in the storage pool equal to the data stored on the volumes hosted on the virtual disk.

- Trim makes it possible for the operating system to reclaim space allocated to a virtual disk when data is deleted from the volumes hosted on the virtual disk.

- Features on Demand make it possible for you to configure Windows Server 2012 and Windows Server 2012 R2 so that the payload files for roles and features are not stored on the computer.
- Tiered storage allows commonly used blocks to be moved to faster disk drives in volumes created in storage pools.

Lesson review

Answer the following questions to test your knowledge of the information in this lesson. You can find the answers to these questions and explanations of each answer choice in the "Answers" section at the end of this chapter.

1. You want to deploy a server that stores centralized information about the iSCSI initiators and iSCSI targets in your organization. Which of the following roles or features would you install to accomplish this goal?

   A. iSCSI target server

   B. BranchCache for Network Files

   C. iSNS server

   D. Server for NFS

2. You want to configure a computer running the Windows Server 2012 R2 operating system so that it can host virtual hard disks that can be accessed by other servers through the iSCSI protocol. Which of the following roles or features would you install to accomplish this goal?

   A. Server for NFS

   B. iSNS server

   C. BranchCache for Network Files

   D. iSCSI target server

3. Which of the following Windows PowerShell commands could you use to remove the payload data for all roles and features not currently installed on a computer running Windows Server 2012 R2?

   A. `Get-WindowsFeature | Where-Object {$_.Installed -eq $True} | Install-WindowsFeature`

   B. `Get-WindowsFeature | Where-Object {$_.Installed -eq $False} | Install-WindowsFeature`

   C. `Get-WindowsFeature | Where-Object {$_.Installed -eq $False} | Uninstall-WindowsFeature -Remove`

   D. `Get-WindowsFeature | Where-Object {$_.Installed -eq $True} | Uninstall-WindowsFeature -Remove`

4. You want to provide server SYD-B with storage through the iSCSI protocol. This storage will be hosted on SYD-A. Which of the following should you configure to accomplish this goal? (Choose two. Each answer forms part of a complete solution.)

A. Install the iSCSI target server on SYD-A.

B. Install the iSCSI target server on SYD-B.

C. Configure the iSCSI initiator on SYD-A.

D. Configure the iSCSI initiator on SYD-B.

Practice exercises

The goal of this section is to provide you with hands-on practice with the following:

- Creating set of properties and rules that automatically assigns a Ready To Archive: Yes value to any file that has not been accessed in more than 365 days.

- Creating an additional iSCSI virtual disk on SYD-DC. Configuring the iSCSI virtual disk so that it can only be accessed by ADL-DC. Connecting, mounting, and formatting the disk.

To perform the exercises in this section, you need access to an evaluation version of Windows Server 2012 R2. You should also have access to virtual machines SYD-DC, MEL-DC, CBR-DC, and ADL-DC, the setup instructions for which are as described in the Introduction. You should ensure that you have a checkpoint of these virtual machines that you can revert to at the end of the practice exercises. You should revert the virtual machines to this initial state prior to beginning these exercises.

Exercise 1: Prepare MEL-DC and ADL-DC

In this exercise, you prepare MEL-DC for practice exercises by joining it to the domain. To complete this exercise, perform the following steps:

1. Power on SYD-DC, MEL-DC, and ADL-DC.

2. Sign on to MEL-DC as MEL-DC\Administrator with the password **Pa$$w0rd**.

3. Click the Windows PowerShell icon on the taskbar.

4. In the Windows PowerShell window, type the following command and press Enter:

   ```
   Add-computer –credential contoso\administrator –DomainName contoso.com
   ```

5. In the Windows PowerShell Credential dialog box, shown in Figure 6-21, type the password **Pa$$w0rd** and click OK.

FIGURE 6-21 Windows PowerShell credentials

6. In the Windows PowerShell window, type the following command and press Enter:

   `Restart-Computer`

7. Sign on to MEL-DC as contoso\don_funk with the password **Pa$$w0rd**.

8. Switch to ADL-DC.

9. Sign on to ADL-DC as ADL-DC\Administrator with the password **Pa$$w0rd**.

10. Click the Windows PowerShell icon on the taskbar.

11. In the Windows PowerShell window, type the following command and press Enter:

    `Add-computer –credential contoso\administrator –DomainName contoso.com`

12. In the Windows PowerShell Credential dialog box, shown in Figure 6-22, type the password **Pa$$w0rd** and click OK.

FIGURE 6-22 Provide Windows PowerShell credentials

13. In the Windows PowerShell window, type the following command and press Enter:

    `Restart-Computer`

14. Sign on to ADL-DC as contoso\don_funk with the password **Pa$$w0rd**.

Exercise 2: Deploy FSRM

In this exercise, you deploy FSRM on MEL-DC. To complete this exercise, perform the following steps:

1. When signed on to MEL-DC as contoso\don_funk, click Add Roles And Features on the Manage menu of the Server Manager console.

2. On the Before You Begin page of the Add Roles And Features Wizard, click Next three times.

3. On the Select Server Roles page, expand File and Storage Services (Installed)\File and iSCSI Services and then select File Server and File Server Resource Manager as shown in Figure 6-23.

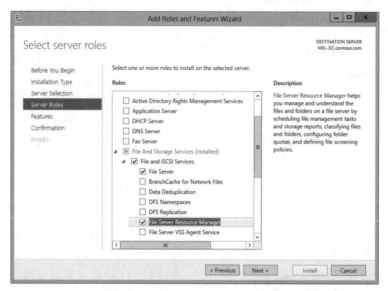

FIGURE 6-23 Install File Server Resource Manager

4. On the Add Roles And Features Wizard menu, click Add Features and then click Next twice. Click Install and click Close.

Exercise 3: Configure quota templates and quotas

In this exercise, you configure quotas and file screens using FSRM. You create and apply both quota templates and file screens templates. To complete this exercise, perform the following steps:

1. When signed in to MEL-DC as contoso\don_funk, click the Windows PowerShell icon on the taskbar.

2. Type the following commands, pressing Enter after each one:

```
Mkdir c:\accounting
kdir c:\research
Mkdir c:\research\backup
Mkdir c:\management
```

3. Click File Server Resource Manager on the Tools menu of the Server Manager console.

4. Expand Quota Management\Quota Templates as shown in Figure 6-24.

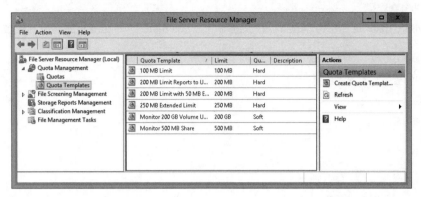

FIGURE 6-24 Quota Templates

5. On the Actions menu, click Create Quota Template.

6. In the Create Quota Template dialog box, enter the following information:

   ■ Template Name: **1 GB Hard Limit**

   ■ Limit: **1 GB**

7. Click Hard Quota: Do Not Allow Users To Exceed Limit.

8. In the Create Quota Template dialog box, click Add.

9. In the Add Threshold dialog box, set the Generate Notifications When Usage Reaches (%) setting to 90 and enable the Send E-Mail To The User Who Exceeded The Threshold option as shown in Figure 6-25. Click OK.

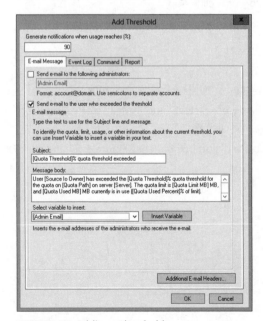

FIGURE 6-25 Adding a threshold

10. In the File Server Resource Manager dialog box warning you about the SMTP server, click Yes.

11. Verify that the Create Quota Template dialog box matches Figure 6-26 and click OK.

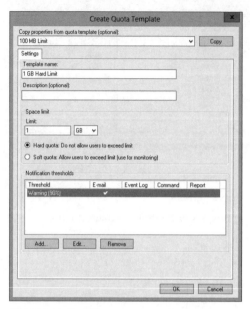

FIGURE 6-26 Creating a quota template

12. On the Actions menu, click Create Quota Template.

13. In the Create Quota Template dialog box, click Add.

14. In the Create Quota Template dialog box, enter the following information:

   ▪ Template Name: **2 GB Soft Limit**

   ▪ Limit: **2 GB**

15. Click Soft Quota: Allow Users To Exceed Limit (Use For Monitoring).

16. Click Add. In the Add Threshold dialog box, select Send E-Mail To The User Who Exceeded The Threshold, click OK, and click Yes.

17. Verify that the Create Quota Template dialog box matches Figure 6-27 and click OK.

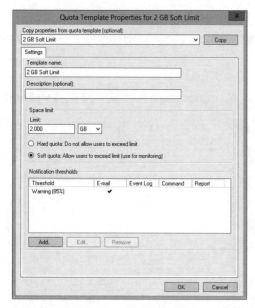

FIGURE 6-27 Quota Template Properties

18. In FSRM, click the Quotas node under the Quota Management node.

19. In the Actions pane, click Create Quota.

20. In the Create Quota dialog box, click Browse.

21. In the Browse For Folder dialog box, expand Local Disk (C), click accounting, and click OK.

22. On the Derive Properties From This Quota Template (Recommended) drop-down menu, click 1 GB Hard Limit as shown in Figure 6-28 and click Create.

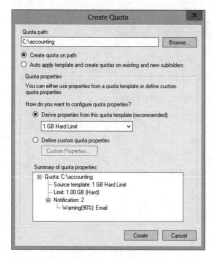

FIGURE 6-28 Selecting the 1 GB hard limit

23. With the Quotas node selected in FSRM, click Create Quota.

24. In the Create Quota dialog box, configure the following settings as shown in Figure 6-29 and click Create.

- Quota Path: **C:\management**
- Derive Properties From This Quota Template (Recommended): **2 GB Soft Limit**

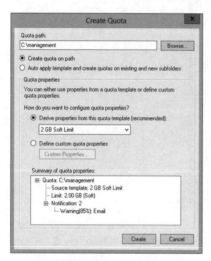

FIGURE 6-29 Apply the 2 GB Soft Limit quota

25. Verify that the quotas listed in FSRM match Figure 6-30 and click Create.

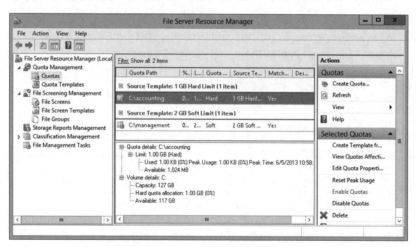

FIGURE 6-30 Verifying the quotas

Exercise 4: Create file groups, file screen templates, apply file screens, and apply file screen exceptions

In this exercise, you use FSRM to modify a file group, create file screen templates, and apply a file screen and a file screen exception. To complete this exercise, perform the following steps:

1. In FSRM on MEL-DC, click the File Groups node under File Screening Management.

2. Click Audio And Video files. On the Actions menu, click Edit File Group Properties.

3. In the File Group Properties For Audio And Video Files dialog box, type ***.mkv** in the Files To Include text box as shown in Figure 6-31. Click Add and then click OK.

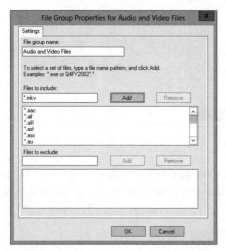

FIGURE 6-31 Adding .mkv files to the file group

4. In FSRM, click File Screen Templates.

5. On the Actions menu, click Create File Screen Template.

6. On the Create File Screen Template dialog box, type **Block Multimedia and Compressed Files** in the Template Name text box, ensure that Active Screening is selected, and select the Audio And Video Files and Compressed Files options as shown in Figure 6-32.

FIGURE 6-32 Creating a file screen template

7. On the E-mail Message tab of the Create File Screen Template dialog box, check Send E-mail To The User Who Attempted To Save An Unauthorized File as shown in Figure 6-33.

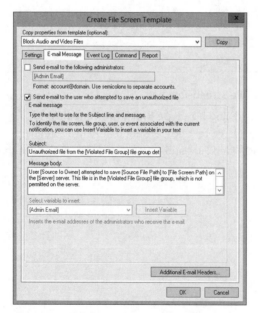

FIGURE 6-33 Configuring an email notification

8. Click OK. In the File Server Resource Manager warning dialog box, click Yes.

9. On the File Screens node, click Create File Screen. In the Actions pane, click Create File Screen.

10. In the Create File Screen dialog box, enter the following details as shown in Figure 6-34 and then click Create:

   - File Screen Path: **C:\research**
   - Derive Properties From This File Screen Template (Recommended): **Block Multimedia and Compressed Files**

FIGURE 6-34 Deploying a file screen

11. In the File Server Resource Manager console, when File Screens is selected, click Create File Screen Exception.

12. In the Create File Screen Exception dialog box, enter the following details as shown in Figure 6-35 and click OK.

   - Exception Path: **C:\research\backup**
   - File Groups: **Backup Files, Compressed Files**

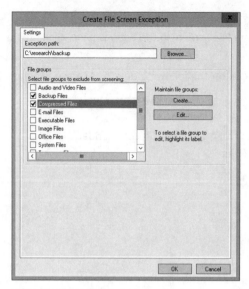

FIGURE 6-35 Configuring an exception

13. Verify that the list of file screens and file screen exceptions matches Figure 6-36.

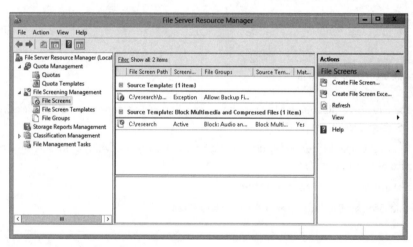

FIGURE 6-36 Verifying the file screens and exceptions

Exercise 5: Configure file classification

In this exercise, you configure a File Classification rule. To complete this exercise, perform the following steps:

1. In FSRM on MEL-DC, click the Classification Properties node under Classification Management.

2. In the Actions pane, click Create Local Property.

3. On the General tab, type the name **Confidential** as shown in Figure 6-37 and click OK.

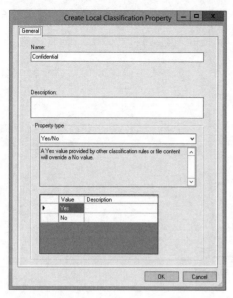

FIGURE 6-37 Configuring a classification property

4. Click the Classification Rules node under Classification Management.

5. In the Actions pane, click Create Classification Rule.

6. On the General tab of the Create Classification Rule dialog box, type the name **Confidential Data.**

7. On the Scope tab, select User Files and click Add.

8. In the Browse For Folder dialog box, click Local Disk (C) and click OK.

9. Verify that the Scope tab matches Figure 6-38.

FIGURE 6-38 Configuring the classification scope

10. On the Classification tab, click Configure.

11. In the Classification Parameters dialog box, set the Expression Type to String and the Expression to Confidential as shown in Figure 6-39. Click OK twice.

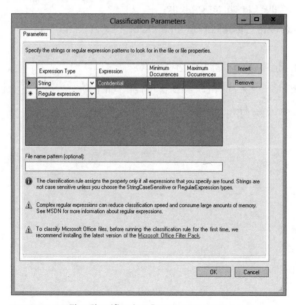

FIGURE 6-39 The Classification Parameters page

Exercise 6: Verify the classification

In this exercise, you verify one of the file classification rules created in the previous exercise. To complete this exercise, perform the following steps:

1. On the taskbar of MEL-DC, click File Explorer.

2. In File Explorer, navigate to the C:\research folder.

3. Create two text files with the following names:

   ■ **Secret.txt**

   ■ **Not-secret.txt**

4. Edit Secret.txt and ensure that the word "Confidential" is present in the body of the text file. Exit and save the file changes.

5. Edit Not-secret.txt. Enter a message, but ensure that it does not contain the word Confidential. Exit and save the file changes.

6. In FSRM, click Classification Rules. In the Actions pane, click Run Classification With All Rules Now.

7. On the Run Classification dialog box, click Wait For Classification To Complete and click OK.

8. Internet Explorer opens and displays an Automatic Classification Report. Scroll to the bottom of the report and ensure that the Secret.txt file is listed as a match for the Confidential Data rule as shown in Figure 6-40.

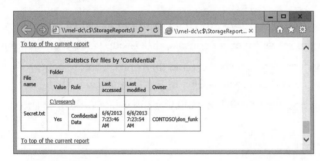

FIGURE 6-40 A storage report

9. In File Explorer, navigate to the C:\research folder.

10. Right-click the Secret.txt file, click Properties, and on the Classification tab ensure that the value of Confidential is set to Yes as shown in Figure 6-41. Click OK to close the Secret Properties dialog box.

FIGURE 6-41 Verifying the classification

Exercise 7: Configure file access auditing

In this exercise, you configure Group Policy to enable auditing, enable auditing on a particular folder, and verify that auditing is functioning. To complete this exercise, perform the following steps:

1. Sign on to SYD-DC as contoso\don_funk with the password **Pa$$w0rd**.

2. On the Tools menu of the Server Manager console, click Group Policy Management.

3. In the Group Policy Management Console, expand the Forest: Contoso.com\Domains, right-click Contoso.com, and click Create A GPO In This Domain and Link It Here.

4. In the New GPO dialog box, type **Auditing-Policy** as shown in Figure 6-42 and click OK.

FIGURE 6-42 The New GPO dialog box

5. Right-click the Auditing-Policy GPO and click Edit.

6. In the Group Policy Management Editor, expand the Computer Configuration\Policies\ Windows Settings\Security Settings\Advanced Audit Policy Configuration\Audit Policies node and select the Object Access node as shown in Figure 6-43.

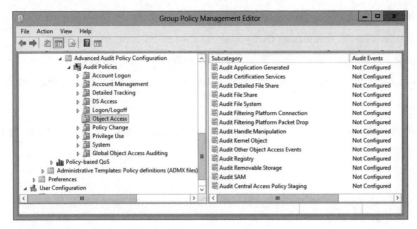

FIGURE 6-43 The Object Access policies

7. Right-click the Audit File Share policy and click Properties.

8. On the Audit File Share Properties dialog box, enable the following options as shown in Figure 6-44 and click OK:

   - Configure The Following Audit Events
   - Success
   - Failure

FIGURE 6-44 Enable auditing of file share access

9. Right-click the Audit File System policy and click Properties.

10. In the Audit File System Properties dialog box, enable success and failure auditing and click OK.

11. Close the Group Policy Management Editor and Group Policy Management Console.

12. Switch to MEL-DC and ensure that you are signed on as contoso\don_funk.

13. Right-click the Windows PowerShell icon on the taskbar and click Run As Administrator.

14. In the Windows PowerShell window, type the following command and press Enter:

    Gpupdate /force

15. Type the following command to verify that the Auditing-Policy policy now applies to the computer as shown in Figure 6-45:

    Gpresult /r /scope:computer

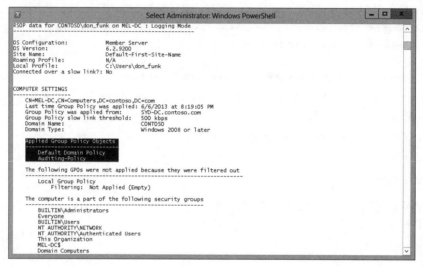

FIGURE 6-45 Viewing the Group Policy results

16. Click the File Explorer icon on the taskbar.

17. In File Explorer, right-click the C:\research folder and click Properties.

18. On the Security tab of the Research Properties dialog box, click Advanced.

19. On the Auditing tab of the Advanced Security Settings For Research dialog box, click Continue and click Add.

20. On the Auditing Entry For Research dialog box, click the Select A Principal link.

21. In the Select User, Computer, Service Account, Or Group dialog box, type **Authenticated Users** and click OK.

22. On the Type drop-down menu, select All.

23. Click the Add A Condition link.

24. Click the User drop-down menu and then select Device.

25. Click Add Items. In the Select Computer Or Group dialog box, type **Domain Computers** and click OK.

26. Verify that the Auditing Entry For Research dialog box matches Figure 6-46 and click OK three times.

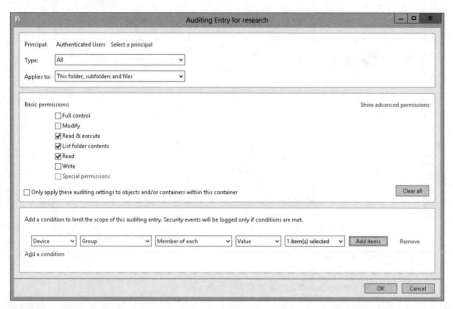

FIGURE 6-46 Configuring auditing

Exercise 8: Create and assign an iSCSI target

In this exercise, you create and assign an iSCSI target on SYD-DC. To complete this exercise, perform the following steps:

1. Sign on to SYD-DC as contoso\don_funk with the password **Pa$$w0rd**.

2. Click Add Roles And Features on the Manage menu of the Server Manager console.

3. On the Before You Begin page of the Add Roles And Features Wizard, click Next three times.

4. On the Select Server Roles page, expand File And Storage Services (Installed), expand File And iSCSI Services (Installed), and select iSCSI Target Server as shown in Figure 6-47.

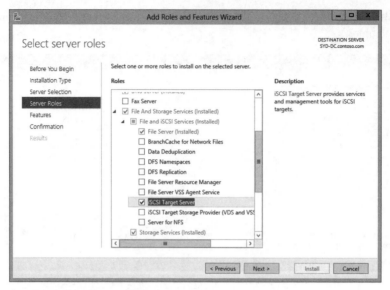

FIGURE 6-47 Installing an iSCSI target server

5. Click Next twice, click Install, and then click Close.

6. In the Server Manager console, click the File And Storage Services node and then click iSCSI as shown in Figure 6-48.

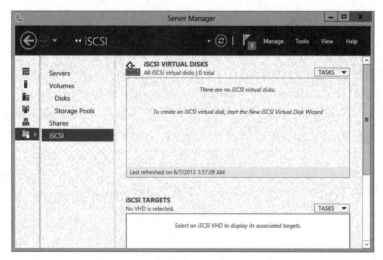

FIGURE 6-48 The iSCSI node of the Server Manager console

7. On the Tasks menu, next to iSCSI Virtual Disks, click New iSCSI Virtual Disk.

8. On the Select iSCSI Virtual Disk Location page of the New iSCSI Virtual Disk Wizard, ensure that volume C: is selected as shown in Figure 6-49 and click Next.

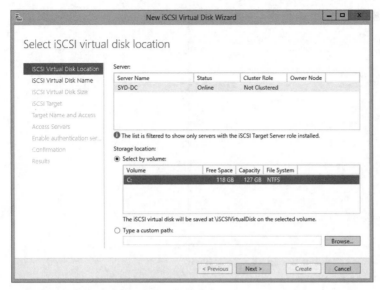

FIGURE 6-49 The New iSCSI Virtual Disk Wizard

9. On the Specify iSCSI Virtual Disk Name page, type the name **iSCSIDisk1** and click Next.

10. On the Specify iSCSI Virtual Disk Size page, type the size **10 GB** and click Next.

11. On the Assign iSCSI Target page, select New iSCSI Target and click Next.

12. On the Specify Target Name page, type **ADL-DC-MEL-DC** and click Next.

13. On the Specify Access Servers page, click Add.

14. On the Add Initiator ID dialog box, click Browse.

15. In the Select Computer dialog box, type **ADL-DC** and click OK.

16. Verify that the Add Initiator ID dialog box matches Figure 6-50 and click OK.

FIGURE 6-50 Add an initiator

17. On the Specify Access Servers page, click Add.

18. In the Add Initiator ID dialog box, type the name **MEL-DC.contoso.com** in the Query Initiator Computer For ID text box and click OK.

19. Verify that the Specify Access Servers page has two IQNs listed as shown in Figure 6-51 and then click Next twice. Click Create and then click Close.

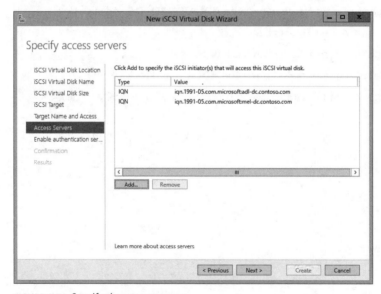

FIGURE 6-51 Specify the access servers

20. Click the Windows PowerShell icon on the taskbar.

21. In the Windows PowerShell window, type the following command and press Enter:

```
New-IscsiVirtualDisk -Path "C:\iSCSIVirtualDisks\ISCSIDisk2.vhd" -Size 10GB
```

22. In the iSCSI node of the Server Manager console, click the Refresh icon, right-click C:\iSCSIVirtualDisk\iSCSIDisk2.vhd, and click Assign iSCSI Virtual Disk.

23. On the Assign iSCSI Target page of the Assign iSCSI Virtual Disk Wizard, ensure that Adl-dc-mel-dc is selected as shown in Figure 6-52 and click Next. Click Assign and click Close.

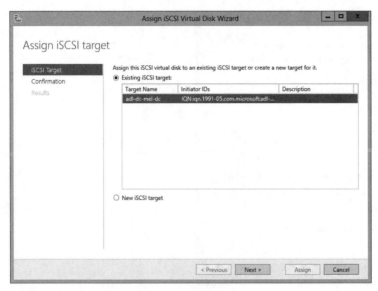

FIGURE 6-52 Selecting an existing iSCSI target

Exercise 9: Connect to an iSCSI target

In this exercise, you connect to the iSCSI target you created on SYD-DC. To complete this exercise, perform the following steps:

1. Ensure that you are signed on to MEL-DC as contoso\don_funk.

2. Click iSCSI Initiator on the Tools menu of the Server Manager console.

3. On the Microsoft iSCSI dialog box, shown in Figure 6-53, click Yes.

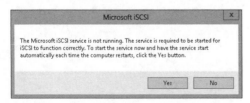

FIGURE 6-53 Starting the iSCSI service

4. In the iSCSI Initiator Properties dialog box, type **SYD-DC.contoso.com** and click Quick Connect.

5. On the Quick Connect dialog box, click Done.

6. Verify that the iSCSI Initiator Properties dialog box matches Figure 6-54 and click OK.

FIGURE 6-54 Properties for the iSCSI initiator

7. Switch to ADL-DC and ensure that you are signed on as contoso\don_funk.

8. Click iSCSI Initiator on the Tools menu of the Server Manager console.

9. In the Microsoft iSCSI dialog box, click Yes.

10. In the iSCSI Initiator Properties dialog box, type **SYD-DC.contoso.com** and click Quick Connect.

11. In the Quick Connect dialog box, shown in Figure 6-55, click Done and click OK.

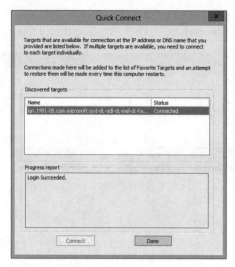

FIGURE 6-55 The Quick Connect dialog box

Exercise 10: Create a new storage pool and thin provisioned virtual disk

In this exercise, you create a new storage pool and then create a new thin provisioned virtual disk. To complete this exercise, perform the following steps:

1. On MEL-DC, ensure that you are signed on as contoso\don_funk.

2. In the Server Manager console, click File And Storage Services and then click Disks under Volumes.

3. In the list of disks, right-click Disk 1 and click Bring Online.

4. In the Bring Disk Online dialog box, shown in Figure 6-56, click Yes.

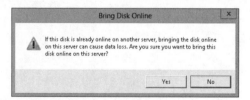

FIGURE 6-56 Bringing the disk online

5. In the list of disks, right-click Disk 2 and click Bring Online.

6. In the Bring Disk Online dialog box, click Yes.

7. Click the Storage Pools node. On the Tasks drop-down menu, click New Storage Pool.

8. On the Before You Begin page of the New Storage Pool Wizard, click Next.

9. On the Specify A Storage Pool Name And Subsystem page, type the name **MEL-SP** and click Next.

10. On the Select Physical Disks For The Storage Pool page, select PhysicalDisk1 and PhysicalDisk2, as shown in Figure 6-57, and click Next. Click Create and click Close.

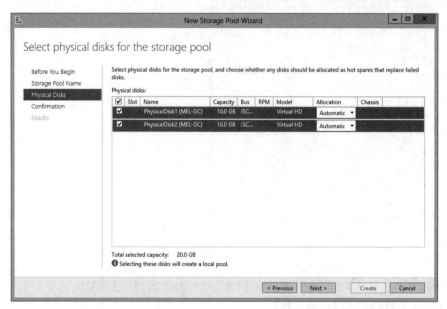

FIGURE 6-57 Creating a storage pool

11. In the Storage Pools node of the Server Manager console, click MEL-SP under Storage Spaces. On the Tasks drop-down menu next to Virtual Disks click New Virtual Disk.

12. On the Before You Begin page of the New Virtual Disk Wizard, click Next twice.

13. On the Specify The Virtual Disk Name page, enter the name **vdisk-alpha** and click Next.

14. On the Select The Storage Layout page, click Mirror as shown in Figure 6-58 and click Next.

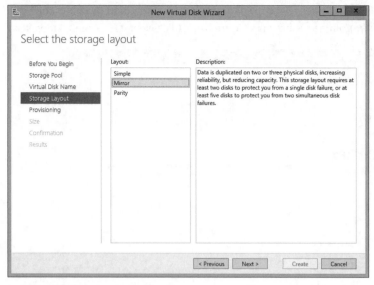

FIGURE 6-58 Choosing the storage layout

15. On the Specify The Provisioning Type page, click Thin as shown in Figure 6-59 and click Next.

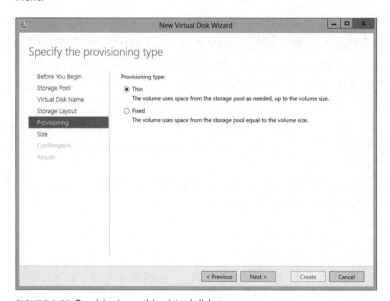

FIGURE 6-59 Provisioning a thin virtual disk

16. On the Specify The Size Of The Virtual Disk page, enter the size **5 GB** and click Next. Click Create and click Close. The New Volume Wizard launches automatically.

17. On the Before You Begin page of the New Volume Wizard, click Next four times.

18. On the Select File System Settings page, set the File System to ReFS and the Volume Label to Thin-Volume as shown in Figure 6-60. Click Next, click Create, and click Close.

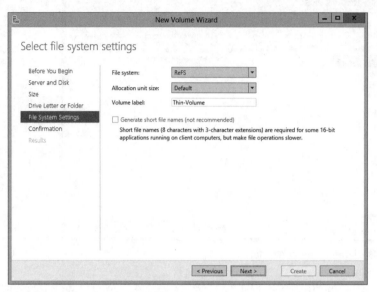

FIGURE 6-60 Choosing the ReFS file system

Exercise 11: Install the iSNS server and register the initiator

In this exercise, you install an iSNS server on SYD-DC and register the initiators on MEL-DC and ADL-DC with the iSNS server. To complete this exercise, perform the following steps:

1. Ensure that you are signed on to SYD-DC as contoso\don_funk.

2. Click the Add Roles And Features on the Manage menu of the Server Manager console.

3. On the Before You Begin page of the Add Roles And Features Wizard, click Next four times.

4. On the Select Features page, click the iSNS Server Service as shown in Figure 6-61. Click Next, click Install, and then click Close.

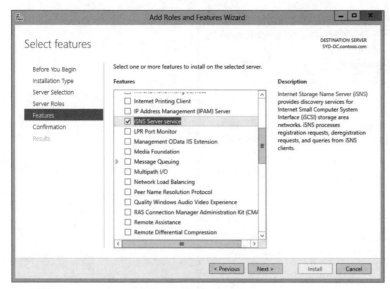

FIGURE 6-61 Installing the iSNS Server service feature

5. Switch to MEL-DC and ensure you are signed on as contoso\don_funk.

6. Click iSCSI Initiator on the Tools menu of the Server Manager console.

7. On the Discovery tab of the iSCSI Initiator Properties dialog box, click Add Server.

8. In the Add iSNS Server dialog box, type **syd-dc.contoso.com** as shown in Figure 6-62 and click OK.

FIGURE 6-62 The Add iSNS Server dialog box

9. On the iSNS Firewall Configuration dialog box, click Yes.

10. Ensure that the Discovery tab of the iSCSI Initiator Properties dialog box matches Figure 6-63 and click OK.

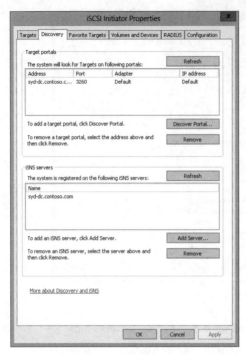

FIGURE 6-63 Verifying the iSNS server configuration

11. Switch to ADL-DC and ensure you are signed on as contoso\don_funk.

12. Click iSCSI Initiator on the Tools menu of the Server Manager console.

13. On the Discovery tab of the iSCSI Initiator Properties dialog box, click Add Server.

14. In the Add iSNS Server dialog box, type **syd-dc.contoso.com** and click OK.

15. On the iSNS Firewall Configuration dialog box, click Yes.

16. Ensure that syd-dc.contoso.com is listed in the iSNS servers area and click OK.

17. Switch to SYD-DC and ensure that you are signed on as contoso\don_funk.

18. Click iSNS Server on the Tools menu of the Server Manager console.

19. Verify that ADL-DC and MEL-DC are shown in the list of Registered iSCSI Initiators And Targets on the General tab of the iSNS Server Properties dialog box as shown in Figure 6-64.

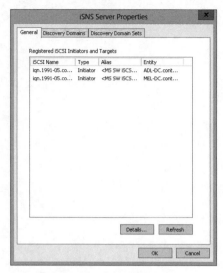

FIGURE 6-64 Viewing the iSCSI targets

20. Click OK to close the iSNS Server Properties dialog box.

Exercise 12: Remove feature files

In this exercise, you remove all role and feature payload files from ADL-DC for roles and features that are not currently installed. To complete this exercise, perform the following steps:

1. Ensure that you are signed on to ADL-DC as contoso\don_funk.

2. Click the File Explorer icon on the taskbar.

3. Click the Computer node, right-click Local Disk (C:), and click Properties.

4. On the Local Disk (C:) Properties dialog box, note the Used Space and the Free Space quantities as shown in Figure 6-65 and click OK

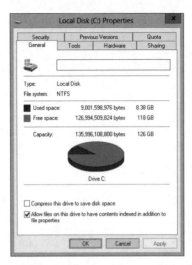

FIGURE 6-65 Viewing the currently used space

5. Right-click the Windows PowerShell icon on the taskbar and click Run As Administrator.

6. On the User Account Control prompt, click Yes.

7. In the Windows PowerShell window, issue the following command and press Enter:

```
Get-WindowsFeature | Where-Object {$_.Installed -eq $False} | Uninstall-
WindowsFeature -Remove
```

8. Issue the following command to verify that the features that weren't installed have been removed as shown in Figure 6-66:

```
Get-WindowsFeature | Where-Object {$_.Installed -eq $False} | Out-GridView
```

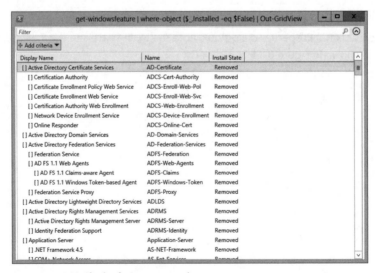

FIGURE 6-66 Verify the feature removal

9. Right-click Local Disk (C:) and click Properties.

10. Verify that space has been made available by removing the role and feature payload files (see Figure 6-67).

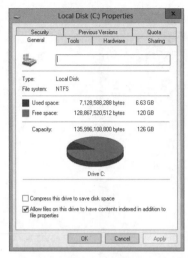

FIGURE 6-67 Verifying that the used space has been reduced.

Exercise 13: Configure BranchCache policies

In this exercise, you configure BranchCache policies. To complete this exercise, perform the following steps:

1. Ensure that you are signed on to SYD-DC with the contoso\don_funk account.

2. Click Group Policy Management on the Tools menu of the Server Manager console.

3. In the Group Policy Management Console, expand the Forest: Contoso.com\Domains node, right-click Contoso.com, and click Create A GPO In This Domain And Link It Here.

4. In the New GPO dialog box, type the name **BranchCachePolicy** as shown in Figure 6-68 and click OK.

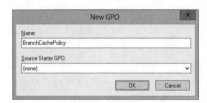

FIGURE 6-68 Creating a new GPO

5. In the Group Policy Management Console, right-click BranchCachePolicy and click Edit.

6. In the Group Policy Management Editor, navigate to Computer Configuration\Policies\Administrative Templates\Network\Branchcache node.

7. Double-click the Turn On BranchCache policy.

8. In the Turn On BranchCache dialog box , click Enabled as shown in Figure 6-69 and click OK.

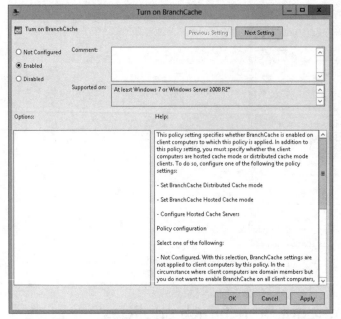

FIGURE 6-69 Turn on the BranchCache policy

9. Double-click the Set BranchCache Distributed Cache Mode policy.

10. In the Set BranchCache Distributed Cache Mode dialog box, click Enabled as shown in Figure 6-70 and click OK.

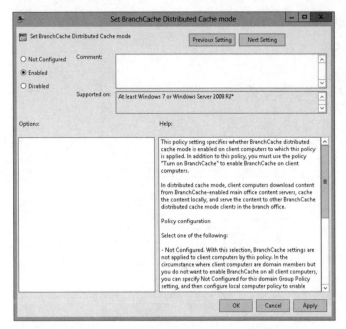

FIGURE 6-70 Set the BranchCache Distributed Cache Mode policy.

11. Double-click the Enable Automatic Hosted Cache Discovery By Service Connection policy.

12. In the Enable Automatic Hosted Cache Discovery By Service Connection Point dialog box, click Enabled as shown in Figure 6-71 and click OK.

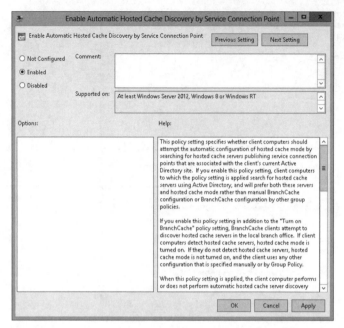

FIGURE 6-71 Enable the Automatic Hosted Cache Discovery By Service Connection Point policy

13. Double-click the Configure BranchCache For Network Files policy.

14. In the Configure BranchCache For Network Files dialog box, click Enabled and set the maximum round-trip network latency to 50 milliseconds as shown in Figure 6-72. Click OK.

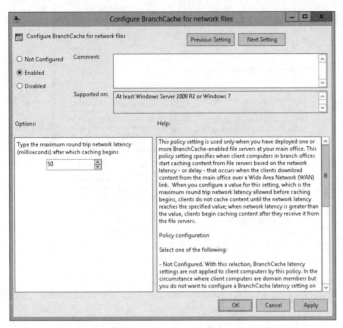

FIGURE 6-72 Configure the BranchCache For Network Files policy

15. Close the Group Policy Management Editor.

Exercise 14: Deploy BranchCache on Windows Server 2012 R2

In this exercise, you configure MEL-DC with BranchCache policies. To complete this exercise, perform the following steps:

1. Ensure that you are signed on to MEL-DC as contoso\don_funk.

2. Click Add Roles And Features on the Manage menu of the Server Manager console.

3. On the Before You Begin page of the Add Roles Aand Features Wizard, click Next three times.

4. Expand File And Storage Services (Installed), expand File And iSCSI Service (Installed), and select BranchCache For Network Files as shown in Figure 6-73 and click Next.

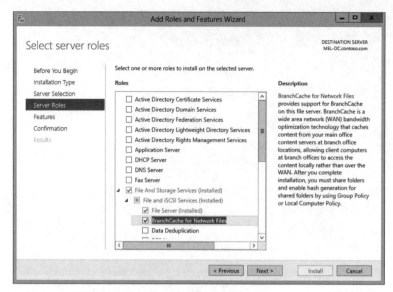

FIGURE 6-73 The BranchCache For Network Files role

5. On the Select Features page, click BranchCache as shown in Figure 6-74 and click Next. Click Install and click Close.

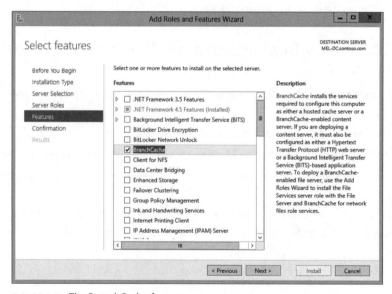

FIGURE 6-74 The BranchCache feature

6. Click the Windows PowerShell item on the taskbar.

7. In the Windows PowerShell window, type the following command and press Enter:

Gpupdate /force

8. Click File Explorer on the taskbar and navigate to Local Disk (C:).

9. Right-click the Research folder and click Properties.

10. On the Sharing tab, click Advanced Sharing.

11. In the Advanced Sharing dialog box, select Share This Folder and click Apply.

12. In the Advanced Sharing dialog box, click Caching.

13. In the Offline Settings dialog box, click Enable BranchCache as shown in Figure 6-75

FIGURE 6-75 Enable BranchCache

14. Click OK two times and click Close.

Suggested practice exercises

The following additional practice exercises are designed to give you more opportunities to practice what you've learned and to help you successfully master the lessons presented in this chapter.

- **Exercise 1** Configure file classification to automatically assign the property Managers: Yes to any file that contains the words Synergy or Paradigm.

- **Exercise 2** Configure MEL-DC to host an iSCSI virtual disk. Configure an iSCSI target that allows ADL-DC to connect to this iSCSI virtual disk.

Answers

This section contains the answers to the lesson review questions in this chapter.

Lesson 1

1. **Correct answer**: A

   A. **Correct**. Server for NFS allows NFS clients to access data hosted on Windows Server 2012 R2 file servers. NFS is commonly used by Linux and UNIX clients. Some also support connecting to Server Message Block (SMB) shares through SAMBA, but that is not an option provided within the available answers.

   B. **Incorrect**. An Internet Storage Name Service (iSNS) server can function as a store of centralized information about iSCSI initiators and iSCSI targets in an environment.

   C. **Incorrect**. BranchCache for Network Files makes it possible for a file server to serve files that can be cached by BranchCache clients.

   D. **Incorrect**. The iSCSI Target Server enables a server running the Windows Server 2012 R2 operating system to host iSCSI targets.

2. **Correct answer**: C

   A. **Incorrect.** An iSNS server can function as a store of centralized information about iSCSI initiators and iSCSI targets in an environment.

   B. **Incorrect**. The iSCSI target server enables a server running the Windows Server 2012 R2 operating system to host iSCSI targets.

   C. **Correct**. BranchCache for Network Files makes it possible for a file server to serve files that can be cached by BranchCache clients.

   D. **Incorrect**. Server for NFS enables NFS clients to access data hosted on Windows Server 2012 R2 file servers.

3. **Correct answer**: D

   A. **Incorrect.** File screens enable you to block files from being written to a specific path based on the file name.

   B. **Incorrect.** File access auditing enables you to track file access.

   C. **Incorrect.** Quotas enable you to control how much data a user can store in a particular location.

   D. **Correct.** File classification enables you to attach metadata to files based on the properties of the file. In this case, you could create a property named Jupiter and have a file classification rule automatically set Jupiter as Yes in the event that the file contained the word Jupiter.

4. **Correct answer**: B

   A. **Incorrect**. File classification enables you to attach metadata to files based on the properties of the file.

   B. **Correct**. File screens enable you to block files from being written to a specific path based on the file name.

   C. **Incorrect.** File access auditing enables you to track file access.

   D. **Incorrect**. Quotas enable you to control how much data a user can store in a particular location.

5. **Correct answer**: C

   A. **Incorrect**. Quotas enable you to control how much data a user can store in a particular location.

   B. **Incorrect**. File screens enable you to block files from being written to a specific path based on the file name.

   C. **Correct**. File access auditing enables you to track file access.

   D. Incorrect. File classification enables you to attach metadata to files based on the properties of the file.

Lesson 2

1. **Correct answer**: C

   A. Incorrect. The iSCSI Target Server makes it possible for a server running the Windows Server 2012 R2 operating system to host iSCSI targets.

   B. **Incorrect**. BranchCache For Network Files enables a file server to serve files that can be cached by BranchCache clients.

   C. **Correct**. An iSNS server can function as a store of centralized information about iSCSI initiators and iSCSI targets in an environment.

   D. **Incorrect**. Server for NFS enables NFS clients to access data hosted on Windows Server 2012 R2 file servers.

2. **Correct answer**: D

   A. **Incorrect.** Server for NFS enables NFS clients to access data hosted on Windows Server 2012 R2 file servers.

   B. **Incorrect**. An iSNS server can function as a store of centralized information about iSCSI initiators and iSCSI targets in an environment.

   C. **Incorrect**. BranchCache for Network Files enables a file server to serve files that can be cached by BranchCache clients.

   D. **Correct**. The iSCSI Target Server makes it possible for a server running the Windows Server 2012 R2 operating system to host iSCSI targets.

3. **Correct answer**: C

   A. **Incorrect**. This command attempts to install roles and features that are already installed.

   B. **Incorrect**. This command installs any role or feature that is not currently installed.

   C. **Correct**. This command removes the payload data of all roles and features not currently installed on the computer.

   D. **Incorrect**. This command removes all installed roles and features as well as removing the payload data.

4. **Correct answer**: A and D

   A. **Correct**. You configure the server that hosts the storage with the iSCSI target server.

   B. **Incorrect**. You configure the server that hosts the storage with the iSCSI target server.

   C. **Incorrect.** You configure the iSCSI initiator on the server that will access the storage.

   D. **Correct**. You configure the iSCSI initiator on the server that will access the storage.

CHAPTER 7

High availability

High availability enables you to ensure that important applications and services are available to users in your organization even if one of the servers that host those applications fails. Windows Server 2012 and Windows Server 2012 R2 offers you several different strategies for ensuring that applications and services are available. The strategy that you choose depends on the nature of the application or service. In this chapter you find out how to configure and manage failover clustering and Network Load Balancing.

Lessons in this chapter:

- Lesson 1: Configuring and managing failover clustering
- Lesson 2: Understanding Network Load Balancing

Before you begin

To complete the practice exercises in this chapter, you need to have deployed computers SYD-DC, MEL-DC, CBR-DC, and ADL-DC as described in the Introduction, by using the evaluation edition of Windows Server 2012 R2.

Lesson 1: Configuring and managing failover clustering

Failover clustering in Windows Server 2012 and Windows Server 2012 R2 is a stateful high availability solution that makes it possible for an application or service to remain available to clients in the event that a host server fails. You can use failover clustering to provide high availability to applications such as SQL Server 2012, scale out file servers, and virtual machines. This lesson explains failover clustering prerequisites, cluster quorum concepts, cluster storage, and Cluster-Aware Updating.

Failover clustering

Failover clustering is supported in both the Standard and Datacenter editions of Windows Server 2012 and Windows Server 2012 R2. In versions of the Windows Server operating system prior to Windows Server 2012, you only gained access to failover clustering if you were using the Enterprise edition of the operating system.

A traditional failover cluster involves two nodes with access to shared storage. With Windows Server 2012 and Windows Server 2012 R2, you can create failover clusters that have up to 64 nodes. A 64-node cluster of computers running Windows Server 2012 or Windows Server 2012 R2 and configured as Hyper-V servers, supports hosting up to 8,000 virtual machines. For comparison, Windows Server 2008 R2 in a similar configuration could only support a maximum of 16 nodes and 1,000 virtual machines per cluster.

Generally all servers in a cluster should be running either a similar hardware configuration or should be similarly provisioned virtual machines. You should use the same edition and same installation option. For example, you should aim to have cluster nodes that are either running the full or server core versions of Windows Server 2012 or Windows Server 2012 R2, but you should avoid having cluster nodes that have a mix of computers running server core and the full graphical user interface (GUI) version. You should use the Datacenter edition of Windows Server 2012 or Windows Server 2012 R2 when building clusters that host a Hyper-V virtual machine because of the virtual machine licensing scheme available with this edition.

To be fully supported by Microsoft, cluster hardware should meet the Certified for Windows Server 2012 or Windows Server 2012 R2 logo requirement. You can use Serial Attached SCSI (SAS), Internet Small Computer Systems Interface (iSCSI), Fibre Channel, or Fibre Channel over Ethernet (FcoE) to host shared storage for a Windows Server 2012 or Windows Server 2012 R2 failover cluster. Failover clustering only supports IPv4-based and IPv6-based protocols. You can install failover clustering by installing the Failover Clustering feature. Installing the Failover Clustering Remote Server Administration Tools (RSAT) enables you to manage other failover clusters in your environment.

Cluster quorum modes

Cluster quorum mode determines how many nodes and *witnesses* must fail before the cluster is in a failed state. Nodes are computers that participate in the cluster. Witnesses can be stored on shared storage or even on file shares, although shared storage is preferred (this recommendation may eventually change as continuously available file shares are more widely adopted). Recommended cluster quorum modes involve an odd number of total votes spread across member nodes and the witness.

There are four cluster quorum modes:

- **Node majority**   This cluster quorum mode is recommended for clusters that have an odd number of nodes. When this quorum type is set, the cluster retains quorum when the number of available nodes exceeds the number of failed nodes. For example, if a cluster has five nodes and three are available, quorum is retained.

- **Node and disk majority**   This cluster quorum node is recommended when the cluster has an even number of nodes. A disk witness, hosted on a shared storage disk (for example iSCSI or Fibre Channel) that is accessible to cluster nodes has a vote when determining quorum as do the quorum nodes. The cluster retains quorum as long as the majority of voting entities remains online. For example, if you had a four-node cluster and a witness disk, a combination of three of those entities would need to remain online for the cluster to retain quorum. The cluster would retain quorum if three nodes were online, or if two nodes and the witness disk were online.

- **Node and file share majority**   This configuration is superficially similar to node and disk majority, but the quorum is stored on a network share rather than a shared storage disk. It is suitable for similar configurations to node and disk majority, although it is not as reliable because file shares generally do not have the redundancy features of shared storage.

- **No Majority: Disk Only**   This model can be used with clusters that have odd numbers of nodes. It is recommended only for testing environments because the disk hosting the witness functions as a single point of failure. When you choose this model, the cluster retains quorum as long as the disk hosting the witness and one node remain available. If the disk hosting the witness fails then quorum is lost, even if all of the other nodes are available.

REAL WORLD ISCSI TARGETS EVERYWHERE

Given that it requires minimal effort to spin up shared storage through the included iSCSI target server role service on Windows Server 2012 or Windows Server 2012 R2, there isn't much more effort involved in providing shared storage than there is in creating a file share to function as a witness.

When you create a cluster, the cluster quorum is configured automatically for you. You might want to alter the quorum mode in the event that you change the number of nodes in your cluster, for example going from a four-node to a five-node cluster. When you change the cluster quorum configuration, the Failover Cluster Manager provides you with a recommended configuration that you can override. The quorum mode is shown in Figure 7-1.

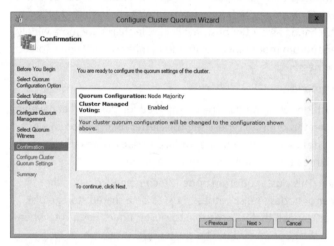

FIGURE 7-1 The quorum configuration

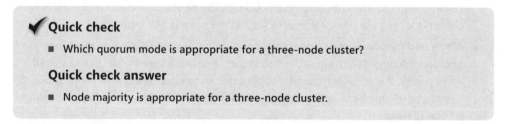

✔ **Quick check**

- Which quorum mode is appropriate for a three-node cluster?

Quick check answer

- Node majority is appropriate for a three-node cluster.

You can perform advanced quorum configuration to specify which nodes are able to participate in the quorum vote. You do this on the Select Voting Configuration page of the Configure Cluster Quorum Wizard as shown in Figure 7-2. When you do this, only the votes of the nodes that are selected are used to calculate quorum. It's possible that fewer nodes would need to fail to cause a cluster to fail than would otherwise be the case if all nodes participated in the quorum vote.

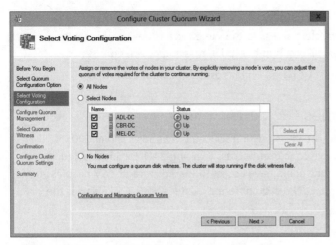

FIGURE 7-2 Quorum voting configuration

> **MORE INFO** **CLUSTER QUORUM**
>
> To learn more about cluster quorum, consult the following article:
> *http://technet.microsoft.com/en-us/library/jj612870.aspx*.

Cluster storage and cluster shared volumes

Almost all failover cluster scenarios require access to some form of shared storage. Windows Server 2012 and Windows Server 2012 R2 failover clusters can use SAS, iSCSI, or Fibre Channel for shared storage. With the inclusion of the iSCSI Target software in Windows Server 2012 and Windows Server 2012 R2, iSCSI is likely to be the simplest and cheapest of these technologies to implement. Figure 7-3 shows the Disks node of the Failover Cluster Manager console.

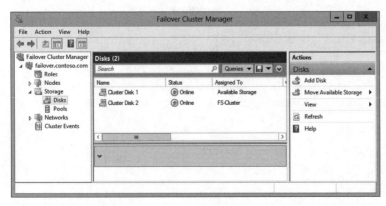

FIGURE 7-3 Cluster disks

Disks used for failover clustering should be configured as follows:

- Volumes should be formatted using the NTFS file system or Resilient File System (ReFS).
- You can use master boot record (MBR) or GUID Partition Table (GPT).
- Avoid allowing different clusters access to the same storage device. This can be accomplished through logical unit number (LUN) masking or zoning.
- Any multipath solution must be based on Microsoft Multipath I/O (MPIO).

Cluster Shared Volumes

Cluster Shared Volumes (CSVs) are a technology introduced in Windows Server 2008 R2 that allow multiple cluster nodes to have concurrent access to a single LUN. Prior to Windows Server 2008 R2, only the active node could have access to shared storage. CSV enables you to have virtual machines on the same LUN run on different cluster nodes. CSV also has the following benefits:

- Support for scale-out file servers
- Support for BitLocker volume encryption
- SMB 3.0 support
- Integration with Storage Spaces
- Online volume scan and repair

You can enable CSV after you have created a failover cluster and then add storage to the CSV. You do this by selecting a disk assigned to Available Storage and selecting Add To Cluster Shared Volumes as shown in Figure 7-4.

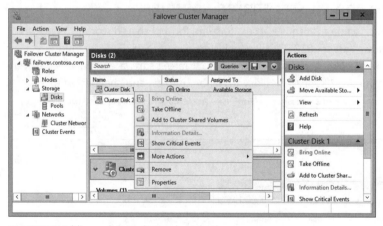

FIGURE 7-4 Adding a disk to cluster shared volumes

Shared virtual hard disks

Windows Server 2012 R2 supports the creation of virtual machine guest failover clusters where shared cluster storage is provided through a shared virtual hard disk rather than SAN storage through iSCSI or Fibre Channel. When using shared virtual hard disks, you configure the virtual machine to use a traditional virtual hard disk to host the operating system and applications. You then attach a specially configured shared virtual hard disk to each virtual machine that participates in the cluster.

Shared virtual hard disks have the following requirements:

- Must use .vhdx format
- Must be connected to a virtual SCSI controller
- Must be hosted on a scale-out file server share or cluster shared volume
- Only supported with guest VMs running Windows Server 2012 or Windows Server 2012 R2
- Is supported when using Generation 1 or Generation 2 virtual machines
- Must be connected to the virtual machine through the virtual machine settings
- Must be configured as shared virtual hard disks as shown in Figure 7-5

FIGURE 7-5 Shared virtual hard disk

> **MORE INFO SHARED VIRTUAL HARD DISKS**
>
> To learn more about shared virtual hard disks, consult the following article:
> *http://technet.microsoft.com/en-us/library/dn281956.aspx.*

Cluster networks

Although you can create failover clusters with nodes that have a single network adapter, best practice is to have separate networks and network adapters for the following:

- A connection for cluster nodes to shared storage
- A private network for internal cluster communication
- A public network that clients use to access services hosted on the cluster

In scenarios where high availability is critical, you might have multiple redundant networks connected through several separate switches. If you have a cluster where everything is connected through one piece of network hardware, you can put money on that piece of network hardware being the first thing that fails. The Networks node of the Failover Cluster Manager console is shown in Figure 7-6.

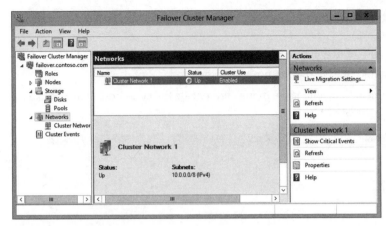

FIGURE 7-6 Cluster networks

You can use IPv4 or IPv6 addresses that are assigned dynamically or statically, but you should not use a mix of dynamically and statically assigned Internet Protocol (IP) addresses for nodes that are members of the same cluster. If you use a mixture of dynamically and statically assigned IP addresses, the Validate A Configuration Wizard generates an error.

> **REAL WORLD DEFAULT GATEWAYS**
>
> Even if the Cluster Validation Wizard only gives you warnings when you perform the test, you won't be able to create a failover cluster unless each node is configured with a default gateway. The default gateway doesn't have to be a host that exists, but if you're having trouble in your virtual machine lab with creating a failover cluster, go back and check whether you've configured a default gateway for each node.

Cluster-Aware Updating

Cluster-Aware Updating (CAU) is a feature included with Windows Server 2012 and Windows Server 2012 R2 that enables you to automate the process of applying software updates to a failover cluster. CAU integrates with Windows Update, Windows Server Update Services (WSUS), System Center Configuration Manager 2012, and other software update management applications.

CAU uses the following process, shown in Figure 7-7:

1. Obtains the update files from the source location.
2. Puts the first node into maintenance mode.
3. Moves any cluster roles off the node to other nodes in the cluster.
4. Installs software updates.
5. Restarts the cluster node if necessary.

6. Checks for additional updates. If found, performs steps 4 through 6 until all updates are applied.

7. Brings the node out of maintenance mode.

8. Reacquires clustered roles that were moved to other nodes.

9. Puts the next node into maintenance mode and repeats the cycle from Step 3 until all nodes have been updated.

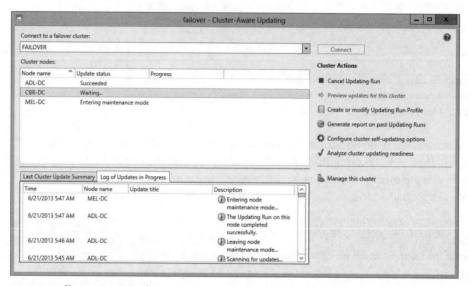

FIGURE 7-7 Cluster-Aware Updating

The main benefit of CAU is that it updates a process that you previously would have had to perform manually. You can configure CAU to work automatically, applying updates to cluster nodes when they are approved through WSUS or System Center Configuration Manager 2012, or you can trigger CAU manually as needed.

You can configure the CAU options, shown in Figure 7-8, so that the updates are rolled back across the cluster in the event that an update fails to install on a node a specified number of times. You can also configure Advanced Options, such as requiring scripts to run before and after the update process has occurred, in the event that services hosted on the cluster require a special shutdown or startup configuration.

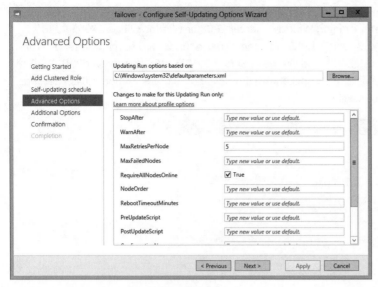

FIGURE 7-8 Cluster-Aware Updating options

> **MORE INFO CLUSTER-AWARE UPDATING**
>
> To learn more about Cluster-Aware Updating, consult the following article:
> *http://technet.microsoft.com/en-us/library/hh831694.aspx.*

Migrating and upgrading clusters

Although computers running Windows Server 2008 and Windows Server 2008 R2 can participate in a failover cluster with computers running Windows Server 2012 and Windows Server 2012 R2, this configuration is not supported except in upgrade scenarios. For example, you might have a two-node Windows Server 2008 R2 cluster. You add two nodes running Windows Server 2012 R2 to the cluster, transfer the workload from the nodes running Windows Server 2008 R2 to the nodes running Windows Server 2012 R2, and then evict the nodes running Windows Server 2008 R2.

Another option, if you do not have the hardware to support additional nodes, is to evict a node from the current cluster, perform an upgrade to (where supported) or a clean installation of Windows Server 2012 R2, and then rejoin the node to the original cluster. You then transfer the cluster workload across to the newly rejoined node, evict the next node running Windows Server 2008 or Windows Server 2008 R2, upgrade or clean install Windows Server 2012 R2, and rejoin until you have upgraded all nodes in the cluster. After you have upgraded all nodes to Windows Server 2012 R2, you should run validation tests to verify the integrity of the configuration.

You can use the Migrate A Cluster Wizard, shown in Figure 7-9, to migrate services or applications from a cluster running Windows Server 2008 or Windows Server 2008 R2 to a cluster running Windows Server 2012 R2. You can also use this wizard to migrate services and applications between clusters running Windows Server 2012 or Windows Server 2012 R2. The wizard only migrates services and applications and does not migrate storage, cluster settings, or networks from the source cluster.

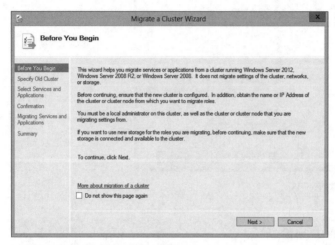

FIGURE 7-9 The Migrate A Cluster Wizard

> **MORE INFO** **MIGRATING CLUSTER ROLES TO SERVER 2012**
>
> The following TechNet blog post has advice about migrating cluster roles to Windows Server 2012: *http://blogs.technet.com/b/hugofe/archive/2012/12/06/best-practices-for-migration-of-cluster-windows-2008-r2-2012-as-melhores-praticas-para-migrar-um-cluster-de-windows-2008-para-windows-2012.aspx.*

Failover and preference settings

With cluster preference settings you can configure the *preferred owner* for a specific cluster role. You can configure different preferred owners for different cluster roles. Where possible, the role is hosted on the preferred owner. You can configure a list of preferred owners. If the most preferred owner isn't available, the next preferred owner hosts the role, and so on. You configure a role-preferred owner in the Cluster Properties dialog box as shown in Figure 7-10.

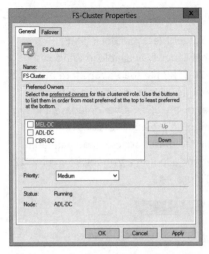

FIGURE 7-10 Configure preferred owners

You configure whether the clustered role fails back to the preferred owner on the Failover tab of the cluster role's Properties dialog box as shown in Figure 7-11. When configuring failback, you need to determine whether you want to prevent failback, to have failback occur automatically as soon as the preferred owner is in a healthy state, or configure failback to occur within a certain number of hours of the preferred owner returning to a healthy state.

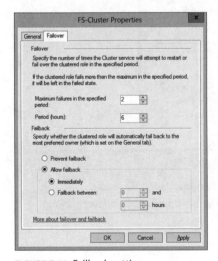

FIGURE 7-11 Failback settings

Continuously available shares

Continuously available file shares allow file shares to use Server Message Block (SMB) Transparent Failover, a feature of the SMB 3.0 protocol that is newly available in Windows Server 2012. Windows Server 2012 and Windows Server 2012 R2 file shares can store both data files and application data. For example, you can configure Hyper-V virtual machines or SQL Server to use a file share to store virtual machine files or the SQL Server database and log files, something that is not possible with file servers running on previous versions of the Windows Server operating system. Continuously available file shares are created by default when you create a file share on a file server that has been installed on a Windows Server 2012 or Windows Server 2012 R2 failover cluster as shown in Figure 7-12.

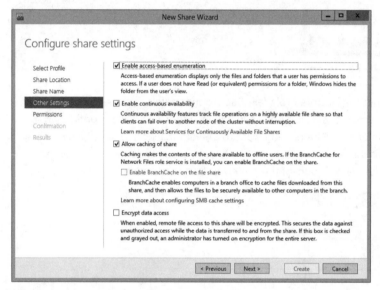

FIGURE 7-12 New share settings

MORE INFO **CONTINUOUSLY AVAILABLE FILE SHARES**

The following TechNet blog post has more on continuously available file shares: *http://blogs.technet.com/b/clausjor/archive/2012/06/07/smb-transparent-failover-making-file-shares-continuously-available.aspx.*

Active Directory detached clusters

Prior to the release of Windows Server 2012 R2, the account used to create a failover cluster required permissions to create computer objects within AD DS. Windows Server 2012 R2 supports the creation of a special type of failover cluster, known as a *detached cluster*, where the cluster name is stored within DNS, but is not stored within AD DS. The computers that will become the nodes that comprise the detached cluster must still be members of an Active Directory domain. You can only create detached clusters using Windows PowerShell.

You are most likely to use detached clusters when you want to automate cluster creation using scripts. Because the account used to run the script does not require permission to create computer objects in AD DS, it doesn't require as many privileges as an account used to create a cluster with Windows Server 2012 cluster nodes.

> **MORE INFO ACTIVE DIRECTORY DETACHED CLUSTERS**
>
> You can learn more about Active Directory detached clusters by consulting the following TechNet article: *http://technet.microsoft.com/en-us/library/dn265970.aspx.*

Lesson summary

- The node majority quorum mode is suitable for clusters with an odd number of nodes.
- The node and disk majority quorum mode is suitable for clusters with an even number of nodes.
- Cluster Shared Volumes allow multiple nodes to have access to shared storage.
- Cluster-Aware Updating enables you to automate the deployment of software updates to failover clusters.
- Failover and preference settings enable you to configure a preferred host for a cluster role.
- Failback settings enable you to configure the length of time it takes after a failover occurs before the workload fails back to the preferred owner.

Lesson review

Answer the following questions to test your knowledge of the information in this lesson. You can find the answers to these questions and explanations of each answer choice in the "Answers" section at the end of this chapter.

1. In which of the following scenarios would you use a witness disk with a failover cluster? (Choose all that apply.)

   A. The cluster has three nodes.

   B. The cluster has four nodes.

   C. The cluster has five nodes.

   D. The cluster has six nodes.

2. With which of the following cluster configurations would you use a node majority quorum model? (Choose all that apply.)

   A. Two-node cluster with witness disk.

   B. Three-node cluster.

   C. Four-node cluster with witness disk.

   D. Five-node cluster.

3. You have a two-node Windows Server 2012 R2 cluster. The cluster must remain operational if only the witness fails. Which of the following quorum modes could you use with this cluster? (Choose all that apply.)

   A. Node majority

   B. Node and disk majority

   C. Node and file share majority

   D. No majority: disk only

4. You want to ensure that a highly available file server returns to node MEL-FS1 in the event that failover occurs and then MEL-FS1 returns to normal operation. What steps would you take to accomplish this goal? (Choose two, each answer forms part of a complete solution.)

   A. Configure MEL-FS1 as the preferred owner

   B. Allow failback

   C. Configure quorum mode

   D. Configure Cluster-Aware Updating

5. Which of the following technologies can you use to manage the process of applying software updates to a four-node failover cluster so that nodes are placed into maintenance mode automatically, updated, and returned to service without disrupting client access to applications hosted on those nodes?

   A. Network Load Balancing

   B. Cluster-Aware Updating

   C. Windows Server Update Services

   D. Windows Intune

Lesson 2: Understanding Network Load Balancing

Network Load Balancing (NLB) is another high availability solution that you can deploy on computers running Windows Server 2012 or Windows Server 2012 R2. You use NLB to host a different type of workload from failover clustering. NLB is suitable for hosting stateless websites, and you can't use it as a high availability solution for virtual machines or SQL Server databases. This lesson explains the prerequisites for NLB, the different cluster operations modes, how to configure port rules, rule filters, and affinity.

> **After this lesson, you will be able to:**
>
> - Determine NLB prerequisites
> - Choose an appropriate NLB cluster operation mode
> - Manage NLB cluster hosts
> - Configure port rules
> - Manage rule filtering and affinity
> - Plan an upgrade of an NLB cluster
>
> **Estimated lesson time: 45 minutes**

Network Load Balancing

Network Load Balancing (NLB) distributes traffic across multiple hosts in a balanced manner. NLB directs new traffic to cluster nodes under the least load. NLB works as a high availability solution as it detects node failures and automatically redistributes traffic to available nodes. NLB is also scalable. This means you can start with a 2-node NLB cluster and keep adding nodes until you reach a maximum of 32 nodes. A node is a computer running the Windows Server 2012 or Windows Server 2012 R2 operating system that participates in the NLB cluster. A computer can only be a member of one Windows NLB cluster.

NLB functions through the creation of a virtual IP and a virtual network adapter with an associated media access control (MAC) address. Traffic to this address is distributed to the cluster nodes. In the default configuration, traffic is distributed to the least utilized node. You can also configure NLB so that specific nodes are preferred and process more traffic than other nodes in the cluster.

NLB is a high availability solution that is suitable for stateless applications. For example, you have a two-tier web application in which you have servers running Internet Information Server (IIS) as the web tier and a server running SQL Server 2012 as the database tier as shown in Figure 7-13. In this scenario, you add Web Server 1, Web Server 2, Web Server 3, and Web Server 4 to an NLB cluster as the web servers host stateless applications. To make the database servers highly available, you would configure a failover cluster or AlwaysOn Availability Groups, but you wouldn't configure NLB as SQL Server is a stateful application.

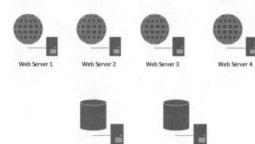

FIGURE 7-13 A two-tier application

NLB is failure aware as long as the failure occurs on the node. For example, if you have a two-node NLB cluster that you use with a web application, and the network card fails on one of the nodes, NLB would be aware of the failure and stop directing traffic to the node. If, instead of the network card failing, the web application fails but everything else remains operational then NLB would remain unaware of the failure and would continue to direct requests to the node that hosts the failed web application. In a real-world environment, you'd set up more sophisticated monitoring that would enable you to detect the failure of the application, not just the failure of the node. Some hardware-based NLB solutions are sophisticated enough to detect the failure of applications rather than just the failure of the host.

MORE INFO **NETWORK LOAD BALANCING**

To learn more about Network Load Balancing, consult the following article: *http://technet.microsoft.com/en-us/library/hh831698.aspx.*

Network Load Balancing prerequisites

In terms of setup, NLB is straightforward, only requiring you to install the feature. Although you can install the feature, you must ensure that a node meets some prerequisites before you can add it to a cluster. Before you add a host to an NLB cluster, you must ensure the following:

- All nodes in the NLB cluster must reside on the same subnet. Although you can configure a subnet to span multiple geographic locations, the cluster is unlikely to converge successfully if the latency between nodes exceeds 250 milliseconds.
- All network adapters must either be configured as unicast or multicast. You can't use Windows NLB to create an NLB cluster that has a mixture of unicast and multicast addresses assigned to network adapters.
- If you choose to use the unicast cluster configuration mode, the network adapter needs to support changing its MAC address.
- The network adapter must be configured with a static IP address.
- Only Transmission Control Protocol/Internet Protocol (TCP/IP) is supported on the network adapter that is used for NLB. You aren't able to bind other protocols such as Internetwork Packet Exchange (IPX) or Banyan Vines on the adapter.

There is no restriction on the number of network adapters in each host. You can have one host with three network adapters in a team and another host with five separate adapters participate in the same NLB cluster. You can run nodes on different editions of Windows Server 2012 or Windows Server 2012 R2, though given that the only difference between the standard and datacenter edition is virtual machine licensing, you are unlikely to be running NLB on the datacenter edition in any case. Although you can have NLB clusters that will work if you are running different versions of Windows Server, such as Windows Server 2008 R2 and Windows Server 2012 R2, you should upgrade all nodes as soon as possible to the same operating system. You should also attempt to ensure that nodes have similar hardware capacity or are running on similarly provisioned virtual machines so that a client doesn't get a radically different experience when connecting to different nodes.

NLB cluster operation modes

When configuring an NLB cluster, you can choose between one of three separate cluster operation modes. The mode that you select depends on the configuration of the cluster nodes and the type of network switch to which the cluster nodes are connected. You can configure the cluster operation mode when creating the cluster as shown in Figure 7-14. The operation modes are as follows:

- **Unicast mode** If you configure an NLB cluster to use the *unicast* cluster operation mode, all nodes in the cluster use the same unicast MAC address. Traffic outbound from node members uses a modified MAC address that is determined by the cluster host's priority settings. The drawback to using unicast mode with nodes that have a single adapter is that you're only able to perform management tasks from computers located on the same TCP/IP subnet as the cluster nodes. This restriction doesn't apply when the cluster nodes have multiple network adapters that are not members of a Network Interface Controller (NIC) team. When you use unicast with multiple network adapters, one adapter is dedicated to cluster communication, and you can connect to any others to perform management tasks. You can improve cluster operation by placing the adapters used for cluster communication on a separate VLAN from the adapters used for management tasks.

- **Multicast mode**   This mode is suitable when each node only has one network adapter. When you configure *multicast* mode, each cluster host keeps the MAC address of its original network adapter, but also is assigned a multicast MAC address. All nodes in the cluster use the same multicast MAC address. You can only use multicast mode if your organization's switches and routers support it. Unless you have very inexpensive network equipment, it's likely that your current network hardware will support multicast mode for NLB.

- **IGMP multicast**   Internet Group Management Protocol (IGMP) multicast mode is an advanced form of multicast mode that reduces the chance that the network switch will become flooded with traffic. It works by only forwarding traffic through the ports that are connected to hosts that participate in the NLB cluster, but it requires a switch that supports this functionality.

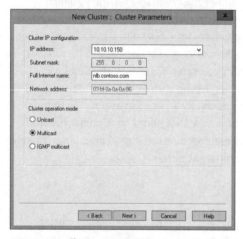

FIGURE 7-14 Cluster parameters

 Quick check

- If each potential NLB cluster node has two network adapters, which cluster operations mode should you select?

Quick check answer

- You should select unicast mode if each cluster node has two network adapters. In this mode, one network adapter is dedicated to cluster communication and the other can be used to manage the cluster.

Managing cluster hosts

You manage NLB clusters through the Network Load Balancing Manager console, shown in Figure 7-15. The NLB console is available as part of the RSAT. This means that you can manage one or more NLB clusters from a computer that is not a member of the cluster. You need to manage clusters using an account that is a member of the local Administrators group on each cluster node. You can use this console to create and manage clusters and cluster nodes.

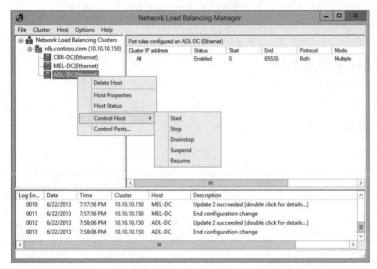

FIGURE 7-15 Control Host options

After the cluster is set up and functioning, most maintenance operations, such as applying software updates, are performed on cluster nodes. When performing maintenance tasks, you should perform the task on one node at a time so that the application that the cluster provides to users continues to remain available. Prior to performing maintenance tasks on a node, you should first stop incoming connections and allow existing connections to be completed naturally. When there are no connections to the node, you can then stop the node, apply the updates, and restart the node. You have the following options for managing cluster nodes as shown in Figure 7-16:

- **Drainstop** Blocks new connections to the cluster node, but doesn't terminate existing connections. Use this prior to planned maintenance to gracefully evacuate the cluster of connections.

- **Stop** Stops the cluster node. All connections to the cluster node from clients are stopped. Use Stop after you use Drainstop so that you can then perform maintenance tasks such as applying updates.

- **Start** Starts a cluster node that is in a stopped state.

- **Suspend**   Pauses the cluster node until you issue the Resume command. Using Suspend does not shut down the cluster service, but it terminates current connections as well as blocks new connections.
- **Resume**   Resumes a suspended cluster node.

> **MORE INFO   MANAGING NLB CLUSTER HOSTS**
>
> To learn more about managing hosts on NLB clusters, consult the following article:
> *http://technet.microsoft.com/en-us/library/cc770870(v=ws.10).aspx.*

FIGURE 7-16 Host Parameters

Port rules

An NLB *port rule* enables you to configure how the NLB cluster responds to incoming traffic on a specific port and protocol, such as TCP port 80 (HTTP) or UDP port 69 (Trivial FTP). Each host in an NLB cluster must use the same port rules. Although it is possible to configure port rules on a per-node basis, it's safer to configure them at the cluster level to ensure that they are consistent. The default port rule redirects traffic on any TCP or User Datagram Protocol (UDP) port to each node in the cluster in a balanced way. If you want to create specific rules, you should delete the default rule. Figure 7-17 shows port rules.

FIGURE 7-17 Port Rules

MORE INFO **PORT RULES**

To learn more about creating port rules, consult the following article:
http://technet.microsoft.com/en-us/library/cc733056(v=ws.10).aspx.

Filtering and affinity

When you create a port rule, you choose a filtering mode, which may also require you to configure *affinity*. Filtering makes it possible for you to determine whether incoming traffic is handled by one, some, or all nodes in the NLB cluster. If you choose to allow multiple nodes to accept incoming traffic, you need to configure affinity. The affinity setting determines whether one node handles all subsequent requests from the same client, or if subsequent requests from the same client will be redistributed across other nodes. Affinity is often important with web applications for which a consistent session must exist between the client and one web server after the session is established. As Figure 7-18 shows, you can configure the following filtering modes:

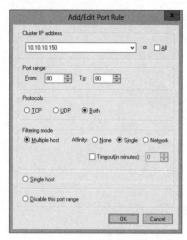

FIGURE 7-18 The Add/Edit Port Rule dialog box

- **Multiple Host**   This is the default filtering mode. This allows traffic to be directed to any node in the NLB cluster. You also need to specify one of the following affinity settings:
  - **Single**   When you configure this option, the incoming request is distributed to one of the cluster nodes. All subsequent traffic from the originating host is directed to that same node for the duration of the session. This is the default multiple host affinity. Don't confuse Multiple Host, Single Affinity with Single Host filtering.
  - **None**   Incoming traffic is distributed to the cluster node under the least load even if there is an existing session. This means that multiple nodes may handle traffic from a single session. Use with applications where it doesn't matter which node handles traffic.
  - **Network**   Directs clients to cluster nodes on the basis of the network address of the requesting client. Use this when wanting to direct traffic to different sites.
- **Single Host**   A single node handles all traffic sent to the cluster on this port rule. In this case, no load balancing occurs. For example, if you have a four-node cluster but you want node three to be the only one that handles traffic on TCP port 25, you configure a port rule with the filtering mode set to Single Host.
- **Disable The Port Range**   When you configure this setting, the NLB cluster drops traffic sent to the cluster that matches the port rule.

Upgrading an NLB cluster

You can upgrade NLB clusters from previous versions of the Windows Server operating system by performing a rolling upgrade. The advantage of the rolling upgrade is that the application hosted on the NLB cluster remains available to users during the upgrade. Rolling upgrades involve taking one host at a time offline, performing the upgrade, and then rejoining them to the cluster. You should use the Drainstop functionality on each node prior to upgrading it to empty it of connected clients.

You can only perform a rolling upgrade if the applications that are running on the cluster nodes support the upgrading of the underlying operating system. If they don't, you might need to take the entire cluster offline when performing the upgrade. It is also possible that you might be attempting an upgrade where a direct operating system upgrade is not possible, for example from an x86 edition of Windows Server 2003 to Windows Server 2012 R2. In this case, you need to determine the best way of migrating the workload. This may involve introducing new Windows Server 2012 R2 cluster nodes and retiring existing Windows Server 2003 cluster nodes.

> **MORE INFO** **UPGRADING NLB CLUSTERS**
>
> To learn more about upgrading NLB clusters, consult the following article:
> *http://technet.microsoft.com/en-us/library/cc731691(v=ws.10).aspx.*

New NLB PowerShell cmdlets

For the most part, NLB hasn't changed much in the last few versions of the Windows Server operating system and if you're used to managing NLB on Windows Server 2003 or Windows Server 2008 you won't find many differences in the user interface (UI) with Windows Server 2012 or Windows Server 2012 R2. Perhaps the most notable change is the inclusion of 35 Windows PowerShell cmdlets.

These cmdlets have the functionality listed in Table 7-1.

TABLE 7-1 NLB PowerShell cmdlets

Noun	Verbs	Function
NlbClusterNode	Add, Get, Remove, Resume, Set, Start, Stop, Suspend	Configure and manage a cluster node
NlbClusterNodeDip	Add, Get, Remove, Set	Configure the cluster node's dedicated management IP address
NlbClusterPortRule	Add, Disable, Enable, Get, Remove, Set	Create and manage port rules
NlbClusterVip	Add, Get, Remove, Set	Configure the cluster's virtual IP address
NlbCluster	Get, New, Remove, Resume, Set, Start, Stop, Suspend	Configure and manage the cluster
NlbClusterDriverInfo	Get	Provides information about the cluster driver
NlbClusterNodeNetworkInterface	Get	Provides information about the node's network interface driver
NlbClusterIpv6Address	New	Configure the cluster's IPv6 address

NlbClusterPortRuleNodeHandlingPriority	Set	Manage priority on a per-port rule basis
NlbClusterPortRuleNodeWeight	Set	Configure the node weight on a per-port rule basis

> **MORE INFO** NETWORK LOAD BALANCING CMDLETS
>
> For a complete list of NLB cmdlets available in Windows Server 2012 or Windows Server 2012 R2, consult the following article: *http://technet.microsoft.com/en-us/library/ hh801274(v=wps.620).aspx.*

Lesson summary

- Use the multicast cluster operation mode when NLB cluster nodes only have a single network adapter. Use IGMP multicast when switches support this technology.
- Use the unicast cluster operation mode when the NLB cluster nodes have multiple network adapters.
- Port rules enable you to determine how NLB clusters process traffic.
- Filtering and affinity determine how traffic is directed to nodes and whether subsequent traffic in the same session will continue to be forwarded to the same NLB cluster node.

Lesson review

Answer the following questions to test your knowledge of the information in this lesson. You can find the answers to these questions and explanations of each answer choice in the "Answers" section at the end of this chapter.

1. You need to apply a critical software update to each node in a six-node NLB cluster that hosts a web application. The critical software update requires each node in the NLB cluster to be restarted. You want to deal with each node in sequence, stopping new sessions from being established and to allow existing sessions to complete before applying the update and restarting each node. Which of the following commands should you apply to each node?

    A. Stop

    B. Drainstop

    C. Suspend

    D. Start

2. You are configuring a port rule for a Windows Network Load Balancing Cluster. You want to ensure that after a client starts a session with a host, all subsequent traffic in that session is directed to that host. Which of the following filtering modes and affinities should you configure to accomplish this goal?

A. Single host, no affinity

B. Multiple host, no affinity

C. Multiple host, single affinity

D. Disable port range

3. You are configuring a port rule for a Windows NLB cluster. You want to ensure that traffic on a specific port is automatically dropped. Which of the following filtering and affinity options should you configure to accomplish this goal?

A. Disable port range

B. Multiple host, single affinity

C. Multiple host, no affinity

D. Single host, no affinity

4. You want to ensure that all TCP traffic on port 25 goes to one host in an eight-node NLB cluster. TCP traffic on port 80 should be shared by all hosts. Which of the following filtering and affinity options should you configure for the rule that deals with TCP traffic on port 25?

A. Multiple host, no affinity

B. Multiple host, single affinity

C. Disable port range

D. Single host, no affinity

5. You are configuring NLB clusters that will be hosted as virtual machines on a Hyper-V server. The NLB cluster and the cluster hosts will be managed from computers running Windows 8 on a separate TCP/IP subnet. For which of the following configurations must you select a multicast mode for the cluster operations mode? (Choose all that apply.)

A. Five-node NLB cluster One network adapter per node.

B. Four-node NLB cluster Two network adapters per node. Network adapters are teamed.

C. Five-node NLB cluster Two network adapters per node. Network adapters not teamed.

D. Four-node NLB cluster One network adapter per node.

Practice exercises

The goal of this section is to provide you with hands-on practice with the following:

- Installing NLB
- Creating an NLB cluster
- Configuring port rules and affinity

- Removing an NLB cluster
- Installing failover clustering
- Creating a two-node failover cluster
- Adding a node to an existing cluster
- Changing failover cluster quorum configuration
- Installing and configuring a highly available file share
- Configuring failover and failback settings
- Configuring and managing Cluster-Aware Updating

To perform the exercises in this section, you need access to an evaluation version of Windows Server 2012 R2. You should also have access to virtual machines SYD-DC, MEL-DC, CBR-DC and ADL-DC, the setup instructions for which are described in the introduction. You should ensure that you have a checkpoint of these virtual machines that you can revert to at the end of the practice exercises. You should revert the virtual machines to this initial state prior to beginning these exercises.

Exercise 1: Prepare ADL-DC, MEL-DC, and CBR-DC for exercises

In this exercise, you prepare ADL-DC, MEL-DC, and CBR-DC for the remaining practice exercises. To complete this exercise, perform the following steps:

1. Ensure that SYD-DC is powered on. After SYD-DC is powered on, power on ADL-DC, CBR-DC, and MEL-DC.

2. Sign on to ADL-DC as administrator with the password **Pa$$w0rd**.

3. Click the Windows PowerShell icon on the task bar. In the Windows PowerShell window, type the following command and press Enter:

   ```
   Add-computer –credential contoso\administrator –domainname contoso.com
   ```

4. In the Windows PowerShell Credential dialog box, type the password **Pa$$w0rd** and click OK.

5. In the PowerShell Window type the following command and press Enter:

   ```
   Restart-computer
   ```

6. Sign on to CBR-DC as administrator with the password **Pa$$w0rd**.

7. Click the Windows PowerShell icon on the task bar. In the Windows PowerShell window, type the following command and press Enter:

   ```
   Add-computer –credential contoso\administrator –domainname contoso.com
   ```

8. In the Windows PowerShell Credential dialog box, type the password **Pa$$w0rd** and click OK.

9. In the PowerShell Window type the following command and press Enter:

```
Restart-computer
```

10. Sign on to MEL-DC as administrator with the password **Pa$$w0rd**.

11. Click the Windows PowerShell icon on the task bar. In the Windows PowerShell window, type the following command and press Enter:

```
Add-computer -credential contoso\administrator -domainname contoso.com
```

12. In the Windows PowerShell Credential dialog box, type the password **Pa$$w0rd** and click OK.

13. In the PowerShell Window type the following command and press Enter:

```
Restart-computer
```

14. Sign on to SYD-DC as contoso\don_funk with the password **Pa$$w0rd**.

15. Click the Windows PowerShell icon on the task bar. In the Windows PowerShell window, type the following command and press Enter. Verify that the output appears similar to that shown in Figure 7-19:

```
Get-ADComputer -filter 'name -like "*DC"' | Out-GridView
```

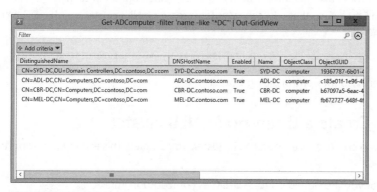

FIGURE 7-19 Verifying domain membership

Exercise 2: Install the Network Load Balancing feature on ADL-DC, CBR-DC, and MEL-DC

In this exercise, you use Windows PowerShell to install the Network Load Balancing feature on ADL-DC, CBR-DC, and MEL-DC. To complete this exercise, perform the following steps:

1. Ensure that you are signed on to SYD-DC as Contoso\don_funk.

2. Click the Windows PowerShell icon on the taskbar, type the following command and press Enter:

```
Invoke-Command -Computername ADL-DC, CBR-DC, MEL-DC -Scriptblock {Install-
WindowsFeature NLB}
```

3. Type the following command and press Enter to verify that the feature has installed on all three computers as shown in Figure 7-20:

```
Invoke-Command -Computername ADL-DC, CBR-DC, MEL-DC -Scriptblock {Get-
WindowsFeature NLB } | Out-GridView
```

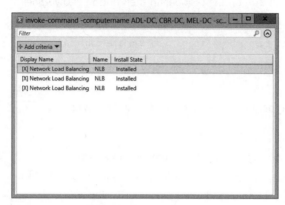

FIGURE 7-20 Verify the feature installation

4. In the Windows PowerShell window, use the following command to install the NLB feature on SYD-DC so that you can remotely create an NLB cluster on MEL-DC, SYD-DC, and ADL-DC:

```
Start-Process PowerShell -verb RunAs {Install-WindowsFeature RSAT-NLB}
```

5. In the User Account Control dialog box, click Yes.

Exercise 3: Create a three-node NLB cluster

In this exercise, you create a three-node NLB cluster. To complete this exercise, perform the following steps:

1. Ensure that you are signed on to SYD-DC as contoso\don_funk.

2. Click Network Load Balancing Manager on the Tools menu of the Server Manager console.

3. On the Cluster Menu of the Network Load Balancing Manager console, click New.

4. On the New Cluster: Connect dialog box, type **MEL-DC** and click Connect as shown in Figure 7-21. Click Next.

FIGURE 7-21 Connecting to the cluster host

5. On the New Cluster: Host Parameter dialog box, ensure that the Default State is set to Started and click Next.

6. On the New Cluster: Cluster IP Addresses dialog box, click Add.

7. In the Add IP Address dialog box, enter the following information and click OK:

   ■ IPv4 Address: **10.10.10.150**

   ■ Subnet Mask: **255.0.0.0**

8. Verify that the New Cluster: Cluster IP Addresses dialog box matches Figure 7-22 and click Next.

FIGURE 7-22 Cluster IP address

9. On the New Cluster: Cluster Parameters dialog box set the Full Internet Name to Nlb. contoso.com and select the Multicast cluster operation mode. Click Next.

10. On the New Cluster: Port Rules dialog box, click Finish.

11. Wait until the cluster reaches convergence (the hourglass icon on MEL-DC(Ethernet) disappears) and the status is set to Enabled as shown in Figure 7-23. Proceed to step 12.

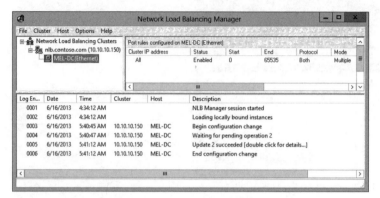

FIGURE 7-23 The cluster node status

12. Right-click the Nlb.contoso.com node and click Add Host To Cluster.

13. On the Add Host To Cluster: Connect dialog box, type **ADL-DC** and click Connect. Verify that the Add Host To Cluster: Connect dialog box matches Figure 7-24 and click Next twice. Click Finish.

FIGURE 7-24 The Add Host To Cluster dialog box

14. When both the MEL-DC and ADL-DC nodes have a status of Converged, as shown in Figure 7-25, right-click Nlb.contoso.com and click Add Host To Cluster.

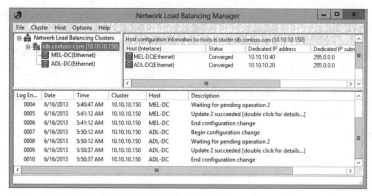

FIGURE 7-25 The Network Load Balancing Manager

15. On the Add Host To Cluster: Connect dialog box, type **CBR-DC i**n the Host text box and click Connect.

16. On the Add Host To Cluster: Connect dialog box, click Next twice and then click Finish.

17. Wait until the status of all three hosts is Converged as shown in Figure 7-26 before starting Exercise 4.

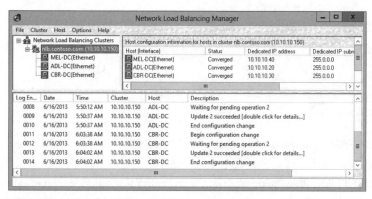

FIGURE 7-26 Cluster status

Exercise 4: Configure port rules and affinity

In this exercise, you configure NLB cluster port rules and affinity. To complete this exercise, perform the following steps:

1. Ensure that you have the Network Load Balancing Manager open on SYD-DC and that you are connected to the NLB cluster Nlb.contoso.com, which you created in Exercise 3.

2. In the Network Load Balancing Manager console, right-click Nlb.contoso.com and click Cluster Properties.

3. On the Port Rule tab of the Nlb.contoso.com(10.10.10.150) Properties dialog box, select the Defined Port Rule All, and click Remove.

4. On the Port Rule tab of the Nlb.contoso.com(10.10.10.150) Properties dialog box, click Add.

5. On the Add/Edit Port Rule dialog box, configure the following settings as shown in Figure 7-27, and then click OK:

   - Cluster IP address: **10.10.10.150** (clear the All check box)
   - Port Range: From **80** to **80**
   - Protocols: **Both**
   - Filtering Mode: **Multiple Host**
   - Affinity: **Single**

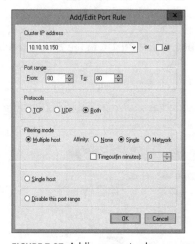

FIGURE 7-27 Adding a port rule

6. On the Port Rule tab of the Nlb.contoso.com(10.10.10.150) Properties dialog box, click Add.

7. On the Add/Edit Port Rule dialog box, set the following settings as shown in Figure 7-28 and then click OK:

   - Cluster IP Address: **10.10.10.150** (clear the All check box)
   - Port Range: From **81** to **81**
   - Protocols: **Both**
   - Filtering Mode: **Single Host**

FIGURE 7-28 Editing a port rule

8. Verify that the Nlb.contoso.com(10.10.10.150) Properties dialog box matches Figure 7-29 and click OK.

FIGURE 7-29 Verifying port rules

9. Wait for the cluster to reach convergence (you might have to refresh the cluster).

Exercise 5: Remove an NLB cluster

In this exercise, you remove the NLB cluster that you installed earlier as well as remove the NLB feature from each of the computers. To complete this exercise, perform the following steps:

1. Ensure that you have the Network Load Balancing Manager open on SYD-DC and that you are connected to the NLB cluster nlb.contoso.com, which you created in Exercise 3.

2. Click Nlb.contoso.com (10.10.10.150). On the Cluster menu, click Delete.

3. On the Network Load Balancing Manager dialog box, shown in Figure 7-30, click Yes.

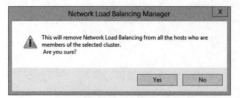

FIGURE 7-30 The NLB Manager Warning dialog box

4. After the cluster has been removed, verify that the Network Load Balancing console shows no cluster present and then close the console.

5. In the Windows PowerShell window, type the following command and press Enter to remove the Network Load Balancing feature from ADL-DC, MEL-DC, and CBR-DC:

```
Invoke-Command –Computername ADL-DC, CBR-DC, MEL-DC –Scriptblock {Remove-
WindowsFeature NLB}
```

6. In the Windows PowerShell window, type the following command and press Enter to restart ADL-DC, MEL-DC, and CBR-DC:

```
Invoke-Command –Computername ADL-DC, CBR-DC, MEL-DC –Scriptblock {restart-
computer}
```

7. After the computers restart, in the Windows PowerShell window, type the following command and press Enter to verify that the NLB feature has been removed from these computers as shown in Figure 7-31:

```
Invoke-Command –Computername ADL-DC, CBR-DC, MEL-DC –Scriptblock {Get-
WindowsFeature NLB} | Out-GridView
```

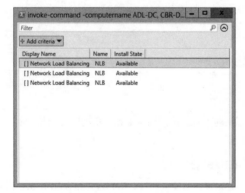

FIGURE 7-31 Network Load Balancing installed

Exercise 6: Create shared storage for failover clustering

In this exercise, you create shared storage on SYD-DC to be used with failover clustering. To complete this exercise, perform the following steps:

1. On SYD-DC, ensure that you are signed in as contoso\don_funk with the password **Pa$$w0rd**.

2. If one is not open already, open a Windows PowerShell window by clicking the Windows PowerShell icon on the taskbar.

3. Type the following command to create a folder to host the virtual disks that will be used for shared storage by the failover cluster you will create in a later exercise:

   ```
   Mkdir c:\shared-disks
   ```

4. Type the following command to install the iSCSI target server role service:

   ```
   Start-Process PowerShell –verb RunAs {Install-WindowsFeature FS-iSCSITarget-
   Server}
   ```

5. In the User Account Control dialog box, click Yes.

6. Type the following command and press Enter to create the first shared storage virtual iSCSI volume:

   ```
   New-iSCSIVirtualDisk –Path "C:\shared-disks\disk-one.vhd" –Size 10GB
   ```

7. Type the following command and press Enter to create the second shared storage virtual iSCSI volume:

   ```
   New-iSCSIVirtualDisk –Path "C:\shared-disks\disk-two.vhd" –Size 10GB
   ```

8. Type the following command and press Enter to create the iSCSI target that you will use to allow access to these iSCSI virtual disks:

   ```
   New-IscsiServerTarget –TargetName "CLUSTER-TGT" –InitiatorIDs DNSName:MEL-DC.
   contoso.com,DNSName:ADL-DC.contoso.com,DNSName:CBR-DC.contoso.com
   ```

9. In the Server Manager console, click File And Storage Services and then click the iSCSI node.

10. Right-click C:\shared-disks\disk-one.vhd and click Assign iSCSI Virtual Disk.

11. On the Assign iSCSI Target page of the Assign iSCSI Virtual Disk Wizard, ensure that CLUSTER-TGT is selected as shown in Figure 7-32. Click Next, click Assign, and click Close.

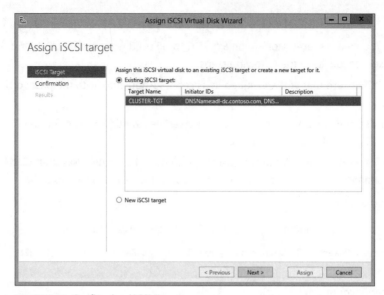

FIGURE 7-32 Configuring iSCSI Target

12. Right-click C:\shared-disks\disk-two.vhd and click Assign iSCSI Virtual Disk.

13. On the Assign iSCSI Target page of the Assign iSCSI Virtual Disk Wizard, ensure that CLUSTER-TGT is selected, click Next, click Assign, and then click Close.

14. Verify that the two iSCSI Virtual Disks appear as shown in Figure 7-33.

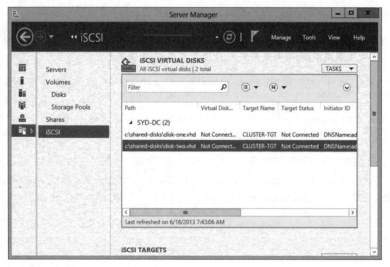

FIGURE 7-33 The iSCSI virtual disks

Exercise 7: Connect potential cluster nodes to shared storage

In this exercise, you start and configure the iSCSI initiator service on MEL-DC, ADL-DC, and CBR-DC. To complete this exercise, perform the following steps:

1. On SYD-DC, ensure that you are signed in as contoso\don_funk with the password **Pa$$w0rd**.

2. If one is not open already, open a Windows PowerShell window by clicking the Windows PowerShell icon on the taskbar.

3. Type the following command and press Enter to set the iSCSI initiator service to use the Automatic startup type:

   ```
   Invoke-Command –Computername ADL-DC, CBR-DC, MEL-DC –Scriptblock {Set-Service
   MSiSCSI –startuptype "Automatic"}
   ```

4. Type the following command and press Enter to start the iSCSI initiator service on ADL-DC, CBR-DC, and MEL-DC:

   ```
   Invoke-Command –Computername ADL-DC, CBR-DC, MEL-DC –Scriptblock {Start-Service
   MSiSCSI}
   ```

5. Type the following command and press Enter to verify that the iSCSI initiator service on ADL-DC, CBR-DC, and MEL-DC is running as shown in Figure 7-34:

   ```
   Invoke-Command –Computername ADL-DC, CBR-DC, MEL-DC –Scriptblock {Get-Service
   MSiSCSI} | Out-GridView
   ```

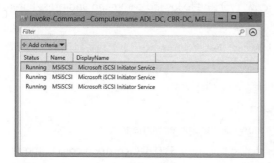

FIGURE 7-34 Verifying service status

6. Sign on to ADL-DC as contoso\don_funk.

7. Click iSCSI Initiator on the Tools menu of the Server Management console.

8. On the iSCSI Initiator Properties dialog, type **SYD-DC.contoso.com** in the Target text box, click Quick Connect, and click Done. Verify that the iSCSI Initiator Properties dialog box matches Figure 7-35 and click OK.

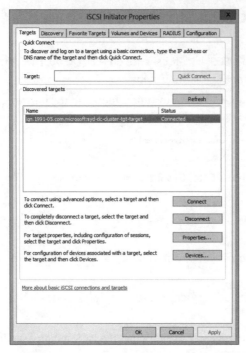

FIGURE 7-35 The iSCSI Initiator Properties dialog box

9. Click the Windows PowerShell icon on the taskbar.

10. In the Windows PowerShell window, type the following command and press Enter to set the default gateway for ADL-DC as 10.10.10.1:

```
Start-Process PowerShell —verb RunAs {Netsh interface ipv4 set address "Ethernet"
static 10.10.10.20 255.0.0.0 10.10.10.1}
```

11. On the User Account Control dialog box, click Yes.

12. Sign on to MEL-DC as contoso\don_funk.

13. Click iSCSI Initiator on the Tools menu of the Server Management console.

14. On the iSCSI Initiator Properties dialog box, type **SYD-DC.contoso.com** in the Target text box and click Quick Connect. Click Done, and click OK.

15. Click the Windows PowerShell icon on the taskbar.

16. In the Windows PowerShell window, type the following command and press Enter to set the default gateway for MEL-DC as 10.10.10.1:

```
Start-Process PowerShell —verb RunAs {Netsh interface ipv4 set address "Ethernet"
static 10.10.10.40 255.0.0.0 10.10.10.1}
```

17. On the User Account Control dialog box, click Yes.

18. Sign on to CBR-DC as contoso\don_funk.

19. Click iSCSI Initiator on the Tools menu of the Server Management console.

20. On the iSCSI Initiator Properties dialog box, type **SYD-DC.contoso.com** in the Target text box and click Quick Connect. Click Done and click OK.

21. Click the Windows PowerShell icon on the taskbar.

22. In the Windows PowerShell window, type the following command and press Enter to set the default gateway for CBR-DC as 10.10.10.1:

```
Start-Process PowerShell -verb RunAs {Netsh interface ipv4 set address "Ethernet"
static 10.10.10.30 255.0.0.0 10.10.10.1}
```

23. On the User Account Control dialog box, click Yes.

24. In the Server Manager console on CBR-DC, click the File And Storage Services node and then click the Disks node under Volumes as shown in Figure 7-36.

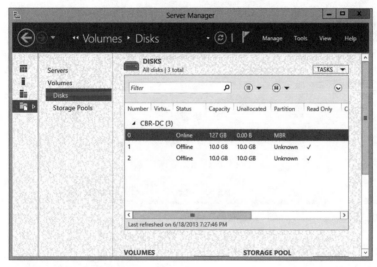

FIGURE 7-36 Available disks

25. Right-click Disk 1 and click Bring Online.

26. In the Bring Disk Online dialog box, click Yes.

27. Right-click Disk 2 and click Bring Online.

28. In the Bring Disk Online dialog box, click Yes.

29. Right-click Disk 1 and click Initialize.

30. In the Initialize Disk dialog box, shown in Figure 7-37, click Yes.

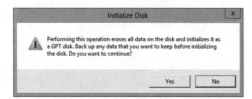

FIGURE 7-37 The Initialize Disk dialog box

31. Right-click Disk 2, and click Initialize.

32. In the Initialize Disk dialog box, click Yes.

33. Right-click Disk 1, and click New Volume.

34. On the Before You Begin page of the New Volume Wizard, click Next four times.

35. On the Select File System Settings page, type the volume label as **Shared-One** as shown in Figure 7-38. Click Next, click Create, and then click Close.

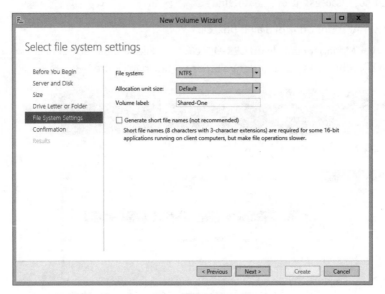

FIGURE 7-38 The settings for volume Shared-One

36. Right-click Disk 2 and click New Volume.

37. On the Before You Begin page of the New Volume Wizard, click Next four times.

38. On the Select File System Settings page, type the volume label as **Shared-Two** as shown in Figure 7-39. Click Next, click Create, and then click Close.

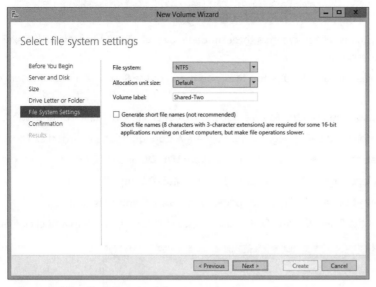

FIGURE 7-39 The file system settings

Exercise 8: Install failover cluster features

In this exercise, you install the failover cluster features and failover cluster management tools. To complete this exercise, perform the following steps:

1. On SYD-DC, ensure that you are signed in as contoso\don_funk with the password **Pa$$w0rd**.

2. If one is not open already, open a Windows PowerShell window by clicking the Windows PowerShell icon on the taskbar.

3. Type the following command and press Enter to install the Failover Clustering role on ADL-DC, CBR-DC, and MEL-DC:

   ```
   Invoke-Command -Computername ADL-DC, CBR-DC, MEL-DC -Scriptblock {Install-WindowsFeature Failover-Clustering}
   ```

4. Type the following command and press Enter to install the cluster administration tools on SYD-DC:

   ```
   Start-Process PowerShell -verb RunAs {Install-WindowsFeature RSAT-Clustering -IncludeAllSubFeature}
   ```

5. On the User Account Control dialog box, click Yes.

Exercise 9: Validate cluster configuration

In this exercise, you install and create a three-node failover cluster. To complete this exercise, perform the following steps:

1. Click Failover Cluster Manager on the Tools menu of the Server Manager console on SYD-DC.

2. On the Action menu of the Failover Cluster Manager, click Validate Configuration.

3. On the Before You Being page of the Validate A Configuration Wizard, click Next.

4. On the Select Servers Or A Cluster page, type **ADL-DC** and click Add.

5. On the Select Servers Or A Cluster page, type **MEL-DC** and click Add.

6. On the Select Servers Or A Cluster page, type **CBR-DC** and click Add.

7. Verify that the Select Servers Or A Cluster page matches Figure 7-40 and click Next.

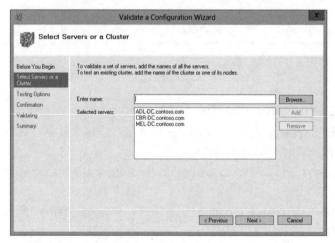

FIGURE 7-40 Potential cluster nodes

8. On the Testing Options page, ensure that Run All Tests (Recommended) is selected and click Next twice.

9. On the Summary page, ensure that warnings only exist in the Validate IP Configuration and Validate Network Communication categories as shown in Figure 7-41 (you might only get one of these warnings).

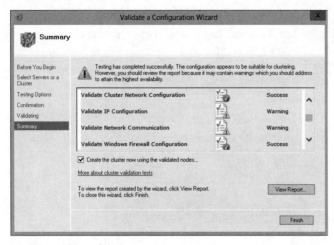

FIGURE 7-41 The validation summary

10. Ensure that Create The Cluster Now Using The Validated Nodes is not selected and click Finish.

Exercise 10: Create a two-node failover cluster

In this exercise, you create a two-node failover cluster. To complete this exercise, perform the following steps:

1. On the Action menu of the Failover Cluster Manager on SYD-DC, click Create Cluster.

2. On the Before You Begin page of the Create Cluster Wizard, click Next.

3. On the Select Servers page, type **ADL-DC** and click Add.

4. On the Select Servers page, type **MEL-DC** and click Add.

5. Verify that the Select Servers page matches Figure 7-42 and click Next.

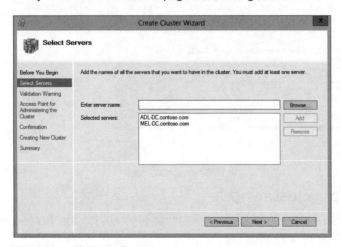

FIGURE 7-42: Cluster nodes

6. On the Validation Warning page, click No, and then click Next.

7. On the Access Point For Administering The Cluster page, type the cluster name as **failover**. Type the IP address as **10.10.10.200** as shown in Figure 7-43 and click Next.

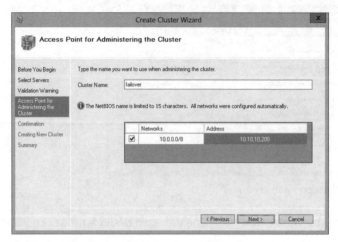

FIGURE 7-43 The access point

8. On the Confirmation page, ensure that Add All Eligible Storage To The Cluster is selected and click Next.

9. On the Summary page, shown in Figure 7-44, click Finish.

FIGURE 7-44 The summary of the Create Cluster Wizard

Exercise 11: Add a cluster node

In this exercise, you add an additional node to the cluster failover.contoso.com. To complete this exercise, perform the following steps:

1. In the Failover Cluster Manager on SYD-DC, select failover.contoso.com and then review the summary information. Verify that the cluster Quorum Configuration is set to Node And Disk Majority (Cluster Disk 1) as shown in Figure 7-45.

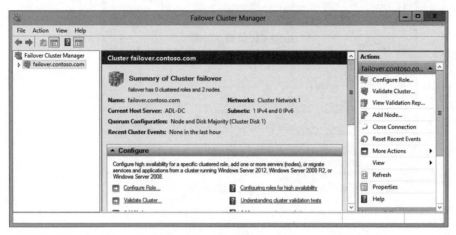

FIGURE 7-45 Cluster quorum configuration

2. In the Actions pane of the Failover Cluster Manager console, click Add Node.

3. On the Before You Begin page of the Add Node Wizard, click Next.

4. On the Select Servers page, type **CBR-DC** and click Add as shown in Figure 7-46. Click Next twice.

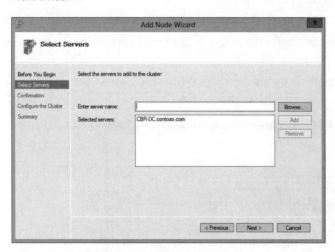

FIGURE 7-46 Adding a cluster node

5. Verify that the node CBR-DC.contoso.com has been added and review the warning about the disk witness shown in Figure 7-47. Click Finish.

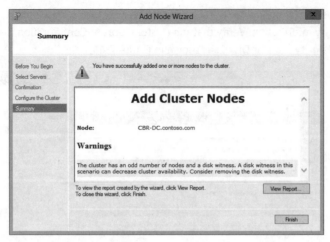

FIGURE 7-47 The Summary page of the Add Node Wizard

Exercise 12: Change the quorum configuration

In this exercise, you change the quorum configuration by removing the disk witness as recommended when you added the third cluster node in Exercise 11. To complete this exercise, perform the following steps:

1. In the Failover Cluster Manager, click More Actions in the Actions pane and then click Configure Cluster Quorum Settings.

2. On the Before You Begin page of the Configure Cluster Quorum Wizard, click Next.

3. On the Select Quorum Configuration Option page, click Add Or Change The Quorum Witness and click Next.

4. On the Select Quorum Witness page, click Do Not Configure A Quorum Witness as shown in Figure 7-48 and click Next twice. Click Finish.

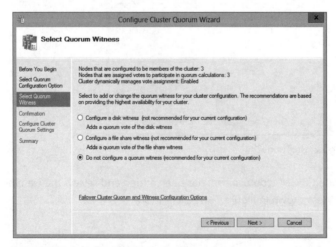

FIGURE 7-48 Selecting the quorum witness

5. Verify that the cluster is set to the Node Majority Quorum Configuration as shown in Figure 7-49.

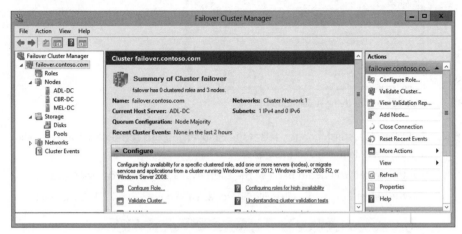

FIGURE 7-49 The Failover Cluster Manager

Exercise 13: Install and configure a highly available file server

In this exercise, you configure the three-node cluster as a highly available file server. To complete this exercise, perform the following steps:

1. Make sure you're signed on to SYD-DC as contoso\don_funk. If one is not already open, open a Windows PowerShell window by clicking the Windows PowerShell icon on the taskbar.

2. Type the following command and press Enter to install the File Server role on MEL-DC, ADL-DC, and CBR-DC:

```
Invoke-Command –Computername ADL-DC, CBR-DC, MEL-DC –Scriptblock {Install-
WindowsFeature FS-FileServer}
```

3. Verify that the File Server role has been installed on ADL-DC, CBR-DC, and MEL-DC by running the following command as shown in Figure 7-50.

```
Invoke-Command –Computername ADL-DC, CBR-DC, MEL-DC –Scriptblock {Get-
WindowsFeature FS-FileServer} | Out-GridView
```

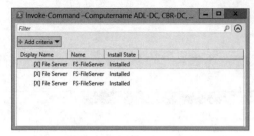

FIGURE 7-50 Verifying installation of role

4. In Failover Cluster Manager, select the Failover.contoso.com\Roles node and click Configure Role in the Actions pane.

5. On the Before You Begin page of the High Availability Wizard, click Next.

6. On the Select Role page, click File Server as shown in Figure 7-51. Click Next.

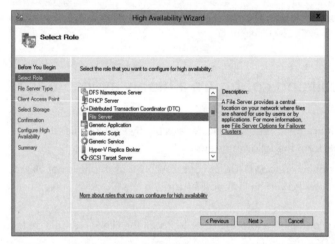

FIGURE 7-51 The Select Role page of the High Availability Wizard

7. On the File Server Type page, ensure that File Server For General Use is selected and click Next.

8. On the Client Access Point page, type the name **FS-Cluster** and type the IP address **10.10.10.220** as shown in Figure 7-52. Click Next.

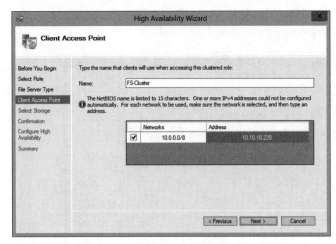

FIGURE 7-52 Specifying the client access point

9. On the Select Storage page, select Cluster Disk 2 as shown in Figure 7-53 and click Next twice. Click Finish.

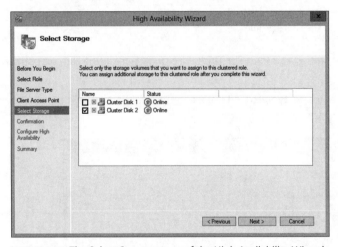

FIGURE 7-53 The Select Storage page of the High Availability Wizard

Exercise 14: Configure a highly available file share

In this exercise, you configure a file share on the highly available file server you deployed in the previous exercise. To complete this exercise, perform the following steps:

1. In the Failover Cluster Manager on SYD-DC, right-click Failover.contoso.com and click Refresh.

2. Click the Roles node, and then click FS-Cluster.

3. In the Actions pane, click Add File Share.

4. On the Select The Profile For This Share page of the New Share Wizard, click SMB Share – Quick as shown in Figure 7-54 and then click Next.

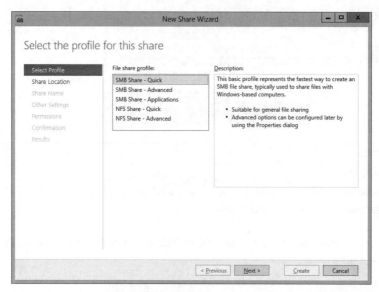

FIGURE 7-54 Selecting the share profile

5. On the Select The Server And Path For This Share page, accept the default path and click Next.

6. On the Share Name page, type **HA-FileShare** in the Share Name text box as shown in Figure 7-55, and click Next.

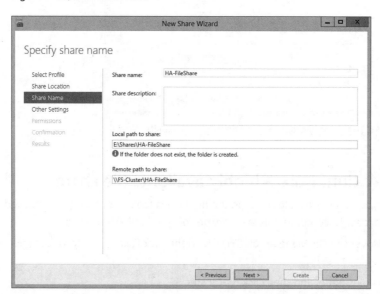

FIGURE 7-55 Specifying the share name

7. On the Configure Share Settings page, select the following options as shown in Figure 7-56 and click Next:

- Enable Access-Based Enumeration
- Enable Continuous Availability
- Allow Caching Of Share

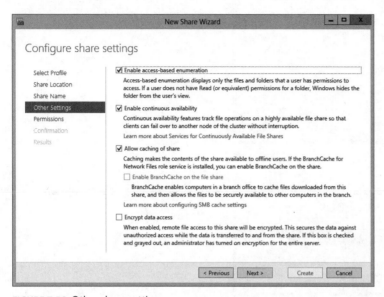

FIGURE 7-56 Other share settings

8. On the Specify Permissions To Control Access page, review the default permissions and click Next. Click Create, and click Close.

Exercise 15: Configure failover settings, failback settings, and move node

In this exercise, you configure failover and failback settings for the highly available file server. To complete this exercise, perform the following steps:

1. In the Failover Cluster Manager console on SYD-DC, expand the Failover.contoso.com node, click Roles, click FS-Cluster, and then click Properties in the Actions pane.

2. On the General tab of the FS-Cluster Properties dialog box, configure MEL-DC as the most Preferred Owner and CBR-DC as the least preferred owner as shown in Figure 7-57. Click Apply.

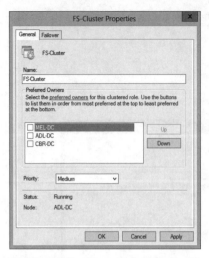

FIGURE 7-57 Configure preferred owners

3. On the Failover tab, click Allow Failback and select the Immediately option as shown in Figure 7-58. Click OK.

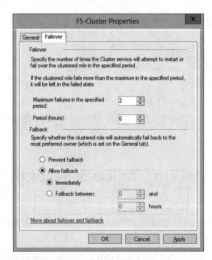

FIGURE 7-58 Configure failover settings

4. On the Actions pane, click Move, and then click Select Node.

5. On the Move Clustered Role dialog box, click MEL-DC as shown in Figure 7-59. Click OK.

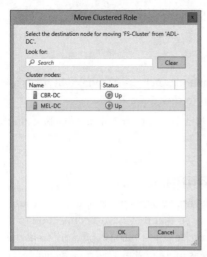

FIGURE 7-59 The Move Clustered Role dialog box

6. When the Roles node is selected, verify that the Owner Node is set to MEL-DC as shown in Figure 7-60.

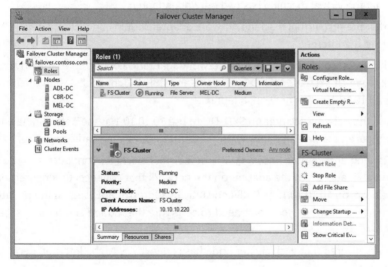

FIGURE 7-60 Cluster roles

Exercise 16: Simulate unplanned failure

In this exercise, you simulate unplanned failure of one of the cluster nodes by restarting MEL-DC, which currently hosts the File Server role. You also verify that the workload returns to the preferred node when the node restarts. To complete this exercise, perform the following steps:

1. On SYD-DC, switch to the Windows PowerShell window and type the following command to restart MEL-DC:

```
Restart-computer -computername MEL-DC -force
```

2. Switch back to the Failover Cluster manager and watch the changes that occur as computer MEL-DC restarts. You might need to click Refresh.

3. Verify that the cluster workload returns to MEL-DC when the virtual machine finishes rebooting.

Exercise 17: Cluster-Aware Updating

In this exercise, you configure Cluster-Aware Updating. This exercise is optional because to perform it you need to set up your virtual machines so that they have a connection to the Internet. Depending on when you perform the exercise, there will also be a different number of updates that apply to each of the cluster nodes as more updates become available. Finally, remember that downloading a substantial number of update files might incur charges from your Internet Service Provider (ISP). To prepare your lab for this exercise, do the following:

1. Install a new virtual machine running Windows Server 2012 R2.

2. Ensure that the virtual machine has two network adapters.

3. Ensure that the first virtual machine network adapter should connect to a network that connects to the Internet.

4. Verify that the second virtual machine network adapter is connected to the private network to which SYD-DC, MEL-DC, ADL-DC, and CBR-DC connect. Assign the IP address 10.10.10.1 to this network adapter.

5. Configure the network adapter on SYD-DC to use 10.10.10.1 as the default gateway (you configured the default gateway on the cluster nodes in an earlier exercise).

6. Install Routing and Remote Access on the new virtual machine. Configure it to use NAT to share the IP address of the adapter on the network that connects to the Internet with the hosts on 10.10.10.1. As DNS and static IP addresses are used on the private virtual machine network, you don't need to configure the routing and remote access server.

After you have ensured that each cluster node has connectivity to the Internet, perform the following steps:

1. Ensure that you are signed on to SYD-DC as contoso\don_funk.

2. If a Windows PowerShell window is not already open, click the Windows PowerShell icon on the taskbar.

3. In the Windows PowerShell window, type the following command and press Enter to install failover clustering management components on each of the cluster nodes:

```
Invoke-Command -Computername ADL-DC, CBR-DC, MEL-DC -Scriptblock {Add-
WindowsFeature RSAT-Clustering}
```

4. Click Cluster-Aware Updating on the Tools menu of the Server Manager console.

5. In the Cluster-Aware Updating dialog box, type **failover** and click Connect as shown in Figure 7-61.

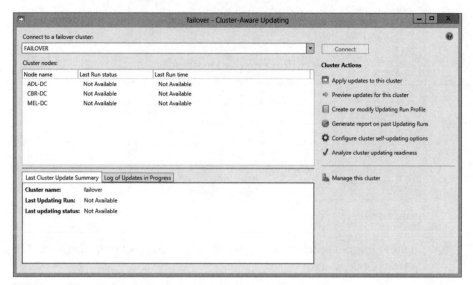

FIGURE 7-61 Viewing the cluster

6. On the Failover – Cluster-Aware Updating dialog box, click Preview Updates For This Cluster.

7. On the Failover – Preview Updates dialog box, shown in Figure 7-62, click Generate Update Preview List. The amount of time this check takes is dependent on available bandwidth.

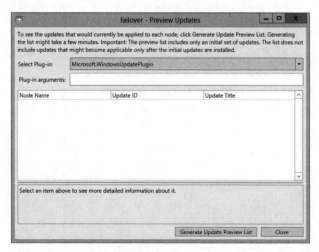

FIGURE 7-62 Previewing the updates

8. Review the list of updates as shown in Figure 7-63 and click Close.

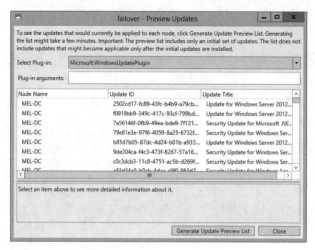

FIGURE 7-63 Available updates

9. On the Failover - Cluster-Aware Updating dialog box, click Configure Cluster Self-Updating Options.

10. On the Getting Started page of the Failover - Configure Self-Updating Options Wizard, click Next.

11. On the Add CAU Clustered Role With Self-Updating Enabled page, select Add The CAU Clustered Role, With Self-Updating Mode Enabled, To This Cluster as shown in Figure 7-64 and click Next.

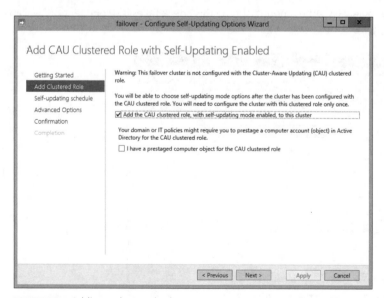

FIGURE 7-64 Adding a clustered role

12. On the Specify Self-Updating Schedule page, select Weekly as shown in Figure 7-65 and click Next.

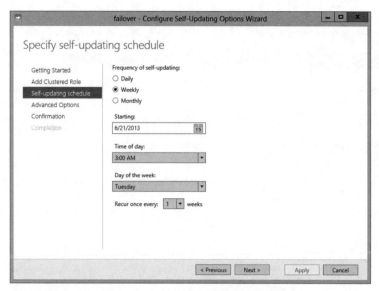

FIGURE 7-65 Configuring the Cluster-Aware Updating schedule

13. On the Advanced Options page, set the MaxRetriesPerNode value to 5 and the RequireAllNodesOnline value to True as shown in Figure 7-66. Click Next twice, click Apply, and then click Close.

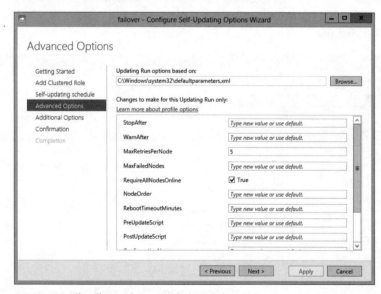

FIGURE 7-66 The Cluster-Aware Updating options

14. On the Cluster Aware Updating dialog box, click Apply Updates To This Cluster.

15. On the Getting Started page of the Cluster-Aware Updating Wizard, click Next three times.

16. On the Confirmation page, shown in Figure 6-67, click Update, and click Close.

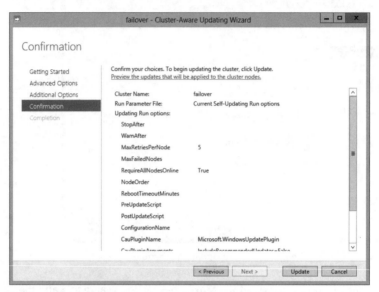

FIGURE 7-67 Confirmation in the Cluster-Aware Updating Wizard

17. Use the Cluster-Aware Updating console to monitor the Cluster-Aware Updating process, noting that each node is updated separately and then brought back online as shown in Figure 7-68.

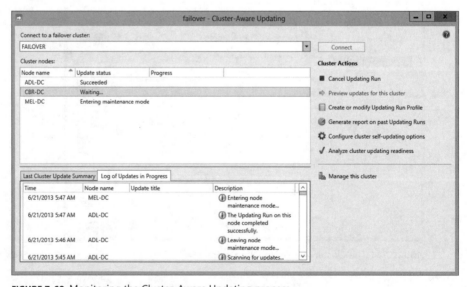

FIGURE 7-68 Monitoring the Cluster-Aware Updating process

Suggested practice exercises

The following additional practice exercises are designed to give you more opportunities to practice what you've learned and to help you successfully master the lessons presented in this chapter.

- **Exercise 1**   Remove node CBR-DC from the failover cluster.
- **Exercise 2**   After removing CBR-DC, re-create a disk witness on the failover cluster and reconfigure the quorum mode to support the new configuration.
- **Exercise 3**   Create an additional highly available file share on the failover cluster.

Answers

This section contains the answers to the lesson review questions in this chapter.

Lesson 1

1. **Correct answers**: B and D

   A. **Incorrect**. You should use a witness disk when a cluster has an even number of nodes. Clusters that have an odd number of nodes don't need a witness disk and use the node majority quorum mode.

   B. **Correct**. You should use a witness disk when a cluster has an even number of nodes. This enables you to use the node and disk majority quorum mode.

   C. **Incorrect**. You should use a witness disk when a cluster has an even number of nodes. Clusters that have an odd number of nodes don't need a witness disk and use the node majority quorum mode.

   D. **Correct**. You should use a witness disk when a cluster has an even number of nodes. This enables you to use the node and disk majority quorum mode.

2. **Correct answer**: B and D

   A. **Incorrect**. Node majority is suited to clusters with odd numbers of nodes.

   B. **Correct**. Node majority is suited to clusters with odd numbers of nodes.

   C. **Incorrect**. Node majority is suited to clusters with odd numbers of nodes.

   D. **Correct**. Node majority is suited to clusters with odd numbers of nodes.

3. **Correct answers**: B and C

   A. **Incorrect**. The node majority quorum mode is unsuitable for clusters with even numbers of nodes and does not use a witness.

   B. **Correct**. You can use this quorum mode with an even number of nodes. If the witness fails, this cluster remains operational.

   C. **Correct.** You can use this quorum mode with an even number of nodes. If the witness fails, this cluster remains operational.

   D. **Incorrect.** This quorum mode does not allow the cluster to remain operational if the witness fails.

4. **Correct answer**: A and B

   A. **Correct**. You need to configure a preferred owner and to configure failback to ensure that the workload returns to the node designated the preferred owner.

   B. **Correct.** You need to configure a preferred owner and to configure failback to ensure that the workload returns to the node designated the preferred owner.

   C. **Incorrect**. Quorum mode determines the number of nodes that must remain operational; it does not control which node is the preferred owner of a workload.

D. **Incorrect.** Cluster-Aware Updating enables you to manage the application of software updates to failover clusters.

5. **Correct answer**: B

A. **Incorrect**. Network Load Balancing is a high availability technology and cannot be used to apply updates to failover clusters.

B. **Correct**. Cluster-Aware Updating enables you to manage the process of applying software updates to clusters, including running an update cycle against each node in succession while ensuring that nodes are in maintenance mode and that workloads have been transferred to other nodes in the cluster.

C. **Incorrect**. Although you can use Windows Server Update Services (WSUS) to approve and deny updates, you can't use WSUS to manage the process of updating failover clusters.

D. **Incorrect**. You can't use Windows Intune to manage the process of applying software updates to failover clusters.

Lesson 2

1. **Correct answer**: B

A. **Incorrect**. Stopping a node drops all current sessions.

B. **Correct**. Using drainstop allows existing sessions to continue while blocking the establishment of new sessions.

C. **Incorrect**. Pausing a node drops all current sessions.

D. **Incorrect**. You use Start to start a stopped node.

2. **Correct answer**: C

A. **Incorrect**. Single host, no affinity is used when you want traffic from a particular port to always go to a specific host and not be shared with the NLB cluster nodes.

B. **Incorrect**. Multiple host, no affinity means that subsequent traffic can go to any host in the cluster.

C. **Correct**. When multiple host, single affinity is configured for a rule, subsequent traffic from a client will be directed to the node that was sent the initial traffic.

D. **Incorrect**. When this option is set, the traffic is dropped.

3. **Correct answer**: A

A. **Correct**. When this option is set, the traffic is dropped.

B. **Incorrect.** When multiple host, single affinity is configured for a rule, subsequent traffic from a client will be directed to the node that was sent the initial traffic.

C. **Incorrect**. Multiple host, no affinity means that subsequent traffic can go to any host in the cluster.

D. **Incorrect**. Single host, no affinity is used when you want traffic from a particular port to always go to a specific host and not be shared with the NLB cluster nodes.

4. **Correct answer**: D

   A. **Incorrect**. Multiple host, no affinity means that subsequent traffic can go to any host in the cluster.

   B. **Incorrect**. When multiple host, single affinity is configured for a rule, subsequent traffic from a client will be directed to the node that was sent the initial traffic.

   C. **Incorrect**. When this option is set, the traffic is dropped.

   D. **Correct**. Single host, no affinity is used when you want traffic from a particular port to always go to a specific host and not be shared with the NLB cluster nodes.

5. **Correct answer**: A, B and D

   A. **Correct.** You should select a multicast mode. You would be unable to manage the cluster hosts from a remote subnet if unicast was selected as the nodes only have a single network adapter.

   B. **Correct.** You should select a multicast mode. You would be unable to manage the cluster hosts from a remote subnet if unicast was selected. Teamed network adapters function as a single network adapter.

   C. **Incorrect**. As the nodes have multiple network adapters, you can use the unicast cluster mode and still manage both the cluster and cluster nodes from remote subnets.

   D. **Correct**. You should select a multicast mode. You would be unable to manage the cluster hosts from a remote subnet if unicast was selected as the nodes only have a single network adapter.

CHAPTER 8

Virtual machine and site resilience

Site resilience enables you to ensure that your organization's access to important virtual servers continue in the event that a critical site goes offline unexpectedly. As virtual servers are data, moving a virtual machine from an offline site to one that is accessible is a lot simpler than putting hardware on a truck and driving it to a new datacenter. You can move servers between sites by transferring the data that constitutes the servers between sites. This lesson explains different techniques to move virtual machines from one Hyper-V server to another, whether it is a node in the same cluster, another Hyper-V server in the same site, or to a Hyper-V server hosting a replica in another country or on another continent.

Lessons in this chapter:

- Lesson 1: Virtual machine movement
- Lesson 2: Site-level fault tolerance

Before you begin

Unlike other practices in this book, moving virtual machines between computers running Windows Server 2012 R2 requires more than one host computer running Windows Server 2012 R2. The instructions at the beginning of the practice exercise describe how you can build servers that make it possible for you to configure virtual machine movement and replication.

Lesson 1: Virtual machine movement

Even when you've planned its placement well, at some point in a virtual machine's operational lifespan, you might need to move it from its original Hyper-V host to a new Hyper-V host. If the virtual machine is providing critical services to the network, you need to move the virtual machine in a manner that doesn't affect the clients that are interacting with it. This lesson describes two technologies that you can use to move virtual machines between Hyper-V nodes. The first involves placing the virtual machine on a Hyper-V failover cluster and accomplishing virtual machine movement by transferring the virtual machine between nodes. The second involves using Shared Nothing Hyper-V Live Migration, a technology new to Windows Server 2012 and improved in Windows Server 2012 R2. The lesson also explains how you can move virtual machines by exporting them and importing them.

> **After this lesson, you will be able to:**
> - Deploy virtual machines on failover clusters
> - Configure Shared Nothing Hyper-V live migration
> - Manage storage migration
> - Understand virtual machine import and export
>
> **Estimated lesson time: 45 minutes**

Virtual machine failover clustering

One of the most common uses for failover clusters is hosting virtual machines. By deploying a workload, such as SQL Server or Exchange on a highly available virtual machine, you can achieve high availability without the application needing to be aware that it is now highly available. The virtual machine functions normally, providing services to clients on the network, and switches between cluster nodes as necessary in the event that the individual cluster node hosting it requires maintenance or experiences some sort of failure. Building a Hyper-V failover cluster involves first creating a failover cluster and then adding the Hyper-V role to each node of the cluster.

You should use *Cluster Shared Volumes* (CSVs) to store virtual machines on a Hyper-V cluster. CSVs allow multiple cluster nodes to manage a single shared storage device. This enables you to put multiple virtual machines on the same-shared storage device but have those virtual machines hosted by different nodes in the failover cluster. Cluster Shared Volumes are mapped under the C:\ClusterStorage folder on cluster nodes as shown in Figure 8-1.

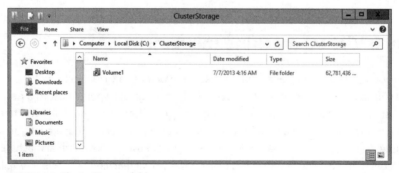

FIGURE 8-1 ClusterStorage folder

When creating a new virtual machine on a failover cluster, you first select which cluster node will host the virtual machine. Figure 8-2 shows the choice between node MEL-HV-1 and MEL-HV-2 when creating a new virtual machine.

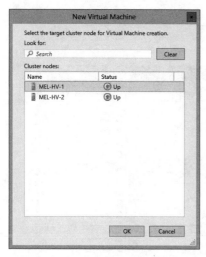

FIGURE 8-2 The New Virtual Machine dialog box

When creating a highly available virtual machine, you specify the Cluster Shared Volume path as the location to store the virtual machine, as shown in Figure 8-3. If you have an existing machine that you want to make highly available, you can move the virtual machine to this path. As an alternative, you also have the option of specifying a Server Message Block (SMB) 3.0 file share as the place to store the highly available virtual machine. The selection of a CSV or an SMB 3.0 file share depends on your organization's storage configuration.

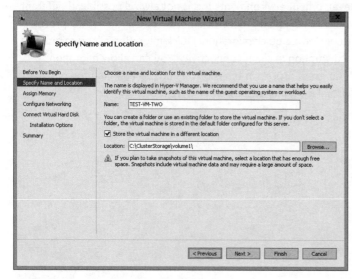

FIGURE 8-3 The New Virtual Machine Wizard

After the virtual machine is created, you can control it using the Failover Cluster Manager console. The move option in the Actions pane enables you to select the cluster node to move the virtual machine to. Figure 8-4 shows a virtual machine named TEST-VM-TWO on the node MEL-HV-2.

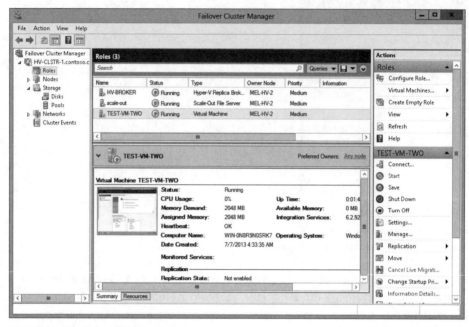

FIGURE 8-4 The Failover Cluster Manager

In production environments you should ensure that each Hyper-V host has an identical hardware configuration. In development environments this is not always possible. If different processor types are used, for example an Intel processor on one node and an AMD processor on another, you might have to perform a quick migration. Quick migration allows migration between nodes, but there is a disruption in client connectivity. You can allow migration between Hyper-V nodes with different processor types or versions by enabling the processor compatibility setting on the virtual machine, as shown in Figure 8-5.

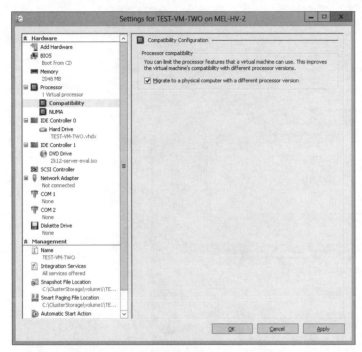

FIGURE 8-5 Processor Compatibility settings

MORE INFO   VIRTUAL MACHINE MIGRATION

To learn more about virtual machine migration, consult the following article:
http://technet.microsoft.com/en-us/library/hh831435.aspx.

Shared Nothing Hyper-V live migration

Hyper-V *live migration* enables you to migrate a virtual machine running on one Hyper-V host to another Hyper-V host without the virtual machine experiencing downtime and without requiring the use of shared storage. You can use Hyper-V live migration to move a virtual machine from one Hyper-V failover cluster to another.

When configuring a computer running Hyper-V to support live migration, you must enable live migrations on the Live Migrations section of the Hyper-V Settings dialog box as shown in Figure 8-6. You must perform this step on both the source and destination Hyper-V servers. When configuring these settings, you must choose an authentication protocol, specify a maximum number of simultaneous live migrations and select which IP addresses can be used for live migration.

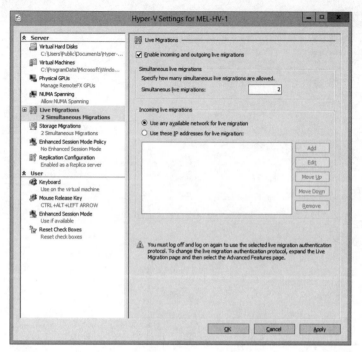

FIGURE 8-6 Enable live migrations

When configuring authentication for live migration you can choose between Credential Security Support Provider (CredSSP) or Kerberos authentication. CredSSP requires local sign on to both the source and destination servers to perform migration. Kerberos enables you to trigger live migration from a remote server, but if you choose Kerberos for live migration authentication, you need to configure constrained delegation for the cifs and Microsoft Virtual System Migration Service services on the computer accounts of the computers that host the Hyper-V role. For example, if you want to be able to perform shared nothing live migration between HV-1 and HV-2, you have to configure delegation for HV-2 for these services on HV-1 and configure delegation for these services on HV-2 for HV-1. Figure 8-7 shows the computer account of MEL-HV-1 configured so that the necessary services are delegated for use by MEL-HV-2.

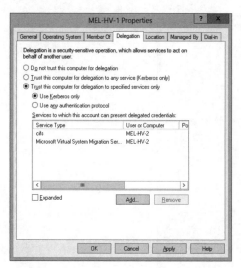

FIGURE 8-7 Configuring delegation

MORE INFO **VIRTUAL MACHINE LIVE MIGRATION**

To learn more about live migration, consult the following article:
http://technet.microsoft.com/en-us/library/jj134199.aspx.

To trigger the shared nothing live migration after you've configured the source and destination servers running Hyper-V, right-click the virtual machines that you want to migrate and select Move The Virtual Machine as shown in Figure 8-8. You then specify the address of the remote server and any additional move options, such as whether you want to move all data to a single location on the destination computer or to multiple locations on the destination computer. You can also indicate that you want to move the storage to a shared storage location.

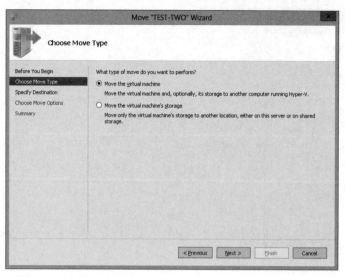

FIGURE 8-8 Choosing the move type

Storage migration

Storage migration enables you to move the virtual machine's storage from one location to another. This includes the virtual hard disk files, configuration files, checkpoint files, and smart paging files. *Checkpoints* are the new term for the virtual machine snapshot technology available in prior versions of Hyper-V. During storage migration, you can move all of this data to one location, or you can move it to many locations as shown in Figure 8-9. For example, you might want to move data from one volume to another, from one directory to another, to a shared storage device, or a shared folder hosted on a computer running Windows Server 2012 or Windows Server 2012 R2. You can perform storage migration while the virtual machine is online.

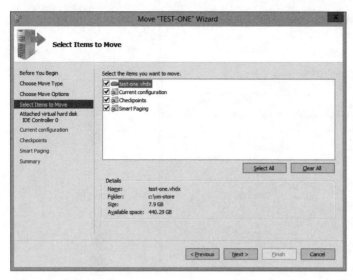

FIGURE 8-9 Selecting items to move

Unlike Hyper-V live migration, which requires you configure the appropriate delegations on the computer accounts, storage migration is simply about moving virtual machine files from one location to another. As long as the storage is accessible to the Hyper-V host, you can use it as a destination during a move operation. For example, in an extreme case, you might attach a temporary universal serial bus (USB 3.0) hard disk drive to a server and move running virtual machines temporarily to this storage device while you modify the configuration of the storage device that normally hosts the virtual machines. When the configuration change is complete, you can then move the virtual machines back to the new storage device without interrupting client access to those virtual machines. To perform storage migration, select Move The Virtual Machine's Storage as shown in Figure 8-10 when you choose to move the virtual machine.

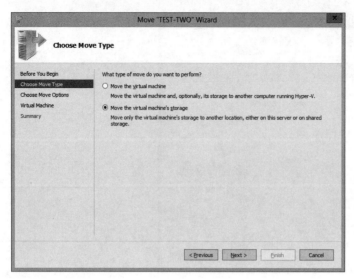

FIGURE 8-10 Moving the virtual machine's storage

When you choose to move the storage, you can consolidate the information in one location or move the virtual hard disk files, configuration files, checkpoint files, and smart paging files to separate locations. As Figure 8-11 shows, you can also choose to move only the virtual machine's hard disk files, keeping the configuration data in its current location.

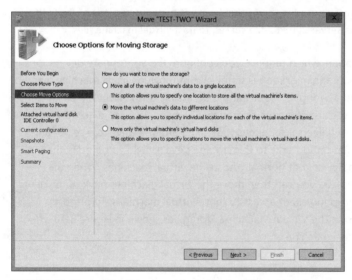

FIGURE 8-11 Moving the virtual machine's data to different locations

Virtual machine import and export

When you export a virtual machine, you can choose to export the virtual machine and all its checkpoints, or you can choose to export the virtual machine in the state of a specific checkpoint. When you export a virtual machine with all its checkpoints, the virtual machine is exported with multiple differencing disks that represent the virtual machine in each different checkpoint state. Windows Server 2012 R2 allows you to perform virtual machine export while the virtual machine is running. Windows Server 2012 only allows you to export a virtual machine that is in a shutdown state. When you import a virtual machine that was running at the time of export, the virtual machine is placed in a saved state. You can resume the virtual machine from this state.

When you import a virtual machine, you have three options as shown in Figure 8-12. You can choose Register The Virtual Machine In Place (Use The Existing Unique ID), Restore The Virtual Machine (Use The Existing Unique ID), or Copy The Virtual Machine (Create A New Unique ID). The differences between these are as follows:

- Registering the virtual machine enables you to import the virtual machine into Hyper-V while keeping the virtual machine files in the current location. This method does not generate a new virtual machine ID, so you need to ensure that the originally exported virtual machine is not present on the Hyper-V host that you are performing the import on. You can register a virtual machine in place and then use storage migration to move the virtual machine files at a later point in time.

- Restoring the virtual machine enables you to import the virtual machine into Hyper-V while moving the virtual machine files to a new location. For example, if you export a virtual machine to a removable disk, you import and restore the virtual machine to move the virtual machine off the removable disk to another location. Restoring uses the existing virtual machine ID, which means you need to ensure that the originally exported virtual machine is not present on the Hyper-V host that you are performing the import on.

- Copying the virtual machine enables you to create a separate clone of the virtual machine. All of the virtual machine files are copied to a new location, and you can go and use those source files to reimport the virtual machine again should you need to. When you copy, a new virtual machine ID is created. This allows copies to run alongside each other as each has a separate ID. It's a good idea to rename virtual machines when you run copies side by side. If you don't, they retain the original name and you might get confused as to which cloned virtual machine is which.

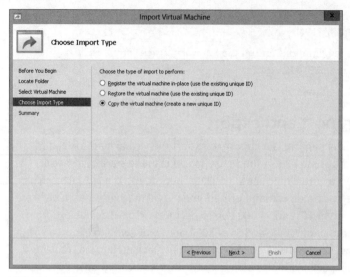

FIGURE 8-12 Choosing the import type

> **MORE INFO** **HYPER-V IMPORT/EXPORT**
>
> To learn more about Hyper-V import and export, consult the following article:
> *http://blogs.technet.com/b/virtualization/archive/2009/05/20/hyper-v-r2-import-export-part-1-the-case-for-new-import-export-functionality.aspx.*

Lesson summary

- Virtual machines hosted on failover clusters use shared storage to store virtual machine configuration and data files.
- Virtual machines hosted on failover clusters move between cluster nodes using live migration.
- Shared Nothing Hyper-V live migration enables you to move a running virtual machine from one Hyper-V server to another without using shared storage and with no disruption to the virtual machine's operation.
- Storage migration enables you to move a running virtual machine's storage to another location that is accessible to the host Hyper-V server.
- You can only export a virtual machine from a Hyper-V server running on the Windows Server 2012 operating system if the virtual machine is shut down.
- When importing a virtual machine, you can import in place using the existing virtual machine ID, import while moving the virtual machine storage, or create a copy of the virtual machine with a new ID. A server cannot host two virtual machines with the same ID.

Lesson review

Answer the following questions to test your knowledge of the information in this lesson. You can find the answers to these questions and explanations of each answer choice in the "Answers" section at the end of this chapter.

1. You have three running virtual machines that are hosted on your Windows Server 2012 R2 Hyper-V server's C: volume. You want to move these three running virtual machines to another storage location without shutting them down. Assuming enough space is available, which of the following volumes could you use as a destination when performing storage migration? (Choose all that apply.)

   A. File share hosted on a computer running Windows Server 2008 R2

   B. iSCSI connected virtual disk

   C. SSD disk connected through USB 3.0

   D. File Share hosted on a computer running Windows Server 2012 R2

2. You have an existing virtual machine named SYD-DB-VM that is hosted through Hyper-V on a computer running the Windows Server 2012 R2 operating system named SYD-HV-1. You want to create a duplicate SYD-DB-VM named SYD-DB-VM-A and also have it hosted on SYD-HV-1. Which of the following steps should you take to accomplish this goal? (Choose two, each answer forms part of a complete solution.)

   A. Export SYD-DB-VM

   B. Import SYD-DB-VM with the Register The Virtual Machine In-Place option

   C. Import SYD-DB-VM with the Restore The Virtual Machine option

   D. Import SYD-DB-VM with the Copy The Virtual Machine option

3. You arze going to use Kerberos as an authentication protocol for live migration. You are configuring delegation for the computer accounts of the Hyper-V hosts that will host the virtual machines that will participate in the live migration process. Which of the following services must you configure delegation for if you want to support moving virtual machine storage and the virtual machines? (Choose all that apply.)

   A. Dcom

   B. cifs

   C. Hyper-V Replica Service

   D. Microsoft Virtual System Migration Service

4. You are configuring a four-node Hyper-V failover cluster. You want to be able to move running Hyper-V virtual machines between any of the nodes as necessary. Which of the following storage devices should you select when configuring the virtual machines that will be hosted on this cluster? (Choose all that apply.)

   A. Cluster Shared Volume

   B. SMB 2.0 File Share

   C. SMB 3.0 File Share

   D. Distributed File System Share

Lesson 2: Site-level fault tolerance

Site-level fault tolerance involves ensuring that an organization has access to critical resources in the event that a site goes unexpectedly offline on a short-term or long-term basis. Hyper-V Replica provides organizations with a method of having critical virtual machines replicated to a second site, allowing both planned and unplanned failover with minimal data loss. Multisite clustering involves configuring a cluster so that the cluster retains quorum in the event that a site goes offline unexpectedly.

> **After this lesson, you will be able to:**
> - Configure and deploy Hyper-V Replica
> - Manage planned and unplanned failover
> - Deploy Hyper-V Replica Broker
> - Determine an appropriate multisite clustering configuration
>
> **Estimated lesson time: 45 minutes**

Hyper-V Replica

Hyper-V Replica makes it possible for a virtual machine to be replicated from one Hyper-V host to another. The computer running Hyper-V hosting the replica can be in the same room or on another continent. Replication is asynchronous and the replica copy is a consistent but lagged version of the original. Hyper-V Replica does not require access to shared storage or that computers be part of the same Active Directory domain. Figure 8-13 shows Hyper-V Replica configured so that the six virtual machines running on one Hyper-V host are replicated to another Hyper-V host.

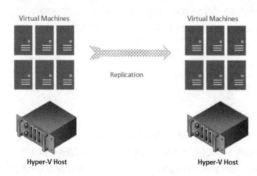

FIGURE 8-13 Hyper-V Replica

You can use Hyper-V Replica to provide site-level fault tolerance for your organization's virtual machines. For example, you could configure replication so that all of the production virtual machines at a primary site automatically replicate to your organization's disaster recovery (DR) site. In the event that a disaster occurred that destroyed the infrastructure at the primary site, you would be able to start up the virtual machines at the DR site. It's important to note that because replication is asynchronous, if failover to the DR site is unplanned then there will be some data loss. The data loss might only be a few seconds or a few minutes, but it's important to remember that the virtual machines at the DR site are lagged copies of the originals.

MORE INFO **HYPER-V REPLICA**

To learn more about Hyper-V replica, consult the following article:
http://blogs.technet.com/b/yungchou/archive/2013/01/10/hyper-v-replica-explained.aspx.

Configuring Hyper-V Replica

Prior to configuring replication for an individual virtual machine, you must perform the following steps on both the source and destination Hyper-V replica servers:

- **Enable replication** This makes it possible for the Hyper-V host to function as a replica server.

- **Choose the authentication method** You can use Kerberos or certificate-based authentication. Kerberos is appropriate if the source and destination servers are part of the same Active Directory environment. Certificate-based authentication is appropriate when the source and destination servers are not members of the same Active Directory environment.

- **Specify which authenticated servers replication can be performed from** The options are to allow replication from any server, or to only allow authentication from specific servers. When configuring server authorization, you also specify the location where replicated files are stored. You can do this on a per-server basis, or have all replicated data stored in a specific folder tree.

You configure these options on the Replication Configuration page of the Hyper-V Settings dialog box as shown in Figure 8-14.

FIGURE 8-14 Enabling this computer as a replica server

After you've configured the replica server to support a specific form of authentication, you also need to configure firewall rules to allow authentication and replica traffic. There are predefined firewall rules available in Windows Firewall with Advanced Security that you enable to support replication. Figure 8-15 shows the built-in firewall rule that you should enable when you use Kerberos authentication. The built-in firewall rule that you use when using certificate-based authentication allows traffic on port 443.

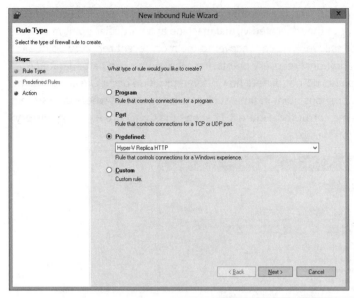

FIGURE 8-15 The Hyper-V Replica HTTP firewall rule

When you have configured the replica configuration and firewall rules on the source and destination servers, you can configure replication for an individual Hyper-V virtual machine. The first step is to select a server to host the replica. As shown in Figure 8-16, you need to specify an authentication type and whether replicated data will be compressed.

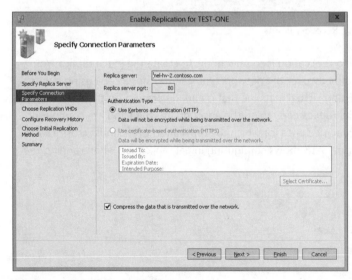

FIGURE 8-16 Specifying connection parameters

You specify which virtual hard disks will be replicated, the replication frequency (an option new to Windows Server 2012 R2 which allows you to configure replication to occur as frequently as every 30 seconds), and the number of recovery points that will be created. A *recovery point* is a checkpoint of the replicated virtual machine at a particular point in time. In the event of an unplanned failover, you can recover to the most recent recovery point, or you can choose one of the additional recovery points. Recovery points can be generated up to once an hour. Recovery points do not dictate how often replication occurs. Recovery points enable you to roll back to a previous point in time, such as prior to a point where data stored on the virtual machine became corrupted. Figure 8-17 shows the Configure Recovery History page of the Enable Replication Wizard.

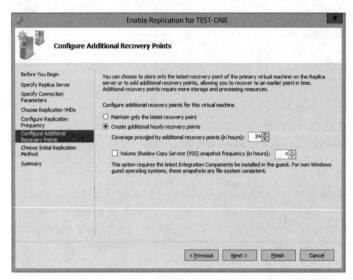

FIGURE 8-17 Configure Additional Recovery Points

The final step in configuring replication is to select how to create the initial replica. You can transfer replicated data directly over the network, you can transfer a copy using external media, or you can use an existing virtual machine that is already present on the replica server. Using media to seed the initial replica copy might be appropriate when you are configuring replication for very large virtual machines for which the replication traffic must cross a wide area network (WAN) link. Figure 8-18 shows configuring initial replication when running the Enable Replication Wizard.

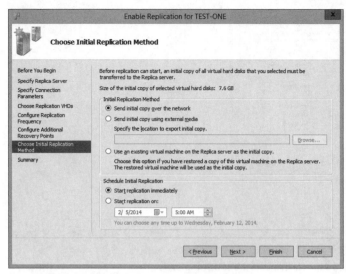

FIGURE 8-18 Choosing the initial replication method

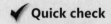
Planned failover

Planned failover involves moving a virtual machine configured for replication from its primary host to the replica server. To ensure that the virtual machine on the replica is up to date, the virtual machine being moved must be in a turned-off state. This is a substantial difference from Hyper-V live migration in which the virtual machine is able to move between hosts while continuing to respond to client requests.

When you perform planned failover, a set of prerequisite checks occur, including checking whether replication back from the replica server to the current primary is allowed. As Figure 8-19 shows, you can also configure planned failover so that the replica virtual machine is automatically started when the failover process completes and that reverse replication is also configured once failover has occurred. You can perform planned failover through the Hyper-V Manager console or by using the Start-VMFailover Windows PowerShell cmdlet.

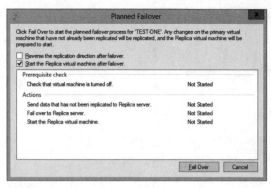

FIGURE 8-19 Planned failover

MORE INFO PLANNED FAILOVER

To learn more about planned failover consult the following article:
http://technet.microsoft.com/en-us/library/jj134194.aspx.

Unplanned failover

Unplanned failover occurs when the primary server has failed unexpectedly. During unplanned failover, you connect to the replica server and trigger failover manually. When you perform an unplanned failover, you need to specify a recovery point to use. You configure the number of available recovery points when initially configuring replication for a virtual machine. By default, when you perform unplanned failover the dialog box suggests the most recent recovery point. Figure 8-20 shows the Failover dialog box. The failover process automatically starts the virtual machine on the replica host.

FIGURE 8-20 The Failover dialog box

After the unplanned failover process is complete and you have restored the original host Hyper-V server, you should configure reverse replication to re-create the replication relationship. This process is almost identical to creating the initial replication relationship, and the wizard is prepopulated with the details of the original relationship when you run it.

MORE INFO **UNPLANNED FAILOVER**

To learn more about unplanned failover, consult the following article:
http://technet.microsoft.com/en-us/library/jj134169.aspx.

Hyper-V Replica Broker

Hyper-V Replica Broker enables you to configure Hyper-V Replica for virtual machines
replicated from or to Windows Server 2012 or Windows Server 2012 R2 Hyper-V failover
clusters. Hyper-V Replica is not necessary if Hyper-V Replica is being performed between
Hyper-V hosts that are not participating in a failover cluster.

To configure the Hyper-V Replica Broker node, perform the following steps:

1. On an existing failover cluster that has the Hyper-V role installed, use Failover Cluster
   Manager to add the Hyper-V Replica Broker role.

2. Verify that the Hyper-V Replica Broker role can be moved across all nodes in the
   cluster

Until you have deployed the Hyper-V Replica Broker role, you are unable to configure
the Hyper-V nodes or virtual machines hosted within the cluster to support replication. The
Hyper-V Replica Broker role is shown deployed on a failover cluster in Figure 8-21.

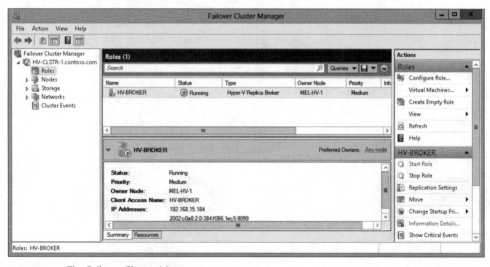

FIGURE 8-21 The Failover Cluster Manager

MORE INFO **HYPER-V REPLICA BROKER**

To learn more about Hyper-V Replica Broker, consult the following article: *http://blogs.
technet.com/b/yungchou/archive/2013/05/05/hyper-v-replica-broker-explained.aspx.*

Multisite clustering

Failover clusters can span multiple sites. When configuring a cluster that spans two sites, you should do the following:

- Ensure that there are an equal number of nodes in each site.

- Allow each node to have a vote.

- Enable dynamic quorum. *Dynamic quorum* makes it possible for quorum to be recalculated when nodes leave the cluster. When nodes leave the cluster, the cluster determines if it still retains quorum. If it does, the cluster recalculates a new quorum based on the number of nodes that remain available. For example, if you have a 7-node cluster and 2 nodes fail, quorum is retained and dynamic quorum will recalculate the quorum requirement based on the 5 remaining nodes. Dynamic quorum also performs a recalculation when nodes return to the cluster. Dynamic quorum is enabled by default on Windows Server 2012 and Windows Server 2012 R2 failover clusters.

- Use a file share witness. As shown in Figure 8-22, the file share witness should be hosted in a third site that has separate connectivity to the two sites that host the cluster nodes. When configured in this manner, the cluster retains quorum in the event that one of the sites is lost.

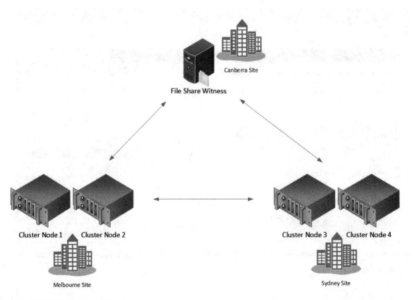

FIGURE 8-22 A multisite cluster

In the event that you only have two sites and are unable to place a file share witness in an independent third site, you can edit the cluster configuration manually to reassign votes so that the cluster recalculates quorum.

Dynamic witness

Dynamic witness is a technology new to Windows Server 2012 R2 that allows the vote of the witness to be ignored when recalculating quorum after a node goes offline if the total number of votes of the remaining nodes and the witness would be an even number. For example, you might configure a 7-node cluster with a witness. In this scenario, the witness would be ignored when calculating quorum. If one node failed and the dynamic quorum process recalculates quorum, then the witness vote would be counted during the next check for quorum. Dynamic witness also minimizes the impact of a witness server failing on quorum calculations by deprecating the failed witness server's vote.

Tie breaker for 50% node split

Tie breaker for 50% node split is a new Windows Server 2012 R2 feature that allows you to configure a cluster node so that its vote is deprecated for quorum calculations when communications between sites that host cluster nodes fail. For example, in the scenario above, Melbourne has two nodes, Sydney has two nodes, and a witness share is present in Canberra. If the witness share in Canberra fails and then the link between Melbourne and Sydney fails, problems will arise as neither the nodes in the Melbourne or Sydney sites will be able to determine if they have quorum. With tie breaker for 50% node split, you can designate a node as having a lower priority than other nodes when it comes to calculating quorum. For example, you designate the second node in Melbourne as having lower priority. When you do this, functionally there will be three quorum votes for the cluster to take into consideration if the Canberra witness fails. If the Canberra witness fails and communication is lost between the Melbourne and Sydney sites, the two nodes in the Sydney site will retain quorum.

Force quorum resiliency

Force quorum resiliency is a new Windows Server 2012 R2 feature designed to minimize the problems related to partitioned or "split brained" clusters. In certain scenarios, you might need to forcibly restart cluster nodes when communication between sites that host cluster nodes is lost. For example, imagine that there are three cluster nodes in Sydney and two cluster nodes in Melbourne. The service hosted on the cluster needs to be available to branch offices in other cities around Australia. A failure occurs that causes communication to the Sydney site to be lost. In this scenario, the three nodes in Sydney would retain quorum. However, it's communication to the Sydney site that is the problem whereas communication to the Melbourne site is still functioning. In this scenario you would forcibly restart the Melbourne cluster nodes so that the service hosted on the cluster would remain available to the other Australian branch offices.

In previous versions of Windows Server, problems would occur when connectivity was restored to the Sydney site as it would host nodes that also believed they had quorum. With Windows Server 2012 R2, when communication is reestablished, the nodes in the Sydney site would detect that the nodes in the Melbourne site were forcibly restarted, and so would restart themselves so that they could automatically rejoin the cluster, avoiding the cluster falling into a partitioned or "split brained" state.

Virtual machine network health detection

Virtual machine network health detection is a Windows Server 2012 R2 feature that provides fault detection and remediation networks used by virtual machines. It allows you to configure a virtual machine so that live migration automatically occurs if a network failure occurs in such a way that the network is not available to the virtual machine on the current virtualization cluster host node but is available to the virtual machine on a different virtualization cluster host node. Virtual machine network health detection requires that you configure multiple network paths between virtualization cluster host nodes.

> **MORE INFO DR CLUSTER CONFIGURATIONS**
>
> To learn more about DR cluster configurations, consult the following article: *http://technet.microsoft.com/en-us/library/jj612870.aspx.*

Lesson summary

- Hyper-V Replica enables you to deploy a replica of a virtual machine on another Hyper-V server.
- You can use Kerberos or certificate-based authentication for Hyper-V Replica.
- You must configure firewall rules for port 80 (Kerberos) or port 443 (certificate-based authentication) when configuring Hyper-V replica.
- You must deploy Hyper-V Replica Broker if you want to use Hyper-V Replica with virtual machines hosted on failover clusters.
- When configuring multisite clustering, ensure that an equal number of nodes are in each site and a file share witness is placed in a third site.

Lesson review

Answer the following questions to test your knowledge of the information in this lesson. You can find the answers to these questions and explanations of each answer choice in the "Answers" section at the end of this chapter.

1. You want to perform a planned failover of a virtual machine that is configured to replicate to another Hyper-V server through Hyper-V Replica. Which of the following steps should you take prior to performing the failover?

    A. Take a checkpoint of the virtual machine.

    A. Pause the virtual machine.

    B. Shut down the virtual machine.

    C. Export the virtual machine.

2. You are planning the deployment of a cluster that should keep functioning in the event that a site is lost. Your organization has three sites. Each site has a connection to the other two sites. The cluster will have six nodes. Which of the following strategies should you implement to ensure that the cluster will remain operational in the event that an entire site becomes unavailable? (Choose two. Each answer forms part of a complete solution.)

   A. Place two nodes in the first site. Place three nodes in the second site.

   B. Place a file share witness in the third site.

   C. Place three nodes in the first site. Place three nodes in the second site.

   D. Place one node in the third site.

3. Which of the following predefined firewall rules would you enable if you were configuring Hyper-V Replica and using Kerberos authentication?

   A. Failover Cluster Manager

   B. Hyper-V Management Clients

   C. Hyper-V Replica HTTP

   D. Hyper-V Replica HTTPS

4. Which of the following predefined firewall rules would you enable if you were configuring Hyper-V Replica and using certificate-based authentication?

   A. Hyper-V Replica HTTPS

   B. Hyper-V Management Clients

   C. Failover Cluster Manager

   D. Hyper-V Replica HTTP

Practice exercises

The goal of this section is to provide you with hands-on practice with the following:

- Preparing servers for shared nothing live migration
- Preparing servers for Hyper-V Replica
- Configuring virtual machine replication
- Performing planned virtual machine replication failover
- Performing shared nothing live migration
- Managing storage migration
- Exporting, importing, and cloning a virtual machine
- Performing unplanned virtual machine replication failover

Unlike other chapters in this book, the practice exercises in this lesson require that you have two reasonably identical computers that will function as Hyper-V hosts. Unlike the other server roles that are addressed by the 70-412 exam, running Hyper-V in a supported configuration requires that you install the operating system on "bare metal." It is possible with some virtualization solutions to trick Windows Server 2012 so that it detects that it is running directly on hardware when in fact it is running in a virtualized state. If you know how to configure a third-party virtualization solution to do this, you can build a lab for this chapter in this manner.

When selecting host computers for MEL-HV-1 and MEL-HV-2, ensure that they meet the following Hyper-V virtualization requirements:

- 1.4 GHz or faster x64 processor with hardware-assisted virtualization. Included with Intel Virtualization Technology (Intel VT) or AMD Virtualization (AMD-V) technology.

- Hardware enforced Data Execution Prevention (DEP). On processors that use Intel architecture, this involves enabling the Intel XP (Execute Disable) bit or the AMD NX (No Execute) bit.

Figure 8-23 serves as a starting point to describe the environment created for this set of practice exercises.

FIGURE 8-23 The lab infrastructure

- The Windows 8.1 Enterprise Edition computer running client Hyper-V and hosting virtual machines SYD-DC, MEL-DC, ADL-DC, and CBR-DC. The client Hyper-V virtual switch is configured with two virtual switches: a private switch and an external switch. Practice exercises in all other chapters of this book assume that SYD-DC, MEL-DC, ADL-DC, and CBR-DC are configured so that network adapters are matched to the private switch.

- SYD-DC.contoso.com is a virtual machine running the evaluation version of Windows Server 2012 R2 and is configured as described in the introduction of this book. The main change is instead of being configured to use a private network on the Hyper-V host, the SYD-DC.contoso.com virtual machine network adapter is configured to use an external network. SYD-DC.contoso.com retains existing Internet Protocol (IP) address information.

- MEL-HV-1 is running the evaluation version Windows Server 2012 R2 Standard Edition. MEL-HV-1 is deployed on computer hardware in a traditional bare metal configuration. MEL-HV1 is configured with the following IP address information and is joined to the contoso.com domain:
  - IP Address: 10.10.10.51
  - Subnet Mask: 255.0.0.0
  - DNS Server Address: 10.10.10.10
- MEL-HV-2 is running the evaluation version Windows Server 2012 Standard Edition. HEL-HV-2 is deployed on computer hardware in a traditional bare metal configuration. MEL-HV2 is configured with the following IP address information and is joined to the contoso.com domain:
  - IP Address: 10.10.10.52
  - Subnet Mask: 255.0.0.0
  - DNS Server Address: 10.10.10.10
- You might wish to enable Remote Desktop on MEL-HV-1 and MEL-HV-2 so that you can manage everything centrally from your workstation.
- Copy the Windows Server 2012 R2 evaluation edition iso file to the folder c:\iso on MEL-HV-1.

Exercise 1: Install the Hyper-V role on MEL-HV-1 and MEL-HV-2

In this exercise, you create identical virtual switches on MEL-HV-1 and MEL-HV-2. To complete this exercise, perform the following steps:

1. Sign on to MEL-HV-1 as contoso\don_funk with the password **Pa$$w0rd**.
2. From the Manage menu of the Server Manager console, click Add Servers.
3. In the Add Servers dialog box, click Find Now. Select MEL-HV-2 and click the arrow key to add it to the list of selected computers as shown in Figure 8-24. Click OK.

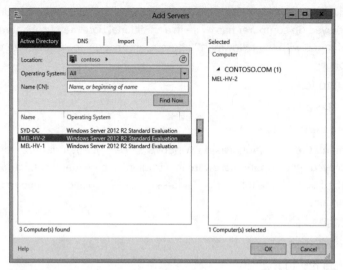

FIGURE 8-24 The Add Servers dialog box

4. Click the All Servers node of the Server Manager console and ensure that MEL-HV-1 and MEL-HV-2 are present as shown in Figure 8-25.

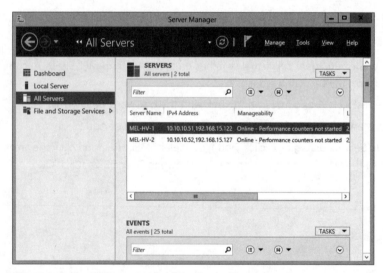

FIGURE 8-25 The All Servers node of the Server Manager

5. From the Manage menu, click Add Roles And Features.

6. On the Before You Begin page of the Add Roles And Features Wizard, click Next twice.

7. On the Select Destination Server page, select MEL-HV-1.contoso.com as shown in Figure 8-26. Click Next.

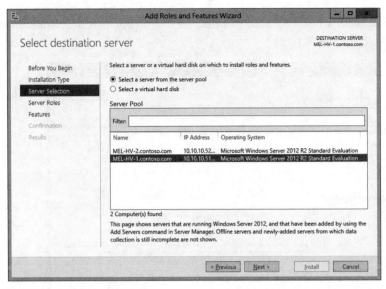

FIGURE 8-26 Server selection

8. On the Select Server Roles page, select Hyper-V. In the Add Roles And Features Wizard pop-up box, click Add Features.

9. Verify that the Hyper-V role is selected as shown in Figure 8-27 and click Next three times.

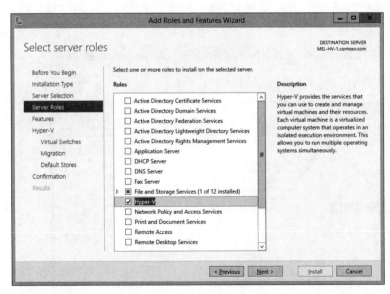

FIGURE 8-27 Selecting server roles

10. On the Virtual Switches page, ensure that no network adapters are selected and click Next.

11. On the Virtual Machine Migration page, ensure that no option is selected as shown in Figure 8-28. Click Next twice.

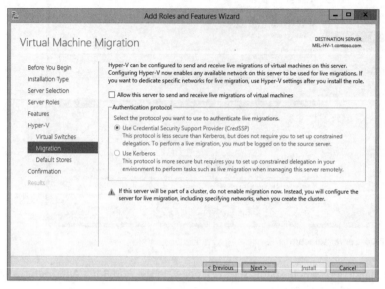

FIGURE 8-28 The Virtual Machine Migration page

12. On the Confirm Installation Selections page, select Restart The Destination Server Automatically If Required as shown in Figure 8-29. In the Add Roles And Features Wizard dialog box, click Yes. Click Install.

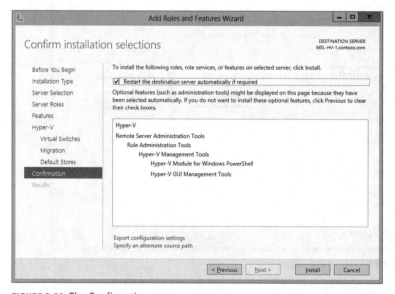

FIGURE 8-29 The Confirmation page

13. MEL-HV-1 might restart a few times. When it completes rebooting, sign in as contoso\ don_funk with the password **Pa$$w0rd**.

14. The Add Roles And Features Wizard restarts, and you are informed that Hyper-V is installed. Click Close.

15. Click the All Servers node on the Server Manager console.

16. In the Manage menu, click Add Roles And Features.

17. On the Before You Begin page of the Add Roles And Features Wizard, click Next twice.

18. On the Select Destination Server page, select MEL-HV-2 as shown in Figure 8-30 and click Next.

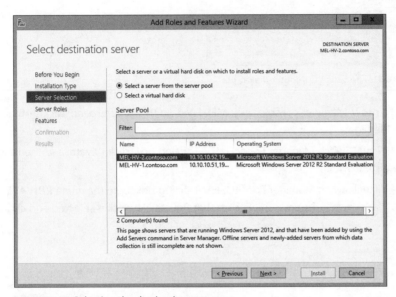

FIGURE 8-30 Selecting the destination server

19. On the Select Server Roles page, click Hyper-V. In the Add Roles And Features Wizard dialog box, click Add Features, and then click Next three times.

20. On the Virtual Switches page, verify that no network adapters are selected and click Next.

21. On the Migration page, ensure that the option to allow the server to send and receive live migrations is not enabled, and click Next twice.

22. On the Confirm Installation Selections page, ensure that the Restart The Destination Server Automatically If Required option is selected and click Install. Server MEL-HV-2 restarts several times during the process of installing Hyper-V.

23. Click Close to dismiss the Add Roles And Features Wizard.

Exercise 2: Configure identical virtual switches on MEL-HV-1 and MEL-HV-2

In this exercise, you configure identical virtual switches MEL-HV-1 and MEL-HV-2. To complete this exercise, perform the following steps:

1. When signed on to MEL-HV-1 as contoso\don_funk, on the Tools menu of the Server Manager console, click Hyper-V Manager.

2. In the Actions pane of the Hyper-V Manager console, click Connect To Server.

3. In the Select Computer dialog box, type **MEL-HV-2** as shown in Figure 8-31. Click OK.

FIGURE 8-31 The Select Computer dialog box

4. In the Hyper-V Manager console, click MEL-HV-1. In the Actions pane, click Virtual Switch Manager.

5. On the Virtual Switch Manager For MEL-HV-1 dialog box, click Private, and then click Create Virtual Switch.

6. On the Virtual Switch Manager For MEL-HV-1 dialog box, type the name **PRIVATE SWITCH** as shown in Figure 8-32. Ensure that Private Network is selected and click OK.

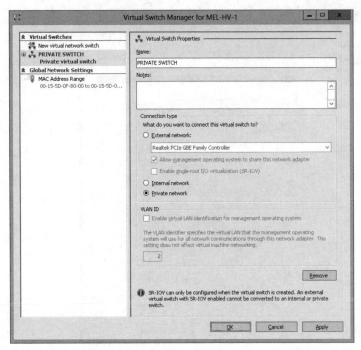

FIGURE 8-32 Private network switch

7. In the Hyper-V Manager console, click MEL-HV-2.

8. In the Actions pane, click Virtual Switch Manager.

9. On the Virtual Switch Manager For MEL-HV-2 dialog box, click Private, and click Create Virtual Switch as shown in Figure 8-33.

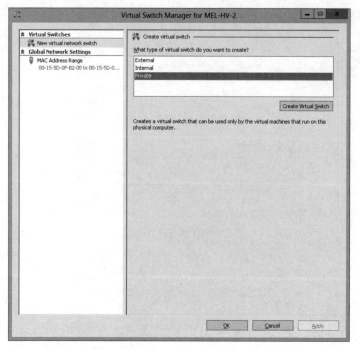

FIGURE 8-33 The private network

10. On the Virtual Switch Manager For MEL-HV-2 dialog box, type the name **PRIVATE SWITCH** and ensure that Private Network is selected. Click OK.

REAL WORLD VIRTUAL SWITCH NAMES

Virtual switch names have to match when you are configuring Hyper-V replication or live migration.

Exercise 3: Prepare servers for live migration

In this exercise, you prepare MEL-HV-1 and MEL-HV-2 for live migration. To complete this exercise, perform the following steps:

1. Sign on to SYD-DC as contoso\don_funk with the password **Pa$$w0rd**.

2. Click Active Directory Users And Computers on the Tools menu of the Server Manager console.

3. Navigate to the Computers container under the contoso.com domain.

4. Right-click the MEL-HV-1 computer account and click Properties.

5. On the Delegation tab of the MEL-HV-1 Properties dialog box, select Trust This Computer For Delegation To Specified Services Only and select Use Kerberos Only as shown in Figure 8-34.

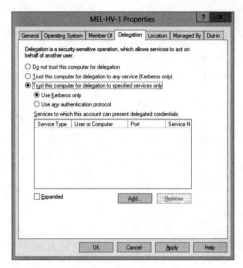

FIGURE 8-34 Configure delegation

6. On the Delegation tab of the MEL-HV-1 Properties dialog box, click Add.

7. On the Add Services dialog box, click Users Or Computers.

8. In the Select Users Or Computers dialog box, type **MEL-HV-2**, click Check Names and click OK.

9. In the list of available services select cifs as shown in Figure 8-35. Scroll down, hold the Ctrl key, and also select the Microsoft Virtual System Migration Service. Click OK.

FIGURE 8-35 Select cifs service

10. Verify that both services are listed as shown in Figure 8-36 and click OK.

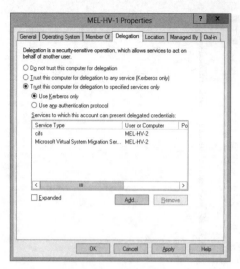

FIGURE 8-36 Service delegation

11. Right-click the MEL-HV-2 computer account and click Properties.

12. On the Delegation tab of the MEL-HV-2 Properties dialog box, select Trust This Computer For Delegation To Specified Services Only and select Use Kerberos Only.

13. On the Delegation tab of the MEL-HV-2 Properties dialog box, click Add.

14. On the Add Services dialog box, click Users Or Computers.

15. In the Select Users Or Computers dialog box, type **MEL-HV-1**, click Check Names and click OK.

16. In the list of available services, hold down the Ctrl key and select cifs and the Microsoft Virtual System Migration Service. Click OK.

17. Verify that both services are listed as shown in Figure 8-37 and click OK.

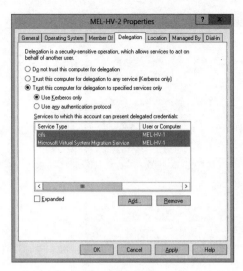

FIGURE 8-37 Service delegation

Exercise 4: Prepare servers for replication

In this exercise, you prepare MEL-HV-1 and MEL-HV-2 for replication by configuring Hyper-V and appropriate firewall rules. To complete this exercise, perform the following steps:

1. Ensure that you are signed on to MEL-HV-1 as contoso\don_funk.

2. In the Search charm, type **Windows Firewall with Advanced Security**. In the list of results, click Windows Firewall With Advanced Security.

3. Right-click the Inbound Rules node and click New Rule.

4. On the Rule Type page of the New Inbound Rule Wizard, click Predefined, and then select Hyper-V Replica HTTP as shown in Figure 8-38. Click Next.

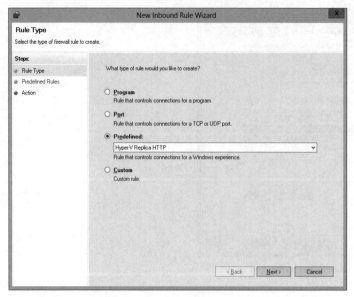

FIGURE 8-38 The New Inbound Rule Wizard

5. On the Predefined Rules page, click Hyper-V Replica HTTP Listener (TCP-In) as shown in Figure 8-39, and click Next.

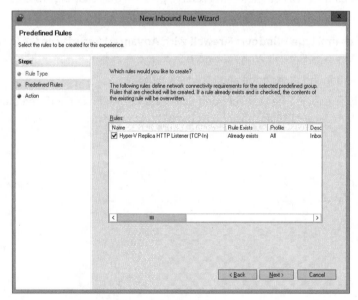

FIGURE 8-39 Enable rule

6. On the Action page of the New Inbound Rule Wizard, click Finish.

7. Sign in to MEL-HV-2 as contoso\don_funk with the password **Pa$$w0rd**.

8. In the Search charm, type **Windows Firewall with Advanced Security**. In the list of results, click Windows Firewall With Advanced Security.

9. Right-click the Inbound Rules node and click New Rule.

10. On the Rule Type page of the New Inbound Rule Wizard, click Predefined, and then select Hyper-V Replica HTTP. Click Next.

11. On the Predefined Rules page, click Hyper-V Replica HTTP Listener (TCP-In) and click Next.

12. On the Action page of the New Inbound Rule Wizard, click Finish.

13. Click the Windows PowerShell icon to open a Windows PowerShell window and issue the following command:

```
Mkdir c:\vm-store
```

14. Switch to MEL-HV-1.

15. In the Hyper-V Manager console, right-click MEL-HV-1 and click Hyper-V Settings.

16. On the Replication Configuration area of the Hyper-V Settings For MEL-HV-1 dialog box, select Enable This Computer As A Replica Server, select Use Kerberos (HTTP), and select Allow Replication From Any Authenticated Server as shown in Figure 8-40. Click OK.

FIGURE 8-40 Enabling the computer as a replica server

17. In the Settings message box, review the message and click OK.

18. In the Hyper-V Manager console, right-click MEL-HV-2 and click Hyper-V Settings.

19. In the Replication Configuration area of the Hyper-V Settings For MEL-HV-2 dialog box, select Enable This Computer As A Replica Server, Use Kerberos (HTTP), and Allow Replication From Any Authenticated Server options as shown in Figure 8-41.

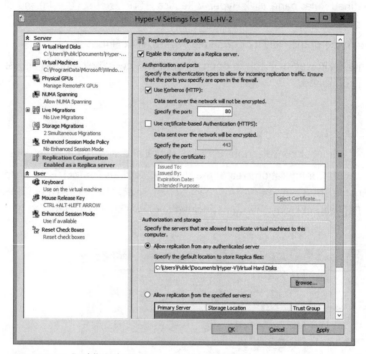

FIGURE 8-41 Enabling the computer as a replica server

20. Review the message in the Settings pop-up box and click OK.

21. Restart MEL-HV-1 and MEL-HV-2.

Exercise 5: Create two virtual machines on MEL-HV-1

In this exercise, you create two virtual machines on MEL-HV-1. You use the first virtual machine to configure Hyper-V replication. You configure the second virtual machine for live migration. This exercise requires that you have access to the Windows Server 2012 evaluation media. This exercise is written assuming this media is stored in the C:\iso folder. To complete this exercise, perform the following steps:

1. Sign on to MEL-HV-1 as contoso\don_funk.

2. Open an elevated Windows PowerShell prompt and type the following command:

   ```
   Mkdir c:\vm-store
   ```

3. Enter the following command to create the virtual machine TEST-ONE:

```
New-VM -NewVHDPath c:\vm-store\test-one.vhdx -NewVHDSizeBytes 20GB -ComputerName
MEL-HV-1 -MemoryStartupBytes 2048MB -Name TEST-ONE -path c:\vm-store -SwitchName
"PRIVATE SWITCH"
```

4. Enter the following command to create the virtual machine TEST-TWO:

```
New-VM -NewVHDPath c:\vm-store\test-two.vhdx -NewVHDSizeBytes 20GB -ComputerName
MEL-HV-1 -MemoryStartupBytes 2048MB -Name TEST-TWO -path c:\vm-store -SwitchName
"PRIVATE SWITCH"
```

5. If the Hyper-V Manager console is not already open, click Hyper-V Manager on the Tools menu of the Server Manager console.

6. In the Hyper-V Manager console, click MEL-HV-1.

7. Verify that virtual machines TEST-ONE and TEST-TWO are listed as shown in Figure 8-42.

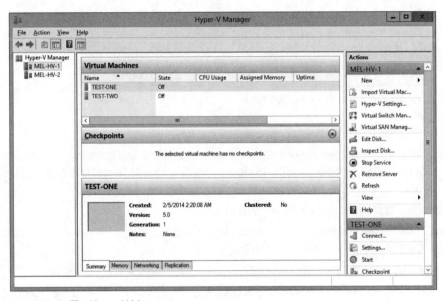

FIGURE 8-42 The Hyper-V Manager

8. Click TEST-ONE. In the Actions pane click Settings.

9. Click the DVD Drive under IDE Controller 1 and set it to use the Windows Server 2012 R2 evaluation media image as shown in Figure 8-43 that you copied to MEL-HV-1 when setting up the computer. Click OK to close the Settings for TEST-ONE on MEL-HV-1 dialog box.

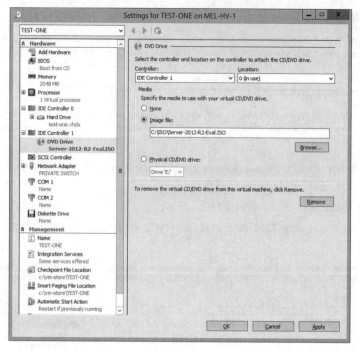

FIGURE 8-43 Settings for the DVD drive

10. Click TEST-TWO. In the Actions pane click Settings.

11. Click the DVD Drive under IDE Controller 1 and set it to use the Windows Server 2012 R2 evaluation media. Click OK to close the Settings for TEST-TWO On MEL-HV-1 dialog box.

12. Click TEST-ONE. In the Actions pane click Start.

13. Perform the installation of the Windows Server 2012 R2 operating system on TEST-ONE by completing the following steps:

   A. On the Windows Setup dialog box, click Next and then click Install Now.

   B. On the Select The Operating System You Want To Install page of the Windows Setup Wizard, click Windows Server 2012 R2 Standard Evaluation (Server With A GUI) and click Next.

   C. On the License Terms page, click I Accept The License Terms and click Next.

   D. On the Which Type Of Installation Do You Want page, click Custom: Install Windows Only (Advanced)

   E. On the Where Do You Want To Install Windows page, click Next. The installation proceeds.

14. In the Hyper-V Manager console, click TEST-TWO. In the Actions pane click Start.

15. Perform the installation of the Windows Server 2012 R2 operating system on TEST-TWO by completing the following steps:

A. On the Windows Setup dialog box, click Next and then click Install Now.

B. On the Select The Operating System You Want To Install page of the Windows Setup Wizard, click Windows Server 2012 R2 Standard Evaluation (Server With A GUI) and click Next.

C. On the License Terms page, click I Accept The License Terms and click Next.

D. On the Which Type Of Installation Do You Want page, click Custom: Install Windows Only (Advanced).

E. On the Where Do You Want To Install Windows Page, click Next. The installation proceeds.

16. Switch back to the TEST-ONE window. When the installation completes, type the password **Pa$$w0rd** twice and click Finish.

17. Sign on to TEST-ONE as Administrator with the password **Pa$$w0rd**.

18. Switch to the TEST-TWO window. When the installation completes, type the password **Pa$$w0rd** twice and click Finish.

19. Sign on to TEST-TWO as Administrator with the password **Pa$$w0rd**.

Exercise 6: Configure TEST-ONE for replication

In this exercise, you configure virtual machine TEST-ONE hosted on MEL-HV-1 so that it replicates to MEL-HV-2. To complete this exercise, perform the following steps:

1. In the Hyper-V Manager console on MEL-HV-1, right-click TEST-ONE and click Enable Replication.

2. On the Before You Begin page of the Enable Replication For TEST-ONE Wizard, click Next.

3. On the Specify Replica Server page, click Browse.

4. In the Select Computer dialog box, type **MEL-HV-2**, click Check Names, and then click OK.

5. Verify that the Specify Replica Server page matches Figure 8-44 and click Next.

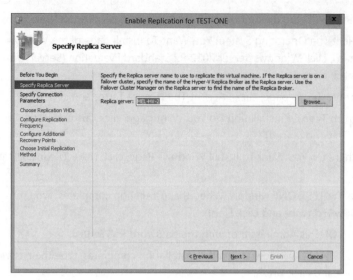

FIGURE 8-44 Specifying the replica server

6. On the Specify Connection Parameters page, ensure that Use Kerberos Authentication (HTTP) And Compress The Data That Is Transmitted Over The Network is selected as shown in Figure 8-45. Click Next.

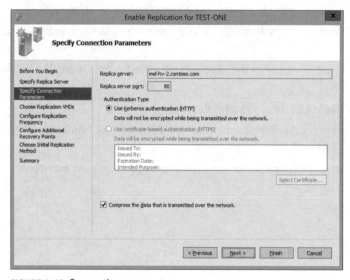

FIGURE 8-45 Connection parameters

7. On the Choose Replication VHDs page, ensure that C:\Vm-store\Test-one.vhdx is selected and click Next.

8. On the Configure Replication Frequency Page, set the frequency to 30 seconds and click Next.

9. On the Configure Recovery History page, select Create Additional Hourly Recovery Points and ensure that the Coverage Provided By Additional Recovery Points (In Hours) is set to 24 as shown in Figure 8-46. click Next.

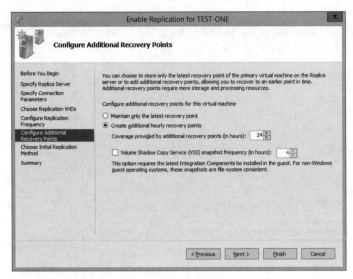

FIGURE 8-46 Configuring the recovery history

10. On the Choose Initial Replication Method page, choose Send Initial Copy Over The Network and Start Replication Immediately as shown in Figure 8-47. Click Finish.

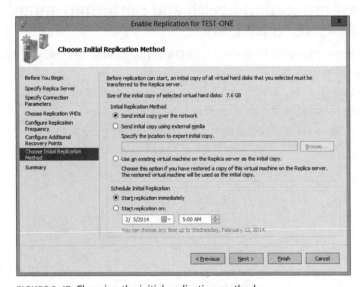

FIGURE 8-47 Choosing the initial replication method

11. In the Hyper-V manager console, click TEST-ONE, and then click the Replication tab. Wait until initial replication completes as shown in Figure 8-48.

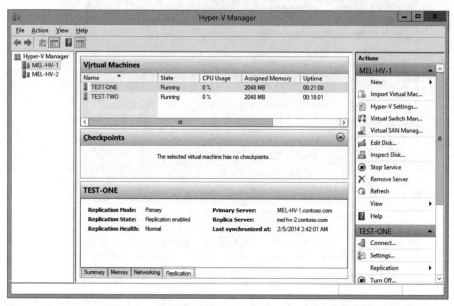

FIGURE 8-48 The Hyper-V Manager console

Exercise 7: View replication health and perform planned failover of TEST-ONE to MEL-HV-2

In this exercise, you trigger a planned failover of TEST-ONE to MEL-HV-2. To complete this exercise, perform the following steps:

1. In the Hyper-V Manager console on MEL-HV-1, right-click the TEST-ONE virtual machine, click Replication, and click View Replication Health.

2. Verify that Replication Health is listed as Normal as shown in Figure 8-49. Click Close.

FIGURE 8-49 The Replication Health dialog box

3. Sign on to TEST-ONE and shut down the virtual machine.

4. In the Hyper-V Manager console, right-click TEST-ONE, click Replication, and click Planned Failover.

5. On the Planned Failover dialog box, ensure that Start The Replica Virtual Machine after Failover option is selected as shown in Figure 8-50 and click Fail Over.

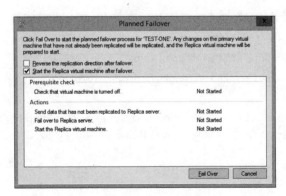

FIGURE 8-50 The Planned Failover dialog box

6. On the Planned Failover dialog box, verify that failover completed successfully.

7. In the Hyper-V Manager console, click MEL-HV-2.

8. Right-click TEST-ONE and verify that TEST-ONE, click Replication and click View Replication Health.

9. Verify that the current Primary Server is listed as MEL-HV-2.contoso.com as shown in Figure 8-51. Click Close.

FIGURE 8-51 The Replication Health dialog box

Exercise 8: Configure Hyper-V to support live migration

In this exercise, you configure MEL-HV-1 and MEL-HV-2 to support virtual machine live migration. To complete this exercise, perform the following steps:

1. In the Hyper-V Manager console on MEL-HV-1, right-click MEL-HV-1 and click Hyper-V Settings.

2. On the Live Migrations page, select Enable Incoming And Outgoing Live Migrations and Use Any Available Networks For Live Migration as shown in Figure 8-52. Click OK.

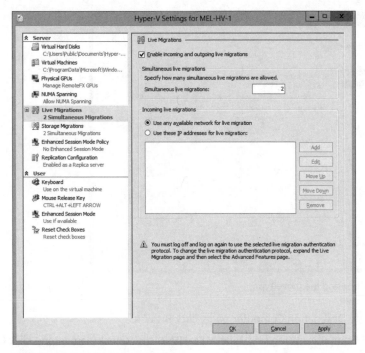

FIGURE 8-52 Enabling live migrations

3. In the Hyper-V Manager console on MEL-HV-1, right-click MEL-HV-2 and click Hyper-V Settings.

4. On the Live Migrations page, select Enable Incoming And Outgoing Live Migrations and Use Any Available Networks For Live Migration. Click OK.

5. Sign out of MEL-HV-1 and then sign on again as contoso\don_funk.

Exercise 9: Perform live migration of TEST-TWO

In this exercise, you perform live migration of TEST-TWO from MEL-HV-1 to MEL-HV-2. To complete this exercise, perform the following steps:

1. Ensure that you are signed on to the TEST-TWO virtual machine as Administrator with the password **Pa$$w0rd**.

2. In the Search charm, type **Notepad** and click Notepad in the results.

3. In the Untitled – Notepad window, type **Open Application with Unsaved Data**.

4. In the Hyper-V Manager console on MEL-HV-1, right-click TEST-TWO and click Move.

5. On the Before You Begin page of the Move "TEST-TWO" Wizard, click Next.

6. On the Choose Move Type page, select Move The Virtual Machine as shown in Figure 8-53. Click Next.

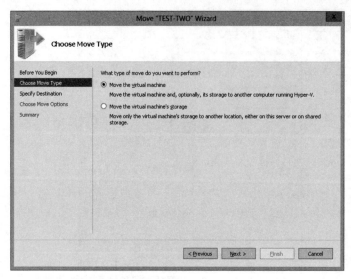

FIGURE 8-53 Choosing the move type

7. On the Specify Destination Computer page, click Browse.

8. In the Select Computer dialog box, type **MEL-HV-2**, click Check Names, and click OK.

9. On the Specify Destination Computer page, click Next.

10. On the Choose Move Options page, select Move The Virtual Machine's Data To A Single Location as shown in Figure 8-54 and click Next.

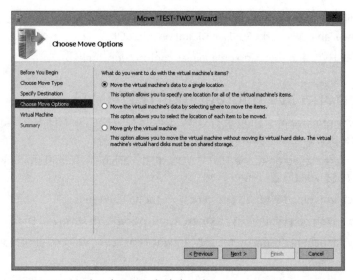

FIGURE 8-54 Moving data to a single location

11. On the Choose A New Location For Virtual Machine page, click Browse.

12. In the Select Folder dialog box, select C:\vm-store on MEL-HV-2.

13. Verify that the Choose A New Location For Virtual Machine Page matches Figure 8-55 and click Finish.

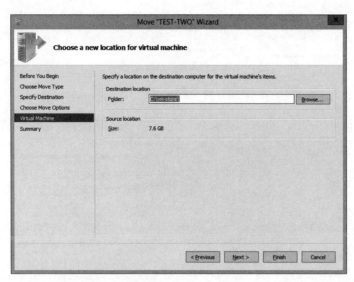

FIGURE 8-55 Specifying a new location

14. When the move completes, verify that the text file with the message is open when the virtual machine is hosted on MEL-HV-2 as shown in Figure 8-56.

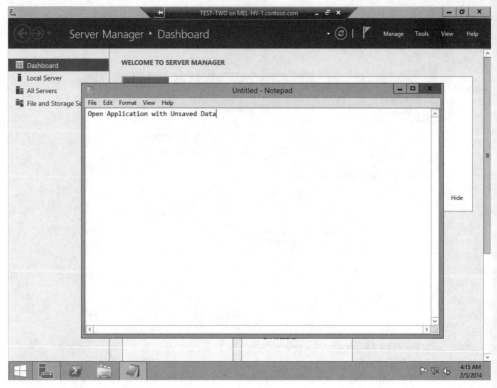

FIGURE 8-56 Notepad with message

Exercise 10: Perform storage migration

In this exercise, you perform storage migration. To complete this exercise, perform the following steps:

1. Sign on to MEL-HV-2 as contoso\don_funk.

2. Click the Windows PowerShell icon to open a Windows PowerShell window.

3. Type the following command and press Enter to create a new folder:

   ```
   Mkdir c:\new-vm-destination
   ```

4. Click Hyper-V Manager on the Tools menu of the Server Manager console.

5. In the Hyper-V Manager console, select MEL-HV-2.

6. Right-click the TEST-TWO virtual machine and click Move.

7. On the Before You Begin page of the Move "TEST-TWO" Wizard, click Next.

8. On the Choose Move Type page, click Move The Virtual Machine's Storage as shown in Figure 8-57 and click Next.

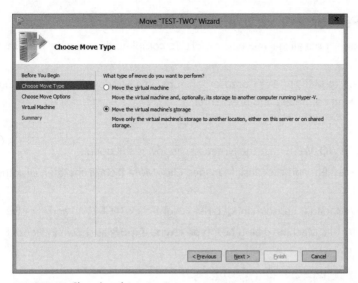

FIGURE 8-57 Choosing the move type

9. On the Choose Move Options page, select Move All Of The Virtual Machine's Data To A Single Location, and click Next.

10. On the Choose A New Location For The Virtual Machine's Items, type **c:\new-vm-destination** as shown in Figure 8-58 and click Finish.

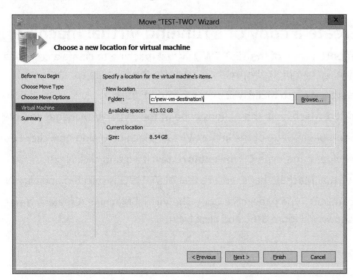

FIGURE 8-58 Specifying the new destination

Exercise 11: Perform a virtual machine export

In this exercise, you perform a virtual machine export. To complete this exercise, perform the following steps:

1. While signed on to MEL-HV-2 as Contoso\don_funk, in a Windows PowerShell window, type the following command and press Enter:

   ```
   Mkdir c:\vm-export
   ```

2. Sign in to TEST-TWO. Verify that the Notepad window is still open.

3. Right-click the taskbar and click Task Manager. Click More Details and then click the Performance tab.

4. In the Hyper-V Manager console on MEL-HV-2, right-click TEST-TWO and click Export.

5. In the Export Virtual Machine dialog box, type **c:\vm-export** as shown in Figure 8-59 and click Export.

FIGURE 8-59 The Export Virtual Machine dialog box

Exercise 12: Create a copy of a running virtual machine

In this exercise, you import a copy of the TEST-TWO virtual machine to create a copy of a running virtual machine. To complete this exercise, perform the following steps:

1. Ensure you are signed on to MEL-HV-2 as contoso\don_funk.

2. Click Import Virtual Machine in the Actions pane of the Hyper-V Manager console.

3. On the Before You Begin page of the Import Virtual Machine dialog box, click Next.

4. On the Locate Folder page, type **C:\vm-explort\test-two** and click Next.

5. On the Select Virtual Machine page, ensure that TEST-TWO is selected and click Next.

6. On the Choose Import Type page, click Copy The Virtual Machine (Create A New Unique ID) as shown in Figure 8-60 and click Next.

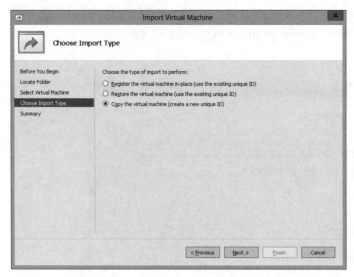

FIGURE 8-60 Choosing Import Type

7. On the Choose Folder For Virtual Machine Files page, click Next twice and then click Finish.

8. When the Import completes, verify that there are now two running virtual machines on MEL-HV-2 and one in a saved state.

9. Right-click the virtual machine in the saved state and click Rename. Rename the VM **TEST-TWO-CLONE**.

10. Right click on TEST-TWO-CLONE and click Start.

11. Sign in to TEST-TWO-CLONE and verify that the Notepad and Task Manager windows are present.

Exercise 13: Enable reverse replication

In this exercise, you perform the steps necessary to configure reverse replication after performing the unplanned failover in the previous exercise. To complete this exercise, perform the following steps:

1. Ensure you are signed on to MEL-HV-1 as contoso\don_funk.

2. On MEL-HV-1, in the Hyper-V Manager console, expand MEL-HV-2. Right-click the TEST-ONE virtual machine and click Shut Down.

3. Expand the MEL-HV-1 node, right-click the TEST-ONE virtual machine, click Replication, and click Reverse Replication.

4. On the Before You Begin page of the Reverse Replication Wizard For TEST-ONE, click Next.

5. On the Specify Replica Server page, ensure that MEL-HV-1.contoso.com has automatically been specified as shown in Figure 8-61. Click Next.

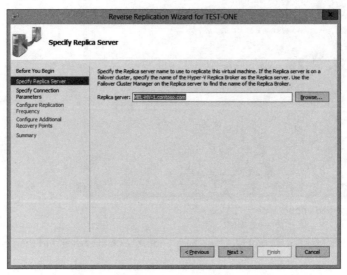

FIGURE 8-61 Specifying the replica server

6. On the Specify Connection Parameters page, ensure that Kerberos Authentication is selected and click Next.

7. On the Configure Replication Frequency page, ensure that 30 seconds is selected and click Next.

8. On the Configure Additional Recovery Points page, ensure that Create Additional Hourly Recovery Points is selected as shown in Figure 8-62. Click Next and click Finish

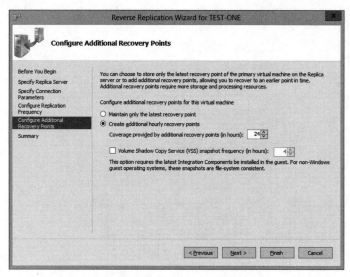

FIGURE 8-62 The Configure Recovery History page

9. Right-click When MEL-VH-2 Is Selected, right-click TEST-ONE, and click Start.

10. Wait five minutes.

Exercise 14: Perform an unplanned failover

In this exercise, you perform an unplanned failover of the TEST-ONE virtual machine. At this point in the practice exercises, the TEST-ONE virtual machine is hosted on MEL-HV-2. You simulate the failure of MEL-HV-2 by shutting down the computer. To complete this exercise, perform the following steps:

1. Ensure you are signed on to MEL-HV-1 as contoso\don_funk.

2. In the Hyper-V Manager console, ensure that the MEL-HV-1.contoso.com is selected. Right-click the TEST-ONE virtual machine, click Replication, and click View Replication Health.

3. On the Replication Health dialog box, ensure that the current primary server is set to MEL-HV-2.contoso.com as shown in Figure 8-63. Click Close to close this dialog box.

FIGURE 8-63 The Replication Health dialog box

4. In the Windows PowerShell window, type the following command and press Enter to force the shutdown of MEL-HV-2:

```
Stop-computer –computername mel-hv-2 -force
```

5. Right-click the TEST-ONE virtual machine, click Replication, and click Failover.

6. On the Failover dialog box, ensure that the most recent recovery point is selected as shown in Figure 8-64 and click Failover.

FIGURE 8-64 Failover dialog box

7. After failover completes, verify that the TEST-ONE virtual machine is running.

Suggested practice exercises

The following additional practice exercises are designed to give you more opportunities to practice what you've learned and to help you successfully master the lessons presented in this chapter.

- **Exercise 1** Configure an iSCSI target on SYD-DC and then configure MEL-HV-1 and MEL-HV-2 to participate in a failover cluster using the iSCSI target on SYD-DC as shared storage.

- **Exercise 2** Deploy a virtual machine on the failover cluster and use the Failover Cluster Manager to move this virtual machine back and forth across the nodes using live migration.

Answers

This section contains the answers to the lesson review questions in this chapter.

Lesson 1

1. **Correct answers**: B, C, and D

    A. **Incorrect**. You cannot use a file share hosted on a computer running Windows Server 2008 R2 to host Hyper-V virtual machines.

    B. **Correct**. You can use storage migration to move a virtual machine from a Hyper-V server's C: volume to an iSCSI-connected virtual disk.

    C. **Correct**. You can use storage migration to move a virtual machine from a Hyper-V server's C: volume to a USB 3.0–connected SSD disk.

    D. **Correct**. You can use storage migration to move a virtual machine from a Hyper-V server's C: volume to a file share hosted on a computer running Windows Server 2012 R2.

2. **Correct answers**: A and D

    A. **Correct**. You must export the SYD-DB-VM virtual machine as the first step in creating a duplicate.

    B. **Incorrect**. The Import/Register option uses the original virtual machine ID. You need to have a new virtual machine ID generated to have the original and the duplicate present on the same server.

    C. **Incorrect**. The Import/Restore option uses the original virtual machine ID. You need to have a new virtual machine ID generated to have the original and the duplicate present on the same server.

    D. **Correct**. The Import/Restore option uses the original virtual machine ID. You need to have a new virtual machine ID generated to have the original and the duplicate present on the same server.

3. **Correct answer**: B and D

    A. **Incorrect**. You do not have to configure delegation for the dcom service to support Hyper-V live migration.

    B. **Correct**. You need to configure delegation for the Cifs service if you want to support moving virtual machine storage using Hyper-V live migration.

    C. **Incorrect**. You do not have to configure delegation for the Hyper-V Replica Service to support Hyper-V live migration.

    D. **Correct**. You need to configure delegation for the Microsoft Virtual System Migration Service to support the movement of virtual machines in live migration.

4. **Correct answer**: A and C

A. Correct. You can use a Cluster Shared Volume file share to host virtual machine files for virtual machines hosted on a Hyper-V failover cluster.

B. Incorrect. Hyper-V does not support hosting virtual machines on SMB 2.0 file shares.

C. Correct. You can use an SMB 3.0 file share to host virtual machine files for virtual machines hosted on a Hyper-V failover cluster.

D. Incorrect. Hyper-V does not support hosting virtual machines on DFS shares.

Lesson 2

1. **Correct answer**: C

   A. Incorrect. You should shut down the virtual machine before performing a planned failover of a virtual machine configured for Hyper-V Replica.

   B. Incorrect. You should shut down the virtual machine before performing a planned failover of a virtual machine configured for Hyper-V Replica.

   C. Correct. You should shut down the virtual machine before performing a planned failover of a virtual machine configured for Hyper-V Replica.

   D. Incorrect. You should shut down the virtual machine before performing a planned failover of a virtual machine configured for Hyper-V Replica.

2. **Correct answers**: B and C

   A. Incorrect. You should place an equal number of nodes in the first and second sites when configuring a cluster that will retain quorum when a site is lost.

   B. Correct. You should place a file share witness in a third site and equal numbers of nodes in the first and second sites when configuring a cluster that will retain quorum in the event of site failure.

   C. Correct. You should place a file share witness in a third site and equal numbers of nodes in the first and second sites when configuring a cluster that will retain quorum in the event of site failure.

   D. Incorrect. You should place a file share witness in the third site when configuring a cluster that will retain quorum when a site is lost.

3. **Correct answer**: C

   A. Incorrect. This rule allows remote failover cluster management.

   B. Incorrect. This rule allows remote Hyper-V management.

   C. Correct. When you choose Kerberos authentication for Hyper-V Replica, you need to enable the Hyper-V Replica HTTP predefined firewall rule to allow authentication and replica traffic.

   D. Incorrect. When you choose Kerberos authentication for Hyper-V Replica, you need to enable the Hyper-V Replica HTTP predefined firewall rule to allow authentication and replica traffic.

4. **Correct answer**: A

   A. **Correct**. When you choose certificate-based authentication for Hyper-V Replica, you need to enable the Hyper-V Replica HTTPS predefined firewall rule to allow authentication and replica traffic.

   B. **Incorrect**. This rule allows remote Hyper-V management.

   C. **Incorrect**. This rule allows remote failover cluster management.

   D. **Incorrect.** You enable this rule when you are using Hyper-V Replica with Kerberos-based authentication, not certificate-based authentication.

DAC and AD RMS

I f you've been following the news in recent years, you're aware that a number of organizations have had sensitive information leaked to the wider world. This is because users have been granted access that they shouldn't have had, or the information wasn't properly protected in the first place. Dynamic Access Control (DAC) provides a way of dynamically assigning access permissions to content based upon the properties of the content and information about the user and device attempting to access that content. Active Directory Rights Management Services (AD RMS) provides a way of securing content through encryption and through rules applied to the operating system and applications on what actions the user can perform with that content. Both technologies, if correctly implemented, can minimize the chance that information that should stay within organizational boundaries doesn't find its way outside of them.

Lessons in this chapter:

- Lesson 1: Implementing Dynamic Access Control (DAC)
- Lesson 2: Installing and configuring Active Directory Rights Management Services (AD RMS)

Before you begin

To complete the practice exercises in this chapter, you need to use the evaluation edition of Windows Server 2012 R2 and deploy computers SYD-DC, MEL-DC, CBR-DC, and ADL-DC as described in the Introduction.federated identity.

Lesson 1: Implementing Dynamic Access Control (DAC)

DAC enables you to configure and apply permissions based upon the properties of files and the users that access them. One example is when you only allow users that have their employee type Active Directory user account attribute set to "Full Time Employee" to access files tagged "confidential." The advantage of DAC is that it allows permissions to change as the properties of the user and file change without requiring you to alter the permissions manually.

Introduction to Dynamic Access Control

If you've worked with New Technology File System (NTFS) permissions for a while, you're aware that they are rarely implemented properly. At a glance the system seems logical. Create a collection of groups that represent ways of describing a user or computer's place in the organization. Use those groups to apply permissions to restrict access to files and folders. This is great in theory, but it requires that security groups are kept up to date and that the permissions themselves are accurately configured. In many organizations, the process of ensuring accurate security group membership is erratic and piecemeal, with users only being added to groups after they lodge a service desk ticket.

 Dynamic Access Control (DAC) enables you to configure security using the properties of a user account or a computer account and the properties of the file. For example, you can configure DAC so that only people who have Don Funk as a manager are able to open files that contain the word "Cake." The way you'd do this is to set up classification rules and claims so that every file is checked to see if it contains the word "Cake." If it does contain the word "Cake," then a custom attribute is configured to reflect that status. Another rule is configured to set permissions on the file so that anyone whose Active Directory user account has the Managed By attribute set to Don Funk has access to open the file. Access is still mediated by NTFS permissions but those NTFS permissions are configured based on the properties of the file and the accessing user, and not set using the traditional method of right-clicking on the file or parent folder and setting them manually.

DAC has the following requirements:

- Windows Server 2012 or Windows Server 2012 R2 with the File Server Resource Manager (FSRM) role service installed on the file servers that will host files protected through DAC. DAC is not supported on Windows Server 2008 R2 and earlier file servers.

- Windows 8 or later client computers to support device claims. Clients using Windows 7 to access files that have security applied through DAC are still able to access files, but device claims are ignored.

- A Windows Server 2012 or Windows Server 2012 R2 domain controller in the domain or an update to the Active Directory Schema if no Windows Server 2012 or Windows Server 2012 R2 domain controllers are present.

Configuring Group Policy to support DAC

Configuring Active Directory to support DAC requires that you configure a Group Policy that applies to all of the domain controllers in the domain. You can do this in a policy that applies to the domain or just to domain controllers. To enable support for DAC, enable the KDC Support For Claims, Compound Authentication And Kerberos Armoring policy as shown in Figure 9-1. You can find this policy in the Computer Configuration\Policies\Administrative Templates\System\KDC node.

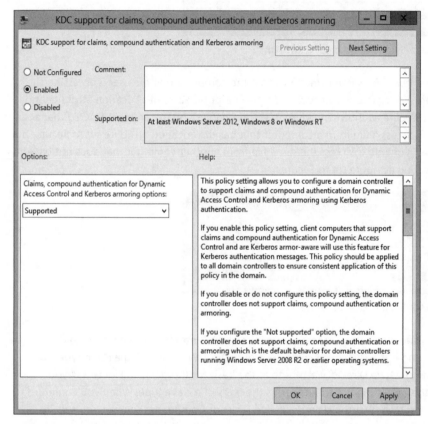

FIGURE 9-1 KDC Support For Claims, Compound Authentication And Kerberos Armoring policy

Configuring user and device claims

Before you can configure access rules, you need to configure claims. Claims are bits of information about users and computers and are usually derived from Active Directory attributes. You can edit Active Directory attributes using the Active Directory Administrative Center as well as with other tools. DAC supports the following types of claims:

■ *User Claim* This is information about the user. It can be based on a user account's attributes, such as EmployeeType, shown in Figure 9-2. You can also use claims related to group membership.

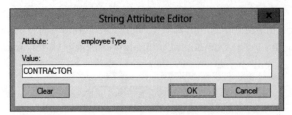

FIGURE 9-2 Set the value to CONTRACTOR

■ *Device Claim* This is information about the computer that the user is accessing the file from. For example, you could edit the computer account's Location attribute and set it to Secure as shown in Figure 9-3. This enables you to configure DAC so that a user can access a file from a computer that has the Location attribute set to Secure, but the user is unable to access the same file from another computer that does not have the location attribute set to Secure.

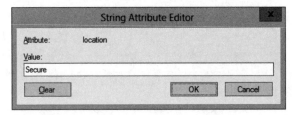

FIGURE 9-3 Set the value to Secure

You create claims in Active Directory Administrative Center by navigating to the Claim Types section under the Dynamic Access Control section. When creating a claim type, you select an existing Active Directory attribute as the basis for the claim. In Figure 9-4 you can see that the Department attribute forms the basis of a claim type. When you configure a claim, you select whether the claim relates to Users or Computers. You can also specify suggested values to associate with the claim. In the case of a claim related to the department attribute, this might be a list of departments within your organization.

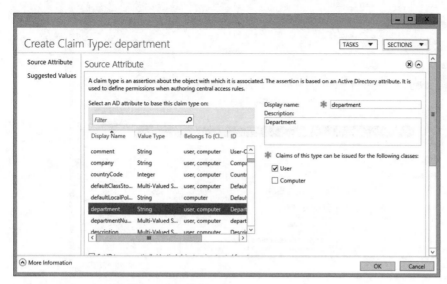

FIGURE 9-4 Creating the Department claim type

Configuring resource properties

Resource properties determine the resource attributes that you can use when configuring central access rules. Windows Server 2012 and Windows Server 2012 R2 ships with a collection of default resource properties, and you can add extra resource properties based on available attributes. Figure 9-5 shows a custom resource property named Project that can have the values Hovercraft or Submarine. You can assign resource properties to files either manually or automatically by configuring File Server Resource Manager File Classification Rules.

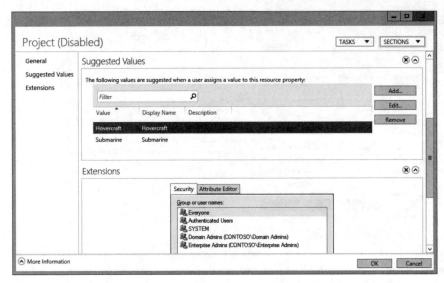

FIGURE 9-5 Hovercraft project

The Global Resource Property List, shown in Figure 9-6, is a list of all resource properties that you can use when configuring Central Access Rules. You can add and remove these properties as necessary. When you publish a property list through Active Directory, you can then assign these properties to files and folders either manually or automatically using File Server Resource Manager.

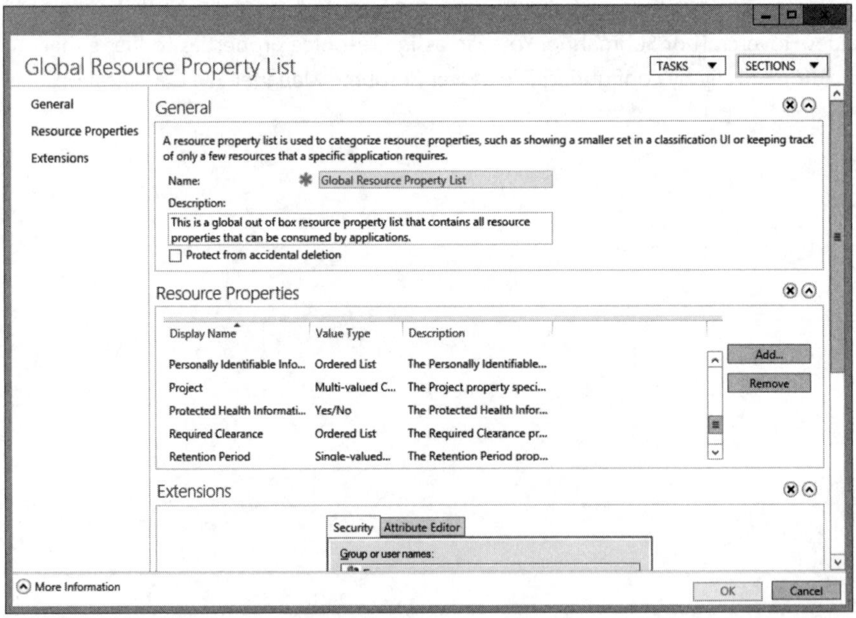

FIGURE 9-6 Global Resource Property List

You use File Server Resource Manager to apply properties to files through file classification rules. You can configure a classification rule to look for a particular string of text in a file and then to assign a particular property to that file based on the string. Figure 9-7 shows the Submarine value will be assigned to the Project property on files that meet the classification requirements, with the classification requirements in this case being any file that contains the text string "Submarine."

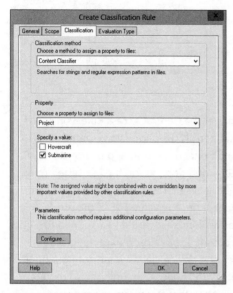

FIGURE 9-7 The Create Classification Rule dialog box

Central access rules

Central access rules include a set of permissions and the conditions under which those permissions are applied. For example, in Figure 9-8, the rule applying the permissions spelled out in the permissions entry will be applied to the file or folder if the file or folder has the Project resource property set to Hovercraft. You can have multiple conditions in a central access rule. You could, for example, require that the Project resource property be set to Hovercraft and the Confidentiality resource property be set to High for the permissions configured in the permissions entry to be applied.

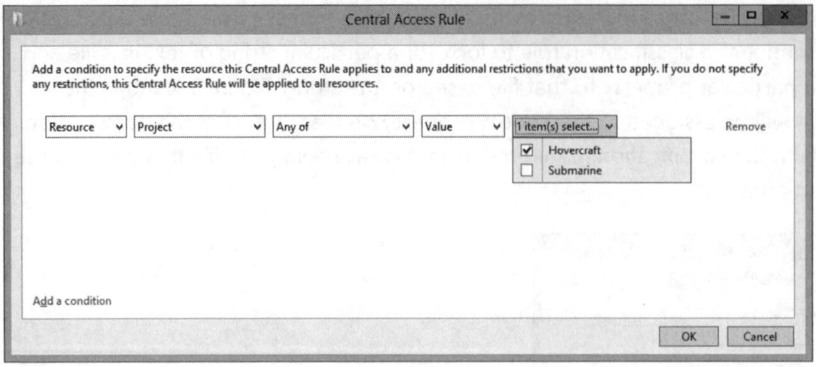

FIGURE 9-8 The Central Access Rule dialog box

After you have configured the conditions that trigger the Central Access Rule, you specify the set of permissions that will be applied. Unlike standard NTFS permissions, permission entries enable you to apply permissions that are conditional upon user and device claims. For example, the permissions entry shown in Figure 9-9 is conditional upon the user attempting access being not only a member of the Hovercraft_Project security group, but also having the EmployeeType attribute on his or her user account set to the value FTE. If the user's EmployeeType attribute isn't set to FTE, then the permissions that would be assigned to the user through his or her membership of the Hovercraft_Project group are not granted. You can configure multiple conditions based on user and device claims when configuring a permissions entry. For example, in the case of sensitive documents, you might also require that the computer account have an attribute set indicating that it is a secure computer.

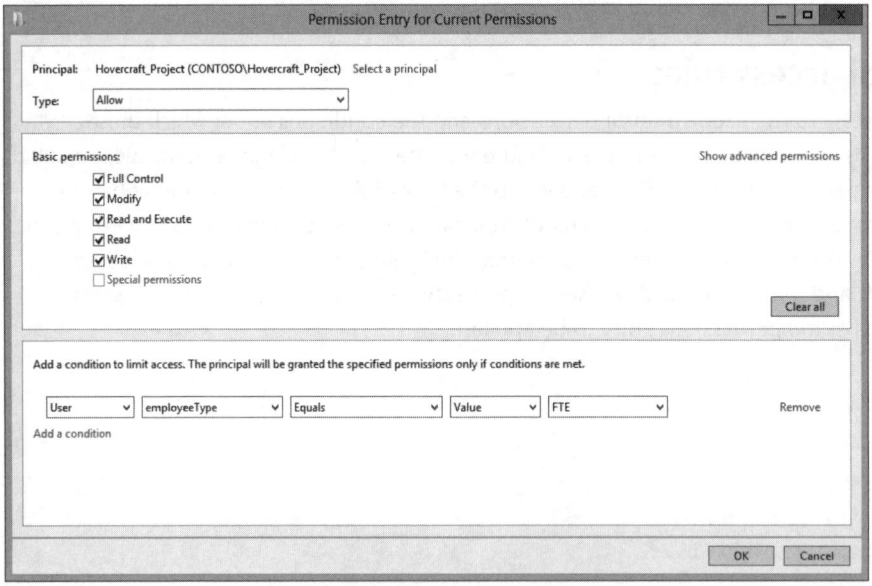

FIGURE 9-9 The Permission Entry For Current Permissions dialog box

Central access policies

A *central access policy* is a collection of central access rules. For example, the Contoso Policy Central Access Policy, shown in Figure 9-10, publishes two central access rules: Research_Projects and Secret_Projects. Only file servers running Windows Server 2012 or later, that are within the scope of the Central Access Policy, apply the rules that are contained within the policy.

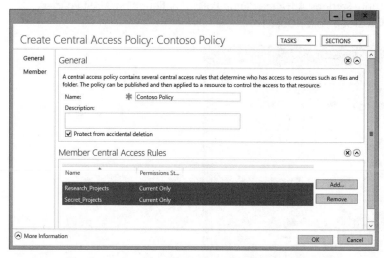

FIGURE 9-10 The Create Central Access Policy: Contoso Policy dialog box

You distribute central access policies through Group Policy. You do this by configuring the Manage Central Access Policies policy, which is located in the Computer Configuration\ Policies\Windows Settings\Security Settings\File System node. This policy is shown in Figure 9-11.

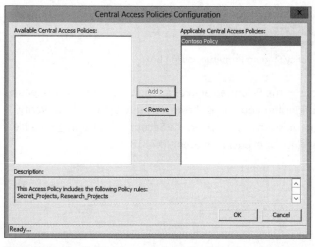

FIGURE 9-11 The Central Access Policies Configuration dialog box

Staging

Staging enables you to configure a set of proposed rather than applied permissions. You use auditing to determine the results of these staged permissions before implementing them. You must enable auditing through group policy to determine the results of staged permissions. The policy that you need to enable is the Audit Central Access Policy Staging Properties policy, shown in Figure 9-12, which is located in the Computer Configuration\Policies\ Windows Settings\Security Settings\Advanced Audit Policy Configuration\Audit Policies\ Object Access node of a Group Policy Object.

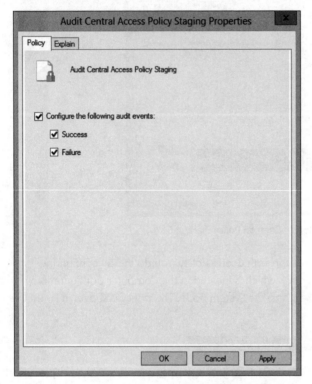

FIGURE 9-12 The Audit Central Access Policy Staging Properties dialog box

You configure staged permissions in the Proposed area of a central access rule by selecting the Enable Permission Staging Configuration option as shown in Figure 9-13. You can verify the functionality of the proposed permissions by checking the Security event sign on the file server that hosts the files and searching for events with event ID 4818.

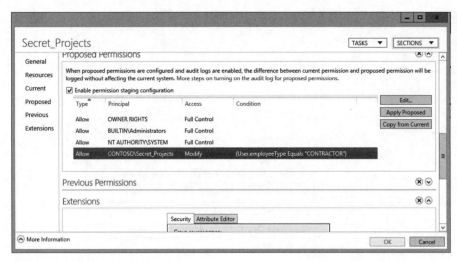

FIGURE 9-13 The Secret_Projects dialog box

Access Denied Assistance

 Access Denied Assistance is a feature available to Windows 8 clients that provides an informational dialog box explaining to users why they are unable to access a file because they do not have appropriate permissions. It's also possible to configure Access Denied Assistance so that an email can be forwarded to the support desk in the event that it is necessary to untangle permissions to allow the user access.

You configure Access Denied Assistance by configuring the Customize Message For Access Denied Errors policy as shown in Figure 9-14. This policy is located in the Computer Configuration\Policies\Administrative Templates\System\Access-Denied Assistance node of a GPO.

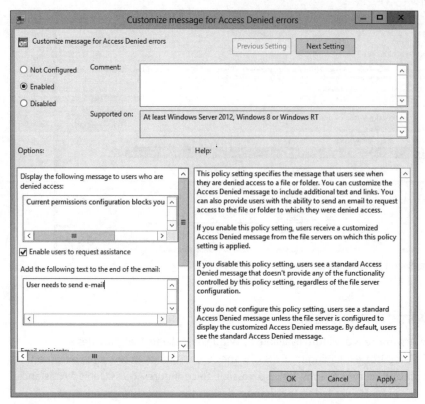

FIGURE 9-14 The Customize Message For Access Denied Errors dialog box

> **MORE INFO** **ACCESS DENIED ASSISTANCE**
>
> To learn more about access denied assistance, consult the following article:
> *http://technet.microsoft.com/en-us/library/jj574182.aspx*.

Lesson summary

- User and device claims provide information about users and devices and are often generated based on the values assigned to Active Directory attributes.
- Resource properties enable you to configure additional information about resources. Default resource properties include values such as Confidentiality and Department. It is possible to create custom resource properties.
- Central access rules determine the permissions that apply based on user and device claims to files that have specific resource properties.
- Central access policies enable you to publish collections of central access rules through Active Directory.

- Access Denied Assistance informs users that they've been denied access to a file because of permissions and enables them to send an email to someone in the IT department to get the issue resolved.

Lesson review

Answer the following questions to test your knowledge of the information in this lesson. You can find the answers to these questions and explanations of each answer choice in the "Answers" section at the end of this chapter.

1. You want to ensure that you are able to configure access to specific files for users that are full-time employees. Which of the following should you configure to extract this information from the user account's Active Directory attribute?

   A. Configure a user or device claim.

   B. Configure a central access policy.

   C. Configure resource properties.

   D. Create a central access rule.

2. You want to apply a set of permissions to the Hovercraft_Project group based on user attributes and the properties of the file. Which of the following would you configure to accomplish this goal?

   A. Configure a central access policy.

   B. Configure resource properties.

   C. Create a central access rule.

   D. Configure a user or device claim.

3. You want to create access rules based on the Confidentiality property of a file. Which of the following do you need to enable so that you can use file confidentiality information in a rule?

   A. Configure resource properties.

   B. Create a central access rule.

   C. Configure a user or device claim.

   D. Configure a central access policy.

4. You want to publish a collection of central access rules to all of the file servers in your domain. Which of the following should you configure to accomplish this goal?

   A. Create a central access rule.

   B. Configure a user or device claim.

   C. Configure a central access policy.

   D. Configure resource properties.

Lesson 2: Installing and configuring Active Directory Rights Management Services (AD RMS)

AD RMS is a technology that allows the assignment of preconfigured rights templates to documents and email messages. For example, you can apply a template to a document so that people are able to open the document, but are unable to copy, print, edit, or save the document. If your organization has deployed Microsoft Exchange, it's possible to apply AD RMS templates to messages to ensure that the messages can't be forwarded, copied, saved, printed, or replied to. In this lesson, you learn how to configure AD RMS infrastructure, configure and manage templates, and apply templates automatically to files based on file properties.

> **After this lesson, you will be able to:**
> - Install a licensing or certificate AD RMS server
> - Manage an AD RMS service connection point (SCP)
> - Manage trusted user domains
> - Configure trusted publishing domains
> - Manage RMS templates
> - Configure exclusion policies
>
> **Estimated lesson time: 45 minutes**

Installing AD RMS

AD RMS uses the term cluster to describe an AD RMS deployment, even though this has nothing to do with failover clustering or network load balancing. When you deploy AD RMS, you first deploy a *root cluster* as shown in Figure 9-15. An AD RMS root cluster is responsible for managing all of the AD RMS licensing and certificate traffic for the forest in which it is installed. You should only have one AD RMS root cluster per forest and organizations that have multiple forests should deploy multiple AD RMS root clusters. After you have deployed a root cluster, you can configure additional licensing-only clusters. Licensing-only clusters distribute licenses that clients use to consume and publish content.

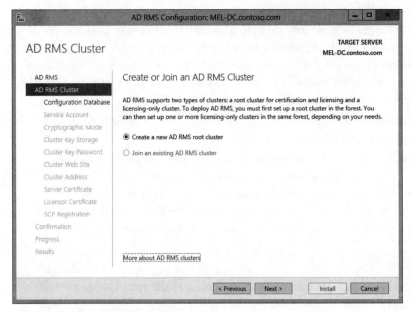

FIGURE 9-15 The AD RMS Cluster page

Installing AD RMS involves performing the following steps:

1. **Specify the database that AD RMS will use to store configuration information**   You can use a Microsoft SQL Server instance to perform this role, or you can deploy the Windows Internal Database. You should only use Microsoft SQL Server in large AD RMS deployments. AD RMS on Windows Server 2012 and Windows Server 2012 R2 can use SQL Server 2008 or later.

2. **Specify a service account**   This account needs to be a domain account and best practice is to use a specially configured group managed service account for this role. Using a group managed service account ensures that the account password is managed by Active Directory and does not need to be manually updated on a periodic basis by an administrator.

3. **Choose a cryptographic mode**   Mode 2 uses RSA 2048-bit keys and SHA-256 hashes. Mode 1 uses RSA 1024-bit keys and SHA-1 hashes. Mode 2 is more secure than mode 1, and is the recommended choice.

4. **Specify the cluster key storage**   This determines where the cluster key is stored. The default is to have the key stored within AD RMS, although you can also use a cryptographic service provider (CSP) if one is available. When you use a CSP, you have to perform manual key distribution when adding additional AD RMS servers.

5. **Specify a cluster key password** This password is used to encrypt the cluster key. You need to provide this password when joining additional AD RMS servers to the cluster. It's also necessary to provide this password when recovering an AD RMS cluster from backup.

6. **Input the cluster address** This is a website address in fully qualified domain name (FQDN) format which is usually hosted on the AD RMS server. Best practice is to configure an SSL certificate with the FQDN of the AD RMS server. Although it is possible to specify a non-SSL-protected address, doing so removes the ability to use AD RMS with identity federation. The cluster address and port cannot be altered after you have deployed AD RMS.

7. **Specify a licensor certificate name** This is the name used with the licensor certificate. It should represent the certificate's functionality.

8. **Determine whether to register the service connection point (SCP) in Active Directory** The SCP enables domain members to locate the AD RMS cluster automatically. A user account must be a member of the Enterprise Admins security group to register an SCP. SCP registration can occur after AD RMS is deployed in the event that the account used to deploy AD RMS is not a member of this security group.

> **MORE INFO DEPLOYING AD RMS**
>
> To learn more about deploying AD RMS, consult the following article: *http://technet.microsoft.com/en-us/library/cc770957.aspx.*

AD RMS certificates and licenses

AD RMS uses four specific types of certificates. These certificates have the following functions:

- **Server licensor certificate (SLC)** This certificate is created when you install the AD RMS role on the first server in the AD RMS cluster. This certificate is valid for 250 years and is used to issue the following certificates and licenses:
  - SLCs to additional servers that join the cluster
  - Rights account certificates
  - Client licensor certificates
  - Publishing licenses
  - Use licenses
  - Rights policy templates

- **AD RMS machine certificate** This certificate identifies a trusted device. The machine certificate public encrypts rights account certificate private keys, and the machine certificate private key decrypts rights account certificates.

- **Rights account certificate (RAC)** This certificate identifies a user. AD RMS can only issue RACs to Active Directory Domain Server (AD DS) users whose user accounts are configured with an email address. By default, a RAC has a validity of 365 days. Temporary RACs are issued with a validity of 15 minutes when a user accesses content from a device that is not a member of a trusted forest.

- **Client licensor certificate**   This certificate allows the publication of AD RMS protected content to computers that are not able to connect directly to the AD RMS cluster. These certificates are tied to a user RAC. Other users of the computer are unable to publish AD RMS–protected documents until a new connection to the AD RMS cluster is established from the computer.

> **MORE INFO AD RMS CERTIFICATES**
>
> To learn more about AD RMS certificates, consult the following article: *http://technet.microsoft.com/en-us/library/cc753886.aspx.*

In addition to the four certificate types, AD RMS uses two license types. These are as follows:

- **Publishing license**   A publishing license determines the rights that apply to AD RMS content. This license contains the content key and the URL and digital signature of the AD RMS server.
- **Microsoft Software License Terms**   This license allows a user to access AD RMS–protected content. The Microsoft Software License Terms are issued per user per document. These licenses are cached by default, though it's possible to disable caching so that the license must be obtained each time the user attempts to access protected content.

AD RMS templates

Rights policy templates enable you to apply rights policies to documents. When an author creates a document or sends an email message, he or she can apply a template to that document. It's also possible to use File Server Resource Manager to automatically apply templates to documents based on the properties of those documents, such as the document having a particular resource property or containing a specific text string. Templates are only used with rights aware applications and you can't open a protected document from an application that is not rights aware.

You create rights policy templates using the AD RMS Management Console. When creating a template, you can enable the following rights on a per-user-group or per-user basis, with any right not granted unavailable to the user:

- **Full Control**   The user has full control over the AD RMS–protected content.
- **View**   Gives a user the ability to view the AD RMS–protected content.
- **Edit**   Allows a user to modify the AD RMS–protected content.
- **Save**   Allows the user to save the AD RMS–protected content.
- **Export**   Allows the user to use the Save As function with the AD RMS–protected content.
- **Print**   Allows the user to print the AD RMS–protected content.

- **Forward** Used with Microsoft Exchange, allows a protected message to be forwarded.
- **Reply** Used with Microsoft Exchange, allows a protected message to be replied to.
- **Reply All** Used with Microsoft Exchange, allows the recipient of a protected message to use the Reply All function.
- **Extract** Allows a user to copy data from the AD RMS–protected content.
- **Allow Macros** Allows the user to use macros with the AD RMS–protected content.
- **View Rights** Allows the user to view rights assigned to the AD RMS–protected content.
- **Edit Rights** Allows the user to modify rights assigned to the AD RMS–protected content

Figure 9-16 shows the rights assigned to the submarine_project@contoso.com group. You can assign different rights to multiple groups. If a user is a member of more than one group, rights are cumulative.

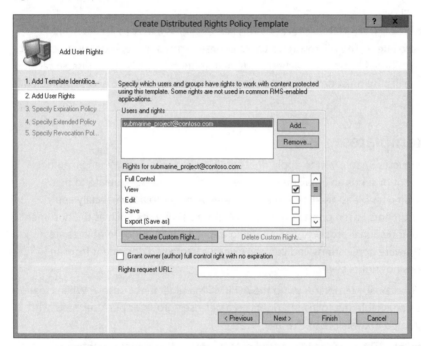

FIGURE 9-16 The Add User Rights page of the Create Distributed Rights Policy Template Wizard

When configuring an AD RMS template, you can configure content expiration settings. Content expiration settings enable you to have content expire either on a certain date or after a certain number of days. Figure 9-17 shows content expiration configured to expire 14 days after content publication. An additional setting enables you to configure use license expiration. This makes it possible for you to configure how often a user must connect to the AD RMS cluster to obtain a new license to access the content.

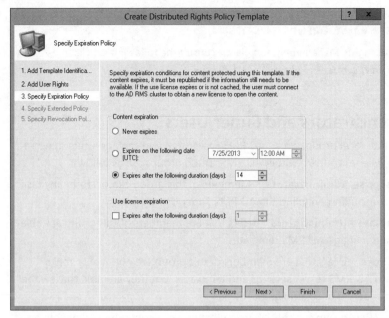

FIGURE 9-17 The Specify Expiration Policy page of the Create Distributed Rights Policy Template Wizard

The Extended Policy settings, shown in Figure 9-18, enable you to configure whether AD RMS content can be viewed using a browser add-on and whether a new license must be obtained each time content is consumed.

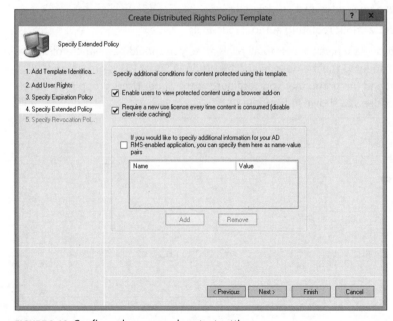

FIGURE 9-18 Configure browser and content settings

AD RMS Administrators and Super Users

There are three separate local groups on an AD RMS server that you can add users to when you want to assign privileges to them within AD RMS. These groups are as follows:

- **AD RMS Enterprise Administrators**   Members of this group can perform any task within AD RMS, including enabling the AD RMS Super Users group.

- **AD RMS Template Administrators**   Users that are members of this group are able to configure and manage AD RMS templates.

- **AD RMS Auditors**   Users that are members of this group are not able to make modifications to AD RMS server settings and templates, but they are able to view the properties of the server and templates.

The AD RMS *Super Users* group is a special group that you can configure and enable on the AD RMS server. Members of the AD RMS Super Users group have full owner rights over all use licenses issued by the AD RMS cluster. Members of the Super Users group are able to do the following:

- Recover expired content

- Recover content when a template is deleted

- Recover content without requiring author credentials

Members of this group are given access to all content, so you should have strict policies about managing and auditing the membership of this group. A Super Users group is not configured by default and the group that you configure as the Super Users group must have an associated email address as shown in Figure 9-19.

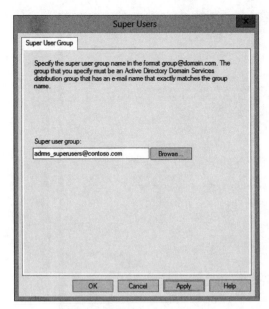

FIGURE 9-19 Super User group

> **MORE INFO** AD RMS ACCOUNTS
>
> To learn more about AD RMS accounts, consult the following article:
> *http://technet.microsoft.com/en-us/library/cc754120.aspx.*

✔ **Quick check**

- Which group should you configure if you want administrative users to be able to access expired content?

Quick check answer

- You configure the Super Users group if you want administrative users to be able to access expired content.

Trusted user and publishing domains

Trusted user domains (TUDs) enable you to configure an AD RMS cluster to manage requests for client licensor certificates (CLCs) for users that have been issued RACs from a different AD RMS cluster. For example, if an organization has two separate Active Directory forests and each forest has its own AD RMS deployment, you'd configure TUDs so that clients from the one forest would be able to issue CLCs to clients with RACs issued by the other forest. TUDs can be one-way or bi-directional. When configuring TUDs, you must export the TUD from the partner before importing the TUD locally. Figure 9-20 shows the Import Trusted User Domain dialog box.

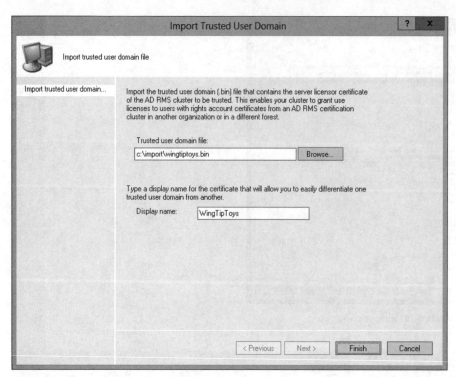

FIGURE 9-20 The Import Trusted User Domain dialog box

Trusted publishing domains (TPDs) allow the AD RMS cluster in one forest to issue end-user licenses to content published with licenses issued by an AD RMS cluster in another forest. You must export the TPD file and have it imported by the partner AD RMS cluster before the AD RMS cluster in the partner forest is able to issue end-user licenses to local AD RMS clients. Figure 9-21 shows exporting a TPD file.

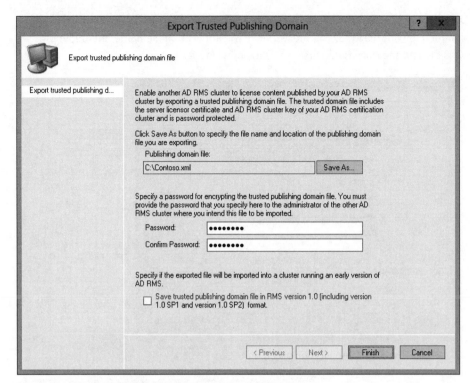

FIGURE 9-21 The Export Trusted Publishing Domain dialog box

> **MORE INFO** TRUSTED USER DOMAINS AND TRUSTED PUBLISHING DOMAINS
>
> To learn more about trusted user domains and trusted publishing domains, consult the following article: *http://technet.microsoft.com/en-us/library/cc754459.aspx.*

Exclusion policies

Exclusion policies enable you to deny specific entities the ability to interact with AD RMS. You can configure exclusions on the basis of application, user, and lockbox version. Exclusion works in the following ways:

- **User Exclusion**   You can exclude a user based on email address or on the basis of the public key assigned to the user's RAC. Use email-based exclusions for users in the forest and public key–based exclusion for external users.

- **Lockbox exclusion**   This enables you to exclude specific client operating systems. Each version of the Windows operating system has a specific lockbox identity. If you want to block clients running Windows Vista or Windows 7 from interacting with AD RMS, you would configure an exclusion where the minimum lockbox version is the version available in Windows 8.

- **Application Exclusion**   This enables you to exclude specific applications from interacting with AD RMS. You must specify the application file name, the minimum version, and the maximum version as shown in Figure 9-22.

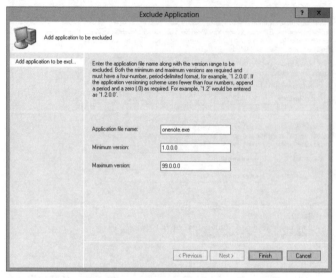

FIGURE 9-22 The Exclude Application dialog box

When you configure an exclusion, the exclusion only applies to new certificate or licensing requests. Licenses and certificates that were issued during the exclusion period still exclude the application, user, or lockbox version. If you remove an exclusion, the removal only applies to new licenses or certificates.

> **MORE INFO EXCLUSION POLICIES**
>
> To learn more about exclusion policies, consult the following article:
> *http://technet.microsoft.com/en-us/library/cc730687.aspx.*

Apply AD RMS templates automatically

1. You can use File Server Resource Manager to automatically apply AD RMS templates to files. You do this by performing the following general steps:

2. Create a new file management task with an appropriate name related to the template.

3. On the Scope tab, set the scope of the task to the folders that host the files to which you want to apply the AD RMS template.

4. On the Condition tab, specify the condition that allows the rule to recognize the files to which you want to apply the AD RMS template. For example, creating a rule that is triggered if the file contains the text "SECRET."

5. On the Action tab of the Create File Management Task dialog box, shown in Figure 9-23, specify RMS Encryption as the action type and the AD RMS template that you want to apply to the file.

6. On the Schedule tab, configure how often the file management task should run, whether it should classify only new files or periodically attempt to reclassify existing files.

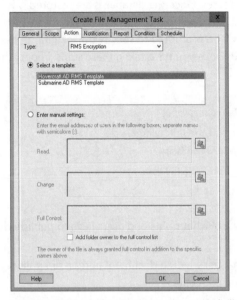

FIGURE 9-23 The Create File Management Task dialog box

Backing up AD RMS

To back up AD RMS in a way that you can perform a recovery in the event that the server hosting AD RMS fails and can't be recovered, requires doing the following:

- Keep a copy of the cluster key password in a safe location. If you do not know the current cluster key password, change it using the AD RMS console and then store the new password in a safe location.

- Export the trusted publishing domain. You can perform this task using the AD RMS console.

- Back up the AD RMS databases.

AD RMS uses three databases. The most important database is the *configuration database*. The configuration database stores information related to account certification, licensing, and publishing for the AD RMS cluster. The other two databases are the *directory services database* and the *logging database*. The directory services database stores cached data from Active Directory, and the logging database stores data about license acquisition and client activity.

If you have deployed AD RMS so that you are using SQL Server to host these databases, use the SQL Server Backup tools or a supported SQL Server backup solution to back up these databases. Recovering a Windows Internal Database is more complicated. You can manage and recover a Windows Internal Database using SQL Server Management Studio. If you're already using SQL Server Management Studio, you should probably use SQL Server to host the AD RMS databases for everything other than a test environment.

To recover AD RMS, first restore the databases. Once the databases are restored, you'll need to redeploy the AD RMS role service. During setup, you should choose the Join An Existing Cluster Option at which time you will be prompted to specify the location of the AD RMS database and the cluster key password. Once you have taken these steps, import the trusted publishing domain.

> **MORE INFO** **AD RMS DISASTER RECOVERY**
>
> To learn more about exclusion policies, consult the following article:
> *http://technet.microsoft.com/en-us/library/cc730687.aspx.*

Lesson summary

- AD RMS templates enable you to control what rights end users have to published content.
- AD RMS templates can be applied manually by the document author, or applied automatically using File Server Resource Manager.
- Trusted user domains allow a local AD RMS server to process CLC requests from users with rights account certificates (RACs) issued by foreign AD RMS clusters.
- Trusted publishing domains allow the local AD RMS server to issue Microsoft Software License Terms for content published using licenses from foreign AD RMS clusters.
- Exclusion policies allow you to block content consumption on the basis of user, application, or lockbox.
- The Super Users group is able to recover expired content, content where the template has been deleted, and content without author credentials.
- When installing AD RMS, you can register the SCP. This provides Active Directory clients with the ability to discover the location of the AD RMS server.

Lesson review

Answer the following questions to test your knowledge of the information in this lesson. You can find the answers to these questions and explanations of each answer choice in the "Answers" section at the end of this chapter.

1. You want a co-worker to be able to recover data from AD RMS–protected documents where the AD RMS template settings have caused that content to expire. To which of the following groups should you add your co-worker's account?

   A. Super Users

   B. AD RMS Enterprise Administrators

   C. AD RMS Template Administrators

   D. AD RMS Auditors

2. You want to allow the AD RMS cluster in the Adatum forest to be able to manage requests for CLCs for users that have been issued RACs from the AD RMS cluster in the Contoso forest. Which of the following should you configure to accomplish this goal?

   A. Trusted user domain

   B. Trusted publishing domain

   C. File Server Resource Manager file management task

   D. File Server Resource Manager classification rule

3. You want to automatically apply an AD RMS template named Submarine_Protection to all documents on a file share that contain the word "Submarine." Which of the following should you configure to accomplish this goal?

   A. File Server Resource Manager classification rule

   B. File Server Resource Manager file management task

   C. Trusted publishing domain

   D. Trusted user domain

4. You want to allow the AD RMS cluster in the Adatum forest to issue license terms to content published with licenses issued by an AD RMS cluster in the Contoso forest. Which of the following should you configure to accomplish this goal?

   A. File Server Resource Manager file management task

   B. Trusted publishing domain

   C. File Server Resource Manager classification rule

   D. Trusted user domain

Practice exercises

The goal of this section is to provide you with hands-on practice with the following:

- Configuring user and device claims
- Configuring resource properties
- Creating central access rules
- Creating central access policies

- Configuring access denied assistance
- Configuring staging
- Installing and configuring AD RMS
- Creating AD RMS templates
- Configuring template distribution
- Configuring application extensions
- Applying AD RMS templates using file classification

To perform the exercises in this section, you need access to an evaluation version of Windows Server 2012 R2. You should also have access to virtual machines SYD-DC, MEL-DC, CBR-DC, and ADL-DC, the setup instructions for which are described in the Introduction. You should ensure that you have a checkpoint of these virtual machines that you can revert to at the end of the practice exercises. You should revert the virtual machines to this initial state prior to beginning these exercises.

Exercise 1: Prepare MEL-DC and ADL-DC

In this exercise, you prepare MEL-DC and ADL-DC for practice exercises by joining them to the domain. To complete this exercise, perform the following steps:

1. Power on SYD-DC, MEL-DC, and ADL-DC.
2. Sign on to MEL-DC as MEL-DC\Administrator with the password **Pa$$w0rd**.
3. Click the Windows PowerShell icon on the taskbar.
4. In the Windows PowerShell window, type the following command and press Enter:

   ```
   Add-computer –credential contoso\administrator –DomainName contoso.com
   ```

5. In the Windows PowerShell Credential dialog box, shown in Figure 9-24, type the password **Pa$$w0rd** and click OK.

FIGURE 9-24 The Windows PowerShell Credentials dialog box

6. In the Windows PowerShell window, type the following command and press Enter:

   ```
   Restart-Computer
   ```

7. Sign on to MEL-DC as contoso\don_funk with the password **Pa$$w0rd**.

8. Switch to ADL-DC.

9. Sign on to ADL-DC as ADL-DC\Administrator with the password **Pa$$w0rd**.

10. Click the Windows PowerShell icon on the taskbar.

11. In the Windows PowerShell window, type the following command and press Enter:

    ```
    Add-computer -credential contoso\administrator -DomainName contoso.com
    ```

12. In the Windows PowerShell Credential dialog box, shown in Figure 9-25, type the password **Pa$$w0rd** and click OK.

FIGURE 9-25 The Windows PowerShell Credentials dialog box

13. In the Windows PowerShell window, type the following command and press Enter:

    ```
    Restart-Computer
    ```

14. Sign on to ADL-DC as contoso\don_funk with the password **Pa$$w0rd**.

Exercise 2: Enable group policy support for DAC

In this exercise, you edit the default domain policy to configure support for DAC. To complete this exercise, perform the following steps:

1. Ensure that you are signed on to SYD-DC as contoso\don_funk.

2. Click Active Directory Administrative Center on the Tools menu of the Server Manager Console.

3. In the Active Directory Administrative Center, right-click Contoso (Local), click New, and click Organizational Unit.

4. On the Create Organizational Unit dialog box, type **FileServers** in the Name text box as shown in Figure 9-26 and click OK.

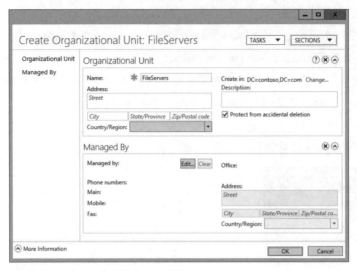

FIGURE 9-26 Create the FileServers OU

5. Click the Contoso (Local) node and then double-click the Computers container.

6. Hold down the Ctrl key and select ADL-DC and MEL-DC. Click Move in the Tasks pane.

7. Click FileServers in the Move dialog box as shown in Figure 9-27 and click OK.

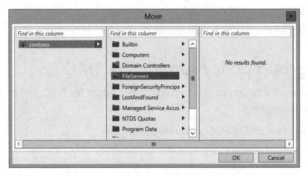

FIGURE 9-27 The Move dialog box

8. Click Group Policy Management on the Tools menu of the Server Manager console.

9. In the Group Policy Management Console, expand the Forest: Contoso.com node, expand the Domains node, expand the Contoso.com node, and then click the Domain Controllers node as shown in Figure 9-28.

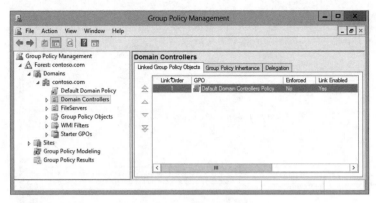

FIGURE 9-28 The Group Policy Management Console

10. Right-click the Default Domain Controllers Policy and click Edit.

11. In the Group Policy Management Editor, under the Computer Configuration node, expand the Policies node, expand the Administrative Templates node, expand the System node, and click the KDC node.

12. Double-click the KDC Support For Claims, Compound Authentication And Kerberos Armoring policy.

13. On the KDC Support For Claims, Compound Authentication And Kerberos Armoring Properties dialog box, click Enabled, and set the Options drop-down list to Supported, as shown in Figure 9-29. Click OK.

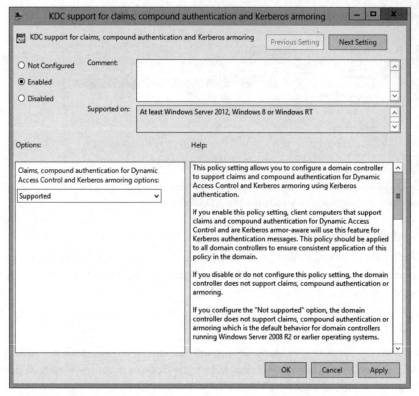

FIGURE 9-29 The KDC Support For Claims, Compound Authentication And Kerberos Armoring Properties dialog box.

14. Close the Group Policy Management Editor and the Group Policy Management Console.

15. Click the Windows PowerShell icon on the taskbar.

16. In the Windows PowerShell window, type the following command and press Enter:

```
Gpupdate /force
```

Exercise 3: Create users and groups

In this exercise, you create two different users that have different account properties that will be used to mediate access through DAC. You also create security groups that will be used in later exercises. To complete this exercise, perform the following steps:

1. On SYD-DC, in the Active Directory Administrative Center console, click Contoso (Local).

2. On the Tasks pane, click New, and then click User.

3. On the Create User dialog box, configure the following settings as shown in Figure 9-30 and click OK:

- Full name: **kim_akers**

- User SamAccountName Logon: **contoso\kim_akers**
- Password: **Pa$$w0rd**
- Confirm password: **Pa$$w0rd**
- Other Password Options: **Enabled**
- Password Never Expires: **Enabled**
- Office: **Melbourne**
- Job Title: **Engineer**
- Department: **Research**

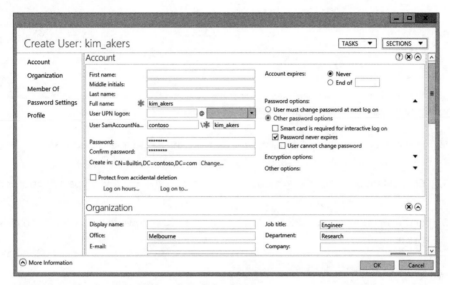

FIGURE 9-30 The Create User: kim_akers dialog box

4. On the Tasks pane, click New, and then click User.

5. On the Create User dialog box, configure the following settings as shown in Figure 9-31 and click OK:

- Full name: **gabe_frost**
- User SamAccountName Logon: **contoso\gabe_frost**
- Password: **Pa$$w0rd**
- Confirm password: **Pa$$w0rd**
- Other Password Options: **Enabled**
- Password Never Expires: **Enabled**
- Office: **Sydney**
- Job Title: **Technician**
- Department: **IT**

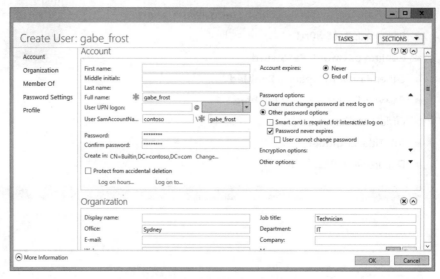

FIGURE 9-31 The Create User: gabe_frost dialog box

6. In the Active Directory Administrative Center console, double-click the Builtin container, click gabe_frost, and click Properties on the Tasks pane.

7. Click Extensions, click the Attribute Editor tab, click the EmployeeType extension, and click Edit.

8. In the String Attribute Editor dialog box, type **FTE** as shown in Figure 9-32 and click OK twice.

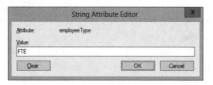

FIGURE 9-32 The String Attribute Editor

9. In the Active Directory Administrative Center console, click the kim_akers user account, and click Properties on the Tasks pane.

10. Click Extensions, click the Attribute Editor tab, click the EmployeeType extension, and click Edit.

11. In the String Attribute Editor dialog box, type **CONTRACTOR** as shown in Figure 9-33 and click OK twice.

FIGURE 9-33 The String Attribute Editor

12. In the Active Directory Administrative Center console, click Contoso (Local) and then double-click the FileServers OU.

13. Select MEL-DC and click Properties in the Tasks pane.

14. Click Extensions and then click the Attribute Editor tab.

15. Click the Location attribute and click Edit.

16. On the String Attribute Editor dialog box, type **Secure** as shown in Figure 9-34 and click OK.

FIGURE 9-34 The String Attribute Editor

17. Click OK to close the MEL-DC dialog box.

18. Click Contoso (Local). On the Tasks pane, click New and click Group.

19. On the Create Group dialog box, type the name **Hovercraft_Project** in the Group Name text box and click OK.

20. Click Contoso (Local). On the Tasks pane, click New and click Group.

21. On the Create Group dialog box, type the name **Submarine_Project** in the Group Name text box and click OK.

22. Right-click the Submarine_Project group and click Properties.

23. On the Members section, click Add. In the Select Users, Contacts, Computers, Service Accounts, Or Groups dialog box, type **kim_akers** and click OK twice.

24. Click Contoso (Local). On the Tasks pane, click New and click Group.

25. On the Create Group dialog box, type the name **Secret_Projects** in the Group Name text box and click OK.

26. Right-click on the Hovercraft_Project group and click Properties.

27. In the Members section, click Add.

28. In the Select Users, Contacts, Computers, Service Accounts, Or Groups dialog box, type **gabe_frost** and click OK twice.

29. Right-click the Secret_Projects group and click Properties.

30. In the Members section, click Add.

31. In the Select Users, Contacts, Computers, Service Accounts, Or Groups dialog box, type **kim_akers; gabe_frost** and click OK.

32. Verify that the Members section of the Secret Projects group matches Figure 9-35 and click OK.

FIGURE 9-35 Secret_Projects

Exercise 4: Configure user and device claims

In this exercise, you configure claims that can be used by DAC based on the attributes configured in the previous exercise. To complete this exercise, perform the following steps:

1. In the Active Directory Administrative Center, click Dynamic Access Control, and double-click Claim Types.

2. On the Tasks pane, click New, and click Claim Type.

3. On the Create Claim Type dialog box, select Department and ensure that User is selected as shown in Figure 9-36. Click Suggested Values.

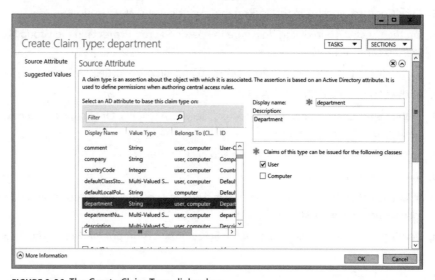

FIGURE 9-36 The Create Claim Type dialog box

4. Click The Following Values Are Suggested and click Add.

5. In the Add A Suggested Value dialog box, type **Research** in the Value and Display Name text boxes as shown in Figure 9-37 and click OK.

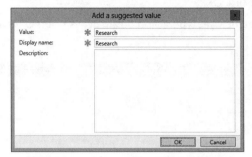

FIGURE 9-37 Add A Suggested Value dialog box

6. On the Create Claim Type: Department dialog box, click Add.

7. On the Add A Suggested Value dialog box, type **IT** in the Value and Display Name text boxes and click OK.

8. Verify that the Create Claim Type: Department dialog box matches Figure 9-38 and click OK.

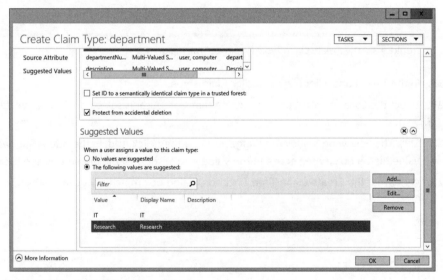

FIGURE 9-38 Create Claim Type dialog box

9. In the Tasks pane, click New and click Claim Type.

10. Click the EmployeeType attribute, ensure User is selected, and click Suggested Values.

11. Click The Following Values Are Suggested and click Add.

12. On the Add A Suggested Value dialog box, type **FTE** in the Value and Display Name text boxes and click OK.

13. Click Add. On the Add A Suggested Value dialog box, type **CONTRACTOR** in the Value and Display Name text boxes and click OK.

14. Verify that the Create Claim Type: EmployeeType dialog box matches Figure 9-39 and click OK.

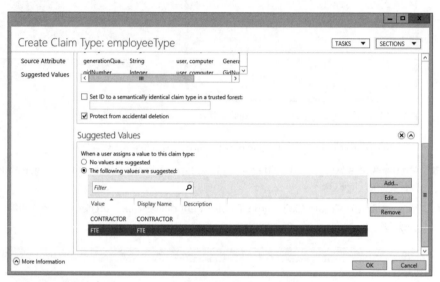

FIGURE 9-39 The Create Claim Type: EmployeeType dialog box

15. In the Tasks pane, click New and click Claim Type.

16. Select the Location attribute and ensure that Computer is selected. Click Suggested Values.

17. Click The Following Values Are Suggested and then click Add. In the Add A Suggested Value dialog box, type **Secure** in the Value And Display Name dialog box and click OK.

18. Verify that the Create Claim Type: Location dialog box matches Figure 9-40 and click OK.

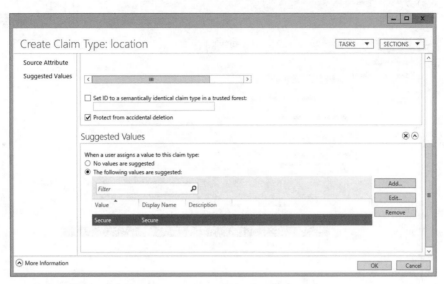

FIGURE 9-40 The Create Claim Type: Location dialog box

19. In the Tasks pane, click New and click Claim Type.

20. Select the PhysicalDeliveryOfficeName attribute, ensure that User is selected, and click Suggested Values.

21. Click The Following Values Are Suggested and click Add. In the Add A Suggested Value dialog box, type **Sydney** in the Value and Display Name text boxes and click OK.

22. Click Add. In the Add A Suggested Value dialog box, type **Melbourne** in the Value and Display Name text boxes and click OK.

23. Verify that the Create Claim Type: PhysicalDeliveryOfficeName dialog box matches Figure 9-41 and click OK.

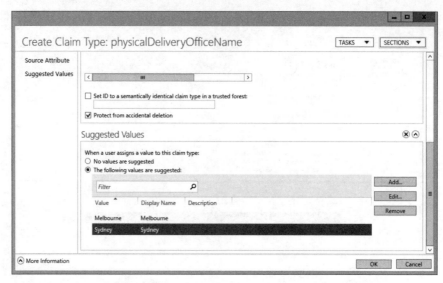

FIGURE 9-41 The Create Claim Type: PhysicalDeliveryOfficeName dialog box

24. In the Tasks pane, click New and click Claim Type.

25. Select the Title attribute, ensure that User is selected and click Suggested Values.

26. Click The Following Values Are Suggested and click Add. In the Add A Suggested Value dialog box, type **Engineer** in the Value and Display Name text boxes and click OK.

27. Click Add. In the Add A Suggested Value dialog box, type **Technician** in the Value and Display Name text boxes and click OK.

28. Verify that the Create Claim Type: Title dialog box matches Figure 9-42 and click OK.

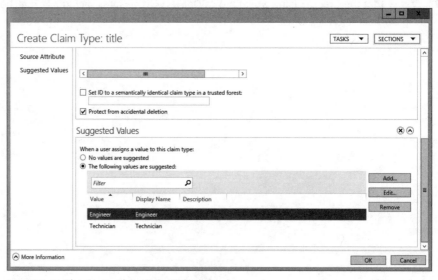

FIGURE 9-42 The Create Claim Type: Title dialog box

29. Verify that the list of Claim Types matches Figure 9-43.

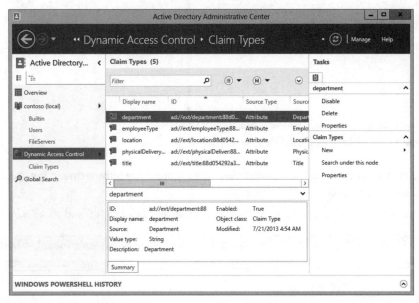

FIGURE 9-43 Claim types

Exercise 5: Configure resource properties

In this exercise, you configure resource properties. To complete this exercise, perform the following steps:

1. In the Active Directory Administrative Center console, click Dynamic Access Control and then double-click Resource Properties.

2. In the list of Resource Properties, click Confidentiality and then click Enable in the Tasks pane.

3. In the list of Resource Properties, click Required Clearance and click Enabled in the Tasks pane.

4. In the list of Resource Properties, click Project and click Properties. Click Suggested Values and click Add.

5. In the Add A Suggested Value dialog box, type **Hovercraft** in the Value and Display Name text boxes as shown in Figure 9-44 and click OK.

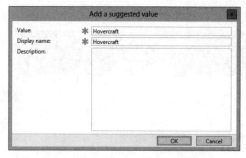

FIGURE 9-44 Add A Suggested Value dialog box

6. Click Add. In the Add A Suggested Value dialog box, type **Submarine** in the Value and Display Name text boxes and click OK.

7. Verify that the Project (Disabled) dialog box matches Figure 9-45 and click OK.

FIGURE 9-45 The Project (Disabled) dialog box

8. Ensure Project is selected in the list of Resource Properties and click Enable.

9. In the Active Directory Administrative Center console, click Dynamic Access Control. In the Dynamic Access Control List, double-click Resource Property Lists and then double-click Global Resource Property List.

10. Verify that Project, Confidentiality, and Required Clearance are present as shown in Figure 9-46 and click Cancel.

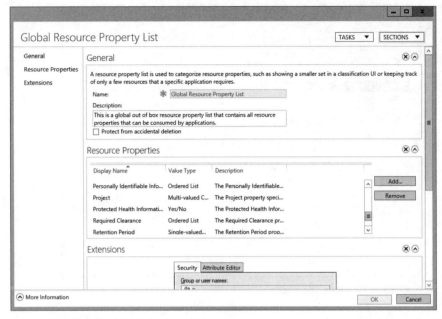

FIGURE 9-46 Global Resource Property List

Exercise 6: Prepare server for file classification

In this exercise, you configure ADL-DC with File Server Resource Manager, create a file share, and create files that you will use for classification. To complete this exercise, perform the following steps:

1. Sign on to ADL-DC as contoso\don_funk.

2. Right-click the Windows PowerShell icon on the desktop and click Run As Administrator to open an elevated Windows PowerShell window. Click Yes on the User Account Control dialog box.

3. Type the following command and press Enter to install the File Server and File Server Resource Manager role services:

   ```
   Install-WindowsFeature FS-FileServer,FS-Resource-Manager –IncludeAllSubFeature
   -IncludeManagementTools
   ```

4. In the Server Manager console, click File And Storage Services, and click Shares.

5. On the Tasks drop-down list, click New Share.

6. On the Select The Profile For This Share page of the New Share Wizard, click SMB Share – Quick and click Next twice.

7. On the Specify Share Name page, type **FileShare** in the Share Name text box as shown in Figure 9-47. Click Next.

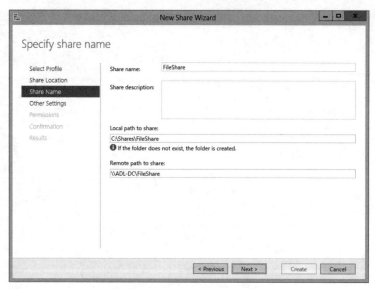

FIGURE 9-47 The New Share Wizard

8. On the Configure Share Settings page, click Enable Access-Based Enumeration as shown in Figure 9-48, click Next twice, click Create, and click Close.

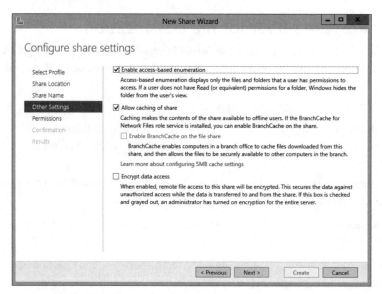

FIGURE 9-48 The New Share Wizard

9. Click the File Explorer icon on the task bar and navigate to the C:\Shares\Fileshare folder.

10. Use Notepad to create five new text files with the following names and properties in the c:\Shares\Fileshare folder:

- **Secret-File.txt** Edit this file so that it contains the text SECRET.

- **Hovercraft-File.txt** Edit this file so that it contains the text HOVERCRAFT.

- **Submarine-File.txt** Edit this file so that it contains the text SUBMARINE AND SECRET.

- **FTE-ONLY.txt** Edit this file so that it contains the text FTE-ONLY.

Exercise 7: Create a file classification rule

In this exercise, you create a file classification rule. To complete this exercise, perform the following steps:

1. On ADL-DC while signed on as contoso\don_funk, click File Server Resource Manager in the Tools menu of the Server Manager console.

2. In the File Server Resource Manager console, expand the Classification Management node and click Classification Properties.

3. Verify that Confidentiality, Project, And Required Clearance are present as shown in Figure 9-49.

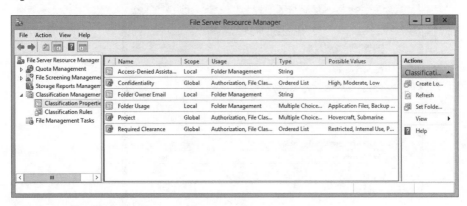

FIGURE 9-49 The File Server Resource Manager

4. Click Classification Rules.

5. In the Actions pane, click Create Classification Rule.

6. On the General tab of the Create Classification Rule dialog box, type the name **Confidentiality_Rule.**

7. On the Scope tab, click Add, select C:\Shares as shown in Figure 9-50, and click OK.

FIGURE 9-50 The Browse For Folder dialog box

8. On the Classification tab, set the Classification Method to Content Classifier, the Property to Confidentiality, and the Value to High as shown in Figure 9-51. Click Configure.

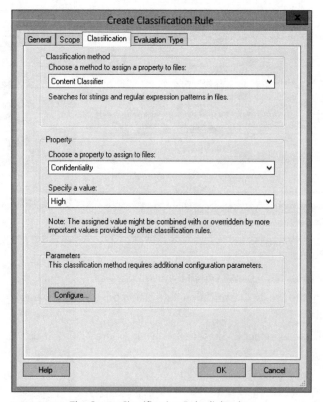

FIGURE 9-51 The Create Classification Rule dialog box

9. On the Classification Parameters dialog box, click the Regular Expression drop-down list and click String. In the Expression text box, type **secret** as shown in Figure 9-52 and click OK.

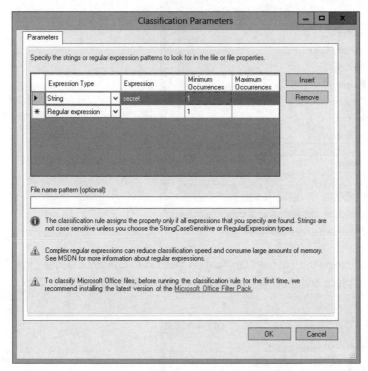

FIGURE 9-52 The Classification Parameters dialog box

10. On the Evaluation Type tab, click Re-Evaluate Existing Property Values, click Overwrite Existing Value, and click OK.

11. In the Actions pane, click Create Classification Rule.

12. On the General tab of the Create Classification Rule dialog box, type the name **Submarine_Rule**.

13. On the Scope tab, click Add, select C:\Shares as shown in Figure 9-53, and click OK.

FIGURE 9-53 The Browse For Folder dialog box

14. On the Classification tab, set the Classification Method to Content Classifier, the Property to Project, and the Value to Submarine as shown in Figure 9-54. Click Configure.

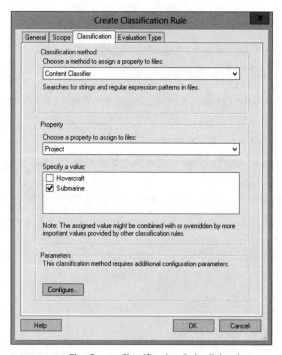

FIGURE 9-54 The Create Classification Rule dialog box

15. On the Classification Parameters dialog box, click the Regular Expression drop-down list and click String. In the Expression text box, type **submarine** as shown in Figure 9-55 and click OK.

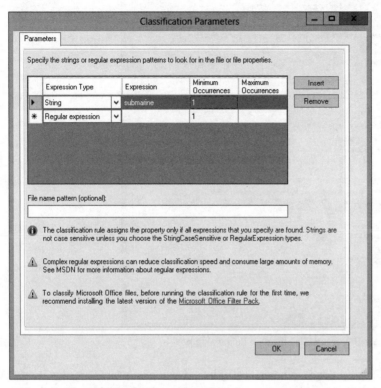

FIGURE 9-55 The Classification Parameters dialog box

16. On the Evaluation Type tab, click Re-Evaluate Existing Property Values, click Overwrite Existing Value, and click OK.

17. In the Actions pane, click Create Classification Rule.

18. On the General tab of the Create Classification Rule dialog box, type the name **Hovercraft_Rule.**

19. On the Scope tab, click Add, select C:\Shares, and click OK.

20. On the Classification tab, set the Classification Method to Content Classifier, the Property to Project, and the Value to Hovercraft as shown in Figure 9-56. Click Configure.

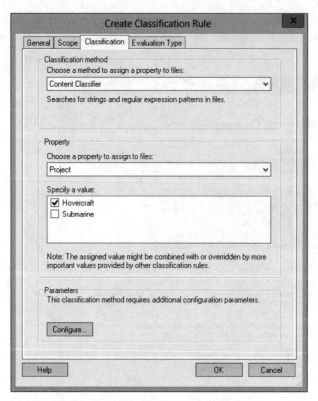

FIGURE 9-56 The Create Classification Rule dialog box

21. On the Classification Parameters dialog box, click the Regular Expression drop-down list and click String. In the Expression text box, type **hovercraft** as shown in Figure 9-57 and click OK.

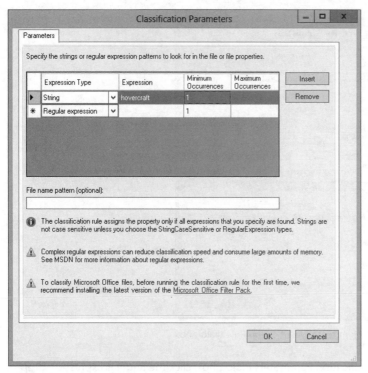

FIGURE 9-57 The Classification Parameters dialog box

22. On the Evaluation Type tab, click Re-Evaluate Existing Property Values, click Overwrite Existing Value, and click OK.

23. In the Actions pane, click Create Classification Rule.

24. On the General tab of the Create Classification Rule dialog box, type the name **FTE_Rule.**

25. On the Scope tab, click Add, select C:\Shares, and click OK.

26. On the Classification tab, set the Classification Method to Content Classifier, the Property to Required Clearance, and the Value to Restricted as shown in Figure 9-58. Click Configure.

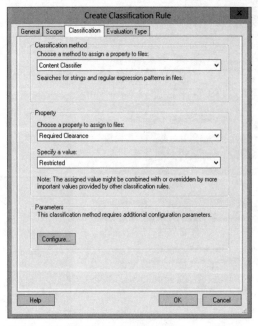

FIGURE 9-58 The Create Classification Rule dialog box

27. On the Classification Parameters dialog box, click the Regular Expression drop-down list and click String. In the Expression text box, type **fte-only** as shown in Figure 9-59 and click OK.

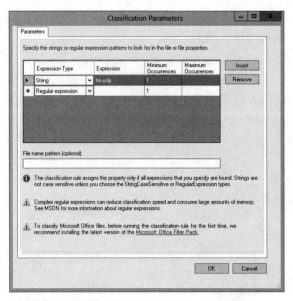

FIGURE 9-59 The Classification Parameters dialog box

28. On the Evaluation Type tab, click Re-Evaluate Existing Property Values, click Overwrite Existing Value, and click OK.

Exercise 8: Run and verify the file classification

In this exercise, you run and verify file classification. To complete this exercise, perform the following steps:

1. In the File Server Resource Manager, ensure that the Classification Rules node is selected and click Run Classification With All Rules Now in the Actions pane.

2. On the Run Classification dialog box, click Wait For Classification To Complete as shown in Figure 9-60 and click OK.

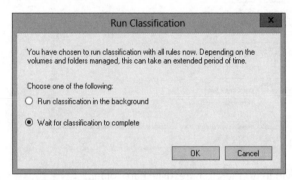

FIGURE 9-60 The Run Classification dialog box

3. Review the Classification Report shown in Figure 9-61 and verify the following:

- Submarine-File.txt was assigned a Confidentiality value of High and a Project value of Submarine.

- Secret-File.txt was assigned a Confidentiality of High.

- Hovercraft-File.txt was assigned a Project of Hovercraft.

- FTE-ONLY.txt was assigned a Required Clearance value of Restricted.

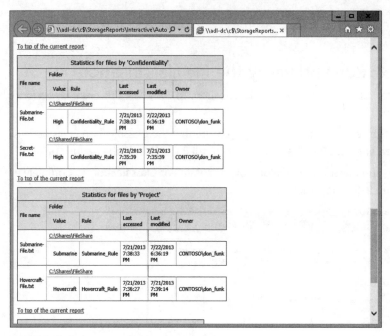

FIGURE 9-61 A storage report

4. Open File Explorer and navigate to the C:\Shares\FileShare folder.

5. Right-click Submarine-File.txt and click Properties.

6. On the Classification tab, verify that Confidentiality is set to High, Project is set to Submarine, and Required Clearance is set to (None) as shown in Figure 9-62. Click OK.

FIGURE 9-62 The Submarine-File Properties dialog box

Exercise 9: Create central access rules

In this exercise, you create access rules. To complete this exercise, perform the following steps:

1. Ensure that you are signed on to SYD-DC as contoso\don_funk.

2. Click Active Directory Administrative Center on the Tools menu of the Server Manger console.

3. Click Dynamic Access Control and then double-click Central Access Rules.

4. On the Tasks pane, click New and click Central Access Rule.

5. In the Name text box, type **Research_Projects**.

6. Click Edit in the Target Resources section.

7. On the Central Access Rule dialog box, click Add A Condition.

8. Click the Confidentiality drop-down list and set it to Project.

9. Click the 0 Items Select drop down-list and click Hovercraft as shown in Figure 9-63. Click OK.

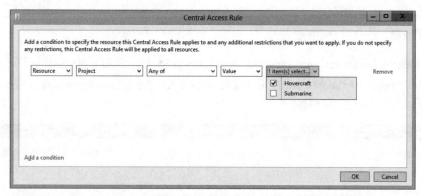

FIGURE 9-63 The Central Access Rule dialog box

10. Click Use The Following Permissions As Current Permissions and click Edit.

11. On the Advanced Security Settings For Permissions dialog box, click Add.

12. On the Permission Entry For Permissions dialog box, click Select A Principal.

13. On the Select User, Computer, Service Account, Or Group dialog box, type **Hovercraft_Project** and click OK.

14. On the Permissions Entry For Permissions dialog box, click Full Control. Click Add A Condition.

15. Click the Group drop-down list and click EmployeeType.

16. Click the blank drop-down list and click FTE.

17. Verify that the Permission Entry For Permissions dialog box matches Figure 9-64 and click OK.

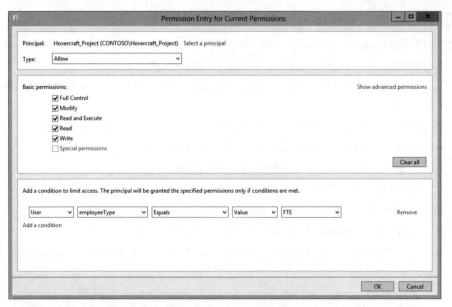

FIGURE 9-64 The Permission Entry For Current Permissions dialog box

18. Click OK to close the Advanced Security Settings For Permissions dialog box.

19. Verify that the Create Central Access Rule: Research_Projects dialog box matches Figure 9-65 and click OK.

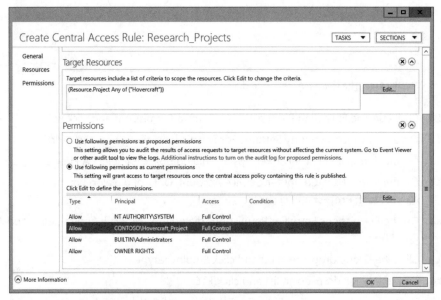

FIGURE 9-65 The Central Access Rule: Research_Projects dialog box

20. On the Tasks pane, click New and click Central Access Rule.

21. In the Name text box, type **Secret_Projects.**

22. Click Edit in the Target Resources section.

23. On the Central Access Rule dialog box, click Add A Condition.

24. On the Central Access Rule dialog box, click the Confidentiality drop-down list and select Required Clearance.

25. On the blank drop-down list click Restricted as shown in Figure 9-66 and click OK.

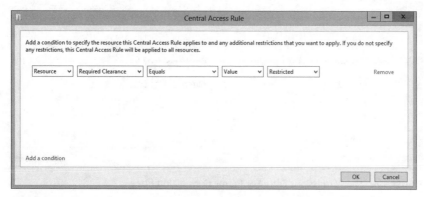

FIGURE 9-66 The Central Access Rule dialog box

26. Click Use The Following Permissions As Current Permissions and click Edit.

27. On the Advanced Security Settings For Permissions dialog box, click Add.

28. On the Permission Entry For Permissions dialog box, click Select A Principal.

29. In the Select User, Computer, Service Account Or Group dialog box, type Secret Projects and click OK.

30. On the Permission Entry For Permissions dialog box, under Basic Permissions, click Full Control and click Add A Condition.

31. Click the Group drop-down list and click EmployeeType.

32. Click the blank drop-down list and click FTE.

33. Verify that the Permission Entry For Permissions dialog box matches Figure 9-67 and click OK three times.

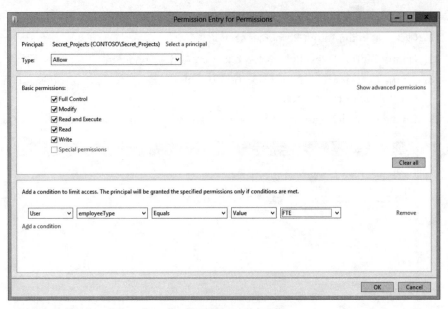

FIGURE 9-67 The Permissions Entry For Permissions dialog box

> **NOTE FTE ONLY**
>
> This permission is configured so that even if a user is a member of the Secret_Projects security group, he or she is only assigned this permission to files that have the Requires Clearance:Restricted classification if the EmployeeType Active Directory attribute is set to FTE.

Exercise 10: Create a central access policy

In this exercise, you create a central access policy. To complete this exercise, perform the following steps:

1. In the Active Directory Administrative Center console, click Dynamic Access Control and click Central Access Policies.

2. On the Tasks pane, click New and click Central Access Policy.

3. In the Create Central Access Policy dialog box, type **Contoso Policy** and click Add.

4. On the Add Central Access Rules, click Research_Projects and Secret_Projects and add them to the Add The Following Central Access Rules list as shown in Figure 9-68. Click OK.

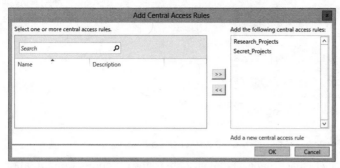

FIGURE 9-68 The Add Central Access Rules dialog box

5. Verify that the Create Central Access Policy: Contoso Policy dialog box matches Figure 9-69 and click OK.

FIGURE 9-69 The Central Access Policy: Contoso Policy dialog box

6. On the Tools menu of the Server Manager console, click Group Policy Management.

7. In the Group Policy Management Console, expand Forest: Contoso.com, expand Domains, expand Contoso.com, and click the FileServers node.

8. In the Action menu, click Create A GPO In This Domain, and Link It Here.

9. On the New GPO dialog box, shown in Figure 9-70, type the name **Contoso DAC Policy** and click OK.

FIGURE 9-70 The New GPO dialog box

10. Right-click the Contoso DAC Policy GPO and click Edit.

11. In the Group Policy Management Editor, navigate to the Computer Configuration\
Policies\Windows Settings\Security Settings\File System node.

12. Click Central Access Policy and on the Action menu click Manage Central Access
Policies.

13. On the Central Access Policies Configuration dialog box, click Contoso Policy and click
Add. Verify that the Central Access Policies Configuration dialog box matches Figure
9-71 and click OK.

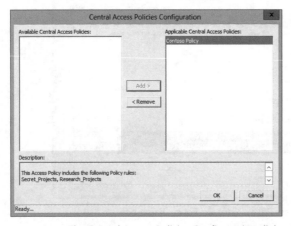

FIGURE 9-71 The Central Access Policies Configuration dialog box

14. Switch to ADL-DC and ensure that you are signed on as contoso\don_funk.

15. Click the Windows PowerShell icon on the taskbar.

16. In the Windows PowerShell window, type the following command and press Enter:

    Gpupdate /force

17. In File Explorer, navigate to the C:\Shares folder. Right-click FileShare and click
Properties.

18. On the Security tab of the FileShare Properties dialog box, click Advanced.

19. On the Advanced Security Settings For FileShare dialog box, click Central Policy tab.

20. On the Central Policy tab of the Advanced Security Settings For FileShare dialog box,
click Change and select Contoso Policy as shown in Figure 9-72. Click Apply.

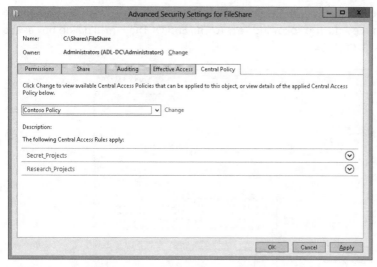

FIGURE 9-72 The Advanced Security Settings For FileShare dialog box

21. Click the Permissions tab and click Replace All Child Object Permission Entries with Inheritable Permission Entries From This Object and click OK.

22. On the Windows Security dialog box, click Yes.

23. Click OK to close the FileShare Properties dialog box.

Exercise 11: Configure Access Denied Assistance

In this exercise, you configure Access Denied Assistance. To complete this exercise, perform the following steps:

1. Switch to SYD-DC and ensure that you are signed on as contoso\don_funk.

2. Click Group Policy Management on the Tools menu of the Server Manager console.

3. In the Group Policy Management Console, expand Forest: Contoso.com, expand Domains, expand Contoso.com, and click FileServers.

4. Right-click the Contoso DAC Policy and click Edit.

5. In the Group Policy Management Editor, expand Computer Configuration, expand Policies, expand Administrative Templates, expand System, and click Access-Denied Assistance.

6. Double-click the Customize Message For Access Denied Errors policy.

7. On the Customize Message For Access Denied Errors dialog box, click Enabled.

8. In the Display The Following Message To Users Who Are Denied Access text box type **Current permissions configuration blocks you from accessing this file.**

9. Select the Enable Users To Request Assistance check box and type **User needs to send e-mail** in the Add The Following Text To The End Of The E-mail dialog box as shown in Figure 9-73. Click OK.

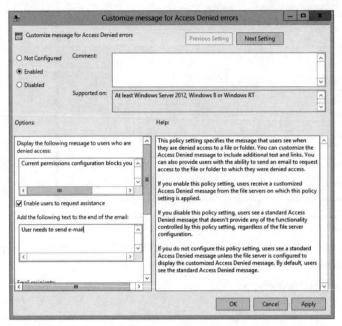

FIGURE 9-73 The Customize Message For Access Denied Errors dialog box

10. Double-click the Enable Access-Denied Assistance on Client For All File Types policy.

11. On the Enable Access-Denied Assistance on Client For All File Types dialog box, click Enabled as shown in Figure 9-74 and click OK.

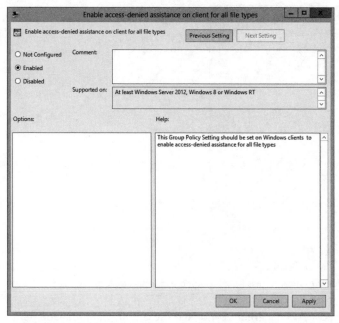

FIGURE 9-74 The Enable Access-Denied Assistance On Client For All File Types dialog box

12. Close the Group Policy Management Editor.

Exercise 12: Configure staging

In this exercise, you configure staging for an existing central access rule. To complete this exercise, perform the following steps:

1. Ensure that you are signed on to SYD-DC as contoso\don_funk.

2. Click Group Policy Management on the Tasks menu of the Server Manager console.

3. In the Group Policy Management Console, expand Forest:contoso.com\Domains\contoso.com. Right-click Default Domain Policy and click Edit.

4. In the Group Policy Management Editor, navigate to the Computer Configuration\Policies\Windows Settings\Security Settings\Advanced Audit Policy Configuration\Audit Policies\Object Access node.

5. Right-click the Audit Central Access Policy Staging policy and click Properties.

6. On the Audit Central Access Policy Staging Properties dialog box, enable Configure The Following Audit Events, Success, And Failure as shown in Figure 9-75 and click OK.

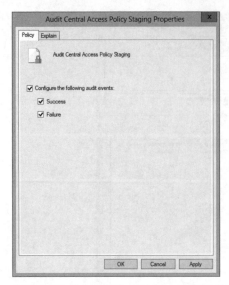

FIGURE 9-75 The Audit Central Access Policy Staging Properties dialog box

7. Close the Group Policy Management Editor and the Group Policy Management Console.

8. Click Active Directory Administrative Center on the Tasks menu of the Server Manager console.

9. In the Active Directory Administrative Center, click Dynamic Access Control and then double-click Central Access Rules.

10. Click Secret_Projects and click Properties in the Tasks pane.

11. In the Secret_Projects dialog box, click Proposed and then click Enable Permission Staging Configuration.

12. Click Contoso\Secret_Projects and click Edit.

13. On the Advanced Security Settings for Proposed Permissions click Secret_Projects and click Edit.

14. On the Permission Entry For Proposed Permissions dialog box, remove the Full Control permission and change FTE to CONTRACTOR as shown in Figure 9-76. Click OK twice.

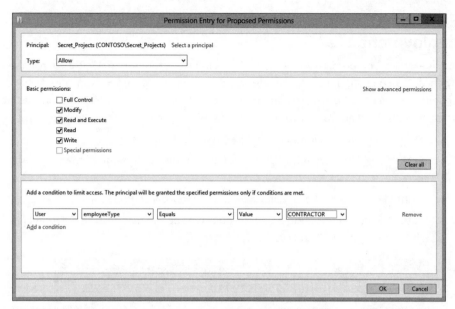

FIGURE 9-76 The Permission Entry For Proposed Permissions dialog box

15. Ensure that the Secret_Projects dialog box matches Figure 9-77 and then click OK.

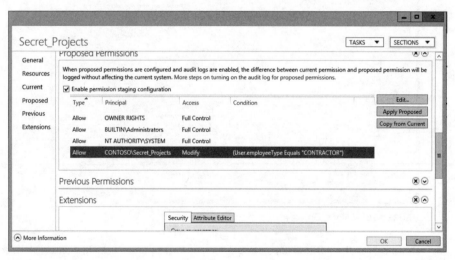

FIGURE 9-77 Secret_Projects

Exercise 13: Prepare infrastructure for an AD RMS deployment

In this exercise, you prepare your organization's infrastructure for an AD RMS deployment by creating and configuring appropriate services, users, and group accounts. As AD RMS depends on email addresses associated with accounts, it is necessary to provision existing accounts with email addresses. To complete this exercise, perform the following steps:

1. Ensure that you are signed on to SYD-DC as contoso\don_funk.

2. Click Active Directory Administrative Center on the Tools menu of the Server Manager console.

3. Right-click Contoso (Local), click New and click Organizational Unit.

4. In the Create Organizational Unit dialog box, type the name **ADRMS_Objects** as shown in Figure 9-78 and click OK.

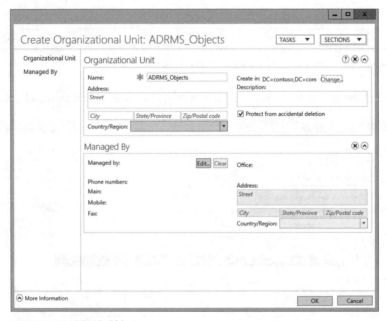

FIGURE 9-78 ADRMS_Objects

5. Double-click the ADRMS_Objects OU. On the Tasks pane, click New and click User.

6. In the Create User dialog box, configure the following as shown in Figure 9-79 and click OK:

   - Full name: **ADRMS_SVC**
   - User UPN logon: **ADRMS_SVC**
   - Password: **Pa$$w0rd**
   - Confirm password: **Pa$$w0rd**

- Other Password Options: **Enabled**
- Password Never Expires: **Enabled**
- User Cannot Change Password: **Enabled**

FIGURE 9-79 The Create User: ADRMS_SVC dialog box

7. In the Tasks pane, click New and click Group.

8. In the Create Group dialog box, configure the following settings as shown in Figure 9-80 and click OK:

- Group name: **ADRMS_SuperUsers**
- E-mail: **ADRMS_SuperUsers@contoso.com**

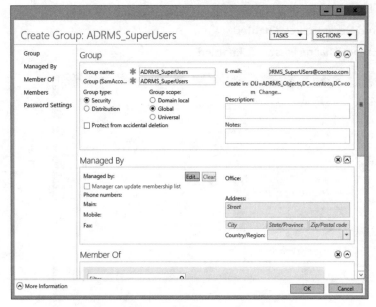

FIGURE 9-80 The Create Group: ADRMS_SuperUsers dialog box

9. Double-click Contoso (Local) and then double-click Builtin.

10. Right-click Gabe_frost and click Properties.

11. On the Gabe_frost dialog box, type the email address **gabe_frost@contoso.com** as shown in Figure 9-81 and click OK.

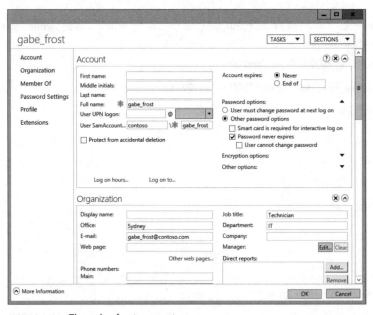

FIGURE 9-81 The gabe_frost account

12. Right-click kim_akers and click Properties.

13. In the Email text box, type **kim_akers@contoso.com** and click OK.

14. Right-click Secret_Projects and click Properties.

15. On the Secret_Projects dialog box, set the Email text box to **secret_projects@contoso.com** as shown in Figure 9-82 and click OK.

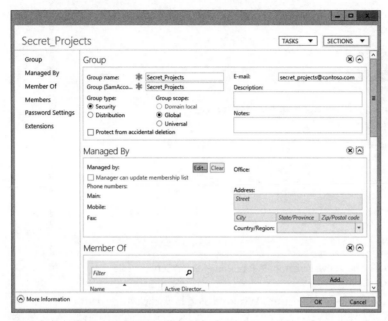

FIGURE 9-82 The Secret_Projects dialog box

16. Right-click Submarine_Project and click Properties.

17. In the Email text box, type **submarine_project@contoso.com** and click OK.

18. Right-click Hovercraft_Project and click Properties.

19. In the Email text box, type **hovercraft_project@contoso.com** and click OK.

20. Right-click the Windows PowerShell icon on the taskbar, click Run As Administrator, and type the following command to create a new host record:

```
Add-DnsServerResourceRecordA –Ipv4Address 10.10.10.40 –Name adrms –ZoneName
contoso.com
```

Exercise 14: Install and configure the AD RMS server role

In this exercise, you install and configure the AD RMS server role. To complete this exercise, perform the following steps:

1. Sign on to MEL-DC as contoso\don_funk with the password **Pa$$w0rd**.

2. On the Manage menu of the Server Manager console, click Add Roles And Features.

3. On the Before You Begin page of the Add Roles And Features Wizard, click Next three times.

4. On the Select Server Roles page, select Active Directory Rights Management Services as shown in Figure 9-83.

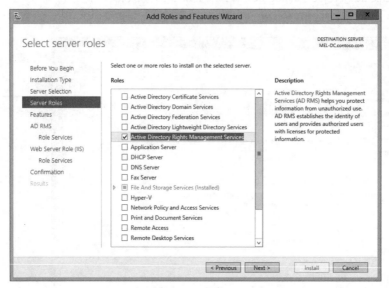

FIGURE 9-83 The Active Directory Rights Management Services role

5. On the Add Roles And Features Wizard dialog box, click Add Features.

6. Click Next six times and click Install. When the Add Roles And Features Wizard completes, click Close.

7. On the Server Manager console, click the notification icon next to the Manage menu.

8. On the Post-Deployment Configuration notification, shown in Figure 9-84, click Perform Additional Configuration.

FIGURE 9-84 Post-Deployment Configuration

9. On the AD RMS page of the AD RMS Configuration Wizard, click Next.

10. On the AD RMS Cluster page, click Create A New AD RMS Root Cluster as shown in Figure 9-85 and click Next.

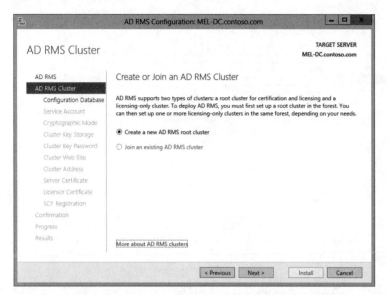

FIGURE 9-85 AD RMS Cluster page of the AD RMS Configuration Wizard.

11. On the Configuration Database page, click Use Windows Internal Database On This Server and click Next.

12. On the Service Account page, click Specify.

13. On the Windows Security dialog box, type **ADRMS_SVC@contoso.com** and the password **Pa$$w0rd** as shown in Figure 9-86, and click OK. Click Next.

FIGURE 9-86 The Windows Security dialog box

14. On the Cryptographic Mode page, select Cryptographic Mode 2 (RSA 2048-bit keys/ SHA-256 hashes) as shown in Figure 9-87 and click Next.

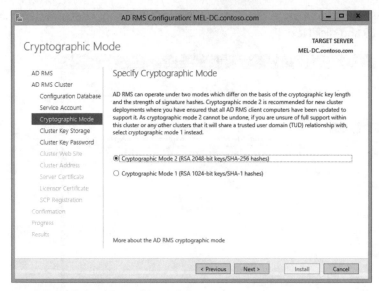

FIGURE 9-87 The Cryptographic Mode page

15. On the Cluster Key Storage page, click Use AD RMS Centrally Managed Key Storage and click Next.

16. On the Cluster Key Password page enter the password **Pa$$w0rd** twice and click Next.

17. On the Cluster Web Site page, click Default Web Site and click Next.

18. On the Cluster Address page, click Use An Unencrypted Connection (http://) and set the Fully Qualified Domain Name to **adrms.contoso.com** as shown in Figure 9-88. Click Next.

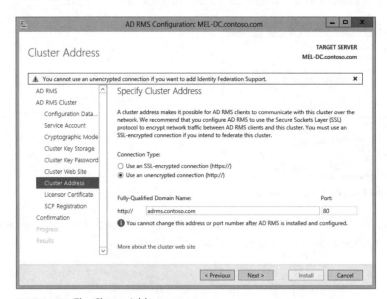

FIGURE 9-88 The Cluster Address page

19. On the Licensor Certificate page, type **Contoso AD RMS** as shown in Figure 9-89 and click Next.

FIGURE 9-89 The Licensor Certificate page

20. On the SCP Registration page, click Register The SCP Now and click Next.

21. On the Confirmation Page, verify that the installation settings match Figure 9-90 and click Install.

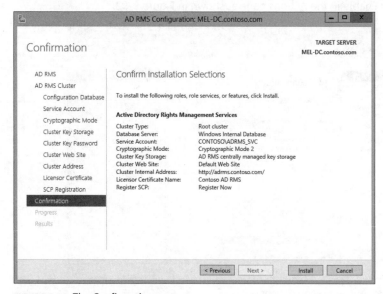

FIGURE 9-90 The Confirmation page

22. Click Internet Information Services (IIS) Manager on the Tools menu of the Server Manager console.

23. Expand the MEL-DC node. Click No to dismiss the Internet Information Services (IIS) Manager dialog box. Expand the Sites node, expand Default Web Site, and click _wmcs as shown in Figure 9-91.

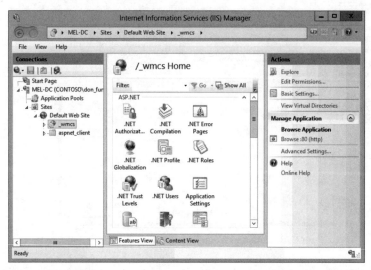

FIGURE 9-91 IIS Manager

24. Under /_wmcs Home, double-click Authentication, click Anonymous Authentication and click Enable in the Actions pane as shown in Figure 9-92.

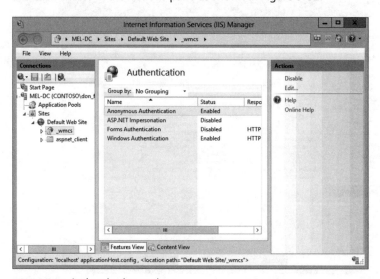

FIGURE 9-92 Authentication options

25. Expand the _wmcs node and click Licensing. Double-click Authentication, right-click Anonymous Authentication, and click Enable as shown in Figure 9-93.

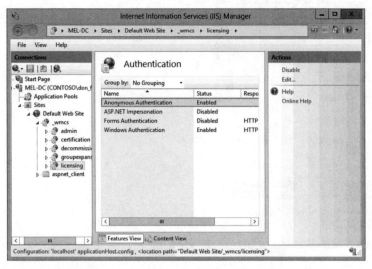

FIGURE 9-93 IIS Manager

26. Restart MEL-DC.

> **MORE INFO** SIGN OUT OR RESTART
>
> After configuring AD RMS, you need to sign off of the server before you can manage it. Asking you to perform a restart accomplishes the same objective and increases the likelihood that you will actually perform the step.

Exercise 15: Create the AD RMS Super Users group

In this exercise, you configure the AD RMS Super Users group. To complete this exercise, perform the following steps:

1. Sign on to MEL-DC as contoso\don_funk.

2. Click Active Directory Rights Management Services on the Tools menu of the Server Manager console.

3. Expand the MEL-DC (local) node and click Security Policies.

4. Click Change Super User settings. In the Actions pane, click Enable Super Users.

5. Click Change Super User Group.

6. On the Super Users dialog box, type **adrms_superusers@contoso.com** as shown in Figure 9-94 and click OK.

FIGURE 9-94 The Super Users dialog box

7. Verify that the Active Directory Rights Management Services console matches Figure 9-95.

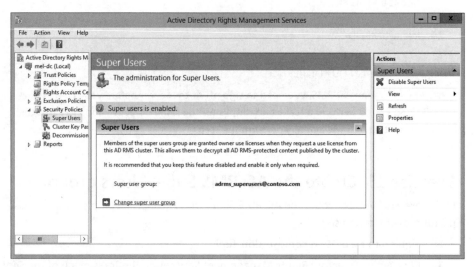

FIGURE 9-95 The AD RMS console

Exercise 16: Create AD RMS templates

In this exercise, you create two AD RMS templates, one for the Submarine project group and one for the Hovercraft project group. To complete this exercise, perform the following steps:

1. In the Active Directory Rights Management Services console on MEL-DC, click the Rights Policy Templates node.

2. In the Actions pane, click Create Distributed Rights Policy Template.

3. On the Add Template Identification Information page of the Create Distributed Rights Policy Template Wizard, click Add.

4. On the Add New Template Identification Information dialog box, type **Submarine AD RMS Template** in the Name box and in the Description section type **Information Protection for Submarine Project** as shown in Figure 9-96. Click Add and click Next.

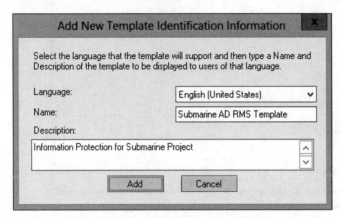

FIGURE 9-96 Add New Template Identification Information dialog box

5. On the Add User Rights page, click Add.

6. On the Add User Or Group page, type **submarine_project@contoso.com** as shown in Figure 9-97 and click OK.

FIGURE 9-97 The Add User Or Group dialog box

7. Select the View permission and ensure that Grant Owner (Author) Full Control Right with No Expiration option is not enabled as shown in Figure 9-98. Click Next.

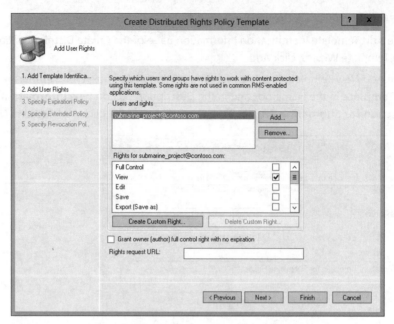

FIGURE 9-98 The Create Distributed Rights Policy Template dialog box

8. On the Specify Expiration Policy page, click Expires After The Following Duration (Days) and enter **14** as shown in Figure 9-99. Click Next.

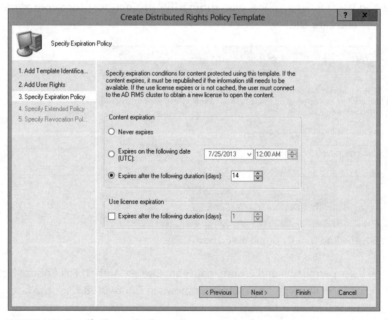

FIGURE 9-99 Specify the expiration policy

9. On the Create Distributed Rights Policy Template, select Enable Users To View Protected Content Using A Browser Add-On and Require A New Use License Every Time Content Is Consumed (Disable Client-Side Caching) as shown in Figure 9-100. Click Next and click Finish.

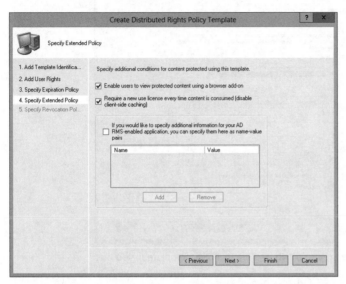

FIGURE 9-100 The Create Distributed Rights Policy Template dialog box

10. On the Actions pane, click Create Distributed Rights Policy Template.

11. On the Add Template Identification page, click Add.

12. On the Add New Template Identification Information Page, type the name as **Hovercraft AD RMS Template** and in the Description section type **Information Protection for Hovercraft Project**. Click Add and then click Next.

13. On the Add User Rights dialog box, click Add.

14. In the Add User or Group dialog box, type **hovercraft_project@contoso.com** and click OK.

15. While hovercraft_project@contoso.com is selected, enable the following rights:

- View
- Edit
- Save
- Print

16. Click Add. In the Add User Or Group dialog box, type **secret_projects@contoso.com** and click OK.

17. Ensure that secret_projects@contoso.com is selected and click Full Control.

18. Clear the Grant Owner (Author) Full Control Right With No Expiration as shown in Figure 9-101 and click Next.

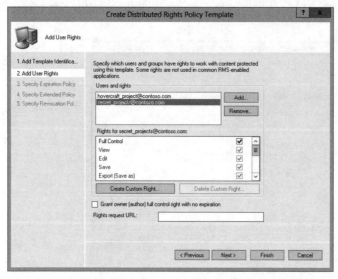

FIGURE 9-101 The Create Distributed Rights Policy Template dialog box

19. On the Specify Expiration Policy page, click Expires On The Following Date, set the date to 1/1/2018 12:00 A.M., and enable Use License Expiration after 3 days as shown in Figure 9-102. Click Next.

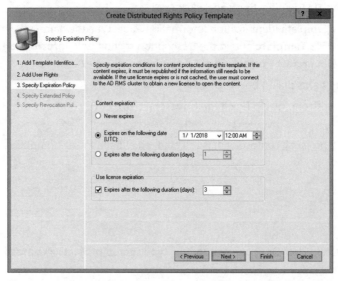

FIGURE 9-102 The Create Distributed Rights Policy Template dialog box

20. On the Specify Extended Policy page, enable the Enable Users To View Protected Content Using A Browser Add-on and Require A New Use License Every Time Content Is Consumed (Disable Client-Side Caching) and click Finish.

Exercise 17: Configure template distribution

In this exercise, you configure AD RMS template distribution. To complete this exercise, perform the following steps:

1. On MEL-DC, right-click the Windows PowerShell icon on the taskbar and click Run As Administrator.

2. On the User Account Control dialog box, click Yes.

3. Type the following commands, pressing Enter after each, to create the templates share:

```
New-Item c:\ADRMS_Templates -ItemType Directory

New-SmbShare -Name ADRMS_Templates -path c:\ADRMS_Templates -FullAccess contoso\
ADRMS_SVC
```

4. In the Active Directory Rights Management Services console, click Change Distributed Rights Policy Templates File Location.

5. In the Rights Policy Templates dialog box, click Enable Export and type **\\MEL-DC\ADRMS_Templates** in the Specify Templates File Location text box as shown in Figure 9-103. Click OK.

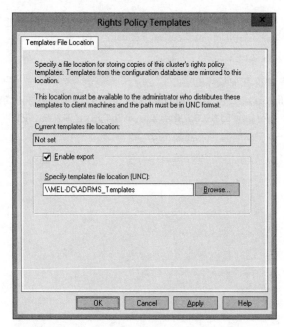

FIGURE 9-103 The Rights Policy Templates dialog box

6. Navigate to the C:\ADRMS_Templates folder and verify the presence of the following two files as shown in Figure 9-104:

   - Hovercraft_AD_RMS_Template
   - Submarine_AD_RMS_Template

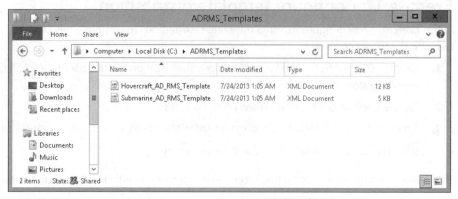

FIGURE 9-104 Exported templates

Exercise 18: Configure application exclusions

In this exercise, you configure application exclusions. To complete this exercise, perform the following steps:

1. On MEL-DC in the Active Directory Rights Management Services console, click the Exclusion Policies node and click Manage Application Exclusion List.

2. In the Actions pane, click Enable Application Exclusion.

3. In the Actions pane, click Exclude Application.

4. In the Exclude Application dialog box, type **onenote.exe** and set the Minimum Version to **1.0.0.0** and the Maximum Version to **99.0.0.0** as shown in Figure 9-105. Click Finish.

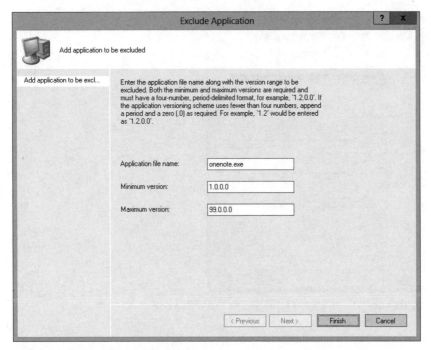

FIGURE 9-105 The Exclude Application text box

Exercise 19: Apply RMS templates using file classification

In this exercise, you apply RMS templates based on file classification. To complete this exercise, perform the following steps:

1. Sign on to ADL-DC as Contoso\don_funk with the password **Pa$$w0rd**.

2. Click File Server Resource Manager on the Tools menu of the Server Manager console.

3. In the File Server Resource Manager console, click File Management Tasks.

4. On the Actions pane, click Create File Management Task.

5. On the General tab of the Create File Management Task dialog box, enter the name **Hovercraft IRM** in the Task Name text box.

6. On the Scope tab, click Add, browse to C:\Shares and click OK.

7. On the Action tab, click the Type drop-down list and set it to RMS Encryption and click the Hovercraft AD RMS Template as shown in Figure 9-106.

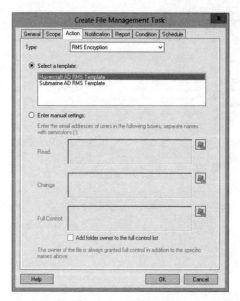

FIGURE 9-106 The Create File Management Task dialog box

8. On the Condition tab, click Add.

9. On the Property Condition dialog box, configure the following settings as shown in Figure 9-107 and then click OK:

- Property: Project

- Operator: Equal

- Value: Hovercraft

FIGURE 9-107 The Property Condition dialog box

10. Click Add. On the Property Condition tab, configure the following settings and then click OK:

- Property: Required Clearance

- Operator: Equal
- Value: Restricted

11. Verify that the Condition tab matches Figure 9-108 and click the Schedule tab.

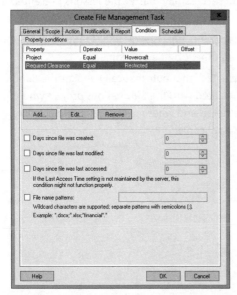

FIGURE 9-108 The Create File Management Task dialog box

12. On the Schedule tab, click Monday, Wednesday, Friday, and Run Continuously on New Files as shown in Figure 9-109. Click OK.

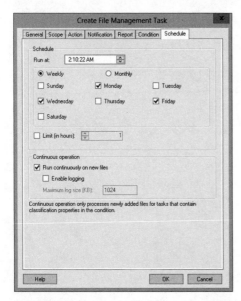

FIGURE 9-109 The Create File Management Task dialog box

Suggested practice exercises

The following additional practice exercises are designed to give you more opportunities to practice what you've learned and to help you successfully master the lessons presented in this chapter.

- **Exercise 1**   Configure a DAC rule that grants full control of files tagged as belonging to the Submarine project to anyone with the job title of Engineer.

- **Exercise 2**   Create a File Management Task that automatically applies the Submarine AD RMS template to files that are associated with the Submarines project where those files have a required clearance of Restricted and where existing files are checked three times a week to see if the template is applicable.

Answers

This section contains the answers to the lesson review questions in this chapter.

Lesson 1

1. **Correct answer**: A

   A. **Correct**. A user or device claim provides information based on the properties, usually contained in Active Directory attributes, of a user or a device.

   B. **Incorrect**. You use a central access policy to publish central access rules.

   C. **Incorrect**. You use resource properties to identify files by characteristics assigned to them, such as Confidentiality.

   D. **Incorrect**. A central access rule enables you to apply permissions to files identified by resource properties to security groups based on user and device claims.

2. **Correct answer**: C

   A. **Incorrect**. You use a central access policy to publish central access rules.

   B. **Incorrect**. You use resource properties to identify files by characteristics assigned to them, such as Confidentiality.

   C. **Correct**. A central access rule enables you to apply permissions to files identified by resource properties to security groups based on user and device claims.

   D. **Incorrect**. A user or device claim provides information based on the properties, usually contained in Active Directory attributes, of a user or a device.

3. **Correct answer**: A

   A. **Correct**. You use resource properties to identify files by characteristics assigned to them, such as Confidentiality.

   B. **Incorrect**. A central access rule enables you to apply permissions to files identified by resource properties to security groups based on user and device claims.

   C. **Incorrect**. A user or device claim provides information based on the properties, usually contained in Active Directory attributes, of a user or a device.

   D. **Incorrect**. You use a central access policy to publish central access rules.

4. **Correct answer**: C

   A. **Incorrect**. A central access rule enables you to apply permissions to files identified by resource properties to security groups based on user and device claims.

   B. **Incorrect**. A user or device claim provides information based on the properties, usually contained in Active Directory attributes, of a user or a device.

   C. **Correct**. You use a central access policy to publish central access rules.

   D. **Incorrect**. You use resource properties to identify files by characteristics assigned to them, such as Confidentiality.

Lesson 2

1. **Correct answer**: A

   A. **Correct**. Members of the Super Users group are able to recover expired content.

   B. **Incorrect**. Although members of this group are able to configure all AD RMS server settings, they are unable to recover expired AD RMS–protected content.

   C. **Incorrect**. Members of this group are able to manage AD RMS templates. They are unable to recover expired AD RMS–protected content.

   D. **Incorrect**. Members of this group are only able to view settings and configuration information. They are unable to recover expired AD RMS–protected content.

2. **Correct answer**: A

   A. **Correct**. TUDs enable you to configure an AD RMS cluster to manage requests for CLCs for users that have been issued RACs from a different AD RMS cluster.

   B. **Incorrect**. TPDs allow the AD RMS cluster in one forest to issue end-user licenses to content published with licenses issued by an AD RMS cluster in another forest.

   C. **Incorrect**. You can use a File Server Resource Manager File Management Task to automatically apply an AD RMS template to a file based on the content of that file or properties associated with that file.

   D. **Incorrect**. A File Server Resource Manager Classification Rule enables you to apply a file classification. It does not enable you to apply AD RMS templates based on the properties of a file.

3. **Correct answer**: B

   A. **Incorrect**. A File Server Resource Manager Classification Rule enables you to apply a file classification. It does not enable you to apply AD RMS templates based on the properties of a file.

   B. **Correct**. You can use a File Server Resource Manager File Management Task to automatically apply an AD RMS template to a file based on the content of that file or properties associated with that file.

   C. **Incorrect**. TPDs allow the AD RMS cluster in one forest to issue end-user licenses to content published with licenses issued by an AD RMS cluster in another forest.

   D. **Incorrect**. TUDs enable you to configure an AD RMS cluster to manage requests for CLCs for users that have been issued RACs from a different AD RMS cluster.

4. **Correct answer**: B

   A. **Incorrect**. You can use a File Server Resource Manager File Management Task to automatically apply an AD RMS template to a file based on the content of that file or properties associated with that file.

   B. **Correct**. TPDs allow the AD RMS cluster in one forest to issue end-user licenses to content published with licenses issued by an AD RMS cluster in another forest.

C. **Incorrect**. A File Server Resource Manager Classification Rule enables you to apply a file classification. It does not enable you to apply AD RMS templates based on the properties of a file.

D. **Incorrect**. TUDs enable you to configure an AD RMS cluster to manage requests for CLCs for users that have been issued RACs from a different AD RMS cluster.

CHAPTER 10

Active Directory Federation Services

Active Directory Federation Services (AD FS) is Microsoft's identity federation solution. Identity federation allows identification, authorization, and authentication to occur across organizational boundaries. When a federated trust is established, users are able to use their local credentials to access resources hosted by another organization. When configured properly, federation also enables users to access resources hosted in the cloud. Although it's possible to configure full forest or domain trust relationships when users in one organization need to use their credentials to access resources in another organization, these trust relationships are often more comprehensive than is necessary. AD FS makes it possible for you to configure highly restricted access to information and resources between partner organizations while still allowing each partner to authenticate using its own credentials.

Lessons in this chapter:

- Lesson 1: Implementing Active Directory Federation Services

Before you begin

To complete the practice exercises in this chapter, you need to have deployed computers SYD-DC, MEL-DC, CBR-DC, and ADL-DC as described in the Introduction, using the evaluation edition of Windows Server 2012 R2.

Lesson 1: Implementing Active Directory Federation Services

Perhaps more than other server roles, AD FS requires you to perform substantial preparation of the environment before deploying the actual server. For example, you have to take into account the type of certificate authority (CA) you will use to sign the AD FS server's certificate, DNS configuration, and how you want partner organizations to be able to interact with your AD FS infrastructure before you deploy the first server. You also have to consider the configuration of claims and attribute stores when deploying AD FS. In this chapter, you discover the basics of deploying AD FS and the configurations that can be used when setting up a federated partnership between organizations.

AD FS Components

AD FS deployments in Windows Server 2012 R2 consist of two components:

- **Federation server**   The computer that hosts the federation server role manages requests involving identity claims. There must be at least one federation server in an Active Directory forest when deploying AD FS.

- **Web Application Proxy**   You deploy the computer that functions as a Web Application Proxy on a perimeter network when you want to provide AD FS functionality to clients on untrusted networks such as the Internet. This server relays connections to the federation server on the internal network. This role can be installed on a stand-alone computer. In Windows Server 2012 and earlier versions of AD FS, this role was known as the federation proxy.

Claims, claim rules, and attribute stores

AD FS provides *claims-based authentication*. Claims-based authentication works on the basis of a claim about the user, such as "allow access to this web application if this user is a full-time employee of the partner organization." AD FS uses the following when building tokens that contain claim data:

- **Claim**   Claims are descriptions made about an object based on the object's attributes. For example, a user account name, employee type, or a security group membership could constitute a claim. Claims are also used with Dynamic Access Control, covered in Chapter 9, "DAC and AD RMS."

- **Claim rules**   These rules determine how a federation server processes a claim. This can be a simple rule such as treating a user's email address as a valid claim. Claim rules can be more complex, with an attribute, such as job title from one organization, being translated into a security group membership in the partner organization.

- **Attribute store** An attribute store holds the values used in claims. AD FS generally uses Active Directory as an attribute store, but can use third party databases from Human Resources management software companies. For example, a lookup of a user's Managed By attribute returns a value that lists the user account assigned as that user's manager.

Figure 10-1 shows the creation of a claim rule where Active Directory is functioning as the attribute store and the Employee-Type attribute is being mapped to an outgoing claim.

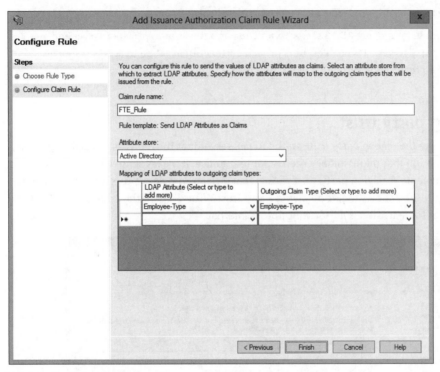

FIGURE 10-1 Claim rule

Claims provider

A *claims provider* is a federation server that provides users with claims. These claims are stored within digitally encrypted and signed tokens. When a user needs a token, the claims provider server contacts the Active Directory deployment in its native forest to determine if the user has authenticated. If the user is properly authenticated against the local Active Directory deployment, the claims provider then builds a user claim using attributes located within Active Directory and other attribute stores. The attributes that are added to the claim are dependent on the attributes required by the partner.

Relying party

The *relying party* server is a member of the Active Directory forest that hosts the resources that the user in the partner organization wants to access. The relying party server accepts and validates the claims contained in the token issued by the claims provider. The relying party server then issues a new token that is used by the resource to determine what access to grant the user from the partner organization.

> **IMPORTANT ROLES ARE NOT EXCLUSIVE**
>
> It is possible for a single AD FS server to function as both a claims provider server and a relying party server. This enables users in each partner organization to access resources in the other organization through a federation trust.

Relying party trust

You configure the *relying party trust* on the AD FS server that functions as the claims provider server. Although that might initially seem counterintuitive, it makes sense when you consider it as a statement: "A relying party trust means that a claims provider trusts a specific relying party." Figure 10-2 shows the Add Relying Party Trust Wizard where the address of the relying party server to be trusted is adl-dc.wingtiptoys.internal.

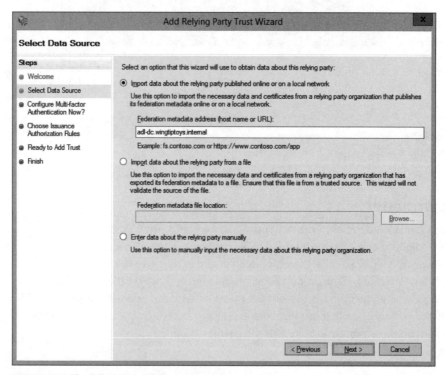

FIGURE 10-2 The Select Data Source page

Claims provider trust

You configure the *claims provider trust* on the Federation Server that functions as the relying party. This also seems counterintuitive until you consider the claims provider trust as a statement: "A claims provider trust means that a relying party trusts a specific claims provider." Figure 10-3 shows setting up a claims provider trust where the address of the claims provider to be trusted is cbr-dc.contoso.com

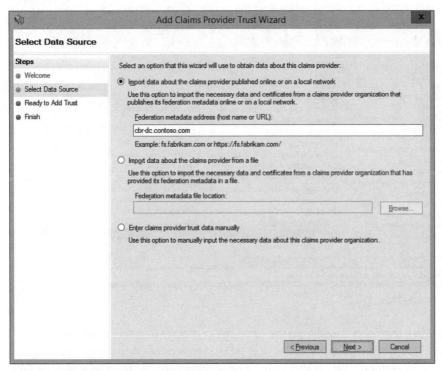

FIGURE 10-3 The Select Data Source page

✔ **Quick check**

- On which server do you configure the claims provider trust: the server functioning as the relying party or the server functioning as the claims provider?

Quick check answer

- You configure the claims provider trust on the server that functions as the relying party.

Configuring certificate relationship

You need to configure partners so that the certificates issued by the opposite partner are trusted. You can accomplish this by using a trusted third-party CA or by configuring CA trusts between partners. To configure a CA trust, you need to import the CA certificate of the partner organization's CA into the Trusted Root CA store as shown in Figure 10-4. You can either do this directly on the AD FS server, or you can configure Group Policy so that all computers within the scope of the policy trust the partner organization's CA.

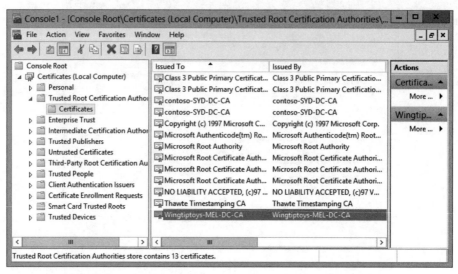

FIGURE 10-4 Trusted root CAs

You can use a certificate issued from the computer certificate template made available through an Active Directory Certificate Services (AD CS) enterprise CA to secure the federation server endpoint. Figure 10-5 shows a certificate generated from an enterprise CA's computer certificate template being used on a federation server. When using a trusted third-party CA, a typical Secure Sockets Layer (SSL) certificate can also be used.

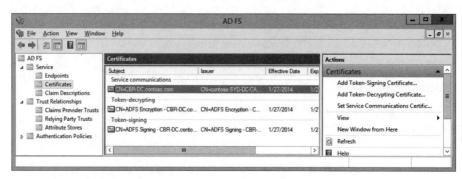

FIGURE 10-5 AD FS certificates

AD FS uses the following certificates:

- **Token-signing certificates**   The Federation server uses the token-signing certificate to sign all tokens that it issues. The server that functions as the claims provider uses the token-signing certificate to verify its identity. The relying party uses the token-signing certificate when verifying that the token was issued by a trusted federation partner.

- **Token-decrypting certificates**   The public key from this certificate is used by the claims provider to encrypt the user token. When the relying party server receives the token, it uses the private key to decrypt the user token.

> *MORE INFO* **FEDERATION SERVER CERTIFICATE REQUIREMENTS**
>
> To learn more about federation server certificate requirements, consult the following article: *http://technet.microsoft.com/en-us/library/dd807040(v=ws.10).aspx.*

Attribute stores

The *attribute store* holds information about users. The AD FS sever uses information contained in the attribute store to build claims after the user has been authenticated. In the majority of AD FS implementations, Active Directory functions as the attribute store. You can configure additional attribute stores based on the following technologies:

- Active Directory Lightweight Directory Services (AD LDS) on computers running Windows Server 2008, Windows Server 2008 R2, Windows Server 2012 and Windows Server 2012 R2.

- Active Directory Application Mode (ADAM) on servers running Windows Server 2003. ADAM is the predecessor to AD LDS.

- All editions of Microsoft SQL Server 2005, SQL Server 2008, SQL Server 2008 R2, and SQL Server 2012.

You add attribute stores to AD FS in the Add An Attribute Store dialog box shown in Figure 10-6.

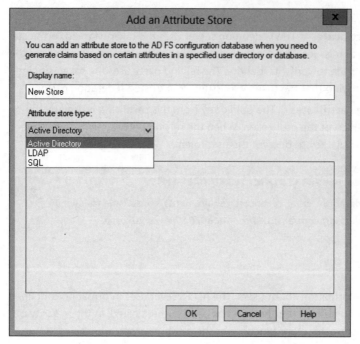

FIGURE 10-6 Attribute stores

Claims rules

Claims rules determine how AD FS servers send and consume claims. AD FS supports two different types of claims rules: relying party trust claims rules and claims provider trust claim rules.

Relying party trust claims rules

Claims rules for a relying party trust determine how the claims about a user are forwarded to the relying party. You configure these claim rules by editing the claim rules of the relying party trust on the AD FS server that functions as the claims provider. There are three types of relying party trust claim rules:

1. **Issuance transform rules**   Determine how claims are sent to the relying party.

2. **Issuance authorization rules**   Determine which users have access to the relying party. An issuance authorization claim rule is shown in Figure 10-7.

3. **Delegation authorization rules**   Determine if users can act on behalf of other users when accessing the relying party.

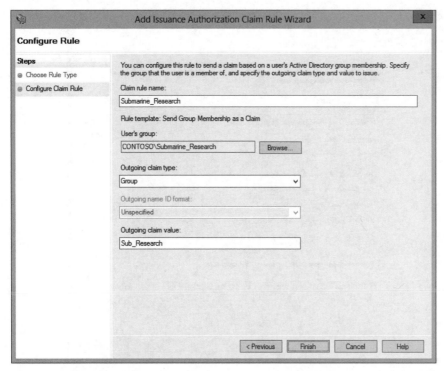

FIGURE 10-7 Choosing a rule type

Claims provider trust claim rules

Claims provider trust rules determine how the relying party filters incoming claims. You configure claims provider trust claim rules by editing the claim rules of the claims provider trust. All claims provider trust claims rules are acceptance transform rules. Figure 10-8 shows an incoming claim type related to group membership.

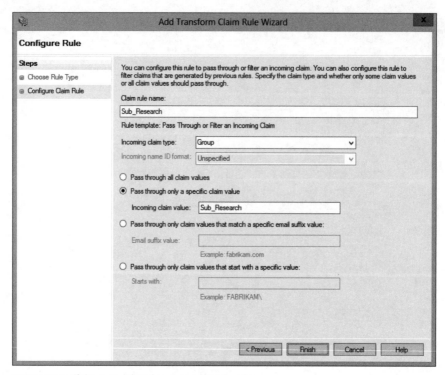

FIGURE 10-8 Claim type related to group membership

Configure Web Application Proxy

Web Application Proxy servers can be deployed on perimeter networks as a way to increase security for AD FS deployment. Clients communicate with the AD FS proxy server, which then communicates with federation servers on the internal network. For example, on the claims provider side of the federated trust, the Web Application Proxy forwards authentication data from the client to the AD FS server, which confirms the authentication and issues the token, which is relayed through the proxy to the relying party Web Application Proxy server. The relying party Web Application Proxy server relays the token to the relying party AD FS server, which issues a new token that is sent back through the proxy to the original client. At no point will a Web Application Proxy server actually create claims or generate tokens. All communication between a Web Application Proxy server and a federation server occurs using the HTTPS protocol.

In Windows Server 2012 and earlier versions of AD FS, the Web Application Proxy server role was performed by an AD FS proxy server. A Web Application Proxy server has the following differences from the AD FS proxy role service available in Windows Server 2012:

- Is deployed as a Remote Access role service
- Provides secure remote access to web-based applications hosted on the internal network

- Functions as a reverse proxy for web-based applications
- Can be used to publish access to Work Folders

When deploying a Web Application Proxy server, you need to ensure that the following certificates are present in the server's certificate store:

- A certificate that includes the federation service name. If the Web Application Proxy server must support Workplace Join, then the certificate must also support the following subject alternative names:
  - <federationservicename>.<domainname>
  - <enterpriseregistration>.<domainname>
- A wildcard certificate, a subject alternative name certificate, or individual certificates to cover each web application that will be accessible through the web application proxy.
- A copy of the certificate used by external servers if you are supporting client certificate preauthentication.

The server hosting the Web Application Proxy role must also trust the certificate authority that issued these certificates. After deploying the Web Application Proxy role service, you run the Web Application Proxy Configuration Wizard. Running the wizard involves specifying the federation service name and the credentials of an account that has AD FS administrative privileges as shown in Figure 10-9.

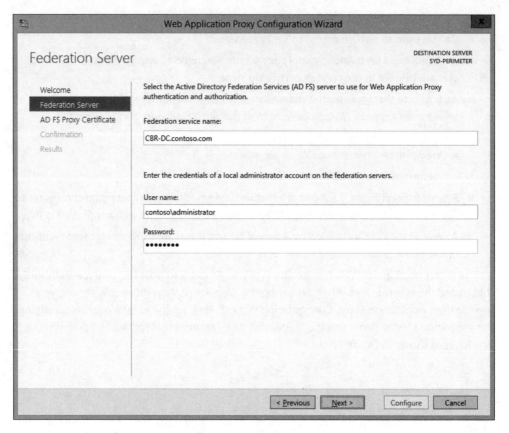

FIGURE 10-9 Web Application Proxy Configuration Wizard

You also need to specify the certificate used by the AD FS proxy component of the Web Application Proxy as shown in Figure 10-10. You'll need to have access to the certificate's private key as well as the public key when configuring the AD FS proxy component of the Web Application Proxy.

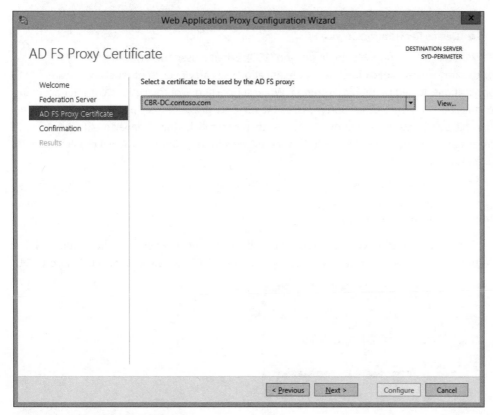

FIGURE 10-10 AD FS Proxy Certificate

MORE INFO WEB APPLICATION PROXY

To learn more about Web Application Proxy, consult the following article:
http://technet.microsoft.com/en-us/library/dn584113.aspx.

Workplace Join

Workplace Join is a Windows Server 2012 R2 feature that you can use to allow non-domain joined devices and computers to access domain resources and claims-enabled applications in a secure manner. When a non-domain joined device or computer performs a Workplace Join, a special object representing the device is created in AD DS. The object stores attributes that describe the device you can use when configuring access rules.

Workplace Join requires the following components:

- Windows 8.1 or iOS 7 or later devices
- Claims-aware application
- AD FS deployment on internal network

- Web Application Proxy deployed on the perimeter network
- Device Registration Service

Workplace Join supports single sign-on (SSO). When a user authenticates to access one claims-aware application, their authentication will carry over to other claims-aware applications hosted by the organization. When supporting Workplace Join, consider acquiring certificates from trusted 3rd party CAs, as the majority of the devices performing Workplace Join will be managed by their owners rather than centrally by the IT department. This means that getting those devices to trust certificates from an internal CA will require extra administrative effort.

You enable Workplace Join by running the following Windows PowerShell cmdlets:

```
Initialize-ADFSDeviceRegistration
Enable-ADFSDeviceRegistration
```

Once you've enabled Workplace Join, you'll be able to enable device authentication by editing the Global Authentication Policy through the AD FS console as shown in Figure 10-11.

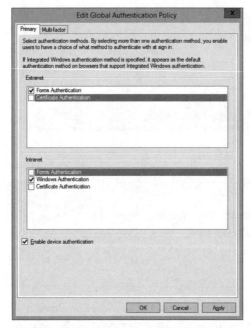

FIGURE 10-11 Enabling device authentication

Users authenticate using their UPNs. When configuring Workplace Join, ensure that you configure your organization's external DNS zone with a record that maps enterpriseregistration.upndomainname.com (where upndomainname.com is the UPN suffix) to the IP address of the Web Application Proxy server or the AD FS server that you've configured to support Workplace Join.

Multi-factor authentication

AD FS supports multi-factor authentication. When you implement multi-factor authentication, more than one form of authentication is required, for example, username, password, and a code from an authenticator application running on a mobile device. You can configure multi-factor authentication in AD FS either globally as shown in Figure 10-12, or on a per-relying party trust basis.

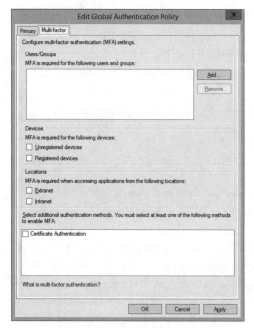

FIGURE 10-12 Multi-factor authentication

You can configure multi-factor authentication using a third party vendor's product or you can integrate Microsoft's Windows Azure multi-factor authentication service. Windows Azure multi-factor authentication allows the following authentication methods:

- **Telephone call**   An automated telephone call is made to the user's registered telephone number. The user enters the data provided in the call when authenticating.

- **Text message**   A text message is sent to the user's registered mobile telephone. The user enters the data provided in the text message when authenticating.

- **Mobile app**   The user installs a mobile authentication app on their mobile device that generates a periodically changing code. The user enters this code when authenticating.

Lesson summary

- The claims provider federation server is a member of the forest that hosts the user accounts that want to gain access to a resource hosted in the partner organization.

- The relying party federation server is a member of the organization that hosts the resource that partner organizations want to access.

- A relying party trust is configured on the claims provider federation server and allows a particular relying party federation server to be trusted.

- A claims provider trust is configured on the relying party federation server and allows a particular claims provider federation server to be trusted.

- Active Directory, AD LDS, ADAM, and SQL Server can function as attribute stores for AD FS.

- A Web Application Proxy server forwards requests from clients on unprotected networks AD FS servers on the internal network.

Lesson review

Answer the following questions to test your knowledge of the information in this lesson. You can find the answers to these questions and explanations of each answer choice in the "Answers" section at the end of this chapter.

1. The Contoso forest hosts a web application that users in Adatum forest want to access. You are one of the systems administrators at Adatum and you are in the process of configuring a federated trust to allow this to occur. A single AD FS server is deployed in each forest. Which of the following statements about this deployment would be true if a solution providing this access through AD FS was implemented? (Choose two.)

    A. The AD FS server in the Contoso forest will function as the claims provider.

    B. The AD FS server in the Contoso forest will function as the relying party server.

    C. You need to configure a relying party trust on the AD FS server on the AD FS server in the Adatum forest.

    D. You need to configure a claims provider trust on the AD FS server in the Adatum forest.

2. The Contoso forest hosts a web application that users in Adatum forest want to access. You are one of the systems administrators at Contoso and you are in the process of configuring a federated trust to allow this to occur. A single AD FS server is deployed in

each forest. Which of the following statements about this deployment would be true if a solution providing this access through AD FS was implemented? (Choose two.)

A. The AD FS server in the Adatum forest will function as the claims provider.

B. The AD FS server in the Adatum forest will function as the relying party server.

C. You will configure a relying party trust on the Contoso AD FS server.

D. You will configure a claims provider trust on the Contoso AD FS server.

3. You are in the process of configuring certificate trusts. You want to ensure that the current and future certificates issued to the Contoso AD FS server by the Contoso CA are trusted by the Adatum AD FS server. You do this by configuring the appropriate certificate to the Computer Configuration\Policies\Windows Settings\Security Settings\ Public Key Policies\Trusted Root Certification Authorities node of the Default Domain Policy in the Adatum domain. Both Adatum and Contoso have a single enterprise root CA. Which of these certificates should you add to this GPO?

A. The CA certificate of the Contoso CA

B. The CA certificate of the Adatum CA

C. The SSL certificate assigned to the Contoso AD FS server

D. The SSL certificate assigned to the Adatum AD FS server

Practice exercises

The goal of this section is to provide you with hands-on practice with the following:

- Configuring a cross-organization CA trust
- Deploying AD FS
- Configuring a relying party trust
- Configuring a claims provider trust
- Configure claim rules

To perform the exercises in this section, you need access to an evaluation version of Windows Server 2012 R2. You should also have access to virtual machines SYD-DC, MEL-DC, CBR-DC, and ADL-DC, the setup instructions for which are described in the Introduction. You should ensure that you have a checkpoint of these virtual machines that you can revert to at the end of the practice exercises. You should revert the virtual machines to this initial state prior to beginning these exercises.

Exercise 1: Prepare separate forests

In this exercise, you configure a new forest using MEL-DC as the domain controller for the root domain wingtiptoys, which has ADL-DC as a member. You also join CBR-DC to the contoso domain. To complete this exercise, perform the following steps:

1. Ensure that SYD-DC is started.

2. Start MEL-DC and sign on as Administrator with the password **Pa$$w0rd**.

3. Right-click the Windows PowerShell icon on the taskbar and click Run As Administrator.

4. In the Windows PowerShell window, type the following command and press Enter to install the Active Directory Domain Services role:

   ```
   Install-WindowsFeature AD-Domain-Services -IncludeManagementTools
   ```

5. In the Windows PowerShell window, type the following command and press Enter to configure MEL-DC as a domain controller in the wingtiptoys.internal domain.

   ```
   Install-ADDSForest -domainname "wingtiptoys.internal"
   ```

6. When prompted for the Safe Mode Administrator Password, enter the password **Pa$$w0rd** twice.

7. When prompted whether you want to configure the operation, click Yes for All, or press A, and press Enter.

8. When MEL-DC restarts, sign on as Wingtiptoys\administrator with the password **Pa$$w0rd**.

9. Switch to ADL-DC and sign on as Administrator with the password **Pa$$w0rd**.

10. Right-click the Windows PowerShell icon on the taskbar and click Run As Administrator.

11. In the Windows PowerShell window, type the following command to configure the network adapter to use the DNS server address on MEL-DC:

    ```
    Set-DNSClientServerAddress EtherNet -ServerAddress 10.10.10.40
    ```

12. In the Windows PowerShell window, type the following command to join ADL-DC to the wingtiptoys.internal domain:

    ```
    Add-Computer -credential wingtiptoys\administrator -DomainName wingtiptoys.internal
    ```

13. On the Windows PowerShell Credential dialog box, shown in Figure 10-13, type **Pa$$w0rd** and click OK.

FIGURE 10-13 Credential dialog box

14. In the Windows PowerShell window, type the following command and press Enter to restart the computer:

    `Restart-Computer`

15. Sign on to ADL-DC as wingtiptoys\administrator with the password **Pa$$w0rd**.

16. Start CBR-DC and sign on as Administrator with the password **Pa$$w0rd**.

17. Right-click the Windows PowerShell icon on the taskbar and click Run As Administrator.

18. In the Windows PowerShell window, type the following command to join CBR-DC to the contoso.com domain:

    `Add-Computer -credential contoso\administrator -DomainName contoso.com`

19. In the Windows PowerShell Credentials dialog box, type **contoso\administrator** and the password **Pa$$w0rd** and then click OK.

20. In the Windows PowerShell window, type the following command and press Enter to restart the computer:

    `Restart-Computer`

21. When the computer restarts, sign on to CBR-DC as contoso\administrator.

Exercise 2: Configure DNS forwarding

In this exercise, you configure DNS forwarding between forests. To complete this exercise, perform the following steps:

1. Sign on to SYD-DC as contoso\administrator with the password **Pa$$w0rd**.

2. Click DNS on the Tools menu of the Server Manager console.

3. In the DNS Manager console, right-click the Conditional Forwarders node and click New Conditional Forwarders.

4. On the New Conditional Forwarder dialog box, type the DNS Domain **wingtiptoys. internal** and set the IP address as 10.10.10.40. Enable the Store This Conditional Forwarder In Active Directory, And Replicate As Follows option as shown in Figure 10-14 and click OK.

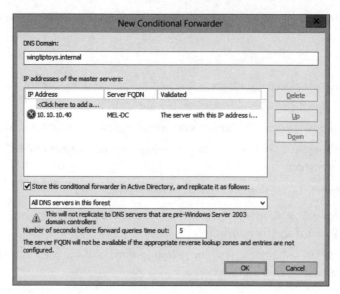

FIGURE 10-14 Setting a conditional forwarder

5. Switch to CBR-DC and click the Windows PowerShell icon on the taskbar.

6. In the Windows PowerShell window, type the following command and press Enter to verify that CBR-DC can resolve names in the wingtip.internal DNS zone as shown in Figure 10-15:

```
nslookup adl-dc.wingtiptoys.internal
```

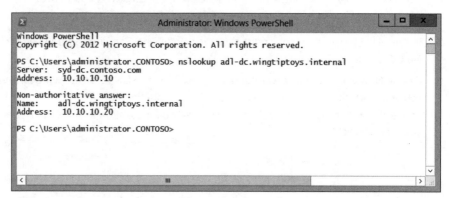

FIGURE 10-15 nslookup

7. Switch to MEL-DC and ensure that you are signed on as wingtiptoys\administrator.

8. From the Tools menu of the Server Manager console, click DNS.

9. In the DNS Manager console, expand MEL-DC, right-click Conditional Forwarders, and click New Conditional Forwarder.

10. On the New Conditional Forwarder dialog box, enter the DNS Domain **contoso.com**, set the IP address to 10.10.10.10 and enable the Store This Conditional Forwarder In Active Directory, And Replicate It As Follows as shown in Figure 10-16. Click OK.

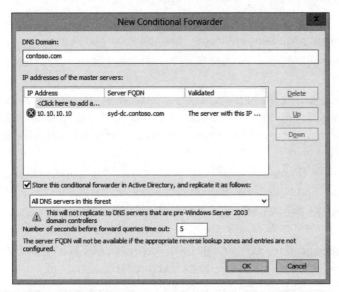

FIGURE 10-16 A conditional forwarder

11. Switch to ADL-DC and click the Windows PowerShell icon on the taskbar.

12. In the Windows PowerShell window, type the following command and press Enter to verify that ADL-DC can resolve names in the contoso.com DNS zone as shown in Figure 10-17:

```
nslookup cbr-dc.contoso.com
```

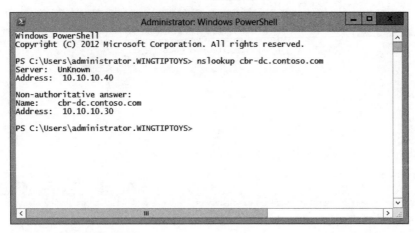

FIGURE 10-17 nslookup

Exercise 3: Deploy AD CS in each forest

In this exercise, you deploy an enterprise root CA in the contoso.com and wingtiptoys.internal forests. To complete this exercise, perform the following steps:

1. Ensure that you are signed on to SYD-DC as contoso\administrator.

2. On the Manage menu of the Server Manager, click Add Roles And Features.

3. On the Before You Begin page of the Add Roles And Features Wizard, click Next three times.

4. On the Select Server Roles page of the Add Roles And Features Wizard, click Active Directory Certificate Services. On the Add Roles And Features Wizard pop-up dialog box, click Add Features. Click Next four times, click Install, and when the installation completes, click Close.

5. In the Server Manager console, click the AD CS node. On the Configuration Required For Active Directory Certificate Services node, click More.

6. On the All Servers Task Details dialog box click Configure Active Directory Certificate Services.

7. On the Credentials page of the AD CS Configuration Wizard, verify that CONTOSO\ Administrator is listed as shown in Figure 10-18 and click Next.

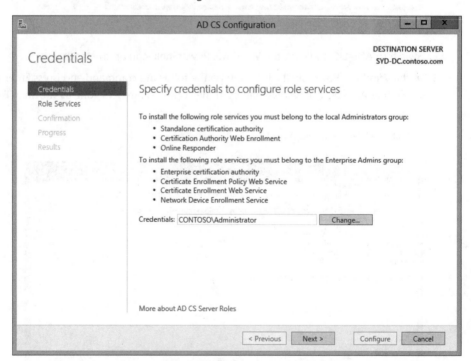

FIGURE 10-18 Specify credentials

8. On the Role Services page, select Certification Authority and click Next.

9. On the Setup Type page, ensure that Enterprise CA is selected and click Next.

10. On the CA Type page, click Root CA and click Next six times. Click Configure.

11. Switch to MEL-DC and ensure that you are signed on as wingtiptoys\administrator.

12. Click the Windows PowerShell icon on the taskbar.

13. In the Windows PowerShell window, type the following command to install the AD CS files:

```
Install-WindowsFeature ADCS-Cert-Authority –IncludeManagementTools
```

14. In the Server Manager console, click Refresh and then click the AD CS node.

15. Click More on the Configuration Required For Active Directory Certificate Services At MEL-DC notification.

16. In the All Servers Task Details dialog box, click Configure Active Directory Certificate Services.

17. On the AD CS Configuration Wizard, ensure that WINGTIPTOYS\Administrator is selected as shown in Figure 10-19 and then click Next.

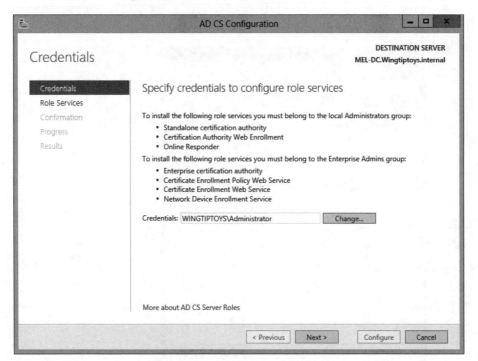

FIGURE 10-19 Specifying credentials

18. On the Role Services page, select Certification Authority and click Next.

19. On the Setup Type page, click Enterprise CA and click Next.

20. On the CA Type page, click Root CA and click Next six times. Click Configure and click Close.

Exercise 4: Prepare SYD-DC for certificate publication

In this exercise, you configure SYD-DC so that clients encountering certificates issued by the CA are able to perform certificate revocation checks. To complete this exercise, perform the following steps:

1. Ensure that you are signed on to SYD-DC as contoso\administrator.

2. Click Group Policy Management on the Tools menu of the Server Manager console.

3. In the Group Policy Management Console, expand Forest: contoso.com\Domains\contoso.com and click Default Domain Policy.

4. Click OK on the Group Policy Management Console dialog box.

5. On the Action menu, click Edit.

6. Expand the Computer Configuration\Policies\Windows Settings\Security Settings\Local Policies\Security Options node.

7. Right-click the Network Access: Let Everyone Permissions Apply To Anonymous Users policy and click Properties.

8. On the Network Access: Let Everyone Permissions Apply To Anonymous Users policy, click Define This Policy Setting and select Enabled as shown in Figure 10-20. Click OK.

FIGURE 10-20 Configuring permissions policy

9. Close the Group Policy Management Editor.

10. Click the Windows PowerShell icon on the taskbar.

11. In the Windows PowerShell window, type the following command and press Enter to update the Group Policy:

```
gpupdate /force
```

12. Click the File Explorer icon on the taskbar, click This PC, double-click Local Disk (C:), click the New Folder icon on the title bar, and name the folder Certs.

13. Right-click the Certs folder, click Share With, and click Specific People.

14. Click the drop-down list, click Everyone, click Add, and click Share as shown in the File Sharing dialog box in Figure 10-21. Click Done.

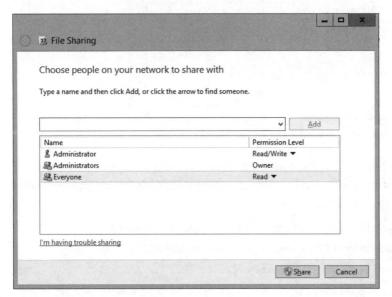

FIGURE 10-21 Configure permissions

15. On the Tools menu of the Server Manager console, click Certification Authority.

16. In the Crtsrv console, right-click Contoso-SYD-DC-CA and click Properties.

17. On the Extensions tab, click Add.

18. On the Add Location dialog box, type the following as shown in Figure 10-22 and click OK:

```
file://<ServerDNSName>/Certs/<CaName><CRLNameSuffix><DeltaCRLAllowed>.crl
```

FIGURE 10-22 Add Location

19. On the Extensions tab, ensure that the address configured in the previous step is selected and then select the following options. Click Apply when you're done.

- Publish CRLs to this location.
- Include in CRLs. Clients use this to find Delta CRL locations.
- Include in the CDP extension of issued certificates.
- Publish Delta CRLs to this location.

20. When prompted to restart Active Directory Certificate Services, click Yes.

21. On the Select Extension drop-down menu, click Authority Information Access (AIA) and then click Add.

22. On the Add Location dialog box, type the following as shown in Figure 10-23 and click OK:

```
file://<ServerDNSName>/Certs/<CaName><CRLNameSuffix><DeltaCRLAllowed>.crl
```

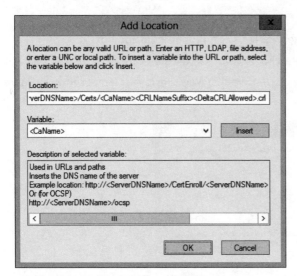

FIGURE 10-23 Configure Adding a location

23. On the Extensions tab, select the Include In The AIA Extension Of Issued Certificates option when the new address is selected as shown in Figure 10-24 and click Apply.

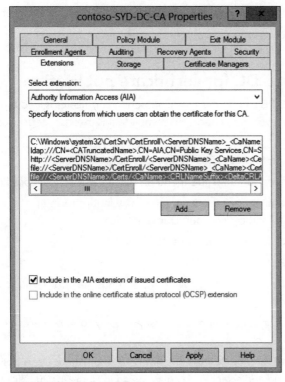

FIGURE 10-24 CA Properties

24. When prompted to restart the Certification Authority click Yes.

25. Click OK to close the Contoso-SYD-DC-CA Properties dialog box.

26. In the Certsrv console, right-click Revoked Certificates, click All Tasks, and click Publish.

27. On the Publish CRL dialog box, ensure that New CRL is selected as shown in Figure 10-25 and click OK.

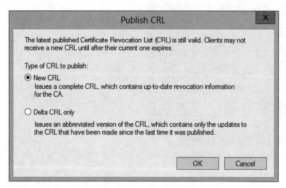

FIGURE 10-25 The Publish CRL dialog box

28. Click the Windows PowerShell icon on the taskbar.

29. In the Windows PowerShell window, type the following command and press Enter:

```
Copy c:\Windows\System32\CertSrv\CertEnroll\*.crt c:\certs
```

Exercise 5: Prepare MEL-DC for certificate publication

In this exercise, you configure MEL-DC so that clients encountering certificates issued by the CA are able to perform certificate revocation checks. To complete this exercise, perform the following steps:

1. Ensure that you are signed on to MEL-DC as wingtiptoys\administrator.

2. Click Group Policy Management on the Tools menu of the Server Manager console.

3. In the Group Policy Management Console, expand Forest: wingtiptoys.internal\ Domains\wingtiptoys.internal and click Default Domain Policy.

4. Click OK on the Group Policy Management Console dialog box.

5. On the Action menu, click Edit.

6. Expand the Computer Configuration\Policies\Windows Settings\Security Settings\Local Policies\Security Options node.

7. Right-click the Network Access: Let Everyone Permissions Apply To Anonymous Users policy and click Properties.

8. On the Network Access: Let Everyone Permissions Apply To Anonymous Users policy, click Define This Policy Setting and select Enabled as shown in Figure 10-26. Click OK.

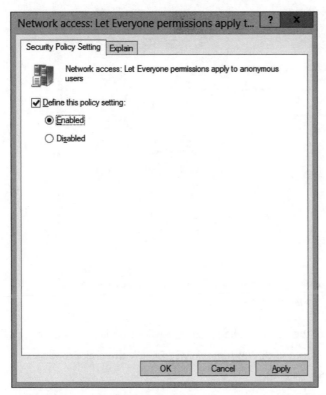

FIGURE 10-26 Enabling anonymous access

9. Close the Group Policy Management Editor.

10. Click the Windows PowerShell icon on the taskbar.

11. In the Windows PowerShell window, type the following command and press Enter to update Group Policy:

```
gpupdate /force
```

12. In the Windows PowerShell window, type the following command and press Enter:

```
Add-KdsRootKey –EffectiveTime ((get-date).addhours(-10))
```

13. Click the File Explorer icon on the taskbar, click This PC, double-click Local Disk (C:), click the New Folder icon on the title bar, and name the folder Certs.

14. Right-click the Certs folder, click Share With, and click Specific People.

15. Click the drop-down list, click Everyone, click Add, and click Share as shown in the File Sharing dialog box in Figure 10-27. Then click Done.

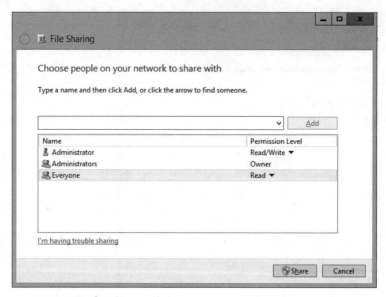

FIGURE 10-27 Configuring permissions

16. On the Tools menu of the Server Manager console, click Certification Authority.

17. In the Crtsrv console, right-click Wingtiptoys-MEL-DC-CA and click Properties.

18. On the Extensions tab, click Add.

19. On the Add Location dialog box, type the following as shown in Figure 10-28 and click OK:

```
file://<ServerDNSName>/Certs/<CaName><CRLNameSuffix><DeltaCRLAllowed>.crl
```

FIGURE 10-28 The Add Location dialog box

20. On the Extensions page, ensure that the address configured in the previous step is selected and then select the following options and click Apply.

- Publish CRLs to this location.

- Include in CRLs. Clients use this to find Delta CRL locations.

- Include in the CDP extension of issued certificates.

- Publish Delta CRLs to this location.

21. When prompted to restart Active Directory Certificate Services, click Yes.

22. On the Select Extension drop-down menu, click Authority Information Access (AIA) and then click Add.

23. On the Add Location dialog box, type the following as shown in Figure 10-29 and click OK:

```
file://<ServerDNSName>/Certs/<CaName><CRLNameSuffix><DeltaCRLAllowed>.crl
```

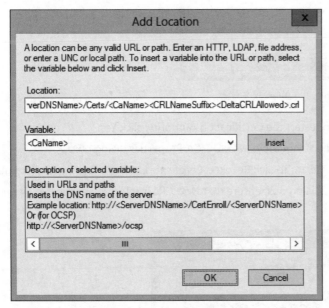

FIGURE 10-29 The Add Location dialog box

24. On the Extensions tab, select the Include In The AIA Extension Of Issued Certificates option when the new address is selected as shown in Figure 10-30. Click Apply.

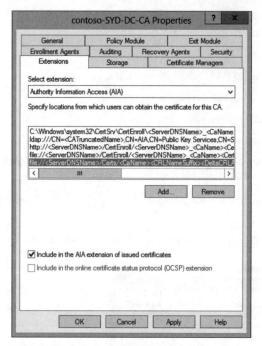

FIGURE 10-30 Configure the AIA extension

25. When prompted to restart the Certification Authority, click Yes.

26. Click OK to close the Wingtiptoys-MEL-DC-CA Properties dialog box.

27. In the Certsrv console, right-click Revoked Certificates, click All Tasks, and click Publish.

28. On the Publish CRL dialog box, ensure that New CRL is selected as shown in Figure 10-31 and click OK.

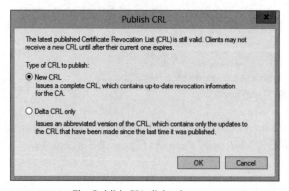

FIGURE 10-31 The Publish CRL dialog box

29. Click the Windows PowerShell icon on the taskbar.

30. In the Windows PowerShell window, type the following command and press Enter:

```
Copy c:\Windows\System32\CertSrv\CertEnroll\*.crt c:\certs
```

Exercise 6: Configure CA trust in each forest

In this exercise, you import each CA's certificate into the partner's Active Directory so that it is trusted by the partner organization. This allows each organization to trust certificates issued by the partner organization's CA. To complete this exercise, perform the following steps:

1. Ensure that you are signed on to SYD-DC as contoso\administrator.

2. Click Group Policy Management on the Tools menu of the Server Manager console.

3. In the Group Policy Management Editor, expand the Forest: contoso.com\Domains\ contoso.com node and click Default Domain Policy.

4. If prompted, click OK.

5. Click the Default Domain Policy. On the Action menu, click Edit.

6. Navigate to the Computer Configuration\Policies\Windows Settings\Security Settings\ Public Key Policies node.

7. Right-click the Trusted Root Certification Authorities node and click Import.

8. On the Welcome To The Certificate Import Wizard, click Next.

9. On the File To Import page of the Certificate Import Wizard, click Browse.

10. Navigate to \\mel-dc.wingtiptoys.internal\certs and click MEL-DC.Wingtiptoys.internal_ Wingtiptoys-MEL-DC-CA as shown in Figure 10-32. Click Open.

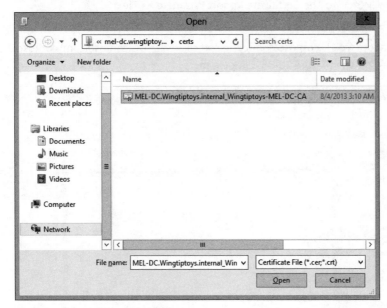

FIGURE 10-32 Importing a certificate

11. On the File To Import page of the Certificate Import Wizard, click Next twice, and click Finish.

12. Click OK on the Certificate Import Wizard dialog box.

13. Verify that Wingtiptoys-MEL-DC-CA is listed under the Trusted Root Certification Authorities node and then close the Group Policy Management Editor.

14. Click the Windows PowerShell icon on the taskbar.

15. In the Windows PowerShell window, type the following command and press Enter:

```
Gpupdate /force
```

16. In the Windows PowerShell window, type the following command and press Enter:

```
Add-KdsRootKey -EffectiveTime ((get-date).addhours(-10))
```

17. Switch to MEL-DC and ensure that you are signed on as wingtiptoys\administrator.

18. Click Group Policy Management on the Tools menu of the Server Manager console.

19. In the Group Policy Management Editor, expand the Forest wingtiptoys.internal\ Domains\wingtiptoys.internal node and click Default Domain Policy.

20. If prompted, click OK.

21. Click the Default Domain Policy. On the Action menu, click Edit.

22. Navigate to the Computer Configuration\Policies\Windows Settings\Security Settings\ Public Key Policies node.

23. Right-click the Trusted Root Certification Authorities node and click Import.

24. On the Welcome To The Certificate Import Wizard, click Next.

25. On the File To Import page of the Certificate Import Wizard, click Browse.

26. Navigate to \\syd-dc.contoso.com\certs and click SYD-DC.contoso.com_contoso-SYD-DC-CA as shown in Figure 10-33. Click Open.

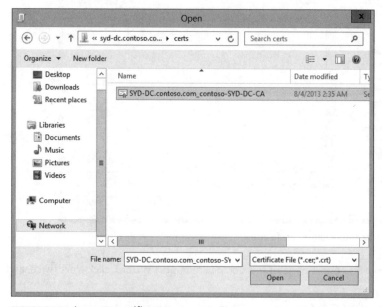

FIGURE 10-33 Import a certificate

27. On the File To Import page of the Certificate Import Wizard, click Next twice and click Finish.

28. Click OK on the Certificate Import Wizard dialog box.

29. Verify that Contoso-SYD-DC-CA is listed under the Trusted Root Certification Authorities node and then close the Group Policy Management Editor.

30. Click the Windows PowerShell icon on the taskbar.

31. In the Windows PowerShell window, type the following command and press Enter:

Gpupdate /force

Exercise 7: Acquire certificates for each server

In this exercise, you acquire computer certificates for CBR-DC and ADL-DC that will be used to identify each server in the AD FS process. To complete this exercise, perform the following steps:

1. Ensure that you are signed on to CBR-DC as contoso\administrator.

2. Click the Windows PowerShell icon on the taskbar.

3. In the Windows PowerShell window, type the following command and press Enter:

Gpupdate /force

4. In the Windows PowerShell window, type the following command and press Enter:

mmc.exe

5. On the File menu of the Console1 – [Console Root], click Add/Remove Snap-In.

6. On the Add Or Remove Snap-Ins dialog box, click Certificates and click Add.

7. On the Certificates Snap-In dialog box, click Computer Account as shown in Figure 10-34. Click Next, click Finish, and click OK.

FIGURE 10-34 Configuring Certificates Snap-In

8. Expand the Certificates (Local Computer) node, click the Personal node and on the Action menu, click All Tasks, and click Request New Certificate.

9. On the Before You Begin page of the Certificate Enrollment Wizard, click Next twice.

10. On the Request Certificates page, click Computer as shown in Figure 10-35 and then click Enroll. Click Finish after enrollment completes.

FIGURE 10-35 Configuring Certificate Enrollment

11. Switch to ADL-DC and ensure that you are signed on as wingtiptoys\administrator.

12. Click the Windows PowerShell icon on the taskbar.

13. In the Windows PowerShell window, type the following command and press Enter:

    Gpupdate /force

14. In the Windows PowerShell window, type the following command and press Enter:

    mmc.exe

15. On the File menu of the Console1 – [Console Root], click Add/Remove Snap-In.

16. On the Add Or Remove Snap-Ins dialog box, click Certificates and click Add.

17. On the Certificates Snap-In dialog box, click Computer Account as shown in Figure 10-36. Click Next, click Finish, and click OK.

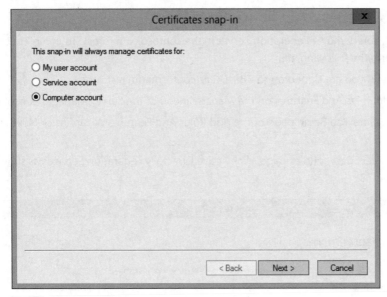

FIGURE 10-36 Selecting Computer Account

18. Expand the Certificates (Local Computer) node, click the Personal node. On the Action menu, click All Tasks and click Request New Certificate.

19. On the Before You Begin page of the Certificate Enrollment Wizard, click Next twice.

20. On the Request Certificates page, click Computer as shown in Figure 10-37 and click Enroll. Click Finish after enrollment completes.

FIGURE 10-37 The Request Certificates page of the Certificate Enrollment Wizard

Exercise 8: Deploy AD FS in each forest

In this exercise, you deploy a Federation Server in the contoso.com forest. To complete this exercise, perform the following steps:

1. Ensure that you are signed on to CBR-DC as contoso\administrator.

2. Click Add Roles And Features on the Manage menu of the Server Manager console.

3. On the Before You Begin page of the Add Roles And Features Wizard, click Next three times.

4. On the Select Server Roles page, click Active Directory Federation Services as shown in Figure 10-38.

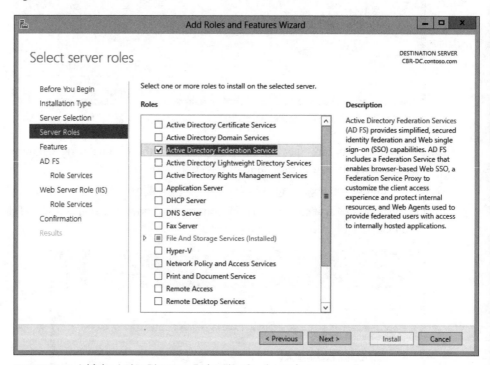

FIGURE 10-38 Add the Active Directory Federation Services role

5. Click Next three times.

6. Click Install, and click Close.

7. In the Server Manager console, click the AD FS node.

8. Click More on the Configuration Required For Federation Service At CBR-DC notification.

9. On the All Servers Task Details dialog box, shown in Figure 10-39, click Configure The Federation Service.

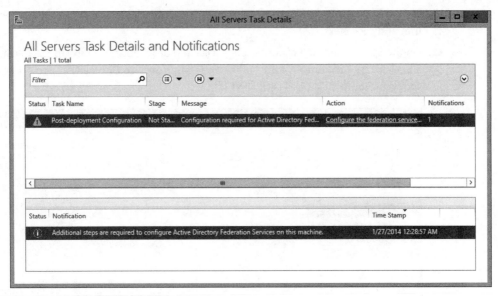

FIGURE 10-39 Post-Deployment Configuration

10. On the Welcome page of the AD FS Federation Server Configuration Wizard, click Create The First Federation Server In A Federation Server Farm as shown in Figure 10-40. Click Next.

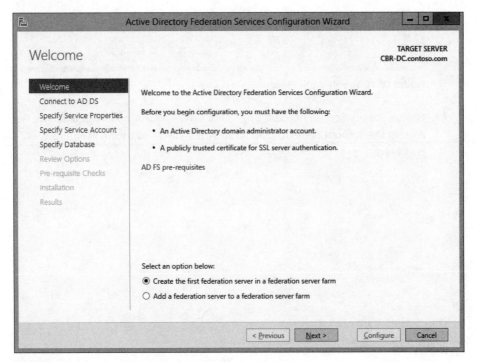

FIGURE 10-40 Creating a new Federation Service

11. On the Connect To AD DS ensure that CONTOSO\Administrator is set to the current user and click Next.

12. On the Specify Service Properties page, click the drop-down list next to SSL Certificate and click CBR-DC.contoso.com. Set the Federation Service Display Name to Contoso as shown in Figure 10-41 and click Next.

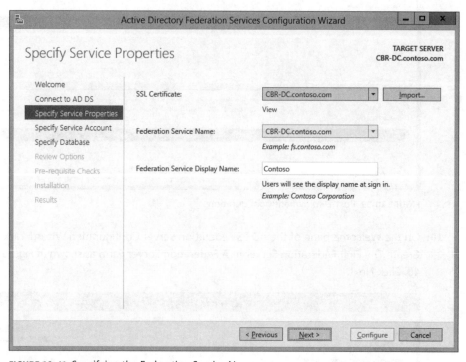

FIGURE 10-41 Specifying the Federation Service Name

13. On the Specify Service Account page, click Create A Group Managed Service Account and set the account name to CONTOSO\ADFS_GMSA as shown in Figure 10-42 and click Next.

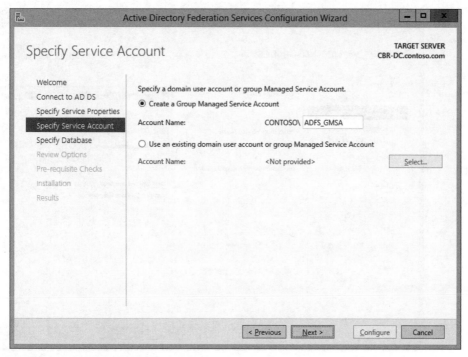

FIGURE 10-42 The Specify Service Account

14. On the Specify Database page, ensure that Create A Database On This Server Using Windows Internal Database is selected and click Next.

15. On the Review Options page, click Next.

16. Verify that the Pre-requisite Checks complete and click Configure and then click Close.

17. Switch to ADL-DC and ensure that you are signed on as wingtiptoys\administrator.

18. Click Add Roles And Features on the Manage menu of the Server Manager console.

19. On the Before You Begin page of the Add Roles And Features Wizard, click Next three times, and click Install. When the installation completes, click Close.

20. In the Server Manager console, click the AD FS node.

21. Click More on the Configuration Required For Federation Service At ADL-DC notification.

22. On the All Servers And Task Details dialog box, click Configure The Federation Service.

23. On the Welcome page of the AD FS Federation Server Configuration Wizard, click Create The First Federation Server In A Federation Server Farm and click Next twice.

24. On the Specify Service Properties page, set the SSL certificate to ADL-DC.wingtiptoys. internal and the Federation Service Display Name to **Wingtip Toys** as shown in Figure 10-43 and click Next.

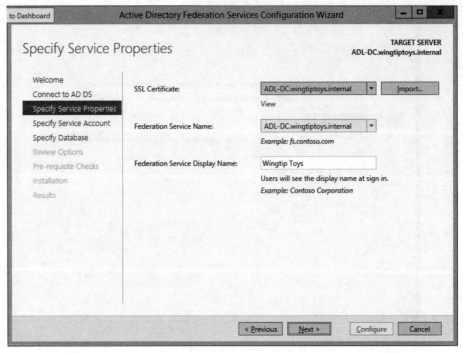

FIGURE 10-43 The Specify Service Properties page

25. On the Specify Service Account page, click Create A Group Managed Service Account and set the account name to WINGTIPTOYS\ADFS_GMSA and click Next three times.

26. On the Pre-requisite Checks page, shown in Figure 10-44, click Configure.

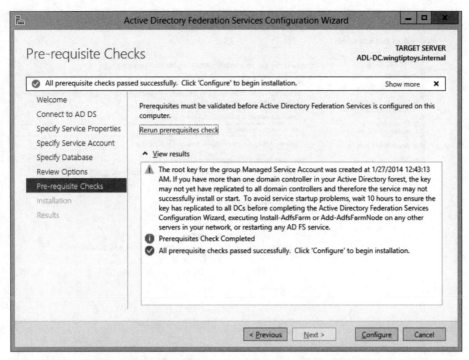

FIGURE 10-44 AD FS Pre-requisite Checks

27. When the installation completes, click Close.

Exercise 9: Configure relying party trust

In this exercise, you configure a relying party trust on CBR-DC. To complete this exercise, perform the following steps:

1. Ensure that you are signed on to CBR-DC as contoso\administrator.

2. In the Tools menu of the Server Manager console, click AD FS Management.

3. In the AD FS console, expand the Trust Relationships node and click Relying Party Trusts.

4. In the Actions pane, click Add Relying Party Trust.

5. On the Welcome To The Add Relying Party Trust Wizard, click Start.

6. On the Select Data Source page, type **adl-dc.wingtiptoys.internal** as shown in Figure 10-45, and then click Next twice.

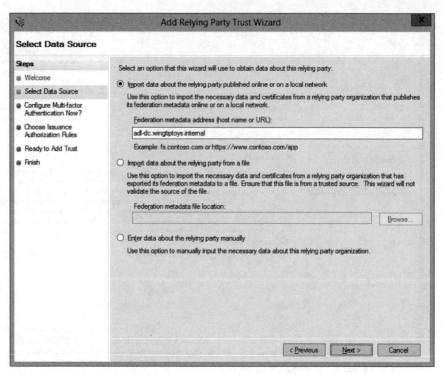

FIGURE 10-45 Selecting a data source

7. On the Configure Multi-factor Authentication page, ensure that I Do Not Want To Configure Multi-factor Authentication Settings For This Relying Party Trust At This Time is selected as shown in Figure 10-46 and click Next.

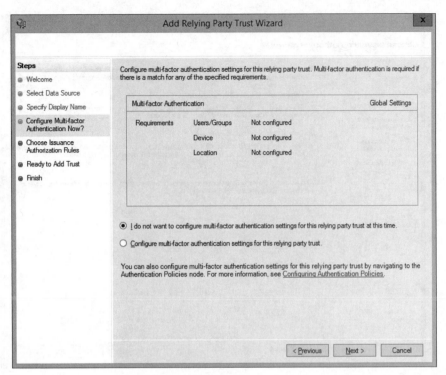

FIGURE 10-46 Configure multi-factor authentication

8. On the Choose Issuance Authorization Rules page, select Deny All Users Access To This Relying Party option as shown in Figure 10-47, and click Next.

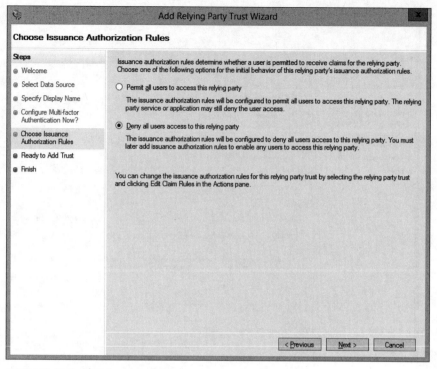

FIGURE 10-47 Configuring permissions

9. On the Ready To Add Trust page, click Next.

10. On the Finish page, remove the check in the Open The Edit Claim Rules Dialog Box For This Relying Party When The Wizard Closes option and click Close.

Exercise 10: Configure a claims provider trust

In this exercise, you configure a claims provider trust on the ADL-DC AD FS Federation Server. To complete this exercise, perform the following steps:

1. Ensure that you are signed in to ADL-DC as wingtiptoys\administrator.

2. In the Tools menu of the Server Manager console, click AD FS Management.

3. In the AD FS console, click the Claims Provider Trusts node under the Trust Relationships node.

4. In the Actions pane, click Add Claims Provider Trust.

5. On the Welcome page of the Add Claims Provider Trust Wizard, click Start.

6. On the Select Data Source page, enter the address **cbr-dc.contoso.com** as shown in Figure 10-48, and click Next three times.

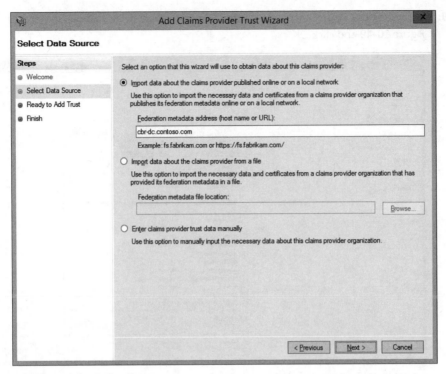

FIGURE 10-48 Importing data

7. On the Finish page of the Add Claims Provider Trust Wizard, clear the check box next to Open The Edit Claim Rules Dialog For This Claims Provider Trust When The Wizard Closes and click Close.

Exercise 11: Prepare claim data

In this exercise, you prepare the contoso.com domain with a security group. To complete this exercise, perform the following steps:

1. Ensure that you are signed on to SYD-DC as contoso\administrator.

2. Click Active Directory Administrative Center on the Tools menu of the Server Manager console.

3. Double-click Contoso (Local) and then double-click the Users container.

4. Click Don Funk and then click Properties on the Tasks pane.

5. In the Don Funk properties dialog box, click Extensions and then click Attribute Editor tab.

6. Click the EmployeeType attribute and click Edit.

7. On the String Attribute Editor dialog box, type **FTE** and click OK.

8. Verify that the Extensions section of the Don Funk properties dialog box matches Figure 10-49 and click OK.

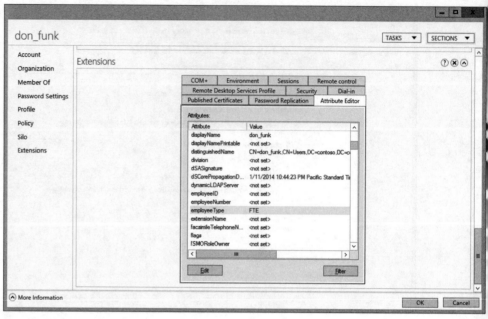

FIGURE 10-49 Employee type FTE

9. Under Users on the Tasks pane in Active Directory Administrative Center, click New and then click Group.

10. In the Create Group dialog box, set the Group Name to Submarine_Research as shown in Figure 10-50 and click OK.

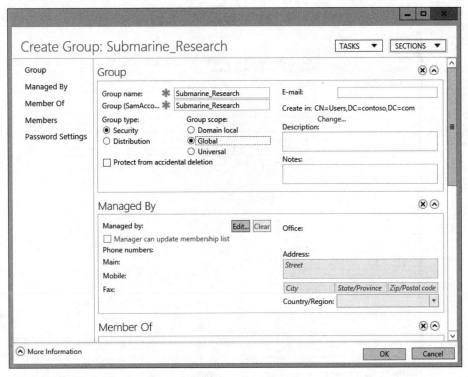

FIGURE 10-50 The Submarine_Research group

Exercise 12: Configure claim rules

In this exercise, you configure claims. To complete this exercise, perform the following steps:

1. Ensure that you are signed on to CBR-DC as contoso\administrator.

2. In the AD FS console, expand the Trust Relationships\Relying Party Trusts node and select the Adl-dc.wingtiptoys.internal trust.

3. On the Actions pane, click Edit Claim Rules.

4. Click the Issuance Authorization Rules tab on the Edit Claim Rules For Adl-dc. wingtiptoys.internal dialog box and then click Add Rule.

5. On the Select Rule Template of the Add Issuance Authorization Claim Rule Wizard, select the Send Group Membership As A Claim Template as shown in Figure 10-51 and click Next.

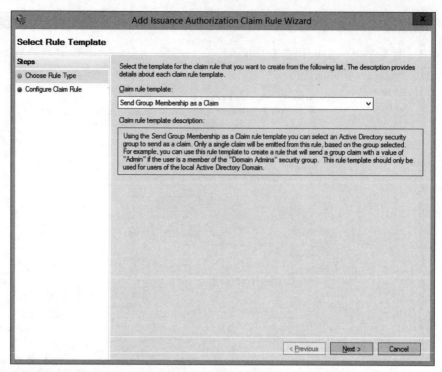

FIGURE 10-51 Configuring the Claim Rule Template

6. On the Configure Rule page, enter the following values as shown in Figure 10-52 and click Finish:

   - Claim Rule Name: **Submarine_Research**
   - User's Group: **CONTOSO\Submarine_Research**
   - Outgoing Claim Type: **Group**
   - Outgoing Claim Value: **Sub_Research**

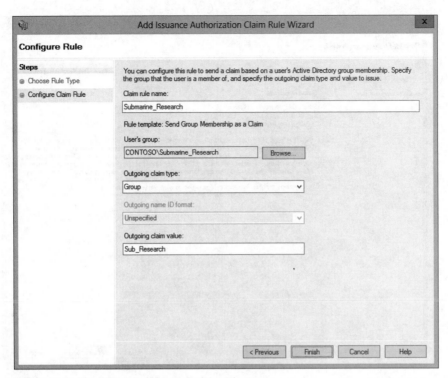

FIGURE 10-52 The Submarine_Research claim rule

7. On the Issuance Authorization Rules tab, click Add Rule.

8. On the Choose Rule Type page, select Send LDAP Attributes As Claims as shown in Figure 10-53 and click Next.

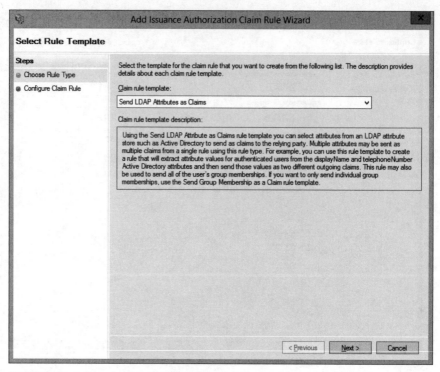

FIGURE 10-53 Configuring the Claim Rule Template

9. On the Configure Rule page, enter the following information as shown in Figure 10-54 and click Finish:

- Claim Rule Name: **FTE_Rule**
- Attribute Store: **Active Directory**
- LDAP Attribute: **Employee-Type**
- Outgoing Claim Type: **Employee-Type**

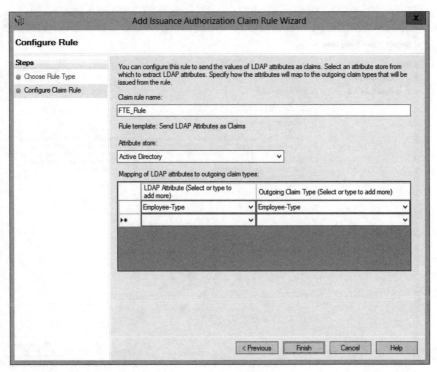

FIGURE 10-54 Specifying FTE_Rule

10. Click OK to close the Edit Claim Rules For Adl-dc.wingtiptoys.internal dialog box.

11. Switch to ADL-DC and ensure that you are signed on as wingtiptoys\administrator.

12. In the AD FS console, click the Trust Relationships\Claims Provider Trusts node.

13. In the list of Claims Provider Trusts, click Cbr-dc.contoso.com and click Edit Claims Rules.

14. On the Edit Claims Rules For dialog box, click Add Rule.

15. On the Select Rule Template page of the Add Transform Claim Rule Wizard, select Pass Through Or Filter An Incoming Claim as shown in Figure 10-55 and click Next.

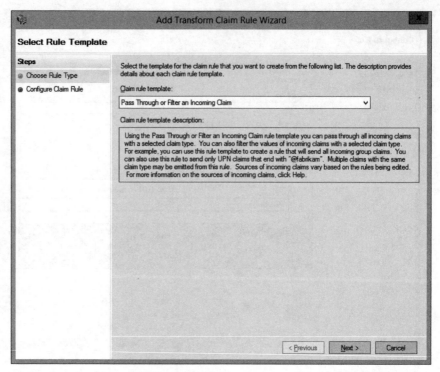

FIGURE 10-55 Pass Through Or Filter claim rule

16. On the Configure Rule page, enter the following data as shown in Figure 10-56 and click Finish:

- Claim Rule Name: **Sub_Research**
- Incoming Claim Type: **Group**
- Pass Through Only A Specific Claim Value: **Sub_Research**

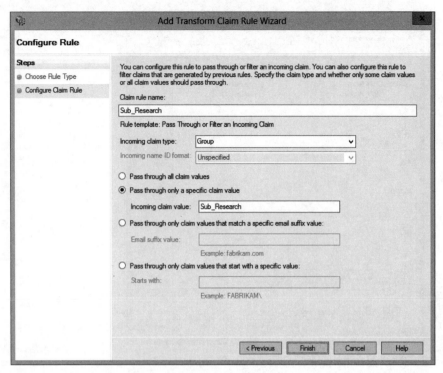

FIGURE 10-56 Specifying Sub_Research claim rule

17. On the Edit Claims Rules For dialog box shown in Figure 10-57, click Add Rule.

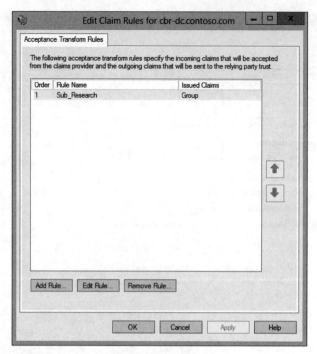

FIGURE 10-57 The Edit Claim Rules dialog box

18. On the Select Rule Template page, select the Send LDAP Attributes As Claims template and click Next.

19. On the Configure Rule page, enter the following information as shown in Figure 10-58 and click Finish:

   - Claim Rule Name: **employeeType claim rule**
   - Attribute Store: **Active Directory**
   - LDAP Attribute: **Employee-Type**
   - Outgoing Claim Type: **Employee-Type**

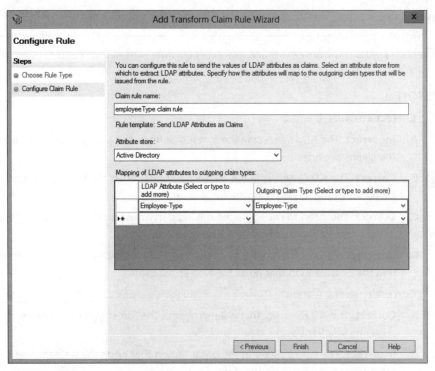

FIGURE 10-58 The EmployeeType Claim Rule

20. Click OK to close the Edit Claim Rules For Cbr-dc.contoso.com dialog box.

Suggested practice exercises

The following additional practice exercises are designed to give you more opportunities to practice what you've learned and to help you successfully master the lessons presented in this chapter.

- **Exercise 1**   Install AD LDS on ADL-DC and configure it as an attribute store for the AD FS instance on that server.
- **Exercise 2**   Deploy a server named BNE-DC and join it to the contoso.com domain. Configure this server as a Web Application Proxy.

Answers

This section contains the answers to the lesson review questions in this chapter.

Lesson 1

1. **Correct answers**: B and C

   A. **Incorrect**. The AD FS server in the forest that hosts the user accounts functions as the claims provider.

   B. **Correct**. The AD FS server in the organization that hosts the web application functions as the relying party server.

   C. **Correct**. You need to configure the relying party trust on the AD FS server that is in the organization that hosts the user accounts.

   D. **Incorrect**. You need to configure the claims provider trust on the AD FS server that is in the organization that hosts the web application.

2. **Correct answers**: A and D

   A. **Correct**. The AD FS server that is a member of the forest that hosts the user accounts functions as the claims provider.

   B. **Incorrect**. The AD FS server in the organization that hosts the web application will function as the relying party server.

   C. **Incorrect**. You configure the relying party trust on the claims provider server.

   D. **Correct**. You configure the claims provider trust on the relying party server.

3. **Correct answer**: A

   A. **Correct**. Because the Contoso CA is the issuing CA, adding the CA certificate to the Trusted Root Certification Authorities policy ensures that certificates from that CA are trusted by all computers in the Adatum domain.

   B. **Incorrect**. The Adatum CA did not issue the certificate to the Contoso AD FS server.

   C. **Incorrect**. An SSL certificate is not a CA certificate and should not be added to the Trusted Root Certification Authorities node.

   D. **Incorrect**. An SSL certificate is not a CA certificate and should not be added to the Trusted Root Certification Authorities node.

Index

A

Access Denied Assistance 577–578
Active Directory And Trusts console 13
Active Directory Application Mode (ADAM) 663
Active Directory Certificate Services 205–300
  installing and configuring 205–218
Active Directory detached clusters 454–455
Active Directory Domains And Trusts console 4, 10
Active Directory Federation Services. *See* AD FS
Active Directory Lightweight Directory Services (AD LDS)
    663
Active Directory Recycle Bin 6
  forest functional levels and 8
Active Directory Rights Management Services. *See* AD
    RMS (Active Directory Rights Management
    Services)
Active Directory Sites And Services console 92
Active Directory Users And Computers console 4
  selective authentication and 17
  UPN suffixes and 10
ADAM (Active Directory Application Mode) 663
AD CS Configuration Wizard 234
address block 148
address range 135, 139, 143, 148, 149
address space 119, 133, 136, 148, 150, 152
address tracking 150–153
Add Roles And Features Wizard dialog box 97, 243
AD FS 657–665
  attribute store 659
  claim 658
  claim rules 658
  claims provider 659
  claims provider trust 661
  claims rules 664–665
  configuring certificate relationship 662–663
  configuring Web Application Proxy 666–667
  multi-factor authentication 671
  relying party 660
  relying party trust 660
  Workplace Join 669–670
AD LDS (Active Directory Lightweight Directory Ser-
    vices) 663
administrative role separation
  certificate permissions and 215
  configuring 264–268
adprep.exe 9
AD RMS (Active Directory Rights Management Ser-
    vices) 580–591
  Administrators 586
  apply templates automatically 590–591
  backing up 591
  certificates and licenses 582–583
  configuration database 591
  Exclusion policies 589–590
  installing and configuring 580–581
  Super Users 586–587
  templates 583–585
  Trusted publishing domains (TPDs) 588–589
  Trusted user domains (TUDs) 587–588
advanced DHCP solution implementation 134–135
  DHCP failover 139–140
  DNS registration 137–138
  Multicast scopes 135–136
  Name Protection 138–139
  Split scopes 136–137
  Superscopes 134–135
Advanced DNS options 126–129
  DNS cache locking 126
  DNS recursion 127
  DNS socket pool 126
  Netmask ordering 128
Advanced Encryption Services (AES). *See* AES
AES (Advanced Encryption Services) 6

affinity 463–464

AIA (Authority Information Access) distribution points 211

Allow Private Key To Be Exported (certificate template settings) 221

application partitions 73

Archive subject's encryption private key 228

Archive Subject's Encryption Private Key (certificate template settings) 221

@ symbol, using UPN suffixes and 10

attribute-level replication 73

attribute store, AD FS 659

authentication
  forest-wide 16
  intraforest 4
  policy silos 7
  selective 16

Authentication Type for CES page (AD CS Configuration Wizard) 239

autoenrollment, certificate management 225–226

Autoenroll permission (certificates) 226

Automatic certificate renewal 224–225

B

backing up AD RMS. *See* AD RMS (Active Directory Rights Management Services)

backup, CAs (certificate authorities) 216–218

bidirectional trust 14

Branch Cache
  Client configuration
    Hosted Cache Server (Uses HTTPS) 384
    Peer Discovery (Uses WSD) 384

BranchCache 61, 380–384
  BranchCache for Network File Server 381–382
  Client configuration 382–384
    Configure Hosted Cache Servers 383
    Content Retrieval (Uses HTTP) 383
    Set BranchCache Hosted Cache Mode 383
    Enable Automatic Hosted Cache Discovery By Service Connection Point 383
  Hosted Cache Server Configuration 380–381

C

CA Compromise issue, revoking a certificate, 231

CA for CES page (AD CS Configuration Wizard) 239

CAs (certificate authorities)
  backup and recovery 216–218

CA Type page (AD CS Configuration Wizard) 236

CDPs (CRL Distribution Points) 212–213

central access policies, (DAC) 575–576

central access rules, (DAC) 573

Certificate Enrollment Policy Web Service 207–208

Certificate Enrollment Web Service 208

Certificate Hold issue, revoking a certificate 231

Certificate Revocation List (CRL)
  Distribution Points 212

certificates
  management
    autoenrollment 225–226
    key archiving and recovery 227–229
    renewal 224–225
  recovery, performing 292–296
  revocation 223, 288–292
  templates 221, 224, 287

Certificate Services 205–300
  CA backup and recovery 216–218
  CDPs (CRL Distribution Points) 212–213
  certificate authority 206–208
  installing and configuring 205–218
    administrative role separation 215–216
    online responders 214–215
  management 224
    autoenrollment 227
    key archiving and recovery 227
    renewal 224–225

Certificate Services Client-Auto-Enrollment group policy 226

Certification authority 207

Certification Authority Backup Wizard 216

Certification Authority Web Enrollment 207

Certutil-backup c:\backup command 217

Change of Affiliation issue, revoking a certificate 231

checkpoints 512

child domains 3

claim rules, AD FS 658

claims, AD FS 658

claims-based authentication 658

claims provider, AD FS 659

claims provider trust, AD FS 661

claims rules, AD FS 664–665

Cluster-Aware Updating (CAU) 449–451

Cluster networks 448–449

Cluster quorum modes 443–445
  Node and disk majority 443
  Node and file share majority 443
  Node majority 443
  No Majority: Disk Only 443

Cluster Shared Volumes 446–447, 506–510
Cluster Shared Volumes (CSVs) 506
Cluster storage and cluster shared volumes 445–446
Compatibility (certificate template settings) 221
Configure file access auditing
   Configure file access auditing 414–417
Configuring advanced file services 373–387
Configuring and managing backups 301–318
Configuring and managing failover clustering 441–455
Configuring and optimizing storage 388–397
Confirmation page (AD CS Configuration Wizard) 238
conflict resolutions 75
Constrained delegation 5
Continuously available file shares 454
Credential page (AD CS Configuration Wizard) 234
Credential Security Support Provider (CredSSP) 510
CRL (Certifcate Revocation List) 212
   CRL Distribution Points (CDPs) and, 212–213
Cryptography for CA page (AD CS Configuration Wizard)
   237

D

DAC (Dynamic Access Control) 567–579
  central access policies 575–577
  central access rules 573–574
  configuring
     Group Policy support 569
     resource properties 571–573
     user and device claims 569–570
  staging 576–577
Data Protection Manager 316–317
Delegated administration 129–130
Delta CRL list 212
device claims (DAC), configuring 570
DFS (Distributed File System) 61, 85
  replicating 5
DHCP failover 139–143
  Hot standby mode 139
  Load sharing mode 140
Distributed File System (DFS) 61, 85
  replicating 5
DNS cache locking 126–127, 132
DNS (Domain Name System)
  SRV record registration, managing 68
  zones, storing 5
DNS event logs 122–123
DNSKEY 121
DNS registration 134, 137, 141

DNSSEC 119–122, 126, 131–132
DNS socket pool 120, 126, 132
domain controllers
  functional levels 6
Domain Name System (DNS). *See* DNS
domain quarantine 21
domains
  configuring 1–11
  controllers, moving 69
  functional levels 4–8
  partitions 73
  trees 3
  trustiong 14
  upgrading 9
Domains And Trusts (Active Directory) console 10
Dynamic Access Control. *See* DAC (Dynamic Access
    Control)
dynamic witness 527

E

Enroll permission (certificates) 226
Enterprise Admins group 7
enterprise root CA
  deploying and configuring 232–241
enterprise root CAs (certificate authorities) 209–212, 218
enterprise subordinate CA 210, 219
  deploying 241
enterprise subordinate CAs deployment 241–246
Exclusion policies. *See* AD RMS (Active Directory Rights
    Management Services)
external trusts 13, 17

F

Failover and preference settings 452–453
Failover clustering 442–443
Features on Demand 396–397
Federation server role 658
File access auditing 385–387
File classification 384–385
File Replication Service (FRS) 85
File screens 374–377
File Server Resource Manager (FSRM) 374
Filtering 463–464
Filtering and affinity 463–464
  Disable The Port Range 464
  Multiple Host 464

Network 464
None 464
Single 464
Single Host 464
fine-grained password policies 6
force quorum resiliency 527
forests
configuring 1–11
functional levels 7
trusts 14, 16
upgrading 9
forest-wide authentication 16
FQDN (full qualified domain name) 3
FRS (File Replication Service) 85
fully qualified domain name (FQDN) 3
functional levels
domain 4–7
forest 7

G

Get-ADTrust cmdlet 21
GlobalNames zones 124–125
group managed service accounts 6

H

hardware security module (HSM) 212
hared Nothing Hyper-V live migration 509
hierarchies, CA 208–209
Hot standby mode (DHCP failover) 139
Hyper-V 6
Hyper-V hosting 518
Hyper-V Replica 518–526
Hyper-V Replica Broker 525–526

I

installation
AD RMS 581–582
Internet Protocol (IP) addresses 60
intraforest authentication 4
IPAM Administrators permissions 152
IPAM ASM Administrators permissions 152
IPAM (IP Address Management) 143–152
Configure IPAM database storage 144–145
Configure server discovery. *See also* Server discovery
Deploy IPAM 144

Introduction to IPAM 144
IPAM administration 152
Managing the IP address space 148
IPAM IP Audit Administrators 152
IPAM MSM Administrators permissions 152
IPAM Users permissions 152
IP (Internet Protocol) addresses 60
iSCSI initiator 392–394
iSCSI target and initiator 389–392
iSCSI targets 388–390
iSNS server 392–394
iSNS Server Properties dialog box 392, 428–429, 429
issuing CAs (certificate authorities) 208

J

K

KCC (knowledge consistency checker) 74
/kcc switch (repadmin) 84
KDC (key distribution center) 6
_kerberos record 68
Kerberos V5
authentication protocol 13
realm 20
key distribution center (KDC) 6
key recovery agent (KRA) certificate 229–231, 277
configuring 268–273
requesting 273–277
Key Signing Key (KSK) 121
knowledge consistency checker (KCC) 74

L

LastLogonTimestamp attribute 5
_ldap SRV record 68
Load sharing mode (DHCP failover) 140

M

Managing cluster hosts 461–462
Drainstop 461
Resume 462
Start 461
Stop 461
Suspend 462
Migrating and upgrading clusters 451–452

Move Server dialog box 70
multicast address 135, 141
Multicast scopes 135, 136, 141
multidomain environments 1–8
multi-factor authentication, AD FS 671–672
multiforest environments 1, 8
   multidomain enviroments and 2
multi-master replication 73
Multisite clustering, site-level fault tolerance 526–527

N

Name Protection 134, 138, 139, 142
name suffix routing 22
netdom.exe 13, 20
Netlogon service on domain controllers 69
Netmask ordering 128, 132, 133
Network Device Enrollment Service 207–209
Network Load Balancing (NLB) 457–458
Network Load Balancing prerequisites 458–459
New-ADReplicationSite Windows PowerShell cmdlet 62
New NLB PowerShell cmdlets 465–466
New Technology File System (NTFS) 568
Next Secure (NSEC/NSEC3) record 121
NLB cluster operation modes 459–460
   IGMP multicast 460
   Multicast mode 460
   Unicast mode 459
NLB clusters, upgrading 465

O

OCSP (Online Certificate Status Protocol) Response
   Signing Certificate template 214
offline root CA 211
Online Responder role service 207
   certificate revocation 214–215
   configuring 257–264

P

partitions, replicating 72
password policies 6
Password Replication Policy tab 77
passwords
   replacated ADL-DC, viewing 107
   RODC replication, configuring 77
perimeter networks, standalone subordinate CAs 211

policy silos 7
Port rules 462–463
practice exercises
   acquiring certificates for each server 691–694
   Add a cluster node 486–488
   apply RMS templates using file classification 649–651
   Backup data to Windows Azure Backup 362–367
   Begin creating a forest trust relationship 37–40
   Boot into Safe Mode 348–350
   Change the quorum configuration 488–489
   Cluster-Aware Updating 496–500
   Complete the creation of the forest trust relationship
         between contoso.com and margiestravel.com
         40–42
   configure Access Denied Assistance 627–629
   Configure a certificate template for autoenrollment
         and key recovery 279–282
   Configure a certificate template to support private key
         archival and recovery and reenroll all certificate
         holders 287–288
   Configure a CRL distribution point 253–257
   Configure additional UPN suffixes 50
   Configure ADL-DC as an RODC 102–105
   Configure administrative role separation 264–268
   Configure a highly available file share 491–493
   Configure a key recovery agent certificate template
         268–273
   Configure and view the DNS event log 165–166
   Configure an Online Responder 257–264
   configure application exclusions 648
   Configure a shortcut trust 50–53
   Configure a standalone CA 250–253
   Configure a standalone computer for use with Win-
         dows Azure Backup 354–358
   Configure BranchCache policies 431–435
   Configure CBR-DC for local backup 330–334
   Configure DHCP failover 184–186
   Configure DHCP Name Protection 180
   Configure DNSSEC 156–158
   Configure failover settings, failback settings, and move
         node 493–495
   Configure file classification 410–411
   Configure Group Policy to support autoenrollment,
         credential roaming, and automatic renewal
         282–286
   Configure Hyper-V to support live migration 552–553
   Configure identical virtual switches on MEL-HV-1 and
         MEL-HV-2 536–538

Configure IPAM GPOs and server discovery 187–189

Configure key recovery 277–278

Configure MEL-DC 155–156

Configure MEL-DC as an additional domain controller 96–100

Configure name suffix routing 43–45

Configure port rules and affinity 473–475

Configure quota templates and quotas 402–407

configure resource properties for DAC 607–608

Configure RODC replication 105–107

Configure selective authentication 45–49

configure staging 629–631

configure template distribution 647–648

Configure TEST-ONE for replication 547–550

Configure the name resolution policy 158–160

configure user and device claims for DAC 602–607

Configure Windows Azure Backup 358–362

configuring a claims provider trust 702–703

configuring CA trust in each forest 689–691

configuring claim rules 705–714

configuring DNS forwarding 675–677

configuring relying party trust 699–701

Connect to an iSCSI target 421–423

create a central access policy 624–626

Create a child domain with a contiguous namespace 27–30

Create a copy of a running virtual machine 558–559

Create Active Directory sites 89–90

Create Active Directory subnets 91–92

Create a DHCP superscope 173–177

create AD RMS templates 642–646

create a file classification rule 611–618

Create and assign an iSCSI target 417–421

Create and manage a GlobalNames zone 163–165

Create a new storage pool and thin provisioned virtual disk 423–426

Create a split scope 177–180

Create a three-node NLB cluster 470–473

Create a two-node failover cluster 485–486

create central access rules 621–624

Create file groups, file screen templates, apply file screens, and apply file screen exceptions 407–410

Create new forest 33

Create new multicast scopes 182–183

Create shared storage for failover clustering 477–478

Create site links 93–94

create the AD RMS Super Users group 641–642

Create two virtual machines on MEL-HV-1 544–547

create users and groups for DAC 598–602

Deploy and configure an enterprise root CA 232–241

Deploy an enterprise subordinate CA 241–246

Deploy BranchCache on Windows Server 2012 R2 435–437

Deploy FSRM 401–402

deploying AD CS in each forest 678–680

deploying AD FS in each forest 694–699

Enable reverse replication 559–561

enabling Group Policy support for DAC 595–598

Increase the size of the DNS socket pool 161

Install and activate the DHCP role 168–173

Install and configure a highly available file server 489–491

install and configure the AD RMS server role 635–641

Install a standalone subordinate CA 246–250

Install failover cluster features 483–485

Install the Hyper-V role on MEL-HV-1 and MEL-HV-2 531–535

Install the IPAM feature 186–187

Install the iSNS server and register the initiator 426–429

Install Windows Server Backup 327–330

Manage servers using IPAM 194–195

Modify Boot Configuration Data store 350–354

Modify DNS Cache Locking 161–163

Modify site link cost and replication schedule 94–95

Monitor replication with repadmin 110–112

nstall the Network Load Balancing feature on ADL-DC, CBR-DC, and MEL-DC 469–470

onnect potential cluster nodes to shared storage 479–483

Perform a backup over the network 336–338

Perform a backup to a local volume 334–335

Perform a full volume recovery using Windows Server Backup 341–345

Perform an unplanned failover 561

Perform a virtual machine export 558

Perform certificate recovery 292–296

Perform certificate revocation 288–291

Perform full server recovery over the network 345–348

Perform live migration of TEST-TWO 553–556

Perform storage migration 556–557

Prepare ADL-DC, MEL-DC, and CBR-DC for exercises 468–469

Prepare a domain controller to host a child domain with a contiguous namespace 25

Prepare a domain controller to host a new forest 32–33

Prepare domain controller to host the wingtiptoys.com tree in the contoso.com forest 30

Prepare for Windows Recovery Environment 344

prepare infrastructure for an AD RMS deployment 632–635

Prepare MEL-DC and ADL-DC 400–401

Prepare MEL-DC and CBR-DC for exercises 326–327

prepare separate forests 673–675

Prepare servers for live migration 538–541

Prepare servers for replication 541–544

Prepare to configure a forest trust relationship 34–37

preparing claim data 703–705

preparing MEL-DC and ADL-DC 594–596

preparing MEL-DC for certificate publication 684–688

preparing SYD-DC for certificate publication 680–684

preparing the server for file classification for DAC 609

Promote domain controller for new tree in contoso. com forest 31–32

Remove an NLB cluster 475–476

Remove feature files 429–431

Remove the RODC and reset accounts 113–114

Request a key recovery agent certificate 273–276

Restore data from Windows Azure Backup 367–369

run and verify the file classification 619

Simulate unplanned failure 495–496

Use IPAM to create a DHCP scope 196

Use IPAM to manage IP addresses 197–198

Use Vssadmin 338–340

Verify netmask ordering and disable recursion 167

Verify site placement and trigger replication 101

Verify the classification 413–414

View account passwords replicated to ADL-DC 107–110

View replication health and perform planned failover of TEST-ONE to MEL-HV-2 550–552

preferred owner 452–453

Private Key 217

Private Key page (AD CS Configuration Wizard) 237

private keys 287

Publish Certificate In Active Directory (certificate template settings) 221

Q

/queue switch (repadmin) 85

Quotas 377–379

Hard Quota 377

Soft Quota 378

R

RDS (Remote Desktop Services) 6, 17

read only domain controllers (RODC) 61, 76
replication, configuring 105

realm trusts 13, 20

Recovering servers 318–324
BCD (Boot Configuration Data store) 324
BCDEdit 324
Restore from backups 318–319
Restore from Windows Azure Backup 320–321
Restore to an alternative location 320
Safe mode, data recovery 322–323
Windows Recovery Environment 321–322

recovery, certificate management 216–218

Recycle Bin (Active Directory) 6
forest functional levels and 8

relative identifiers (RIDs) 2

relying party server, AD FS 660

relying party trust, AD FS 660

RemoteApp 6

Remote Desktop Services. *See* RDS

renewal, certificate management 224–225

Renewal Period (certificate template settings) 221

Repadmin tool 83–85

Replicate Now dialog box 101

/replicate switch (repadmin) 85

replication 59–118, 72–88
monitoring and managing 81
multi-master 73

Resource Record Signature (RRSIG) record 120

/replsingobj switch (repadmin) 85

revocation, certificate management, 223–225

Revoked Certificates Properties, 257

Revoked Certificates Properties dialog box 223

RIDs (relative identifiers) 2

/rodcpwdrepl option (repadmin) 85

RODC (read only domain controllers) 61, 76
replication, configuring 105

Role specifc backups 312–313

root CAs (certificate authority) 208
enterprise root CA 232–241
offline root CAs 211

root domain names 3

Rsers And Computers (Active Directory) console
selective authentication, configuring 17

S

Safe mode, data recovery 322–323
  Safe mode 323
  Safe mode with command prompt 323
  Safe mode with networking 323
schemas
  mulitforest environments and 8
  partitions 73
Security (certificate template settings) 221
selective authentication 5
  configuring 16
Select Role Services to Configure page (AD CS Configu-
    ration
Wizard) 234
Server discovery 145–148
Server for NFS 379–380
  Server for NFS Data Store 379
SetADDomainMOde Windows PowerShell cmdlet 4
Set-ADForestMode Window PowerShell cmdlet 7
Setup Type page (AD CS Configuration Wizard) 236
Shared virtual hard disks 447–448
shortcut trusts 13, 18
/showutdvec switch (repadmin) 85
SID filtering 21
silos (policy) 7
site-level fault tolerance 518–529
  dynamic witness 527
  Force quorum resiliency 527
  Hyper-V Replica 518–526
    planned failover 523–524
    unplanned failover 524–525
  Hyper-V Replica Broker 525–526
  multisite clustering 526–527
  tie breaker for 50% node split 527
  virtual machine network health detection 528
site links 64
  bridges 66
sites 59–118
  configuring 60–68
Split scopes 136, 137, 141
SRV records registration 68
staging (DAC) 576–577
standalone root CAs 210–211
  configuring 250
  subordinates 246
Storage tiers 398–399
subnets

configuring 60–68
Superscopes 134, 135, 141
Superseded reason, revoking a certificate (certificate
    template settings) 231
Superseded Templates 221
System Center 2012 R2 Configuration Manager, Ex-
    change Server 61
SYSVOL replication, upgrading 85

T

templates, AD RMS 583–584
thin provisioned virtual disk 396
Thin provisioning and trim 394–396
tie breaker for 50% node split 527
Tiered storage 398–399
token-decrypting certificates, AD FS 663
token-signing certificates, AD FS 663
transtitve trust 14
trigger replication 101
Trim 396
Trust anchor 121
Trusted publishing domains (TPDs). *See* AD RMS (Active
    Directory Rights Management Services)
Trusted user domains (TUDs). *See* AD RMS (Active Direc-
    tory Rights Management Services)
trusting domains/forests 14
trust relationships 4
trusts 13–21
two-way trust 14

U

Understanding Network Load Balancing 456–466
unidirectional trust 14
update sequence numbers (USNs) 75
Upgrading an NLB cluster 464–465
UPN (user principal names) suffixes 10
USB (Universal Serial Bus) ports 212
   hardware security module (HSM) 212
user claims (DAC), configuring 570
user principal names (UPN) suffixes 10
Users And Computers (Active Directory) console 4
   selective authentication and 17
   UPN suffixes and 10
USNs (update sequence numbers) 75

V

Validity Period (certificate template settings) 221
Validity Period page (AD CS Configuration Wizard) 220
virtual desktops 6
virtual machine network health detection 528
virtual machines
   movement 505–516
      failover clustering 506–508
      Hyper-V live migration 509–511
      import/export 515–516
      storage migration 512–514
Vssadmin 313–316

W

WAN (wide-area network) 61
Web Application Proxy 658
Web Application Proxy server 667–668
wide-area network (WAN) 61
Windows Azure Backup 306–315
   Backing up data 310
   Preparing 308
   Recovery Services 312
   Restore from 320–321
Windows PowerShell Credential pop-up 241
Windows Server 2003 domain functional level 5
Windows Server 2008 domain functional level 5
Windows Server 2008 R2 domain functional level 5, 6
Windows Server Backup 302–306
   Backing up data 306
   Backup locations 304

PowerShell cmdlets 305–306
Workplace Join, AD FS 669–670

Z

Zone level statistics 131
   Cache statistics 131
   DNSSEC statistics 131
   Error statistics 131
   Master statistics 131
   Query statistics 131
   Record statistics 131
   Recursion statistics 131

About the author

ORIN THOMAS is an MVP, an MCT and has a string of Microsoft
MCSE and MCITP certifications. He has written more than 25 books
for Microsoft Press and is a contributing editor at Windows IT Pro
magazine. He has been working in IT since the early 1990's. He
regularly speaks at events like TechED in Australia and around the
world on Windows Server, Windows Client, System Center and security
topics. Orin founded and runs the Melbourne System Center, Security,
and Infrastructure Group. You can follow him on twitter at
http://twitter.com/orinthomas.

Training Guide: Configuring Advanced Windows Server 2012 R2 Services and Exam 70-412

This book is designed to help build and advance your job-role expertise. In addition it covers some of the topics and skills related to Microsoft Certification Exam 70-412, and might be useful as a complementary study resource. If you are preparing for the exam, use additional materials such as Exam Ref 70-412: Configuring Advanced Windows Server 2012 R2 Services (9780735673618) to help bolster your readiness in conjunction with real-world experience.

EXAM OBJECTIVES/SKILLS	SEE TOPIC-RELATED COVERAGE HERE
CONFIGURE AND MANAGE HIGH AVAILABILITY	
Configure Network Load Balancing	Chapter 7, Lesson 2
Configure failover clustering	Chapter 7, Lesson 1
Manage failover clustering roles	Chapter 7, Lesson 2
Manage virtual machine (VM) movement	Chapter 8, Lesson 1
CONFIGURE FILE AND STORAGE SOLUTIONS	
Configure advanced file services	Chapter 6, Lesson 1
Implement Dynamic Access Control (DAC)	Chapter 9, Lesson 1
Configure and optimize storage	Chapter 6, Lesson 2
IMPLEMENT BUSINESS CONTINUITY AND DISASTER RECOVERY	
Configure and manage backups	Chapter 5, Lesson 1
Recover servers	Chapter 5, Lesson 2
Configure site-level fault tolerance	Chapter 8, Lesson 2
CONFIGURE NETWORK SERVICES	
Implement an advanced Dynamic Host Configuration Protocol (DHCP) solution	Chapter 3, Lesson 2
Implement an advanced DNS solution	Chapter 3, Lesson 1
Deploy and manage IP Address Management (IPAM)	Chapter 3, Lesson 3
CONFIGURE THE ACTIVE DIRECTORY INFRASTRUCTURE	
Configure a forest or a domain	Chapter 1, Lesson 1
Configure trusts	Chapter 1, Lesson 2
Configure sites	Chapter 2, Lesson 1
Manage Active Directory and SYSVOL replication	Chapter 2, Lesson 2

CONFIGURE ACCESS AND INFORMATION PROTECTION SOLUTIONS

Implement Active Directory Federation Services (AD FS)	Chapter 10, Lesson 1
Install and configure Active Directory Certificate Services (AD CS)	Chapter 4, Lesson 1
Manage certificates	Chapter 4, Lesson 2
Install and configure Active Directory Rights Management Services (AD RMS)	Chapter 9, Lesson 2

Now that you've read the book...

Tell us what you think!

Was it useful?
Did it teach you what you wanted to learn?
Was there room for improvement?

Let us know at http://aka.ms/tellpress

Your feedback goes directly to the staff at Microsoft Press,
and we read every one of your responses. Thanks in advance!

 Microsoft